WordPress®
ALL-IN-ONE
FOR
DUMMIES®

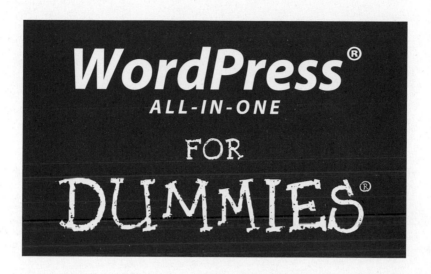

by Lisa Sabin-Wilson, Cory Miller, Kevin Palmer, Andrea Rennick, and Michael Torbert

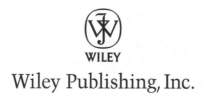

Wiley Publishing, Inc.

WordPress® All-in-One For Dummies®

Published by
Wiley Publishing, Inc.
111 River Street
Hoboken, NJ 07030-5774
www.wiley.com

Copyright © 2011 by Wiley Publishing, Inc., Indianapolis, Indiana

Published by Wiley Publishing, Inc., Indianapolis, Indiana

Published simultaneously in Canada

For general information on our other products and services, please contact our Customer Care Department within the U.S. at 877-762-2974, outside the U.S. at 317-572-3993, or fax 317-572-4002.

For technical support, please visit www.wiley.com/techsupport.

Wiley also publishes its books in a variety of electronic formats. Some content that appears in print may not be available in electronic books.

Library of Congress Control Number: 2011924142

ISBN: 978-0-470-87701-2

Manufactured in the United States of America

10 9 8 7 6 5 4 3 2 1

WILEY

About the Authors

Lisa Sabin-Wilson (*WordPress For Dummies*, *BuddyPress For Dummies*, *WordPress Web Design For Dummies*) has 8 years experience working with the WordPress platform, having adopted it early in its first year of release in 2003. Lisa is the owner of a successful design studio, E.Webscapes (http://ewebscapes.com), and a WordPress Web hosting company, BlogsAbout (http://blogsabout.com), and is a regular speaker on topics related to design and WordPress at several national conferences. Additionally, she hosts WordPress workshops around the country, teaching people how to use the WordPress platform to publish their own sites on the World Wide Web. You can find Lisa online at her personal blog (http://lisasabin-wilson.com) and Twitter (@LisaSabinWilson).

Cory Miller is a former newspaper journalist and public relations practitioner, turned freelance web designer, turned full-time entrepreneur. In January 2008, Cory founded iThemes (http://ithemes.com), a provider of premium WordPress themes, and in the summer of 2009, he and his team launched WebDesign.com (http://webdesign.com), a premium provider of web design training with WordPress. You can find Cory online on his personal blog: http://corymiller.com and on Twitter: @CoryMiller303.

Kevin Palmer is the founder of Social Media Answers, a consulting firm that helps companies create and foster a social media marketing strategy, improve their SEO, and drive traffic through organic and paid marketing in the B2B and B2C spaces. Kevin has successfully helped Internet startups and Fortune 500 companies. Kevin resides in Portland, OR and is attempting to prove you are never too old to play ice hockey. You can read Kevin's blog at http://socialmediaanswers.com/blog and follow him on Twitter (@kevinpalmer).

Andrea Rennick is self-taught in all things WordPress since 2005. She is also a mom of four homeschooled, mostly grown children, and grandmother to one. She thinks if she can do it, you can, too. When not building things with WordPress or writing about how to do things with WordPress, she's usually quilting. Often, Andrea populates the WordPress support forums with answers to your questions about WordPress, particularly her area of expertise: WordPress Multisite. She also runs a multisite resource Web site, WordPress Must Use Tutorials, at http://wpmututorials.com. You can find Andrea online at her personal blog (http://ronandandrea.com) and Twitter (@Andrea_R).

Michael Torbert is the developer of the popular WordPress All in One SEO Pack plugin and owner of Semper Fi Web Design (http://semperfiwebdesign.com). Michael's expertise includes WordPress plugin development and best SEO practices.

Dedication

Lisa Sabin-Wilson: To WordPress . . . and all that entails from the developers, designers, forum helpers, bug testers, educators, consultants, plugin makers, and theme bakers.

Cory Miller: I would like to dedicate my part of the book to my family — my mom, Charleen, and my dad, David, who loved and supported me and simply encouraged me that I could do anything I set my mind to do, and my grand-father and fellow entrepreneur, Leo Chaney, who inspired me to live my dreams and to use business as a tool to provide a great, fulfilling life for my family and team.

Kevin Palmer: For my parents, Alex and Sue Guerra, who tend to have no idea what I'm doing, but who morally support me anyway.

Andrea Rennick: I would like to dedicate my portion of this book to my grandfather, Alfred Thomas Thornton, who introduced me to this new thing called a computer. My only wish is that you and Nanny could hold this book in your hands.

Authors' Acknowledgments

Lisa Sabin: Every person involved in the WordPress community plays a vital role in making this whole thing work, and work well. Kudos to all of you! Also, big thanks to my wonderful husband, Chris Wilson, for his incredible support, backbone, and ability to put up with my crazy days of writing — I could *not* have done it without you!

Cory Miller: I would not be involved in this project without the help and support of my amazing team at iThemes, and in particular Chris Jean and Matt Danner — it is an honor to work with you all and I count you as some of my best friends in life! Big thanks to my business partners, Scott Day and Jay Chapman, for simply being who you are — amazing and encouraging every step of the way. Last but certainly not least, I want to thank Lisa Sabin-Wilson — your personal friendship and support has meant more to me than you might ever realize. I cherish your presence in my life and thank you for inviting me to be part of this project. To all the above: #boom.

Kevin Palmer: I would like to thank Lisa Sabin-Wilson for inviting me to contribute to this book and for answering numerous WordPress questions throughout the years. I would also like to thank my friends: Michelle, Kelly, Chrissy, Mark, Kurt, Kris, Tiffany, Nina, Tim, Chris, Lorna, Shawn, Karl, Tom, and numerous others who have listened, given advice, and helped me down my path.

Andrea Rennick: None of this would have been possible if Lisa hadn't asked me to write my section on the multisite feature, so a huge thanks to her for making that call. Thanks to the editors for making me look good, and my fellow co-authors for being awesome. It was great to have someone to commiserate with. A lot of my knowledge comes from the great folks who shared what they knew, via both the old WordPress MU forums and blogs. Some of the people are drmike, lunabyte, David Sader, Deanna Schneider, Tim Moore, SteveAtty, MrBrian, venturemaker, sulciman, Jim Groom and probably many others. Also, WordPress people like Matt Mullenweg, Donncha O'Caoimh, Jane Wells, Pete Mall, John James Jacoby, Boone Gorges, Andy Peatling, and more. Everyone is so wonderful at embracing new faces; big hugs all around at the next WordCamp. Thanks to my mom, who always knew I could do something like this; Addison and Sarah for not minding too much when their mom does something cool; Meaghan for reminding me to eat; and Emma for reminding me to play. And, finally, my husband Ron for being there to talk me down, to read over my work, to put up with me, to bounce ideas off of, and to be in this together. I love you so much — here's to another twenty years. I would be remiss if I didn't mention how much Ron has also brought to my knowledge base and how much work he has done within the multisite area.

Michael Torbert: Thanks go out to the WordPress community.

Publisher's Acknowledgments

We're proud of this book; please send us your comments at http://dummies.custhelp.com. For other comments, please contact our Customer Care Department within the U.S. at 877-762-2974, outside the U.S. at 317-572-3993, or fax 317-572-4002.

Some of the people who helped bring this book to market include the following:

Acquisitions, Editorial

Sr. Project Editor: Christopher Morris

Acquisitions Editor: Amy Fandrei

Copy Editors: Brian Walls, Jennifer Riggs, and Laura Miller

Technical Editors: Paul Chaney, Tom Myers

Editorial Manager: Kevin Kirschner

Editorial Assistant: Amanda Graham

Sr. Editorial Assistant: Cherie Case

Cartoons: Rich Tennant
(www.the5thwave.com)

Composition Services

Project Coordinator: Katie Crocker

Layout and Graphics: SDJumper, Corrie Socolovitch

Proofreaders: Melissa Cossell, Bonnie Mikkelson

Indexer: BIM Indexing & Proofreading Services

Publishing and Editorial for Technology Dummies

    Richard Swadley, Vice President and Executive Group Publisher

    Andy Cummings, Vice President and Publisher

    Mary Bednarek, Executive Acquisitions Director

    Mary C. Corder, Editorial Director

Publishing for Consumer Dummies

    Diane Graves Steele, Vice President and Publisher

Composition Services

    Debbie Stailey, Director of Composition Services

Contents at a Glance

Table of Contents

Introduction

WordPress is the most popular blogging software on the planet. Between the hosted service at WordPress.com and the self-hosted software available at WordPress.org, millions of bloggers use WordPress today! That's impressive. And with WordPress, you can truly tailor a blog to your own tastes and needs.

With no cost for using the benefits of the WordPress platform to publish content on the Web, WordPress is as priceless as it is free. WordPress makes writing, editing, and publishing content on the Internet a delightful, fun, and relatively painless experience whether you're a publisher, designer, developer — or just blogging as a hobby.

About This Book

Because WordPress is free and accessible to all, however, doesn't make it inherently easy for everyone. For some, the technologies, terminology, and coding practices can be a little intimidating or downright daunting. *WordPress All-in-One For Dummies* eliminates any intimidation about using WordPress. With a little research, knowledge, and time, you'll soon have a blog that suits your needs and gives your readers an exciting experience that keeps them coming back for more.

WordPress All-in-One For Dummies — a complete guide to WordPress — covers the basics: installation and configuration, the Dashboard, publishing content, creating themes, and developing plugins. Additionally, *WordPress All-in-One For Dummies* provides advanced information about security, the WordPress tools, using the multisite features, and optimizing your blog for search engines.

Foolish Assumptions

We make some inescapable assumptions about you and your knowledge, including the following:

✦ You're comfortable using a computer, mouse, and keyboard.

✦ You have a good understanding of how to access the Internet, use e-mail, and use a Web browser to access Web pages.

✦ You have a basic understanding of what a blog is; perhaps you already maintain your own blog.

✦ You want to use WordPress for your online publishing, or use the various WordPress features to improve your online publishing.

If you consider yourself an advanced user of WordPress, or if your friends refer to you as an all-knowing WordPress guru, chances are you'll find the information in this book elementary. However, this book is for the beginner, intermediate, and advanced user — there is something for everyone.

Conventions Used in This Book

Throughout the book, we apply the following typography conventions to guide you through some of the information we present:

✦ When we ask you to type something, the text you're supposed to type is **bold.**

✦ We also use **bold** in step list instructions.

✦ When we suggest a keyword that you may want to enter in a search engine, the term appears in *italics*.

✦ Text that appears in this `special font` is certain to be a URL (Web address), e-mail address, filename, folder name, or code.

✦ We apply *italics* to terms we think you may not be familiar with to let you know that we're defining it.

✦ In some instances, we provide blocks of code to use on your WordPress Web site. Code looks like this:

```
<html>
<head>
<title>This is my Web site</title>
</head>
```

✦ When the text that you see may be different, depending on your settings and preferences, we apply *italics* to that text.

What You Don't Have to Read

WordPress All-In-One For Dummies is eight books in one. Each minibook could easily stand alone, but combined, they give you a comprehensive WordPress reference guide.

This book isn't designed to be read from cover to cover, unless you want to! Reading the entire book from start to finish will surely give you an excellent and comprehensive understanding of WordPress. However, there may be aspects of the WordPress software that you are already familiar with and can safely ignore; whereas, you may feel you need to read other sections of the book to get the information you need. Feel free to take what you want and leave the rest!

You can also flip to the comprehensiveindex of this book to find out what information is covered or search for the topics you want to read about.

How This Book Is Organized

This book is divided into eight minibooks containing information on topics related to WordPress, including installing WordPress on a Web server, creating customized themes and plugins, and extending the functionality of the software.

Book 1: WordPress Basics

This book gives you a complete understanding of the WordPress software, including a brief introduction into blogging and such blogging technologies as RSS, comments, trackbacks, and archiving content. Additionally, you explore the differences between using WordPress as a blogging platform and a full-blown content management system.

Because WordPress is an open source project, it is good for users to have a basic understanding of open source and the licensing involved; therefore, this book also helps you understand GPL and open source basics.

After the introduction into WordPress, blogging, and licensing, you read about WordPress development and release cycles, important for any user because they affect the future of your WordPress-powered Web site. You also gain an understanding of WordPress versions and are introduced to the famous and helpful WordPress user community.

Book II: Setting Up the WordPress Software

This book is a must read for those wanting to wrap their head around some of the more technical aspects of getting a WordPress site running. It introduces you to a basic understanding of PHP and MySQL, the programming software that runs the framework of your Web site. You also discover information about domain name registration, obtaining a Web server from a Web hosting provider, and the basic Web hosting requirements to run WordPress. From there, you discover all the information you need to know about FTP, or File Transfer Protocol, a technology included in almost all Web hosting accounts.

After discovering some of the more geeky aspects of Web servers and programming languages, you start to get your hands dirty by digging in and installing WordPress on your Web server by using two different installation methods. Find out some great tips and tricks to improve the performance of your WordPress Web site and discover what it means to upgrade WordPress when new versions of the software are released.

This book also contains vital information about securing your WordPress installation against hackers and malicious Internet users. Additionally, we provide information on making a secure backup of your WordPress Web site and restoring the backup in the event of a disaster or if you simply want to transfer your WordPress Web site to a different hosting provider.

Book III: Exploring the WordPress Dashboard

This book takes you on a guided tour of the WordPress Dashboard, from logging in to the tools and features you use on a regular basis to administer your site. You discover how WordPress makes customizing your Dashboard to create a unique work space optimized for how you work easy to accomplish.

You explore the different tools and features available within the WordPress Dashboard, including a comprehensive run-through of how to configure the settings for optimal performance and to create a great user experience on your Web site.

In this book, you find out how to deal with comments and discover how to tackle comment spam; run a multi-author blog where you invite others to publish with you, build link lists to your favorite resources and Web sites, and discover ways to archive your content with categories and tags.

Book IV: Publishing Your Site with WordPress

This book takes you through the mechanics of publishing content with WordPress. You write a new post on your blog and discover the options for posting to your site, including categorizing and tagging your post, using post excerpts, setting discussion options, and creating a unique work space for your publishing efforts.

From there, you dig into more detail by discovering how to save drafts of your posts, edit existing posts, and even schedule posts for a future publishing date. In this book, you also get the differences between a blog post and a static page, taking you toward using WordPress as a content management tool, not just a blogging platform.

After discovering the ways and wonders of publishing content, you dig into how to include multimedia files on your site, including photos, photo galleries, videos, and audio files for a more interactive experience.

You work with custom fields for your site to make publishing unique information easier, and you discover a great feature in WordPress called Custom Post Types that allows you to create different content types for publishing such items as dedicated photo galleries, video blogs, podcasts, and more.

Book V: Examining SEO and Social Media

Most site owners are very interested in how to attract more traffic to their sites through search engine optimization and networking through popular social-media sites, such as Twitter and Facebook. This book takes a multifaceted approach to search engine optimization and social-media involvement.

You discover how to improve your social-media reach by making it easy for visitors to share your content on social-media networks. This book also helps you determine which social networks to participate in by helping you discover your niche, find influencers on the Internet, and involve users in what you're doing.

In this book, you use WordPress to create a social-media hub in your WordPress Dashboard by creating a one-stop social-media shop and using several different tools to stay aware of your brand and online reputation.

You obtain practical information on creating content that is search engine aware; that is, helping search engines discover and list your content and Web site in the various search engine directories and databases. We show you how to take advantage of the built-in features that make WordPress SEO ready, and provide the tools, plugins, and tips you can use along the way. This book also takes you into understanding the importance of site analytics and setting goals for optimal site performance in search engines and traffic.

Book VI: Customizing the Look of Your Site

Read this book if you're at all interested in customizing the look, feel, and layout of your site with WordPress themes. This book starts by taking you through a comprehensive and in-depth look at the default WordPress Twenty Ten theme and using its features to customize the presentation on your site.

If the default Twenty Ten theme isn't quite what you're looking for, this book takes you through the method of searching for, finding, previewing, installing, and activating one of thousands of free WordPress themes available to every WordPress user.

If you are ready to really dig in and get your hands dirty, this book gives you the details needed to tweak the look of existing themes, as well as a comprehensive look into the structure of a WordPress theme, including the information and tools you need to create your own theme from scratch.

As if that weren't enough, this book polishes off the topic of WordPress themes and customization with more advanced practices for creating WordPress themes, including parent/child theme relationships, WordPress template tags and parameters, adding new templates, using hooks, actions, and filters, and enhancing themes with built-in features.

Finally, this book takes you through the concept of WordPress theme frameworks, including how they work and why you might want to use them. We give you some great references on where to find some fantastic frameworks, too.

Book VII: Using and Developing Plugins

Plugins are to WordPress what that cool new App is to your iPhone; they're not completely necessary but they make the experience a lot more fun by extending the functionality of your WordPress Web site. This book starts by explaining what plugins are, the circumstances under which you want to use plugins, and how plugins can improve your visitors' experiences on your site.

After introducing the basics (including how to find, explore, and install plugins on your WordPress site), this book explores plugin options and settings and how you can navigate your way through different plugin setups.

For the very brave, this book takes you through the mechanics of modifying existing plugin base code to customize a plugin to do what you want it to do. From there, you create a basic plugin from scratch and discover plugin development best practices, including security concepts, naming techniques, localization, optimization, and tips from the pros on how to avoid common mistakes and pitfalls when developing plugins for the WordPress software.

As a bonus, this book looks at the WordPress API, how to use a plugin template, digging into actions and hooks and how you can avoid re-inventing the wheel by using already present filters and hooks. The last four chapters of this book contain some pretty geeky stuff should you be up for the challenge!

Book VIII: Running Multiple Sites with WordPress

Very new to the WordPress software (as recent as 2010), is the ability to run multiple sites with one installation of WordPress. This book takes you through setting up the multisite feature built into the WordPress software and includes circumstances under which you would use the multisite feature to determine whether it's right for you.

This book starts out with setting up and configuring the multisite feature after you install WordPress on your Web server and gives you the Web server configurations you need to run the multisite feature successfully on your site.

With the multisite feature set up, you become more than just a mere site owner; you become what WordPress calls a super admin! Super admins can access various features and settings that help you run the multisite feature on your Web site. If the multisite feature interests you at all, this book is a must read, providing you with practical tips, tricks, and advice. Running a multisite installation of WordPress is a lot different from running a regular WordPress installation on your site, so read this book to discover what you need to know.

Icons Used in This Book

Those little pictures in the margins of the book emphasize a point to remember, a danger to be aware of, or information that we think you may find helpful. This book uses the following icons:

Tips are little bits of information that you may find useful — procedures that aren't necessarily obvious to the casual user or beginner.

When your mother warned you, "Don't touch that pan — it's hot!", but you touched it anyway, you discovered the meaning of "Ouch!" We use this icon for situations like that. Out of curiosity, you may very well touch the hot pan, but you can't say that we didn't warn you!

All geeky stuff goes here. We use this icon when talking about technical information. You can skip it, but we think you'll find some great nuggets of information next to these icons. You may even surprise yourself and find you enjoy them. Be careful — you may turn into a geek overnight!

When you see this icon, brand the text next to it into your brain so that you remember whatever it was we thought you should remember.

Where to Go from Here

From here, you can go anywhere you please! *WordPress All-in-One For Dummies* is designed so that you can read one book, or all books, between the front and back cover, depending on what topics interest you.

Book I is a great place to get a good introduction into the world of WordPress, if you've never used it before and would like to find out more. Book II is also extremely helpful in giving you insight into the programming techniques and terminology involved with running a WordPress Web site — and that information is extremely helpful when you move forward to the other minibooks in *WordPress All-in-One For Dummies*.

Above all else, have fun with the information contained within these pages! Read the books on topics you think you already know about — you might just come across something new! Then dig into the books that contain topics that you really want to discover more about.

Book I

WordPress Basics

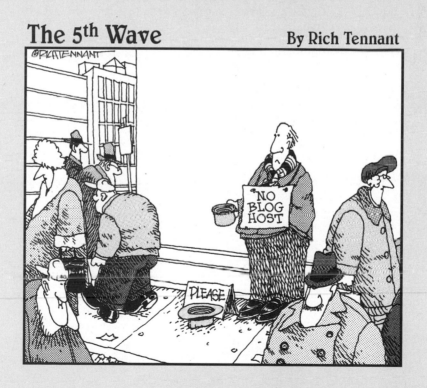

The 5th Wave — By Rich Tennant

Contents at a Glance

Chapter 1: Exploring Basic WordPress Concepts

In This Chapter

✔ **Introducing blogging**

✔ **Publishing and archiving content**

✔ **Interaction through comments**

✔ **Syndication through RSS**

✔ **Using WordPress as a content management tool**

✔ **Creating different types of sites with WordPress**

By providing regular, nontechnical Internet users the ability to publish content on the World Wide Web quickly and easily, blogging has taken the world by storm. These days, blogging is considered mainstream. Regular Internet users are blogging, but so are major corporations, news organizations, and educational institutions. Over the past decade, the question went from "What the heck is a blog?" to "What do you mean you don't have a blog?" Blogs have become a part of everyday life.

Nowadays, you can choose from several software platforms. For many bloggers, WordPress has the best combination of options. WordPress is unique in that it offers a variety of ways to run your Web site — WordPress is not only a blogging platform, but also a full-featured content management system (CMS) that includes all the tools and features you need to publish a blog or a complete Web site on your own, without a whole lot of technical expertise or understanding.

In this chapter, we introduce you to such blogging basics as publishing and archiving content, interacting with readers through comments, and providing ways for readers to have access to your content through syndication, or RSS technologies. This chapter also helps you sort the differences between a blog and a Web site, and introduces how WordPress, as a CMS, can help you build an entire Web site. Finally, we show you some Web sites that you can build with the WordPress platform.

Introducing the World of Blogging

Blogging is an evolutionary process, and blogs have evolved beyond personal journals to become tools for real journalism, business, and authorship.

A blog is a fabulous tool for publishing your diary of thoughts and ideas; however, blogs also serve as excellent tools for business, editorial journalism, news, and entertainment. Here are some ways that people use blogs:

✦ **Personal:** A blogger can use a blog as a journal or diary. You're considered a personal blogger if you use your blog mainly to discuss topics related to you or your life — your family, your cats, your children, or your interests (for example, technology, politics, sports, art, or photography). Lisa's blog, which you find at `http://lisasabin-wilson.com`, is an example of a personal blog.

✦ **Business:** A blogger can use a blog to promote her company's business services or products. Blogs are very effective tools for promotion and marketing, and business blogs usually offer helpful information to readers and consumers, such as sales events and product reviews. Business blogs also let readers provide feedback and ideas, which can help a company improve its services. A good example of a business blog is ServerBeach, which you can find on the hosted WordPress.com service at `http://serverbeach.wordpress.com`.

✦ **Media/journalism:** Popular news outlets, such as Fox News, MSNBC, and CNN, are using blogs on their Web sites to provide information on current events, politics, and news on a regional, national, and international level. These news organizations often have editorial bloggers, too. CNN's Anderson Cooper, for example, maintains a blog on CNN's Web site at `http://ac360.blogs.cnn.com`, with news and commentary from the *Anderson Cooper 360°* television show. Readers are invited to join in, too, by leaving comments about the news stories.

✦ **Government:** Number 10 (`www.number10.gov.uk`) is the official site of the British Prime Minister from his headquarters at 10 Downing Street in London. (See Figure 1-1.) The Prime Minister and his staff provide content by way of blog posts, photos, and videos, and integrate feeds from their Twitter and Facebook accounts. Governments use blogs to post news and updates to the web quickly, as well as integrate social-media tools as a means and way to interact with their citizens and representatives.

✦ **Citizen journalism:** Blogging has provided people opportunities to report and analyze news and information on a national and international level. Citizens are using blogs with the intention of keeping the media and politicians in check by fact-checking news stories and exposing inconsistencies. Major cable news programs interview many of these bloggers because the mainstream media recognize the importance of the citizen voice that's emerging via blogs. An example of citizen journalism is Power Line at `http://powerlineblog.com`.

Figure 1-1:
Number 10,
the official
blog of
the British
Prime
Minister, is
powered by
WordPress.

✦ **Professional:** Professional bloggers, a category that's growing every day, can blog for companies or Web sites. Blog networks, such as WeblogsInc.com, hire bloggers to write about certain topics. Additionally, several services match advertisers with bloggers, and the advertisers pay the bloggers to post about their products. Check out Darren Rowse's ProBlogger blog at `http://problogger.net`. Darren is considered the grandfather of all professional bloggers.

The Web sites and blogs we provide in this list run on the WordPress platform. A wide variety of organizations and individuals choose WordPress to run their blogs and Web sites.

Understanding Blogging Technologies

The WordPress software is a personal publishing system that uses a PHP-and-MySQL platform, which provides you everything you need to create your blog and publish your content dynamically without having to program the pages yourself. In short, with this platform, all your content is stored in a MySQL database in your hosting account.

PHP (which stands for *PHP Hypertext Preprocessor*) is a server-side scripting language for creating dynamic Web pages. When a visitor opens a page built in PHP, the server processes the PHP commands and then sends the results to the visitor's browser. MySQL is an open source relational database management system (RDBMS) that uses Structured Query Language (SQL), the most popular language for adding, accessing, and processing data in a database. If that all sounds Greek to you, think of MySQL as a big filing cabinet where all the content on your blog is stored.

Every time a visitor goes to your blog to read your content, he makes a request that's sent to your server. The PHP programming language receives that request, obtains the requested information from the MySQL database, and then presents the requested information to your visitor through his Web browser.

Book II, Chapter 1 gives you more in-depth information about the PHP and MySQL requirements you need to run WordPress. Book II, Chapter 3 introduces you to the basics of PHP and MySQL and provides information about how they work together with WordPress to create your blog or Web site.

Content, as it applies to the data that's stored in the MySQL database, refers to your blog posts, comments, and options that you set up on the WordPress Dashboard, or the control/administration panel of the WordPress software where you manage your site settings and content (Book III, Chapters 1 and 2). The theme (design) you choose for your blog (whether it's the default theme, one you create, or one that you have custom designed) isn't part of the content. Those files are part of the file system and aren't stored in the database. Therefore, it's a good idea to create a backup of any theme files you're using. See Book VI for further information on WordPress theme management.

When you look for a hosting service, keep an eye out for hosts that provide daily backups of your site so that your content will not be lost if a hard drive fails or someone makes a foolish mistake. Web hosting providers that offer daily backups as part of their services can save the day by restoring your site to a previous form.

Archiving your publishing history

WordPress maintains chronological and categorized archives of your publishing history automatically. This archiving process happens with every post you publish to your blog. WordPress uses PHP and MySQL technology to organize what you publish so that you and your readers can access the information by date, category, author, tag, and so on. When you publish to your WordPress blog, you can file that post under any category you specify — a nifty archiving system in which you and your readers can then find posts in specific categories. The archives page on Lisa's blog (`http://lisasabin-wilson.com/archives`) contains a Posts by Category section, where you find a list of categories she's created for her blog posts. Clicking the Blog Design link below the Posts by Category heading takes you to a listing of posts on that topic (see Figure 1-2).

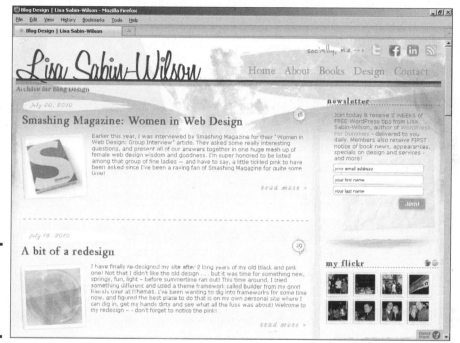

Figure 1-2:
A page with
posts in the
Blog Design
category.

WordPress lets you create as many categories as you want for filing your blog posts. We've seen blogs that have just one category and blogs that have up to 1,800 categories — when it comes to organizing your content, WordPress is all about personal preference. On the other hand, using WordPress categories is your choice. You don't have to use the category feature if you'd rather not.

Interacting with your readers through comments

An exciting aspect of blogging with WordPress is receiving feedback from your readers after you post to your blog. Feedback, or *blog comments,* is akin to having a guestbook on your blog. People can leave notes for you that publish to your site, and you can respond and engage your readers in conversation (see Figure 1-3). These notes can expand the thoughts and ideas you present in your blog post by giving your readers the opportunity to add their two cents' worth.

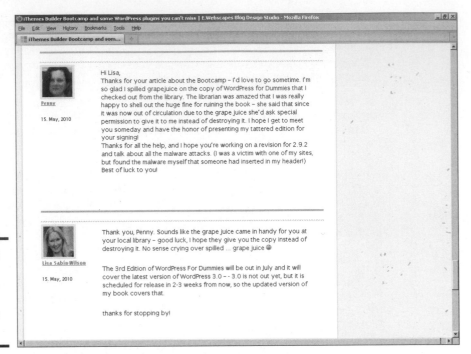

Figure 1-3:
Blog
comments
and
responses
on a blog.

On the WordPress Dashboard, you have full administrative control over who can leave comments. Additionally, if someone leaves a comment with questionable content, you can edit the comment or delete it. You're also free to not allow comments on your blog.

The blogging community says that a blog without comments isn't a blog at all because exchanging views with visitors is part of what makes blogging popular. Allowing comments on your blog invites your audience members to involve themselves in your discussion. However, publishing a blog without comments lets your readers partake of your published words passively and, sometimes, that's okay. For example, if your content on a controversial topic may attract visitor insults, it would be reasonable to publish a post without enabling the comment feature. Mostly, readers find commenting to be a satisfying experience when they visit blogs because comments make them part of the discussion. Still, it's up to you.

Feeding your readers

RSS stands for *Really Simple Syndication*. An *RSS feed* is a standard feature that blog readers have come to expect. So what is RSS, really?

RSS is written to the Web server in XML — Extensible Markup Language, as a small, compact file that can be read by RSS readers (such as I outline in Table 1-1). Think of an RSS feed as a syndicated, or distributable, auto-updating list of "What's New" for your Web site.

By using tools called *feed readers,* readers can download your feed automatically — that is, they can set their feed readers to automatically discover new content (such as posts and comments) from your blog and download that content for their consumption. Table 1-1 lists some of the most popular feed readers.

Table 1-1	Popular RSS Feed Readers	
Reader	**Source**	**Description**
Bloglines	`http://bloglines. com`	Bloglines is a free online service for searching, subscribing to, and sharing RSS feeds. You have no software to download or install; Bloglines is all Web based. You need to sign up for an account to use this service.
Google Reader	`http://google. com/reader`	This free online service is provided by Internet search giant Google. With Google Reader, you can keep up with your favorite blogs and Web sites that have syndicated (RSS) content. You have no software to download or install, but you need to sign up for an account with Google.
FeedDemon	`http://feeddemon. com`	This free service requires that you download the RSS reader application to your computer.

For blog readers to stay up-to-date with the latest and greatest content you post, they need to subscribe to your RSS feed. Most blogging platforms allow RSS feeds to be *autodiscovered* by the various feed readers. The reader needs only to enter your site's URL, and the program automatically finds your RSS feed.

 Most Web browsers alert visitors to the RSS feed on your site by displaying the universally recognized orange RSS feed icon, shown in the margin.

WordPress has RSS feeds in several formats. Because the feeds are built into the software platform, you don't need to do anything to provide your readers an RSS feed of your content.

Tracking back

The best way to understand *trackbacks* is to think of them as comments, except for one thing: Trackbacks are comments left on your blog by other blogs, not people. Sounds perfectly reasonable, doesn't it? After all, why wouldn't inanimate objects want to participate in your discussion?

Actually, maybe it's not so crazy after all. A trackback happens when you make a post on your blog, and within that post, you provide a link to a post made by another blogger on a different blog. When you publish that post, your blog sends a sort of electronic memo to the blog you linked to. That blog receives the memo and posts an acknowledgment of receipt in the form of a comment to the post that you linked to on their site. The information that is contained within the trackback includes a link back to the post on your site that contains the link to theirs — along with the date and time, as well as a short excerpt of your post. Trackbacks are displayed within the comments section of the individual posts.

The memo is sent via a *network ping* (a tool used to test, or verify, whether a link is reachable across the Internet) from your site to the site you link to. This process works as long as both blogs support trackback protocol. Almost all major blogging platforms support the trackback protocol.

Sending a trackback to a blog is a nice way of telling the blogger that you like the information she presented in her blog post. Every blogger appreciates trackbacks to their posts from other bloggers.

Dealing with comment and trackback spam

Ugh. The absolute bane of every blogger's existence is comment and trackback spam. When blogs became the "It" things on the Internet, spammers saw an opportunity. If you've ever received spam in your e-mail program, you know what we mean. For bloggers, the concept is similar and just as frustrating.

Before blogs, you often saw spammers filling Internet guestbooks with their links but not relevant comments. The reason is simple: Web sites receive higher rankings in the major search engines if they have multiple links coming in from other sites. Enter blog software with comment and trackback technologies, and blogs become prime breeding ground for millions of spammers.

Because comments and trackbacks are published to your site publicly — and usually with a link to the commenter's Web site — spammers got their site links posted on millions of blogs by creating programs that automatically seek Web sites with commenting systems and then hammer those systems with tons of comments that contain links back to their sites.

No blogger likes spam. Therefore, blogging services, such as WordPress, spend untold hours in the name of stopping these spammers in their tracks, and for the most part, they're successful. Occasionally, however, spammers sneak through. Many spammers are offensive, and all of them are frustrating because they don't contribute to the conversations that occur in blogs.

All WordPress systems have one important thing in common: Akismet, which kills spam dead. Akismet is a WordPress plugin brought to you by Automattic, the maker of WordPress.com. We cover the Akismet plugin, and comment spam in general, in Book III, Chapter 5.

Using WordPress as a Content Management System

You hear it a lot if you browse different Web sites that publish posts about WordPress: "WordPress is more than a blogging platform; it's a full content management system." What does that mean?

A *content management system (CMS)* is a platform that lets you run a full Web site on your domain. This means that WordPress, in addition to a blog, allows you to create pages and build additional features into your Web site that have nothing to do with the content on your blog.

A Web site and a blog are two different things. Although a Web site can contain a blog, a blog cannot contain a full Web site. We know it sounds confusing, but after you read this section and explore the differences between the two, you'll have a better understanding.

A *blog* is a chronological display of content — most often, written by the blog author. The posts are published and, usually, categorized into topics and archived by date. Blog posts can have comments activated so readers can leave their feedback and the author can respond, creating a dialogue about the blog post.

A *Web site* is a collection of published pages and different sections that offer the visitor a different experience. A Web site can incorporate a blog but usually contains other sections and features. These other features include

✦ **Photo galleries:** Albums of photos uploaded and collected in a specific area so that visitors can browse through and comment on them.

✦ **E-commerce stores:** Fully integrated shopping area into which you can upload products for sale and from which your visitors can purchase them.

✦ **Discussion forums:** Where visitors can join, create discussion threads, and respond to one another in specific threads of conversation.

✦ **Social communities:** Where visitors can become members, create profiles, become friends with other members, create groups, and aggregate community activity.

✦ **Portfolios:** Photographers, artists, or Web designers can devote sections of their sites to displaying their work.

✦ **Feedback forms:** Contact forms that your visitors fill out with information that then gets e-mailed to you directly.

✦ **Static pages (such as a Bio, FAQ, or Services page):** Pages that don't change as often as a blog page. Blog pages change each time you publish a new post.

The preceding list isn't exhaustive; it's just a listing of some of the most often seen Web site sections.

For example, Figure 1-4 shows the front page of Lisa's blog at `http://lisasabin-wilson.com`. Notice that the site displays a chronological listing of her most recent blog posts. Primarily, this blog uses WordPress as a blogging tool.

Figure 1-4: Lisa's blog uses WordPress as a blogging tool.

Comparatively, Lisa's business Web site at `http://ewebscapes.com`
uses WordPress as a CMS to publish a full Web site. This full site includes a
static front page of information that acts as a portal to the rest of the site, on
which you can find a blog, a portfolio of work, a contact form, an order form,
and various other static pages, including Services, FAQ (Frequently Asked
Questions), Terms of Service, Privacy Policy and more. Check out Figure 1-5
for a look at the front page of Lisa's E.Webscapes site; it's quite a bit different from her personal blog site.

Figure 1-5:
Lisa's
business
Web
site uses
WordPress
as a content
manage-
ment
system.

Using WordPress as a CMS means that you're creating more than just a blog;
you're creating an entire Web site full of sections and features that offer a
different experience for your visitors.

Chapter 2: Exploring the World of Open Source Software

In This Chapter

✔ **Exploring open source concepts**

✔ **Discovering examples of open source projects**

✔ **Understanding WordPress licensing**

✔ **Applying WordPress licensing**

*O*pen source software is a movement that started in the software industry in the 1980s. Its origins are up for debate, but most believe that the concept came about in 1983 when a company called Netscape released its Navigator Web browser source code to the public, making it freely available to anyone who wanted to dig through it, modify it, or redistribute it.

WordPress software users need a basic understanding of the open source concept and the licensing upon which WordPress is built because WordPress's open source policies affect you as a user — and greatly affect you if you plan to develop plugins or themes for the WordPress platforms. A basic understanding helps you conduct your practices in accordance with the license at the heart of the WordPress platform.

In this chapter, we introduce you to open source, the Open Source Initiative, and the GPL (General Public License), which is the specific license that WordPress is built upon (GPLv2, to be exact). You also discover how the GPL license applies to any projects you may release (if you are a developer of plugins or themes) that depend on the WordPress software and how you can avoid potential problems by abiding by the GPL as it applies to WordPress.

IANAL — *I Am Not a Lawyer* — is an acronym you find in articles about WordPress and the GPL. I use it here because I am not a lawyer and the information found in this chapter shouldn't be construed as legal advice. Rather, you should consider the chapter an introduction to the concepts of open source and the GPL. The information presented here is meant to inform and introduce you to the concepts as they relate to the WordPress platform.

Defining Open Source

Open source software is software whose source code is freely available to the public and can be modified and redistributed by anyone without restraint or consequence. This is a very simple, watered-down version of the definition of open source. An official organization called the Open Source Initiative (http://opensource.org), founded in 1998 to organize the open source software movement in an official capacity, has provided a very clear and easy-to-understand definition of open source. During the course of writing this book, I obtained permission from the OSI Board to include it here.

Open source doesn't just mean access to the source code. The distribution terms of open source software must comply with the following criteria:

1. **Free Redistribution**

The license shall not restrict any party from selling or giving away the software as a component of an aggregate software distribution containing programs from several different sources. The license shall not require a royalty or other fee for such sale.

2. **Source Code**

The program must include source code, and must allow distribution in source code as well as compiled form. Where some form of a product is not distributed with source code, there must be a well-publicized means of obtaining the source code for no more than a reasonable reproduction cost preferably, downloading via the Internet without charge. The source code must be the preferred form in which a programmer would modify the program. Deliberately obfuscated source code is not allowed. Intermediate forms such as the output of a preprocessor or translator are not allowed.

3. **Derived Works**

The license must allow modifications and derived works, and must allow them to be distributed under the same terms as the license of the original software.

4. **Integrity of the Author's Source Code**

The license may restrict source-code from being distributed in modified form only if the license allows the distribution of "patch files" with the source code for the purpose of modifying the program at build time. The license must explicitly permit distribution of software built from modified source code. The license may require derived works to carry a different name or version number from the original software.

5. **No Discrimination Against Persons or Groups**

The license must not discriminate against any person or group of persons.

6. **No Discrimination Against Fields of Endeavor**

   The license must not restrict anyone from making use of the program in a specific field of endeavor. For example, it may not restrict the program from being used in a business, or from being used for genetic research.

7. **Distribution of License**

   The rights attached to the program must apply to all to whom the program is redistributed without the need for execution of an additional license by those parties.

8. **License Must Not Be Specific to a Product**

   The rights attached to the program must not depend on the program's being part of a particular software distribution. If the program is extracted from that distribution and used or distributed within the terms of the program's license, all parties to whom the program is redistributed should have the same rights as those that are granted in conjunction with the original software distribution.

9. **License Must Not Restrict Other Software**

   The license must not place restrictions on other software that is distributed along with the licensed software. For example, the license must not insist that all other programs distributed on the same medium must be open-source software.

10. **License Must Be Technology-Neutral**

    No provision of the license may be predicated on any individual technology or style of interface.

The preceding items comprise the definition of open source, as provided by the Open Source Initiative; the definition is found at http://opensource.org/docs/osd, and shown in Figure 2-1.

Open source software source code must be freely available, and any licensing of the open source software must abide by this definition. Based on the OSI definition, WordPress is an open source software project. Its source code is accessible and publicly available for anyone to view, build on, and distribute at no cost anywhere, at anytime, or for any reason.

Several examples of high profile software enterprises, such as the ones in the following list, are also open source. You'll recognize some of these names:

✦ **Mozilla (http://mozilla.org):** Projects include the popular Firefox Internet browser and Thunderbird, a popular e-mail client. All projects are open source and considered public resource.

✦ **PHP (http://php.net):** An HTML-embedded scripting language. Stands for PHP Hypertext Preprocessor and is a popular software that runs on most Web servers today. Actually, WordPress requires the presence of PHP on your Web server for you to run the WordPress platform successfully on your site.

✦ **MySQL (`http://mysql.com`):** The world's most popular open source database. Used by your Web server to store all the data from your WordPress installation, including your posts, pages, comments, links, plugin options, theme option, widgets, and more.

✦ **Linux (`http://www.linux.org`):** A free and open source operating system used by Web hosting providers, among other organizations.

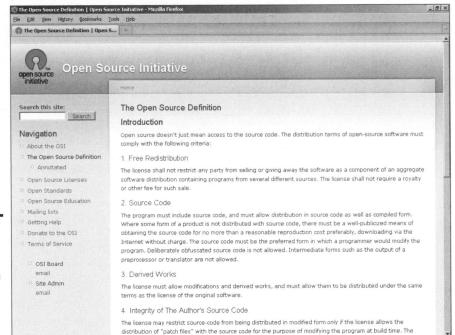

Figure 2-1: Definition of open source from the Open Source Initiative.

As open source software, WordPress is in some fine company. Open source itself is not a *license* — I cover licenses in the next section. Rather, open source is a movement — some consider it a philosophy — created and promoted as a way to provide software as a public resource open to community collaboration and peer review. WordPress development is clearly community driven and focused. You can read about the WordPress Community in Book II, Chapter 4.

Understanding WordPress Licensing

If you are bored, read the GPL text at `http://www.gnu.org/licenses/gpl-2.0.html`. Licensing language on any topic can be a difficult thing to navigate and understand. Mostly, have just a basic understanding of the concept of GPL and let the lawyers, if necessary, sort out the rest.

A complete copy of the GPL is included in every copy of the WordPress download package in the `license.txt` file. The directory listing of the WordPress software files shown in Figure 2-2 lists the `license.txt` file.

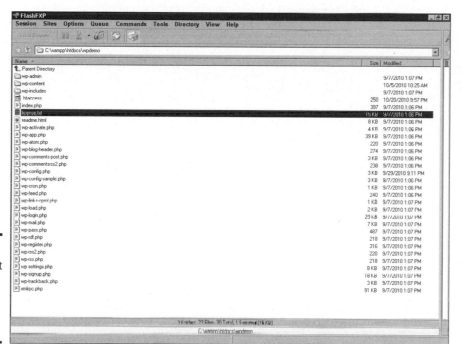

Figure 2-2:
The GPL text is included in every copy of WordPress.

Simply put, any iteration of a piece of software developed and released under the GPL must be released under the very same license in the future. Check out the nearby "The origins of WordPress" sidebar that tells the story of how the WordPress platform came to existence. Essentially, it was *forked* — meaning, the original software (in this case, a blogging platform called b2) was abandoned by its original developer, and the founders of WordPress took the b2 platform, called it WordPress, and began a new project with a new plan, outlook, and group of developers.

The origins of WordPress

Once upon a time, there was a simple PHP-based blogging platform called b2. This software, developed in 2001, slowly gained a bit of popularity among geek types as a way to publish content on the Internet. Its developer, Michel Valdrighi, kept development active until early 2003, when users of the software noticed that Valdrighi seemed to have disappeared. They became a little concerned about b2's future.

Somewhere deep in the heart of Texas, one young man in particular was very concerned, because b2 was his software of choice for publishing his own content on the World Wide Web. He didn't want to see his favorite publishing tool become obsolete. You can view the original post to his own blog in which he wondered what to do (`http://ma.tt/2003/01/the-blogging-software-dilemma`).

In that post, he talked briefly about some of the other software that was available at the time, and he tossed around the idea of using the b2 software to "to create a fork, integrating all the cool stuff that Michel would be working on right now if only he was around."

Create a fork he did. In the absence of b2's developer, this young man developed from the original b2 codebase a new blogging application called WordPress.

That blog post was made on January 24, 2003, and the young man's name was (and is) Matt Mullenweg. On December 26, 2003, with the assistance of a few other developers, Mullenweg announced the arrival of the first official version of the WordPress software. The rest, as they say, is history. The history of this particular piece of software surely is one for the books, as it is the most popular blogging platform available today.

Because the b2 platform was originally developed and released under the GPL, the WordPress software (all current and future iterations of the platform) must also abide by the GPL, by law. Because of the nature of the GPL, you, your next-door neighbor, or I could do the very same thing with the WordPress platform. There is nothing stopping you, or anyone, from taking WordPress, giving it a different name and re-releasing it as a completely different project. Typically, open source projects are forked when the original project development stalls or is abandoned (as was the case with b2) or (in rare cases) when the majority of the development community is at odds with the leadership of the open source project. We certainly aren't suggesting you do that because WordPress has one of the most active development communities of any open source project we've come across.

Applying WordPress Licensing to Your Projects

Regular users of WordPress software need never concern themselves with the GPL of the WordPress project at all. Regular users of the platform have to do nothing special to abide by the GPL. You don't have to pay to use the WordPress software, and you aren't required to acknowledge that you're using the WordPress software on your site. (That said, providing on your site at least one link back to the WordPress Web site is common courtesy and a great way of saying thanks.)

Most regular users of WordPress aren't even aware of the software licensing because it doesn't affect the day-to-day business of blogging and publishing their sites with the platform. However, it's not a bad idea to educate yourself on the basics of the GPL and try to be certain that any plugins and themes you use with your WordPress installation abide by the GPL so that you have peace of mind that all applications and software you're using are in compliance.

Knowledge of the GPL must increase dramatically if you develop plugins or themes for the WordPress platform. We cover WordPress themes in Book VI, and WordPress plugins in Book VII.

The public licensing that pertains to WordPress plugins and themes wasn't decided in a court of law. The current opinion of the best (legal) practices is just that, opinion. The opinion of the WordPress core development team, as well as the opinion of the Software Freedom Law Center (`http://en.wikipedia.org/wiki/Software_Freedom_Law_Center`), is that WordPress plugins and themes are derivative works of WordPress and, therefore, must abide by the GPL by releasing the development works under the same license that WordPress has.

A *derivative work,* as it relates to WordPress, is a work that contains programming whose functionality depends on the core WordPress files. Because plugins and themes contain PHP programming that call WordPress core functions, they rely on the core WordPress framework to work properly and, therefore, are extensions of the software.

The text of the opinion from James Vasile from the Software Freedom Law Center is available at `http://wordpress.org/news/2009/07/themes-are-gpl-too`.

To maintain compliance with the GPL, plugin or theme developers cannot release development work under any (restrictive) license other than the GPL. Nonetheless, many plugin and theme developers have tried to release material under other licenses, and some have been successful (from a moneymaking standpoint). However, the WordPress community generally doesn't support these developers and their plugins and themes. Additionally, the core WordPress development team considers such works noncompliant with the license, and therefore, the law.

WordPress has made it publicly clear that they will not support or promote any theme or plugins not in 100 percent compliance with the GPL. If you are not 100 percent compliant with the GPL, then you cannot include your plugin or theme in the WordPress Plugin Directory hosted at `http://wordpress.org`. If you develop plugins and themes for WordPress, or are considering dipping your toe into that pool, do it in accordance with the GPL so that your works are in compliance and your good standing in the WordPress community is protected. Table 2-1 gives you a quick review of what you can (and cannot) do as a WordPress plugin and theme developer.

Table 2-1 Development Practices Compliant with GPL License

Development/Release Practice	GPL Compliant?
Distribute to the public for free with GPL	Yes
Distribute to the public for a cost with GPL	Yes
Restrict the number of users of one download with GPL	No
Split portions of your work between different licenses (PHP files are GPL; JavaScript or CSS files are licensed with the Creative Commons license)	Yes (however, WordPress.org will not promote works that are not 100 percent GPL across all files)
Released under a different license, such as the PHP License	No

The one and only way to make sure that your plugin or theme is 100 percent compliant with the GPL is to take the following few steps before you release your development work to the world:

✦ Include a statement in your work that indicates the work is released under the GPLv2 license in the `license.txt` file, which WordPress does (refer to Figure 2-2). Alternatively, you can include this statement in the header of your plugin file:

```
<?php

    This program is free software; you can redistribute it and/or modify
    it under the terms of the GNU General Public License, version 2, as
    published by the Free Software Foundation.

    This program is distributed in the hope that it will be useful,
    but WITHOUT ANY WARRANTY; without even the implied warranty of
    MERCHANTABILITY or FITNESS FOR A PARTICULAR PURPOSE.  See the
    GNU General Public License for more details.

    You should have received a copy of the GNU General Public License
    along with this program; if not, write to the Free Software
    Foundation, Inc., 51 Franklin St, Fifth Floor, Boston, MA 02110-1301
    USA
*/
?>
```

+ Do not restrict the use of your works by the number of users per download.

+ If you charge for your work, which is compliant with the GPL, the licensing doesn't change and users still have the freedom to modify your work and rerelease it under a different name.

+ Do not split the license of other files included in your work, such as CSS or graphics. Although this practice complies with the GPL, it won't be approved for inclusion in the WordPress Plugin Directory.

Chapter 3: Understanding Development and Release Cycles

In This Chapter

✓ Delving into WordPress release cycles

✓ Exploring betas, release candidates, and final release versions

✓ Navigating WordPress release archives

✓ Tracking WordPress development

✓ Using bleeding-edge builds

*I*f you're planning to dip your toe into the WordPress waters (or you've already dived in and gotten completely wet) the WordPress platform's development cycle is really good to know about and understand because it affects every WordPress user on a regular basis.

WordPress and its features form the foundation of your Web site. WordPress is a low-maintenance way to publish content on the Web and the software is free in terms of cost. However, WordPress isn't 100 percent *maintenance* free, and part of maintenance is ensuring that your WordPress software is up-to-date to keep your Web site secure and safe.

This chapter explains the development cycle for the WordPress platform and shows you how you can stay up-to-date and informed about what's going on. This chapter also gives you information on WordPress release cycles and shows you how you can track ongoing WordPress development on your own.

Discovering WordPress Release Cycles

In Book I, Chapter 2, we introduce you to the concept of open source software and discuss the WordPress development community being primarily volunteer developers who donate their time and talents to the WordPress platform. The development of new WordPress releases is a collaborative effort, sometimes requiring contributions from more than 300 developers.

The public schedule for WordPress updates is, roughly, one new release every 120 days. As a user, you can expect a new release of the WordPress software about four times per year. We can attest that the WordPress development team sticks to that schedule closely, with exceptions only here and there. When they make exceptions to the 120-day rule, they usually make a public announcement about it so that users know what to expect and when to expect it.

Mostly, interruptions to the 120-day schedule occur because the development of WordPress is primarily on a volunteer basis. A few developers — employees of Automattic, the company behind WordPress.com — are paid to develop for WordPress, but most developers are volunteers. Therefore, the progress of WordPress development depends on the developers' schedules.

I'm confident in telling you that you can expect to update your WordPress installation at least three, if not four, times per year.

Upgrading your WordPress experience

Don't be discouraged or frustrated by the number of times you'll upgrade your WordPress installation. The WordPress development team is constantly striving to improve the user experience and bring exciting and fun new features to the WordPress platform. Each upgrade improves security and adds new features to enhance your (and your visitors') experience on your Web site. WordPress also makes the upgrades easy to perform, which we discuss in Book II, Chapter 6.

The following list gives you some good reasons why you should upgrade your WordPress software each time a new version becomes available:

✦ **Security:** When WordPress versions come and go, outdated versions are no longer supported and are vulnerable to malicious attacks and hacker attempts. Most WordPress security failures occur when a user is running an outdated version of WordPress on his Web site. To make sure that you're running the most up-to-date and secure version, upgrade to the latest release as soon as you can.

✦ **New features:** Major WordPress releases (I discuss the difference between major versus minor, or point, releases later in the chapter), offer great new features that are fun to use, improve your experience, and boost your efficiency and productivity. Upgrading your WordPress installation ensures that you always have access to the latest and greatest tools and features that WordPress has to offer.

✦ **Plugins and themes:** Most plugin and theme developers work hard to make sure that their product is up-to-date with the latest version of WordPress. Generally, plugin and theme developers don't worry about backwards compatibility, and they tend to ignore out-of-date versions of WordPress. To be sure that the plugins and themes you've chosen are current and not breaking your site, make sure that you're using the latest version of WordPress and the latest versions of your plugins and themes.

Understanding the cycles of a release

By the time the latest WordPress installation becomes available, that version has gone through several iterations, or *versions*. This section helps you understand what it takes to get the latest version to your Web site, and explains some of the WordPress development terminology.

The steps and terminology involved in the release of a new version of WordPress include

✦ **Alpha:** This is the first developmental phase of a new version. This is typically the "idea" phase in which developers gather ideas, including ideas from users and community members. During the alpha phase, developers determine which features to include in the new release and then develop an outline and project plan. After features are decided, developers start developing and testers start testing until they reach a "Feature Freeze" point in the development cycle where all new features are considered complete. The development moves on to perfecting new features through user testing and bug fixes.

✦ **Beta:** This phase is to fix bugs and clear any problems that testers report. Beta cycles can last up to four to six weeks, if not more. WordPress often releases several different beta versions with such names as WordPress version 3.0 Beta, WordPress version 3.0 Beta 1, and so on. The beta process continues until the development team decides that the software is ready to move into the next phase in the development cycle.

✦ **Release Candidate:** A version becomes a release candidate (RC) when the bugs from the beta versions are fixed and the version is nearly ready for final release. You sometimes see several release candidate iterations, referred to as RC-1, RC-2, and so on.

✦ **Final Release:** After a version has gone through full testing in several (hopefully all) types of environments, use cases, and user experiences, any bugs from the alpha, beta, and RC phases have been squashed, and no major bugs are being reported, the development team releases the final version of the WordPress software.

Major versus point releases

You may have noticed that WordPress versions are numbered. These numbers show the progress of the development of the software, but the numbers also serve a purpose and tell you something else about the version you are using. *Software versioning* is a method of assigning unique numbers to each version release. Generally, the two types of versioning are

✔ **Point Release:** Point releases usually only increase the numbered version by a decimal point or two, indicating a relatively minor release. Such releases include insignificant updates or minor bug fixes. For example, when the version number jumps from 3.0 to 3.0.1, you can be certain that the new version was released to fix existing minor bugs or to clean up the source code rather than to add new features.

✔ **Major Release:** A major release most often contains new features, and jumps by a more seriously incremented version number. For example, WordPress going from 2.9.2 to 3.0 (release 2.9 versioned into 2.9.1 and 2.9.2 before jumping to 3.0), was considered a major release because it jumped a whole number, rather than incrementally going up another decimal point. A large jump is a sign to users that new features are included in this version, rather than just bug fixes or clean up of code. The bigger the jump in version number, the more major the release. For example, a release jumping from 3.0 to 3.5 is an indication of some major new features.

After the WordPress development team issues a final release version, they start again in the alpha phase, gearing up and preparing to go through the development cycle for the next major version.

Typically, a development cycle lasts 120 days. However, this is an approximation because any number of things can happen (from developmental problems to difficult bugs) to delay the process.

Finding WordPress release archives

WordPress keeps a historical archive of all versions they've ever released at `http://wordpress.org/download/release-archive`, as shown in Figure 3-1. On that page, you find releases dating back to version 0.17 from 2003.

 None of the releases found on the WordPress Web site is safe for you to use except for the latest release in the 3.0.x series. WordPress just likes to have a recorded history of every release for posterity's sake.

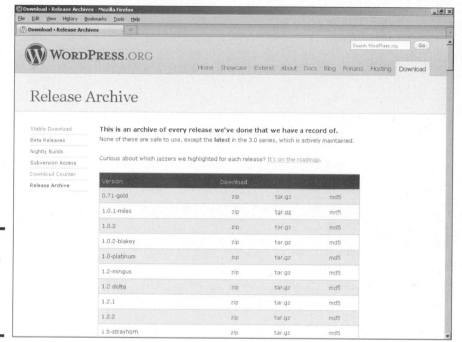

Figure 3-1:
The archive
of every
WordPress
release on
record.

Keeping Track of WordPress Development

If you know where to look, keeping track of the WordPress development
cycle is easy, especially because the WordPress development team tries to
make the development process as transparent as possible. You can track
updates by reading about them in various spots on the Internet and by listening to conversations between developers. If you're so inclined, you can
jump in and lend the developers a hand, too.

You have several ways to stay up-to-date on what's going on in the world
of WordPress development, including blog posts, live chats, development
meetings, tracking tickets, and bug reports, just to name a few. The following
list gives you a solid start on where you can go to stay informed:

✦ **WordPress Development Updates (`http://wpdevel.wordpress.
com`):** The WordPress development team's blog is where you can follow
and keep track of the progress of the WordPress software project while
it happens (see Figure 3-2). You find agendas, schedules, meeting minutes, and discussions surrounding the development cycles.

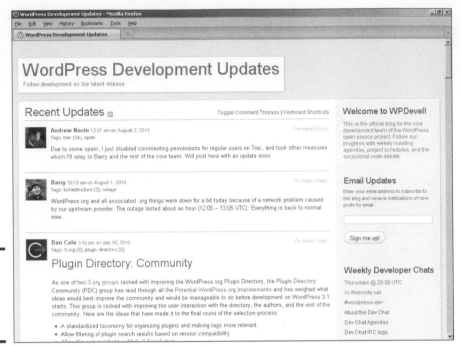

Figure 3-2:
The
WordPress
develop-
ment blog.

✦ **WordPress developers' chats (`irc.freenode.net` in `#wordpress-dev`):** Using an Internet chat program called IRC (Internet Chat Relay), WordPress developers gather weekly to discuss a predetermined agenda of items that need to be addressed during the development cycle. You're invited to join the IRC chat room to listen in, or participate, if you want to. (You can download a free IRC program called mIRC from `www.mirc.com` for PC users, or a program called Ircle from `www.ircle.com` for Mac users. Follow the program's user manual for instructions on how to use IRC to chat via the Internet).

✦ **WordPress Trac (`http://trac.wordpress.org`):** Here are ways to stay informed about the changes in WordPress development:

   • Follow the timeline: `http://core.trac.wordpress.org/timeline`

   • View the road map: `http://core.trac.wordpress.org/roadmap`

   • Read reports: `http://core.trac.wordpress.org/report`

   • Perform a search: `http://core.trac.wordpress.org/search`

✦ **WordPress mailing lists (`http://codex.wordpress.org/Mailing_Lists`):**

   Join mailing lists focused on different aspects of WordPress development, such as bug testing, documentation, and hacking WordPress. (We provide specifics about mailing lists in Book II, Chapter 4.)

Downloading Nightly Builds

WordPress development moves pretty fast. Often, changes in the WordPress software's development cycle occur daily. While the developers are working on alpha and beta versions and release candidates, they will commit the latest core changes to the repository and make those changes available to the public to download, install, and test on their own sites. The changes are released in a full WordPress software package called a *nightly build* — which contains the latest core changes submitted to the project, changes that have not yet released as a full and final version, yet.

Using nightly builds is not a safe practice for a live site. We strongly recommend creating a test environment to test the nightly builds. Many times, especially during alpha and beta phases, the core code may break and cause problems with your existing installation, so use nightly builds in a test environment only and leave your live site intact until the final release is available.

Hundreds of members of the WordPress community help in the development phases, even though they aren't developers or programmers. They help by downloading the nightly builds, testing them in various server environments, and reporting to the WordPress development team by way of Trac tickets (shown in Figure 3-3; check out `http://core.trac.wordpress.org/report`) any bugs and problems they find with that version of the software.

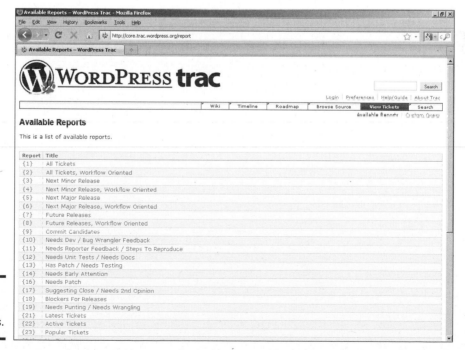

Figure 3-3: WordPress Trac tickets.

You can download the latest nightly build from the WordPress repository at `http://wordpress.org/download/nightly`. For information about installing WordPress, see Book II, Chapter 4.

WP Beta Tester (`http://wordpress.org/extend/plugins/wordpress-beta-tester`) is a super plugin that allows you to use the automatic upgrade tool in your WordPress Dashboard to download the latest nightly build. For information about installing and using WordPress plugins, check out Book VII, Chapter 1.

Running the latest nightly build on your Web site is referred to as using *bleeding-edge* software because it's an untested version requiring you to take risks just to run it on your Web site.

Chapter 4: Introducing the WordPress Community

In This Chapter

✔ Finding WordPress users

✔ Locating users on social networks

✔ Members helping members in support forums

✔ Participating in testing and bug squashing

✔ Discovering professional consultants and services

✔ Attending and organizing local WordCamps

*A*llow me to introduce you to the fiercely loyal folks who make up the WordPress user base, better known as the WordPress community. This band of merry ladies and gentlemen comes from all around the globe, from California to Cairo, Florida to Florence, and all points in between.

In March 2005, Matt Mullenweg of WordPress proudly proclaimed that the number of WordPress downloads had reached 900,000 — an amazing landmark in the history of the software. By August 2006, WordPress had logged more than 1 million downloads, and by 2007, more than 3 million. The number of downloads of WordPress continues to grow with each passing day. 2010 was a landmark year for WordPress when Microsoft announced that they would be transferring their 30 million+ users of their Windows Live service to WordPress. This makes for a rather large community of users, to say the least.

This chapter introduces you to the WordPress community and the benefits of membership within that community, such as where to find support, how to locate other WordPress users on various social networks, getting support and assistance from other users, how you can participate in WordPress development, and hooking up with WordPress users face to face at WordPress events, such as WordCamp.

Finding Other WordPress Users

Don't let the sheer volume of users intimidate you: WordPress has bragging rights to the most helpful blogging community on the Web today. Thousands of Web sites exist that spotlight everything from WordPress news, resources, updates, tutorials, training — the list is endless. Do a quick Google search for *WordPress* and you'll get at least 180,000,000 results.

Point is, WordPress users are all over the Internet from Web sites to discussion forums and social networks to podcasts, and more; and for many people, the appeal of the WordPress platform lies not only in the platform itself — but in its passionate community of users.

Finding WordPress news and tips on community Web sites

WordPress-related Web sites cover an array of different topics related to the platform, including everything from tutorials to news, and even a little gossip, if that's your flavor. The Internet has no shortage of Web sites related to the popular WordPress platform; here are few that stand out:

✦ **WP Candy (http://wpcandy.com):** Covers everything from soup to nuts: news, resources, tools, tutorials, and interviews with standout WordPress personalities. You can pretty much count on WP Candy to be on top of what's new and going on in the WordPress community.

✦ **WP Tavern (http://wptavern.com):** There is nothing like walking into a pub where everyone knows your name. WP Tavern is a Web site that offers the latest in WordPress news and discussion surrounding related topics, as well as an interactive discussion forum of WordPress software fans — all wrapped in an inviting tavern atmosphere (without the beer).

✦ **WordCast (http://wordcastnet.com):** A weekly podcast (or Internet radio show) that features WordPress-related topics, blogging, and social media.

✦ **Blog Herald (http://blogherald.com):** The Blog Herald covers a variety of Internet technology and blogging topics aside from just WordPress, however; their WordPress coverage is quite extensive and includes a wealth of WordPress news, resources, and tips.

Locating users on social networks

In addition to WordPress, many bloggers use different microblogging tools, like Twitter (http://twitter.com), or social-media networks, like Facebook (http:/facebook.com), to augment their online presence and market their blog, services, and products. Within these different networks, you can find WordPress users, resources, and links, including the following:

✦ **WordPress Twitter Lists:** Twitter, the popular microblogging network, allows users to create lists of people and their tweets who have the same interests, like WordPress. You can find a few of these lists here:

- WeFollow WordPress: `http://wefollow.com/twitter/wordpress`

- Listorious WordPress People and Lists: `http://listorious.com/tags/wordpress`

- Lisa Sabin-Wilson's WordPress list: `http://twitter.com/LisaSabinWilson/twibes-wordpress`

✦ **Facebook Pages on WordPress:** Facebook users create pages and groups around their favorite topics of interest, like WordPress. You will find some interesting WordPress pages and groups here:

- WordPress.org Fan Page: `http://www.facebook.com/WordPress`

- WordPress For Dummies Fan Page: `http://www.facebook.com/pages/WordPress-For-Dummies/47542644546`

- Matt Mullenweg on Facebook (founder of WordPress): `http://www.facebook.com/matt.mullenweg`

You can also include Twitter Lists of interest to you on your site by using the handy Twitter Lists for WordPress plugin at `http://wordpress.org/extend/plugins/twitter-lists-for-wordpress`.

Users Helping Users

Don't let the volume of users fool you: WordPress has bragging rights to the most helpful blogging community on the Web. Don't worry if you're not a member of the WordPress community. Joining is easy: Simply start your own blog by using the WordPress platform. If you're already blogging on a different platform, such as Blogspot or Movable Type, WordPress makes migrating your data from that platform to a new WordPress setup simple. (See Book II, Chapter 7 for information on migrating to WordPress from a different platform.)

WordPress support forums

The WordPress Forums page (shown in Figure 4-1) can be found at `http://wordpress.org/support`. This is where you find users helping other users in their quest to use and understand the platform. The support forums are hosted on the WordPress.org Web site, but don't expect to find any official form of support from the WordPress developers. Instead, you find a large community of people from all walks of life seeking answers and providing solutions.

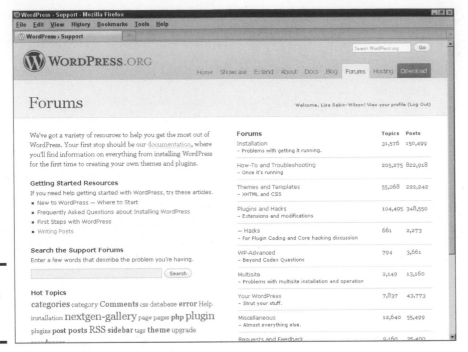

Figure 4-1:
WordPress
Forums
page.

Users from beginner and novice level to the most advanced level browse the forums providing support for one another. Each user has their own experiences, troubles, and knowledge level with WordPress, and the support forums are where they share those experiences and seek out the experiences of other users.

It is important to remember that the people you find and interact with on these official forums are offering their knowledge on a volunteer basis only — so, as always, common courtesy rules apply. Using "please" and "thank you" go a long, long way in the forums.

If you find solutions and assistance in the WordPress support forums, consider browsing through the forum entries to see whether you can help someone else by answering a question or two.

WordPress user manual

You can also find users contributing to the very helpful WordPress Codex (a collection of how-to documents) at `http://codex.wordpress.org`. *Codex,* by the way, is Latin for *book.*

The WordPress Codex is a collaborative effort to document the use of the WordPress software. All contributors to the Codex are WordPress users who donate their time as a way of giving back to the free, open source project that has given them a dynamic piece of software for publishing freely on the Web.

WordPress mailing lists

You can subscribe to various mailing lists, too. These lists offer you the opportunity to become involved in various aspects of the WordPress community as well as future development of the software. All the available WordPress mailing lists are on the Automattic Web site at `http://lists.automattic.com/mailman/listinfo`. The most popular ones include

- ✦ **wp-hackers (`http://lists.automattic.com/mailman/listinfo/wp-hackers`):** Subscribe to this mailing list to interact and talk to other WordPress users about hacking WordPress; otherwise known as altering WordPress code to make it do what you want it to do.

- ✦ **wp-testers (`http://lists.automattic.com/mailman/listinfo/wp-testers`):** This mailing list is filled with people who are testing new releases (as well as Beta versions) of WordPress and reporting any bugs or problems that they find.

- ✦ **wp-edu (`http://lists.automattic.com/pipermail/wp-edu/`):** A mailing list dedicated to educating people on the use of the WordPress platform.

Discovering Professional WordPress Consultants and Services

You have big plans for your blog, and your time is valuable. Hiring a professional to handle the back-end design and maintenance of your blog enables you to spend your time creating the content and building your readership on the front end.

Many bloggers who decide to go the custom route by hiring a design professional do it for another reason: They want the designs/themes of their blogs to be unique. Free themes are nice, but you run the risk that your blog will look like hundreds of other blogs out there.

A *brand,* a term often used in advertising and marketing, refers to the recognizable identity of a product — in this case, your blog. Having a unique brand or design for your site sets yours apart from the rest. If your blog has a custom look, people will associate that look with you. You can accomplish branding with a single logo or an entire layout and color scheme of your choosing.

Many consultants and design professionals put themselves up for hire. Who are these people? We get to that topic in just a second. First, you want to understand what services they offer, which can help you decide whether hiring a professional is the solution for you.

Here are some of the many services available:

✦ Custom graphic design and CSS styling for your blog

✦ Custom templates

✦ WordPress plugin installation and integration

✦ Custom WordPress plugins

✦ WordPress software installation on your Web server

✦ Upgrades of the WordPress software

✦ Web hosting and domain registration services

✦ Search engine optimization and site marketing

Some bloggers take advantage of the full array of services provided, whereas others use only a handful. The important thing to remember is that you aren't alone. Help is available for you and your blog.

Table 4-1 pairs the three types of blog experts — designers, developers, and consultants — with the services they typically offer.

Many of these folks are freelancers with self-imposed titles, but we've matched titles to typical duties. Keep in mind that some of these professionals wear all these hats; others specialize in only one area.

Table 4-1	Types of WordPress Professionals
Title	*Services*
Designers	These folks excel in graphic design, CSS, and the development of custom WordPress themes.
Developers	These guys and gals are code monkeys. Some of them don't know a stitch about design; however, they can provide you custom code to make your blog do things you never thought possible. Usually, you'll find these people releasing plugins in their spare time for the WordPress community to use free.
Consultants	If you're blogging for a business, these folks can provide you a marketing plan for your blog or a plan for using your blog to reach clients and colleagues in your field. Many of these consultants also provide search engine optimization to help your domain reach high ranks in search engines.

We wish we could tell you what you could expect to pay for any of these services, but the truth is the levels of expertise — and expense — vary wildly. We see services range from $5 per hour to $300 per hour — and all points in between and beyond. As with any purchase, do your research, and make an informed decision before you buy. That advice is the absolute best we can give.

Listing all the professionals who provide WordPress services is impossible, but we do list some of the most popular ones in Tables 4-2 through 4-4. Our goal is to cover a diverse level of services so that you have the knowledge to make an informed decision about which professional to choose.

WordPress designers

WordPress designers can take a simple blog and turn it into something dynamic, beautiful, and exciting. These people are experts in the graphic design, CSS styling, and template tagging needed to create a unique theme for your Web site. Often, WordPress designers are skilled in installing and upgrading WordPress software and plugins; sometimes, they're even skilled in creating custom PHP or plugins. These folks are the ones you want to contact when you're looking for someone to create a nice, unique design for your Web site that is an individual, visual extension of you or your company, such as my own Premium WordPress theme business shown in Figure 4-2.

Figure 4-2:
The design of E.Webscapes premium WordPress themes site.

Some blog designers post their rates on their Web sites because they offer design *packages,* whereas other designers quote projects on a case-by-case basis because every project is unique. When you're searching for a designer, if the prices aren't displayed on the site, just drop the designer an e-mail and ask for an estimate. Armed with this information, you can do a little comparison shopping while you search for just the right designer.

The designers and design studios listed in Table 4-2 represent a range of styles, pricing, services, and experience. All of them excel in creating custom WordPress blogs and Web sites. This list is by no means exhaustive, but it's a nice starting point.

Table 4-2	Established WordPress Designers
Who They Are	*Where You Can Find Them*
Blueprint Design Studio	`http://blueprintds.com`
Convertiv	`http://convertiv.com`
E.Webscapes - Lisa Sabin-Wilson	`http://ewebscapes.com`
Lamplight Media	`http://www.lamplightmedia.net`
Pixelita Designs	`http://pixelita.com`
Web Dev Studios	`http://webdevstudios.com`

Developers

The WordPress motto sits at the bottom of the WordPress home page:

> Code is poetry.

No one knows this better than the extremely talented blog developers in the core WordPress development team. A developer can take some of the underlying code, make a little magic happen between PHP and the MySQL database that stores the content of your blog, and create a dynamic display of that content for you. Most likely, you'll contact a developer when you want to do something with your blog that's a little out of the ordinary and you can't find a plugin that does the trick.

If you've gone through all the available WordPress plugins and still can't find the exact function that you want your WordPress blog to perform, contact one of these folks. Explain what you need. The developer can tell you whether it can be done, whether she is available to do it, and how much it will cost (don't forget that part!). You may recognize some of the names in Table 4-3 as developers/authors of some popular WordPress plugins.

Table 4-3	Established WordPress Developers
Who They Are	*Where You Can Find Them*
Crowd Favorite	`http://crowdfavorite.net/wordpress`
eHermits Inc	`http://ehermitsinc.com`
Mark Jaquith	`http://coveredwebservices.com`
Pluginize	`http://ewebscapes.com/pluginize`
Voce Communications	`http://vocecommunications.com`

Consultants

Blog consultants may not be able to design or code for you, but they're probably connected to people who can. Consultants can help you achieve your goals for your blog in terms of online visibility, marketing plans, and search engine optimization. Most of these folks can help you find out how to make money with your blog and connect you with various advertising programs. Quite honestly, you can do what blog consultants do by investing just a little time and research in these areas. As with design and coding, however, figuring everything out and then implementing it takes time. Sometimes, it's easier — and more cost effective — to hire a professional rather than do it yourself.

Who hires blog consultants? Typically, a business that wants to incorporate a blog into its existing Web site or a business that already has a blog but wants help taking it to the next level. Table 4-4 lists some people and organizations that offer this kind of consulting.

Table 4-4	Established Blog Consultants	
Who They Are	*Where You Can Find Them*	*Type of consulting*
Copyblogger Media	`http://www.copyblogger.com`	SEO, Marketing
Kevin Palmer	`http://convertiv.com`	WordPress Design and Development; Social Media Consulting
WebDesign.com	`http://webdesign.com`	WordPress Training

Contributing to WordPress

WordPress is a project driven by its user base, and contributing to the WordPress project is easier than you might think. Contributing code to the core WordPress software is only one way of participating in the WordPress project. You do not need to be a coder or developer to contribute to WordPress. Here are several ways you can contribute to the project, including, but not limited to, code:

✦ **Code:** One of the more obvious ways users can contribute to WordPress is by providing code to be used in the core files. The WordPress project has several hundred developers who contribute code at one time or another. You submit code through the WordPress Trac at `http://core.trac.wordpress.org`. Within the Trac, you can follow current development and track changes. To contribute, you can use the Trac to download and test a code patch or look at reported bugs to see whether you can offer a fix or submit a patch. Required skills include, at the very least, PHP programming, WordPress experience, and MySQL database administration (but not an exhaustive list, mind you).

✦ **Testing:** Earlier in this chapter, we mention the wp-testers mailing list you can join to test beta versions of WordPress and report your own user experience, known as testing. WordPress developers monitor this mailing list and try to fix any true bugs or problems.

✦ **Documentation:** Previously, we discuss the WordPress Codex, which is the user documentation for WordPress. Anyone can submit documentation to the Codex; all you need to do is visit `http://codex.wordpress.org`, create an account, and dig in! Be sure to check out the article in the Codex titled "Codex: Contributing" (`http://codex.wordpress.org/Codex:Contributing`), which provides good tips on how to get started, including guidelines for documentation contributions.

✦ **Tutorials:** Do you feel like you have a few tips and tricks you want to share with other WordPress users? Take it to your blog! What better way to contribute to WordPress than sharing your knowledge with the rest of the world? Write up your how-to tutorial and publish it on your Web site — then promote your tutorial on Twitter and Facebook.

✦ **Support Forums:** Volunteer your time and knowledge on the WordPress support forums at `http://wordpress.org/support`. Involvement of WordPress users donating their time and talents in the support forum is an essential part of the WordPress experience.

✦ **Presentations:** In the next section of this chapter, we discuss live WordPress events called MeetUps or WordCamps. Consider offering to speak at one of those events to share your knowledge and experience with other users — or host one in your local area.

Participating in Live WordPress Events

Not only can you find out about WordPress and contribute to the project online via the Internet, but you can get involved in WordPress offline, too. Live WordPress events, called MeetUps and WordCamps, are where WordPress users and fans get together to discuss, learn, and share about their favorite platform. The two events are somewhat different:

✦ **WordPress MeetUps:** Generally, these local WordPress events occur monthly in small groups of people from the same geographical location. Typically, speakers, organizers, and attendees are from the same area and enjoy gathering on a monthly or bimonthly basis.

✦ **WordCamps:** These annual WordPress events are usually much larger than MeetUps and are attended by people from all over the country. WordCamps are hosted in almost every major city in the United States and abroad. Usually, WordCamps cost a small amount to attend and speakers at WordCamps are well-known personalities from the WordPress community.

You can find a WordPress MeetUp near your community by visiting the MeetUp Web site at `http://meetup.com` or by performing a search, using the keyword *WordPress* and your city or zip code.

You can also find a WordCamp event close to you by visiting the WordCamp Web site at `http://wordcamp.org` and browsing through the upcoming WordCamps.

If there is not a MeetUp or WordCamp near your area, consider getting involved and organizing one! Some great tips and information about organizing WordCamps can be found at `http://wordcamp.org`.

Chapter 5: Discovering Different Versions of WordPress

In This Chapter

✔ **Getting hosted with WordPress.com**

✔ **Self-hosting with WordPress.org**

✔ **Running a network of blogs with the multisite feature**

✔ **Exploring enterprise options and VIP services**

*B*loggers have a wealth of software platforms to choose from. You want to be sure that the platform you choose has all the options you're looking for. WordPress is unique in that it offers two versions of its software. Each version is designed to meet the various needs of bloggers.

One version is a hosted platform available at WordPress.com that meets the needs of bloggers who do not want to worry about installing or dealing with software; the other is the self-hosted version of the WordPress software available at `http://wordpress.org`, which offers users a bit more freedom and flexibility, as described throughout this chapter.

This chapter introduces you to both versions of the WordPress platform in order to enable to you choose which version suits your particular needs the best.

Comparing the Two Versions of WordPress

The two versions of WordPress are

+ The hosted version at WordPress.com

+ The self-installed and self-hosted version available at WordPress.org

Certain features are available to you in every WordPress blog setup, whether you're using the self-hosted software from WordPress.org or the hosted version at WordPress.com. These features include (but aren't limited to)

+ Quick-and-easy installation and setup

+ Full-featured blogging capability, letting you publish content to the Web through an easy-to-use Web-based interface

✦ Topical archiving of your posts, using categories

✦ Monthly archiving of your posts, with the ability to provide a listing of those archives for easy navigation through your site

✦ Comment and trackback tools

✦ Automatic spam protection through Akismet

✦ Built-in gallery integration for photos and images

✦ Media Manager for video and audio files

✦ Great community support

✦ Unlimited number of static pages, letting you step out of the blog box and into the sphere of running a fully functional Web site

✦ RSS capability with RSS 2.0, RSS 1.0, and Atom support

✦ Tools for importing content from different blogging systems (such as Blogger, Movable Type, and LiveJournal)

Table 5-1 compares the two WordPress versions.

Table 5-1	Exploring the Differences between the Two Versions of WordPress	
Feature	*WordPress.org*	*WordPress.com*
Cost	Free	Free
Software download	Yes	No
Software installation	Yes	No
Web hosting required	Yes	No
Custom CSS control	Yes	$15/year
Template access	Yes	No
Sidebar widgets	Yes	Yes
RSS syndication	Yes	Yes
Access to core code	Yes	No
Ability to install plugins	Yes	No
WP themes installation	Yes	No
Multi-author support	Yes	Yes
Unlimited number of blog setups with one account (multisite)	Yes*	Yes
Community-based support forums	Yes	Yes

*with the multisite feature enabled only

Choosing the hosted version from WordPress.com

WordPress.com (see Figure 5-1) is a free service. If downloading, installing, and using software on a Web server sounds Greek to you, and are things you'd rather avoid, the WordPress folks provide a solution for you at WordPress.com.

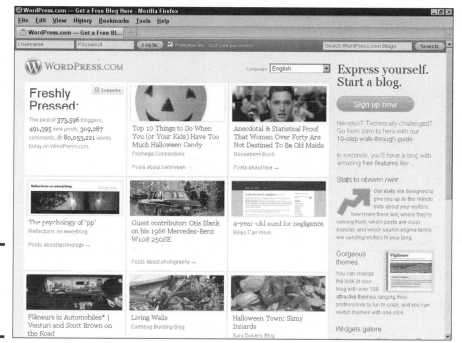

Figure 5-1:
The
WordPress.
com Web
site.

WordPress.com is a *hosted solution,* which means it has no software requirement, no downloads, and no installation or server configurations. Everything's done for you on the back end, behind the scenes. You don't even have to worry about how the process happens; it happens quickly, and before you know it, you're making your first blog post by using a WordPress.com blog solution.

WordPress.com has some limitations, however. It won't let you install plugins or custom themes, for example, or customize the base code files. WordPress.com offers some customization with its custom CSS feature — but that isn't a free service; you have to pay for the upgrade. WordPress.com offers several upgrades (see Figure 5-2) to help make your blogging life easier. Here's a list of upgrades you can purchase to enhance your WordPress.com account, with prices reflecting the annual cost:

✦ **Add a Domain:** This upgrade allows you to add your own domain name to your WordPress.com account; see Book II, Chapter 1. This service costs $5.00 for the domain registration and $12.00 for the domain mapping.

✦ **VideoPress:** This upgrade equips you with the ability to upload, store, and share your videos from your WordPress.com account. This service covers the storage space that your video files take up on the WordPress.com servers. $59.97 per year.

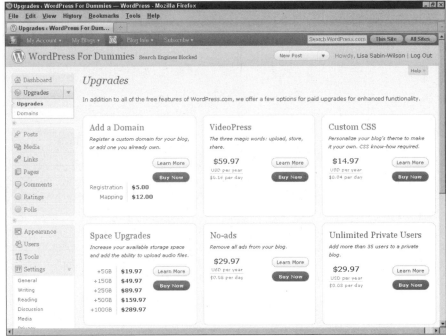

Figure 5-2: Several paid upgrades available on the WordPress.com free service.

✦ **Custom CSS:** This upgrade lets you customize the Cascading Style Sheet (CSS) for the theme you're using in the WordPress.com system. Recommended for users who understand CSS. $14.97 per year.

✦ **Space Upgrades:** With the free WordPress.com blog, you have 3GB of hard drive space in your upload directory. The various space upgrades add more, letting you upload more files (images, videos, audio files, and so on). You can add 5GB for $19.97 per year, 15GB for $49.97 per year, 25GB for $89.97 per year, 50GB for $159.97 per year, and 100GB for $289.97 per year.

✦ **No Ads:** For $29.97 per year, you can ensure that your WordPress.com blog is ad free. Occasionally, WordPress.com does serve ads on your blog pages to defray the costs of running a popular service. If you'd rather not have those ads appearing on your blog, pay for the No Ads upgrade and you'll be ad free!

✦ **Unlimited Private Users:** With a free account, you're limited to 35 private users — if you choose to publish your WordPress.com blog as a private blog — giving access to only those users whom you authorize. This upgrade removes that limit, letting you have unlimited private users for your blog (provided that those users are already WordPress.com account holders). $29.97 per year.

✦ **Offsite Redirect:** Allows you to forward your WordPress.com URL to an offsite domain; this is helpful if you choose to move away from WordPress.com to your own domain with the WordPress.org software — you can forward the traffic that you have built for $12 per year.

✦ **Text Messaging:** Gives you the ability to use SMS text messages on your mobile phone to administer your blog by moderating comments, authenticating your login and more. $20.00 per year.

Even with its limitations, WordPress.com is an excellent starting point and introduction to the world of WordPress, if you're new to blogging and a little intimidated by the configuration requirements of the self-installed WordPress.org software.

The good news is that if you outgrow your WordPress.com-hosted blog and want to move to the self-hosted WordPress.org software, you can. You can even take all the content from your WordPress.com-hosted blog with you and easily import it into your new setup with the WordPress.org software.

Therefore, in the grand scheme of things, your options aren't really that limited.

Self-hosting with WordPress.org

The self-installed version from WordPress.org is the primary focus of *WordPress All-in-One For Dummies*. Using WordPress.org requires you to download the software from the WordPress Web site at `http://wordpress.org` (shown in Figure 5-3).

The WordPress.org Web site is an excellent repository of tools and resources for you throughout the lifespan of your WordPress-powered blog, so be sure to bookmark it for future reference! Here's a list of helpful things that you can find on the Web site:

✦ **Plugins (`http://wordpress.org/extend/plugins`):** The Plugin page of the WordPress.org Web site houses a full directory of plugins available for WordPress. You can search for and find the plugins you need for SEO enhancement, comment management, and social-media integration, among many others.

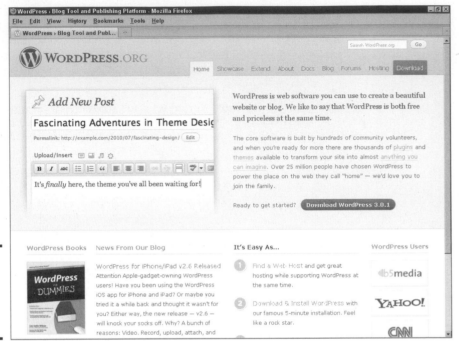

Figure 5-3:
The
WordPress.
org Web
site.

✦ **Themes (http://wordpress.org/extend/themes):** The Free Themes Directory page, shown in Figure 5-4, is a repository of WordPress themes free for the taking. In this section of the WordPress.org Web site, you can browse more than 1,500 themes for you to use on your site to dress up your content.

✦ **Docs: (http://codex.wordpress.org):** Almost every piece of software released comes with documentation and user manuals. The Docs section of the WordPress.org Web site contains the WordPress Codex, which tries to help you answer questions about the use of WordPress and its various features and functions.

✦ **Forums (http://wordpress.org/support):** The WordPress.org Web site hosts support forums where you find people from all walks of WordPress experience, from beginners to very advanced level users. The support forums at WordPress.org consist of WordPress users from all over with one goal — learning how to use WordPress to suit their particular needs. The support forums are very much a community of users helping other users, and you can generally obtain a solution to your WordPress needs here from other users of the software.

✦ **Roadmap (http://wordpress.org/about/roadmap):** This section of the WordPress.org Web site doesn't contain support information or tools that you can download; it offers an at-a-glance peek at what's new and upcoming for WordPress. In Chapter 3 of this minibook, we talk about the WordPress development and release cycle. The Roadmap page gives you a pretty accurate idea of when WordPress will release the next version of its software. (Hint: Click the version number to visit the WordPress Trac and see what features developers are working on and adding.)

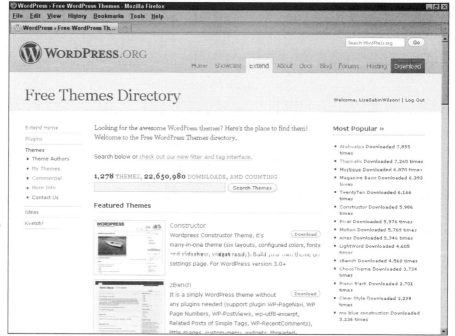

Figure 5-4:
The Free Themes Directory on WordPress. org.

WordPress.org is the self-installed, self-hosted software version of WordPress you install on a Web server that you have set up on a domain you have registered. Unless you own your own Web server, you need to lease one. Leasing space on a Web server is *Web hosting,* and unless you know someone who knows someone, hosting generally isn't free.

That said, Web hosting doesn't cost a whole lot, either. You can usually obtain a good Web hosting service for anywhere from $5 to $10 per month. (Book II, Chapters 1 and 2 give you some great information on Web hosting accounts and tools.) However, you need to make sure that any Web host you choose to work with has the required software installed on the Web server. The recommended minimum software requirements for WordPress include

✦ PHP version 5.0 or greater

✦ MySQL version 5.0 or greater

After you have WordPress installed on your Web server (see the installation instructions in Book II, Chapter 4), you can start using it to blog to your heart's content. With the WordPress software, you can install several plugins that extend the functionality of the blogging system, which we describe in Book VII. You also have full control of the core files and code that WordPress is built on. If you have a knack for PHP and knowledge of MySQL, you can work within the code to make changes that you think would be good for you and your blog.

You don't need design or coding ability to make your blog look great. Members of the WordPress community have created more than 1,600 WordPress themes (designs), and you can download them free and install them on your WordPress blog (Book VI, Chapter 2). Additionally, if you're creatively inclined, like to create designs on your own, and know Cascading Style Sheets (CSS), you have full access to the template system within WordPress and can create your own custom themes (See Book VI, Chapters 3 through 7).

Hosting Multiple Sites with One WordPress Installation

The self-hosted WordPress.org software lets you run an unlimited number of blogs on one installation of its software platform, on one domain. When you configure the options within WordPress to enable a multisite interface, you become administrator of a network of blogs. All the options remain the same, but with the multisite options configured, you can add additional blogs and domains, and allow registered users of your Web site to host their own blog within your network. More information about the multisite feature in WordPress is found in Book VIII.

The following types of sites use the Network options within WordPress:

✦ **Blog networks**, which can have more than 150 blogs. The popular electronics retail store, Best Buy, uses WordPress to power 1,050 local store blogs (example: `http://stores.bestbuy.com/577`).

✦ **Newspapers and magazines**, such as *The New York Times,* and universities, such as Harvard Law School, use WordPress to manage the blog sections of their Web sites.

✦ **Niche-specific blog networks**, such as Edublogs.org, use WordPress to manage their full networks of free blogs for teachers, educators, lecturers, librarians, and other education professionals.

Extensive information on running a network of sites by using the multisite feature in WordPress is found in Book VIII. The chapters there take you through everything: setting it up, maintaining it, and using it to run a network of sites with one WordPress installation.

Anyone using a WordPress platform prior to version 3.0 may recognize *WordPress MU*, the separate piece of software you needed in order to run multiple sites with WordPress. The multisite feature that replaced WordPress MU was introduced into WordPress version 3.0. All you old dogs out there need to forget WordPress MU and embrace the multisite feature in version 3.0+ because WordPress MU no longer exists.

With the multisite features enabled, users of your network can run their own sites within your installation of WordPress. They also have access to their own Dashboard with the same options and features you read about in Book III. Heck, it would probably be a great idea to buy a copy of this book for every member within your network so everyone can become familiar with the WordPress Dashboard and features, too. At least have a copy on hand so people can borrow yours!

If you plan to run just a few of your own sites with the WordPress multisite feature, then your current hosting situation is probably well suited (see Book II, Chapter 1 for information on Web hosting services). However, if you plan to host a large network with hundreds of blogs and multiple users, you should consider contacting your host and increasing your bandwidth and the disk space limitations on your account.

The best example of a large blog network with hundreds of blogs and users (actually, more like millions) would be the hosted service at WordPress.com (as we discuss earlier in this chapter). At WordPress.com, people are invited to sign up for an account and start a blog by using the multisite feature within the WordPress platform on the WordPress server. When you enable this feature on your own domain and enable the user registration feature (covered later in this chapter), you invite users to:

✦ Create an account

✦ Create a blog on your WordPress installation (on your domain)

✦ Create content by publishing blog posts

✦ Upload media files, such as photos, audio, and video

✦ Invite their friends to view their blog or sign up for their own account

In addition to the necessary security measures, time, and administrative tasks that go into running a community of blogs, you have a few things to worry about. Creating a community increases the resource use, bandwidth, and disk space on your Web server. In many cases, if you go over the allotted limits given to you by your Web host, you will incur great cost. Make sure that you anticipate your bandwidth and disk space needs before running a large network on your Web site! (Don't say we didn't warn you.)

Many WordPress network communities start with grand dreams of being a large and active community — be realistic on how your community will operate in order to make the right hosting choice for yourself and your community.

Small blogging communities are handled easily with a shared-server solution; larger, more active communities should really consider a dedicated server solution for operation. The difference between the two lies in their names:

✦ **Shared-server solution:** You have one account on one server that has several other accounts on it. Think of this as apartment living. One building has several apartments under one roof.

✦ **Dedicated server:** You have one account on one server. The server is dedicated to your account and your account is dedicated to the server. Think of this as owning a home where you don't share your living space with anyone else.

A dedicated-server solution is a more expensive investment for your blog community; a shared-server solution is the most economical. Base your decision regarding which solution to go with for your WordPress network on how big and how active you estimate your community will be. You can move from a shared-server solution to a dedicated-server solution if your community becomes larger than you expect; however, starting with the right solution for your community from day one is best.

Discovering WordPress VIP Services

The company behind the WordPress.com service, Automattic, is owned and operated by WordPress cofounder, Matt Mullenweg. Although Automattic doesn't own the WordPress.org software (as an open source platform, WordPress.org is owned by the community and hundreds of developers that contribute to the core code), Automattic is a driving force behind all things WordPress.

Have a look at the Automattic Web site at `http://automattic.com` (shown in Figure 5-5). The folks behind WordPress own and operate a number of different properties and services, including

✦ **WordPress.com (`http://wordpress.com`):** A hosted WordPress blogging service, discussed previously in this chapter.

✦ **PollDaddy (`http://polldaddy.com`):** A polling and survey software that easily plugs into the WordPress platform.

✦ **VaultPress (`http://vaultpress.com`):** Premium backup and restore service for your blog.

✦ **Akismet (http://akismet.com):** Spam protection for your blog (discussed in Book III, Chapter 5).

✦ **VideoPress (http://videopress.com):** Video hosting and sharing application for WordPress.

✦ **IntenseDebate (http://intensedebate.com):** An integrated commenting system for your WordPress blog.

✦ **Gravatar (http://gravatar.com):** Photos or graphical icons for comment authors (discussed in Book III, Chapter 3).

✦ **Plinky (http://plinky.com):** Even great authors get writer's block from time to time; Plinky gives a daily source of inspiration.

✦ **VIP (http://vip.wordpress.com):** Enterprise level Web hosting and WordPress support starting at $15,000 per year (usually reserved for heavy hitters, such as CNN, BBC, and *Time*, for example).

✦ **P2 (http://p2theme.com):** A unique, free WordPress theme with such features as in-line comments, real-time updates, and a posting form right on the home page so users don't ever touch the Dashboard.

✦ **After the Deadline (http://afterthedeadline.com):** A fancy and useful spelling and grammar checker for WordPress with such features as contextual spell checking, advanced style checking, and intelligent grammar checking.

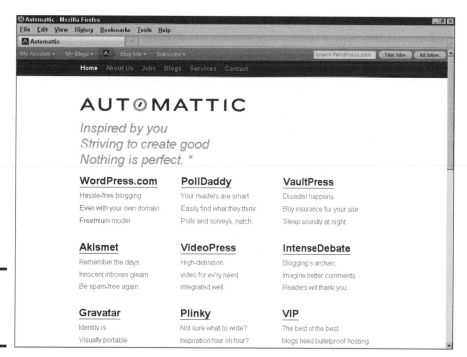

Figure 5-5:
The
Automattic
Web site.

Book II

Setting Up the WordPress Software

Contents at a Glance

Chapter 1: Understanding the System Requirements

In This Chapter

- ✔ **Registering a domain name**
- ✔ **Exploring Web hosting environments**
- ✔ **Basic requirements for PHP and MySQL**
- ✔ **Web hosting recommendations for WordPress**
- ✔ **Understanding bandwidth and disk space needs**

Before you can start blogging with WordPress, you have to set up your base camp. Doing so involves more than simply downloading and installing the WordPress software. You also need to establish your *domain* (your blog address) and your *Web hosting service* (the place that houses your blog). Although you initially download your WordPress software onto your hard drive, you install it on a Web host.

Obtaining a Web server and installing software on it is something you may already have done on your site; in which case, you can move on to the next chapter. If you haven't installed WordPress, you must first consider many factors, as well as cope with a learning curve, because setting up your blog through a hosting service involves using some technologies that you may not feel comfortable with. This chapter takes you through the basics of those technologies, and by the last page of this chapter, you'll have WordPress successfully installed on a Web server with your own domain name.

Establishing Your Domain

You've read all the hype. You've heard all the rumors. You've seen the flashy blogs on the Web powered by WordPress. But where do you start?

The first steps toward installing and setting up a WordPress blog are making a decision about a domain name and then purchasing the registration of that name through a domain registrar. A *domain name* is the *unique* Web address that you type in a Web browser's address bar to visit a Web site. Some examples of domain names are `WordPress.org` and `Google.com`.

Domain names: Do you own or rent?

When you "buy" a domain name, you don't really own it. Rather, you're purchasing the right to use that domain name for the time specified in your order. You can register a domain name for one year or up to ten years. Be aware, however, if you don't renew the domain name when your registration period ends, you lose it — and most often, you lose it right away to someone who preys on abandoned or expired domain names. Some people keep a close watch on expiring domain names, and as soon as the buying window opens, they snap the names up and start using them for their own Web sites, in the hope of taking full advantage of the popularity that the previous owners worked so hard to attain for those domains.

I emphasize *unique* because no two domain names can be the same. If someone else has registered the domain name you want, you can't have it. With that in mind, it sometimes takes a bit of time to find a domain that isn't already in use.

Understanding domain name extensions

When registering a domain name, be aware of the *extension* that you want. The .com, .net, .org, .info, or .biz extension that you see tagged on to the end of any domain name is the *top-level domain extension*. When you register your domain name, you're asked to choose the extension you want for your domain (as long as it's available, that is).

A word to the wise here: Just because you registered your domain as a .com doesn't mean that someone else doesn't, or can't, own the very same domain name with a .net. Therefore, if you register MyDogHasFleas.com, and the site becomes hugely popular among readers with dogs that have fleas, someone else can come along, register MyDogHasFleas.net, and run a similar site to yours in the hope of riding the coattails of your Web site's popularity and readership.

If you want to avert this problem, you can register your domain name with all available extensions. My business Web site, for example, has the domain name EWebscapes.com; however, I also own EWebscapes.net, EWebscapes.biz, and EWebscapes.info.

Considering the cost of a domain name

Registering a domain costs you anywhere from $3 to $30 per year, depending on what service you use for a registrar and what options (such as privacy options and search engine submission services) you apply to your domain name during the registration process.

When you pay the domain registration fee today, you need to pay another registration fee when the renewal date comes up again in a year, or two, or five — however many years you chose to register your domain name for. (See the nearby "Domain names: Do you own or rent?" sidebar.) Most registrars give you the option of signing up for a service called Auto Renew to automatically renew your domain name and bill the charges to the credit card you set up on that account. The registrar sends you a reminder a few months in advance, telling you it's time to renew. If you don't have Auto Renew set up, you need to log in to your registrar account before it expires and manually renew your domain name.

Registering your domain name

Domain registrars are certified and approved by the Internet Corporation for Assigned Names and Numbers (ICANN). Although hundreds of domain registrars exist, the ones in the following list are popular because of their longevity in the industry, competitive pricing, and the variety of services they offer in addition to domain name registration (such as Web hosting and Web site traffic builders):

✦ **GoDaddy:** `http://godaddy.com`

✦ **Register.com:** `http://register.com`

✦ **Network Solutions:** `http://networksolutions.com`

✦ **NamesDirect:** `http://namesdirect.com`

No matter where you choose to register your domain name, here are the steps you can take to accomplish this task:

1. **Decide on a domain name.**

Doing a little planning and forethought here is necessary. Many people think of a domain name as a *brand* — a way of identifying their Web sites or blogs. Think of potential names for your site and then proceed with your plan.

2. **Verify the domain name's availability.**

In your Web browser, enter the URL of the domain registrar of your choice. Look for the section on the registrar's Web site that lets you enter the domain name (typically, a short text field) to see whether it's available. If the domain name isn't available as a `.com`, try `.net` or `.info`.

3. **Purchase the domain name.**

Follow the domain registrar's steps to purchase the name, using your credit card. After you complete the checkout process, you receive an e-mail confirming your purchase, so be sure to use a valid e-mail address during the registration process.

The next step is obtaining a hosting account, which we cover in the next section.

 Some of the domain registrars have hosting services that you can sign up for, but you don't have to use those services. Often, you can find hosting services for a lower cost than most domain registrars offer. It just takes a little research.

Finding a Home for Your Blog

After you register your domain, you need to find a place for it to live — a Web host. Web hosting is the second piece of the puzzle that you need to complete before you begin working with WordPress.org.

A *Web host* is a business, a group, or an individual that provides Web server space and bandwidth for file transfer to Web site owners who don't have it. Usually, Web hosting services charge a monthly or annual fee — unless you're fortunate enough to know someone who's willing to give you server space and bandwidth free. The cost varies from host to host, but you can obtain quality Web hosting services for $3 to $10 per month to start.

When discussing Web hosting considerations, it is important to understand where your hosting account ends and WordPress begins. Support for the WordPress software may or may not be included in your hosting package.

Some Web hosts consider WordPress to be a *third-party application*. This means that the host typically won't provide technical support on the use of WordPress (or any other software application) because software support generally isn't included in your hosting package. The Web host supports your hosting account but, typically, doesn't support the software you choose to install.

On the other hand, if your Web host supports the software on your account, it comes at a cost: You have to pay for that extra support. To find whether your chosen host supports WordPress, ask first. If your host doesn't offer software support, you can still find WordPress support in the support forums at `http://wordpress.org/support`, as shown in Figure 1-1.

 Several Web hosting providers also have WordPress-related services available for additional fees. These services can include technical support, plugin installation and configuration, and theme design.

Generally, hosting services provide (at least) these services with your account:

✦ Hard drive space

✦ Bandwidth (transfer)

✦ Domain e-mail with Web mail access

✦ File Transfer Protocol (FTP) access

✦ Comprehensive Web site statistics

✦ MySQL database(s)

✦ PHP

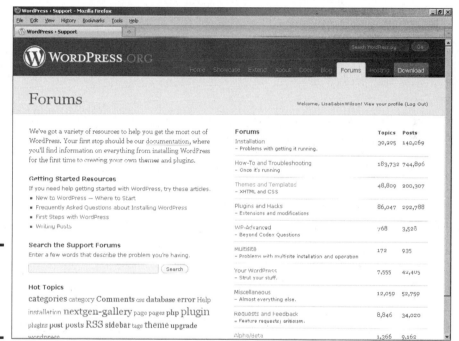

Figure 1-1:
The
WordPress
support
forums.

Because you intend to run WordPress on your Web server, you need to look for a host that provides the *minimum* requirements needed to run the software on your hosting account, which are

✦ PHP version 4.3 (or greater)

✦ MySQL version 4.0 (or greater)

The easiest way to find whether a host meets the minimum requirement is to check the FAQ (Frequently Asked Questions) section of the host's Web site, if it has one. If not, find the contact information for the hosting company, and fire off an e-mail requesting information on exactly what it supports. Any Web host worth dealing with will answer your e-mail within a reasonable amount of time (12–24 hours is a good barometer).

If the technojargon confuses you — specifically, all that talk about PHP, MySQL and FTP in this section — don't worry! Chapter 2 of this minibook gives you an in-depth look into what FTP is and how you will use it on your Web server; Book II, Chapter 3 introduces you to the basics of PHP and MySQL. Become more comfortable with these topics because we discuss them frequently.

Getting help with hosting WordPress

The popularity of WordPress has given birth to Web services — including WordPress designers, WordPress consultants, and (yes) Web hosts — that specialize in using WordPress.

Many of these hosts offer a full array of WordPress features, such as an automatic WordPress installation included with your account, a library of WordPress themes, and a staff of support technicians who are very experienced in using WordPress.

Here is a list of some of those providers:

✦ **Blogs About Hosting:** `http://blogs-about.com` (shown in Figure 1-2)

✦ **Laughing Squid:** `http://laughingsquid.net`

✦ **BlueHost:** `http://bluehost.com`

✦ **DreamHost:** `http://dreamhost.com`

A few Web hosting providers offer free domain name registration when you sign up for hosting services. Research this topic and read their terms of service because that free domain name may come with conditions. Many of our clients have gone this route, only to find out a few months later that the Web hosting provider has full control of the domain name, and the client can't move that domain off the host's servers, either for a set period (usually, a year or two) or for infinity. It's always best to have the control in *your* hands, not someone else's, so try to stick with an independent domain registrar, such as Network Solutions.

Dealing with disk space and bandwidth

Web hosting services provide two very important things with your account:

✦ **Disk space:** The amount of space you can access on the Web servers' hard drive; generally measured in megabytes (MB) or gigabytes (GB).

✦ **Bandwidth transfer:** The amount of transfer your site can do per month; typically, traffic is measured in gigabytes (GB).

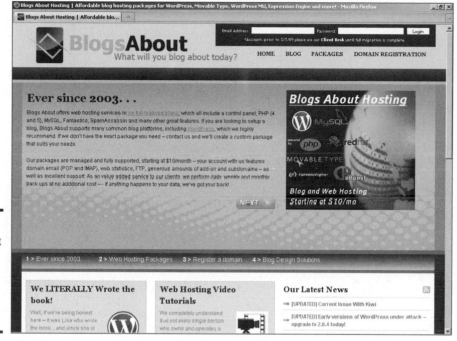

Book II
Chapter 1

Understanding
the System
Requirements

Figure 1-2:
Blogs About
Hosting
run by your
author,
Lisa Sabin-
Wilson.

Think of your Web host as a garage that you pay to park your car in. The garage gives you the place to store your car (disk space). It even gives you the driveway so that you, and others, can get to and from your car (bandwidth). It won't, however, fix your rockin' stereo system (WordPress or any other third-party software application) that you've installed — unless you're willing to pay a few extra bucks for that service.

Most Web hosting providers give you access to a hosting account manager that allows you to log in to your Web hosting account to manage services. cPanel is perhaps the most popular management interface, but Plesk and NetAdmin are still widely used. These management interfaces give you access to your server logs where you can view such things as bandwidth and hard disk usage. Get into a habit of checking those things occasionally to make sure that you stay informed about how much usage your site is using. Typically, I check monthly.

Managing disk space

Disk space is nothing more complicated than the hard drive on your own computer. Each hard drive has the capacity, or space, for a certain amount of files. An 80GB (gigabyte) hard drive can hold 80GB of data — no more. Your hosting account provides you a limited amount of disk space, and the same concept applies. If your Web host provides you 10GB of disk space, that's the absolute limit you have. If you want more disk space, you need to upgrade your space limitations. Most Web hosts have a mechanism in place for you to upgrade your allotment.

Starting with a self-hosted WordPress blog doesn't take much disk space at all. A good starting point for disk space is between 3–5GB of storage space. If you find that you need additional space, contact your hosting provider for an upgrade in space.

Choosing the size of your bandwidth pipe

Bandwidth refers to the amount of data that is carried from point A to point B within a specific period (usually, only a second or two). I live out in the country — pretty much the middle of nowhere. The water that comes to my house is provided by a private well that lies buried in the backyard somewhere. Between my house and the well are pipes that bring the water to my house. The pipes provide a free flow of water to our home so that everyone can enjoy their long, hot showers while I labor over dishes and laundry, all at the same time. Lucky me!

The very same concept applies to the bandwidth available with your hosting account. Every Web hosting provider offers a variety of bandwidth limits on the accounts it offers. When I want to view your Web site in my browser window, the bandwidth is essentially the pipe that lets your data flow from your "well" to my computer. The bandwidth limit is similar to the pipe connected to my well: It can hold only a certain amount of water before it reaches maximum capacity and won't bring the water from the well any longer. Your bandwidth pipe size is determined by how much bandwidth your Web host allows for your account — the larger the number, the bigger the pipe. A 50MB bandwidth limit makes for a smaller pipe than a 100MB limit.

Web hosts are pretty generous with the amount of bandwidth they provide in their packages. Like disk space, bandwidth is measured in gigabytes (GB). Bandwidth provision of 10–50GB is generally a respectable amount to run a Web site with a blog.

Web sites that run large files — such as video, audio, or photo files — generally benefit from higher disk space compared with sites that don't involve large files. Keep this point in mind when you're signing up for your hosting account. Planning now will save you a few headaches down the road.

Be wary of hosting providers that offer things like unlimited bandwidth, domains, and disk space. That is a great selling point, but what they don't tell you outright (you may have to look into the fine print of their agreement) is that although they may not put those kinds of limits on you, they will limit your site's CPU usage.

CPU stands for *central processing unit* and is the part of a computer (or Web server in this case) that handles all the data-processing requests sent to your Web servers whenever anyone visits your site. Although you may have unlimited bandwidth to handle a large amount of traffic, if a high spike in traffic increases your site's CPU usage, your host will throttle your site because they limit the CPU use.

What do I mean by *throttle*? I mean they shut it down — they turn it off. Not permanently, though; maybe for only a few minutes to an hour. They do this to kill any connections to your Web server causing the spike in CPU use. They eventually turn your site back on — but the inconvenience happens regularly with many clients across various hosting environments.

When looking into different Web hosting providers, ask about their policy on CPU use and what they do to manage a spike in processing. It's better to know about it upfront, than to find out about it after your site's been throttled.

**Book II
Chapter 1**

Understanding
the System
Requirements

Chapter 2: Using File Transfer Protocol

In This Chapter

✓ Introducing FTP

✓ Understanding file transfer

✓ Exploring easy-to-use FTP clients

✓ Making sense of FTP terminology

✓ Editing files by using FTP

✓ Changing file permissions

Throughout this entire book, you run into the term FTP. FTP (File Transfer Protocol) is a network protocol used to copy files from one host to another over the Internet. With FTP, you can perform various tasks, including uploading and downloading WordPress files, editing files, and changing permissions on files.

Read this chapter to familiarize yourself with FTP, understand what it is and how to use it, and discover some free, easy-to-use FTP clients or programs that make your life as a WordPress Web site owner much easier. If you run across sections in this book that ask you to perform certain tasks by using FTP, you can refer to this chapter to refresh your memory on how to do it, if needed.

Introducing FTP Concepts

This section introduces you to the basic elements of File Transfer Protocol (FTP). The ability to use FTP with your hosting account is a given for almost every Web host on the market today. FTP is a way of moving files from one place to another, such as:

✦ **Uploading:** Transferring files from your local computer to your Web server

✦ **Downloading:** Transferring files from your Web server to your local computer

You can do several other things with FTP, including the following, which we discuss later in this chapter:

✦ **View files:** After you log in via FTP, you can see all the files that are located on your Web server.

✦ **View Date Modified:** You can see the date a file was last modified, which can sometimes be helpful when trying to troubleshoot problems.

✦ **View file size:** You can see the size of each file on your Web server, which is helpful if you need to manage the disk space on your account.

✦ **Edit files:** Almost all FTP clients allow you to open and edit files through the client interface, which is a convenient way to get the job done.

✦ **Change permissions:** Commonly referred to as CHMOD, it controls what type of read/write/execute permissions the files on your Web server have.

FTP is a convenient utility that gives you access to the files located on your Web server, making managing your WordPress Web site a bit easier.

Setting Up FTP on Your Hosting Account

Many Web hosts today offer FTP as part of their hosting packages, so just confirm that your hosting provider makes FTP available to you for your account. In Book II, Chapter 1, we mention the hosting account management interface called cPanel. cPanel is by far the most popular hosting account management software used by hosts on the Web, eclipsing other popular tools, such as Plesk and NetAdmin.

In this chapter, we use cPanel as the example. If your hosting provider gives you a different interface to work with, the concepts are still the same, but you'll need to refer to your hosting provider for the specifics to adapt these directions to your specific environment.

Mostly, the FTP for your hosting account is set up automatically. Figure 2-1 shows you the FTP Accounts page in cPanel — follow these steps to get to this page and set up your FTP account:

1. **Log in to the cPanel for your hosting account.**

Typically, you'll browse to http://*yourdomain*.com/cpanel to bring up the login screen for your cPanel. Enter your specific hosting account username and password in the login fields and click OK.

2. **Browse to the FTP Accounts page.**

Click the FTP Accounts link or icon in your cPanel to open the FTP Accounts page shown in Figure 2-1.

3. View the existing FTP account.

If your hosting provider automatically sets you up with an FTP account, then you will see it listed in the Account Management section. Ninety-nine percent of the time, the default FTP account uses the same username and password combination as your hosting account or the login information you used to log in to your cPanel in Step 1.

**Book II
Chapter 2**

Using File Transfer Protocol

Figure 2-1:
The FTP
Accounts
page within
cPanel.

If the FTP Accounts page doesn't display a default FTP user in the Account Management section, you can create one easily in the Add FTP Account section:

1. Type your desired username in the Login field.

This creates the username of *username@yourdomain*.com (where *username* is the desired username you typed and *yourdomain*.com is your specific domain name).

2. Type your desired password in the Password field.

You can choose to type in your own password or click the Password Generator button to have the server generate a secure password for you. Retype the password in the Password (Again) field to validate.

3. **Check the Strength indicator.**

   The server tells you if your password is Very Weak, Weak, Good, Strong, or Very Strong (refer to Figure 2-1). You want to have a very strong password for your FTP account that's very hard for hackers and malicious Internet users to guess and crack.

4. **Type the directory access for this FTP user.**

   Leaving this field blank gives this new FTP user access to the root level of your hosting account, which, as the site owner, you want. So leave this field blank. (In the future, if you set up FTP accounts for other users, you can lock down their access to your hosting directory by indicating which directory the FTP user has access to.)

5. **Indicate the space limitations in the Quota field.**

   Because you're the site owner, leave the radio button selection to Unlimited. (In the future, if you add a new FTP user, you can limit the amount of space, in Megabytes (MB) by selecting the radio button to the left of the text field and typing the numeric amount in the text box; for example: 50MB.)

6. **Click the Create FTP Account button.**

   A new screen with a message that the account was created successfully appears. Additionally, the settings for this new FTP account appear, which you should copy and paste into a blank text editor window (like Notepad for PC, or TextMate for Mac users). The settings for the FTP account are the connection details you need to connect to your Web server via FTP.

7. **Set the following settings:**

   FTP Username, Password, and FTP Server are specific to your domain and the information you entered in the preceding steps.

   - FTP Username: *username@yourdomain*.com

   - Password: *yourpassword*

   - FTP Server: ftp.*yourdomain*.com

   - FTP Server Port: 21

   - Quota: Unlimited MB

Ninety-nine point nine percent of the time, the FTP Server Port will be 21 — be sure to double-check your FTP settings to make sure that this is the case.

At any time, you can revisit the FTP Accounts page to delete the FTP accounts you've created, change the quota, change the password, and find the connection details specific to that account.

Finding and Using Free and Easy FTP Programs

FTP programs are referred to as FTP *clients* or FTP *client software*. Whatever you decide to call it, an FTP client is software that you use to connect to your Web server to view, open, edit, and transfer files to and from your Web server.

Using FTP to transfer files requires an FTP client. Many FTP clients are available for download. Here are some good (and free) ones:

✦ **WS_FTP:** www.ipswitch.com/_download/wsftphome.asp

✦ **SmartFTP:** www.smartftp.com/download

✦ **FileZilla:** http://sourceforge.net/projects/filezilla

✦ **Cyberduck (for Mac users):** http://cyberduck.ch

✦ **FTP Explorer:** www.ftpx.com

In Book II, Chapter 1, you discover how to obtain a hosting account, and in the previous section of this chapter, you discover how to create an FTP account on your Web server. By following the steps in the previous section, you also have the FTP username, password, server, and port information you need to connect your FTP client to your Web server so you can begin transferring files.

Connecting to the Web Server via FTP

For the purposes of this chapter, we use the FileZilla FTP client (http://sourceforge.net/projects/filezilla) because it's very easy to use, and the cost is free ninety-nine (that's open source geek-speak for free!).

Figure 2-2 shows a FileZilla client that's not connected to a server. By default, the left side of the window displays a directory of files and folders on the local computer.

The right side of the window displays content when the FileZilla client is connected to a Web server, specifically, directories of the Web server's folders and files.

If you use a different FTP client software than FileZilla, the steps and look of the software will differ, and you will need to adapt your steps and practice for the specific FTP client software you are using.

Connecting to a Web server is an easy process. Remember the FTP settings you saved from Step 7 in the previous section? As a reminder, here are the FTP settings from the previous example:

FTP Username: *username@yourdomain*.com

Password: *yourpassword*

FTP Server: ftp.*yourdomain*.com

FTP Server Port: 21

Quota: Unlimited MB

Figure 2-2:
Mozilla
FileZilla
FTP client
software.

This is where you need that information. To connect to your Web server via the FileZilla FTP client, follow these few steps:

1. **Open the FTP client software on your local computer.**

Locate the program on your computer and click (or double-click) the program icon to launch the program.

2. **Choose File⇨Site Manager to open the Site Manager utility.**

The Site Manger utility appears, as shown in Figure 2-3.

3. **Click the New Site button.**

You can give the new site a name, so type a name that helps you identify the site. This site name can be anything you want it to be because it isn't part of the connection data you add in the next steps. (In Figure 2-4, you see My Site — original, we know.)

Figure 2-3:
The Site Manager utility in the FileZilla FTP client software.

4. Enter the FTP server in the Host field.

Host is the same as the FTP server information provided to you when you set up the FTP account on your Web server. In the example, the FTP server is ftp.*yourdomain*.com, so that's entered in the Host field, as shown in Figure 2-4.

5. Enter the FTP port in the Port field.

In the previous example, the FTP port is 21. Typically, in most hosting environments, FTP uses port 21 and this never changes. However, double-check your port number and enter it in the Port field, as shown in Figure 2-4.

6. Select the server type.

FileZilla asks you to select a server type (as do most FTP clients). Select FTP - File Transfer Protocol from the Server Type drop-down menu, as shown in Figure 2-4.

7. Select the logon type.

FileZilla gives you several different logon types to choose from (as do most FTP clients). Select Normal from the Logon Type drop-down menu.

8. Enter your username in the Username field.

This is the username given to you in the FTP settings. In the example, the username is *lisa@yourdomain*.com

9. Type your password in the Password field.

This is the password given to you in the FTP settings. In the example, the password is {W?$s((7Tqi.

Figure 2-4:
FileZilla Site
Manager
utility with
FTP account
information
filled in.

10. **Click the Connect button.**

This connects your computer to your Web server. The directory of folders and files from your local computer display on the left side of the FileZilla FTP client window, and the directory of folders and files on your Web server display on the right side, as shown in Figure 2-5.

Now you can take advantage of all the tools and features FTP has to offer you!

Figure 2-5:
FileZilla
displays
local files on
the left and
server files
on the right.

Transferring files from point A to point B

Now that your local computer is connected to your Web server, transferring files between the two couldn't be easier. Within the FTP client software, you can browse the directories and folders on your local computer on the left side and browse the directories and folders on your Web server on the right side.

FTP clients make it easy to transfer files from your computer to your hosting account by using a drag-and-drop method. Two methods of transferring files are

+ **Uploading:** Generally, transferring files from your local computer to your Web server. To upload a file from your computer to your Web server, click the file you want to transfer from your local computer and drag and drop it onto the right side (the Web server side).

+ **Downloading:** Transferring files from your Web server to your local computer. To download a file from your Web server to your local computer, click the file you want to transfer from your Web server and drag and drop it onto the left side (the local computer side).

Downloading files from your Web server is a very efficient, easy, and smart way of backing up files to your local computer. It's always a good idea to keep your files safe, especially things like theme files and plugins, which we cover in Books VI and VII.

Editing files by using FTP

You will run into situations where you need to edit certain files that live on your Web server. You can use the methods described in the preceding section to download a file, open it, edit it, save it, and then upload it back to your Web server. That is one way to do it. Another way is to use the built-in edit feature that exists in most FTP client software, by following these steps:

1. **Connect the FTP client to your Web server.**

2. **Locate the file you want to edit.**

3. **Open the file by using the internal FTP editor.**

Right-click the file with your mouse and choose View/Edit. (Remember I'm using FileZilla; your FTP client may name it differently, such as Open or Edit.) Usually, the FTP client will use a program that already exists on your computer — such as Notepad for a PC or TextMate for Mac — to edit the files. In some rare cases, your FTP client software may have its own internal text editor. FileZilla uses a program designated for text editing that already exists on your computer.

4. **Edit the file to your liking.**

5. **Save the changes you made to the file.**

   Click the Save icon or choose File⇨Save.

6. **Upload the file to your Web server.**

   After you save the file, FileZilla alerts you that the file has changed and asks whether you want to upload the file to the server. Click the Yes button; the newly edited file will replace the old one.

That's all there is to it. Use the FTP edit feature to edit, save, and upload files as you need to.

When you edit files by using the FTP edit feature, you are editing files in a "live" environment; meaning that when you save the changes and upload the file, the changes take effect immediately and affect your live Web site. For this reason, we strongly recommend downloading a copy of the original file to your local computer before making changes. That way, if you happen to make a typo on the saved file and your Web site goes haywire, you have a copy of the original to upload to restore it to its original state.

Changing file permissions

Every file and folder on your Web server has a set of assigned attributions, called *permissions,* that tells the Web server three things about the folder or file. On a very simplistic level, these permissions include:

✦ **Read:** This setting determines whether the file/folder is readable by the Web server.

✦ **Write:** This setting determines whether the file/folder is writable by the Web server.

✦ **Execute:** This setting determines whether the file/folder is executable by the Web server.

Each set of permissions has a numeric code assigned to it, identifying what type of permissions are assigned to that file or folder. There are a lot of them, so here are the most common ones that you run into when running a WordPress Web site:

✦ **644:** Files with permissions set to 644 are readable by everyone and writable only by the file/folder owner.

✦ **755:** Files with permissions set to 755 are readable and executable by everyone, but only writable by the file/folder owner.

✦ **777:** Files with permissions set to 777 are readable, writable, and executable by everyone. For security reasons, you should not use this set of permissions on your Web server unless absolutely necessary.

Typically, folders and files within your Web server are assigned permissions of either 644 or 755. Usually, you'll see PHP files, or files that end with the .php extension, with permissions set to 644 if the Web server is configured to use PHP Safe Mode.

This is a very basic look at file permissions because, usually, you will not need to mess with file permissions on your Web server. In case you do need to dig further, you can find a great reference on file permissions from Elated.com at http://www.elated.com/articles/understanding-permissions.

You may run across a situation where you're asked to edit and change the file permissions on a particular file on your Web server. With WordPress sites, this usually happens when dealing with plugins or theme files that require files or folders to be writable by the Web server. This practice is referred to as *CHMOD*, an acronym for Change Mode. When someone says, "You need to CHMOD that file to 755," you'll know what they are talking about.

Here are some quick and easy steps for using your FTP program to CHMOD a file, or edit its permissions on your Web server:

1. **Connect the FTP client to your Web server.**

2. **Locate the file you want to CHMOD.**

3. **Open the file attributes for the file.**

Right-click the file on your Web server and choose File Permissions. (Your FTP client, if not FileZilla, may use different terminology.)

4. **The Change File Attributes window appears, as shown in Figure 2-6.**

5. **Type the correct file permissions number in the Numeric Value field.**

This is the number assigned to the permissions you want to give the file. Most often, the plugin or theme developer provides you which permissions number to assign to the file or folder; typically, it will be either 644 or 755. (The permissions in Figure 2-6 are assigned the value of 755.)

6. **Click OK to save the file.**

Book II
Chapter 2

Using File Transfer Protocol

Figure 2-6:
The Change File Attributes window in FileZilla.

Chapter 3: Introducing PHP and MySQL

In Book VI, you dig into the code necessary to create functions and features on your Web site. Many, if not all, of these functions and features use Hypertext Preprocessor (PHP) tags. When combined with the WordPress code, these tags make things happen (such as displaying post content, categories, archives, links, and more) on your Web site.

One of the reasons WordPress is the most popular content management system (CMS) is that you don't need to know PHP code to use it. That's to say, you can use WordPress easily without ever looking at any of the code or template files contained within it. However, if you want to tweak the settings of your WordPress theme (flip to Book VI) or the code of a particular plugin (see Book VII), you need to understand some basics of how PHP works. But don't worry; you don't need to be a PHP programmer.

This chapter introduces you to the very basics of PHP and *MySQL,* which is the database system that stores your WordPress data. After you read this chapter, you'll understand how PHP and MySQL work together with the WordPress platform to serve up your Web site in visitors' browsers.

This book doesn't turn you into a PHP programmer or MySQL database administrator, but it gives you a glimpse of how PHP and MySQL work together to help WordPress build your Web site. If you're interested in finding out how to program PHP or become a MySQL database administrator, check out *PHP and MySQL For Dummies* by Janet Valade (Wiley).

Understanding How PHP and MySQL Work Together

WordPress uses a PHP/MySQL platform, which provides everything you need to create your own blog and publish your own content dynamically, without knowing how to program those pages. In short, all your content is stored in a MySQL database in your hosting account.

PHP is a server-side scripting language for creating dynamic Web pages. When a visitor opens a page built in PHP, the server processes the PHP commands and then sends the results to the visitor's browser. *MySQL* is an open source relational database management system (RDBMS) that uses *Structured Query Language (SQL),* the most popular language for adding, accessing, and processing data in a database. If that all sounds like Greek to you, just think of MySQL as a big file cabinet where all the content on your blog is stored.

Every time a visitor goes to your blog to read your content, he makes a request that's sent to a host server. The PHP programming language receives that request, makes a call to the MySQL database, obtains the requested information from the database, and then presents the requested information to your visitor through his Web browser.

Here *content* refers to the data stored in the MySQL database; that is, your blog posts, pages, comments, links, and options that you set up in the WordPress Dashboard. However, the *theme* (or design) you choose to use for your blog — whether it's the default theme, one you create, or one you have custom designed — isn't part of the content in this case. Theme files are part of the file system and aren't stored in the database. Therefore, it's a good idea to create and keep a backup of any theme files that you're currently using. See Book VI for further information on WordPress theme management.

When you look for a hosting service, keep an eye out for the hosts that provide daily backups of your site so that your content (data) won't be lost in case something happens. Web hosting providers who offer daily backups as part of their services can save the day by restoring your site to its original form. Additionally, Book II, Chapter 5 covers important information about backing up your Web site.

Exploring PHP Basics

WordPress requires PHP in order to work; therefore, your Web hosting provider must have PHP enabled on your Web server. If you already have WordPress up and running on your Web site, you know PHP is running and working just fine. Currently, the PHP version required for WordPress is version 4.3 or later.

In the very near future, WordPress will drop support for PHP version 4. When this happens, version 5 will be the only version supported by the WordPress platform. Ask your Web host to upgrade you to PHP version 5 sooner rather than later because most WordPress developers (for plugins, themes, and so on) base their development practices on PHP version 5.

Before you play around with template tags (covered in Book VI) in your WordPress templates or plugin functions, you need to understand what makes up a template tag and why, as well as the correct syntax, or function, for a template tag as it relates to PHP. Additionally, have a look at the WordPress files contained within the download files. Many of the files end with the .php file extension — an extension required for PHP files, which separates them from other file types, such as JavaScript (.js) or CSS (.css).

As we state earlier, WordPress is based in *PHP* (a scripting language for creating Web pages) and uses PHP commands to pull information from the MySQL database. Every tag begins with the function to start PHP and ends with a function to stop it. In the middle of those two commands lives the request to the database that tells WordPress to grab the data and display it.

A typical template tag, or function, looks like this:

```
<?php get_info(); ?>
```

This example tells WordPress to do three things:

✦ **Start PHP: <?php**

✦ **Use PHP to get information from the MySQL database and deliver it to your blog: get_info();**

✦ **Stop PHP: ?>**

In this case, get_info() represents the tag function, which grabs information from the database to deliver it to your blog. The information retrieved depends on what tag function appears between the two PHP commands.

Every PHP command you start requires a stop command. For every <?php, you must include the closing ?> command somewhere later in the code. PHP commands structured improperly cause ugly errors on your site, and they've been known to send programmers, developers, and hosting providers into loud screaming fits. You find a lot of starting and stopping of PHP throughout the WordPress templates and functions. The process seems as though it would be resource intensive, if not exhaustive, but it really isn't.

Always, always make sure that the PHP start and stop commands are separated from the function with a single space. You must have a space after <?php and a space before ?> — if not, the PHP function code doesn't work. So make sure that the code looks like this: <?php get_info(); ?> — not like this: <?phpget_info();?>

Trying Out a Little PHP

To test some PHP code, follow these steps to create a simple HTML Web page with an embedded PHP function:

1. **Open a new, blank file in your default text editor — Notepad (Windows) or TextMate (Mac) — type** <html>**, and then press Enter.**

The <html> tag tells the Web browser that this is an HTML document and should be read as a Web page.

2. **Type** <head> **and then press Enter.**

The <head> HTML tag contains elements that tell the Web browser about the document; this information is read by the browser but hidden from the Web page visitor.

3. **Type** <title>This is a Simple PHP Page</title> **and then press Enter.**

The <title> HTML tag tells the browser to display the text between two tags as the title of the document in the browser title bar. (***Note:*** All HTML tags need to be opened and then closed, just like PHP tags that we describe in the preceding section. In this case the <title> tag opens the command, and the </title> tag closes it and tells the Web browser that you're finished dealing with the title).

4. **Type** </head> **to close the <head> tag from Step 2 and then press Enter.**

5. **Type** <body> **to define the body of the Web page and then press Enter.**

Anything that appears after this tag displays in the Web browser window.

6. **Type** <?php **to tell the Web browser to start a PHP function and then press Enter.**

See the preceding section on starting and stopping PHP functions.

7. **Type** echo '<p>Testing my new PHP function</p>'; **and then press Enter.**

This is the function that you want PHP to execute on your Web page. This particular function echoes the text "Testing my new PHP function" and displays it on your Web site.

8. **Type** ?> **to tell the Web browser to end the PHP function and then press Enter.**

9. **Type </body> to close the <body> HTML tag from Step 5 and then press Enter.**

   This tells the Web browser that you're done with the body of the Web page.

10. **Type </html> to close the <html> tag from Step 1 and then press Enter.**

    This tells the Web browser that you're at the end of the HTML document.

When you're done with Steps 1–10, double-check that the code in your text editor looks like this:

```
<html>
<head>
<title>This is a Simple PHP Page</title>
    </head>
    <body>
    <?php echo '<p>Testing my new PHP function</p>'; ?>
    </body>
    </html>
```

**Book II
Chapter 3**

Introducing PHP
and MySQL

After you write your code, follow these steps to save and upload your file:

1. **Save the file to your local computer as testing.php.**

2. **Upload the testing.php file.**

   Via File Transfer Protocol, upload testing.php to the root directory of your Web server. If you need a review on how to use FTP to transfer files to your web server, review the information presented in Book II, Chapter 2.

3. **Open a Web browser and type the address (**http://*yourdomain*.com/ testing.php**) in the Web browser's address bar (where *yourdomain* is your actual domain name).**

   A single line of text displays: Testing my new PHP function, as shown in Figure 3-1.

If the testing.php file displays correctly in your browser, congratulations! You programmed PHP to work in a Web browser!

If the testing.php file doesn't display correctly in your browser, a PHP error message will give you an indication of the errors in your code. (Usually included with the error message is the line number where the error exists in the file.)

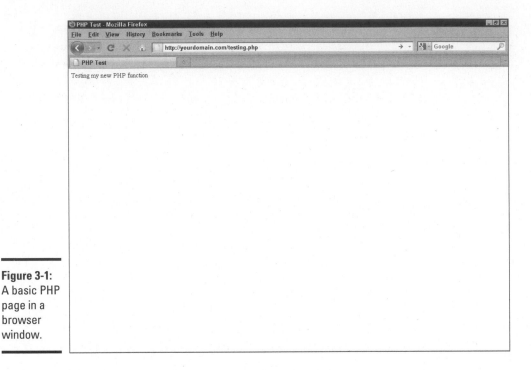

Figure 3-1:
A basic PHP page in a browser window.

Managing Your MySQL Database

Many new WordPress users are intimidated by the MySQL database, perhaps because it seems to be way above their technical skills or abilities. Truth be told, regular users of WordPress — those who just use it to publish content — don't really ever have to dig into the database unless they want to. You only need to explore the database if you're dealing with theme or plugin development, or with contributing code to the WordPress project. In this section, we give you a basic overview of the WordPress database stored in MySQL so that you have an understanding of the structure and know where items are stored.

Currently, WordPress requires MySQL version 4.1.2 (or greater) in order to work correctly. If your Web hosting provider doesn't have 4.1.2 (or greater) installed on your Web server, kindly ask to upgrade.

After WordPress is installed on your server (which I discuss in Chapter 4 of this minibook), the database gets populated with 11 tables that exist to store different types of data from your WordPress blog. Figure 3-2 displays the structure of the tables, as follows:

✦ **wp_commentmeta:** This table stores every comment published to your site contains information, or *metadata,* that includes

- A unique comment ID number

- A comment meta key, meta value, and meta ID (unique numerical identifiers assigned to each comment left by you, or visitors, on your site)

✦ **wp_comments:** This table stores the body of the comments published to your site, including

- A post ID that specifies which post the comment belongs to

- The comment content

- The comment author's name, URL, IP address, and e-mail address

- The comment date (day, month, year, and time)

- The comment status (approved, unapproved, or spam)

✦ **wp_links:** This stores the name, URL, and description of all Links you create by using the WordPress Link Manager. It also stores all the advanced options for the links you created, if any.

✦ **wp_options:** This stores all the option settings that you set for WordPress after you install it, including all theme and plugin option settings.

✦ **wp_postmeta:** This includes all posts or pages published to your site and contains metadata that includes

- The unique post ID number. (Each blog post has a unique ID number to set it apart from the others.)

- The post meta key, meta value (unique numerical identifiers for each post created on your site), and any custom fields you've created for the post.

✦ **wp_posts:** This table features the body of any post or page you've published to your blog, including autosaved revisions and post option settings, such as

- The post author, date, and time

- The post title, content, and excerpt

- The post status (published, draft, or private)

- The post comment status (open or closed)

- The post type (page, post, or custom post type)

- The post comment count

✦ **wp_terms:** This stores the categories you've created for posts and links as well as tags that have been created for your posts.

Figure 3-2:
The
WordPress
database
structure.

✦ **wp_term_relationships:** This stores the relationships among the posts as well as the categories and tags that have been assigned to them.

✦ **wp_term_taxonomies:** WordPress has three types of taxonomies by default: category, link, and tag. This table stores the taxonomy associated for the terms stored in the wp_terms table.

✦ **wp_usermeta:** This table features metadata from every user with an account on your WordPress Web site. This metadata includes

   • A unique user ID

   • A user meta key, meta value, and meta ID, which are unique identifiers for users on your site

✦ **wp_users:** The list of users with an account on your WordPress Web site is maintained within this table and includes

   • The username, first name, last name, and nickname

   • The user login

   • The user password

- The user e-mail

- The registration date

- The user status and role (subscriber, contributor, author, editor, or administrator)

Most Web hosting providers give you a *utility,* or an interface, to view your MySQL database, and the most common one is phpMyAdmin (as shown in Figure 3-2). If you're unsure how you can view your database on your hosting account, get in touch with your hosting provider to find out.

When the Multisite feature in WordPress is activated (check out Book VIII for information about the Multisite feature), WordPress adds six additional tables in the database:

✦ `wp_blogs:` This table stores information about each blog created in your network, including

- A unique blog numerical ID

- A unique site ID number (determines the ID of the site the blog belongs to)

- The blog domain

- The blog server path

- The date the blog was registered

- The date the blog was updated

- The blog status (public, private, archived, spam; see Book VIII for more information on blog status)

✦ `wp_blog_versions:` This table stores general information about each network blog ID, database version, and date of last update.

✦ `wp_registration_log:` This table stores information about registered users, including

- Unique user numerical ID

- User e-mail address

- Users IP address

- Users Blog ID

- The date the user registered

✦ **wp_signups:** This table stores information about user sign-ups that includes all the information from the `wp_registration_log` table, the date the user account was activated, and the unique activation key the user accessed during the sign-up process.

✦ **wp_site:** This table stores information about your main installation site including the site ID, domain, and server path.

✦ **wp_sitemeta:** This table stores all the information about the Multisite configurations set after you install the Multisite feature. See Book VIII.

Chapter 4: Installing WordPress on Your Web Server

In This Chapter

✔ **Installing WordPress via Fantastico**

✔ **Manually installing WordPress**

✔ **Running installation scripts**

*T*his chapter takes you through two installation methods for WordPress — an automatic, one-click installation with the Fantastico script installer, which is available from your Web hosting provider, and manual installation.

I also show you how to set up a MySQL database by using the cPanel Web hosting management interface. By the time you're done reading this chapter, you'll be logged in to and looking at your brand-spanking-new WordPress Dashboard, ready to start publishing content right away (if you already have WordPress installed, go ahead and skip to Chapter 5 in this minibook, which contains great information about configuring WordPress for optimum performance and security).

Installing the WordPress Files

Before you're ready to install WordPress, the following needs to be done:

✦ Purchase the domain name registration for your account (Chapter 1 of this minibook).

✦ Obtain a hosting service on a Web server for your blog (Chapter 1 of this minibook).

✦ Establish your hosting account username, password, and File Transfer Protocol (FTP) address (Chapters 1 and 2 of this minibook).

✦ Acquire an FTP client for transferring files to your hosting account (Chapter 2 of this minibook).

If you omitted any of the preceding items, flip to the chapter listed to complete the step.

Using Fantastico to install WordPress

Fantastico is a very popular script installer that several Web hosting providers make available to their clients. Fantastico contains different types of scripts and programs that you can install on your hosting account, notably, the WordPress software.

Here we make a few assumptions about your hosting environment:

✦ Your hosting provider has Fantastico available for your use.

✦ Your hosting account has the cPanel account management interface.

If your hosting provider doesn't give you access to an installation script, such as Fantastico, skip to the next section in this chapter for the steps to install WordPress manually, via FTP.

Follow these steps to install WordPress with Fantastico:

1. **Log in to the cPanel for your hosting account:**

   a. *Browse to* `http://yourdomain.com/cpanel` *(where* yourdomain. com *is your actual domain name) to bring up the cPanel login screen.*

   b. *Enter your specific hosting account username and password in the login fields and then click OK. The page refreshes and displays the cPanel for your account.*

2. **Click the Fantastico icon.**

   The Fantastico page loads in your browser window and displays a list of available scripts on the left side of the page, as shown in Figure 4-1.

3. **Click the WordPress link in the Blogs heading.**

   The WordPress page loads, displaying a short description of WordPress and the version that's available with Fantastico. (See Figure 4-2.)

Fantastico is a third-party script that exists as an add-on to cPanel. Web hosts subscribe to Fantastico and add it to your cPanel as an extra service for you to take advantage of; however, Web hosting providers do not control which scripts, or which versions of scripts, are available within Fantastico. Web hosts are completely dependent upon the makers of Fantastico as to what scripts and script versions are available. Fantastico is usually about a month or so behind the game when updating the programs in its script installer.

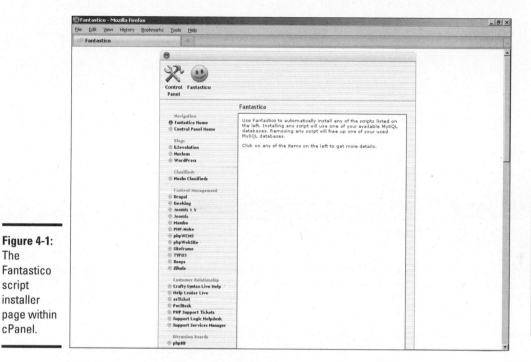

Figure 4-1:
The
Fantastico
script
installer
page within
cPanel.

Figure 4-2:
The
WordPress
page in
Fantastico.

4. **Click the New Installation link.**

The Install WordPress (1/3) page, shown in Figure 4-3, displays.

5. **Select the WordPress installation location by choosing the domain you want to install WordPress on from the Install on Domain drop-down list.**

6. **Type the directory name for installation in the Install in Directory text field.**

Leave this text field empty to install WordPress in the root directory (`http://yourdomain.com`), or enter the name of the directory you want to install WordPress into, such as `http://yourdomain.com/wordpress`. If you type in this text field, the directory should *not* exist on your Web server; if it does, Fantastico tells you that WordPress can't be installed.

7. **Provide the Admin Access Data info by typing the desired username in the Administrator Username text field and then typing your desired password in the Password text field.**

These two items are the username and password for the WordPress administrator, and you use them to log in to the WordPress Dashboard after it's installed (See Book III, Chapter 1).

Figure 4-3:
WordPress access and administrator data in Fantastico.

8. **Provide the Base Configuration info for WordPress.**

The information you enter in this section can be changed later in the general settings of the WordPress Dashboard (after it's installed and you've logged in). Enter the info as follows:

a. Type your desired nickname in the Admin Nickname text field.

This name displays on your Web site after you start publishing to your WordPress blog.

b. Type your e-mail address in the Admin E-Mail text field.

This e-mail address is used for your administrator user account in WordPress, after it's installed on your Web server in Step 9.

c. Type your site name in the Site Name text field.

The site name displays on your site, and can be changed later, if you want.

d. Type a short description of your site in the Description text field.

The description displays on your site, and can be changed later, if you want.

9. **Click the Install WordPress button.**

The Install WordPress (2/3) page displays with several messages. The Fantastico script installer creates the MySQL database for you and displays the name of the database. This page also displays a confirmation message on the domain and directory that WordPress is installed into.

10. **Click the Finish Installation button.**

The page refreshes in your browser and Fantastico displays a message confirming the success of the WordPress installation and displays the login URL, username, and password.

If you enter your own e-mail address in the Email the Details of This Installation To text field and then click the Send E-mail button, the URL, username, and password are sent to your inbox for safe storage. (This is an optional feature, but we strongly recommend doing this in case your browser crashes and you lose the information.)

Your WordPress installation via Fantastico is complete, and you're ready to start using WordPress on your Web server. If you installed WordPress by using the Fantastico method and don't want to review the steps to install WordPress manually, flip to Chapter 5 in this minibook to optimize your WordPress installation for performance and security.

Installing WordPress manually

If you install WordPress manually, here's where the rubber meets the road — that is, you're putting WordPress's famous five-minute installation to the test. Set your watch and see whether you can meet that deadline.

The famous five-minute installation includes only the time it takes to install the software. This doesn't include the time to register a domain name; the time to obtain and set up your Web hosting service; or the time to download, install, configure, and figure out how to use the FTP software.

Setting up the MySQL database

The WordPress software is a personal publishing system that uses a PHP/MySQL platform, which provides everything you need to create your own blog and publish your own content dynamically without knowing how to program those pages. In short, all your content (options, posts, comments, and other pertinent data) is stored in a MySQL database in your hosting account.

Every time visitors go to your blog to read your content, they make a request that's sent to your server. The PHP programming language receives that request, obtains the requested information from the MySQL database, and then presents the requested information to your visitors through their Web browsers.

Every Web host is different in how it gives you access to set up and manage your MySQL database(s) for your account. In this section, we use the popular hosting cPanel interface. If your host provides a different interface, the same basic steps apply; however, the setup in the interface that your Web host provides may be different.

To set up the MySQL database for your WordPress site with cPanel, follow these steps:

1. **Log in to the cPanel for your hosting account:**

   a. *Browse to* `http://yourdomain.com/cpanel` *(where* yourdomain. com *is your actual domain name) to bring up the login screen for your cPanel.*

   b. *Enter your specific hosting account username and password in the login fields, and then click OK. The page refreshes and displays the cPanel for your account.*

2. **Locate the MySQL Databases icon.**

   Click the MySQL Databases icon to load the MySQL Databases page in your cPanel.

3. **Enter a name for your database in the Name text box.**

   Be sure to make note of the database name because you need it to install WordPress.

4. **Click the Create Database button.**

   A message appears confirming that the database was created.

5. **Click the Go Back link or the Back button on your browser toolbar.**

   The MySQL Databases page displays in your browser window.

6. **Locate MySQL Users on the MySQL Databases page.**

   Scroll to the approximate middle of the page to locate this section.

7. **Choose a username and password for your database, enter them in the Username and Password text boxes, and then click the Create User button.**

   A confirmation message appears stating that the username was created with the password you specified.

For security reasons, make sure that your password isn't something that sneaky hackers can easily guess. Give your database a name that you'll remember later. This practice is especially helpful if you run more than one MySQL database in your account. For instance, if you name a database *WordPress* or *wpblog,* you can be reasonably certain a year from now when you want to access your database to make some configuration changes that you know exactly which credentials to use.

Make sure that you note the database name, username, and password that you set up during this process. You need them in the section "Running the installation script" later in this chapter before officially installing WordPress on your Web server. Jot them down on a piece of paper, or copy and paste them into a text editor window; either way, make sure that you have them handy.

8. **Click the Go Back link or the Back button on your browser toolbar.**

   The MySQL Databases page displays in your browser window.

9. **In the Add Users to Database section of the MySQL Databases page, choose the user you just set up from the User drop-down list and then choose the new database from the Database drop-down list.**

   The MySQL Account Maintenance, Manage User Privileges page appears in cPanel.

10. **Assign user privileges by selecting the All Privileges check box.**

    Because you're the *administrator* (or owner) of this database, you need to make sure that you assign all privileges to the new user you just created.

11. **Click the Make Changes button.**

    A page opens with a confirmation message that you've added your selected user to the selected database.

12. **Click the Go Back link or the Back button on your browser toolbar.**

    You return to the MySQL Databases page.

The MySQL database for your WordPress Web site is complete and you're ready to proceed to the final step of installing the software on your Web server.

Downloading the WordPress software

Without further ado, get the latest version of the WordPress software at `http://wordpress.org/download`.

WordPress gives you two compression formats for the software: `.zip` and `.tar.gz`. We recommend getting the Zip file because it's the most common format for compressed files and both Windows and Mac operating systems can use the format. Generally, the `.tar.gz` file format is used for Unix operating systems.

Download the WordPress software to your computer and then *decompress* (unpack or unzip) it to a folder on your computer's hard drive. These steps begin the installation process for WordPress. Having the program on your own computer isn't enough, however. You also need to *upload* (or transfer) it to your Web server account (the one you obtained in Chapter 1 of this minibook).

Before you install WordPress on your Web server, you need to make sure that you have the MySQL database set up and ready to accept the WordPress installation. Be sure that you've followed the preceding steps to set up your MySQL database before proceeding.

Uploading the WordPress files via FTP

To upload the WordPress files to your host, return to the /wordpress folder (shown in Figure 4-4) on your computer where you unpacked the WordPress software that you downloaded earlier. If you need a review on using FTP (File Transfer Protocol) to transfer files from your computer to your Web server, review Chapter 2 in this minibook.

Using your FTP client, connect to your Web server, and upload all these files to your hosting account, into the root directory.

Figure 4-4:
WordPress
installation
files to be
uploaded to
your Web
server.

If you don't know what your root directory is, contact your hosting provider and ask, "What is my root directory for my account?" Every hosting provider's setup is different. On Lisa's Web server, her root directory is the `public_html` folder; some of her clients have a root directory in an `httpdocs` folder. The answer really depends on what type of setup your hosting provider has. When in doubt, ask!

Here are a few things to keep in mind when you upload your files:

✦ **Upload the *contents* of the /wordpress folder to your Web server —
   not the folder** itself. Most FTP client software lets you select all the files and drag and drop them to your Web server. Other programs have you highlight the files and click a Transfer button.

✦ **Choose the correct transfer mode.** File transfers via FTP have two forms: ASCII and binary. Most FTP clients are configured to autodetect the transfer mode. Understanding the difference as it pertains to this WordPress installation is important so that you can troubleshoot any problems you have later:

   • *Binary transfer mode* is how images (such as JPG, GIF, BMP, and PNG files) are transferred via FTP.

- *ASCII transfer mode* is for everything else (text files, PHP files, JavaScript, and so on).

  For the most part, it's a safe bet to make sure that the transfer mode of your FTP client is set to autodetect. But if you experience issues with how those files load on your site, retransfer the files by using the appropriate transfer mode.

✦ **You can choose a different folder from the root.** You aren't required to transfer the files to the root directory of your Web server. You can choose to run WordPress on a subdomain or in a different folder on your account. If you want your blog address to be `http://yourdomain.com/blog`, you transfer the WordPress files into a `/blog` folder (where *yourdomain* is your domain name).

✦ **Choose the right file permissions.** *File permissions* tell the Web server how these files can be handled on your server — whether they're files that can be written to. Generally, PHP files need to have a permission (`Chmod` is explained in Chapter 2 of this minibook) of 666, whereas file folders need a permission of 755. Almost all FTP clients let you check and change the permissions on the files, if you need to. Typically, you can find the option to change file permissions within the menu options of your FTP client.

Some hosting providers run their PHP software in a more secure format — *safe mode.* If this is the case with your host, you need to set the PHP files to 644. If you're unsure, ask your hosting provider what permissions you need to set for PHP files.

Running the installation script

The final step in the installation procedure for WordPress is connecting the WordPress software you uploaded to the MySQL database. Follow these steps:

1. **Type the URL of your Web site into the address bar in your Web browser.**

   If you chose to install WordPress in a different folder from the root directory of your account, make sure you indicate that in the URL for the install script. For example, if you transferred the WordPress software files to the `/blog` folder, for example, you point your browser to the following URL to run the installation: `http://yourdomain.com/blog/wp-admin/install.php`. If WordPress is in the root directory, use the following URL to run the installation: `http://yourdomain.com/wp-admin/install.php` (where *yourdomain* is your domain name).

   Assuming that you did everything correctly (see Table 4-1 for help with common installation problems), you see the message shown in Figure 4-5.

There doesn't seem to be a `wp-config.php` file. I need this before we can get started. Need more help? We got it. You can create a `wp-config.php` file through a web interface, but this doesn't work for all server setups. The safest way is to manually create the file.

Create a Configuration File

2. **Click the Create a Configuration File button.**

    The Welcome to WordPress page appears, giving you the information you need to proceed with the installation.

3. **Click the Let's Go button at the bottom of that page.**

4. **Dig out the database name, username, and password that you saved in the earlier section "Setting up the MySQL database," and use that information to fill in the following fields, as shown in Figure 4-6:**

    • *Database Name:* Type the database name you used when you created the MySQL database before this installation. Because hosts differ in configurations, you need to enter the database name by itself or a combination of your username and the database name, separated by an underscore mark (_).

      If you named your database *wordpress,* for example, you enter that in this text box. If your host requires you to append the database name with your hosting account username, you enter **username_ wordpress**, substituting your hosting username for *username.* Lisa's username is *lisasabin,* so she enters lisasabin_wordpress.

    • *User Name:* Type the username you used when you created the MySQL database before this installation. Depending on what your host requires, you may need to enter a combination of your hosting account username and the database username separated by an underscore mark (_). In Figure 4-6, you can see both: `lisasabin_username`.

    • *Password:* Type the password you used when you set up the MySQL database. You don't need to append the password to your hosting account username here.

Figure 4-6:
Entering the
database
name,
username,
and
password.

- *Database Host*: Ninety-nine percent of the time, you leave this field set to `localhost`. Some hosts, depending on their configurations, have different hosts set for the MySQL database server. If `localhost` doesn't work, you need to contact your hosting provider to find out the MySQL database host.

- *Table Prefix*: Leave this field set to `wp_`.

  You can change the table prefix to create an environment secure from outside access. See Chapter 5 for more information.

5. **After you fill in that information, click the Submit button.**

   You see a message that says, "All right, sparky! You've made it through this part of the installation. WordPress can now communicate with your database. If you're ready, time to run the install!"

6. **Click the Run the Install button.**

   Another welcome page appears with a message welcoming you to the famous five-minute WordPress installation process.

7. **Enter the following information, as shown in Figure 4-7:**

   - *Site Title*: Enter the title you want to give your site. The title you enter isn't written in stone; you can change it later, if you like. The site title also displays on your site.

- *Username*: This is the name you use to log in to WordPress. By default, the username is *admin,* and you can leave it that way. However, for security reasons, I recommend you change your username to something unique to you. This username is different from the one you set for the MySQL database in previous steps. You use this username when you log in to WordPress to access the Dashboard (see Book III), so be sure to make it something you'll remember.

- *Password, Twice*: Type your desired password in the first text box and then type it again in the second to confirm that you've typed it correctly. If the two versions of your password don't match, WordPress alerts you with an error message. If you don't enter a password, one is generated automatically for you. For security reasons, it's a good thing to set a different password here than the one you set for your MySQL database in the previous steps — just don't get them confused.

For security reasons (and so other people can't make a lucky guess), passwords should be at least seven characters long and use as many different characters in as many combinations as possible. Use a mixture of uppercase and lowercase letters, numbers, and symbols (such as ! " ? $ % ^ &).

Figure 4-7:
Finishing the
WordPress
installation.

![WordPress Installation screen]

WORDPRESS

Welcome

Welcome to the famous five minute WordPress installation process! You may want to browse the ReadMe documentation at your leisure. Otherwise, just fill in the information below and you'll be on your way to using the most extendable and powerful personal publishing platform in the world.

Information needed

Please provide the following information. Don't worry, you can always change these settings later.

Site Title	Your Site Name Goes Here
Username	LisaSW
	Usernames can have only alphanumeric characters, spaces, underscores, hyphens, periods and the @ symbol.
Password, twice	••••••••••••••••
A password will be automatically generated for you if you leave this blank.	••••••••••••••••
	Strong
	Hint: The password should be at least seven characters long. To make it stronger, use upper and lower case letters, numbers and symbols like ! " ? $ % ^ &).

- *Your E-Mail*: Enter the e-mail address you want to use to be notified of administrative information about your blog. You can change this address later, too.

- *Allow My Blog to Appear in Search Engines Like Google and Technorati*: By default, this check box is selected, which lets the search engines index the content of your blog and include your blog in search results. To keep your blog out of the search engines, deselect this check box (see Book III).

8. **Click the Install WordPress button.**

The WordPress installation machine works its magic and creates all the tables within the database that contain the default data for your blog. WordPress displays the login information you need to access the WordPress Dashboard. Make note of this username and password before you leave this page. Scribble them on a piece of paper or copy them into a text editor, such as Notepad.

After you click the Install WordPress button, you're sent an e-mail with the login information and login URL. This information is handy if you're called away during this part of the installation process. So go ahead and let the dog out, answer the phone, brew a cup of coffee, or take a 15-minute power nap. If you somehow get distracted away from this page, the e-mail sent to you contains the information you need to log in to your WordPress blog.

9. **Click the Log In button to log in to WordPress.**

If you happen to lose this page before clicking the Log In button, you can always find your way to the login page by entering your domain followed by the call to the login file (for example, `http://yourdomain.com/wp-login.php` — where *yourdomain* is your domain name).

You know that you're finished with the installation process when you see the login page, as shown in Figure 4-8. Check out Table 4-1 if you experience any problems during this installation process; it covers some of the common problems users run into.

So do tell — how much time does your watch show for the installation? Was it five minutes? Stop by Lisa's blog sometime at `http://lisasabin-wilson.com` and let Lisa know whether WordPress stood up to its famous five-minute installation reputation. She's a curious sort.

The good news is — you're done! Were you expecting a marching band? WordPress isn't that fancy . . . yet. Give them time, though. If anyone can produce it, the folks at WordPress can.

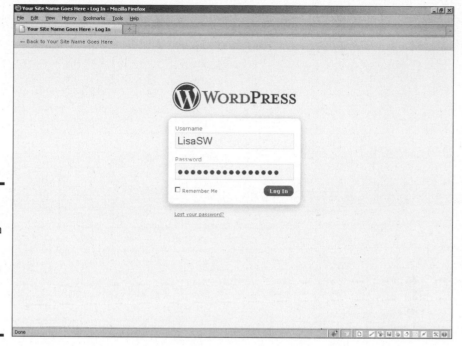

Figure 4-8:
You know
you've run a
successful
WordPress
installation
when you
see the
login page.

Table 4-1	**Common WordPress Installation Problems**	
Error Message	*Common Cause*	*Solution*
`Error Connecting to the Database`	The database name, user-name, password, or host was entered incorrectly.	Revisit your MySQL data-base to obtain the database name, username, and pass-word and then reenter that information.
`Headers Already Sent Error Messages`	A syntax error occurred in the `wp-config.php` file.	Open the `wp-config.php` file in a text editor. The first line needs to contain only this line: `<?php`. The last line needs to contain only this line: `?>`. Make sure that those lines contain nothing else — not even white space. Save the file changes.

(continued)

Table 4-1 *(continued)*

Error Message	Common Cause	Solution
500: Internal Server Error	Permissions on PHP files are set incorrectly.	Try setting the permissions (chmod) on the PHP files to 666. If that change doesn't work, set them to 644. Each Web server has different settings for how it lets PHP execute on its servers.
404: Page Not Found	The URL for the login page is incorrect.	Double-check that the URL you're using to get to the login page is the same as the location of your WordPress installation (such as http://*yourdomain*.com/wp-login.php).
403: Forbidden Access	An index.html or index.htm file exists in the WordPress installation directory.	WordPress is a PHP application, so the default home page is index.php. Look in the WordPress installation folder on your Web server. If an index.html or index.htm file is there, delete it.

Let us be the first to congratulate you on your newly installed WordPress blog! When you're ready, log in and familiarize yourself with the Dashboard, which we describe in Book III.

Chapter 5: Configurations for Optimum Performance and Security

In This Chapter

✔ **Exploring the configuration file**

✔ **Caching data to increase speed and performance**

✔ **Using text editors and browsers to edit and test your site**

*I*n Chapter 3 of this minibook, I show you the basics of *PHP (Hypertext Preprocessor),* the programming language that WordPress is built on, as well as the MySQL database system that stores the data for your Web site. These two programs, PHP and MySQL, combined with JavaScript, images, Cascading Style Sheet (CSS), and other scripts can create a slow load time for your Web site, especially if your Web site is on a mediocre Web host or if your Web site experiences high traffic volumes. Additionally, WordPress is somewhat vulnerable to hacking attempts; however, you can take a few steps to make it much more difficult (if not impossible) for hackers to exploit the files on your Web server and improve the overall security of your WordPress Web site.

In this chapter, I introduce you to a very important file in your WordPress installation: `wp-config.php`. This configuration file contains important system information needed for WordPress to function correctly on your Web site. We also show you some tweaks you can include in the configuration file to change or remove certain features of WordPress to improve your visitors' experience on your Web site.

Later in this chapter, we recommend some tools, such as text editors to make your file-editing experiences easier, and various browsers you can choose from. We also cover cross-browser compatibility and development tools you can use to view different aspects of your Web site or to test your site for performance.

Discovering the Configuration File

Every WordPress installation contains a configuration file that holds essential data for your Web site to work. The file, wp-config.php, is located in your WordPress installation directory (see Chapter 4 of this minibook). Simply put, your Web site doesn't work if this file is missing or if the data found within the file is incorrect.

More than likely, you haven't even looked at your wp-config.php file yet because when you download the WordPress software, the file is actually wp-config-sample.php. When you install WordPress, the file is renamed wp-config.php and is populated by WordPress with the following information, some of which you may remember from when you installed WordPress, and some that we explain later in this chapter:

+ **Database name**
+ **Database username**
+ **Database password**
+ **Database host**
+ **WordPress language:** English is the default.
+ **WordPress database table prefix:** wp_
+ **Secret keys**
+ **Absolute path to the WordPress files on your Web server**

All this information must be present in the wp-config.php file for your installation to work correctly. If WordPress already works on your site, most likely, your wp-config.php file is correct and functioning beautifully. (See Chapter 4 in this minibook for how to install WordPress.)

Securing the configuration file

As you can probably already guess, hackers find the valuable information stored in the wp-config.php file attractive. If someone with nefarious intent were to get your database username and password, he could log in and undo everything that you've built! Therefore, take whatever steps you can to secure that file so that no one, but you, has access to it. One quick and easy way to do that is to disallow any bots (automated software applications that run on the Internet) access to it and to change the file permissions. To do so, follow these steps:

1. **Log in to your Web server via FTP, and then locate and open the**
   .htaccess file to edit it.

   See Chapter 2 of this minibook for information on File Transfer
   Protocol (FTP).

   Most FTP programs allow you to open and edit a file on the server by
   right-clicking the filename and choosing Edit. This opens the file in the
   default text editor on your computer (either Notepad for Windows or
   TextMate for Mac).

2. **Add the Deny from all code to the top of the .htaccess file.**

   This secures the file from being seen by any bots or search engines
   on the Web:

   ```
   <Files wp-config.php>
   Order Allow,Deny
   Deny from all
   </Files>
   ```

3. **Save the new .htaccess file and upload it to your Web server.**

   Your wp-config.php file is hidden from any outside bots or
   search engines.

4. **Change file permission (chmod) on wp-config.php to 640.**

   See Chapter 2 of this minibook for information on file permissions and
   how to change permissions (chmod) via FTP.

   Changing the file permission to 640 ensures that the file can be written
   (or changed/edited) only by the owner of the file, not by the public; or
   worse yet, by any automated bots or script programs run by hackers.

Book II
Chapter 5

Configurations
for Optimum
Performance and
Security

Exploring main configuration settings

After the wp-config.php file is nice and secure, you need to know what's
stored within it so you can reference it and understand how WordPress
hooks into, or communicates with, the database you configured and set
up in Chapter 4 of this minibook. Open the wp-config.php file by using
your default text editor and have a look inside. The next sections take you
through, in detail, the information stored within.

Database information

The database information section of the wp-config.php file contains the
database credentials that are required for WordPress to connect to your
database. During installation, the WordPress installation script populates

this data after you input the database name, username, password, and host in the installation form (see Book II, Chapter 4). The following lines of code show you what this section of the file looks like in its default form:

```
// ** MySQL settings - You can get this info from your Web host ** //

/** The name of the database for WordPress */
define('DB_NAME', 'database_name_here');

/** MySQL database username */
define('DB_USER', 'username_here');

/** MySQL database password */
define('DB_PASSWORD', 'password_here');

/** MySQL hostname */
define('DB_HOST', 'localhost');
```

Secret keys (salts)

Secret keys enhance WordPress security through user authentication with the placement of a cookie in the user's Web browser. They are also referred to as *salts,* a word commonly used in cryptography to represent random keys, such as in a password. Secret keys in your wp-config.php file make your site harder for outside sources to gain access to because they add random keys to the user password.

These keys aren't populated during the WordPress installation, so after the installation is complete, you need to visit the wp-config.php file to set the keys so that your WordPress installation has unique keys that are different from any other installation — making it more secure because the keys are specific only to your site. By default, the code in the file looks like this:

```
/**#@+
 * Authentication Unique Keys and Salts.
 *
 * Change these to different unique phrases!
 * You can generate these with the {@link https://api.wordpress.org/secret-key/1.1/
     salt/ WordPress.org secret-key service}. You can change these at any point in
     time to invalidate all existing cookies. This will force all users to have to
     log in again.
 *
 * @since 2.6.0
 */
define('AUTH_KEY',         'put your unique phrase here');
define('SECURE_AUTH_KEY',  'put your unique phrase here');
define('LOGGED_IN_KEY',    'put your unique phrase here');
define('NONCE_KEY',        'put your unique phrase here');
define('AUTH_SALT',        'put your unique phrase here');
define('SECURE_AUTH_SALT', 'put your unique phrase here');
define('LOGGED_IN_SALT',   'put your unique phrase here');
define('NONCE_SALT',       'put your unique phrase here');
```

Follow the directions in the file and visit the WordPress secret-key service Web page (https://api.wordpress.org/secret-key/1.1/salt; be sure to refresh this page a few times to make sure that you get unique keys) to obtain the keys that you need to replace the existing defaults (represented in the wp-config.php file by the lines that start with define. Copy the keys from the Web page and then replace the eight lines of default (blank) keys in your wp-config.php file. After you do that, this section of the file looks like this (except with your own, unique secret keys):

```
/**#@+
 * Authentication Unique Keys and Salts.
 *
 * Change these to different unique phrases!
 * You can generate these with the {@link https://api.wordpress.org/secret-key/1.1/
     salt/ WordPress.org secret-key service}. You can change these at any point in
     time to invalidate all existing cookies. This will force all users to have to
     log in again.
 *
 * @since 2.6.0
 */
define('AUTH_KEY','OkjsE|hTe1A#ıyK*;zWOh_-we{X}(uX-TUXtV`WC9Owz_eA@c_
    LKH-Le;qKDPcn');

define('SECURE_AUTH_KEY','mGt;>cS&Gn,weoFIoJts[.+8bm$Qk|+|a|]>u<TLQRJBH2_
    eb>$TDk{ru&:|$5b');

define('LOGGED_IN_KEY','N13G3G^n8w%B4Nge)|V6TyI!S^Td!u|6_]}8kVSDB]p|@fTu=%>)
    M<s>%|t<qJb');

define('NONCE_KEY','pOj/Uj?&ıAJVO9SnRhr<e8:d0ıA8>XgSO5SuUYpvkjy@%O:Hi
    < Z->|!-YIA+Yq');

define('AUTH_SALT','8c%^y1/Kts3(I|N9/:`DM(j+qx.rKQh+I##E~e!Oq7|
    @p5j^D1:Yic+GQtlX>d');

define('SECURE_AUTH_SALT','!$Fi=K0jtK([;1x~EzN,QQOja_y5a|oxl_On~7AIT&8<dE:)
    M|DGc?Cb:sQiTor');

define('LOGGED_IN_SALT','N&j*A6khkJb}DhN>)+||e2}(:^Oo+mw!~DVOV;3W:75C|KCrHK[)
    7th_w:3%Fqe');

define('NONCE_SALT','xscOi.7I=%1;=-{mWjN=+gN03].RjLR6|ZpvbZt@
    bqK{p$2p;M.%,&i#9U8SLZ');
```

You can change the secret keys any time by editing the wp-config.php file and replacing the keys with new ones. Doing so doesn't affect the functioning of your Web site, but it does require that users log in to your site again, if they were already logged in, because changing the keys changes user authentication and retires the cookies that had already been placed in their browsers.

**Book II
Chapter 5**

Configurations
for Optimum
Performance and
Security

Default language

English is the default language for every WordPress installation; however, you can use any of the language translations currently available for WordPress by changing the WPLANG parameter in the wp-config.php file. By default, the WPLANG parameter looks like this:

```
/**
 * WordPress Localized Language, defaults to English.
 *
 * Change this to localize WordPress. A corresponding MO file for the chosen
 *     language must be installed to wp-content/languages. For example, install
 *     de.mo to wp-content/languages and set WPLANG to 'de' to enable German
 *     language support.
 */
define ('WPLANG', '');
```

We don't have the room to list the all the available languages, but you can find the specifics at the WordPress Codex page (http://codex.wordpress.org/WordPress_in_Your_Language), which lists all the languages you have access to, including the language code. If you want WordPress translated into French, for example, look up the language code on the Codex page. You can see that the code is fr_FR. To use French rather than English, you change the WPLANG parameter to:

```
define ('WPLANG', 'fr_FR');
```

Then save the file and upload it to your server. Your WordPress Dashboard (see Book III) displays in the French language, rather than the default English.

Database table prefix

By default, when installing WordPress, you're asked for the database table prefix and given the wp_ default prefix. This is how the tables in the database are defined and called by the different WordPress functions in the code. Figure 5-1 shows Lisa's WordPress database displayed in phpMyAdmin (a database administration interface), which displays all the tables in Lisa's WordPress installation with the wp_ prefix.

Here's how the database table prefix definition looks in the wp-config.php file:

```
/**
 * WordPress Database Table prefix.
 * You can have multiple installations in one database if you give each a unique
 *     prefix. Only numbers, letters, and underscores please!
 */
$table_prefix = 'wp_';
```

Figure 5-1:
phpMyAdmin
displaying
WordPress
database
tables.

Book II
Chapter 5

Configurations
for Optimum
Performance and
Security

During the installation process, you can change the default `wp_` prefix to anything you want. In fact, most security experts recommend that you change the database prefix because WordPress is a big target for hacking (malicious scripts, spam, and so on). Web bots and spiders can be set to look for the usual WordPress default settings and attempt to exploit them. The `wp_` database table prefix is one of those obvious default settings, so to safeguard your installation, change the prefix to anything you choose. However, keep in mind that if you change the prefix, you need to change it to something very difficult for a script or an automated program to guess. Treat the prefix like a password and make it a random string of letters and numbers — something like `sd30df43xxi54_`. Just be sure that it's unique and difficult to guess.

If you didn't change the table prefix during installation, you can go back and do it later if you want to. You will need to edit the `$table_prefix` line in the `wp-config.php` file. Also, you'll need to alter the table names in your database by accessing the database administration interface provided by your Web hosting provider (like phpMyAdmin, for example) and by renaming the tables to replace the `wp_` prefix with the one you defined in the `wp-config.php`.

The underscore after the table prefix isn't required but is recommended practice to make the database tables easier to read and sort. Refer to Figure 5-1 and you see that the tables are named like this: `wp_commentmeta`, `wp_comments`, and so on. Placing the underscore after the prefix makes for easier reading and a more organized looking database. Reading a database can be confusing enough, so make it easy on yourself and use the underscore if you choose to change the database table prefix.

Absolute WordPress path

The configuration file defines the absolute path, or the full directory path on your web server, to the WordPress files on your Web server. This is called once when WordPress is executed and tells the Web server where, within your directory, it needs to look for the core files to successfully run WordPress on your site. The code that defines the absolute path in the `wp-config.php` file looks like this:

```
/** Absolute path to the WordPress directory. */
if ( !defined('ABSPATH') )
define('ABSPATH', dirname(__FILE__) . '/');

/** Sets up WordPress vars and included files. */
require_once(ABSPATH . 'wp-settings.php');
```

Moving the /wp-content directory

Another directory in your WordPress installation that's attractive to hackers is the `/wp-content` folder. Hackers sometimes attack this directory because it holds all your theme and plugin files. If a hacker can exploit any of the code found within those files, she can gain control of your Web site, or at the very least, mess it up a lot.

You can move the `/wp-content` directory to a location on your Web server outside the WordPress installation directory, making it a lot harder, if not impossible, for outside hackers to locate. To move the folder, create a new folder on your Web server outside the WordPress installation directory and then, using your FTP program, drag and drop the `/wp-content` folder to the new one you just created. In most popular FTP programs, you can right-click with your mouse and choose New Folder, which allows you to create a new folder and give it a name.

When you move the `/wp-content` folder, you need to define the new location in the `wp-config.php` file so that WordPress knows where to find those necessary files. You can define the new path to the `/wp-content` folder by adding these lines of code to the `wp-config.php` file (replacing *newfolder* with the name of the folder you just created):

```
define ('WP_CONTENT_DIR', $_SERVER['DOCUMENT_ROOT'].' /newfolder/wp-content');
define ('WP_CONTENT_URL', 'http://yourdomain.com/newfolder/wp-content');
```

Tweaking the configuration file for optimization

Adding a few bits of code to your `wp-config.php` file can change some of WordPress's default behaviors and improve the speed at which your site loads. In this section, I describe a few of the most popular configuration tweaks.

Post revisions, autosave, and trash handling

WordPress autosaves revisions of your posts and pages, and you can send posts and pages to the trash can, instead of completely deleting them. You visit the trash can and permanently delete your posts or pages. This extra step is a safeguard in case of mistakes. (We give you the details about this in Book IV.)

**Book II
Chapter 5**

Configurations
for Optimum
Performance and
Security

In terms of the post revisions, by default, WordPress saves unlimited revisions and sometimes, depending on how often you edit and reedit posts and pages, the saved revision list can get pretty long. You can limit the number of revisions that WordPress will save by adding the following line to the `wp-config.php` file:

```
define ('WP_POST_REVISIONS', 3); // limit number of revisions to 3
```

You can also completely disable the default revision feature by adding this line to the `wp-config.php` file, on its own line:

```
define ('WP_POST_REVISIONS', false); // disable post revisions
```

WordPress creates these revisions through the Autosave feature. By default, WordPress automatically saves a post revision every minute. If you take a long time to write a post, you could rack up dozens of post revisions, which are stored in the database and take up room. You can change the autosave interval by adding this code to the `wp-config.php` file on its own line (this code changes the autosave interval to 160 seconds, specifically — you can choose any time interval you want):

```
define ('AUTOSAVE_INTERVAL', 160); // in seconds
```

The Trash feature in WordPress gives you a safeguard against permanently deleting posts by mistake. In Book IV, you find that you can send a post or a page to the trash and that this action doesn't permanently delete it; instead, WordPress stores it in a virtual trash can. (Windows users can think of it as the Recycle Bin.) You can visit the trash can any time and permanently delete the post or page, or you can leave it there and WordPress automatically empties the trash can every 30 days. If you want to adjust this time interval, you can add the first line of code to force WordPress to empty the trash weekly, or the second line to disable the trash feature, completely, as follows (on its own line):

```
define('EMPTY_TRASH_DAYS', 7); // empty trash weekly
define('EMPTY_TRASH_DAYS', 0); // disable trash
```

Site and WordPress installation Web address

As we discuss in Book VI, one of the most common template tags for use in a theme is the `bloginfo()`; tag, which has several parameters you can use to call different bits of information about your site (like the site name and description, for example). You then can call in different theme template files and graphics (or images) into your theme. For example, the URL of your Web site can be defined in your template files with the following template tag:

```
<?php bloginfo('url'); ?> // Site URL
```

In Book VI, we cover template tags and parameters in detail.

That template tag tells WordPress to communicate with the site database, locate the site URL, and return it back to the template or plugin file that's making that database call. You can greatly reduce the number of database calls (thereby, speeding up your site) by defining the site URL in the `wp-config.php` file by inserting the following two lines on their own lines (replacing *yourdomain*.com with your actual domain name, of course):

```
define ('WP_HOME', 'http://yourdomain.com'); // site address
define ('WP_SITEURL', 'http://yourdomain.com'); // wordpress address
```

With these two lines in place in the `wp-config.php` file, whenever WordPress comes across a template tag that requests your site URL, it won't need to reach out to your database to discover what that URL is because it's defined in the file structure within the `wp-config.php` file. This reduces the number of calls to the database, which, in turn, reduces the resources your site uses on the Web server to display your Web site to your visitors.

Template and stylesheet path

Just as with the site URL from the preceding section, many themes and the WordPress core code look for your WordPress theme template and stylesheet directory through the following WordPress template tags:

```
<?php bloginfo('template_directory'); ?> // template directory
<?php bloginfo('stylesheet_directory'); ?> // stylesheet directory
```

Once again, you can significantly reduce the number of calls to the database for the template and stylesheet directories by directly defining them in your wp-config.php file. To do so, add these two lines of code (replace *absolute/ path/* with your own server path and replace */themefolder* with the name of the theme folder you use currently) on their own separate lines:

```
define('TEMPLATEPATH', '/absolute/path/to/wp-content/themes/themefolder');
define('STYLESHEETPATH, '/absolute/path/to/wp-content/themes/themefolder');
```

As with the site URL in the preceding section, having these two lines of code in your wp-config.php file defines the file path within the file structure in the wp-config.php file, so that WordPress doesn't need to make an additional call to the database to discover what the absolute and stylesheet paths are.

Increasing PHP memory limits

Most Web hosting providers limit the amount of memory any one PHP script or program file can use on the Web server at any given time. PHP is at the core of WordPress (see Book II, Chapter 3), and by default, WordPress attempts to set the PHP memory limit to 32MB. However, if you see PHP memory limit errors on your Web site, such as

```
PHP Fatal error: Allowed memory size of 33554432 bytes exhausted
    (tried to allocate 6233929 bytes) …
```

The PHP memory limit needs to be increased to run the PHP script or file. That memory limit error tells you that the PHP script was attempting to allocate 64MB of memory; however, the allowed memory size set by the server is limited to 32MB, which is the reason for the error.

To help resolve the PHP memory limit errors, within the wp-config.php, define the maximum amount of memory that PHP can use by writing one of these three lines of code, depending on how much memory you allow PHP to use on your site, and adding it to the wp-config.php file on its own line:

```
define ('WP_MEMORY_LIMIT', '64m'); // increase limit to 64M
define ('WP_MEMORY_LIMIT', '96M'); // increase limit to 96M
define ('WP_MEMORY_LIMIT', '128M'); // increase limit to 128M
```

Some hosting providers disable the ability to increase PHP memory limits on your Web hosting account, so depending on your hosting environment, your attempts to increase the memory limit may not work. If you discover this is the case for your particular hosting account, you can contact your host and ask him to increase the PHP memory limit for your account or switch to a different hosting provider.

**Book II
Chapter 5**

Configurations
for Optimum
Performance and
Security

Using a Caching System for Speed and Performance

A good way to improve the speed of your Web site is through caching different types of content. *Caching* content means to store it transparently so that it can be used for future loads of your Web site. A good caching system for your Web site collects all the Web pages on your site and copies, stores, and delivers the files to visitors of your Web site. This significantly reduces the server load because without it, WordPress creates pages on your Web site *dynamically* — each time a visitor loads your Web site, calls are made to the database and code is complied and executed each time to create the page in her browser. If you use a good caching program, those files are already built and displayed, so your Web server doesn't need to rebuild those pages each time.

The following are the different types of caching that can improve your site performance:

✦ **Page:** Builds and stores (in your Web server memory) all the pages on your Web site. Page caches generally have an expiration date. In case you update content on your Web pages, the cache will eventually rebuild itself to capture changes you make.

✦ **Database:** Reduces Web server overhead by storing and remembering database tables and queries made by WordPress.

✦ **Browser:** Stores Web pages on the visitor's local storage so when she revisits your site, her browser displays the page from her hard drive memory, instead of rebuilding it and calling it from your server. Browser caches have an expiration date, so any changes you make can be captured again in the future (your site visitors can also set their browser settings to disable cache — so this may not work for everyone who visits your site).

✦ **Object:** Stores data objects or HTML structures, which can increase server load because, without a caching system, they need to be rebuilt each time the site is loaded in a visitor's Web browser. Object caching helps the overall caching system by storing complete Web pages and saving them for future loads of your site.

Minifying JavaScript, CSS, and HTML

You can also improve the speed of your Web site through *minifying* — making some of the files, like JavaScript, CSS, and HTML, smaller. This involves taking all the files of your Web site and reducing the size by doing things like

✦ Removing all line breaks and spaces in the file.

✦ Removing all code comments in the file.

✦ Removing unnecessary characters in the file.

✦ Using code shorthand, where possible, to decrease the amount of characters in the file.

✦ Combining the files into one file, wherever possible; therefore, instead of having ten JavaScript files, you could reduce the number to four or five.

Minifying JavaScript, CSS, and HTML files reduces the overall file size, making them load faster on your Web site. Obviously, adjusting each of the existing files on your site to make them smaller would take quite a lot of time and programming skills that you may or may not possess. Therefore, you may prefer to use a plugin or program to adjust these files. A good plugin or program used to minify files can reduce the file to 30–40 percent of its original size, which greatly improves the response time of your Web site.

Figure 5-2 shows the HTML source code from Lisa's Web site in its regular state, and Figure 5-3 displays it in a minified state. You can see how minifying shrinks the size of the overall file by removing spaces and line breaks, and shortening the characters used.

Book II
Chapter 5

Configurations for Optimum Performance and Security

Use a WordPress plugin (such as W3 Total Cache (`http://wordpress.org/extend/plugins/w3-total-cache`) that has a feature that minifies files, such as JavaScript, CSS, and HTML, by caching the minified files. This leaves the original files intact so they are easily readable and editable by you.

Figure 5-2:
The HTML source code from Lisa's Web site.

Figure 5-3:
The HTML source code from Lisa's Web site, minified.

Using a content delivery network

A *content delivery network (CDN)* stores your Web site data within different points on a network and can deliver that data to Web site visitors with a decreased amount of bandwidth. A CDN can choose to deliver this data from the nearest geographical location, making the transfer faster. Because of this, visitors don't access the data from the same place at the same time, which lightens the load on your server significantly.

To use a CDN, you need to sign up for a service that provides a network and a series of computers to store and serve your data on your Web site. The CDN can include items like images and CSS, JavaScript, and media files. Using a CDN reduces the load on your server because the files are delivered through the CDN, not through your Web server. This is especially helpful if you use a significant amount of bandwidth on your current hosting account.

CDN services are relatively inexpensive, particularly if you don't have a lot of media files, images, and data to store on their servers. A few popular CDN providers include

✦ **Amazon Web Services:** http://aws.amazon.com

✦ **Akamai:** www.akamai.com

+ **CacheFly:** www.cachefly.com

+ **PEER 1:** www.peer1.com/managed/content_delivery_network.php

+ **MaxCDN:** www.maxcdn.com

The benefits of running a content delivery network include the following:

+ Improved speed of your Web site

+ Improved visitor experience

+ Improved scalability for your Web site and database data delivery

+ Resistant to Web site crashes during times of high traffic volumes

In the next section of this chapter, we give you a couple of plugins that provide a user interface to help you set up a CDN on your Web site. Just remember that CDN services aren't free, and the costs vary depending on the service provider that you use.

Using plugins to make caching easier

We recommend these two plugins, which provide you with the best and easiest ways to make sure that your WordPress site has a caching system in place:

+ **W3 Total Cache:** Install this plugin to easily optimize your Web site and user experience with page, browser, database, and object caching. W3 Total Cache also includes features like HTML, CSS, and JavaScript minify, as well as CDN configurations to improve your Web site's speed and performance (http://wordpress.org/extend/plugins/w3-total-cache).

+ **WP Super Cache:** This plugin generates static HTML files from your dynamic WordPress blog posts and pages. The static HTML files are then served to your Web site visitors instead of the dynamically generated PHP files, without affecting the look or function of your site. This reduces the load on your server and increases the speed of your Web site. Unlike the W3 Total Cache plugin, WP Super Cache (http://wordpress.org/extend/plugins/wp-super-cache) doesn't have minify or CDN configurations.

Editing Files and Testing Performance with WordPress Tools

Over the course of Lisa's journey with WordPress, which began in 2003, she's learned a lot of lessons from editing WordPress files, building themes,

**Book II
Chapter 5**

Configurations
for Optimum
Performance and
Security

and using different browsers and browser tools to help her view, test, and diagnose certain problems (such as speed, error messages, and CSS rendering) on her Web site.

One important thing she's learned is that when she sits at the computer to begin to work on any WordPress project, large or small, it's vital that she have the right tools readily available. Having the right tools makes a world of difference in the quality, efficiency, and overall experience in designing and developing a Web site for her or a client.

This section of the chapter introduces you to tools for things like editing HTML, CSS, and PHP, as well as using various Web browser platforms, such as Internet Explorer and Mozilla Firefox. For example, we include different tools and add-ons that you can add to the browser to make it work better for your Web site and be easier for you to maintain it.

In some cases, the tools we mention here aren't necessarily required — however, you'll be very thankful when you find tools that make your Web site managing a lot easier!

Choosing the text editor that's right for you

In Book VI, you dig into WordPress themes, work with CSS and HTML, and type template tags and a bit of PHP; this chapter arms you with the tools you need to gather to prepare for a smooth and efficient experience later.

Next to good ol' pen and paper, nothing beats a good, solid text editor. We admit, we're a little old school, so for things like grocery lists and jotting down ideas, we stick with a pad of paper and a pen. Unfortunately, writing code is difficult with a pen and paper, and it doesn't translate very well when we need to publish it to the Internet. That's when a basic text editor program comes in very handy — we always have one open on the computer (usually several instances of a favored text editor, actually) and use it daily for writing CSS and HTML, and for coding WordPress templates and themes.

Make sure that you use a *text editor* and not a *word processor,* such as Microsoft Word, to write any code. A word processing program automatically inserts formatting, characters, and hidden spaces because it assumes that you want the document formatted. When you're writing code, this sort of formatting is the last thing you want — so stick with a basic text editor.

The text editors listed and described in this section are programs that are installed on your computer. Some of them are available only for Windows, some only for Mac users — we specify this in their descriptions.

Notepad (Windows)

Notepad is a basic plain-text editor that you can use to write code without the fuss and worry of text formatting; it doesn't support any special document formatting or characters at all, which is what makes it great for writing code and Web documents.

Notepad is the go-to text editor for most Windows users because it's a Microsoft product packaged in every Windows operating system. Notepad is typically used for viewing and editing text files with the .txt extension, but many people, including myself, use it to create basic CSS and HTML files as well.

Notepad, by default, saves files with a .txt extension. With WordPress templates and theme files, you typically save files with a .php or .css extension, so you want to take care and make sure that you save files correctly. To save as a .php or .css extension with Notepad, follow these quick steps:

1. **Open Notepad by clicking the Start button and then choosing Programs⇨Accessories⇨Notepad.**

2. **Create your CSS or PHP document.**

   Check out Chapter 3 of this minibook for a simple PHP document you can create.

3. **Choose File⇨Save As and then select the location to save the document in the Save In drop-down list in the dialog box that appears.**

4. **Type the name of the file, including the extension, in the File Name field.**

   In Figure 5-4, the name of the file is header.php. If you're saving a CSS document, the extension is .css (for example: style.css).

5. **Choose All Files in the Save as Type drop-down list.**

   By default, Notepad wants to save it as a text document (.txt).

6. **Leave ANSI selected in the Encoding field and then click the Save button.**

By following the preceding steps, you save a .php or css document by using the Notepad text editor program.

**Book II
Chapter 5**

Configurations
for Optimum
Performance and
Security

Figure 5-4:
Saving
a PHP
document in
Notepad.

Notepad++ (Windows)

Notepad++ is a text editor for Windows users and is often referred to as
"Notepad on steroids." The interface of Notepad++ looks a lot like the regular Notepad but that's where the similarities end. Notepad++ is a text editor
with advanced features, such as color-coded syntax (see the nearby sidebar,
"Code syntax highlighting," for information on syntax highlighting), code
indentation, and line numbering, which make it an extremely useful and
helpful application for writing and editing code. Figure 5-5 demonstrates
the color-coded syntax where the functions of the code are represented
by colors, making it easier for you (or the programmer) to pick different
sections of the code (such as functions or HTML).

Notepad++ supports many programming languages, including the main ones
you use for this book: CSS, HTML, and PHP. Notepad++ is free and open
source software; you can download it to your Windows computer from its
Website at `http://notepad-plus-plus.org`.

Figure 5-5:
Notepad++
with color-
coded
syntax.

Book II
Chapter 5

Configurations
for Optimum
Performance and
Security

Code syntax highlighting

Except for Notepad, all the text editors we mention in this chapter are *syntax editors*. They follow code-syntax highlighting formats for different types of code, such as PHP, JavaScript, HTML, and CSS. Lines of code are highlighted with colors to make it easy for you to read and separate the type of code and markup you're looking at, such as JavaScript from HTML markup, for example. This doesn't affect the way code executes; it's purely a readability feature that makes it easier on the eyes, and on the brain, when reading lines and lines of code.

TextMate (Mac)

TextMate is an Apple product and, as such, can be used only on a Mac; it's the most popular text editor for Mac users and is referred to as "the missing editor" for Macs. Like Notepad++, TextMate is a syntax editor that color-codes the markup and code that you write. Additionally, TextMate can

✦ Easily search and replace

✦ Auto-indent mark up and code

✦ Open several documents, each in their own tab

✦ Work as an external editor for FTP programs

TextMate is not free, however. You can download a free 30-day trial from its Website: `http://macromates.com`. After using TextMate for 30 days, you can buy a single-user license for $56.

Understanding and choosing a Web browser

Knowing which Web browser to use as your primary browser can be confusing because there are so many browser systems available. Everyone has a favorite browser, and if you don't already, you'll find one that emerges as your favorite for one reason or another. Each browser system has a different look and feel, as well as different features and tools that make one of them your preferred browser of choice.

One thing you need to keep in mind, however, is that it doesn't matter which browser you use as your preferred browser for Internet surfing. However, having access to all major browsers is essential so you can test and view your Web designs in different browsers to make sure that they render and look the same.

 If you can, download and install all the browsers in this chapter to your computer so you have them readily available to test your designs across them. Some browsers work only on a Mac or a Windows system, so use the ones that are for your system.

Discovering different browsers and tools

Multitudes of different browser systems are available on the Web. This section takes you through five browsers that are the most popular among Internet users. Additionally, you find some helpful tools and add-ons to assist you with your Web design efforts in the different browser systems, including some of the must-have tools we use on a regular basis.

As far as the design and development community is concerned, the choice over which Web browser to use typically falls on how compliant the browser is with open Web standards developed by the *World Wide Web Consortium (W3C),* an international community that develops Web standards to ensure long-term Web growth (www.w3.org). As a designer, you need to at least have a working knowledge of what the W3C is and the standards it supports and promotes. You can read about the W3C vision and mission statement at www.w3.org/Consortium/mission.html.

Internet Explorer

Internet Explorer (IE), owing to the fact that it's part of all Windows operating systems, is by far one of the most popular browsers. Over the years, IE has struggled with its reputation of not keeping up and being noncompliant with Web standards and CSS rendering that the development and design community has come to love and expect from other browser systems. This is largely due to the layout engine (the method used to display Web sites by translating CSS and HTML markup) in use at the foundation of the IE browser.

One of the challenges that designers come across is the different versions of Internet Explorer that are widely used across the Web. With each new version, Microsoft's flagship browser comes closer and closer to compliance with open Web standards; however, because Internet Explorer is the browser present across millions of operating systems across the world, not every individual user or company is quick to adopt the new versions as they're released. This results in several versions of IE in use across the world, and designers generally make an effort to make sure that their designs render correctly on, at least, the last two to three recent versions of Internet Explorer.

Currently, the major versions of Internet Explorer that are supported by the majority of designers are versions 7 and 8, with most designers gradually dropping support for version 6 (commonly referred to as IE6). At the time of this writing, Microsoft has released a version 9 beta, with the final version of IE9 expected in late 2011 or early 2012.

Trying to test your Web site on different versions of Internet Explorer is difficult because attempting to install different versions on your computer can cause some big problems, if you don't know exactly what you're doing. We use a few tools for overall browser testing (see the section "Understanding cross-browser compatibility" later in this chapter); however, *IETester* comes in handy specifically for testing on different versions of IE. In Figure 5-6, the buttons across the top right are labeled for specific versions of Internet Explorer: IE5.5, IE6, IE7, and IE8. The WordPress Web site is shown in version 7 of the IE browser.

Figure 5-6:
Test in different versions of Internet Explorer with IETester.

IETester allows you to test Web site designs across several versions of Internet Explorer, going all the way back to version 5 (IE5). We highly recommend checking this out and using it to help test your Web site designs across different versions of Internet Explorer. Download IETester from `www.my-debugbar.com/wiki/IETester`.

Mozilla Firefox

Firefox, shown in Figure 5-7, is the second most popular browser on the Web and has emerged over the years to be a solid competitor for IE. Designers and developers tend to prefer Firefox to Internet Explorer because Mozilla (the makers of Firefox) use a solid layout engine that adheres closely to open Web standards and supports and renders CSS better.

Firefox is available for download and usage on Windows, Mac, and Linux operating systems in 76 languages. You can download it from the official Mozilla Web site at `http://mozilla.com`.

Book II
Chapter 5

Configurations for Optimum Performance and Security

Figure 5-7:
The Mozilla Firefox Web browser.

One of the main reasons why Firefox is our personal browser of choice is because it's an open source software project with a development community that releases very helpful add-ons and tools to extend its capabilities beyond a Web browser, turning it into a Web development tool, in many cases.

You can find Firefox add-ons at `https://addons.mozilla.org/firefox`. You can find add-ons for just about everything from the appearance of your Firefox browser to browser-based games. At the time of writing, Mozilla reports that 2,139,478,273 add-ons have been downloaded from its Web site.

Obviously, we can't cover all the add-ons available for Firefox in this chapter because this is a book, not an encyclopedia. However, here are three add-ons for Firefox that we use on a daily basis to make our days as full-time Web designers and developers easier, more efficient, and just more fun:

✦ **Firebug:** *Firebug* (`https://addons.mozilla.org/firefox/addon/1843`) is an add-on that integrates into the Firefox browser and provides you with a host of tools for Web development, including the ability to edit, debug, and monitor the behaviors of CSS, HTML, and JavaScript live for any Web page you view. We can't live without this tool mainly because of the CSS editing capabilities. We can open a Web page in Firefox, activate the CSS editing tool in Firebug, and do live CSS editing, which makes our Web site development go much faster.

✦ **YSlow:** To use YSlow (`https://addons.mozilla.org/en-US/firefox/addon/5369`), you have to install the Firebug add-on. *YSlow* analyzes Web pages and makes suggestions as to how you can improve the speed and load time of your Web site by incorporating things like image size optimization, JavaScript, or CSS, or by reducing the overall size of your Web page. We use this tool every time we deploy a WordPress site to get recommendations on how to improve the site loading time.

✦ **Web Developer:** *Web Developer* (`https://addons.mozilla.org/firefox/addon/60`) adds a very helpful toolbar in your Firefox browser that gives you access to several types of Web development tools, such as CSS viewing, CSS editing, image information, browser resizing, HTML and CSS validation tools, HTML viewing and editing, and more. We use the Web Developer toolbar on a constant basis to help us develop, test, and debug Web sites that we create.

As much as we prefer the Mozilla Firefox browser, many users consider it somewhat of a resource/memory hog. We've experienced this as well, but it isn't enough to make us stop using it. However, we have to shut down and restart the Mozilla Firefox browser at least two times during a normal workday to prevent it from crashing our system with its resource use.

Other browsers

Three other Web browsers are used regularly, and although they aren't quite as popular as IE or Firefox, they're worth checking out:

✦ **Google Chrome:** Google developed and released this Web browser (`www.google.com/chrome`). You can download this browser only for Windows operating systems, at this time. Chrome has a smaller development community and has add-ons, dubbed *extensions,* that you can download and install, just like Firefox — although not as many . . . yet. You can find Web development extensions for Google Chrome on the Web site here: `https://chrome.google.com/extensions/featured/Web_dev`.

✦ **Opera:** The Opera browser (www.opera.com) is available for Windows, Mac, and Linux operating systems and markets itself as being fast, secure, and completely in line with open Web standards, including cutting edge development languages like HTML5 and CSS3. Opera has add-ons available as well, which you can find on its Web site here: www. opera.com/addons.

✦ **Safari:** Safari (www.apple.com/safari) is installed on every Mac operating system from the large iMacs to MacBook laptops to iPads and iPhones. In short, Safari is an Apple product; however, Safari can be installed on a Windows operating system. Rather than a bunch of add-ons or extensions that you can download and install for Web development, Safari has built-in Web developer tools, including

- A Developer toolbar with tools used for Web site manipulation, testing, and debugging

- A Web Inspector with a wealth of Web development tools, including an Elements pane where you can inspect CSS and HTML markup

- A Resources pane that displays Web site resources by date, size, and speed

- A JavaScript debugger

- A Timeline pane that analyzes a Web site's behavior over time

- A JavaScript Profiler that lists the performance characteristics of scripts that run on a Web site

- A Console pane for debugging

- A Snippet Editor to test HTML markup

**Book II
Chapter 5**

**Configurations
for Optimum
Performance and
Security**

Understanding cross-browser compatibility

Cross-browser compatibility is the practice of testing designs across all major browser systems and is important in Web design because you don't just design Web sites for yourself, but for an entire audience on the Web. Because you have no idea which browser your audience uses, it's essential that you test your designs in all the different systems to ensure that all the visitors to your Web site have the same experience.

The problem that Web designers run into with Web browsers is that each browser system uses a different layout engine that renders CSS differently. The difference in CSS rendering can sometimes make adjusting your CSS styling to account for the different layout engines a challenge. Additionally, not every layout engine supports all versions of CSS. Table 5-1 illustrates the different layout engines, the browsers, and the CSS version it supports to give you an idea of what you're dealing with when it comes to the different browser systems. More information on CSS versions, support, and validation is in Book VI.

Table 5-1	Layout Engines, Browser Types, and CSS Version Support	
Layout Engine	*Browser System*	*Supports CSS Version*
Gecko	Mozilla Firefox	CSS v1, v2, v3 (partially) *
Presto	Opera	CSS v1, v2, v3 (partially) *
Trident	Internet Explorer	CSS v1, v2, v3 (slightly) *
WebKit	Google Chrome, Safari	CSS v1, v2, v3 (partially) *

*Partially and slightly indicate that the layout engines listed don't fully support CSS v3, at this time. Partial support indicates that the layout engine understands CSS v3 properties, but they aren't supported entirely. Slight support indicates that the layout engine is understood by the browser, but support is incomplete, and at times, buggy.

The absolute best way to test your Web site across the various browser systems is to download the browser to your computer and then load your Web site in it, checking for correct rendering as you go. However, if you only have a Windows computer, you can't really test your Web site on a Mac, and vice versa. Don't fret, though, because here are two alternatives for you:

✦ **Browsershots.org:** This is an online, browser-based tool. Visit the Browsershots.org Web site (`http://browsershots.org`), enter your desired URL in the Enter URL Here field at the top of the site, and then choose your desired browsers and operating systems. Browsershots. org takes a screenshot of your Web site in each of the browsers that you indicated so you can see what your Web site looks like in each. From there, you can fix any problems and retest again, if needed.

✦ **BrowserCam:** BrowserCam (`www.browsercam.com`) is another online cross-browser compatibility-testing tool that captures your Web site and takes a picture of it in different browsers. BrowserCam even has a tool that allows you to access its computers remotely so you can see your Web site in a live browser environment, instead of just getting a screenshot of your Web site. This service isn't free; the cost starts at $39.95 per month.

Chapter 6: Upgrading WordPress

In This Chapter

✔ Finding upgrades notifications

✔ Backing up your database before upgrading

✔ Deactivating plugins

✔ Upgrading from the dashboard

✔ Upgrading manually

In Book I, Chapter 3, the schedule of WordPress development and release cycles shows you that WordPress releases a new version (upgrade) of its platform roughly once every 120 days (or every 4 months). That chapter also explains why you need to keep your WordPress software up-to-date by using the most recent version for security purposes, mostly, but also to make sure you're taking advantage of all the latest features the WordPress developers pack within every major new release.

In this chapter, you discover the WordPress upgrade notification system and find out what to do when WordPress notifies you that a new version is available. This chapter also covers the best practices to upgrade the WordPress platform on your site to ensure the best possible outcome (that is, how not to break your Web site after a WordPress upgrade).

Getting Notified of an Available Upgrade

After you install WordPress and log in for the first time, you can see the version number at the bottom-right corner of the WordPress Dashboard, as shown in Figure 6-1. Therefore, if anyone asks what version you're using, you know exactly where to look to find out.

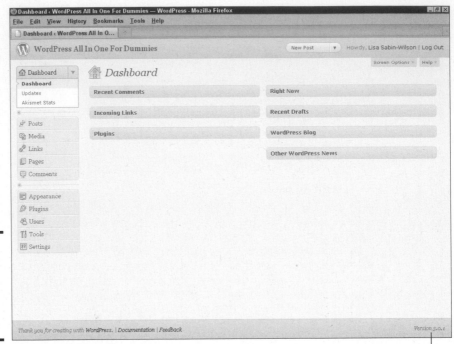

Figure 6-1:
WordPress
version
displayed
in the
Dashboard.

Version number

Say you have WordPress installed and you've been happily publishing content to your Web site with it for several weeks, maybe even months, then one day you log in to your Dashboard and see a message at the top of your screen you've never seen before that reads, "WordPress X.X.X is available! Please update now." (Figure 6-2 shows the message and a small black circle, or *notification bubble,* on the left side of the page.)

Both the message at the top of the page and the notification bubble in the Dashboard menu are visual indicators that you're using an outdated version of WordPress and that you can (and need to) upgrade the software.

The message at the top of your Dashboard includes two links that you can click for more information. (Refer to Figure 6-2.) The first is a link called WordPress 3.0.1. Clicking this link takes you to the WordPress Codex page titled Version 3.0.1, which is filled with information about the version upgrade, including

✦ Installation/upgrade information

✦ Summary of the development cycle for this version

✦ List of files that have been revised

Notification bubble   Update notification

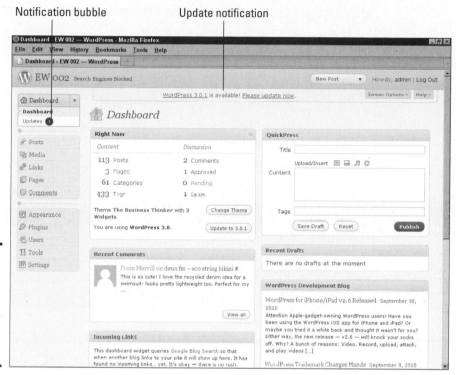

Figure 6-2:
Dashboard
notification
of an
available
WordPress
upgrade.

The second link, Please Update Now, takes you to another page in the
WordPress Dashboard — the WordPress Updates page, as shown in Figure 6-3.

At the very top of the WordPress Updates page is another important
message for you:

```
Important: before updating, please backup your database and files. For help with
    updates, visit the Updating WordPress Codex page.
```

Both links in the message take you to pages in the WordPress Codex that
contain helpful information on creating backups and updating WordPress.

Book II, Chapter 7 has extensive information on how to back up your
WordPress Web site, content, and files.

The WordPress Updates page tells you that an update version of WordPress
is available. You can update two ways:

✦ Automatically, by using the built-in WordPress updater

✦ Manually, by downloading the files and installing them on your server

These ways to update are discussed later in the chapter.

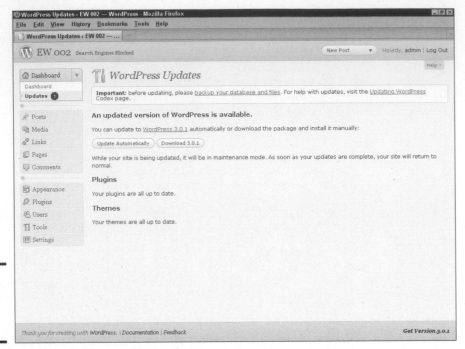

Figure 6-3:
WordPress
Updates
page.

Backing Up Your Database

Before upgrading your WordPress software installation, make sure you back up your database. This step isn't required, of course, but it's a smart step to take to safeguard your Web site and ensure you have a complete copy of your Web site data in the event that your upgrade goes wrong.

The best way to back up your database is to use the MySQL administration interface provided to you by your Web hosting provider. (Book II, Chapter 5 takes you through the steps of creating a new database by using the phpMy-Admin interface.)

cPanel is a Web hosting interface provided by many Web hosts as a Web hosting account management tool that contains phpMyAdmin as the preferred tool to use to manage and administer databases. Not all Web hosts use cPanel or phpMyAdmin, however, so if yours doesn't, you need to consult the user documentation for the tools that your Web host provides. The instructions in this chapter are provided by using cPanel and phpMyAdmin.

The following takes you through the steps of creating a database backup, using the same phpMyAdmin interface:

1. **Log in to the cPanel for your hosting account.**

   Typically, browse to http://yourdomain.com/cpanel to bring up the login screen for your cPanel. Enter your specific hosting account username and password in the login fields and click OK to log in.

2. **Click the phpMyAdmin icon.**

   The phpMyAdmin interface opens and displays your database.

3. **Click the name of the database that you want to back up.**

   If you have more than one database in your account, the left-side menu in phpMyAdmin displays the names of all of them. Click the one you want to back up; the database loads in the main interface window.

4. **Click the Export tab at the top of the screen.**

   The page refreshes and displays the backup utility page.

5. **Select the Save as File box.**

6. **Select the "zipped" option.**

   This compiles the database backup file in a .zip file and prepares it for download.

7. **Click the Go button.**

   A pop-up window appears, allowing you to select a location on your computer to store the database backup file.

8. **Click the Save button to download it and save it to your computer.**

Book II, Chapter 7 contains in-depth information on making a complete backup of your Web site, including all your files, plugins, themes, and images. For the purposes of upgrading, a database backup is sufficient, but be sure to check out that chapter for valuable information on extensive backups, including how to restore a database backup in case you ever need to go through that process.

Upgrading WordPress Automatically

To update WordPress automatically, follow these steps:

1. **Back up your WordPress Web site.**

   Backing up your Web site before updating is an important step in case something goes wrong with the upgrade. Give yourself some peace of mind knowing that you have a full copy of your Web site that can be restored, if needed. My advice is not to skip this step under any circumstances.

2. **Deactivate all plugins.**

This prevents any plugin conflicts caused by the upgraded version of WordPress from affecting the upgrade process, and ensures that your Web site won't break after the upgrade is completed. More information on working with and managing plugins can be found in Book VII; for the purposes of this step, you can deactivate plugins by following these steps:

a. *Choose Plugins⇨Plugins on the Dashboard.*

   The Plugins page appears.

b. *Select all plugins by checking the box to the left of the plugin names listed on that page (see Figure 6-4).*

c. *In the drop-down menu at the top, select Deactivate.*

d. *Click the Apply button.*

3. **Choose Dashboard⇨Updates.**

The WordPress Updates page appears.

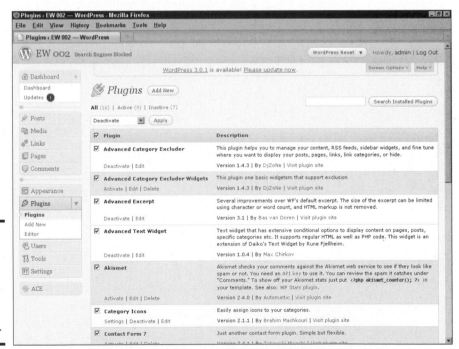

Figure 6-4: Plugins page with all plugins selected, ready to de-activate.

4. **Click the Update Automatically button.**

   The Update WordPress page appears with a series of messages (as shown in Figure 6-5).

5. **Click the Go to Dashboard link.**

   The Dashboard page appears in your Web browser. Notice that both the update alert message at the top of the site, and the notification bubble on the Dashboard menu are no longer visible. Your WordPress installation is now using the latest version of WordPress.

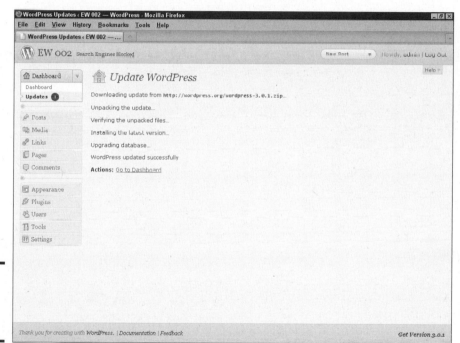

Figure 6-5:
WordPress
update
messages.

Upgrading WordPress Manually

The second and least used method of upgrading WordPress is the manual method. The method is least used mainly because the automatic method, discussed in the preceding section, is so quick and easy to accomplish. However, certain circumstances — probably related to the inability of your hosting environment to accommodate the automatic method — exist where you can manually upgrade WordPress, so we include the description of the process here.

To upgrade WordPress manually:

1. **Back up your WordPress Web site and deactivate all plugins.**

   Refer to Steps 1 and 2 in the preceding "Upgrading WordPress Automatically" section.

2. **Navigate to the WordPress Updates page by clicking the Please Update Now link.**

3. **Click the Download button.**

   This opens a dialog box that allows you to save the `.zip` file of the latest WordPress download package to your local computer, as shown in Figure 6-6.

Figure 6-6:
Down-
loading the
WordPress
files to your
local
computer.

4. **Select a location to store the download package and click Save.**

   The `.zip` file downloads to your selected location on your computer.

5. **Browse to the `.zip` file on your computer.**

6. **Unzip the file.**

   Use a program like WinZip (`www.winzip.com`).

7. **Connect to your Web server via FTP.**

   See Book II, Chapter 2 for a refresher on how to use FTP.

8. **Delete all the files and folders in your existing WordPress installation directory *except* the following:**

   - `/wp-content` folder
   - `.htaccess`
   - `wp-config.php`

9. **Upload the contents of the /wordpress folder to your Web server — not the folder itself.**

   Most FTP client software lets you select all the files to drag and drop them to your Web server. Other programs have you highlight the files and click a Transfer button.

10. **Navigate to the following URL on your Website: http:// yourdomain.com/wp-admin.**

    Don't panic — your database still needs to be upgraded to the latest version; so instead of seeing your Web site on your domain, you see a message telling you that a database upgrade is required, as shown in Figure 6-7.

11. **Click the Upgrade WordPress Database button.**

    WordPress initiates the upgrade of the MySQL database associated with your Web site. When the database upgrade is complete, the page refreshes and displays a message that the process has finished.

12. **Click the Continue button.**

    Your browser loads the WordPress login page. The upgrade is complete and you can continue using WordPress with the newly upgraded features.

Figure 6-7:
Press the
button to
upgrade
your
WordPress
database.

The upgrade process occurs on a regular basis, at least three or four times per year. For some users, this is a frustrating reality of using WordPress; however, this active development environment is part of what makes WordPress the most popular platform available. Because WordPress is always adding great new features and functions to the platform, upgrading always ensures that you're on top of the game and using the latest tools and features.

If you're the type of person who is uncomfortable with performing administrative tasks, such as upgrading and creating database backups, you can hire someone to perform these tasks for you — either a member of your company (if you are a business) or a WordPress consultant skilled in the practice of performing these tasks. Book I, Chapter 4 includes a listing of experienced consultants who can lend a hand.

Chapter 7: Backing Up, Packing Up, and Moving to a New Host

In This Chapter

✔ **Moving to WordPress from a different platform**

✔ **Database backup management**

✔ **Backing up plugins and themes**

✔ **Storing images and media files**

✔ **Exporting data from WordPress**

✔ **Using plugins to make backups and moving easier**

As a WordPress Web site owner, you may need to move your site to a different home on the Web; either to a new Web host or into a different account on your current hosting account. Or maybe you're an owner who needs to move your site right now.

This chapter covers the best way to migrate a blog that exists within a different blogging platform (like Movable Type or TypePad) to WordPress. This chapter also takes you through how to back up your WordPress files, data, and content and move them to a new hosting provider, or different domain.

Migrating Your Existing Blog to WordPress

So you have a blog on a different blogging system and want to move your blog to WordPress? This chapter helps you accomplish just that. WordPress makes it relatively easy to pack up your data and archives from one blog platform and move to a new WordPress blog.

WordPress lets you move your blog from such platforms as Blogspot, TypePad, and Movable Type. It also gives you a nifty way to migrate from any blogging platform via RSS feeds, as long as the platform you're importing from has an RSS feed available. Some platforms, such as MySpace, have some limitations on RSS feed availability, so be sure to check with your platform provider. In this chapter, you discover how to prepare your blog for migration and how to move from the specific platforms for which WordPress provides importer plugins.

For each blogging platform, the WordPress.org platform provides you with a quick and easy way to install plugins that allows you to import and use your content right away. The importers are packaged in a plugin format because most people use an importer just once, and some people don't use the importer tools at all. The plugins are there for you to use if you need them. WordPress.com, on the other hand, has the importers built into the software. Note the differences for the version you are using.

Movin' on up

Bloggers have a variety of reasons to migrate from one system to WordPress:

✦ **Curiosity:** There is a *lot* of buzz around the use of WordPress and the whole community of WordPress users. People are naturally curious to check out something that all the cool kids are doing.

✦ **More control of your blog:** This reason applies particularly to those who have a blog on Blogspot, TypePad, or any other hosted service. Hosted programs limit what you can do, create, and mess with. When it comes to plugins, add-ons, and theme creation, hosting a WordPress blog on your own Web server wins hands down. Additionally, you have complete control of your data, archives, and backup capability when you host your blog on your own server.

✦ **Ease of use:** Many people find the WordPress interface easier to use, more understandable, and a great deal more user-friendly than many of the other blogging platforms available today.

The hosted version of WordPress.com and the self-hosted version of WordPress.org allow you to migrate your blog to their platforms; however, WordPress.com does not provide as many options for import as WordPress.org does. The following is a list of blogging platforms that have built-in importers, or import plugins, for migration to WordPress:

✦ Blogger

✦ Movable Type

✦ TypePad

✦ Vox

✦ Posterous

✦ TextPattern

✦ RSS Feeds

✦ GreyMatter

✦ DotClear

✦ Blogware

✦ WordPress.com

In the WordPress.org software (self-hosted), the importers are added to the installation as plugins. The importer plugins included in the preceding list are plugins packaged within the WordPress.org software or found by searching in the Plugins Directory at `http://wordpress.org/extend/plugins/tags/importer`. You can import content from several other platforms by installing other plugins from the WordPress Plugins Directory, but you may have to search a bit on Google to find them.

Preparing for the big move

Depending on the size of your blog (that is, how many posts and comments you have), the migration process can take anywhere from 5 to 30 minutes. As with any major change or update you make, no matter where your blog is hosted, the very first thing you need to do is create a backup of your blog. You should back up the following:

✦ **Archives:** Posts, comments, and trackbacks

✦ **Template:** Template files and image files

✦ **Links:** Any links, banners, badges, and elements you have in your current blog

✦ **Images:** Any images you use in your blog

Table 7-1 gives you a few tips on creating the export data for your blog in a few major blogging platforms. *Note:* This table assumes that you are logged in to your blog software.

Book II Chapter 7

Backing Up, Packing Up, and Moving to a New Host

Table 7-1	Backing Up Your Blog Data on Major Platforms
Blogging Platform	*Backup Information*
Movable Type	Click the Import/Export button in the menu of your Movable Type Dashboard and then click the Export Entries From link. When the page stops loading, save it on your computer as a `.txt` file.
TypePad	Click the name of the blog you want to export and then click the Import/Export link in the Overview menu. Click the Export link at the bottom of the Import/Export page. When the page stops loading, save it on your computer as a `.txt` file.
Blogspot	Back up your template by copying the text of your template to a text editor, such as Notepad. Save it on your computer as a `.txt` file.

(continued)

Table 7-1 *(continued)*

Blogging Platform	Backup Information
LiveJournal	Browse to `http://livejournal.com/export.bml` and enter your information; choose XML as the format. Save this file on your computer.
WordPress	Choose Tools⇨Export on the Dashboard; choose your options on the Export page and then click the Download Export File button. Save this file on your computer.
RSS feed	Point your browser to the URL of the RSS feed you want to import. Wait until it loads fully (you may need to set your feed to display all posts). View the source code of the page, copy and paste that source code into a `.txt` file, and save the file on your computer.

This import script allows for a maximum file size of 128MB. If you get an "out of memory" error, try dividing the import file into pieces and uploading them separately. The import script is smart enough to ignore duplicate entries, so if you need to run the script a few times to get it to take everything, you can do so without worrying about duplicating your content. (You could also attempt to, temporarily, increase your PHP memory limit by making a quick edit of the `wp-config.php` file; more information on this is found in Book II, Chapter 5 and Chapter 6.)

Converting templates

Every blogging program has a unique way of delivering content and data to your blog. Template tags vary from program to program; no two are the same, and each template file requires conversion if you want to use *your* template with your new WordPress blog. In such a case, you have two options:

✦ **Convert the template yourself.** To accomplish this task, you need to know WordPress template tags and HTML. If you have a template that you're using on another blogging platform and want to convert it for use with WordPress, you need to swap the original platform tags for WordPress tags. The information provided in Book VI gives you the rundown on working with themes, as well as basic WordPress template tags; you may find that information useful if you plan to attempt a template conversion yourself.

✦ **Hire an experienced WordPress consultant to do the conversion for you.** See Book I, Chapter 4 for a list of WordPress consultants.

To use your own template, make sure that you saved *all* the template files, the images, and the stylesheet from your previous blog setup. You need them to convert the template(s) for use in WordPress.

Hundreds of free templates are available for use with WordPress, so it may be a lot easier to abandon the template you're currently working with and find a free WordPress template that you like. If you paid to have a custom design done for your blog, contact the designer of your theme, and hire him to perform the template conversion for you. Alternatively, you can hire several WordPress consultants to perform the conversion for you — including yours truly.

Moving your blog to WordPress

You've packed all your stuff, and you have your new place prepared. Moving day has arrived!

This section takes you through the steps for moving your blog from one blog platform to WordPress. This section assumes that you already have the WordPress software installed and configured on your own domain.

Find the import function that you need by following these steps:

1. **On the Dashboard, choose Tools⇨Import.**

   The Import page appears, listing blogging platforms, such as Blogger and Movable Type, from which you can import content. (See Figure 7-1.)

**Book II
Chapter 7**

**Backing Up,
Packing Up,
and Moving to
a New Host**

Figure 7-1: The Import feature of the (self-hosted) WordPress.org Dashboard.

2. **Click the link for the blogging platform you're working with.**

   Click the Install Now button to install the importer plugin to begin using it.

The following sections provide some import directions for a few of the most popular blogging platforms (other than WordPress, that is). Each platform has its own content export methods, so be sure to check the documentation for the blogging platform that you are using.

Importing from Blogspot, er Blogger

I call it Blogspot; you call it Blogger — a rose by any other name would smell as sweet. The blogging application owned by Google is referenced either way. In the end, we're talking about the same application.

To begin the import process, first complete the steps in the "Moving your blog to WordPress" section, earlier in this chapter. Then follow these steps:

1. **Click the Blogger link on the Import page and install the plugin for importing from Blogger.**

   Click the Activate Plugin & Install Importer link and the Import Blogger page loads with instructions to import your file, as shown in Figure 7-2.

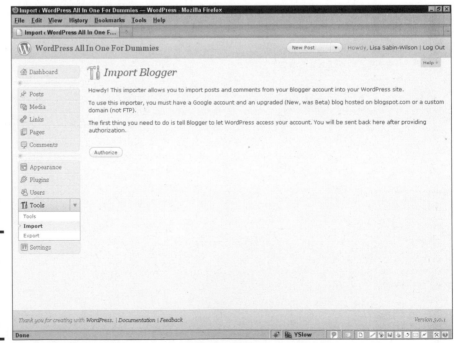

Figure 7-2: Import Blogger page in the WordPress Dashboard.

2. **Click the Authorize button to tell WordPress to access your account.**

   A page from Google opens with a message that says your WordPress blog is trying to access your Google account.

3. **Enter the e-mail address and password you use for Google; then click the Sign In button.**

   The Access Request page in your Google Account opens. When you have successfully logged in, you receive a message from Google stating that your blog at WordPress is requesting access to your Blogger account so that it can post entries on your behalf.

4. **Give your permission by clicking the Grant Access button on the Access Request page.**

   If you have many posts and comments in your Blogger blog, the import can take 30 minutes or more.

   After the import script has performed its magic, you're redirected to your WordPress Dashboard, where the name of your Blogger blog is listed.

5. **To finish importing the data from Blogger, click the Import button (below the Magic Button header).**

   The text on the button changes to *Importing . . .* while the import takes place. When the import is complete, the text on the button changes to *Set Authors* (no wonder it's called the Magic Button!).

6. **Click the Set Authors button to assign the authors to the posts.**

   The Blogger username appears on the left side of the page; a drop-down menu on the right side of the page displays the WordPress login name.

7. **Assign authors by using the drop-down menu.**

   If you have just one author on each blog, the process is especially easy: Use the drop-down menu on the right to assign the WordPress login to your Blogger username. If you have multiple authors on both blogs, each Blogger username is listed on the left side with a drop-down menu to the right of each username. Select a WordPress login for each Blogger username to make the author assignments.

8. **Click Save Changes.**

   You're done!

Importing from LiveJournal

Both WordPress.com and WordPress.org offer an import script for LiveJournal users, and the process of importing from LiveJournal to WordPress is the same for each platform.

Book II
Chapter 7

Backing Up,
Packing Up,
and Moving to
a New Host

To export your blog content from LiveJournal, log in to your LiveJournal blog and then type this URL in your browser's address bar: www.livejournal.com/export.bml.

LiveJournal lets you export the XML files one month at a time, so if you have a blog with several months' worth of posts, be prepared to be at this process for a while. First, you have to export the entries one month at a time, and then you have to import them into WordPress — yep, you guessed it — one month at a time.

To speed the process a little, you can save all the exported XML LiveJournal files in one text document by copying and pasting each month's XML file into one plain-text file (created in a text editor such as Notepad), thereby creating one long XML file with all the posts from your LiveJournal blog. Then you can save the file as an XML file to prepare it for import into your WordPress blog.

After you export the XML file from LiveJournal, return to the Import page in your WordPress Dashboard, and follow these steps:

1. Click the LiveJournal link and install the plugin for installing from LiveJournal.

Click the Activate Plugin & Install Importer link and the Import LiveJournal page loads with instructions to import your file, as shown in Figure 7-3.

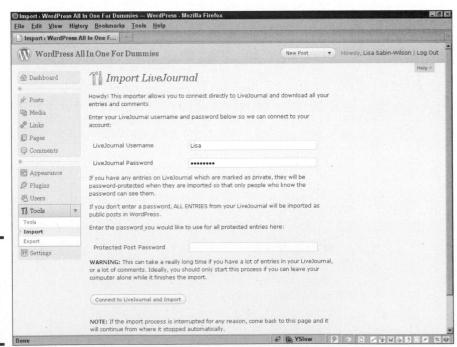

Figure 7-3:
Import LiveJournal page on the WordPress Dashboard.

2. **Click the Browse button.**

   A window opens, listing files on your computer.

3. **Double-click the name of the XML file you saved earlier.**

4. **Click the Upload and Import button.**

   When the import script finishes, it reloads the page with a confirmation message that the process is complete. Then WordPress runs the import script and brings over all your posts from your LiveJournal blog.

Importing from Movable Type and TypePad

Six Apart created both Movable Type and TypePad. These two blogging platforms run on essentially the same code base, so the import/export procedure is the same for both. Refer to Table 7-1, earlier in this chapter, for details on how to run the export process in both Movable Type and TypePad. This import script moves all your blog posts, comments, and trackbacks to your WordPress blog.

Go to the Import page on your WordPress Dashboard by following Steps 1 and 2 in the "Moving your blog to WordPress" section, earlier in this chapter. Then follow these steps:

1. **Click the Movable Type and Typepad link and install the plugin for importing from Movable Type and Typepad.**

   Click the Activate Plugin & Install Importer link and the Import Movable Type or TypePad page loads with instructions to import your file, as shown in Figure 7-4.

2. **Click the Browse button.**

   A window opens, listing your files.

3. **Double-click the name of the export file you saved from your Movable Type or TypePad blog.**

4. **Click the Upload File and Import button.**

   Sit back and let the import script do its magic. When the script finishes, it reloads the page with a confirmation message that the process is complete.

Book II
Chapter 7

Backing Up,
Packing Up,
and Moving to
a New Host

Figure 7-4:
Import
Movable
Type or
TypePad
page on the
WordPress
Dashboard.

When the import script finishes, you can assign users to the posts, matching the Movable Type or TypePad usernames with WordPress usernames. If you have just one author on each blog, this process is easy; you simply assign your WordPress login to the Movable Type or TypePad username by using the drop-down menu. If you have multiple authors on both blogs, match the Movable Type or TypePad usernames with the correct WordPress login names and then click Save Changes. You're done!

Importing from WordPress

With the WordPress import script, you can import one WordPress blog into another; this is true for both the hosted and self-hosted versions of WordPress. WordPress imports all your posts, comments, custom fields, and categories into your blog. Refer to Table 7-1, earlier in this chapter, to find out how to use the export feature to obtain your blog data.

When you complete the export, follow these steps:

1. **Click the WordPress link on the Import page and install the plugin to import from WordPress.**

   Click the Activate Plugin & Install Importer link and the Import WordPress page loads with instructions to import your file, as shown in Figure 7-5.

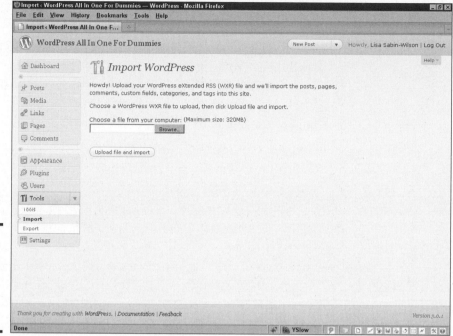

Book II
Chapter 7

Backing Up,
Packing Up,
and Moving to
a New Host

Figure 7-5:
Import
WordPress
page on the
WordPress
Dashboard.

2. **Click the Browse button.**

   A window opens, listing the files on your computer.

3. **Double-click the export file you saved earlier from your WordPress blog.**

4. **Click the Upload File and Import button.**

   The import script gets to work, and when it finishes, it reloads the page with a confirmation message that the process is complete.

Importing from an RSS feed

If all else fails, or if WordPress doesn't provide an import script that you need for your current blog platform, you can import your blog data via the RSS feed for the blog you want to import. With the RSS import method, you can import posts only; you can't use this method to import comments, track-backs, categories, or users. WordPress.com currently doesn't let you import blog data via an RSS feed; this function works only with the self-hosted WordPress.org platform.

Refer to Table 7-1, earlier in this chapter, for the steps to create the file you need to import via RSS. Then follow these steps:

1. **On the Import page in the WordPress Dashboard, click the RSS link and install the plugin to import from an RSS feed.**

   Click the Activate & Install link and the Import RSS page loads with instructions to import your RSS file, as shown in Figure 7-6.

2. **Click the Browse button on the Import RSS page.**

   A window opens, listing the files on your computer.

3. **Double-click the export file you saved earlier from your RSS feed.**

4. **Click the Upload File and Import button.**

   The import script does its magic and then reloads the page with a confirmation message that the process is complete.

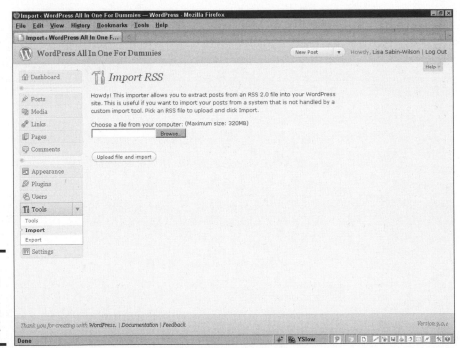

Figure 7-6:
Import RSS page in the WordPress Dashboard.

Finding other import resources

The WordPress Codex has a long list of other available scripts, plugins, workarounds, and outright hacks for importing from other blog platforms. You can find that information at `http://codex.wordpress.org/Importing_Content`.

Note, however, that volunteers run the WordPress Codex. When you refer to the Codex, be aware that not everything listed in it is necessarily up-to-date or accurate, including import information (or any other information about running your WordPress blog).

Moving Your Web Site to a Different Host

Book II
Chapter 7

Backing Up,
Packing Up,
and Moving to
a New Host

There may come a time that you decide you need to switch from your current hosting provider to a new one. There are reasons why someone would have to do this — either you're unhappy with your current provider and want to move to a new one, or your current provider is going out of business and you're forced to move. Transferring from one host to another is a reality that some Web site owners must face, and transferring an existing Web site, with all of its content, files, and data, from one host to another can seem a very daunting task. This section of the chapter should make it easier for you.

You can go about it two ways:

✦ Manually through backing up your database and downloading essential files

✦ Using a plugin to automate as much of the process as possible

Obviously, using a tool to automate the process for you to make it easier is the more desirable way to go, but just in case you need to do it manually, In the next section of this chapter, I provide you with the instructions for doing it both ways.

Creating a backup and moving manually

In Book II, Chapter 5, we provide you with step-by-step instructions on how to take a backup of your database by using phpMyAdmin. Follow the steps available in that chapter and you'll have a backup of your database with all the recent content you've published to your blog. However, when we say *content,* we mean what you've (or someone else has) written or typed into your blog via the WordPress Dashboard, including

✦ Blog posts, pages, and custom post types

✦ Links, categories, and tags

✦ Post and page options, such as excerpts, time and date, custom fields, categories, tags, and passwords

✦ WordPress settings you configured under the Settings menu in the Dashboard

✦ All widgets that you created and configured

✦ All plugin options that you configured for the plugins you installed

Other elements of your Web site aren't stored in the database, which you need to download, via FTP, from your Web server. The following is a list of those elements, including instructions on where to find them and how to download them to your local computer:

✦ **Media files:** The files you uploaded by using the WordPress media upload feature, including images, videos, audio files and documents. Media files are located in the `/wp-content/uploads` folder. Connect to your Web server via FTP and download that folder to your local computer.

✦ **Plugin files:** Although all the plugin settings are stored in the database, the actual, physical plugin files are not. The plugin files are located in the `/wp-content/plugins` folder. Connect to your Web server via FTP and download that folder to your local computer.

✦ **Theme files:** Widgets and options you've set for your current theme are stored in the database; however, the physical theme template files, images, and stylesheets are not. They're stored in the `/wp-content/themes` folder. Connect to your Web server via FTP and download that folder to your local computer.

Now you have your database and WordPress files stored safely on your local computer; moving them to a new host just involves reversing the process:

1. **Create a new database on your new hosting account.**

The steps for creating a database are found in Book II, Chapter 4.

2. **Import your database backup into the new database you just created:**

   a. *Log in to the cPanel for your hosting account.*

   b. *Click the phpMyAdmin icon and click the name of your new database in the left menu.*

   c. *Click the Import tab at the top.*

   d. *Click the Browse button and select the database backup from your local computer.*

   e. *Click the Go button; the old database imports into the new.*

3. **Install WordPress on your new hosting account.**

   The steps for installing WordPress are found in Book II, Chapter 4.

4. **Edit the `wp-config.php` file to include your new database name, username, password, and host.**

   Information on editing the information in the `wp-config.php` file is found in Book II, Chapter 5 and Chapter 6.

5. **Upload all that you downloaded from the `/wp-content` folder to your new hosting account.**

6. **Browse to your domain in your Web browser.**

   Your Web site should work and you can log in to the WordPress Dashboard by using the same username and password as before because that information is stored in the database you imported.

Using a plugin to back up and move to a new host

BackupBuddy is a plugin that moves a WordPress Web site from one hosting environment to another. This plugin is not free or available in the WordPress Plugin Directory, but it's worth every penny because it takes the entire backup and migration process and makes mincemeat out of it — meaning, it makes moving the site easy to accomplish and can be done in minutesrather than hours. Follow these steps to use this plugin to move your site to a new hosting server:

1. **Purchase and download the BackupBuddy plugin from `http://ewebscapes.com/backupbuddy`.**

   At this time, the cost for the plugin starts at $45.

Book II
Chapter 7

Backing Up,
Packing Up,
and Moving to
a New Host

2. **Install the plugin on your current WordPress Web site.**

   By *current,* I mean the old one, not the new hosting account yet.

3. **Activate the plugin on your WordPress Dashboard.**

   Choose Plugins in the navigation menu and then click the Activate link under the BackupBuddy plugin name.

4. **Navigate to the Backups section on the BackupBuddy options page.**

   Click the Backups link in the BackupBuddy menu.

5. **Click the Full Backup button.**

   This initiates a full backup of your database, files, and content and wraps it neatly into one `.zip` file for you to store on your local computer.

6. **Download the `importbuddy.php` file.**

   Click the `importbuddy.php` file on the Backups page and download it to your local computer, preferably in the same directory as the backup file you downloaded in Step 5.

7. **Connect to your new Web server via FTP.**

8. **Upload the `backup.zip` file and the `importbuddy.php` file.**

   These files should be uploaded in the root, or top level, directory on your Web server (on some Web servers this is the `/public_html` folder; on others it might be the `/httpdocs` folder — if you're unsure what your root directory is, your hosting provider should be able to tell you).

9. **Create a new database on your new hosting account.**

   The steps for creating a database are found in Book II, Chapter 4.

10. **Navigate to the `importbuddy.php` file in your Web browser.**

    The URL for this looks similar to `http://yourdomain.com/importbuddy.php`.

11. **The BackupBuddy page loads in your Web browser.**

    Follow the steps to import the backup file and install WordPress, including the database information needed: database username, name, password, and host. This entire process takes about five to ten minutes, maybe more depending on the size of your Web site.

12. **Load your Web site in your Web browser.**

    After BackupBuddy does its thing, your Web site is ready to use like always.

Book III

Exploring the WordPress Dashboard

The 5th Wave   By Rich Tennant

"Are you using that 'clone' tool again?!"

Contents at a Glance

Chapter 1: Logging In and Taking a Look Around

*W*ith WordPress.org successfully installed, you can explore your new blogging software. This chapter guides you through the preliminary setup of your new WordPress blog by using the Dashboard. When you blog with WordPress, you spend a lot of time in the Dashboard, which is where you make all the exciting, behind-the-scenes stuff happen. In this panel, you can find all the settings and options that enable you to set up your blog just the way you want it. (If you still need to install and configure WordPress, check out Book II, Chapter 4.)

Feeling comfortable with the Dashboard sets you up for successful entrance into the WordPress blogging world. You'll tweak your WordPress settings several times throughout the life of your blog. In this chapter, while we go through the various sections, settings, options, and configurations available to you, understand that nothing is set in stone. You can set options today and change them at any time.

Logging In to the Dashboard

The direct approach (also known as jumping in) usually works best when you want to get familiar with a new software tool. To that end, just follow these steps to log in to WordPress and look at the guts of the Dashboard:

1. **Open your Web browser and type the WordPress login page address (or URL) in the address box.**

The login page's address looks something like this (exchange that `.com` for a `.org` or a `.net`, as needed):

```
http://www.yourdomain.com/wp-login.php
```

If you installed WordPress in its own folder, include that folder name in the login URL. If you installed WordPress in a folder ingeniously named `wordpress`, the login URL becomes `http://www.yourdomain.com/wordpress/wp-login.php`.

2. **Type your username in the Username text box and your password in the Password text box.**

In case you forget your password, WordPress has you covered. Click the Lost Your Password link (located near the bottom of the page), enter your username and e-mail address, and then click the Submit button. WordPress resets your password and e-mails the new password to you.

3. **Select the Remember Me check box if you want WordPress to place a cookie in your browser.**

The cookie tells WordPress to remember your login credentials the next time you show up. The cookie set by WordPress is harmless and stores your WordPress login on your computer. Because of the cookie, WordPress remembers you the next time you visit. Additionally, because this option tells the browser to remember your login, we don't advise checking this option on public computers. Avoid selecting Remember Me when you're using your work computer or a computer at an Internet café.

Note: Before you set this option, make sure that your browser is configured to allow cookies. (If you aren't sure how to do this configuration, check the help documentation of the Internet browser you're using.)

4. **Click the Log In button.**

After you log in to WordPress, the Dashboard page appears.

Navigating the Dashboard

You can consider the Dashboard to be a control panel of sorts because it offers several quick links and areas that provide information about your blog, starting with the actual Dashboard page, as shown in Figure 1-1.

You can change how the WordPress Dashboard looks, at least in terms of the order the modules appear on it. You can expand (open) and collapse (close) the individual modules by clicking your mouse anywhere within thegray title bar of the module. This feature is really nice because you can use the Dashboard for just those modules that you use regularly. The concept is easy: Keep the modules you use all the time open and close the ones that you use only occasionally — you can open those modules only when you really need them. You save space and can customize your Dashboard to suit your needs.

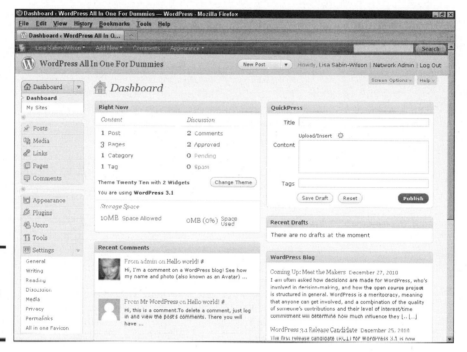

Figure 1-1: The WordPress Dashboard page.

Book III Chapter 1

Logging In and Taking a Look Around

When you view your Dashboard for the very first time, all the modules in the Dashboard appear in the expanded (open) position by default (refer to Figure 1-1).

The navigation menu in the WordPress Dashboard appears on the left side of your browser window. When you need to get back to the WordPress Dashboard, click the Dashboard link that appears at the top of the navigation menu of any of the pages within your WordPress Dashboard.

In the following sections, we cover the Dashboard page as it appears when you log in to your WordPress Dashboard for the very first time; later we show you how to configure the appearance of your Dashboard so that it best suits how you use the available modules. Also, check out the nearby "Discovering the admin bar" sidebar that covers the menu located at the top of every page in your Dashboard and site.

Right Now

The Right Now module in the Dashboard shows what's going on in your blog right now — right this very second! Figure 1-2 shows the expanded Right Now module in a brand-spanking-new WordPress blog.

Discovering the admin bar

New to WordPress 3.1 is a navigation menu, the admin bar, which you see across the top of Figure 1-1. The admin bar appears at the top of every page on your site, by default, and across the top of every page of the Dashboard if you set it to do so in your profile settings (Chapter 3 of this minibook). The nice thing is that the only person who can see the admin bar is you because it displays only for the user who is logged in. The admin bar contains shortcuts that take you to the most frequently viewed areas of your WordPress Dashboard. Across the top, from left to right you find that your photo and name display with a drop-down menu when you hover on them. The drop-down menu provides you with quick links to three areas in your Dashboard: Edit Your Profile, Dashboard, and Log Out. The next link in the admin bar is

called New; hover on that and you find links to Post and Page, which you click to go to either the Add New Post page or the Add New Page screen. The next link is Comments; click that and visit the Manage Comments page in your Dashboard. The last link is Appearance; hover on that link and the Widgets and Menus links appear. When you click one, you can visit either the Widgets page or the Custom Menu page in your Dashboard. Additionally, on the right side of the admin bar is a search form that you can use to search for items on your site by using keywords.

Again, the admin bar is seen only by you at the top of your site, no matter what page you're on, as long as you are logged in to your WordPress site.

Figure 1-2:
The Right Now module in the Dashboard, expanded so that you can see the available features.

The Right Now module shows the following default information below the Content and Discussion headers:

✦ **The number of posts you have:** This number reflects the total number of posts you currently have in your WordPress blog; the blog in Figure 1-2 has one post. The number is blue, which means it's a clickable link. When you click the link, you go to the Edit Posts page, where you can edit the posts on your blog. We cover editing posts in Book IV, Chapter 1.

✦ **The number of pages:** The number of pages on your blog, which changes when you add or delete pages. (*Pages,* in this context, refer to the static pages you create in your blog.) Figure 1-2 shows that the blog has three pages.

Clicking this link takes you to the Edit Pages page, where you can view, edit, and delete your current pages. (Find the difference between WordPress posts and pages in Book IV, Chapter 2.)

✦ **The number of categories:** The number of categories on your blog, which changes when you add and delete categories. Figure 1-2 shows that this blog has one category.

Clicking this link takes you to the Categories page, where you can view, edit, and delete your current categories or add brand-new ones. (For details about the management and creation of categories, see Book III, Chapter 7.)

**Book III
Chapter 1**

**Logging In
and Taking a
Look Around**

✦ **The number of tags:** The number of tags in your blog, which changes when you add and delete categories. Figure 1-2 shows that this blog has one tag.

Clicking this link takes you to the Tags page, where you can add new tags and view, edit, and delete your current tags. (You can find more information about tags in Book III, Chapter 7.)

✦ **The number of comments:** The number of comments on your blog. Figure 1-2 shows that this blog has two comments, two approved comments, 0 (zero) pending comments, and 0 (zero) comments marked as spam.

Clicking any of these four links takes you to the Edit Comments page, where you can manage the comments on your blog. We cover the management of comments in Book III, Chapter 5.

The last section of the Dashboard's Right Now module shows the following information:

✦ **Which WordPress theme you're using:** Figure 1-2 shows that the example blog is using the theme Twenty Ten. The theme name is a link that, when clicked, takes you to the Manage Themes page, where you can view and activate themes on your blog.

✦ **How many widgets you've added to your blog:** The number of WordPress widgets you're using in your blog. Figure 1-2 shows that this blog has two widgets. The number 2 is a link that, when clicked, takes you to the Widgets page, where you can change your widget options by editing them, moving them, or removing them. (Widgets are covered in detail in Book VI, Chapter 1.)

✦ **Change Theme:** Clicking this button takes you to the Manage Themes page, which lists currently active and all available themes for your WordPress blog. Your active theme (the theme that's visible on your active blog) appears at the top of the page, below the Current Theme header. All other available themes are listed below Available Themes. Click any theme on this page to use it on your blog.

✦ **The version of WordPress you're using:** The last statement in the Right Now section. Figure 1-2 shows that this blog is using WordPress version 3.1. This version announcement changes if you're using an earlier version of WordPress. When WordPress software is upgraded, this statement tells you that you're using an outdated version of WordPress and encourages you to upgrade to the latest version.

Recent Comments

The module below the Right Now module is the Recent Comments module, as shown in Figure 1-3. Within this module, you find

+ **The most recent comments published to your blog:** WordPress displays a maximum of five comments in this area.

+ **The author of each comment:** The name of the person who left the comment. This section also displays the author's picture (or avatar), if he or she has one.

+ **A link to the post the comment was left on:** The post title appears to the right of the commenter's name. Click the link, and you go to that post in the Admin panel.

+ **An excerpt of the comment:** A short snippet of the comment left on your blog.

+ **Comment management links:** When you hover on the comment with your mouse cursor, five links appear below the comment. These links give you the opportunity to manage those comments right from your Dashboard: The first link is Unapprove, which appears only if you have comment moderation turned on. (Find out more about moderating comments in Book III, Chapter 5). The other four links are Edit, Reply, Spam, and Trash.

+ **View All button:** This button invites you to see all the comments on your blog. Clicking the View All button takes you to the Edit Comments page, where you can view, edit, moderate, or delete any comments on your blog.

Book III
Chapter 1

Logging In
and Taking a
Look Around

Figure 1-3:
The Recent
Comments
module
in the
Dashboard.

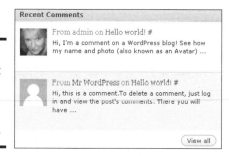

You can find even more information on managing your comments in Book III, Chapter 5.

Incoming Links

The module below the Recent Comments module in the Dashboard is Incoming Links. It lists all the blog-savvy people who wrote a blog post that links to your blog. When your blog is brand new, you won't see any incoming links listed in this section. Don't despair, however; as time goes on, you'll see this listing of links fill up while more and more people discover you and your inspired writings!

In the meantime, the Incoming Links module shows, "This dashboard widget queries Google Blog Search so that when another blog links to your site it will show up here. It has found no incoming links . . . yet. It's okay — there is no rush." The phrase *Google Blog Search* is a link; when you click it, you go to the Google Blog Search directory, which is a search engine for blogs only.

Follow these steps to edit the Incoming Links module:

1. Hover your mouse on the title of the Incoming Links module.

A new link labeled Configure appears directly to the right of the Incoming Links title.

2. Click the Configure link.

The Incoming Links module expands and you see settings that you can configure (see Figure 1-4).

Figure 1-4: Changing the settings of the Incoming Links module by clicking the Configure link.

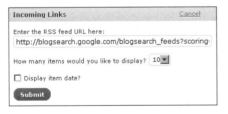

3. Add a URL in the Enter the RSS Feed URL Here text box.

You can enter the URL of any RSS feed that you want to display incoming links to your site. Examples of feeds you can use include such sources as Technorati (`http://technorati.com`), Yahoo! Search (`http://search.yahoo.com`), or Social Mention (`www.socialmention.com`). You're not restricted to using the Google Blog Search engine (`http://blogsearch.google.com`) to provide your Incoming Links information.

4. **Select how many items you want to display from the drop-down list.**

    The default is 5, but you can display up to 20 items (incoming links).

5. **Check the Display Item Date box if you want each incoming link to display the date the link was created.**

    If you don't want the date display, leave that box blank.

6. **Click the Submit button to save all your preferences.**

    Clicking Submit resets the Incoming Links module with your new settings saved.

Plugins

We get into the management and use of WordPress plugins in detail in Book VII; however, for the purposes of this section, we discuss the functions of the Plugins module in the Dashboard.

The Plugins module includes three titles of WordPress plugins that are linked to its individual plugin page within the WordPress Plugin Directory. The Plugins module pulls information via RSS feed from the official WordPress Plugin Directory at `http://wordpress.org/extend/plugins`. This module displays a plugin from three different plugin categories in the official WordPress Plugin Directory: Most Popular, Newest Plugins, and Recently Updated, as shown in Figure 1-5.

Figure 1-5:
The Plugins module in the Dashboard

Plugins

Most Popular
Fast Secure Contact Form (Install)
A super customizable contact form that lets your visitors send you email. Blocks all automated spammers. Packed with settings and features.

Newest Plugins
Rating-Widget (Install)
Create and manage Rating-Widget ratings from within WordPress.

Recently Updated
Contact Form 7 Customfield in mail (Install)
This plugin provides a new tag type for the Contact Form 7 Plugin. It allows the use of customfields from a post to be used in the mail section

**Book III
Chapter 1**

Logging In and Taking a Look Around

The Plugins module doesn't have an Edit link, so you can't customize the information that it displays. Use this module to discover new plugins that can help you do some fun and exciting things with your blog.

The Plugins module does have a very exciting feature that you can use to install, activate, and manage plugins on your blog. Just follow these steps to make it happen:

1. **Click the Install link next to the title of the plugin.**

   The Plugin Information pop-up window opens. It displays the various bits of information about the plugin you chose, such as title, description, version, author, date last updated, and the number of times the plugin was downloaded.

2. **Click the Install Now button.**

   This button appears at the top right of the Plugin Information window.

   The Plugin Information window closes, and the Install Plugins page in your WordPress Dashboard opens, displaying a confirmation message that the plugin has been downloaded, unpacked, and successfully installed.

3. **Specify whether to activate the plugin or proceed to the Plugins page.**

   Two links appear below the confirmation message:

   - *Activate Plugin:* Activate the plugin you just installed on your blog.
   - *Return to Plugins Page:* Go to the Manage Plugins page.

   We cover the installation and activation of WordPress plugins in further depth in Book VII.

4. **Click the Dashboard link to return to the Dashboard.**

   The Dashboard link appears at the top of the left menu on every page of your WordPress Dashboard.

QuickPress

The QuickPress module, shown in Figure 1-6, is a handy form that allows you to write, save, and publish a blog post right from your WordPress Dashboard. The options are similar to the ones we cover in Book IV, Chapter 1.

Figure 1-6: The QuickPress module in the Dashboard.

QuickPress

Title

Upload/Insert

Content

Tags

Save Draft   Reset   Publish

Recent Drafts

If you're using a brand-new WordPress blog and this is a new installation, the Recent Drafts module displays the message There Are No Drafts at the Moment because you haven't written any drafts. As time goes on, however, and you write a few posts in your blog, you may save some of those posts as drafts — to be edited and published later. Those drafts show up in the Recent Drafts module.

The Recent Drafts module displays up to five drafts, showing for each the title of the post, the date it was last saved, and a short excerpt. A View All link also appears; click that link to go the Manage Posts page, where you can view, edit, and manage your blog posts (check out Book IV, Chapter 2 for more information). Figure 1-7 displays the Recent Drafts module, with five posts in draft status, awaiting publication.

Figure 1-7: The Recent Drafts module in the Dashboard

WordPress Blog

When you first install WordPress, by default, the WordPress Development Blog module displays the two most recent updates from the official WordPress Development Blog at `http://wordpress.org/news`. You see the title of the last post, the date it was published, and a short excerpt of the post. Click a title to go directly to that post on the WordPress Development Blog.

We highly recommend following the updates of the WordPress Development Blog. Every single time you log in to your WordPress Dashboard, a glance at this section informs you about any news, updates, or alerts from the makers of WordPress. You can find out about any new versions of the software, security patches, or other important news regarding the software you're using to power your blog.

Although we recommend that you keep the WordPress Development Blog updates in this section, the WordPress platform lets you change this module to display posts from another blog of your choosing. You can accomplish this change by following these steps:

1. **Hover your mouse over the WordPress Development Blog module title and click the Configure link that appears to the right.**

The module changes to display several options for adjusting the information contained in the module (see Figure 1-8).

Figure 1-8: Options to change the feed title and URL of the WordPress Blog module.

2. **Type your preferred RSS feed in the Enter the RSS Feed URL Here text box.**

3. **Type your preferred title in the Give the Feed a Title (Optional) text box.**

4. **Select a number from the How Many Items Would You Like to Display drop-down list.**

The default is 2, but you can display up to 20 by making a different selection from the drop-down list.

5. **Specify whether you want to display the item's content.**

Item content refers to the text content of the post. If you don't select the Display Item Content check box, WordPress doesn't display an excerpt of the post — only the post title.

6. **Specify whether you want to display the name of the person who wrote the post.**

Leave the Display Item Author if Available check box unchecked if you don't want the author's name displayed.

7. **Specify whether you want to display the date.**

   Leave the Display Item Date check box unchecked if you don't want the date displayed.

8. **Click the Submit button to save your changes.**

   The Dashboard page refreshes with your new changes.

If you change your mind, click the Cancel link that appears to the right of the WordPress Development Blog title. Clicking Cancel discards any changes you made and keeps the original settings intact.

The title of the WordPress Development Blog module changes to the title you chose in Step 3 of the preceding list. Figure 1-9 shows that we changed the title to Lisa's Blog, which now displays the RSS Feed from Lisa's blog, using the Feed URL: http://lisasabin-wilson.com/feed.

Figure 1-9: The WordPress Blog module changes based on the options you set.

Lisa's Blog
Atlanta Bound 2011 December 30, 2010
Have Yourself A Merry Little Christmas December 24, 2010
Free Live Webinar: Tips on Running a Successful Web Studio December 15, 2010
Metrodome Collapse December 12, 2010
Tumbl, Tumbl, Tumbl December 12, 2010

Other WordPress News

The Other WordPress News module of the Dashboard pulls in posts from a site called WordPress Planet (http://planet.wordpress.org). By maintaining the default setting in this area, you stay in touch with several posts made by folks who are involved in WordPress development, design, and troubleshooting. You can find many interesting and useful tidbits if you keep this area intact. Quite often, we find great information about new plugins or themes, problem areas and support, troubleshooting, and new ideas, so we tend to stick with the default setting.

WordPress is all about user experience, however, so you can change the options to specify what appears in this area. You can change the items in this module in the same way that you change the options for the WordPress Development Blog module (see the preceding section).

Chapter 2: Customizing Your Dashboard

In This Chapter

✔ Arranging the elements of your Dashboard

✔ Using inline documentation and help

✔ Specifying Dashboard options

✔ Making the Dashboard into your own workspace

*W*hether you work in a cubicle at your local post office or in the comfort of your own home office, you create a workspace individualized to your tastes and needs. Your pens and pencils are in one spot, papers and note cards in another, and your computer monitor and keyboard are placed in a position comfortable and convenient for you. It's your space, and you make it work the best you can with the space you have.

One of the features we've really become quite fond of in WordPress is the ability to create your own workspace within the Dashboard. In this chapter, you can find out how to customize your WordPress Dashboard to fit your own individual needs, including the layout of the Dashboard, changing links and RSS feed information, and even rearranging the modules in the different pages of the Dashboard. Armed with this information, you can open up your Dashboard and create your very own workspace.

Arranging the Dashboard to Your Tastes

You can arrange the order of the modules in your Dashboard to suit your tastes. WordPress places a great deal of emphasis on user experience, and a big part of that effort results in your ability to create a Dashboard that you find most useful. You can very easily change the modules to display and the order in which they display.

Follow these steps to move the Right Now module so that it appears on the right side of your Dashboard page:

1. **Hover your mouse on the title bar of the Right Now module.**

When hovering over the title, your mouse cursor changes to the Move cursor (a cross with arrows on a PC or the hand cursor on a Mac).

2. **Click and hold your mouse button and drag the Right Now module to the right side of the screen.**

While you drag the module, a light-gray box with a dotted border appears on the right side of your screen. That gray box is a guide that shows you where you can drop the module. See Figure 2-1.

Figure 2-1: A light gray box appears as a guide when you drag and drop modules in the WordPress Dashboard.

3. **Release the mouse button when you have the Right Now module in place.**

The Right Now module is positioned on the right side of your Dashboard page.

The other modules on the right side of the Dashboard have shifted down, and the Recent Comments Module is the module in the top left of the Dashboard page.

4. (Optional) Click the title bar of the Right Now module.

The module collapses. Click the title bar again to expand the module. You can keep that module open or closed based on your own preference.

Repeat these steps with each module that you want to move on the Dashboard by dragging and dropping them so that they appear in the order you prefer.

When you navigate away from the Dashboard, WordPress remembers the changes you made. When you return, you still see your customized Dashboard, and you don't need to redo these changes in the future.

Removing Dashboard Modules

If you find that your Dashboard contains a few modules that you just never use, you can get rid of them altogether by following these steps:

1. Click the Screen Options button at the top of the Dashboard.

The Screen Options pop-up menu opens, displaying the title of each module with a check box to the left of each title.

2. Deselect the check box for the module you want to hide on your Dashboard.

The check mark disappears from the box, and the module disappears from your Dashboard.

If you want a module that you hid to reappear, you can simply enable that module by selecting the module's check box in the Screen Options menu.

Changing the Dashboard layout

We're positive that everyone works differently, in terms of how we like our workspace laid out. Personally, Lisa likes to have one long column of items so that she can scroll through and focus on one area, in particular, without other things to the right and left of her periphery.

In the same Screen Options area where you can remove modules (as discussed in the preceding section), you can also change the format of your Dashboard by choosing to have one, two, three, or four columns displayed on your Dashboard — just follow these few steps:

**Book III
Chapter 2**

**Customizing Your
Dashboard**

1. **Click the Screen Options button at the top of the Dashboard.**

The Screen Options pop-up menu opens.

2. **In the Screen Layout Options section of the menu, choose the number of columns you want displayed.**

You have the choice of one, two, three, or four columns — check the radio button to the left of the number you want, and your Dashboard display changes immediately.

3. **Click the Screen Options button again to close the Screen Options menu.**

You can see that Lisa likes all her stuff in one long column, which her personal blog's Dashboard shows in Figure 2-2, where she chose to display her Dashboard in a one-column layout. In Figure 2-2, almost all of Lisa's Dashboard modules are closed — you can open and close them when you need to, based on what you need to see and do within your Dashboard at any given time.

By using the features that enable you to customize your Dashboard, you can create your own, individualized workspace that works best for you, based on how you use WordPress. With these features, everyone can customize his own WordPress experience, and no two WordPress user experiences are necessarily the same — like snowflakes!

Figure 2-2: Lisa's WordPress Dashboard displays a one-column layout.

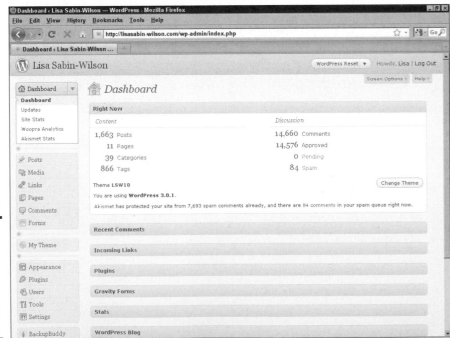

Finding Inline Documentation and Help

The developers of the WordPress software really put in time and effort to provide users with tons of inline documentation that provides several tips and hints right inside the Dashboard. You can generally find inline documentation for nearly every WordPress feature you'll use.

Inline documentation refers to those small sentences or phrases that you see alongside or below a feature in WordPress that give a short, but very helpful, explanation about what the feature is. Figure 2-3 shows the General Settings page, where a lot of inline documentation and guiding tips correspond with each feature. These tips can clue you into what the features are, how to use them, and some basic recommended settings.

In addition to the inline documentation that you find scattered throughout the Dashboard, a helpful Help tab is located in the upper-right corner of your Dashboard. Click this tab to open a panel that contains a lot of text — that text is documentation relevant to the page you're currently viewing in your Dashboard. For example, if you're viewing the General Settings page, the Help tab displays documentation relevant to the General Settings page. Likewise, if you're viewing the Add New Post page, then the Help tab displays documentation with topics relevant to the settings and features you find on the Add New Post page within your Dashboard.

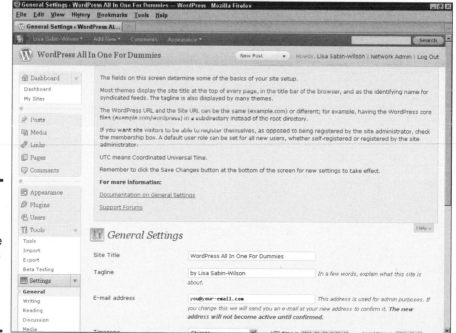

Figure 2-3:
Inline documentation on the General Settings page in the WordPress Dashboard.

The inline documentation, and the topics and text you find in the Help tab, exist to assist users while they work with the WordPress platform, helping make the experience as easy to understand as possible. Other places on the Web that you can visit to find help and useful support for WordPress include the WordPress Support Forums at `http://wordpress.org/support`.

Creating Your Own Workspace

Throughout the different pages of your WordPress Dashboard, you can apply the customization features that we cover for the main Dashboard page in the section "Arranging the Dashboard to Your Tastes," earlier in this chapter. Every section of the WordPress Dashboard is customizable, with drag-and-drop modules, screen options, and inline help and documentation.

Figure 2-4 displays the Posts page in the WordPress Dashboard (the Posts page is covered in greater detail in Book IV, Chapter 1), with the Screen Options menu displayed, showing the different options for customization, including

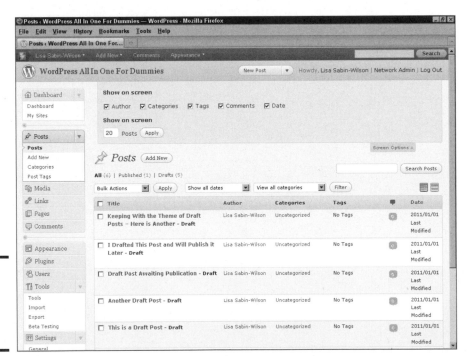

Figure 2-4:
Screen options on the Posts page.

✦ Check boxes that you can to select or deselect to display or hide, respectively, the Author, Categories, Tags, Comments, and Date of the posts listed on the Posts page

✦ A text box in which you can input the number of posts you want displayed on the Posts page

Figure 2-5 shows the Help topics on the Posts page that appear when you click the Help tab at the top of the page to display the inline documentation for the page.

In the Help menu on each page of the WordPress Dashboard, you can find links that lead you to other areas on the Internet that contain additional help and support topics and resources so that you can find out more about the different WordPress features.

**Book III
Chapter 2**

**Customizing Your
Dashboard**

Figure 2-5:
Click the
Help tab on
the Posts
page to
display inline
documen-
tation.

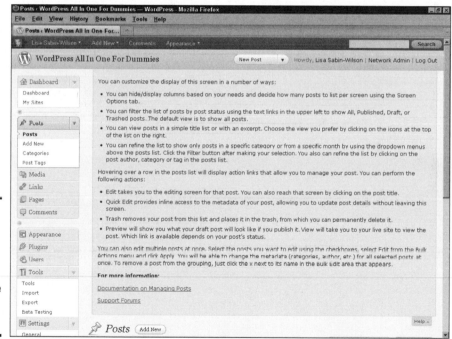

Chapter 3: Exploring Tools and Settings

In This Chapter

✔ Configuring your WordPress general settings

✔ Putting together your personal profile

✔ Formatting your blog

A s exciting as it is to dig right in and start blogging right away, you should attend to a few housekeeping items first, including adjusting the settings that allow you to personalize your Web site or blog. These settings are the first settings that we cover in this chapter because these settings create your readers' experience with your Web site.

In this chapter, you can completely explore the Settings menu in the WordPress Dashboard and discover how to configure items such as date and time settings, site titles, and e-mail notification settings. This chapter also covers important aspects of your Web site configuration, such as permalinks, discussion options, and privacy settings.

Some of the menu items, such as creating and publishing new posts, are covered in detail in other chapters, but they're well worth a mention here, as well. (Each section in this chapter contains a cross-reference telling you where you can find more in-depth information on that topic in this book.)

Configuring the Settings

At the very bottom of the navigation menu, you can find the Settings option. Click Settings, and a menu list opens that contains the following links, which we discuss in the sections that follow:

✦ General

✦ Writing

✦ Reading

✦ Discussion

✦ Media

✦ Privacy

✦ Permalinks

General

After you install the WordPress software and log in, you can put a personal stamp on your blog by giving it a title and description, setting your contact e-mail address, and identifying yourself as the author of the blog. You take care of these and other settings on the General Settings page.

To begin personalizing your blog, start with your general settings by following these steps:

1. **Click General link in the Settings menu list.**

The General Settings page appears (see Figure 3-1).

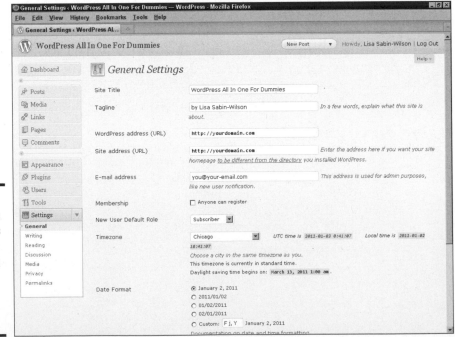

Figure 3-1: Personalize the settings of your WordPress blog on the General Settings page.

2. Enter the name of your blog in the Site Title text box.

The title you enter here is the one that you gave your blog to identify it as your own. In Figure 3-1, Lisa gave the new blog the title *WordPress All-In-One For Dummies,* which appears on the blog, as well as in the title bar of the viewer's Web browser.

Give your blog an interesting and identifiable name. You can use *Fried Green Tomatoes,* for example, if you're blogging about the topic, the book, or the movie, or even anything remotely related to the lovely Southern dish.

3. In the Tagline text box, enter a five- to ten-word phrase that describes your blog.

Figure 3-1 shows that the tagline is *by Lisa Sabin-Wilson.* Therefore, this blog displays the blog title, followed by the tagline: *WordPress All-in-One For Dummies by Lisa Sabin-Wilson.*

The general Internet-surfing public can view your blog title and tagline, which various search engines (such as Google, Yahoo!, and MSN) grab for indexing, so choose your words with this fact in mind. (You can find more information about search engine optimization, or SEO, in Book V.)

4. In the WordPress Address (URL) text box, enter the location where you installed your WordPress blog software.

Be sure to include the `http://` portion of the URL and the entire path to your WordPress installation — for example, `http://yourdomain.com`. If you installed WordPress in a folder in your directory — in a folder called `wordpress`, for example — you need to make sure to include it here. If we installed WordPress in a folder called `wordpress`, the WordPress address would be `http://yourdomain.com/wordpress` (where *yourdomain.com* is your domain name).

5. In the Site Address (URL) text box, enter the Web address where people can find your blog by using their Web browsers.

Typically, what you enter here is the same as your domain name (`http://yourdomain.com`). If you install WordPress in a subdirectory of your site, the WordPress installation URL is different from the blog URL. If you install WordPress at `http://yourdomain.com/wordpress/` (WordPress URL), you need to tell WordPress that you want the blog to appear at `http://yourdomain.com` (the blog URL).

6. Enter your e-mail address in the E-Mail Address text box.

WordPress sends messages about the details of your blog to this e-mail address. When a new user registers for your blog, for example, WordPress sends you an e-mail alert.

**Book III
Chapter 3**

**Exploring Tools
and Settings**

7. **Select a Membership option.**

   Select the Anyone Can Register check box if you want to keep registration on your blog open to anyone. Keep the check box unchecked if you'd rather not have open registration on your blog.

8. **From the New User Default Role drop-down list, select the role that you want new users to have when they register for user accounts in your blog.**

   You need to understand the differences among the user roles because each user role is assigned a different level of access to your blog, as follows:

   - *Subscriber:* The default role. You may want to maintain this role as the one assigned to new users, particularly if you don't know who's registering. Subscribers have access to the Dashboard page, and they can view and change the options in their profiles on the Your Profile and Personal Options page. (They don't have access to your account settings, however — only to their own.) Each user can change his username, e-mail address, password, bio, and other descriptors in his user profile. Subscribers' profile information is stored in the WordPress database, and your blog remembers them each time they visit, so they don't have to complete the profile information each time they leave comments on your blog.

   - *Contributor:* In addition to the access Subscribers have, Contributors can upload files and write, edit, and manage their own posts. Contributors can write posts, but they can't publish the posts; the Administrator reviews all Contributor posts and decides whether to publish them. This setting is a nice way to moderate content written by new authors.

   - *Author:* In addition to the access Contributors have, Authors can publish and edit their own posts.

   - *Editor:* In addition to the access Authors have, Editors can moderate comments, manage categories, manage links, edit pages, and edit other Authors' posts.

   - *Administrator:* Administrators can edit all the options and settings in the WordPress blog.

9. **In the Timezone section, select your UTC time from the drop-down list.**

This setting refers to the number of hours that your local time differs from Coordinated Universal Time (UTC). This setting ensures that all the blog posts and comments left on your blog are time-stamped with the correct time. If you're lucky enough, like Lisa, to live on the frozen tundra of Wisconsin, which is in the Central Standard Time (CST) Zone, you choose – from the drop-down list because that time zone is 6 hours off UTC.

If you're unsure what your UTC time is, you can find it at the Greenwich Mean Time (http://wwp.greenwichmeantime.com) Web site. GMT is essentially the same thing as UTC. WordPress also lists some major cities in the Timezone drop-down list so that you can more easily choose your time zone if you don't know it.

10. **In the Date Format text box, enter the format in which you want the date to appear in your blog.**

This setting determines the style of the date display. The default format displays time like this: January 1, 2011.

Select a different format by clicking the radio button to the left of the option you want. You can also customize the date display by selecting the Custom option and entering your preferred format in the text box provided. If you're feeling adventurous, you can find out how to customize the date format at http://codex.wordpress.org/Formatting_ Date_and_Time.

11. **In the Time Format text box, enter the format for how you want time to display in your blog.**

This setting is the style of the time display. The default format displays time like this: 12:00 a.m.

Select a different format by clicking the radio button to the left of the option you want. You can also customize the date display by selecting the Custom option and entering your preferred format in the text box provided; find out how at http://codex.wordpress.org/ Formatting_Date_and_Time.

You can format the time and date in several ways. Go to http:// us3.php.net/date to find potential formats at the PHP Web site.

12. **From the Week Starts On drop-down list, select the day on which the week starts in your calendar.**

    Displaying the calendar in the sidebar of your blog is optional. If you choose to display the calendar, you can select the day of the week on which you want your calendar to start.

Click the Save Changes button at the bottom of any page where you set new options. If you don't click Save Changes, your settings aren't saved, and WordPress reverts to the preceding options. Each time you click the Save Changes button, WordPress reloads the current page, displaying the new options that you just set.

Writing

Click Writing in the Settings menu list; the Writing Settings page opens (see Figure 3-2).

Figure 3-2:
The Writing
Settings
page.

This page lets you set some basic options for writing your posts. Table 3-1 gives you some information on choosing how your posts look and how WordPress handles some specific conditions.

After you set your options, be sure to click the Save Changes button; otherwise, the changes won't take effect.

Table 3-1	Writing Settings Options	
Option	*Function*	*Default*
Size of the Post Box	Determines the size of the text box on the Write Post page. The bigger the number, the taller the box.	Ten lines
Formatting	Determines whether WordPress converts emoticons to graphics and whether WordPress corrects invalidly nested XHTML automatically. In general, we recommend selecting this option. (You can find more information about valid XHTML code at `http://validator.w3.org/docs/#docs_all`.)	Converts emoticons — such as :-) and :-P — to graphics and corrects invalidly nested XHTML
Default Post Category	Select the category that WordPress defaults to any time you forget to choose a category when you publish a post.	Uncategorized
Default Post Format	Select the format that WordPress defaults to any time you create a post and do not assign a post format. (This is theme specific, not all themes support post formats; see Book VI, Chapter 6.)	Standard
Default Link Category	Select the category that WordPress defaults to any time you forget to categorize a link.	Uncategorized
Press This	Drag and drop the Press This link to the bookmark toolbar of your Web browser, and then use it to easily publish content that you find around the Internet directly to your blog.	N/A
Post via E-Mail	Publish blog posts from your e-mail account by entering the e-mail and server information for the account you'll be using to send posts to your WordPress blog.	N/A

(continued)

Table 3-1 *(continued)*

Option	Function	Default
Remote Publishing	Enable Atom Publishing Protocol or one of the XML-RPC publishing interfaces that enable you to post to your WordPress blog from a remote Web site or desktop publishing application.	Disabled
Update Services *Note:* This option is available only if your blog is made public in the Privacy settings, covered in the "Privacy" section, later in this chapter.	Indicate which ping service you want to use to notify the world that you've made updates, or new posts, to your blog. The default, XML-RPC (`http://rpc.pingomatic.com`), updates all the popular services simultaneously.	`http://rpc.pingomatic.com`

Go to `http://codex.wordpress.org/Update_Services` for comprehensive information on update services.

Reading

The third item in the Settings drop-down list is Reading. Click the Reading link to open the Reading Settings page (see Figure 3-3).

You can set the following options in the Reading Settings page:

✦ **Front Page Displays:** Select the radio button for what you want to appear on the front page of your blog: your latest posts or a static page. You can find detailed information about using a static page for your front page in Book IV, Chapter 2, including information on how to set it up by using the drop-down menus in this section.

✦ **Blog Pages Show at Most:** In the text box, enter the maximum number of posts you want to appear on each blog page.

✦ **Syndication Feeds Show the Most Recent:** In the text box, enter the maximum number of posts that you want to appear in your RSS feed at any time.

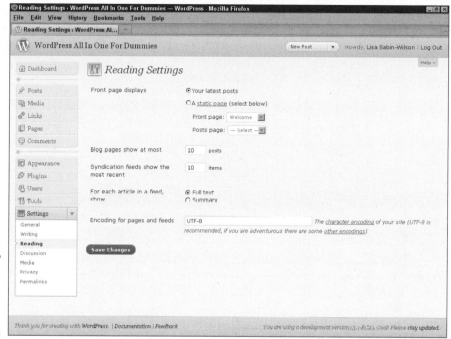

Figure 3-3:
The Reading
Settings
page.

✦ **For Each Article in a Feed, Show:** Select the radio button for either Full Text or Summary. Full Text publishes the entire post to your RSS feed, whereas Summary publishes only an excerpt. (Check out Book I, Chapter 1 for more information on WordPress RSS feeds.)

✦ **Encoding for Pages and Feeds:** UTF-8 is the default, and recommended, character encoding for your blog. *Character encoding* is code that handles the storage and transmission of the text from your blog through the Internet connection. Your safest bet is to leave the default setting in place because UTF-8 is the most commonly accepted character encoding and supports a wide range of languages.

Be sure to click the Save Changes button after you set all your options in the Reading Settings page to make the changes take effect.

**Book III
Chapter 3**

**Exploring Tools
and Settings**

Discussion

Discussion is the fourth item in the Settings menu list; click it to open the Discussion Settings page (see Figure 3-4). The sections on this tab let you set options for handling comments and publishing posts to your blog.

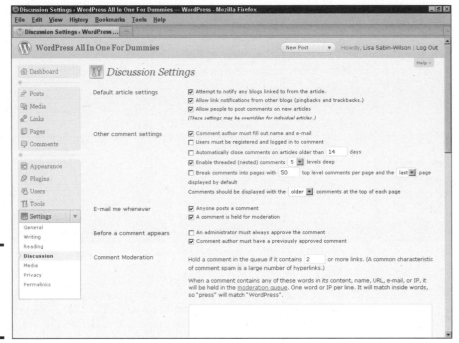

Figure 3-4:
The
Discussion
Settings
page.

The following sections cover the options available to you in the Discussion Settings page, which deals mainly with how comments and trackbacks are handled in your blog.

Default Article Settings

With the Default Article Settings options, you can tell WordPress how to handle post notifications. Here are your options:

✦ **Attempt to Notify Any Blogs Linked to from the Article:** If you select this check box, your blog sends a notification (or *ping*) to any site you've linked to in your blog posts. This notification is also commonly referred to as a *trackback* (we discuss trackbacks in Book III, Chapter 5). Deselect this check box if you don't want these notifications sent.

✦ **Allow Link Notifications from Other Blogs (Pingbacks and Trackbacks):** By default, this check box is selected, and your blog accepts notifications via pings or trackbacks from other blogs that have linked to yours. Any trackbacks or pings sent to your blog appear on your site in the Comments section of the blog post. If you deselect this check box, your blog doesn't accept pingbacks or trackbacks from other blogs.

✦ **Allow People to Post Comments on New Articles:** By default, this check box is selected, and people can leave comments on your blog posts. If you deselect this check box, no one can leave comments on your blog. (You can override these settings for individual articles — you can find more information about this process in Book IV, Chapter 1.)

Other Comment Settings

The Other Comment Settings section tells WordPress how to handle comments:

✦ **Comment Author Must Fill Out Their Name and E-Mail:** Enabled by default, this option requires all commenters on your blog to fill in the Name and E-Mail fields when leaving comments. This option can really help you combat comment spam. (See Book III, Chapter 5 for information on comment spam.) Deselect this check box to disable this option.

✦ **Users Must Be Registered and Logged In to Comment:** Not enabled by default, this option allows you to accept comments on your blog from only people who are registered and logged in as a user on your blog. If the user isn't logged in, she sees a message that reads, "You Must Be Logged in in Order to Leave a Comment."

✦ **Automatically Close Comments on Articles Older Than *X* Days:** Select the check box next to this option to tell WordPress you want comments on older articles to be automatically closed. Fill in the text box provided with the number of days you want to wait before WordPress closes comments on articles.

Many bloggers use this very effective anti-spam technique to keep the comment and trackback spam on their blog down.

✦ **Enable Threaded (Nested) Comments *X* Levels Deep:** From the drop-down list, you can select the level of threaded comments you want to have on your blog. The default is one; you can choose up to ten levels. Instead of all comments being displayed on your blog in chronological order (as they are by default), nesting them allows you and your readers to reply to comments within the comment itself.

**Book III
Chapter 3**

Exploring Tools
and Settings

✦ **Break Comments into Pages with *X* Comments Per Page:** Fill in the text box with the number of comments you want to appear on one page. This setting can really help blogs that receive a large number of comments. It provides you with the ability to break the long string of comments into several pages, which makes them easier to read and helps speed up the load time of your site because the page isn't loading such a large number of comments at once.

✦ **Comments Should Be Displayed with the Older/Newer Comments at the Top of Each Page:** From the drop-down list, select Older or Newer. Selecting Older displays the comments on your blog in the order of oldest to newest. Selecting Newer does the opposite: displays the comments on your blog in the order of newest to oldest.

E-Mail Me Whenever

The two options in the E-Mail Me Whenever section are enabled by default:

✦ **Anyone Posts a Comment:** Enabling this option means that you receive an e-mail notification whenever anyone leaves a comment on your blog. Deselect the check box if you don't want to be notified by e-mail about every new comment.

✦ **A Comment Is Held for Moderation:** This option lets you receive an e-mail notification whenever a comment is awaiting your approval in the comment moderation queue. (See Book III, Chapter 5 for more information about the comment moderation queue.) You need to deselect this option if you don't want to receive this notification.

Before a Comment Appears

The two options in the Before a Comment Appears section tell WordPress how you want WordPress to handle comments before they appear in your blog:

✦ **An Administrator Must Always Approve the Comment:** Disabled by default, this option keeps every single comment left on your blog in the moderation queue until you, the administrator, log in and approve it. Select this check box to enable this option.

✦ **Comment Author Must Have a Previously Approved Comment:** Enabled by default, this option requires comments posted by all first-time commenters to be sent to the comment moderation queue for approval by the administrator of the blog. After comment authors have been approved for the first time, they remain approved for every comment thereafter (this cannot be changed). WordPress stores their e-mail addresses in the database, and any future comments that match any stored e-mails are approved automatically. This feature is another measure that WordPress has built in to combat comment spam.

Comment Moderation

In the Comment Moderation section, you can set options to specify what types of comments are held in the moderation queue to await your approval.

To prevent spammers from spamming your blog with a *ton* of links, enter a number in the Hold a Comment in the Queue If It Contains *X* or More Links text box. The default number of links allowed is two. Try that setting, and if you find that you're getting a lot of spam comments that contain links, consider dropping that number down to 1, or even 0, to prevent those comments from being published on your blog. Sometimes, legitimate commenters will include a link or two in the body of their comment; after a commenter is marked as approved, she is no longer affected by this method of spam protection.

The large text box in the Comment Moderation section lets you type keywords, URLs, e-mail addresses, and IP addresses so that if they appear in comments, you want to hold those comments in the moderation queue for your approval.

Comment Blacklist

In this section, type a list of words, URLs, e-mail addresses, and/or IP addresses that you want to flat-out ban from your blog. Items placed here don't even make it into your comment moderation queue; the WordPress system filters them as spam. We'd give examples of blacklist words, but the words we've placed in our blacklists aren't family-friendly and have no place in a nice book like this one.

What are avatars, and how do they relate to WordPress?

An *avatar* is an online graphical representation of an individual. It's a small graphic icon that people use to visually represent themselves on the Web in areas they participate in conversations, such as discussion forums and blog comments. *Gravatars* are globally recognized avatars; they are avatars that you can take with you wherever you go. They appear alongside blog comments, blog posts, and discussion forums as long as the site you're interacting with is Gravatar-enabled. In October 2007, Automattic, the core group behind the WordPress platform, purchased the Gravatar service and integrated it into WordPress so that all could enjoy and benefit from the service. Gravatars are not automatic; you need to sign up for an account with Gravatar so that you can receive an avatar, via your e-mail address. Find out more about Gravatar by visiting `http://gravatar.com`.

Avatars

The final section of the Discussion Settings page is Avatars. (See the nearby sidebar, "What are avatars, and how do they relate to WordPress?," for information about avatars.) In this section, you can select different settings for the use and display of avatars on your site:

1. **In the Avatar Display section (see Figure 3-5), decide how to display avatars on your site.**

   You have two options:

   - *Don't Show Avatars:* Select this radio button if you don't want your blog to display avatars.
   - *Show Avatars:* Select this radio button to have your blog display avatars.

2. **In the Maximum Rating section, select the radio button for the maximum avatar rating you want to allow for the avatars that do appear on your site.**

   This feature works much like the American movie-rating system. You can select G, PG, R, and X ratings for the avatars that appear on your site, as shown in Figure 3-5. If your site is family-friendly, you probably don't want it to display R- or X-rated avatars, so select G or PG.

3. **Select the radio button for a default avatar in the Default Avatar section (see Figure 3-5).**

4. **Click the Save Changes button.**

Avatars appear in a couple of places:

- ✦ **The Comments page in the Dashboard:** In Figure 3-6, the first two comments display either the commenter's avatar or the default avatar if the commenter hasn't created his or her own.
- ✦ **The comments on individual blog posts in your blog:** Figure 3-7 shows a list of comments on a blog post. If the user doesn't have an avatar assigned from `http://gravatar.com`, the default avatar appears.

To enable the display of avatars in comments on your blog, the Comments template (`comments.php`) in your active theme has to contain the code to display them. Hop on over to Book VI to find information about themes and templates, including template tags that allow you to display avatars in your comment list.

Click the Save Changes button after you set all your options on the Discussion Settings page to make the changes take effect.

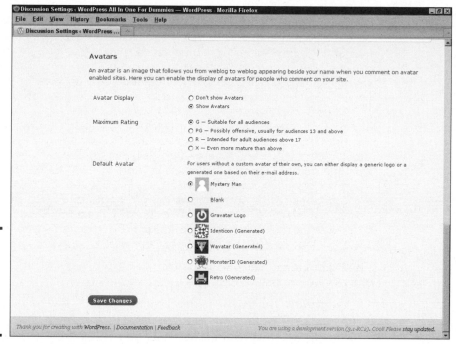

Figure 3-5:
Default
avatars that
you can
display in
your blog.

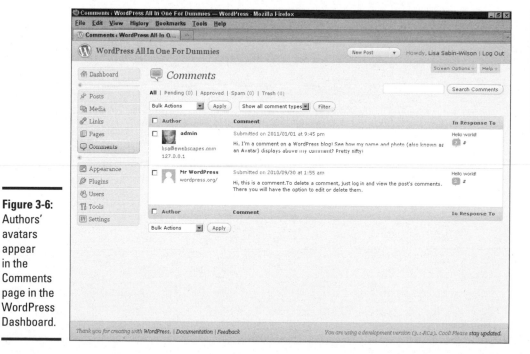

Figure 3-6:
Authors'
avatars
appear
in the
Comments
page in the
WordPress
Dashboard.

Media

The next menu item in the Settings menu list is Media; click the Media link to make the Media Settings page open (see Figure 3-7).

On the Media Settings page, you can configure the options for how your image files (graphics and photos) are resized for use in your blog.

The first set of options on the Media Settings page deals with images. WordPress automatically resizes your images for you in three different sizes. The dimensions are referenced in pixels by width, and then height. (For example, 150 x 150 means 150 pixels in width by 150 pixels in height.)

✦ **Thumbnail Size:** The default is 150 x 150; enter the width and height of your choice. Select the Crop Thumbnail to Exact Dimensions check box to resize the thumbnail exactly to the width and height you specify. Deselect this check box to make WordPress resize the image proportionally.

✦ **Medium Size:** The default is 300 x 300; enter the width and height numbers of your choice.

✦ **Large Size:** The default is 1024 x 1024; enter the width and height numbers of your choice.

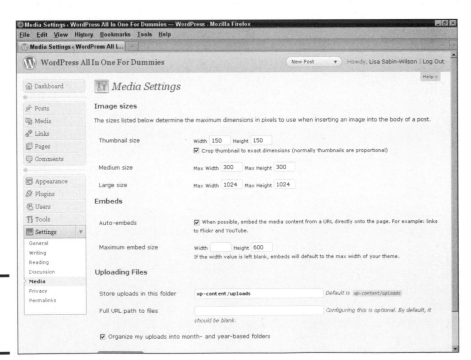

Figure 3-7: The Media Settings page.

In Book VI, we go into detail about WordPress themes and templates, including how you can add image sizes other than just these three. You can use these additional images sizes in and around your Web site, as well as a feature called Featured Image for your posts and articles.

The second set of options on the Media Settings page deals with embedded links and files, such as video and audio files. Select the check box that says Attempt to Automatically Embed All Plain Text URLs if you want your WordPress blog to automatically attach a hyperlink to a text-based URL that you type into your posts or pages. Activating this option means that you don't have to copy and paste the full code given to you by services such as YouTube — instead, you simply paste the hyperlink to the video, and WordPress automatically does the video embedding for you.

Next, set the width and height for the maximum size you want embedded files to be within your post and pages. Embedded items include video players and audio players that appear within your post or page.

Finally, the last set of options on the Media Settings page is the Uploading Files section. Here, you can tell WordPress where to store your uploaded media files:

✦ **Store Uploads in This Folder:** Type the server path to the folder on your Web server where you want your file uploads to be stored. The default is `wp-content/uploads`. You can specify any folder you want. Just be sure that the folder you specify has permissions (`chmod`) set to 755 so that it's writable. (See Book II, Chapter 2 for more information on setting file permissions.)

✦ **Full URL Path to Files (Optional):** You can also type the full URL path to the Uploads folder as an optional setting. (The full URL path is something like `http://yourdomain.com/wp-content/uploads`.)

✦ **Organize My Files into Month and Year-Based Folders:** Select this check box to have WordPress organize your uploaded files in folders by month and by year. Files you upload in September 2010, for example, would be in the following folder: `/wp-content/uploads/2010/09/`. Likewise, files you upload in October 2010, would be in `/wp-content/uploads/2010/10/`.

This check box is selected by default; uncheck it if you don't want WordPress to organize your files by month and year.

Be sure to click the Save Changes button to save your configurations!

In Book IV, Chapter 3, we detail how to insert images in your WordPress posts and pages.

**Book III
Chapter 3**

Exploring Tools
and Settings

Privacy

The next Settings menu item list is Privacy; click it to display the Privacy Settings page, as shown in Figure 3-8.

This page contains only two options, both of which concern visibility on your blog:

✦ **I Would Like My Blog to Be Visible to Everyone, Including Search Engines (Like Google, Bing, Technorati) and Archivers:** This option is the default setting; you're freely allowing search engines to visit your blog and list you in their search results, and letting your site be indexed in blog archive services, such as Technorati.

✦ **I Would Like to Block Search Engines, but Allow Normal Visitors:** If you are one of those rare bloggers who *doesn't* want that type of exposure for your blog, but you do want to let normal visitors (read: no search engines) see your blog, select this option.

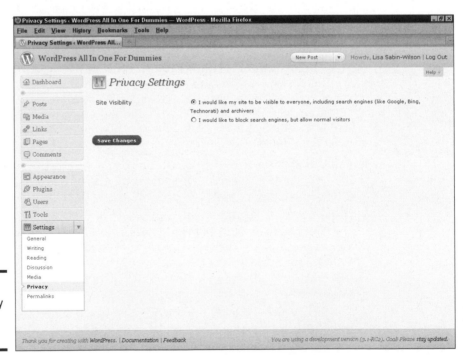

Figure 3-8:
The Privacy
Settings
page.

Generally, you want search engines to be able to find your blog. However, if you have special circumstances, you may want to enforce your privacy settings. For example, we blocked search engines for the site we're using to create the figures in this book because we don't want search engines to find it. At the top of the site, to the right of the site title, a note says *Search Engines Blocked.* This note exists only when you have your privacy settings set to block search engines. When you have privacy enabled, search engines and other content bots can't find your Web site.

Be sure to click the Save Changes button after you set all your options on the Privacy Settings page to make the changes take effect.

Permalinks

The next link on the Settings menu list is Permalinks; click the Permalinks link to view the Permalink Settings page, as shown in Figure 3-9.

Book III Chapter 3

Exploring Tools and Settings

Figure 3-9: The Permalink Settings page.

Each WordPress blog post is assigned its own Web page, and the address (or URL) of that page is called a *permalink*. Posts that you see in WordPress blogs usually have the post permalink in four typical areas:

+ The title of the blog post

+ The Comments link below the post

+ A Permalink link that appears (in most themes) below the post

+ The titles of posts appearing in a Recent Posts sidebar

Permalinks are meant to be permanent links to your blog posts (which is where the *perma* part of that word comes from, in case you're wondering). Other bloggers can use a post permalink to refer to that particular blog post. Ideally, the permalink of a post never changes. WordPress creates the permalink automatically when you publish a new post.

By default, a blog post permalink in WordPress looks like this:

`http://yourdomain.com/?p=100/`

The p stands for *post,* and 100 is the ID assigned to the individual post. You can leave the permalinks in this format, if you don't mind letting WordPress associate each post with an ID number.

WordPress, however, lets you take your permalinks to the beauty salon for a bit of makeover so that you can create pretty permalinks. You probably didn't know that permalinks could be pretty, did you?

Making your post links pretty

Pretty permalinks are links that are more pleasing to the eye than standard links and, ultimately, more pleasing to search-engine spiders. (See Book V for an explanation of why search engines like pretty permalinks.) Pretty permalinks look something like this:

`http://yourdomain.com/2011/01/01/pretty-permalinks`

Break down that URL, and you see the date when the post was made, in year/month/day format. You also see the topic of the post.

To choose how your permalinks look, click Permalinks in the Settings drop-down list. The Permalink Settings page opens (refer to Figure 3-9).

In this page, you can find several options for creating permalinks:

✦ **Default** (ugly permalinks): WordPress assigns an ID number to each blog post and creates the URL in this format: `http://yourdomain.com/?p=100`.

✦ **Day and Name** (pretty permalinks): For each post, WordPress generates a permalink URL that includes the year, month, day, and post slug/title: `http://yourdomain.com/2008/01/01/sample-post/`.

✦ **Month and Name** (also pretty permalinks): For each post, WordPress generates a permalink URL that includes the year, month, and post slug/title: `http://yourdomain.com/2008/01/sample-post/`.

✦ **Numeric** (not so pretty): WordPress assigns a numerical value to the permalink. The URL is created in this format: `http://yourdomain.com/archives/123`.

✦ **Custom Structure:** WordPress creates permalinks in the format you choose. You can create a custom permalink structure by using tags or variables, as we discuss in the following section.

To create the pretty-permalink structure, select the Day and Name radio button; then click the Save Changes button at the bottom of the page.

Customizing your permalinks

A *custom permalink structure* is one that lets you define which variables you want to see in your permalinks by using the tags in Table 3-2.

Table 3-2	Custom Permalinks
Permalink Tag	*Results*
`%year%`	Four-digit year (such as `2007`)
`%monthnum%`	Two-digit month (such as `02` for February)
`%day%`	Two-digit day (such as `30`)
`%hour%`	Two-digit hour of the day (such as `15` for 3 p.m.)
`%minute%`	Two-digit minute (such as `45`)
`%second%`	Two-digit second (such as `10`)
`%postname%`	Text — usually, the post name — separated by hyphens (such as `making-pretty-permalinks`)
`%post_id%`	The unique numerical ID of the post (such as `344`)
`%category%`	The text of the category name in which you filed the post (such as `books-i-read`)
`%author%`	The text of the post author's name (such as `lisa-sabin-wilson`)

If you want your permalink to show the year, month, day, category, and post name, select the Custom Structure radio button in the Customize Permalink Structure page and type the following tags in the Custom Structure text box:

`/%year%/%monthnum%/%day%/%category%/%postname%/`

By using this permalink format, the link for a post made on February 1, 2011, called WordPress All in One For Dummies and filed in the Books I Read category, would look like this:

`http://yourdomain.com/2011/02/01/books-i-read/wordpress-all-in-one-for-dummies/`

 Be sure to include the slashes before tags, between tags, and at the very end of the string of tags. This format ensures that WordPress creates correct, working permalinks by using the correct `re_write` rules located in the `.htaccess` file for your site. (See the following section for more information on `re_write` rules and `.htaccess` files.)

 Changing the structure of your permalinks in the future affects the permalinks for all the posts on your blog . . . new and old. Keep this fact in mind if you ever decide to change the permalink structure. An especially important reason: Search engines (such as Google and Yahoo!) index the posts on your site by their permalinks, so changing the permalink structure makes all those indexed links obsolete.

Don't forget to click the Save Changes button at the bottom of the Customize Permalink Structure page; otherwise, your permalink changes aren't saved!

Making sure that your permalinks work with your server

After you set the format for the permalinks for your site by using any options other than the default, WordPress writes specific rules, or directives, to the `.htaccess` file on your Web server. The `.htaccess` file in turn communicates to your Web server how it should serve up the permalinks, according to the permalink structure you chose to use.

To use an `.htaccess` file, you need to know the answers to two questions:

✦ Does your Web server configuration use and give you access to the `.htaccess` file?

✦ Does your Web server run Apache with the `mod_rewrite` module?

If you don't know the answers, contact your hosting provider to find out.

If the answer to both questions is yes, proceed to the following section. If the answer is no, check out the "Working with servers that don't use Apache mod_rewrite" sidebar, in this chapter.

Creating .htaccess files

You and WordPress work together in glorious harmony to create the
`.htaccess` file that lets you use a pretty permalink structure in your blog.
Follow these steps to create an `.htaccess` file on your Web server and
create a new permalink structure:

1. **Using a plain-text editor (such as Notepad for Windows or TextEdit for
    a Mac), create a blank file; name it `htaccess.txt` and upload it to
    your Web server via FTP.** (See Book II, Chapter 2 for more information
    about FTP.)

2. **After the file is uploaded to your Web server, rename the file
    `.htaccess` (notice the period at the beginning), and make sure
    that it is writable by the server by changing permissions to either
    755 or 777.** (See Book II, Chapter 2 for information on changing
    permissions on server files.)

   If `.htaccess` already exists, you can find it in the root of your directory
   on your Web server — that is, the same directory where you find your
   `wp-config.php` file. If you don't see it in the root directory, try changing the options of your FTP client to show hidden files. (Because the
   `.htaccess` file starts with a period [.], it may not be visible until you
   configure your FTP client to show hidden files.)

3. **Create the permalink structure in the Customize Permalink Structure
    page in your WordPress Dashboard.**

4. **Click the Save Changes button at the bottom of the Customize
    Permalink Structure page.**

   WordPress inserts into the `.htaccess` file the specific rules necessary
   for making the permalink structure functional in your blog.

If you follow the preceding steps correctly, you have an `.htaccess` file on
your Web server that has the correct permissions set so that WordPress
can write the correct rules to it. Your pretty permalink structure works
flawlessly. Kudos!

If you open the `.htaccess` file and look at it now, you see that it's no longer
blank. It should have a set of code in it called *rewrite rules,* which looks
something like this:

```
# BEGIN WordPress
<IfModule mod_rewrite.c>
RewriteEngine On
RewriteBase /
RewriteCond %{REQUEST_FILENAME} !-f
RewriteCond %{REQUEST_FILENAME} !-d
RewriteRule . /index.php [L]
</IfModule>

# END WordPress
```

Working with servers that don't use Apache mod_rewrite

Using permalink structures requires that your Web-hosting provider has a specific Apache module option called mod_rewrite activated on its servers. If your Web-hosting provider doesn't have this item activated on its servers, or if you're hosting your site on a Windows server, the custom permalinks work only if you type **index.php** in front of any custom permalink tags.

For example, create the custom permalink tags like this:

```
/index.php/%year%/%month%/
%date%/%postname%/
```

This format creates a permalink like this:

```
http://yourdomain.com/index.
php/2008/02/01/wordpress-all-
in-one-for-dummies
```

You don't need an .htaccess file to use this permalink structure.

We could delve deeply into .htaccess and all the things you can do with this file, but we're restricting this chapter to how it applies to WordPress permalink structures. If you want to unlock more mysteries about .htaccess, check out "Comprehensive Guide to .htaccess" at http://javascriptkit.com/howto/htaccess.shtml.

Creating Your Personal Profile

To personalize your blog, visit your Profile page in your WordPress Dashboard.

To access your Profile page, click the down arrow to the right of Users to open the Users menu list, and then click the Your Profile link. The Profile page appears, as shown in Figure 3-10.

Here are the settings on this page:

✦ **Personal Options:** In the Personal Options section, you can set three preferences for your blog:

   • *Visual Editor:* Select this check box to indicate that you want to use the Visual Editor when writing your posts. The Visual Editor refers to the formatting options you find in the Write Post page (discussed in detail in Book IV, Chapter 1). By default, the check box is selected, which means that the Visual Editor is on. To turn it off, clear the check box.

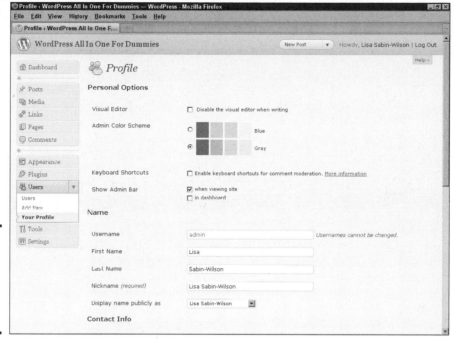

Figure 3-10:
Establish your profile details on the Profile page.

**Book III
Chapter 3**

Exploring Tools and Settings

- *Admin Color Scheme:* These options set the colors in your Dashboard. The default is the Gray color scheme. If you've been using WordPress since before March 2007, the Blue color scheme will be familiar to you because previous versions of the Dashboard used those colors.

- *Keyboard Shortcuts:* Enables you to use keyboard shortcuts for comment moderation. To find out more about keyboard shortcuts, click the More Information link; you're taken to the Keyboard Shortcuts page (http://codex.wordpress.org/Keyboard_Shortcuts) in the WordPress Codex, which offers some helpful information.

- *Show Admin Bar:* Allows you to control where the admin bar (see Book III, Chapter 1) is shown on your site. By default, the admin bar displays on the top of every page of your site when you are viewing it in your browser. You can also set it to display on the top of every Dashboard page by checking the In Dashboard check box. You can completely disable the admin bar by removing the checks in the check boxes.

✦ **Name:** Input personal information, such as your first name, last name, and nickname, and specify how you want your name to appear publicly. Fill in the text boxes with the requested information.

✦ **Contact Info:** Provide your e-mail address and other contact information to tell your visitors who you are and where they can contact you. Aside from e-mail, you can provide your username for various Internet chat programs such as Yahoo! IM, AIM (AOL Instant Messenger), and Jabber/Google Talk.

  Your e-mail address is the only required entry in this section. This address is the one WordPress uses to notify you when you have new comments or new user registrations on your blog. Make sure to use a real e-mail address so that you get these notifications.

✦ **About Yourself:** Provide a little bio for yourself and change the password for your blog, if you want, including

  • *Biographical Info:* Type a short bio in the Biographical Info text box. This information can appear publicly if you're using a theme that displays your bio, so be creative!

  • *New Password:* When you want to change the password for your blog, type your new password in the first text box in the New Password section. To confirm your new password, type it again in the second text box.

When your profile is published to your Web site, not only can anyone view it, but also search engines, such as Google and Yahoo!, can pick it up. Always be careful with the information in your profile. Think hard about the information you want to share with the rest of the world!

Directly below the two New Password text boxes is a little password helper. WordPress helps you create a secure password. It alerts you if the password you chose is too short or not secure enough by telling you that it's Bad. When creating a new password, use a combination of letters, numbers, and symbols to make it hard for anyone to guess (for example, `aty89!#4j`). When you create a password that WordPress thinks is a good one, it lets you know by saying that the password is Strong.

Change your password frequently. We can't recommend this practice strongly enough. Some people on the Internet make it their business to attempt to hijack blogs for their own malicious purposes. If you change your password monthly, you lower your risk by keeping hackers guessing.

When you finish setting all the options on the Profile page, don't forget to click the Update Profile button to save your changes.

Setting Your Blog's Format

In addition to setting your personal settings in the Dashboard, you can manage the day-to-day maintenance of your blog. The following sections take you through the links to these pages in the Dashboard navigation menus.

Posts

Click the down arrow to the right of Pages in the navigation menu to open a drop-down list with four links: Posts, Add New, Tags, and Categories. Each link gives you the tools you need to publish content to your blog:

✦ **Posts:** Opens the Posts page, where a listing appears of all the saved posts you've written on your blog. On this page, you can search for posts by date, category, or keyword. You can view all posts, only posts that have been published, or just posts that you've saved but haven't published *(drafts)*. You can also edit and delete posts from this page. Check out Book IV, Chapter 1 for more information on editing posts on your blog.

✦ **Add New:** Opens the Add New Post page, where you can compose your blog posts, set the options for each post (such as assigning a post to a category, or making it a private or public post), and publish the post to your blog. You can find more information on posts, post options, and publishing in Book IV, Chapter 1.

You can also get to the Add New Post page by clicking the Add New button on the Posts page.

✦ **Categories:** Opens the Categories page, where you can view, edit, add, and delete categories on your blog. Find more information on creating categories in Book III, Chapter 7.

✦ **Post Tags:** Opens the Post Tags page in your WordPress Dashboard, where you can view, add, edit, and delete tags on your blog. Book III, Chapter 7 provides you with more information about tags and using them on your blog.

Media

Click Media to expand the drop-down list of links for this section:

✦ **Library:** Opens the Media Library page. On this page, you can view, search, and manage all the media files you've ever uploaded to your WordPress blog.

**Book III
Chapter 3**

Exploring Tools
and Settings

✦ **Add New:** Opens the Upload New Media page, where you can use the built-in uploader to transfer media files from your computer to the media directory in WordPress. Book IV, Chapters 3 and 4 take you through the details of how to upload images, videos, and audio files by using the WordPress upload feature.

You can also get to the Upload New Media page by clicking Add New button on the Media Library page.

Links

The next item in the navigation menu is Links. Expand the Links drop-down list by clicking the down arrow to the right of Links:

✦ **Links:** Opens the Links page, where you can view, search, edit, and delete existing links in your WordPress blog. Book III, Chapter 6 gives you detailed information about links, link lists, and blogrolls.

✦ **Add New:** Opens the Add New Link page, where you can add new links to your link lists. (You can find more information about creating and managing link lists in Book III, Chapter 6.)

You can also get to the Add New Link page by clicking the Links menu.

✦ **Link Categories:** Opens the Link Categories page, where you can add new and view, edit, and delete existing link categories (see Book III, Chapter 6).

Pages

People use this feature to create pages on their sites such as an About Me or Contact Me page. Flip to Book IV, Chapter 2 for more information on pages. Click Pages to reveal the drop-down list:

✦ **Pages:** Opens the Pages page, where you can search, view, edit, and delete pages in your WordPress blog.

✦ **Add New:** Opens the Add New Page page, where you can compose, save, and publish a new page on your blog. Book IV, Chapter 2 describes the difference between a post and a page — it's subtle, but posts and pages are very different from one another!

You can also get to the Add New Page page by clicking the Add New button on the Pages page.

Comments

Comments in the navigation menu don't have a drop-down list of links. You simply click Comments to open the Comments page, where WordPress gives you the options to view

✦ **All:** Shows all comments that currently exist on your blog, including approved, pending, and spam comments

✦ **Pending:** Shows comments that you haven't yet approved but are pending in the moderation queue

✦ **Approved:** Shows all comments that you previously approved

✦ **Spam:** Shows all the comments that are marked as spam

✦ **Trash:** Shows comments that you marked as Trash but haven't deleted permanently from your blog

In Book III, Chapter 5, we give you details on how to use the Comments section of your WordPress Dashboard.

Appearance

When you click Appearance in the navigation menu, a drop-down list opens, displaying the following links:

✦ **Themes:** Opens the Manage Themes page, where you can manage the themes available on your blog. Check out Book VI, Chapter 2 to find out about using themes on your WordPress blog and managing themes on this page.

✦ **Widgets:** Opens the Widgets page, where you can add, delete, edit, and manage the widgets that you use on your blog.

✦ **Menus:** Opens the Menus page, where you can build navigation menus that will appear on your site. Book VI, Chapter 1 provides information on creating menus by using this feature.

✦ **Background:** Opens the Custom Background page, where you can upload an image to use as the background of your WordPress blog design. Like the Custom Header option (discussed in the next bullet), the Custom Background option exists in the Appearances menu only if you have a theme that has activated the custom background feature (covered in Book VI).

✦ **Header:** Opens the Your Header Image page, where you can upload an image to use in the *header* (or top) of your WordPress blog; however, this menu item and page exist only if you are using a theme that has activated the custom header feature (covered in Book VI). The Twenty Ten theme is activated by default on all new WordPress blogs, which is why we include this menu item in this list. Not all WordPress themes use the Customize Header feature, so you don't see this menu item if your theme doesn't take advantage of that feature.

✦ **Editor:** Opens the Theme Editor page, where you can edit your theme templates. Book VI has extensive information on themes and templates.

Uploading custom header and background images helps you individualize the visual design of your blog or Web site. You can find more information on tweaking and customizing your WordPress theme in Book VI, as well as a great deal of information about how to use WordPress themes (including where to find, install, and activate them in your WordPress blog) and detailed information about using WordPress widgets to display the content you want.

Book VI provides information about WordPress themes and templates. You can dig deep into WordPress template tags and tweak an existing WordPress theme by using Cascading Style Sheets (CSS) to customize your theme a bit more to your liking.

Plugins

The next item in the navigation menu is Plugins. Click Plugins to expand the drop-down list:

✦ **Plugins:** Opens the Plugins page, where you can view all the plugins currently installed on your blog. On this page, you also have the ability to activate, deactivate, and delete plugins on your blog (see Book VII).

✦ **Add New:** Opens the Install Plugins page, where you can search for plugins from the official WordPress Plugin Directory by keyword, author, or tag. You can also install plugins directly to your blog from the WordPress Plugin Directory — you can find out all about this exciting feature in Book VII, Chapter 1.

✦ **Editor:** Opens the Edit Plugins page, where you can edit the plugin files in a text editor. We very strongly advise against editing plugin files unless you know what you're doing (meaning that you're familiar with PHP and WordPress functions). Head over to Book VII, Chapter 4 to read more information on editing plugin files.

Users

The Users drop-down list has three links:

✦ **Users:** Go to the Users page, where you can view, edit, and delete users on your WordPress blog. Each user has a unique login name and password, as well as an e-mail address assigned to his account. You can view and edit a user's information on the Users page.

✦ **Add New:** Opens the Add New User page, where you can add new users to your WordPress blog. Simply type the user's username, first name, last name, e-mail (required), Web site, and a password in the fields provided and click the Add User button. You can also select whether you want WordPress to send login information to the new user by e-mail. If you want, you can also assign a new role for the new user. Turn to the section "Configuring the Settings," earlier in this chapter, for more info about user roles.

✦ **Your Profile:** Turn to the "Creating Your Personal Profile" section, earlier in this chapter, for more information about creating a profile page.

Tools

The last item in the navigation menu (and subsequently in this chapter!) is Tools. Click Tools to open a drop-down list of links that includes

✦ **Tools:** Opens the Tools page in your Dashboard. WordPress comes packaged with two extra features that you can use on your blog, if needed. They're Press This and Category/Tag Conversion.

✦ **Import:** Clicking this link opens the Import page in your Dashboard. WordPress gives you the ability to import from a different blog platform. This feature is covered in depth in Book II, Chapter 7.

✦ **Export:** Clicking this menu item opens the Export page in your Dashboard. WordPress allows you to export your content from WordPress so that you can import it into a different platform or to another WordPress blog.

Chapter 4: Managing Users and Multiple Authors

In This Chapter

✔ Deciding what roles to assign users

✔ Allowing new users to register

✔ Adding a new user

✔ Making changes to user profiles

✔ Using tools to manage multi-author sites

*M*ulti-author blogging means inviting others to coauthor, or contribute articles, posts, pages, or other content to your blog. You can expand the offerings on your Web site or blog by using multi-author blogging because you can have several different people writing on different topics or offering different perspectives on the same topic. Many people use it to create a collaborative writing space on the Web, and WordPress doesn't limit you in the number of authors you can add to your blog.

Additionally, bloggers can invite other people to register as *subscribers,* who don't contribute content but are registered members of the blog, which can have benefits, too (for example, some sites make content available to registered users only).

This chapter takes you through the steps of adding users to your blog, takes the mystery out of the different user roles and capabilities, and gives you some tools for managing a multi-author Web site by using WordPress.

Understanding User Roles and Capabilities

Before you start adding new users to your site, you need to understand the differences among the user roles because each user role is assigned a different level of access and grouping of capabilities to your blog, as follows:

✦ **Subscriber:** The default role. Maintain this role as the one assigned to new users, particularly if you don't know who's registering. Subscribers get access to the Dashboard page, and they can view and change the options in their profiles on the Your Profile and Personal Options page.

(They don't have access to your account settings, however — only to their own.) Each user can change her username, e-mail address, password, bio, and other descriptors in her user profile. The WordPress database stores subscribers' profile information, and your blog remembers them each time they visit, so they don't have to complete the profile information each time they leave comments on your blog.

✦ **Contributor:** In addition to the access Subscribers have, Contributors can upload files and write, edit, and manage their own posts. Contributors can write posts, but they can't publish the posts; the administrator reviews all Contributor posts and decides whether to publish them. This setting is a nice way to moderate content written by new authors.

✦ **Author:** In addition to the access Contributors have, Authors can publish and edit their own posts.

✦ **Editor:** In addition to the access Authors have, Editors can moderate comments, manage categories, manage links, edit pages, and edit other Authors' posts.

✦ **Administrator:** Administrators can edit all the options and settings in the WordPress blog.

✦ **Super Admin:** This role exists only when you have the Multisite feature activated in WordPress — see Book VIII for more about the Multisite feature.

Table 4-1 gives you a quick, at-a-glance reference for the basic differences in roles and capabilities for WordPress users.

Table 4-1	WordPress User Roles and Capabilities					
	Super Admin	*Administrator*	*Editor*	*Author*	*Contributor*	*Subscriber*
Manage Multisite features	Yes	No	No	No	No	No
Add/edit users	Yes	Yes	No	No	No	No
Add/edit/install plugins	Yes	Yes	No	No	No	No
Add/edit/install themes	Yes	Yes	No	No	No	No
Manage comments	Yes	Yes	Yes	No	No	No
Manage categories, tags, and links	Yes	Yes	Yes	No	No	No

	Super Admin	Administrator	Editor	Author	Contributor	Subscriber
Publish posts	Yes	Yes	Yes	Yes	No (moderated)	No
Edit published posts	Yes	Yes	Yes	No	No	No
Edit others' posts	Yes	Yes	Yes	No	No	No
Edit own posts	Yes	Yes	Yes	Yes	Yes	No
Publish pages	Yes	Yes	Yes	No	No	No
Read	Yes	Yes	Yes	Yes	Yes	Yes

Table 4-1 doesn't offer exhaustive information, by any means. However, it covers the basic user roles and capabilities for WordPress, or the most common capabilities for each user role. For a full listing of user roles and capabilities, check out the WordPress Codex at `http://codex.word-press.org/Roles_and_Capabilities`.

Allowing New User Registration

As you can see in Table 4-1, each user level has a different set of capabilities. In Book III, Chapter 3, we discuss the General Settings in the WordPress Dashboard, in which you set the default role for users who register on your Web site. Keep the default role set to Subscriber because when you open registration to the public, you don't always know who's registering until after they register — and you don't want to arbitrarily hand out higher levels of access to the settings of your Web site unless you know and trust the user.

When users register on your Web site, you, as the Administrator, get an e-mail notification (sent to the e-mail address you set on the General Settings page), so you always know when new users register, and you can then go into your Dashboard and edit the user to set his role any way you see fit.

New users can register on your site only after you enable the Anyone Can Register option on the General Settings page within your Dashboard (Book III, Chapter 3). If you don't have it enabled, then users see a message on the Registration page that tells them registration isn't allowed, as shown in Figure 4-1.

Figure 4-1:
The
message to
users that
registration
isn't
allowed.

By the way, the direct URL for registration on a blog that has registration enabled is `http://yourdomain.com/wp-register.php`. With registration enabled (in the General Settings), a user sees a form inviting her to input her desired username and e-mail address. After she does, she gets a confirmation notice in her inbox that includes an authorization link that she must click in order to authenticate her registration.

After a user has registered, you, as the site Administrator, can manage her user account and assign a user role (refer to Table 4-1).

Adding New Users

Allowing new users to register by using the WordPress registration interface is only one way to add users to your site. As the site Administrator, you have the ability to add new users manually by following these steps:

1. **Log in to your WordPress Dashboard by inputting your username and password in the form at `http://yourdomain.com/wp-admin`.**

2. **Click the Add New link in the Users menu on the Dashboard.**

   The Add New User page, shown in Figure 4-2, loads.

3. **Enter the username in the Username text box.**

   You can't skip this text box. The new user types in this username when he's prompted to log in to your site.

4. **Enter the user's e-mail address in the E-Mail text box.**

   You can't skip this text box, either. The user receives notifications from you and your site at this e-mail address.

5. **Enter the user's first name in the First Name text box.**

6. **Enter the user's last name in the Last Name text box.**

7. **Enter the URL for the user's Web site in the Website text box.**

8. **Enter the desired password in the Password text box.**

   WordPress asks you to type the password twice as a way of *authenticating* the password (making sure that you typed it correctly the first time). WordPress provides a strength indicator that gives you an idea of how *strong,* or secure, your chosen password is. You want secure passwords so that no one can easily guess them, so make the password at least seven characters long and use a combination of letters, numbers, and symbols (such as @, #, $, and ^).

9. **If you want the user to receive his password by e-mail, select the Send This Password to the New User by Email check box.**

10. **Select Subscriber, Contributor, Author, Editor, or Administrator from the Role drop-down list.**

11. **Click the Add User button.**

   The Add New User page loads and the e-mail notification is sent to the user you just added. When the page loads, all the fields are cleared, allowing you to add another new user, if you want.

**Book III
Chapter 4**

**Managing Users and
Multiple Authors**

Figure 4-2:
The Add
New User
page in the
WordPress
Dashboard.

Editing User Details

After users register and settle into their accounts on your site, you, as the site Administrator, have the ability to edit their accounts. You may never have to edit user accounts at all; however, you have the option if you need it. Most often, users can access the details of their own accounts and change e-mail addresses, names, passwords, and so on; however, circumstances under which a site administrator may need to edit user accounts would be to do things such as

✦ **Edit user roles.** When a user registers, you may want to increase her role, or level of access, to your site; promote an existing user to Administrator; or conversely, demote an existing Administrator or Editor down a notch or two.

✦ **Edit user e-mails.** If a user loses access to the e-mail account that she registered with, she may ask you to change his account e-mail address so that she can access her account notifications again.

✦ **Edit user passwords.** If a user loses access to the e-mail account with which she registered, she can't use WordPress's Lost Password feature, which allows users to gain access to their account password through e-mail recovery. In that case, a user may ask you to reset her password for her so that she can log in and access her account again.

In any of these circumstances, you can make the necessary changes by clicking the Users link in the Users menu on your WordPress Dashboard, which loads the Users page shown in Figure 4-3.

Figure 4-3 shows you the Users page on a site that has multiple users who have different levels of access, or roles (we blurred out the usernames and e-mail addresses in Figure 4-3 to protect the users' privacy).

When you hover over the name of the user, an Edit link appears below the user listing. Click that Edit link to access the Edit User page, where you can edit different pieces of information for that user, including

✦ **Personal Options:** These options include Visual Editor and Color Scheme preferences.

✦ **Name:** Specify a user's role, first and last name, and nickname.

✦ **Contact Info:** Includes users' e-mail addresses; Web sites; and AIM, Yahoo IM, and Google Talk IDs.

✦ **Biographical Info:** A few lines of biographical info for the user (optional, but some WordPress themes display authors' biographies).

✦ **New Password:** Change the password for the user.

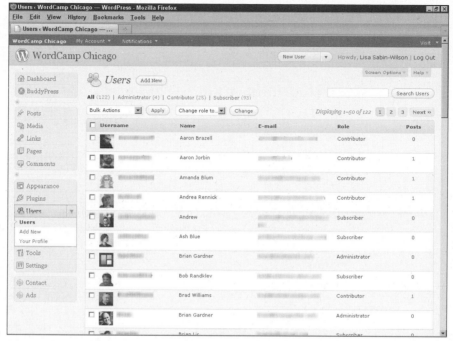

Figure 4-3:
The Users page lets you manage all the users on your site.

The Edit User page looks the same, and has the very same features, as the Profile page that you deal with in Book III, Chapter 3 — feel free to visit that chapter to get the lowdown on the different options and settings on this page.

Managing a Multi-Author Site

You may love running a multi-author site, but it has its challenges. The minute you become the owner of a multi-author site, you immediately assume the role of manager for the authors you invited into your space. At times, those authors look to you for support and guidance, not only on their content management, but also for tips and advice about how to use the WordPress interface — it's a good thing you have this book at the ready so that you can offer up the gems of information you're finding within these pages!

You can find many tools available to assist you in managing a multi-author site, as well as making your site more interactive by adding some features, which can make it a more rewarding and satisfying experience not only for you and your readers, but for your authors, as well.

The tools we list in the following sections come by way of plugins, which are add-ons that extend the scope of WordPress by adding different functionality and features. You can find information on the use and installation of plugins in Book VII.

Tools that help authors communicate

When you're running a multi-author site, communication is crucial for sharing information, giving and receiving inspiration, and making certain that no two authors are writing the same (or a similar) article on your site. Use the following tools to help you manage the flow of communication between everyone involved:

✦ **WP Status Notifier (`http://wordpress.org/extend/plugins/wp-status-notifier`):** In the section "Understanding User Roles and Capabilities," earlier in this chapter, we mention that the role of Contributor can write and save posts to your site, but those posts don't get published to the site until an Administrator approves them. This plugin notifies the Contributor author, via e-mail, when his post is published to (or rejected by) your site.

✦ **Editorial Calendar (`http://wordpress.org/extend/plugins/editorial-calendar`):** This plugin gives you an overview of scheduled posts, post authors, and the dates when you scheduled the posts to publish to your blog. This plugin can help you prevent multiple author posts from publishing too close together or, in some cases, right on top of one another by enabling you to reschedule posts by using a drag-and-drop interface.

✦ **Email Users (`http://wordpress.org/extend/plugins/email-users`):** This plugin allows you to send e-mails out to all registered users of your blog, and users can send e-mails back and forth to one another by using the plugin interface in the Dashboard. This tool provides the authors and users on your multi-author blog the ability to keep in touch and communicate with one another.

✦ **Subscribe to Authors Post Feed (`http://wordpress.org/extend/plugins/subscribe-to-author-posts-feed`):** This plugin adds an RSS feed to each author's post archives, which allows you, other users, and site visitors to subscribe to that author's RSS feed so that you receive immediate notification through your RSS feed reader when the author publishes new content.

✦ **Dashboard Notepad (`http://wordpress.org/extend/plugins/dashboard-notepad`):** This plugin gives you a widget that appears on your main Dashboard page and allows you and other users (depending on the user role that you set in the plugin options) to leave notes for each other. You can use this plugin to ask and answer questions, and to create to-do lists for your authors.

Tools to promote author profiles

One way to operate a successful multi-author blog involves taking every opportunity to promote your authors and their information as much as possible. Authors often get involved in posting content on other Web sites, in addition to yours, for exposure, and the plugins in this list give you tools to promote authors bios, links, social network feeds, and more:

✦ **Author Information Widget (`http://wordpress.org/extend/plugins/author-info-widget`):** This plugin gives you a widget that you can place in the sidebar of a single post page, displaying the post author's name, biography (from the About Me section of the Author Profile page in the Dashboard), Avatar (author's photo) and Social Network and Contact links.

✦ **List Authors (`http://wordpress.org/extend/plugins/list-authors`):** This plugin provides a widget that displays a list of the authors on your site, where the author's name is a link to her post archive. Figure 4-4 displays the List Authors widget with the different options that you can set for it.

Figure 4-4: The List Authors widget options.

Book III
Chapter 4

Managing Users and
Multiple Authors

✦ **Profile Pic (`http://wordpress.org/extend/plugins/profile-pic`):** This plugin gives your authors the ability to add their own photos to their profiles on your site, and it provides you with a widget that can display each author's photo, as well as his name and a link to his post archive.

✦ **Author Spotlight (`http://wordpress.org/extend/plugins/author-profile`):** This plugin provides a widget that you can place in your sidebar, displaying the profile of the author of the post being viewed — the author information automatically appears on only a single post page and displays the profile of the author of the post.

✦ **Author Based Twitter (`http://wordpress.org/extend/plugins/author-based-twitter-widget`):** This plugin gives your authors the ability to show their own Twitter feeds in the sidebar by using a handy widget. The author's Twitter feed information appears on her post page only — so authors can promote their own Twitter accounts on your Web site.

Tools to manage multi-author blog posts

The plugins listed in this section can help you, the site Administrator, manage your group of authors and registered users by giving you some tools to track users' activity, list their posts, and stay up-to-date and notified when your authors publish new content:

✦ **Co-Authors Plus (`http://wordpress.org/extend/plugins/co-authors-plus/faq`):** This plugin allows you to assign multiple authors to one post, which you may find especially helpful when you have more than one author collaborating on one article, allowing the authors to share the byline and credit.

✦ **Author Complete Post List (`http://wordpress.org/extend/plugins/author-complete-post-list`):** This plugin provides a very easy way to show a complete list of an author's posts, enabling you to display an archive page per author.

✦ **Custom Author Byline (`http://wordpress.org/extend/plugins/custom-author-byline`):** This plugin adds a custom author byline module below the Post Editor on the Add New Posts page, which enables you to include the name of an author who's not a registered member of your site (helpful when you need to give credit to collaborators).

✦ **Pending Post Notifier (`http://wordpress.org/extend/plugins/wp-pending-post-notifier`):** This plugin simply sends an e-mail to the site Administrator whenever posts are ready for review. For example, when a user who has the role of Contributor writes and saves a post, an e-mail is sent to the Administrator, telling him that new posts are awaiting his review.

✦ **Audit Trail (`http://wordpress.org/extend/plugins/audit-trail`):** This plugin records the actions of the registered users on your site, such as when they log in or log out, when they publish posts and pages, and when they visit pages within your site. As the site Administrator, you can keep track of the actions your authors and users take on your Web site.

Chapter 5: Dealing with Comments and Spam

In This Chapter

✔ Making the decision to allow comments

✔ Working with comments and trackbacks

✔ Recognizing and dealing with spam

✔ Using Akismet to help combat spam

*O*ne of the most exciting aspects of blogging with WordPress is getting feedback from your readers the moment you make a post to your blog. Feedback, also known as *blog comments,* is akin to having a guestbook on your blog.

People leave notes for you that are published to your site, and through these notes, you can respond and engage your readers in conversation about the topic. Having this function in your blog allows you to expand the thoughts and ideas you present in your blog posts by giving readers the opportunity to add their two cents' worth.

In this chapter, you can decide whether to allow comments on your site, figure out how to manage those comments, use trackbacks, and discover the negative aspects of allowing comments (such as spam).

Deciding to Allow Comments on Your Site

Some blog users say that a blog without comments isn't a blog at all because the point of having a blog, in some minds, is to foster communication and interaction between the site authors and the readers. This belief is common in the blogging community because experiencing visitor feedback via comments is part of what's made blogging so popular. However, allowing comments is a personal choice, and you don't have to do it if you don't want to.

Positive aspects of allowing comments

Allowing comments on your blog lets audience members actively involve themselves in your blog by creating a discussion and dialogue about your content. Mostly, readers find commenting a satisfying experience when they visit blogs because comments make them part of the discussion.

Depending on the topic you write about on your blog, allowing comments sends the message that you, as the author/owner of the site, are open to the views and opinions of your readers. Having a comment form on your site that readers can use to leave their feedback on your articles (such as the one shown in Figure 5-1) is like having a great big Welcome to My Home sign on your site — it invites users in to share thoughts and participate in discussions.

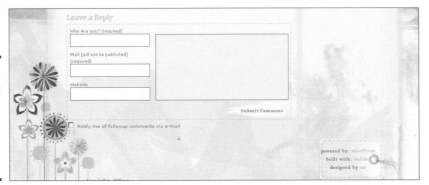

Figure 5-1:
Readers use the Leave a Reply form to share their comments.

If you want to build a community of people who come back to your site frequently, respond to as many comments that your readers leave on your blog as possible. When people take the time to leave you a comment on your content, they like to know that you're reading it and they appreciate hearing your feedback to them. Plus, it keeps discussions lively and active on your site. Figure 5-2 illustrates what comments look like after they're published to your site. (*Note:* The actual design and layout of the comments on sites varies from theme to theme; you can find information on theme design in Book VI).

Exploring reasons to disallow comments

Under certain circumstances, you may not want to allow readers to leave comments freely on your site. For example, if you wrote a blog post on a topic that is considered very controversial, you may not want to invite comments because the topic may incite flame wars, or comments that are insulting to you, or your readers. If you're not interested in the point of view or feedback of readers on your site, or if your content doesn't really lend itself to reader feedback, you may decide to disallow comments entirely.

In making the decision to have comments, you have to be prepared for the fact that not everyone is going to agree with what you write; especially if you're writing on a topic that invites a wide array of opinions, such as politics, religion, or op-ed pieces. As a site owner, you make the decision, ahead of time, whether you want readers dropping in and leaving their own views, or even disagreeing with you on yours (sometimes vehemently!).

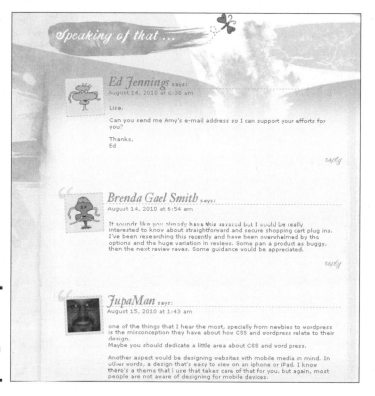

**Book III
Chapter 5**

Dealing with Comments and Spam

Figure 5-2:
Blog
readers
comment on
a blog.

If you're on the fence about whether to allow comments, the WordPress platform allows you to toggle that decision on a per-post basis. Therefore, each time you publish a post or article on your Web site, you can indicate in the Post Options (on the Add New Post page in your Dashboard) whether this particular post should allow discussion. You may choose to disallow comments entirely on your site, which you can configure in the Discussion Settings in the Dashboard, or disallow them on only certain posts, which you can configure in the Dashboard on the Edit Post page, which we talk about in Book IV, Chapter 1.

Interacting with Readers through Comments

People can leave notes for you that are published to your site, and you can respond and engage your readers in conversation about the topic at hand (refer to Figure 5-1 and Figure 5-2). Having this function in your blog creates the opportunity to expand the thoughts and ideas that you present in your blog post by giving your readers the opportunity to share their own thoughts.

In the WordPress Dashboard, you have full administrative control over who can and can't leave comments. In addition, if someone leaves a comment that has questionable content, you can edit the comment or delete it. You're also free to disallow comments on your blog. The Discussion Settings page in your Dashboard contains all the settings for allowing, or disallowing, comments on your site; flip back to Book III, Chapter 3 to dig into those settings, what they mean, and how you can use them to configure the exact interactive environment that you want for your site.

Tracking back

The best way to understand trackbacks is to think of them as comments, except for one thing: *Trackbacks* are comments left on your blog by other blogs, not by actual people. Although this process may sound mysterious, it's actually perfectly reasonable.

A trackback happens when you make a post on your blog and, within that post, you provide a link to a post made by another blogger in a different blog. When you publish that post, your blog sends a sort of electronic memo to the blog you linked to. That blog receives the memo and posts an acknowledgment of receipt in a comment within the post that you linked to on their site.

That memo is sent via a *network ping* (a tool used to test, or verify, whether a link is reachable across the Internet) from your site to the site you link to. This process works as long as both blogs support trackback protocol. Trackbacks can also come to your site by way of a *pingback* — which, really, is the same thing as a trackback, but the terminology varies from blog platform to blog platform.

Sending a trackback to a blog is a nice way of telling the blogger that you like the information she presented in her blog post. Every blogger appreciates the receipt of trackbacks to their posts from other bloggers. Figure 5-3 shows one trackback link, below the Who's Linking Here header.

Comment and trackback display

Almost every single WordPress theme displays comments at the bottom of each post published in WordPress. You can do custom styling of the comments so that they match the design of your site by using several items:

✦ **WordPress template tags:** Tags related to the display of comments and trackbacks. For more on these tags, see Book VI, Chapter 3.

✦ **Basic HTML:** Using HTML markup helps you provide unique styles to display content. For information about the use of basic HTML, check out Book VI.

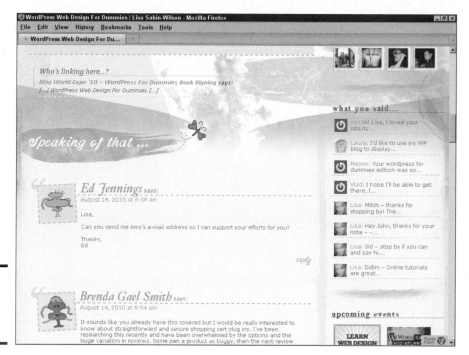

Figure 5-3:
Trackback
links on a
blog.

✦ **CSS:** Every WordPress theme has a Cascading Style Sheet (CSS) template called `style.css`. Within this CSS template, you define the styles and CSS markup that creates a custom look and feel for the comment and trackback display on your site. You can find more information about using CSS in Book VI.

✦ **Graphics:** Using graphics to enhance and define your branding, style, and visual design is an integral part of Web design. Because we can't fully cover graphic design in a single chapter, you may want to check out *WordPress Web Design For Dummies*, which Lisa wrote, for great information on graphic and Web-site design with WordPress (published by Wiley).

✦ **WordPress widgets:** WordPress has a built-in widget to display the most recent comments published to your site by your visitors. You also can find several plugins that display comments in different ways, including top comments, most popular posts based on the number of comments, comments that display the author's photo, and more. For information about widgets and plugins for these purposes, flip to Book VI, Chapter 1 and Book VII, Chapters 1 and 2, respectively.

**Book III
Chapter 5**

**Dealing with
Comments and
Spam**

Managing Comments and Trackbacks

When you invite readers to comment on your site, you, as the site administrator, have full access to manage and edit those comments through the Comments page, which you can access on your WordPress Dashboard.

To find your comments, click the Comments link on the Comments menu; the Comments page opens (see Figure 5-4).

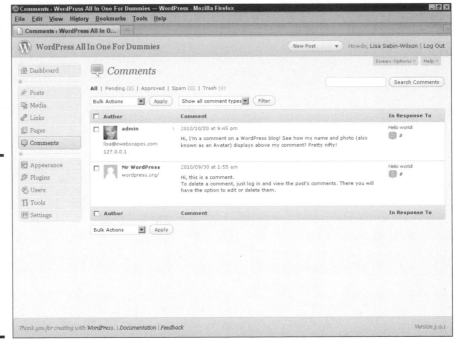

Figure 5-4:
The Comments page contains all the comments and trackbacks on your blog.

When you hover over a comment with your mouse, several links appear that give you the opportunity to manage the comment:

✦ **Unapprove:** This link appears only if you have comment moderation turned on. Also, it appears only on approved comments. The comment is placed in the moderation queue, which you can get to by clicking the Pending link that appears below the Comments page header. The moderation queue is kind of a holding area for comments that haven't yet been published to your blog.

✦ **Reply:** Makes a text box drop down, where you can type and submit your reply to this person. This feature eliminates the need to load your live site in order to reply to a comment.

✦ **Quick Edit:** Opens the comment options inline, without ever leaving the Comments page. You can configure options such as name, e-mail address, URL, and comment content. Click the Save button to save your changes.

✦ **Edit:** Opens the Edit Comment page, where you can edit the different fields, such as name, e-mail address, URL, and comment content (see Figure 5-5).

✦ **Spam:** Marks the comment as spam and marks it as spam in the database, where it will never be heard from again! (Actually, it's stored in the database as spam; you just don't see it in your comments list unless you click the Spam link at the top of the Comments page.)

✦ **Trash:** This link does exactly what it says; it sends the comment to the trash can and deletes it from your blog. You can access comments that have been sent to the trash to permanently delete them from your blog, or restore them.

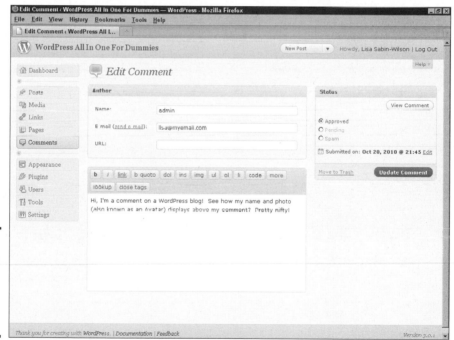

Figure 5-5:
Edit a user's comment on the Edit Comment page.

If you have a lot of comments listed on the Comments page and want to bulk-edit them, select the check boxes to the left of all the comments you want to manage; then select one of the following from the Bulk Actions drop-down list at the top left of the page: Approve, Mark as Spam, Unapprove, or Delete.

If you have your options set so that comments aren't published to your blog until you approve them, you can approve comments from the Comments page, as well. Just click the Pending link to list the comments that are pending moderation. If you have comments and/or trackbacks awaiting moderation, they appear on this page, and you can approve them, mark them as spam, or delete them.

WordPress immediately notifies you of any comments sitting in the moderation queue, awaiting your action. This notification, which appears on every single page, is a small circle, or bubble, in the left navigation menu, to the right of Comments. Figure 5-6 shows that Lisa has 20 comments pending moderation. She'd better get busy and deal with those comments!

20 comments pending

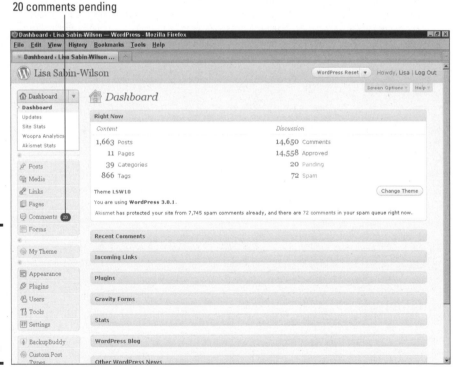

Figure 5-6:
A small circle tells Lisa that she has 20 comments pending moderation.

Dealing with Comment and Trackback Spam

Ugh. The absolute bane of every blogger's existence is comment and track-back spam. When blogs became the "It" things on the Internet, spammers saw an opportunity. If you've ever received spam e-mail, the concept is similar and just as frustrating.

Before blogs came onto the scene, you often saw spammers filling Internet guest books with their links but not leaving any relevant comments. The reason is simple: Web sites receive higher rankings in the major search engines if they have multiple links from other sites. Enter blog software, with comment and trackback technologies — prime breeding ground for millions of spammers.

Because comments and trackbacks are published to your site publicly — and usually with links to the commenters' Web sites — spammers got their site links posted on millions of blogs by creating programs that automatically seek Web sites that have commenting systems, and then hammer those systems with tons of comments that contain links back to their own sites.

No blogger likes spam. In fact, blogging services such as WordPress have spent untold hours in the name of stopping these spammers in their tracks, and for the most part, they've been successful. Occasionally, however, spammers sneak through. Many spammers are offensive, and all of them are frustrating because they don't contribute to the ongoing conversations that occur in blogs.

All WordPress installations have one significant thing in common: Akismet, a WordPress plugin.

Tackling Spam with Akismet

It's our humble opinion that Akismet is the mother of all plugins and that no WordPress blog is complete without a fully activated version of Akismet running in it.

Apparently, WordPress agrees because the plugin is packaged in every WordPress software release beginning with version 2.0. Akismet was created by the folks at Automattic, the same folks who brought you the WordPress.com-hosted version.

Akismet is the answer to combating comment and trackback spam. Matt Mullenweg of Automattic says Akismet is a "collaborative effort to make comment and trackback spam a non-issue and restore innocence to blogging, so you never have to worry about spam again" (from the Akismet Web site at http://akismet.com).

Lisa has been blogging since 2002. She started blogging with the Movable Type blogging platform and moved to WordPress in 2003. While blogging became more and more popular, comment and trackback spam became more and more of a nuisance. One morning in 2004, she found that 2,300 pieces of disgusting comment spam had been published to her blog. Something had to be done! The folks at Automattic did a fine thing with

Akismet. Since the emergence of Akismet, she's barely had to think about comment or trackback spam except for the few times a month she checks her Akismet spam queue.

We cover the use of plugins in Book VII. However, this chapter wouldn't be complete if we didn't show you how to activate and use the Akismet plugin on your site. Book VII covers the use, installation, and management of other plugins for your WordPress site.

Akismet is already included in every WordPress installation, so you don't have to worry, at this point, about downloading and installing it because it's already there. Follow these steps to activate and begin using Akismet:

1. **Click the Plugins link in the left navigation menu of the Dashboard to load the Plugins page.**

2. **Click the Activate link below the Akismet plugin name and description.**

   A yellow box appears at the top of the page, saying Akismet Is Almost Ready. You Must Enter Your WordPress.com API Key for It to Work (see Figure 5-7). An *API key* is a string of numbers and letters that functions like a unique password given to you by WordPress.com; it's the key that allows your WordPress.org application to communicate with your WordPress.com account.

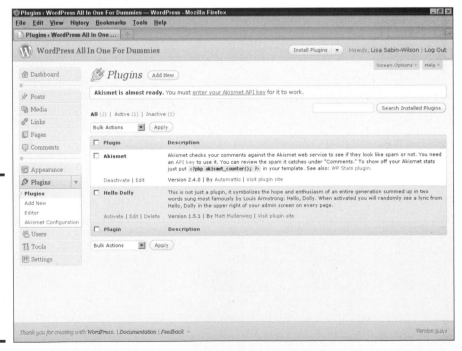

Figure 5-7: After you activate Akismet, WordPress tells you that the plugin isn't quite ready to use.

3. **Click the link in the yellow box to navigate to the Akismet Configuration page.**

   The Akismet Configuration page asks you to enter your Akismet API key. You can obtain an API key free from your WordPress.com account. If you're a professional or corporate user, click the Get Your Key link to visit the Akismet Web site, where you can purchase an API key.

   You need to register for an account on WordPress.com (`http://word-press.com`) in order to get access to a free API key. Be sure to visit the WordPress.com Web site to register your account before you proceed with the following steps.

4. **In a new browser window, log in to your WordPress.com account and click the Edit My Profile link in the WordPress.com menu.**

   The My Public Profile page opens in your Web browser.

5. **Click the API Key and Other Personal Settings link.**

   The Personal Settings page appears in your WordPress.com Dashboard. Your WordPress.com API key appears at the top of that page, as shown in Figure 5-8. (We blurred out Lisa's API key in Figure 5-8 because — shhhh — it's a secret, and we're not supposed to share it!)

Book III
Chapter 5

Dealing with
Comments and
Spam

Figure 5-8:
You can find your WordPress API key on the Personal Settings page in the Dashboard.

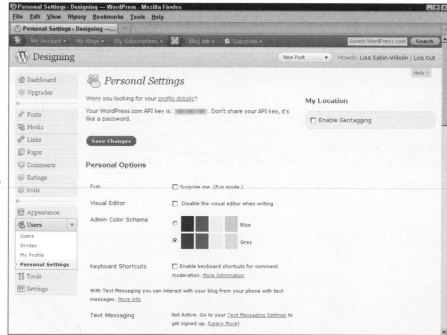

6. **In your Dashboard on the Akismet Configuration page, enter the API key in the WordPress.com API Key text box and click the Update Options button to activate the Akismet plugin fully.**

A message appears, telling you that your Akismet API key has been verified (see Figure 5-9). You're now protected against comment spam because you're using the Akismet plugin.

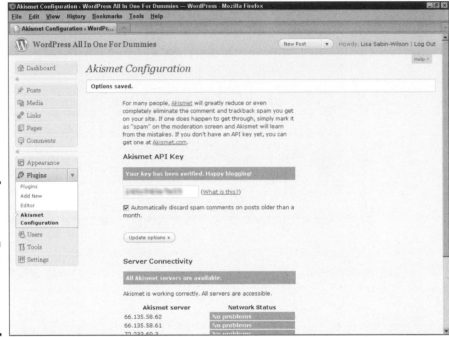

Figure 5-9:
Akismet
verification
confirmation
message on
the Akismet
Config-
uration
page.

Akismet catches spam and throws it into a queue, holding the spam for 15 days and then deleting it from your database. It's probably worth your while to check the Akismet Spam page once a week to make sure that the plugin hasn't captured any legitimate comments or trackbacks.

You can rescue those non-spam captured comments and trackbacks by following these steps (after you log in to your WordPress Dashboard):

1. **Click Comments in the left navigation menu.**

The Comments page appears, displaying a list of the most recent comments on your blog.

2. **Click the Spam link.**

The Comments page now displays all spam comments that the plugin caught.

3. **Browse through the list of spam comments, looking for any comments or trackbacks that are legitimate.**

4. **If you locate a comment or trackback that's legitimate, select the Approve link directly below the entry.**

   The comment is marked as legitimate. In other words, WordPress recognizes that you don't consider this comment to be spam. WordPress then approves the comment and publishes it on your blog.

Check your spam filter often. Lisa just found four legitimate comments caught in her spam filter; she was able to de-spam them, releasing them from the binds of Akismet and unleashing them upon the world.

Chapter 6: Building Link Lists

In This Chapter

✔ **Creating a link list**

✔ **Discovering link options**

✔ **Creating a link directory on your site**

A *link list,* commonly referred to as a *blogroll,* is a list of links to other Web sites and blogs that you want to share with your readers. The link list usually displays in a sidebar on your blog (by using widgets) or on a dedicated page if your theme offers a links page template (see Book VI to find out how to create a template).

You can use a link list in various ways:

✦ Share links with other blogs that have linked to your blog.

✦ Provide additional resources for your readers.

✦ Provide links to other sites that you own.

This chapter takes you through the mechanics of building and categorizing link lists, understanding link relationships, and discovering the different options you can set for the link lists on your site.

Organizing Your Links

Sometimes, having a large list of links below the Blogroll heading is just too generic, and you may want to display groups of links with different headings that further define them. Like with posts, you can create multiple categories for your links in the WordPress Dashboard if you want to have more than one link list.

By default, WordPress provides one link category called Blogroll. You can keep this name as-is or change it by using the same method you use to change a post category name (for more on changing the name of a category, see Book III, Chapter 7) — simply click the name of the link category to view the Edit Link Category page and edit the details however you want.

You can organize your links by creating link categories in the Dashboard and then assigning links to the appropriate categories. To create link categories, follow these steps:

1. **Click the down arrow to the right of Links menu title in the left navigation menu, and then select Link Categories from the drop-down list that appears.**

The Link Categories page opens, as shown in Figure 6-1. The left side of the Link Categories page displays the Add Link Category section.

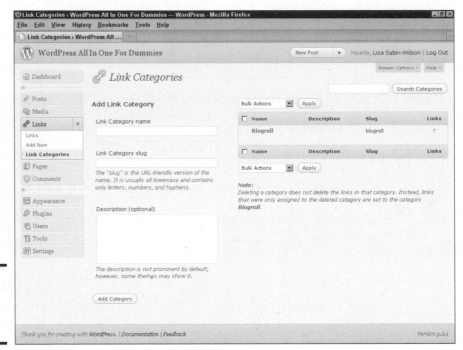

Figure 6-1:
The Link
Categories
page.

2. **Type the name of the link category in the Link Category Name text box.**

3. **Type the slug of the link category in the Link Category Slug text box.**

The term *slug* refers to the word(s) used in the Web address for the specific category.

4. **(Optional) Type a description of the link category in the Description text box.**

Providing a description further defines the category for your readers. You can make the description as short or as long as you want. Some WordPress themes are set up to actually display the category description directly beneath the category name (check out Book VI for information on template tags that allow you to add category descriptions).

5. Click the Add Category button.

The Link Categories page refreshes and displays your new link category.

You can create an unlimited amount of link categories to sort your link lists by topics. (We know one blogger who has 50 categories for his links.) Revisit the Link Categories page any time you want to add, edit, or delete a link. To edit or delete a link category, hover your mouse over the link category you want to manage, and then click one of the three links that appears below the link category name:

+ **Edit:** Open the Edit Category page, where you can edit the name, slug, and description of the category.

+ **Quick Edit:** Opens an inline menu (the menu drops down without leaving the Link Categories page) on the Link Categories page, where you can edit the name and slug of the category.

+ **Delete:** Delete the link category completely, but not before confirming your decision to delete the category in question by clicking OK on the message that pops up.

Adding new links

After you create your link categories, you just need to add some new links! To add a new link, follow these steps:

1. Click Add New in the Links drop-down list.

The Add New Link page opens, as shown in Figure 6-2.

2. Type the name of the link in the Name text box.

Enter the actual name of the site that you're adding to your link list.

3. Type the URL of the link in the Web Address text box.

You want your visitors to go to this destination when they click the name of the site. Don't forget to include the `http://` part of the Web address (`http://lisasabin-wilson.com`, for example).

4. (Optional) Type a description of the site in the Description text box.

Providing a description helps further define the site for your readers. Some WordPress templates display the link description directly below the link name by using a specific WordPress template tag.

5. (Optional) Assign your new link to a category by selecting the check box to the left of the category in the Categories module.

If you don't select a category for your new link, that link is automatically assigned to the default category. Figure 6-3 shows the list of link categories that Lisa has in her blog.

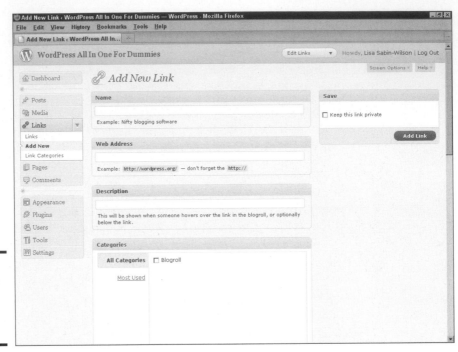

Figure 6-2:
Add a new
link on the
Add New
Link page.

Figure 6-3:
You can
assign a
link to an
existing
category or
add a new
category
on the Add
New Link
page.

If you don't use the Link Category option regularly, you can collapse
(close) this module by clicking anywhere in the Categories title bar. You
can also move the Categories module to a different position on the Add
New Link page by dragging and dropping it to a new location.

6. **(Optional) Select a target for your new link by selecting a radio button
in the Target module.**

Select one of the following radio buttons:

- *_blank:* Loads the link in a new browser window

- *_top:* Loads the link in the top frame (if your site is designed with frames)

- *_none:* Loads the link in the same browser window as the one you are currently browsing in

The third option — None — is the standard/default option here — leaving your visitors to decide how they want to open links on your site. If they want to open a link in a new browser window, they can use their browser tools to make that happen.

You can reposition the Target module by dragging and dropping it to a new location on the Add New Link page. You can also collapse this module.

7. **(Optional) Set the Link Relationship (XFN) options.**

XFN stands for XHTML Friends Network and allows you to indicate the relationship you have with the people you're linking to by defining how you know, or are associated with, them. Table 6-1 lists the different relationships you can assign to your links.

You can reposition the Link Relationship module by dragging and dropping it to a new location on the Add New Link page. You can also collapse (close) this module.

Table 6-1	Link Relationships
Link Relationship	*Description*
Identity	Select this check box if the link is to a Web site you are the owner of.
Friendship	Select the option (Contact, Acquaintance, Friend, or None) that most closely identifies the friendship, if any.
Physical	You've met the person you're linking to face to face. Sharing pictures over the Internet doesn't count; this selection identifies a person you've physically met.
Professional	The person you're linking to is a co-worker or colleague.
Geographical	Select Co-Resident if the person you're linking to lives with you; or select Neighbor or None, depending on which option applies to your relationship with the person you're linking to.
Family	If the blogger you're linking to is a family member, select the option that tells how the person is related to you.
Romantic	Select the option that applies to the type of romantic relationship, if any, you have with the person you're linking to. Do you have a crush on him? Is she your creative muse or someone you consider a sweetheart?

8. **Set the advanced options for your new link (see Figure 6-4).**

Advanced

Image Address

RSS Address

Notes

Rating   0   (Leave at 0 for no rating.)

Figure 6-4:
Advanced
link options
further
manage the
individual
links in your
blogroll.

You have four options in the Advanced module:

- *Image Address:* In this text box, enter the URL of the picture that you want to appear next to the link in your link list.

  This option associates an image with the link. To use it, you need to know the direct URL to the image source (such as `http://your domain.com/images/image.jpg`). Figure 6-5 displays the Resources page on a business Web site; that page uses the WordPress Links feature to assign image addresses to links.

  To find the URL for an image that appears on a Web site, right-click the image and choose Properties from the pop-up menu that appears. Copy the image address (URL). The image's URL starts with http:// and looks like a Web address. Then paste it into the Image Address text box in the Add New Link page.

- *RSS Address:* Add the site's RSS feed alongside the link that appears on your site. (Not all WordPress themes accommodate this feature.)

  To find the RSS URL of the site you're linking to, visit that site and locate the RSS link. (It's usually listed in the sidebar or footer of the site.) Right-click the link, and from the pop-up menu that appears, choose Copy Shortcut (in Internet Explorer) or Copy Link Location (in Firefox). Then in WordPress, paste the link in the RSS Address field.

- *Notes:* Type your notes in the Notes field.

  These notes don't appear on your site, so feel free to enter whatever notes you need to define the details of this link further. A month from now, you may not remember who this person is or why you linked to her, so add notes here to remind yourself.

Figure 6-5:
A Web site's
Resources
page
that uses
WordPress
Links.

- *Rating:* Select a number from the Rating drop-down list to rate how well you like the link from 0 to 10, 0 being the worst and 10 being the best. Some WordPress themes display your link list in the order in which you rate your links, from best to worst.

  You can reposition the Advanced module by dragging and dropping it to a new location on the Add New Link page. You can also collapse (close) this module.

9. **In the Save module, choose whether to make the link public or private.**

   To keep the link private, select the Keep This Link Private check box. No one can see the link. If you want the link to appear publicly on your blog, leave that check box deselected.

   You can reposition the Save module by dragging and dropping it to a new location on the Add New Link page. You can also collapse (close) this module.

10. **To save your changes, scroll to the top of the Add New Links page and click the Add Link button.**

    The Add New Link page refreshes and displays a message to you that your new link has been added.

Editing existing links

You can edit the links in your blog by clicking the name of the link you want to edit on the Links page; the Edit Links page opens.

When you first view the Links page, some links are already assigned to your blog. By default, WordPress provides seven links in your link list. These links go to some helpful Web sites that contain information and resources for the WordPress software. You can delete these links, but we recommend saving them for future reference.

Here's what you can do with your links:

✦ **Edit an existing link.** Click the name of the link you want to edit. The Edit Link page opens. Edit the fields you need to change, and then click the Save button at the top right of the page.

✦ **Sort the links.** Select Link ID, Name, Address, or Rating from the Order by Name drop-down list. Likewise, you can sort your links by category by selecting the Link Category you want from the View All Categories drop-down list.

✦ **Search for specific links by using keywords and phrases.** Enter your keyword in the text box at the top-right side of the Edit Links page and click the Search Links button. If any links match the keywords and/or phrase you typed, those links appear on the page.

Displaying Link Lists on Your Site

With the different options you have available with the Link feature (categories, images, RSS feeds, and so on), you can display a simple listing of links in your sidebar by using widgets, or you can create a full page dedicated to your links in your Dashboard's link lists.

Some site owners use the Link feature to create a full-blown link directory on their sites, which you can easily do by using link categories, images, descriptions, and so on. Following the instructions provided in this chapter, you can create your link categories, add your links to the categories, and then display them on a page by using different template tags that are available in WordPress (covered in Book VI).

Figure 6-5 shows you a page of resource links on a business Web site. You can create this kind of page by using the Image Address on the Add New Link page in your Dashboard, discussed previously in this chapter. Figure 6-6 shows another way of displaying a listing of links that appears more like a directory than just a simple list. This page was made possible by creating several link categories, assigning links to the categories, and then (with a simple WordPress template tag and a little CSS magic) creating the page to display the links like a directory page.

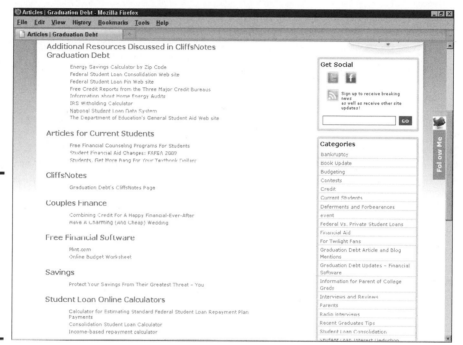

Figure 6-6:
Using
WordPress
links
and link
categories
to create
a Link
Directory
page.

Book VI gives you information on how to display your link lists on your Web site by using WordPress widgets, as well as information about different ways you can display your link lists by using template tags.

Chapter 7: Creating Categories and Tags

In This Chapter

✔ **Exploring content archive options in WordPress**

✔ **Creating and editing categories**

✔ **Creating tags and editing them**

*W*ordPress provides you with so many different ways to organize, categorize, and archive content on your Web site or blog. Packaged within the WordPress software is the capability to automatically maintain chronological, categorized archives of your publishing history, which provides your Web site visitors with different ways to find your content. WordPress uses PHP and MySQL technology to sort and organize everything you publish in an order that you and your readers can access by date and category. This archiving process occurs automatically with every post you publish to your blog.

In this chapter, you can find out all about WordPress archiving, from categories to tags and more. You also can discover how to take advantage of the category description feature to improve your search engine optimization, how to distinguish between categories and tags, and how to use categories and tags to create topical archives of your site content.

Archiving Content with WordPress

When you create a post on your WordPress blog, you can file that post under a category that you specify. This feature makes for a nifty archiving system in which you and your readers can find articles/posts that you've placed within a specific category. Articles you post are also sorted and organized by date (day/month/year) so that you can easily locate articles that you posted at a certain time. The archives page on Lisa's Web site (see it at `http://ewebscapes.com/sitemap`) contains a Chronological Archive section, which has a list of months followed by the content she published in that particular month and year. If you click a date on that page, a listing of articles from that month drops down, and each article title is linked to that article (see Figure 7-1).

You can easily create an archive listing like the one on Lisa's Sitemap page (shown in Figure 7-1) by using a WordPress plugin called Clean Archives Reloaded, which you can find in the WordPress Plugin Directory at `http://wordpress.org/extend/plugins/clean-archives-reloaded`. This plugin is easy to install, and to use it, you just need to create a page and add a short code segment (`[cleanarchivesreloaded]`) to the page content; that code automatically builds a Chronological Archives page that links to all the content you've published on your site. Easy archives!

Figure 7-1:
An archive listing of posts by month and year on Lisa's Web site.

WordPress archives and organizes your content for you in more ways than by date and by category. In this section, I give you an overview of the several other ways — then later in this chapter, I show you how you can leverage those archive types to create a dynamic Web site that's easy to navigate for your readers. The different types of archives and content include

✦ **Categories:** Create categories of topics in which you can file your articles so that you can easily archive relevant topics. Many Web sites display content by category — typically referred to as a *magazine theme,* in which all content is displayed by topic, rather than in a simple chronological listing. Figure 7-2 shows an example of a magazine theme. You can find out how to create one of your own by using the information in Book VI; also be sure to check out Book VI, Chapter 6 to discover how to use template tags and category templates to display category-specific content — exciting stuff!

Figure 7-2:
A magazine
theme
created with
WordPress
(Syndicate
News
Theme by
iThemes.
com).

✦ **Tags:** Tagging your posts with microkeywords, called *tags,* further defines related content within your site, which can improve your site for SEO purposes by assisting the search engines in finding related and relevant content, as well as provide additional navigation to help your readers find relevant content on your site.

✦ **Date Based:** Your content is automatically archived by date based on the day, month, year, and time of day you publish it.

✦ **Author:** Content is automatically archived by author based on the author of the post and/or page — you can create an author archive if your site has multiple content contributors.

✦ **Keyword (or Search):** WordPress has a built-in search function that allows you and your readers to search for keywords, which presents an archive listing of content that's relevant to your chosen keywords.

✦ **Custom Post Types:** You can build custom post types based on the kind of content your site offers — you can find detailed information on custom post types and how to create them in Book VI, Chapter 7.

✦ **Attachments:** WordPress has a built-in media library where you can upload different media files such as photos, images, documents, videos, and audio files (to name a few). You can build an archive of those files to create things such as photo galleries, eBook archives (PDFs), or video galleries.

✦ **Links:** Build your own link directory of resources by using the built-in Link Manager in the WordPress Dashboard, and then create a page to display the links on your site. You can find more information on links and link categories in Book III, Chapter 6.

Building categories

In WordPress, a *category* is what you determine to be the main topic of a blog post. By using categories, you can file your blog posts into topics by subject. To improve your readers' experiences in navigating through your blog, WordPress organizes posts by the categories you assign to them. Visitors can click the categories they're interested in to see the blog posts you've written on those particular topics. You can display the list of categories you set up on your blog in a few different places, including the following:

✦ **Body of the post:** In most WordPress themes, you see the title followed by a statement, such as Filed In: *Category 1, Category 2.* The reader can click the category name to go to a page that lists all the posts you've made in that particular category. You can assign a single post to more than one category.

✦ **Sidebar of your blog theme:** You can place a full list of category titles in the sidebar by using the Categories widget included in your WordPress installation. A reader can click any category to open a page on your site that lists the posts you made within that particular category.

Subcategories (also known as *category children*) can further refine the main category topic by listing specific topics related to the main *(parent)* category. In your WordPress Dashboard, on the Manage Categories page, subcategories appear directly below the main category. Here's an example:

> Books I Enjoy (main category)
>> Fiction (subcategory)
>>
>> Nonfiction (subcategory)
>>
>> Trashy romance (subcategory)
>>
>> Biographies (subcategory)
>>
>> *For Dummies* (subcategory)

You can create as many levels of categories as you like. For example, Biographies and For Dummies could be subcategories of Nonfiction, which is a subcategory of the Books category. You aren't limited to the number of category levels you can create.

Changing the name of a category

When you install WordPress, it gives you one default category called Uncategorized (see the Categories page shown in Figure 7-3). This category name is pretty generic, so you definitely want to change it to one that applies to you and your blog. (On Lisa's blog, she changed it to Life in General. Although that name's still a bit on the generic side, it doesn't sound quite so . . . well, uncategorized.)

REMEMBER

The default category also serves as kind of a fail-safe. If you publish a post to your blog and don't assign that post to a category, the post is assigned to the default category automatically, no matter what you name the category.

The default category

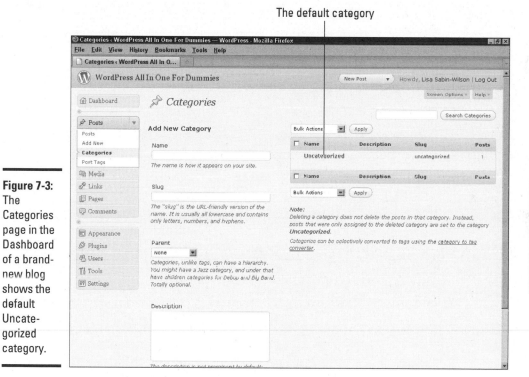

Figure 7-3: The Categories page in the Dashboard of a brand-new blog shows the default Uncategorized category.

Book III
Chapter 7

Creating Categories and Tags

So, how do you change the name of that default category? When you're logged in to your WordPress Dashboard, just follow these steps:

1. **Click Categories in the Posts drop-down list.**

The Categories page opens, containing all the tools you need to set up and edit category titles for your blog.

2. **Click the title of the category that you want to edit.**

   If you want to change the Uncategorized category, click the word Uncategorized to open the Edit Category page (see Figure 7-4).

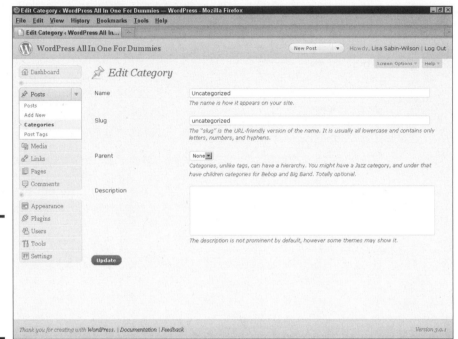

Figure 7-4: Editing a category in WordPress on the Edit Category page.

3. **Type the new name for the category in the Name text box.**

4. **Type the new slug in the Slug text box.**

   The term *slug* refers to the word(s) used in the Web address for the specific category. For example, the category of Books has a Web address of `http://yourdomain.com/category/books`; if you change the Category Slug to Books I Like, then the Web address is `http://your domain.com/category/books-i-like` (WordPress automatically inserts a dash between the slug words in the Web address).

5. **Select a parent category from the Parent drop-down list.**

   If you want this category to be a main category, not a subcategory, select None.

6. **(Optional) Type a description of the category in the Description text box.**

   Use this description to remind yourself what your category is about. Some WordPress themes display the category description right on your site, too, which your visitors may find helpful. (See Book VI for more about themes.) You know that your theme is coded in this way if your site displays the category description on the category page(s).

7. **Click the Update button.**

   The information you just edited is saved, and the Categories page reloads, showing your new category name.

Creating new categories

Today, tomorrow, next month, next year — while your blog grows in size and age, continuing to add new categories further defines and archives the history of your blog posts. You aren't limited in the number of categories and subcategories you can create in your blog.

Creating a new category is as easy as following these steps:

1. **Click Categories in the Posts drop-down list.**

   The Categories page opens.

2. **The left side of the Categories page displays the Add New Category section (see Figure 7-5).**

Figure 7-5:
Create
a new
category on
your blog.

3. Type the name of your new category in the Name text box.

Suppose that you want to create a category in which you file all your posts about the books you read. In the Name text box, type something like **Books I Enjoy**.

4. Type a name in the Slug text box.

The slug creates the link to the category page that lists all the posts you made in this category. If you leave this field blank, WordPress automatically creates a slug based on the category name. If the category is Books I Enjoy, WordPress automatically creates a category slug like `http://yourdomain.com/category/books-i-enjoy`. If you want to shorten it, however, you can! Type **books** in the Category Slug text box, and the link to the category becomes `http://yourdomain.com/category/books`.

5. Select the category's parent from the Parent drop-down list.

Select None if you want this new category to be a parent (or top-level) category. If you want to make this category a subcategory of another category, select the category that you want to be the parent of this one.

6. (Optional) Type a description of the category in the Description text box.

Some WordPress templates are set up to actually display the category description directly beneath the category name (see Book VI). Providing a description further defines the category intent for your readers. The description can be as short or as long as you want.

7. Click the Add New Category button.

That's it! You've added a new category to your blog. Armed with this information, you can add an unlimited number of categories to your blog.

You can delete a category on your blog by hovering your mouse pointer on the title of the category you want to delete, and then clicking the Delete link that appears below the category title.

Deleting a category doesn't delete the posts and links in that category. Instead, posts in the deleted category are reassigned to the Uncategorized category (or whatever you've named the default category).

If you have an established WordPress blog that has categories already created, you can convert some or all of your categories to tags. To do so, look for the Category to Tag Converter link on the right side of the Category page in your WordPress Dashboard — click it to convert your categories to tags. (See the nearby sidebar, "What are tags, and how/why do I use them?," for more information on tags.)

What are tags, and how/why do I use them?

Don't confuse tags with categories (a lot of people do). *Tags* are clickable, comma-separated keywords that help you micro-categorize a post by defining the topics in it. Unlike WordPress categories, tags don't have a hierarchy; you don't assign parent tags and child tags. If you write a post about your dog, for example, you can put that post in the Pets category — but you can also add some specific tags that let you get a whole lot more specific, such as *poodle* or *small dogs.* If someone clicks your poodle tag, he finds all the posts you ever made that contain the poodle tag.

Besides defining your post topics for easy reference, you have another reason to use tags: Search-engine spiders harvest tags when they crawl your site, so tags help other people find your site when they search for specific words.

You can manage your tags in the WordPress Administration panel by clicking Tags on the Pages drop-down list. The Tags page, where you can view, edit, delete, and add new tags, opens.

Book VI, Chapter 6 takes you through the steps of really taking advantage of categories in WordPress to build a dynamic theme that displays your content in a way that highlights the different topics available on your site. Book VI describes how to use WordPress template tags to manipulate category archives for display and distribution on your Web site.

**Book III
Chapter 7**

Creating Categories and Tags

Creating and Editing Tags

In Book IV, Chapter 1, you can find out all about publishing your posts in WordPress and how you can assign different tags to your content. This section takes you through the steps of managing tags, which is similar to the way you manage categories. To create a new tag, follow these steps:

1. **Click Post Tags in the Posts drop-down list.**

The Post Tags page opens, as shown in Figure 7-6.

Unlike categories and links, WordPress doesn't create a default tag for you, so when you visit the Post Tags page for the first time, no tags are listed on the right side of the page.

2. **The left side of the Post Tags page displays the Add New Tag section (refer to Figure 7-6).**

3. **Type the name of your new tag in the Name text box.**

Suppose that you want to create a tag in which you file all your posts about the books you read. In the Name text box, type something like **Fictional Books**.

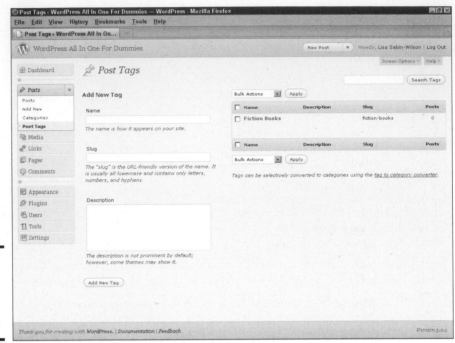

Figure 7-6:
The Post
Tags page
in the
Dashboard.

4. **Type a name in the Slug text box.**

The *slug* is the permalink of the tag and can help identify tag archives on your site by giving them their own URL, such as `http://yourdomain.com/tag/fictional-books`. By default, the tag slug adopts the words from the tag name.

5. **(Optional) Type a description of the tag in the Description text box.**

Some WordPress templates are set up to actually display the tag description directly beneath the tag name. Providing a description further defines the category intent for your readers. The description can be as short or as long as you want.

6. **Click the Add New Tag button.**

That's it! You've added a new tag to your blog. The Add New Tag page refreshes in your browser window with blank fields, ready for you to add another tag to your site.

7. **Repeat Steps 2 through 7 to add an unlimited number of tags to your blog.**

You use the Tags and the Categories pages in your Dashboard to manage, edit, and create new tags and categories to which you assign your posts when you publish them. Book IV, Chapter 1 contains a lot of information about how to go about assigning tags and categories to your posts, as well as a few good tips on how you can create new categories and tags right on the Edit Posts page itself.

Many WordPress Web sites have a cool feature called a *tag cloud,* which is a unique way to display a list of tags used on your site to give your readers navigation options to view your content. Figure 7-7 shows the tag cloud displayed on the sidebar of Lisa's design blog.

Tag cloud

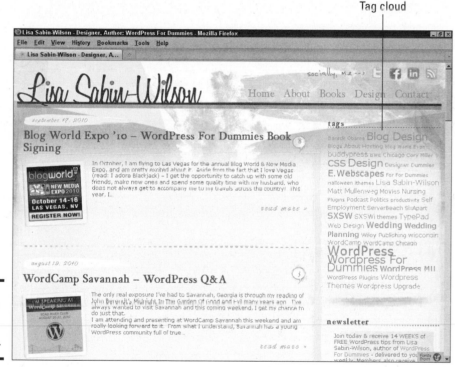

Figure 7-7: A tag cloud on Lisa's design blog.

Book III
Chapter 7

Creating Categories
and Tags

At the top of the right sidebar in Figure 7-7, the tag cloud gives you an at-a-glance peek at the topics Lisa writes about. You can tell the topic she writes about most often because that tag appears in the largest text; likewise, the topics displayed in small text aren't written about quite as often. You can tell by her tag cloud that Lisa's quite a fan of WordPress.

Book IV

Publishing Your Site with WordPress

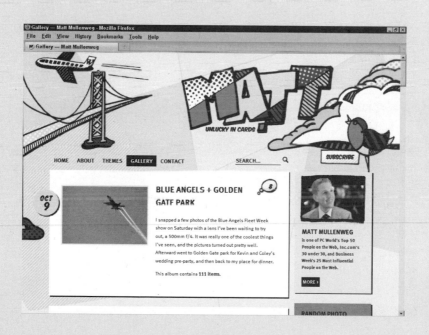

Contents at a Glance

Chapter 1: Writing Your First Post

In This Chapter

✔ **Navigating the Add New Post page**

✔ **Writing and publishing your posts**

✔ **Creating a unique work space for writing**

*1*t's time to write your first post in your new WordPress blog! The topic you choose to write about and the writing techniques you use to get your message across are all up to you; we have our hands full writing this book! We *can* tell you, however, all about the techniques you'll use to write the wonderful passages that can bring you blog fame. Ready?

This chapter covers everything you need to know about the basics of publishing a blog post on your site, from writing a post to formatting, categorizing, tagging, and publishing it to your site.

Composing Your Blog Post

Composing a blog post is a lot like typing an e-mail: You give it a title, you write the message, and you click a button to send your words into the world. This section covers the steps you take to compose and publish a blog post on your site. By using the different options that WordPress provides — like discussion options, categories and tags, for example — you can configure each post however you like.

 You can collapse or reposition all the modules on the Add New Posts page to suit your needs. The only part of the Add New Posts page that can't be collapsed and repositioned is the actual Title and Post text boxes (where you write your blog post).

Follow these steps to write a basic blog post:

1. **Click Add New on the Posts drop-down list.**

   The Add New Post page opens, as shown in Figure 1-1.

2. **Type the title of your post in the Enter Title Here text box at the top of the Add New Post page.**

3. **Type the content of your post in the large text box below the Enter Title Here text box.**

You can use the Visual Text Editor to format the text in your post. We explain the Visual Text Editor, and the buttons and options, later in this section.

4. **Click the Save Draft button in the Publish module, located at the top right of the Add New Post page.**

The page refreshes with your post title and content saved, but not yet published to your blog.

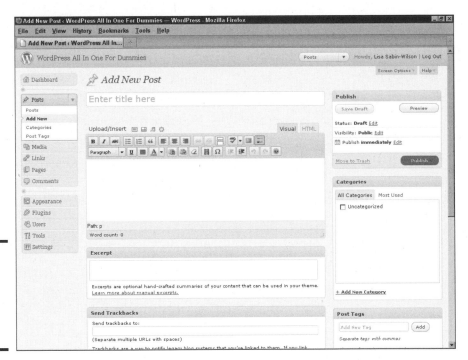

Figure 1-1:
Give your blog post a title and write your post body.

By default, the area in which you write your post is in Visual Editing mode, as indicated by the Visual tab that appears above the text. Visual Editing mode provides WYSIWYG (What You See Is What You Get) options for formatting. Rather than have to embed HTML code in your post, you can simply type your post, highlight the text you want to format, and click the buttons (shown in Figure 1-1) that appear above the text box in which you type your post.

If you've ever used a word processing program, such as Microsoft Word, you'll recognize many of these buttons:

✦ **Bold:** Embeds the `<strong> </strong>` HTML tag to emphasize the text in bold. Example: **Bold Text.**

✦ **Italic:** Embeds the `<em> </em>` HTML tag to emphasize the text in italic. Example: *Italic Text.*

✦ **Strikethrough:** Embeds the `<strike> </strike>` HTML tag that puts a line through your text. Example: ~~Strikethrough Text~~.

✦ **Unordered List:** Embeds the `<ul><li> </li></ul>` HTML tags that create an unordered, or bulleted, list.

✦ **Ordered List:** Embeds the `<ol><li> </li></ol>` HTML tags that create an ordered, or numbered, list.

✦ **Blockquote:** Inserts the `<blockquote> </blockquote>` HTML tag that indents the paragraph or section of text you selected.

✦ **Align Left:** Inserts the `<p align="left"> </p>` HTML tag that lines up the paragraph or section of text you selected against the left margin.

✦ **Align Center:** Inserts the `<p align="center"> </p>` HTML tag that positions the paragraph or section of text you selected in the center of the page.

✦ **Align Right:** Inserts the `<p align="right"> </p>` HTML tag that lines up the paragraph or section of text you selected against the right margin.

✦ **Insert/Edit Link:** Inserts the `<a href=" "> </a>` HTML tag around the text you selected to create a hyperlink.

✦ **Unlink:** Removes the hyperlink from the selected text, if it was previously linked.

✦ **Insert More Tag:** Inserts the `<!--more-->` tag, which lets you split the display on your blog page. It publishes the text written above this tag with a Read More link, which takes the user to a page with the full post. This feature is good for really long posts.

✦ **Toggle Spellchecker:** Perfect for typo enthusiasts! Checking your spelling before you post is always a good idea.

✦ **Toggle Full Screen Mode:** Lets you focus purely on writing, without the distraction of all the other options on the page. Click this button to make the Post text box expand to fill the full height and width of your browser screen. To bring the Post text box back to its normal state, click the Toggle Full Screen button again. Voilà — it's back to normal!

✦ **Show/Hide Kitchen Sink:** Lisa saw this button and thought, "Wow! WordPress does my dishes, too!" Unfortunately, the button's name is a metaphor that describes the advanced formatting options available with the Visual Text Editor. Click this button to make a new formatting list drop down, providing options for underlining, font color, custom characters, undo and redo, and so on — a veritable kitchen sink full of options, such as

- *Format:* This drop-down list allows you to select the different text formatting available.

- *Underline:* Inserts the `<u>  </u>` HTML tags around the text to display it as underlined.

- *Text Color:* Displays the text in the color chosen.

- *Paste as Plain Text:* Useful if you copy text from another source, this option removes all formatting and special/hidden characters from the text and adds it to your post as unformatted text.

- *Paste from Word:* Useful if you're copying text from a Microsoft Word document because Word inserts a lot of hidden HTML and characters that could make your post text look funny on your Web site. Use the Paste from Word feature to transfer posts from Word to WordPress to preserve formatting without the hidden mess.

- *Remove Formatting:* Removes all formatting inside the post.

- *Insert/Edit Embedded Media:* Easily embeds media (video or movie) files such as Flash, Quicktime, Shockwave, Windows Media or Real Media video files from outside, third-party sources. Here, you can configure options for the size of the embedded media, alignment within your post (top, right, bottom or left) and background color (optional), for example.

- *Insert Custom Character:* If you click this option, a pop-up window appears, offering different characters (see Figure 1-2) such as $, % &, and ©. In the pop-up window, click the symbol that you want to include to add it to your post.

Figure 1-2: Custom characters.

- *Outdent:* Moves indented the text to the left one preset level with each click.

- *Indent:* Moves text in to the right one preset level with each click.

- *Undo:* Click to undo your last formatting action.

- *Redo:* Click to redo your last formatting action.

- *Help:* Pops open a window that displays helpful information about using the text editor, including timesaving keyboard shortcuts (as shown in Figure 1-3).

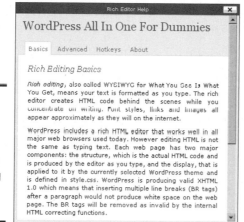

Figure 1-3:
The Help window displays information about using the text editor.

 You can turn off the Visual Text Editor by clicking Your Profile in the Users drop-down list. Deselect the Use the Visual Editor When Writing check box to turn off this editor if you want to insert the HTML code in your posts yourself.

 If you want to embed your own HTML code and skip the Visual Text Editor, click the HTML tab that appears to the right of the Visual tab. If you're planning to type HTML code in your post — for a table or video files, for example — you have to click the HTML tab before you can insert that code. If you don't, the Visual Text Editor formats your code, and it most likely looks nothing like you intended it to.

WordPress has a nifty, built-in autosave feature that saves your work while you're typing and editing a new post. If your browser crashes or you accidentally close your browser window before you manually save your post, you can access it again when you get back.

Directly above and to the left of the Visual Text Editor row of buttons, an Add Media area has a row of four icons. These icons let you insert images/photos, photo galleries, videos, and audio files into your posts. WordPress has an entire Media Library capability, which we describe in great detail in Chapters 2 and 3 of this minibook.

**Book IV
Chapter 1**

Writing Your First
Post

Refining Your Post Options

After you write the post, you can choose a few extra options before you publish it for the entire world to see. These settings apply to the post you're currently working on — not to any future or past posts. You can find these options below and to the right of the Post text box (see Figure 1-4). Click the title of each option — the settings for that specific option expand.

You can reposition the different post option modules on the Add New Post page to fit the way you use this page.

Figure 1-4:
Several options are available for your blog post.

Here are the options that appear below the Post text box:

✦ **Excerpt:** Excerpts are short summaries of your posts. Many bloggers use snippets to show teasers of their blog posts, thereby encouraging the reader to click the Read More links to read the posts in their entirety. Type your short summary in the Excerpt box. Excerpts can be any length, in terms of words; however, the point is to keep it short and sweet, and tease your readers into clicking the Read More link. Figure 1-5 shows a blog post published to Lisa's site; however, it displays only an excerpt of the post on the front page — requiring the reader to click the Continue Reading link to view the post in its entirety.

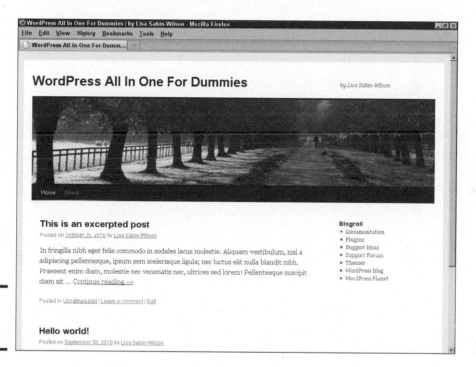

Figure 1-5:
A post
excerpt.

✦ **Send Trackbacks:** If you want to send a trackback to another blog, enter the blog's trackback URL in the Send Trackbacks To text box. You can send trackbacks to more than one blog; just be sure to separate trackback URLs with a space between each. For more on trackbacks, refer to Book III, Chapter 5.

✦ **Custom Fields:** Custom fields add extra data to your posts, and you can fully configure them. You can read more about the Custom Fields feature in WordPress in Book IV, Chapter 6.

✦ **Discussion:** Decide whether to let readers submit comments through the comment system by selecting the Allow Comments on this Post check box. By default, the box is checked; uncheck it to disallow comments on this post.

✦ **Author:** If you're running a multi-author blog, you can select the name of the author who wrote this post. By default, your own author name appears selected in the Author drop-down menu.

Here are the options that appear to the right of the Post text box:

✦ **Publish:** Publishing and privacy options for your post, which we cover in more detail in the following section of this chapter.

✦ **Categories:** You can file your posts in different categories to organize them by subject. (See more about organizing your posts by category in Book III, Chapter 7.) Select the check box to the left of the category you want to use. You can toggle between listing all categories or seeing just the categories that you use the most by clicking the All Categories or Most Used links, respectively.

Don't see the category you need? Click Add New Category, and you can add a category right there on the Add New Post page that appears.

✦ **Post Tags:** Type your desired tags in the Add New Tag text box. Be sure to separate each tag with a comma so that WordPress knows where each tag begins and ends. `Cats, Kittens, Feline` represents three different tags, for example, but without the commas, WordPress would consider those three words to be one tag. See Book III, Chapter 7 for more information on tags and how to use them.

✦ **Featured Image:** Some WordPress themes are configured to use an image (photo) to represent each post that you have on your blog. The image can appear on the home/front page, blog page, archives, or anywhere within the content display on your Web site. If you're using a theme that has this option, you can easily define the post thumbnail by clicking Set Featured Image below the Featured Image module on the Add New Post page. More information about using Featured Images can be found in Book VI, Chapter 6.

When you finish setting the options for your post, don't navigate away from this page; you haven't yet fully saved your options. The following section on publishing your post covers all the options you need for saving your post settings!

Publishing your post

After you give your new post a title; write the content of your new blog post; maybe add an image or other type of media file to your blog post (see Book IV, Chapter 4); and configure the tags, categories, and other options, now the question is: Publish? Or not to publish (yet)?

WordPress gives you three options for saving or publishing your post when you're done writing it. The Publish module is located on the right side of the Add New (or Edit) Post page. Just click the title of the Publish module to expand the settings you need. Figure 1-6 shows the available options in the Publish module.

Figure 1-6:
The publish status for your blog posts.

The Publish module has several options:

✦ **Save Draft:** Click this button to save your post as a draft. The Add New Post page reloads with all your post contents and options saved; you can continue editing it now, tomorrow, the next day, or next year — the post is saved as a draft until you decide to publish it or delete it. To access your draft posts, click the Posts link on the Posts menu.

✦ **Preview:** Click the Preview button to view your post in a new window, as it would appear on your live blog if you'd published it. Previewing the post doesn't publish it to your site yet. It gives you the opportunity to view it on your site and check it for any formatting or content changes you want to make.

✦ **Status:** Click the Edit link to open the settings for this option. A drop-down list appears, from which you can select Draft or Pending Review:

   • *Draft:* Save the post in draft form but don't publish it to your blog.

   • *Pending Review:* The post shows up in your list of drafts next to a Pending Review header. This option lets the administrator of the blog know that contributors have entered posts that are waiting for administrator review and approval (helpful for blogs that have multiple authors).Generally, only contributors use the Pending Review option.

   Click the OK button to save your Status setting.

✦ **Public:** Select this option to make the post viewable to everyone who visits your site.

✦ **Stick This Post to the Front Page:** Select this check box to have WordPress publish the post to your blog and keep it at the very top of all blog posts until you change this setting for the post.

This option is otherwise known as a *sticky post*. Typically, posts are displayed in chronological order on your blog, displaying the most recent post on top. If you make a post sticky, it remains at the very top, no matter how many other posts you make after it. When you want to unstick the post, deselect the Stick This Post to the Front Page check box.

✦ **Password Protected:** By assigning a password to a post, you can publish a post to your blog that only you can see. You can also share the post password with a friend, who can see the content of the post after he or she enters the password. But why would anyone want to password-protect a post? Imagine that you just ate dinner at your mother-in-law's house and she made the *worst* pot roast you've ever eaten. You can write all about it! Protect it with a password and give the password to your trusted friends so that they can read all about it without offending your mother-in-law. Figure 1-7 shows a published post that's private; visitors see that a post exists, but they need to enter a password in the text box and then click Submit in order to view it.

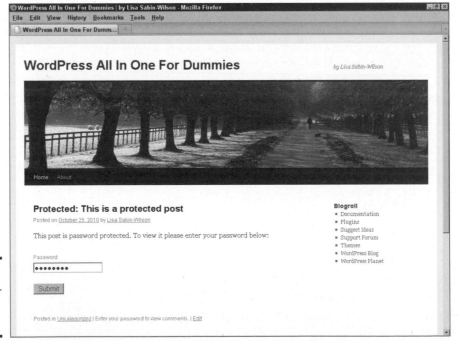

Figure 1-7: A password-protected post.

✦ **Private:** Publish this post to your blog so that only you can see it — no one else will be able to see it, ever. You may want to protect personal and private posts that you write only to yourself (if you're keeping a personal diary, for example).

✦ **Publish Immediately:** Click the Edit link to make the publish date options appear, where you can set the timestamp for your post. If you want the post to have the current time and date, ignore this setting altogether.

If you want to future-publish this post, you can set the time and date for anytime in the future. This feature has come in handy for Lisa many times. For example, when you have a vacation planned and you don't want your blog to go without updates while you're gone, you can write a few posts and set the date for a time in the future. Those posts are published to her blog while you're somewhere tropical, diving with the fishes.

✦ **Publish:** This button wastes no time! It bypasses all the previous draft, pending review, and sticky settings, and publishes the post directly to your blog immediately.

After you select an option from the Publish drop-down list, click the Update button. The Write Post page saves your publishing-status option.

If you click Publish and for some reason don't see the post appear on the front page of your blog, you probably left the Status drop-down list set to Unpublished. Your new post appears in the draft posts, which you can find by clicking Edit in the Posts drop-down list.

Being your own editor

While we write this book, we have editors looking over our shoulders, making recommendations, correcting typos and grammatical errors, and helping us by telling us when we get too long winded. You, on the other hand, are not so lucky! You're your own editor and have full control of what you write, when you write it, and how you write it. You can always go back and edit previous posts to correct typos, grammatical errors, and other mistakes by following these steps:

1. **Find the post that you want to edit by clicking Posts in the Posts drop-down list.**

The Posts page opens and lists the 20 most recent posts you've made to your blog.

To filter that listing of posts by date, select a date from the Show All Dates drop-down list at the top of the Posts page. For example, if you select February 2011, the Posts page reloads, displaying only those posts that were published in the month of February in 2011.

You can also filter the post listing by category. Select your desired category from the View All Categories drop-down list.

**Book IV
Chapter 1**

Writing Your First Post

2. **When you find the post you need, click its title.**

   Alternatively, you can click the Edit link that appears below the post title.

   The Edit Post window opens. In this window, you can edit the post and/or any of its options.

   If you need to edit only the post options, click the Quick Edit link. A drop-down Quick Edit menu appears, displaying the post options that you can configure, such as the title, status, password, categories, tags, comments, and timestamp. Click the Save button to save your changes.

3. **Edit your post; then click the Update Post button.**

   The Edit Post window refreshes with all your changes saved.

Creating Your Own Workspace for Writing

Back in Book III, Chapter 2, you can discover how to organize the Dashboard to create your own customized workspace by rearranging modules and screen options for your Dashboard. The Add New Post page, where you write, edit, and publish your post, has the same options available, allowing you to fully control the workspace arrangement to create your own custom, unique space that suits your writing needs.

To start customizing your workspace, open the Add New Post page by clicking Add New in the Posts drop-down list on the Dashboard.One of the first things we do when we visit this page on a new WordPress site is make the Post text box (where you write the content of your post) bigger. You just need to click your mouse in the bottom corner of the box, and while holding down your mouse button, drag it until it's the length you want, and then release your mouse button (conversely, you can make the box smaller by dragging it up, rather than down). Figure 1-8 shows a large Post text box on Lisa's Add New Post page.

Adjusting screen options

Several items appear on the Add New Post page, as described in the section, "Composing Your Blog Post," earlier in this chapter. You may not use all these items, and in fact, you may find that simply removing them from the Add New Post page (and the Edit Post page) makes writing your posts easier and more efficient. To remove an item, follow these steps:

1. **Click the Screen Options tab at the top of the screen.**

   The Screen Options panel drops down, as shown in Figure 1-9.

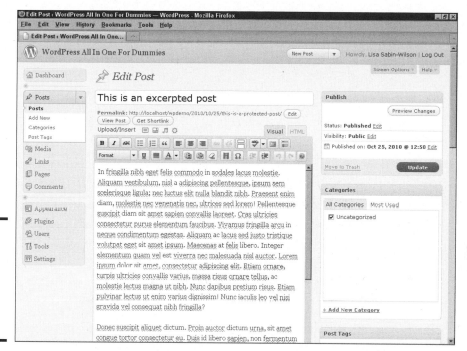

Figure 1-8:
Adjust the size of the Post text box on the Add New Post page.

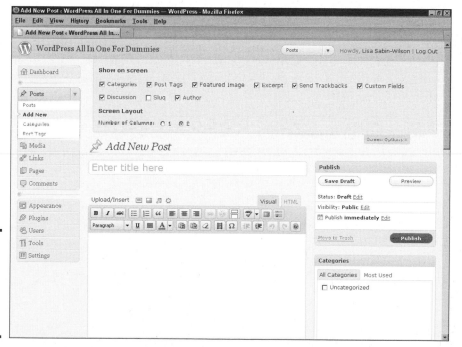

Figure 1-9:
The Screen Options panel on the Add New Post page.

2. **Select or deselect items below the Show on Screen heading.**

Select an item by placing a check mark in the check box to the left of its name; deselect it by removing the check mark. Selected items appear on the page, and deselected items are removed from the page.

If you deselect an item that you want to include again on the Add New Post page, it's not gone forever! Revisit the Screen Options panel and reselect its check box to make that item appear on the page once again.

3. **Select your preferred Screen Layout.**

You can choose whether the layout appears in one column or two columns (the default option).

4. **Click the Screen Options tab when you're done.**

The Screen Options panel closes and the options you've chosen are saved and remembered by WordPress.

Arranging post modules

Aside from being able to make the Post text box bigger (or smaller), as we discuss in the section "Creating Your Own Workspace for Writing," earlier in this chapter, you can't edit the Post text box module. You can configure all other modules on the Add New Post page (and the Edit Post page); you can remove them (in the Screen Options panel, as we discuss in the preceding section), expand and collapse them, and drag them around to place them in a different spot on your screen.

Collapse, or close, any of the modules by hovering your mouse over the module title and then clicking the down arrow that appears to the right of the module name, as shown in Figure 1-10 for the Categories module (likewise, you can expand, or open, a module by doing the same when it's collapsed).

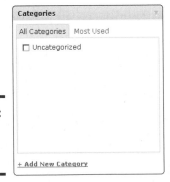

Figure 1-10: Expand or collapse modules.

You can also drag and drop a module on the Add New Post screen to position it wherever you want. Just click a module and, while holding down the mouse button, drag it to different area on the screen. WordPress displays a dashed border around the area when you have the module hovering over a spot where you can drop it. Because Lisa uses the Featured Image module on every post she publishes, she's dragged that module to the top right of her writing space, as shown in Figure 1-11.

Figure 1-11: Drag and drop modules on the Add New Post page.

You can really configure your own custom workspace on the Post page within your Dashboard that suits your style, work habits, and needs. WordPress remembers all the changes you make to this page, including the screen options and modules, so you have to set up this page only once. You can drag and drop modules on any Dashboard page in the same way you do on the main Dashboard page, as covered in Book III, Chapter 2.

Chapter 2: Examining the Difference between Posts and Pages

*I*n Book III, Chapter 7, we discuss the different ways that content gets archived by WordPress, and in Book III, Chapter 2, we give you a very brief introduction to the concept of pages and where to find them in the WordPress Dashboard.

This chapter takes you through the full concept of pages in WordPress, including how to write and publish them. This chapter also fully explains the differences between posts and pages in WordPress so that you know which to publish for different situations.

Understanding the Difference between Posts and Pages

In Book III, Chapter 7, we go into great detail about how WordPress archives your published content on your site by filing it under categories and tags, as well as by date (year/month/day/time of day), and through the use of pages, rather than posts.

Pages, in WordPress, are different from posts because they don't get archived the way your blog posts/articles do: They aren't categorized or tagged, don't appear in your listing of recent blog posts or date archives, and aren't syndicated in the RSS feeds available on your site — because content within pages generally doesn't change. Pages are considered static or stand-alone content and exist separately from the archived post content on your site.

With the page feature, you can create an unlimited amount of static pages separate from your blog posts. People commonly use this feature to create About Me or Contact Me pages, among other things. Table 2-1 illustrates the differences between posts and pages by showing you the different ways the WordPress platform handles them.

Table 2-1	Differences between a Post and a Page	
WordPress Options	*Page*	*Post*
Appears in blog post listings	No	Yes
Appears as a static page	Yes	No
Appears in category archives	No	Yes
Appears in monthly archives	No	Yes
Appears in Recent Posts listings	No	Yes
Appears in site RSS feed	No	Yes
Appears in search results	Yes	Yes

Creating the Front Page of Your Web Site

For the most part, when you visit a blog powered by WordPress, the blog appears on the main page. Lisa's personal blog at `http://lisasabin-wilson.com`, powered by WordPress (of course), shows her latest blog posts on the front page, along with links to the post archives (by month or by category). This setup is typical of a site run by WordPress (see Figure 2-1).

But the front page of Lisa's business site at `http://ewebscapes.com`, also powered by WordPress, contains no blog and displays no blog posts (see Figure 2-2). Instead, it displays the contents of a static page that Lisa created in the WordPress Dashboard. This static page serves as a portal to her design blog, her portfolio, and other sections of her business site. The site includes a blog, but also serves as a full-blown business Web site, with all the sections Lisa needs to provide her clients the information they want.

Both of Lisa's sites are powered by the self-hosted version of WordPress.org, so how can they differ so much in what they display on the front page? The answer lies in the templates in the WordPress Dashboard.

You use static pages in WordPress to create content that you don't want to appear as part of your blog but do want to appear as part of your overall site (such as a bio page, a page of services, and so on).

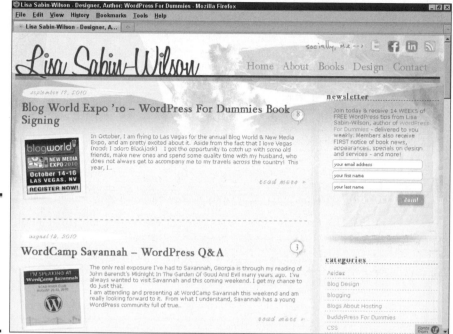

Figure 2-1:
Lisa's personal blog, set up like a typical site powered by WordPress.

Figure 2-2:
Lisa's business site, set up as a business Web site, rather than a blog.

Creating a front page is a three-step process: Create a static page, designate that static page as the front page of your site, and tweak the page to look like a Web site, rather than a blog.

By using this method, you can create unlimited numbers of static pages to build an entire Web site. You don't even need to have a blog on this site, unless you want one.

Creating the static page

To have a static page appear on the front page of your site, you need to create that page. Follow these steps:

1. **Click Add New in the Pages drop-down list.**

   The Add New Page page opens, where you can write a new page for your WordPress blog, as shown in Figure 2-3.

2. **In the Title text box, type a title for the page.**

3. **Type the content of your page in the large text box.**

4. **Set the options for this page.**

   We explain the options on this page in the following section.

5. **Click the Publish button.**

   The page is saved to your database and published to your WordPress site with its own, individual URL (or *permalink*). The URL for the static page consists of your blog URL and the title of the page. For example, if you titled your page About Me, then the URL of the page is `http://yourdomain.com/about-me`. (See Book III, Chapter 3 for more information about permalinks.)

The Page Template option is set to Default Template. This setting tells WordPress that you want to use the default page template (`page.php` in your theme template files) to format the page you're creating. The default page template is the default setting for all pages you create; you can assign a different page template to pages you create, if your theme has made different page templates available for use. In Book VI, Chapter 6, you can find extensive information on advanced WordPress themes, including information on page templates and how to create and use them on your site.

Setting page options

Before you publish a new page to your site, you can change options to use different features available in WordPress. These features are similar to the ones available for publishing posts, which you can read about in Book IV, Chapter 1:

✦ **Custom Fields:** Custom fields add extra data to your page, and you can fully configure them. You can read more about the Custom Fields feature in WordPress in Book IV, Chapter 5.

✦ **Discussion:** Decide whether to let readers submit comments through the comment system by selecting or deselecting the Allow Comments text box. By default, the box is checked; uncheck it to disallow comments on this page.

Typically, you don't see a lot of static pages that have the Comments feature enabled because pages offer static content that doesn't generally lend itself to a great deal of discussion. There are exceptions, however, such as a Contact page, which might use the Comments feature as a way for readers to get in touch with the site owner through that specific page. Of course, the choice is yours to make based on the specific needs of your Web site.

✦ **Author:** If you're running a multi-author site, you can select the name of the author you want to be attributed to this page. By default, your own author name appears selected here.

✦ **Publish:** The publishing and privacy options for your post, which we cover in Book IV, Chapter 1.

✦ **Page Attributes:** Select a parent for the page you're publishing. In Book III, Chapter 7, we cover the different archiving options, including the ability to have a hierarchical structure for pages that create a navigation of main pages and subpages (called parent and child pages).

✦ **Page Template:** Mentioned in the section "Creating the Front Page of Your Web Site," earlier in this chapter. You can assign the page template if you're using a template other than the default one (Book VI, Chapter 7 contains more information about themes and templates, including using page templates on your site).

✦ **Page Order:** By default, this option is set to 0 (zero). You can enter in a number, however, if you want this page to appear in a certain spot on the page menu of your site. (If you're using the built-in menu feature in WordPress, you can use this option; but you don't have to use it because you can define the order of pages and how they appear in your menu by assigning a number to the page order — for example, a page with the page order of 1 will appear first in your navigation menu, where a page with the page order of 2 will appear second, and so on. Book VI, Chapter 1 covers the Menu feature in greater detail.)

✦ **Featured Image:** Some WordPress themes are configured to use an image (photo) to represent each post that you have on your blog. The image can appear on the home/front page, blog page, archives, or any-where within the content display on your Web site. If you're using a theme that has this option, you can easily define a post's thumbnail by clicking the Set Featured Image link below the Featured Image module on the Add New Post page. Then you can assign an image that you've uploaded to your site as the featured image for a particular post.

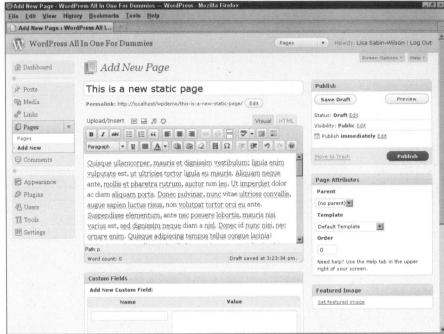

Figure 2-3:
Create the
static page
that you
want to use
as your front
page.

Assigning a static page as the front page

After you create the page you want to use for the front page of your web site,
tell WordPress that you want the static page to serve as the front page of
your site. Follow these steps:

1. **Click Reading in the Settings drop-down list to display the Reading
   Settings page.**

2. **In the Front Page Displays section, select the A Static Page radio
   button.**

3. **From the Front Page drop-down list, select the static page that you
   want to serve as your front page.**

   In Figure 2-4, we chose to display a static page, and the Welcome page is
   the one we want to appear on the front page of the Web site.

4. **Click the Save Changes button at the bottom of the Reading Settings
   page.**

   WordPress displays the page you selected in Step 4 as the front page of
   your site. Figure 2-5 shows Lisa's site displaying the page she created as
   her front page.

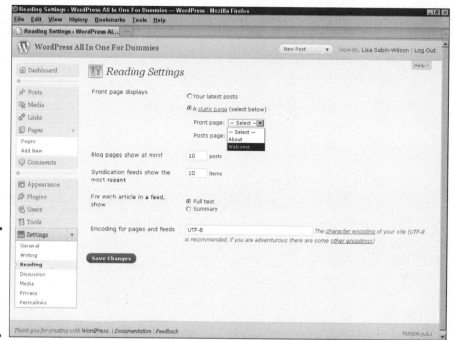

Figure 2-4:
Choosing
which page
to display
as the front
page.

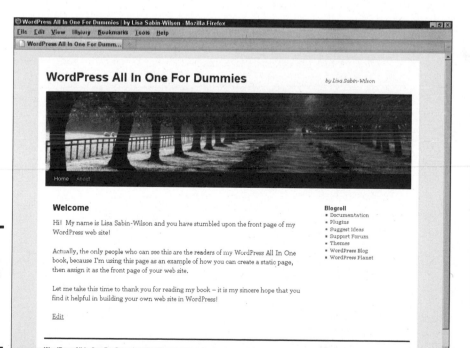

Figure 2-5:
WordPress
displays the
page you
selected as
your front
page.

Adding a Blog to Your Web Site

If you want a blog on your site but don't want to display the blog on the front page, you can add one from the WordPress Dashboard. To create the blog for your site, first follow these steps:

1. **Click Add New link in the Pages drop-down list.**

   The page where you can write a new post to your WordPress blog opens.

2. **Type** Blog **in the Title text box.**

   The page slug is automatically set to /blog. (Read more about slugs in Book III, Chapter 3.)

3. **Leave the Page Content text box blank.**

4. **Click the Publish button.**

   The page is saved to your database and published to your WordPress site.

   Now, you have a blank page that redirects to http://*yourdomain.* com/blog. Next, you need to assign the page you just created as your blog page.

5. **Click Reading in the Settings drop-down list.**

   The Reading Settings page opens.

6. **From the Posts Page drop-down list, select the page that you created in the preceding step list.**

   The page is set as your blog page, as shown in Figure 2-6.

7. **In the Blog Pages Show at Most section, type the number of posts that you want to appear in the Posts text box.**

   If you enter **5**, for example, the blog page shows the last five posts you made to your blog.

8. **Click the Save Changes button.**

   The options you just set are saved, and your blog is now at http:// *yourdomain.*com/blog (where *yourdomain.com* is the actual domain name of your site).

When you navigate to http://*yourdomain.*com/blog, a listing of your blog posts appears.

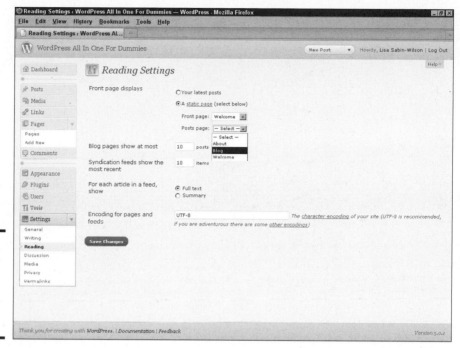

Figure 2-6:
Selecting
the page to
display for
your blog
posts.

This method of using the /blog page slug works only if you're using custom permalinks with your WordPress installation. (See Book III, Chapter 3 if you want more information about permalinks.) If you're using the default permalinks, the URL for your blog page is different; it looks something like http://yourdomain.com/?p=4 (where 4 is the ID of the page you created for your blog).

Chapter 3: Uploading and Displaying Photos and Galleries

Adding images and photos to your posts can really dress up the content. By using images and photos, you give your content a dimension that you can't express in plain text. Through visual imagery, you can call attention to your post and add depth to it. With WordPress, you can insert single images or photographs, or (by using a few nifty plugins) you can turn some of the pages in your site into a full-fledged photo gallery.

In this chapter, you can discover how to add some special touches to your blog posts by adding images and photo galleries, using the built-in image upload feature and image editor in WordPress.

Inserting Images into Your Blog Posts

You can add images to a post pretty easily by using the WordPress image uploader. Jump right in and give it a go by clicking the Upload an Image icon on the Add New Post page. The Add an Image window that appears lets you choose images from your hard drive or from a location on the Web (see Figure 3-1).

The interface that WordPress uses for file uploads is based on Adobe Flash. Flash is a specific set of multimedia technologies programmed to handle media files on the Web. Some browsers and operating systems aren't configured to handle Flash-based applications. If you experience difficulties with the Add an Image window, WordPress gives you an easy alternative: Click the Browser Uploader link in the Add an Image window to use a non–Flash-based uploader to transfer your files.

Figure 3-1:
The
WordPress
Add an
Image
window.

Adding an image from the Web

To add an image from the Web after you click the Add an Image icon, follow these steps:

1. **Click the From URL tab in the Add an Image window.**

The Add Media File from URL window opens.

2. **Type the URL (Internet address) of the image in the Image URL text box.**

Type the full URL, including the http:// and www portion of the address. You can easily find the URL of any image on the Web by right-clicking (PC) or Command-clicking (Mac), and then selecting Properties from the pop-up menu that appears.

3. **Type a title for the image in the Image Title text box.**

4. **Type a description of the image in the Alternate Text text box.**

The alternative text appears in a browser for visually impaired people who use text readers or if, for some reason, the image doesn't load properly. Although alternate text gives the visitors to your site a description of what the image is, it can also improve your SEO (search engine optimization) efforts. Search engines read the alternative text (also called ALT tags) to further categorize and define your site in listings and directories.

5. **(Optional) Type the caption of the image in the Image Caption text box.**

    The words you type here appear below the image on your blog, as a caption.

6. **Specify an alignment option by selecting the None, Left, Center, or Right radio button.**

7. **Type the URL to which you want the image linked.**

    The option you select determines where your readers go when they click the image you uploaded:

    - *None:* You don't want the image to be clickable.

    - *Link to Image:* Readers can click through to the actual image itself, where the image file loads in their browser window.

8. **Click the Insert into Post button.**

    WordPress inserts the appropriate HTML markup in the body of your post so that the image gets displayed when visitors to your site view your post.

Adding an image from your computer

To add an image from your own hard drive after you click the Add an Image Icon, follow these steps:

1. **Click the From Computer tab, and then click the Select Files button.**

    A dialog box, from which you can select an image (or multiple images) from your hard drive, opens.

2. **Select your image(s), and then click Open.**

    The image is uploaded from your computer to your Web server. WordPress displays a progress bar on the upload and displays an Image Options window when the upload is finished.

3. **Edit the details for the image(s) by clicking the Show link that appears to the right of the image thumbnail (the Show link appears for each image if you uploaded multiple images at once — if you uploaded only one image, the Image options automatically appear).**

    When you click Show, the Add an Image window appears (see Figure 3-2), which contains several image options:

    - *Title:* Type a title for the image.

    - *Alternate Text:* Type the alternate text (see preceding section) for the image.

    - *Caption:* Type a caption for the image (such as **This is a flower from my garden**).

    - *Description:* Type a description of the image.

- *Link URL:* If you want the image linked to a URL, type that URL in this text box. Alternately, select the appropriate option button to determine where your readers go when they click the image you uploaded: Selecting None means the image isn't clickable, File URL directs readers through to the image itself, and Post URL directs readers through to the post in which the image appears.

- *Alignment:* Select None, Left, Center, or Right. (See Table 3-1, later in this chapter, for styling information regarding image alignment.)

- *Size:* Select Thumbnail, Medium, Large, or Full Size.

WordPress automatically creates small- and medium-sized versions of the images you upload through the built-in image uploader. A thumbnail is a smaller version of the original file. You can edit the size of the thumbnail by clicking the Settings link and then clicking the Media menu link. In the Image Sizes section of the Media Settings page, designate your desired height and width of the small and medium thumbnail images generated by WordPress.

Edit Image button

Figure 3-2:
You can
set several
options for
your images
after you
upload
them.

If you're uploading more than one image, skip to the "Inserting a Photo Gallery" section, later in this chapter.

4. **Click the Edit Image button (shown in Figure 3-2) to edit the appearance of the image.**

   The image editor (see Figure 3-3) options are represented by icons shown across the top of the image editor window and include

   - *Crop:* Cut the image down to a smaller size.
   - *Rotate Counter-Clockwise:* Rotate the image to the left.
   - *Rotate Clockwise:* Rotate the image to the right.
   - *Flip Vertically:* Flip the image upside down and back again
   - *Flip Horizontally:* Flip the image from right to left and back again.
   - *Undo:* Undo any changes you made.
   - *Redo:* Redo images edits that you've undone.
   - *Scale Image:* The option drop-down list appears, giving you the ability to set a specific width and height for the image.

5. **Click the Insert into Post button.**

Figure 3-3:
The
WordPress
image editor
options.

The Add an Image window closes, and the Add New Post page (or the Add New Page page, if you're writing a page) reappears. WordPress has inserted the HTML to display the image in your post, as shown in Figure 3-4; you can continue editing your post, save it, or publish it.

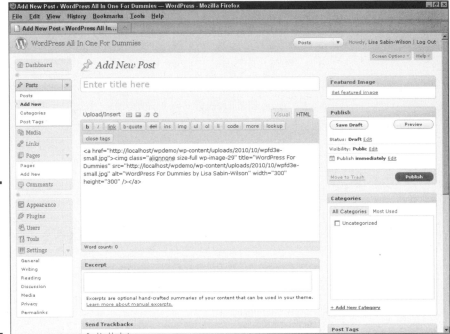

Figure 3-4: WordPress inserts the correct HTML code for your uploaded image into your post.

To see the actual image, and not the code, click the Visual tab just above the Post text box.

Aligning your images

When you upload your image, you can set its alignment as None, Left, Center, or Right. The WordPress theme you're using, however, may not have these alignment styles accounted for in its stylesheet. If you set the alignment to Left, for example, but the image on your blog doesn't appear to be aligned at all, you may need to add a few styles to your theme's stylesheet.

Themes and templates are discussed in greater detail in Book VI; however, for purposes of making sure that you have the correct image alignment for your newly uploaded images, follow these steps for a quick-and-dirty method:

1. **Click Editor in the Appearance drop-down list.**

The Edit Themes page opens. All the template files for your active theme are listed on the right side of the page.

2. **Click the Stylesheet template.**

The Stylesheet (`style.css`) template opens in the text box on the left side of the page.

3. **Add your desired styles to the stylesheet.**

Table 3-1 shows the styles you can add to your stylesheet to make sure that image-alignment styling is present and accounted for in your theme.

Table 3-1	Styling Techniques for Image Alignment
Image Alignment	*Add This to Your Stylesheet* (`style.css`)
None	`img.alignnone {float:none; margin: 5px 0 5px 0;}`
Left	`img.alignleft {float:left; margin: 5px 10px 5px 0px;}`
Center	`img.aligncenter {display:block; float:none; margin: 5px auto;}`
Right	`img.alignright {float:right; margin: 5px 0 5px 10px;}`

These styles are just examples of what you can do. Get creative with your own styling. You can find more information about using CSS (Cascading Style Sheets) to add style to your theme(s) in Book VI, Chapter 4.

Inserting a Photo Gallery

You can also use the WordPress Add an Image window to insert a full photo gallery into your posts. Upload all your images; then instead of clicking the Insert into Post button, click the Save All Changes button at the bottom of the Add an Image window (refer to Figure 3-1), and then click the Gallery link at the top of the Add an Image window (the Gallery link appears only on posts that have images uploaded to it). (See Figure 3-5.) This tab displays thumbnails of all the images you uploaded for your post.

Figure 3-5:
The Gallery
tab of the
Add an
Image
window.

Follow these steps to insert a photo gallery into a blog post:

1. **(Optional) On the Gallery tab, below the Actions column, type the order that you want the images to appear in the gallery.**

Type the number of the sequence in which you want this image displayed. (If you want this image displayed first, for example, type the number 1.)

2. **Set options for your gallery.**

You can specify the following options:

- *Link Thumbnails To:* Image File or Attachment Page.
- *Order Images By:* Menu Order, Name, or Date/Time.
- *Order:* Ascending or Descending.
- *Gallery Columns:* Select how many columns of images you want to appear in your gallery.

3. **Click the Save All Changes button.**

All the changes you made to each individual image listed in the gallery are saved.

4. **Click the Insert Gallery button.**

WordPress inserts into your post a piece of short code that looks like this: [gallery].

Table 3-2 shows some gallery short codes that you can use to manually specify the display settings for your photo gallery.

5. **(Optional) Change the order of appearance of the images in the gallery, as well as the markup (HTML tags or CSS selectors).**

Use the WordPress gallery short code to change different aspects of the display of the gallery in your post, such as the caption, order of image appearance and HTML markup tags that help you control the style of the gallery within your CSS file:

- *captiontag:* Change the markup that surrounds the image caption by altering the gallery short code. Here are some examples: [gallery captiontag="div"] places <div></div> tags around the image caption (the <div> tag is considered a block-level element and creates a separate container for the content — see more about div tags and CSS in Book VI, Chapter 4); to have the gallery appear on a line of its own, the [gallery captiontag="p"] code places <p class="gallery-caption"></p> tags around the image caption. The default markup for the captiontag option is dd.

- *icontag:* Defines the HTML markup around each individual thumbnail image in your gallery. Change the markup around the icontag (thumbnail icon) of the image by altering the gallery short code to something like [gallery icontag="p"], which places <p class="gallery-icon"></p> tags around each thumbnail icon. The default markup for icontag is dt.

- *itemtag:* Defines the HTML markup around each item in your gallery. Change the markup around the itemtag (each item) in the gallery by altering the gallery short code to something like [gallery itemtag="span"], which places <span class= "gallery-item"></span> tags around each item in the gallery. The default markup for the itemtag is dl.

- *captiontag:* Define the HTML markup around the image caption for each image in your gallery. Change the markup around the captiontag (caption) for each image by altering the gallery short code to something like [gallery captiontag="p"], which places <p></p> tags around the image caption. The default markup for captiontag is dd.

- *orderby:* Defines the order in which the images are displayed within your gallery. Change the order used to display the thumbnails in the gallery by altering the gallery short code to something like `[gallery orderby="menu_order ASC"]`, which displays the thumbnails in ascending menu order. Another parameter you can use is `ID_order ASC`, which displays the thumbnails in ascending order according to their IDs.

Table 3-2	Gallery Short Code Examples
Gallery Short Code	*Output*
`[gallery columns="4" size="medium"]`	A four-column gallery containing medium-sized images
`[gallery columns="10" id="215" size="thumbnail"]`	A ten-column gallery containing thumbnail images pulled from the blog post with the ID 215
`[gallery captiontag="p" icontag="span"]`	A three-column (default) gallery in which each image is surrounded by `<span></span>` tags and the image caption is surrounded by `<p></p>` tags

6. **Define the style of the `<span>` tags in your CSS stylesheet.**

   The `<span>` tags create an inline element. An element contained within a `<span>` tag stays on the same line as the element before it; there's no line break. You need a little knowledge of CSS to alter the `<span>` tags. Click the Design tab in your WordPress Dashboard, and then click the Theme Editor subtab to edit the stylesheet for your theme. Here's an example of what you can add to the stylesheet (`style.css`) for your current theme:

   ```
   span.gallery-icon img {
   padding: 3px;
   background: white;
   border: 1px solid black;
   margin: 0 5px;
   }
   ```

   Placing this bit of CSS in the stylesheet (`style.css`) of your active theme automatically places a 1-pixel black border around each thumbnail, with 3 pixels of padding and a white background. The left and right margins are 5 pixels wide, creating nice spacing between images in the gallery.

7. **Click the Update File button to save changes to your Stylesheet (`style.css`) template.**

WordPress gallery plugins

Here are a handful of great gallery plugins:

- **NextGEN Gallery by Alex Rabe** (`http://wordpress.org/extend/plugins/nextgen-gallery`): Creates sort-able photo galleries and more

- **Organizer by Imthiaz** (`http://wordpress.org/extend/plugins/organizer`): Organizes, renames, resizes, and manages image files

- **Random Image widget by Marcel Proulx** (`http://wordpress.org/extend/plugins/random-image-widget`): Displays images at random from your image-upload folder

- **Mini-Slides by Roland Rust** (`http://wordpress.org/extend/plugins/mini-slides`): Creates inline slide shows

---

Figure 3-6 shows Lisa's post with her photo gallery displayed, using the preceding steps and CSS example in the default WordPress theme: Twenty Ten. This code is the gallery short code that she used for the gallery shown in Figure 3-6 — `[gallery icontag="span" size="thumbnail"]`.

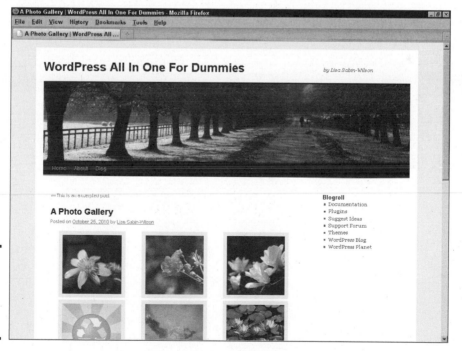

Figure 3-6:
A photo gallery displayed in a post.

Matt Mullenweg, cofounder of the WordPress platform, created a very extensive photo gallery by using the built-in gallery options in WordPress. Check out the fabulous photo gallery at `http://ma.tt/category/gallery`, as shown in Figure 3-7.

Figure 3-7:
A photo gallery created with WordPress by founder Matt Mullenweg.

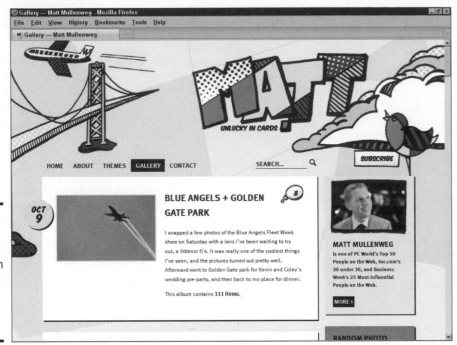

Chapter 4: Exploring Podcasting and Video Blogging

In This Chapter

✔ **Uploading and embedding videos in posts**

✔ **Adding audio files to posts**

✔ **Exploring podcasting and vlogging**

✔ **Using the Media Library**

Many Web site owners want to go beyond just offering written content for the consumption of their visitors by offering different types of media, including audio and video files. WordPress makes it pretty easy to include these different types of media files in your posts and pages by using the built-in file-upload feature.

The audio files you add to your site can include music or voice in formats such as .mp3, .midi, or .wav (to name just a few). Some Web site owners produce their own audio files in regular episodes, called *podcasts*, to create an Internet radio show. Often, you can find these audio files available for syndication through RSS and can subscribe to them in a variety of audio programs, such as iTunes.

You can include videos in blog posts or pages by embedding code offered by popular third-party video providers such as YouTube (www.youtube.com) or Vimeo (www.vimeo.com). Web site owners can also produce and upload their own video shows, an activity known as vlogging (video blogging).

This chapter takes you through the steps to upload and embed audio and video files within your content, and provides you with some tools that can help you more easily embed those files without having to use elaborate coding techniques.

Inserting Video Files into Your Blog Posts

Whether you're producing your own videos for publication or embedding other people's videos, placing a video file in a blog post has never been easier with WordPress.

Check out a good example of a video blog at `http://1938media.com`. Loren Feldman and his team produce video for the Web and for mobile devices.

Several video galleries on the Web today allow you to add videos to blog posts — Google's YouTube service (`www.youtube.com`) is a good example of a third-party video service that allows you to share their videos.

Adding video from the Web

To add video from the Web, click the Add Video icon, then click the From URL tab, shown in Figure 4-1, on the Add Video pop-up window and follow these steps:

> **Add Video**   ✕
>
> From Computer | From URL | Media Library
>
> Add media file from URL
>
> **Video URL**   * [   ]
>
> **Title**   * [   ]
>
> *Link text, e.g. "Lucy on YouTube"*
>
> (Insert into Post)

Figure 4-1:
Add Video
from URL.

1. **Type the URL (Internet address) of the video in the Video URL text box.**

Type the full URL, including the `http://` and www portion of the address. Video providers, such as YouTube, usually list the direct links for the video files on their sites; you can copy and paste one of those links into the Video URL text box.

2. **(Optional) Type the title of the video in the Title text box.**

Giving a title to the video allows you to provide a bit of a description of the video. Provide a title if you can so that your readers know what the video is about.

3. **Click the Insert into Post button.**

   A link to the video is inserted into your post. WordPress doesn't embed the actual video in the post; it inserts only a link to the video. Your blog visitors click the link to load another page in which the video plays.

The preceding steps give you the ability to insert a hyperlink that your readers can click to view the video on another Web site (such as YouTube). However, if you activate WordPress's nifty Auto-Embed feature, WordPress can automatically embed many of these videos within your posts and pages.

With this feature, WordPress automatically detects that a URL you typed in your post is a video (from YouTube, for example) and wraps the correct HTML embed code around that URL to make sure that the video player appears in your post (in a standards, XHTML-compliant way).

Before WordPress can embed a video, however, you must enable the Auto-Embed feature on the Media Settings page by following these steps:

1. **Click Media in the Settings drop-down list on your WordPress Dashboard.**

   The Media Settings page loads in the Dashboard.

2. **Select the Auto-Embed check box.**

   The Auto-Embed feature is now enabled and WordPress will attempt to embed a video player from a video URL from third-party video services like YouTube or Flickr within your post.

3. **Set the dimensions of the video in which you want the (video) to appear on your site in the Maximum Embed Size field.**

   Enter size (width and height) that you want the videos to appear in your posts and pages.

4. **Click the Save Changes button.**

   You're ready to automatically embed links into your WordPress posts.

Currently, WordPress automatically embeds videos from YouTube, Vimeo, DailyMotion, blip.tv, Flickr, Hulu, Viddler, Qik, Revision3, Scibd, PhotoBucket, PollDaddy, and Google Videom, as well as VideoPress-type videos from WordPress.tv.

Adding video from your computer

To upload and post to your blog a video from your computer, click the Add Video icon on the Edit Post or Add New Post page. Then follow these steps:

Book IV
Chapter 4

Exploring
Podcasting and
Video Blogging

1. **Click the Choose Files to Upload button.**

   An Open dialog box appears.

2. **Select the video file that you want to upload and click Open (or simply double-click the filename).**

   The file uploader window in WordPress appears, which shows a progress bar while your video uploads. When the upload is complete, a dialog box that contains several options opens.

3. **Type a title for the file in the Title text box.**

4. **Type a caption for the file in the Caption text box.**

5. **Type a description of the file in the Description text box.**

6. **Click the File URL button.**

   Clicking this button provides a direct link in your post to the video file itself.

7. **Click Insert into Post.**

   WordPress doesn't embed a video player in the post, it inserts only a link to the video; however, if you have the Auto-Embed feature activated, WordPress attempts to embed the video within a video player. If WordPress cannot embed a video player, it displays the link that your visitors will have to click in order to open the video in a new window to view it.

Inserting Audio Files into Your Blog Posts

Audio files can be music files or voice recordings, such as recordings of you speaking to your readers. These files add a nice personal touch to your blog. You can easily share audio files on your blog by using the Upload Audio feature in WordPress. After you insert an audio file in a blog post, your readers can listen to it on their computers, or download it onto an MP3 player and listen to it on their drives to work, if they want.

Click the Add Audio icon on the Edit Post or Add New Post page, and then follow these steps to upload an audio file to your blog post:

1. **Click the Select Files button.**

   An Open dialog box appears, as shown in Figure 4-2.

2. **Select the file that you want to upload and click Open (or simply double-click the filename).**

   The file uploader window reappears in WordPress, which shows a progress bar while your audio file uploads. When the upload is complete, a dialog box that contains several options opens.

Figure 4-2:
Add Audio
Files
from your
computer.

3. **Type a title for the file in the Title text box.**

4. **Type a caption for the file in the Caption text box.**

5. **Type a description of the file in the Description text box.**

6. **Click the File URL button.**

   Clicking this button provides a direct link in your post to the video file itself.

7. **Click Insert into Post.**

   A link to the audio file is inserted into your post. WordPress doesn't embed an actual audio player in the post; it only inserts a link to the audio file. Visitors click the link to open another page, where they can play the audio file.

Some great WordPress plugins for audio-handling can enhance the functionality of the file uploader and help you manage audio files in your blog posts. Check out Book VII for information on how to install and use WordPress plugins in your blog.

Podcasting with WordPress

As we explain in the introduction to this chapter, to podcast, the Web site owner provides regular episodes of an audio show that visitors can download to their computer and listen to on their favorite audio player. Think of podcasting as a weekly radio show that you tune into, except that it's hosted on the Internet, rather than on a radio station.

In the sidebar "WordPress video and audio plugins" in this chapter, we mention a few plugins that allow you to more easily insert audio files in your WordPress posts and pages — however, a few plugins are dedicated to podcasting, and they provide features to podcasters that go beyond just embedding audio files in a Web site. Some of the more important of these features include

✦ **Archives:** Create an archive of your audio podcast files so that your listeners can catch up on your show by listening to past episodes.

✦ **RSS Feed:** An RSS feed of your podcast show gives visitors the opportunity to subscribe to your syndicated content so that they can be notified when you publish future episodes.

✦ **Promotion:** A podcast isn't successful without listeners, right? Podcasters like to promote their shows by including their audio files in the iTunes (`www.apple.com/itunes`) library so that when people search iTunes for podcasts by subject, they find the podcasters' podcasts and subscribe to them.

These three plugins go beyond just audio-file management, they're dedicated to podcasting and all the features a podcaster is looking for:

✦ **PowerPress (`http://wordpress.org/extend/plugins/ powerpress`):** PowerPress has many of the features podcasters are looking for, including full iTunes support; audio players; multiple file-format support (`.mp3`, `.m4a`, `.ogg`, `.wma`, `.ra`, `.mp4a`, `.m4v`, `.mp4v`, `.mpg`, `.asf`, `.avi`, `.wmv`, `.flv`, `.swf`, `.mov`, `.divx`, `.3gp`, `.midi`, `.wav`, `.aa`, `.pdf`, `.torrent`, `.m4b`, `.m4r`); statistics to track the popularity of your different podcast offerings; and tagging, categorizing, and archiving of podcast files.

✦ **Podcast Channels (`http://wordpress.org/extend/plugins/ podcast-channels`):** WordPress provides some of the basic stuff needed for podcasting, such as media-file embedding, archiving, and RSS feed handling. The Podcast Channels plugin gives you iTunes metadata that enables you to specify channels for your podcast files and include them in the iTunes library.

✦ **Podcasting Plugin (`http://wordpress.org/extend/plugins/ podcasting`):** Enhances the built-in WordPress audio-management features by adding iTunes support, compatible RSS feeds, and media players. This plugin also allows you to have multiple podcasting feeds, in case you have different podcast shows that cover a range of different topics.

We discuss Web hosting requirements in Book II. If you're a podcaster and intend to store audio files on your Web hosting account, you may need to add increased storage and bandwidth to your account so that you don't run out of space or incur higher fees from your Web hosting provider. Discuss these issues with your Web hosting provider to find out upfront what you have to pay for increased disk space and bandwidth needs.

Keeping Media Files Organized

If you've been running your blog for any length of time, you can easily forget what files you've uploaded by using the WordPress uploader. Lisa used to have to log in to her Web server via FTP and view the Uploads folder to see what she had in there.

Now, the WordPress Media Library allows you to conveniently and easily discover which files are in your Uploads folder.

To find an image, video, or audio file you've already uploaded by using the file uploader and to use that file in a new post, follow these steps:

1. **Click the Upload Media icon to open the File Uploader window.**

2. **Click the Media Library link at the top of the window.**

All the files you've ever uploaded to your blog appear because of the File Uploader feature (see Figure 4-3). Files you uploaded through other methods, such as FTP, don't appear in the Media Library.

3. **Select the file that you want to reuse and click the Show link.**

4. **In the settings menu that appears, set the options for that file: Title, Caption, Description, Link URL, Order, Alignment, and Size.**

5. **Click the Insert into Post button.**

The correct HTML code is inserted into the Post text box.

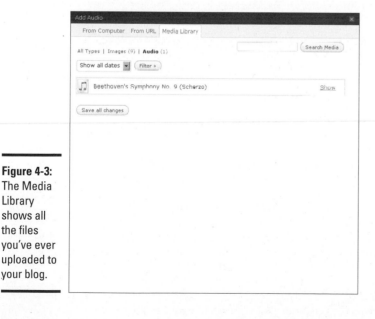

Figure 4-3:
The Media Library shows all the files you've ever uploaded to your blog.

WordPress video and audio plugins

You can find some great WordPress plugins for audio and video handling. Check out Book VII for information on how to install and use WordPress plugins.

Here are a handful of great plugins for audio:

- **Audio Player by Martin Laine** (`http://wordpress.org/extend/plugins/audio-player`): Embeds a Flash MP3 player in your blog posts without any special HTML

- **1 Bit Audio Player by Mark Wheeler** (`http://wordpress.org/extend/plugins/1-bit-audio-player`): Autodetects MP3 files on your site and inserts a stylish player

- **Podcasting Plugin by TSG** (`http://wordpress.org/extend/plugins/podcasting`): Supports several media formats and automatically creates a podcast RSS feed

Here are a handful of great plugins for video:

- **wordTube by Alex Rabe** (`http://wordpress.org/extend/plugins/wordtube`): Creates a YouTube-like player when you insert video files within your posts without any special HTML

- **Smart YouTube by Vladimir Prelovacn** (`http://wordpress.org/extend/plugins/smart-youtube`): Inserts YouTube videos into blog posts, comments, and RSS feeds

- **WP-Vidavee by Vidavee Labs** (`http://wordpress.org/extend/plugins/wp-vidavee-film-manager`): Uploads, manages, organizes, and displays video in your blog

- **Video Embedder by Kristoffer Forsgren** (`http://wordpress.org/extend/plugins/video-embedder`): Embeds video from various sources

If you want to view only the files you've uploaded, click the Edit link in the Media menu, found in the left navigation menu of the Dashboard, which opens the Media Library page.

The Media Library page lists all the files you've ever uploaded to your WordPress blog. By default, the page displays all types of files, but you can click the Images, Audio, or Video link to specify which file type you want to see (as shown in Figure 4-4).

You can do the following tasks on the Media Library page:

✦ **Filter media files by date.** If you want to view all media files that were uploaded in July of 2010, select that date from the drop-down list and click the Filter button; the page reloads and displays only the media files uploaded in the month of July, 2010.

✦ **Search media files by using a specific keyword.** If you want to search your Media Library for all files that reference kittens, then you type the word **kittens** in the Search box in the upper-right side of the Media Library page. Then click the Search Media button; the page reloads and displays only media files that contain the keyword or tag *kittens*.

✦ **Delete media files.** To delete files, click the small white box that appears to the left of the file's thumbnail on the Manage Media page; then click the Delete button, which appears at the top left of the page. The page reloads, and the media file you just deleted is now gone.

✦ **View media files.** On the Manage Media page, click the thumbnail of the file you want to view. The actual file opens in your Web browser. If you need the URL of the file, you can copy the permalink of the file from your browser's address bar.

Figure 4-4:
The WordPress Media Library, displaying only audio files.

Chapter 5: Working with Custom Fields

In This Chapter

✔ Understanding what Custom Fields can do for you

✔ Working with the Custom Fields interface

✔ Adding custom field codes to your templates

✔ Using custom fields in a variety of ways

In Book IV, Chapter 2, we discuss all the different elements you can add to your blog posts and pages when you publish them. By default, WordPress allows you to give your posts and pages titles and content, to categorize and tag posts, to select a date and time for publishing, and to control the discussion options on a per-post or per-page basis.

However, you may sometimes want to add extra items to your posts — items you may not want to add to every post, necessarily, but that you add often enough to make manually adding them each time you publish a nuisance. These items can include a multitude of things, from telling your readers your current mood to what you're currently listening to or reading — to pretty much anything you can think of.

WordPress gives you the ability to create and add *metadata* (additional data that can be added to define you and your post) to your posts by using a feature called Custom Fields. In Book IV, Chapter 2, we briefly touch on the Custom Field interface on the Write Post screen in the Dashboard, and in this chapter, we go through Custom Fields in depth by explaining what they are and how to implement them, as well as offering some cool ideas for using Custom Fields on your site.

Understanding Custom Fields

A WordPress template contains static pieces of data that you can count on to appear on your site. These static items include elements such as the title, the content, the date, and so on. But what if you want more? Say you write a weekly book-review post on your site and want to include a listing of recent reviews and accompanying thumbnails of the books; you can, through the use of Custom Fields, without having to retype the list each time you do a review. You can add literally thousands of auto-formatted pieces of data like this (such as book reviews or movie reviews, for example) by adding Custom Fields on your WordPress blog.

You create Custom Fields on a per-post or per-page basis, which means that you can create an unlimited amount of them and add them only to certain posts. They help you create extra data for your posts and pages by using the Custom Fields interface, which is covered in the following section.

So, what can you do with Custom Fields? Really, the only right answer is: Anything you want. Your imagination is your only limit when it comes to the different types of data you can add to your posts by using Custom Fields. Custom Fields allow the site owner the flexibility of defining certain pieces of data for each post.

To use Custom Fields, you do need a bit of knowledge about how to navigate through WordPress theme templates because you have to insert a WordPress function tag, with specific parameters, in the body of the template file. Book VI takes you through all the information you need to know in order to understand WordPress themes, templates, and template tags — so you may want to hit that minibook before you attempt to apply what we discuss in the rest of this chapter. If you're already comfortable and familiar with WordPress templates and tags, then you probably won't have any trouble with this chapter at all.

Exploring the Custom Fields Interface

The Custom Fields module appears on both the Write Post and Write Page (See Book IV, Chapters 2 and 3) pages in the WordPress Dashboard, below the Post text box, as shown in Figure 5-1.

Figure 5-1: The Custom Fields module on the Write Post page in the Dashboard.

The Custom Fields module has two different text boxes:

✦ **Name:** Also known as the Key, you give this name to the Custom Field you're planning to use. The Name needs to be unique: It's used in the template tag that you can read about in the section "Adding Custom Fields to Your Template File," later in this chapter. In Figure 5-2, you can see that Lisa's Custom Field has the name mood.

✦ **Value:** Assigned to the Custom Field name and displayed in your blog post on your site if you use the template tag that you can also read about in the section "Adding Custom Fields to Your Template File," later in this chapter. In Figure 5-2, the Value assigned to the mood (the Custom Field name) is Happy.

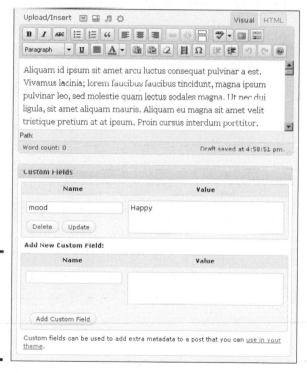

**Book IV
Chapter 5**

**Working with
Custom Fields**

Figure 5-2:
Custom
Fields that
have Name
and Value
assigned.

Simply fill out the Name and Value text boxes, and then click the Add Custom Field button to add the data to your post or page. Figure 5-2 shows a Custom Field that Lisa added to her post with the Name of mood and with the assigned Value Happy. In the section "Adding Custom Fields to Your Template File," later in this chapter, we show you the template tag you need to add to your WordPress theme template in order to display this Custom Field, which appears in her post like this: My Current Mood is: Happy, shown in Figure 5-3, where the Custom Field appears at the end of Lisa's post.

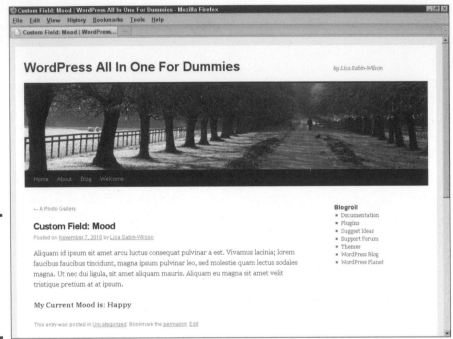

WordPress All In One For Dummies

by Lisa Sabin-Wilson

Home   About   Blog   Welcome

← A Photo Gallery

Custom Field: Mood

Posted on November 7, 2010 by Lisa Sabin-Wilson

Aliquam id ipsum sit amet arcu luctus consequat pulvinar a est. Vivamus lacinia; lorem faucibus faucibus tincidunt, magna ipsum pulvinar leo, sed molestie quam lectus sodales magna. Ut nec dui ligula, sit amet aliquam mauris. Aliquam eu magna sit amet velit tristique pretium at at ipsum.

My Current Mood is: Happy

This entry was posted in Uncategorized. Bookmark the permalink. Edit

Blogroll
- Documentation
- Plugins
- Suggest Ideas
- Support Forum
- Themes
- WordPress Blog
- WordPress Planet

Figure 5-3:
A Custom Field output appears in Lisa's published post.

You can add multiple Custom Fields to one post. To do so, simply add the Name and the Value of the Custom Field in the appropriate text boxes on the Write Post page, and then click the Add Custom Field button in order to assign the data to your post. You will do this for each Custom Field you want to add to your post.

After you add a particular Custom Field (such as the mood Custom Field Lisa added in Figure 5-2), you can always add it to future posts. So, you can make a post tomorrow and use the mood Custom Field but assign a different value to it. If tomorrow you assign the value Sad, your post displays My Current Mood is: Sad. You can easily use just that one Custom Field on subsequent posts. After you create a Custom Field (such as the mood Custom Field), you can access it in a drop-down list below the Name field, as shown in Figure 5-4 — so you can easily select it again and assign a new Value to it in the future.

Custom Fields are considered extra data, separate from the post content itself, for your blog posts, and WordPress refers to them as *metadata*. The Custom Field Name and Value get stored in the database in the wp_post-metadata table, which keeps track of which Names and Values are assigned to each post. See Book II, Chapter 7 for more information about the WordPress database structure and organization of data.

Figure 5-4:
Custom
Field
Names are
saved and
displayed
in a drop-
down list for
future use.

You can find a Custom Fields module on the Write Page screen in the Dashboard, as well; so, you can add Custom Fields to either your posts or pages, as needed.

Adding Custom Fields to Your Template File

If you followed along in theprevious sections and added the mood Custom Field to your own site, notice that the data doesn't appear on your site the way it does on Lisa's. To get the data to display properly, you must open the template files and dig into the code a little bit. If the idea of digging into the code of your template files intimidates you, you can put this section aside and read up on WordPress themes, template files, and template tags in Book VI.

You can add Custom Fields, in several ways, to your templates in order to display the output of the fields you've set; we think the easiest way involves using the get_post_meta(); template tag function, which looks like this:

```
<?php $key="NAME"; echo get_post_meta($post->ID, $key, true); ?>
```

Here's how that function breaks down:

✦ **<?php:** Part of the functions begins PHP. (Every template tag or function needs to first start PHP with <?php. You can read more about basic PHP in Book II, Chapter 3.)

✦ **$key="*NAME*";:** Defines the name of the key that you want to appear. You define the Name when you add the Custom Field to your post.

✦ **echo get_post_meta:** Grabs the Custom Field data and displays it on your site.

✦ **$post->ID,:** A parameter of the get_post_meta function that dynamically defines the specific ID of the post being displayed so that WordPress knows which metadata to display.

✦ **$key,:** A parameter of the get_post_meta function that gets the value of the Custom Field based on the name, as defined in the $key="NAME"; setting earlier in the code string.

✦ **true);:** A parameter of the get_post_meta function that tells WordPress to return a single result, rather than multiple results. (By default, this parameter is set to true; typically, don't change it unless you're using multiple definitions in the Value setting of your Custom Field.)

✦ **?>:** Ends the PHP function.

Based on the preceding code, to make our mood Custom Field example, you define the key name as mood (replace the *NAME* in the preceding code with the word mood); it looks like this:

```
<?php $key="mood"; echo get_post_meta($post->ID, $key, true); ?>
```

The part of the functions that says $key="mood"; tells WordPress to return the Value for the Custom Field with the Name field of mood.

Entering the code in the template file

So that you can see how to enter the code in your template file, we use the default WordPress theme called Twenty Ten. If you're using a different theme (and you can find thousands of different WordPress themes available), then you need to adapt these instructions to your particular theme. If you really want to follow along in this chapter, activate the Twenty Ten theme on your site, for now, just so that you can follow along and know that you're seeing the same code in the places we describe (you can find information on the Twenty Ten theme and how to activate it in Book VI).

We use Lisa's mood Custom Field as the example here. When you're done with these steps, WordPress displays your current mood at the bottom of the posts to which you've added the mood Custom Field. Keep in mind that this example is just one type of Custom Field that you can add to your posts (and it's an easy one for the purposes of introducing you to the concept).

If you're ready to give it a go, then you're in luck because you can follow these steps to add the template tag, along with a little HTML code to make it look nice, to your theme (these steps assume that you've already added the mood Custom Field to your blog post and have assigned a Value to it):

1. **Log in to your WordPress Dashboard.**

2. **Click Editor in the Appearances drop-down list.**

   The Edit Themes page loads in the Dashboard, as shown in Figure 5-5.

3. **Locate the template files for the Twenty Ten theme.**

   The available templates are listed on the right side of the Edit Themes page, as shown in Figure 5-5.

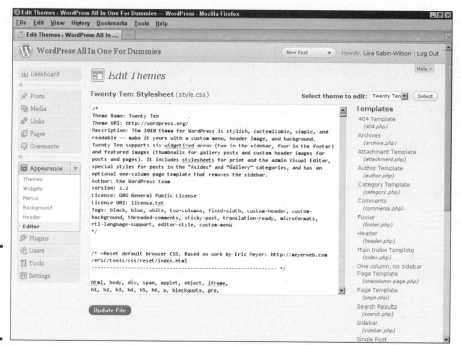

Figure 5-5:
The Edit Themes page in the Dashboard.

4. **Click Single Post in the list of templates.**

   The Single Post (`single.php`) file opens in the text editor on the left side of the screen, where you can edit the template file.

5. **Scroll down and locate the template tag that looks like this: `<?php the_content() ?>`.**

6. **On the new line underneath the preceding one, type:** `<p><strong>My Current Mood is:`.

<p> and <strong> open the HTML tags for paragraph and bold text, respectively; followed by the words to display in your template (My Current Mood is:).

7. **Type the code that we discuss in the preceding section.**

```
<?php $key="mood"; echo get_post_meta($post->ID, $key, true); ?>
```

8. **Type** </strong></p>.

   This code closes the HTML tags you opened in Step 6.

9. **Click the Update File button.**

   Located at the bottom of the Edit Themes page, this step saves the changes you made to the Single Post (single.php) file and reloads the page with a message that says your changes have been successfully saved.

10. **View your post on your site to see your Custom Field data displayed.**

    The data should look just like the "My Current Mood is: Happy" shown in Figure 5-3.

The entire code, put together, should look like this in your template:

```
<p><strong>My Current Mood is: <?php $key="mood"; echo get_post_meta($post->ID,
    $key, true); ?></strong></p>
```

The code is case sensitive, which means that the words you input for the Key in your Custom Field need to match case with the $key in the code. For example, if you input mood in the Key field, then the code needs to be lowercase, as well: $key="mood", if you attempt to change the case like this: $key="Mood", the code will not work.

You have to add this code for the mood Custom Field only one time; after you add the template function code to your template for the mood Custom Field, you can define your current mood in every post you publish to your site by using the Custom Fields interface.

Getting WordPress to check for your Custom Field

The previous sections show you how to add the necessary code to your template file to display your Custom Field; however, what if you want to publish a post on which you don't want the mood Custom Field to appear? If you leave your template file as you set it up by following the steps in the previous sections, even if you don't add the mood Custom Field, your blog post displays My Current Mood is: — without a mood because you didn't define one.

IF, ELSE

In our daily lives, we deal with IF, ELSE situations every day, like in these examples:

✔ **IF** I have a dollar, then I'll buy coffee, or **ELSE** I won't.

✔ **IF** it's warm outside, then I'll take a walk, or **ELSE** I won't.

✔ **IF** I understand this code, then I'll be happy, or **ELSE** I won't.

But you can easily make WordPress check first to see whether the Custom Field is added. If it finds the Custom Field, WordPress displays your mood; if it doesn't find the Custom Field, then WordPress doesn't display anything.

If you followed along in the previous sections, the code in your template looks like this:

```
<p><strong>My Current Mood is: <?php $key="mood"; echo get_post_meta($post->ID,
    $key, true); ?></strong></p>
```

To make WordPress check to see whether the mood Custom Field exists, add this code to the line above your existing code:

```
<?php if ( get_post_meta($post->ID, 'mood', true) ) : ?>
```

Then add this line of code to the line below your existing code:

```
<?php endif; ?>
```

Put together, the lines of code in your template should look like this:

```
<?php if ( get_post_meta($post->ID, 'mood', true) ) : ?>
<p><strong>My Current Mood is: <?php $key="mood"; echo get_post_meta($post->ID,
    $key, true); ?></strong></p>
<?php endif; ?>
```

The first line is an IF statement and, basically, asks the question: Does the mood metadata exist for this post? If it does, the data gets displayed. If it doesn't, then WordPress skips over the code, ignoring it completely so that nothing gets displayed for the mood Custom Field. The final line of code simply puts an end to the IF question. Refer to the "IF, ELSE" sidebar, in this chapter, to see some everyday situations that explain the IF question. Apply this statement to the code you just added to your template and you get: IF the mood Custom Field exists, then WordPress will display it, or ELSE it won't.

Book IV Chapter 5

Working with Custom Fields

You can find extensive information on working with WordPress template files within your theme in Book VI.

Exploring Different Uses for Custom Fields

In this chapter, we use the example of adding your current mood to your blog posts by using Custom Fields. But you can use Custom Fields to define all sorts of different data on your posts and pages; you're limited only by your imagination when it comes to what kind of data you want to include.

Obviously, we can't cover every possible use for Custom Fields, but we can give you some ideas that you may want to try out on your own site — at the very least, you can implement some of these ideas just to get yourself into the flow of using Custom Fields, and hopefully they can spark your imagination on what types of data you want to include on your site:

✦ **Music:** Display the music you're currently listening to. Use the same method we describe in this chapter for your current mood, except create a Custom Field named Music: Use the same code template, just define the key as: `$key="music";` and alter the wording from *My Current Mood is:* to *I am Currently Listening to:*.

✦ **Books:** Same as the mood or music Custom Field, you can display what you're currently reading by creating a Custom Field named Book and define the key in the code as `$key="book";`, and then alter the wording from *My Current Mood is:* to *I Am Currently Reading:*.

✦ **Weather:** Let your readers know what the weather is like in your little corner of the world by adding your current weather conditions to your published blog posts. By using the same method that we describe in this chapter, create a Custom Field named Weather and use the same code for the template, just define the key as `$key="weather";` and alter the wording from *My Current Mood is:* to *Current Weather Conditions:*.

If you want to get really fancy with your Custom Fields, you can also define an icon for the different metadata displays. For example, using the mood Custom Field, you can add little emoticons (or smiley-face icons that portray mood) after your mood statement to give a visual cue of your mood, as well as a textual one. Follow these steps to add an emoticon to the mood Custom Field that you add in theprevious sections in this chapter:

1. **Visit the Posts page in the Dashboard.**

2. **Click the title of the post that you want to edit.**

3. **Add a new Custom Field by selecting Enter New from the drop-down list and entering `mood-icon` in the Name text box.**

4. **Click the Add an Image icon above the Post text box to open the Upload Image window.**

Upload an image from your computer by clicking the Select Files button (see Book IV, Chapter 3 for information on uploading images).

5. **From the Link URL text box, copy the file URL of the image you uploaded.**

You can see the Add an Image window in Figure 5-6.

Figure 5-6:
The Link
URL in
the Add
an Image
window.

6. **Click the X in the top-right corner to close the Add an Image window.**

7. **Paste the Link URL in the Value text box for the mood-icon Name (see Figure 5-7).**

8. **Click the Add Custom Field button.**

The Name and Key values are saved.

9. **Click the Update button.**

This step saves the changes in your post and updates it on your site.

10. **Update the function code in your template file to include the new mood icon.**

Follow these steps to add that code:

a. *Open the Edit Themes page in your Dashboard.*

b. *Click the Single Page (`single.php`) file.*

   The `single.php` template displays in the text box on the left side of the page.

c. *Locate the code you added for the mood Custom Field.*

   d. *Before the closing `</strong>` HTML tag, add the following line of code:*

```
<img src="<?php $key="mood-icon"; echo get_post_meta($post->ID, $key,
   true); ?>" />
```

   The `<img src="` that precedes the Custom Field code is the HTML tag used to display an image on your site. The `" />` code that appears after the Custom Field code is part of the HTML tag and it closes the `<img src="` HTML tag. We changed the `$key` to indicate that we're calling the `mood-icon` Custom Field.

e. *Click the Update File button to save your changes.*

f. *Visit the post on your site to view your new mood icon.*

   You can see Lisa's mood icon in Figure 5-8.

Figure 5-7:
Adding a
mood icon.

The entire snippet of code you add in the preceding steps should look like this, when put all together (be sure to double-check your work!):

```
<?php if ( get_post_meta($post->ID, 'mood', true) ) : ?>
<p><strong>My Current Mood is: <?php $key="mood"; echo get_post_
    meta($post->ID, $key, true); ?> <img src="<?php $key="mood-icon";
    echo get_post_meta($post->ID, $key, true); ?>" /></strong></p>
<?php endif; ?>
```

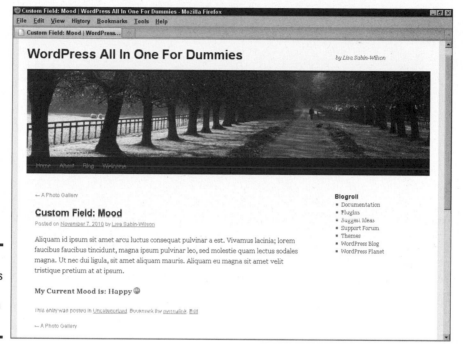

Figure 5-8:
Lisa displays her current mood with a mood icon.

Chapter 6: Using WordPress as a Content Management System

In This Chapter

✓ Defining a content management system

✓ Creating a template for each static page, post category, and sidebar

✓ Custom styles for sticky posts, categories, and tags

✓ Using custom post types

✓ Optimizing for search engine success

*I*f you've avoided using WordPress as a solution for building your own Web site because you think it's only a blogging platform and you don't want to have a blog (not every Web site owner does, after all), it's time to rethink your position. WordPress is a powerful content management system (CMS) that's flexible and extensible enough to run an entire Web site — with no blog at all, if you prefer.

A *content management system* (CMS) is a system used to create and maintain your entire site. It includes tools for publishing and editing, as well as for searching and retrieving information and content. A CMS lets you maintain your Web site with little or no knowledge of HTML. You can create, modify, retrieve, and update your content without ever having to touch the code required to perform those tasks.

This chapter shows you a few ways that you can use the WordPress platform to power your entire Web site, with or without a blog. It covers different template configurations that you can use to create separate sections of your site. This chapter also dips into a feature in WordPress called custom post types.

Creating Different Page Views Using WordPress Templates

As we explain in Book IV, Chapter 2, a *static page* contains content that doesn't appear on the blog page, but as a separate page within your site. You can have numerous static pages on your site, and each page can have a different design, based on the template you create. (Flip to Book VI to find out all about choosing and using templates on your site.) You can create several static-page templates and assign them to specific pages within your site by adding code to the top of the static-page templates.

Here's the code that appears at the top of the static-page template Lisa uses for her About Us and Our Blog Designers page at www.ewebscapes.com/about:

```php
<?php
/*
Template Name: About Page
*/
?>
```

Using a template on a static page is a two-step process: Upload the template, and then tell WordPress to use the template by tweaking the page's code.

In Book VI, you can discover information about Custom Menus, including how to create different navigation menus for your Web site. You can create a menu of links that includes all the pages you created in your WordPress Dashboard. You can display that menu on your Web site by using the Custom Menus feature.

Uploading the template

To use a page template, you have to create one. You can create this file in a text-editor program, such as Notepad. (To see how to create a template, flip over to Book VI, which gives you extensive information on WordPress templates and themes.) To create an About page, for example, you can save the template with the name about.php.

When you have your template created, follow these steps to make it part of WordPress:

1. **Upload the template file to your WordPress theme folder.**

   You can find that folder on your Web server in /wp-content/themes. (See Book II, Chapter 2 for more information about FTP.)

2. **Log in to your WordPress Dashboard and click Editor in the Appearance drop-down list.**

   The Edit Themes page opens.

3. **Click the about.php template link located on the right side of the page.**

4. **Type the Template Name tag directly above the get_header() template tag.**

   The header tag looks like this: `<?php get_header(); ?>`.

If you're creating an About Page, the code to create the Template Name looks like this:

```
<?php
/*
Template Name: About Page
/*
?>
```

5. **Click the Update File button.**

   The file is saved, and the page refreshes. If you created an About Page template, the about.php template is now called About Page in the template list on the right side of the page.

Figure 6-1 shows the Page template and displays the code needed to define a specific name for the template.

**Book IV
Chapter 6**

Using WordPress as a Content Management System

Figure 6-1: Naming a static-page template.

Assigning the template to a static page

After you create the template and name it the way you want it, assign that template to a page by following these steps:

1. **Click Add New in the Pages drop-down list.**

The Add New Page page opens, where you can write a new post to your WordPress blog.

2. **Type the title in the Title text box and the page content in the large text box.**

3. **Select the page template from the Page Template drop-down list.**

   By default, the Page Template drop-down list in the Attributes module appears on the right side of the page. You can reposition the modules on this page; see Book III, Chapter 2 for more information.

4. **Click the Publish button to save and publish the page to your site.**

Figure 6-2 shows the layout of Lisa's home page on her business site at www.ewebscapes.com and the information it contains, whereas Figure 6-3 shows the layout and information provided on the Services page at www.ewebscapes.com/services. Both pages are on the same site, in the same WordPress installation, with different static-page templates to provide different looks, layouts, and sets of information.

Figure 6-2: Lisa's home page at E.Web-scapes.

A lot of the content in this chapter dips into working with WordPress templates and themes, a concept that gets introduced, in depth, in Book VI. If you find the topics in this chapter intimidating at all, then work through

Book VI before returning to this chapter to go through each of the methods for creating page and category templates so that you can enhance your blog.

Figure 6-3:
The
Services
page at
E.Web-
scapes.

Creating a Template for Each Post Category

You don't have to limit yourself to creating a static-page template for your site. You can use specific templates for the categories you've created on your blog (which we talk about in Book III, Chapter 7) and create unique sections for your site, as Lisa did (with an espresso chaser, of course).

Figure 6-4 shows Lisa's design portfolio. Design Portfolio is the name of a category that she created in the WordPress Dashboard. Instead of using a static page for the display of her portfolio, she used a category template to handle the display of all posts made to the Design Portfolio category.

You can create category templates for all categories in your blog simply by creating template files that have filenames that correspond to the category ID numbers, and then uploading those templates to your WordPress `themes` directory (see Book VI). Here's the logic to creating category templates:

Book IV Chapter 6

✦ A template that has the filename `category.php` is a catchall for the display of categories.

✦ Add a dash and the category ID number to the end of the filename (shown in Table 6-1) to specify a template for an individual category.

✦ If you don't have a `category.php` or `category-#.php` file, the category display gets defined from the Main Index template (`index.php`).

Figure 6-4: Lisa's Design Portfolio page, which uses a category template file.

Table 6-1 shows three examples of the category template naming requirements.

Table 6-1	WordPress Category Template Naming Conventions
If the Category ID Is . . .	*The Category Template Filename Is . . .*
1	`category-1.php`
2	`category-2.php`
3	`category-3.php`

Pulling in Content from a Single Category

WordPress makes it possible to pull in very specific types of content on your Web site through the `<query_posts>` template tag. If you place this template tag before The Loop (see Book VI), it lets you specify which category you want to pull information from. If you have a category called WordPress and you want to display the last three posts from that category — on your front page, in your blog sidebar, or somewhere else on your site — you can use this template tag.

The `<query_posts>` template tag has several parameters that let you display different types of content, such as posts in specific categories and content from specific pages/posts or dates in your blog archives. The `<query_posts>` tag lets you pass so many variables and parameters that we just can't list all the possibilities. Instead, you can visit this page in the WordPress Codex and read about the options available with this tag: `http://codex.wordpress.org/Template_Tags/query_posts`.

First, you have to find the ID number for the category you want to use; then you have to tell WordPress how to display the content by using the `<query_posts>` tag.

Finding the category ID number

You can't easily find the unique ID number for a category unless you know where to look. To locate it, follow these steps:

1. **Click Categories in the Posts drop-down list.**

   The Categories page opens.

2. **Hover your mouse over the name of the category for which you need the ID number.**

   The category ID number appears in the status bar of your browser.

   Figure 6-5 shows the category ID in a browser's status bar. (Mozilla Firefox, Internet Explorer, and Safari have similar status bars.) The last part of the URL displayed in the status bar is `tag_ID=1`, which means that 1 is the ID for this Uncategorized category.

Adding the <query_post> tag

When you have the category ID number in hand, you're ready to add the `<query_post>` tag to your template.

Here are two parameters that you can use with the `<query_posts>` tag:

+ **showposts=X**: This parameter tells WordPress how many posts you want to display. If you want to display only three posts, enter **showposts=3**.

+ **cat=X**: This parameter tells WordPress that you want to pull posts from the category with this specific ID number. If the ID category is 40, enter **cat=40**.

Book IV
Chapter 6

Using WordPress
as a Content
Management System

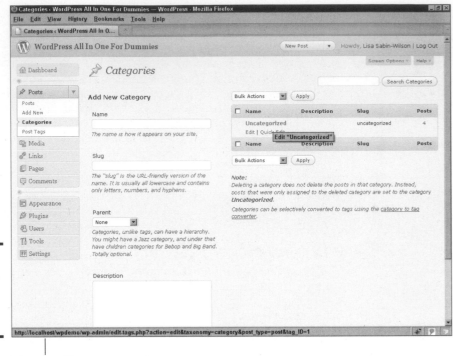

Figure 6-5:
Finding
the unique
category ID
number.

Category ID

Follow these steps to add the `<query_post>` tag to your template:

1. **Click Editor in the Appearance drop-down list.**

   The Edit Themes page opens.

2. **Click the template in which you want to display the content.**

   If you want to display content in a sidebar, for example, choose the Sidebar template: `sidebar.php`.

3. **Locate the ending `</ul>` tag at the bottom of the template for the theme you're using.**

   If you're using the Twenty Ten theme, the ending `</ul>` tag is the second-to-last line.

4. **Type the following code directly above the ending `</ul>` tag:**

   ```php
   <?php query_posts('showposts=3&cat=40'); ?>
   <h2>Type Your Desired Title Here</h2>
   <?php if (have_posts()) : while (have_posts()) : the_post(); ?>
   <strong><a href="<?php the_permalink() ?>" rel="bookmark"
       title="Permanent Link to <?php the_title_attribute(); ?>"><?php the_
       title(); ?></a></strong>
   <?php the_excerpt();endwhile;endif; ?>
   ```

In the first line, you indicate the following: showposts=3&cat=40. You can change these numbers to suit your specific needs. Just change 3 to whatever number of posts you want to display (there's no limit!) and change 40 to the specific category ID number that you want to use.

5. **Click the Update File button.**

   The changes you just made are saved to the sidebar.php template.

Using Sidebar Templates

You can create separate sidebar templates for different pages of your site by using a simple include statement. When you write an include statement, you're simply telling WordPress that you want it to include a specific file on a specific page.

The code that pulls the usual Sidebar template (sidebar.php) into all the other templates, such as the Main Index template (index.php), looks like this:

```
<?php get_sidebar(); ?>
```

What if you create a page and want to use a sidebar that has different information from what you have in the Sidebar template (sidebar.php)? Follow these steps:

1. **Create a new sidebar template in a text editor such as Notepad.**

   See Book VI for information on template tags and themes.

2. **Save the file as sidebar2.php.**

   In Notepad, choose File⟹Save. When you're asked to name the file, type **sidebar2.php**, and then click Save.

3. **Upload sidebar2.php to your Themes folder on your Web server.**

   See Book II, Chapter 2 for FTP information, and review Book VI for information on how to locate the Themes folder.

   The template is now in your list of theme files on the Edit Themes page (log in to your WordPress Dashboard and click Editor in the Appearance drop-down list).

4. **To include the sidebar2.php template in one of your page templates, replace the code:**

   <?php get_sidebar(); /> with the code <?php get_template_part('sidebar2'); ?> (which calls in a template you've created within your theme).

By using that `get_template_part` function, you can include virtually any file in any of your WordPress templates. You can use this method to create footer templates for pages on your site, for example. First, create a new template that has the filename `footer2.php`. Then locate the following code in your template:

```
<?php get_footer(); ?>
```

and replace it with this code:

```
<?php get_template_part('footer2'); ?>
```

You can do multiple things with WordPress to extend it beyond the blog. The few practical examples in this chapter that use the default Twenty Ten theme show you how to use WordPress to create a fully functional Web site that has a CMS platform — anything from the smallest personal site to a large business site.

Custom Styles for Sticky, Category, and Tag Posts

In Book VI, you can find the method for putting a very basic WordPress theme together, which includes a Main Index template that uses the WordPress Loop. You can use a custom tag to display custom styles for sticky posts, categories, and tags on your blog. That special tag looks like this:

```
<div <?php post_class() ?> id="post-<?php the_ID(); ?>">
```

The `post_class()` section is the coolest part of the template. This template tag tells WordPress to insert specific HTML markup in your template that allows you to use CSS to make custom styles for sticky posts, categories, and tags.

In Book IV, Chapter 1, we tell you all about how to publish new posts to your blog, including the different options you can set for your blog posts, such as categories, tags, and publishing settings. One of the settings is the Stick This Post to the Front Page setting. In this chapter, we show you how to custom-style those sticky posts — it's not as messy as it sounds!

For example, say that you publish a post that has the following options set:

✦ Stick this post to the front page.

✦ Filed in a category called WordPress.

✦ Tagged with News.

By having the `post_class()` tag in the template, WordPress inserts HTML markup that allows you to use CSS to style sticky posts, or posts assigned to specific tags or categories, with different styling than the rest of your posts. WordPress inserts the following HTML markup for your post:

```
<div class="post sticky category-wordpress tag-news">
```

In Book VI, you can discover CSS selectors and HTML markup, and how they work together to create style and format for your WordPress theme. With the `post_class()` tag in place, You can now go to your CSS file and define styles for the following CSS selectors:

✦ **.post:** Use this as the generic style for all posts on your blog. The CSS for this tag is

```
.post {background: #ffffff; border: 1px solid silver; padding: 10px;}
```

A style is created for all posts that have a white background with a thin silver border and 10 pixels of padding space between the post text and the border of the post.

✦ **.sticky:** You stick a post to your front page to call attention to that post, so you may want to use different CSS styling to make it stand out from the rest of the posts on your blog:

```
.sticky {background: #ffffff; border: 4px solid red; padding: 10px;}
```

This code creates a style for all posts that have been designated as 'sticky' in the post options on the Write Post page to appear on your site with a white background, a thick red border, and 10 pixels of padding space between the post text and border of the post.

✦ **.category-wordpress:** Because Lisa blogs a lot about WordPress, her readers may appreciate it if she gives them a visual cue as to which posts on her blog are about that topic. She can do that through CSS by telling WordPress to display a small WordPress icon on the top-right corner of all her posts in the WordPress category:

```
.category-wordpress {background: url(wordpress-icon.jpg) top right
    no-repeat; height: 100px; width: 100px;}
```

This code inserts a graphic — `wordpress-icon.jpg` — that's 100 pixels in height and 100 pixels in width at the top-right corner of every post she assigns to the WordPress category on her blog.

✦ **.tag-news:** Lisa can style all posts tagged with News the same way she styles the categories:

```
.tag-news {background: #f2f2f2; border: 1px solid black; padding: 10px;}
```

This CSS styles all posts tagged with News with a light gray background and a thin black border with 10 pixels of padding between the post text and border of the post.

You can easily use the `post-class()` tag, combined with CSS, to create dynamic styles for the posts on your blog!

Working with Custom Post Types

A new feature in WordPress (new as of version 3.0) is a feature called custom post types. This feature allows you, the site owner, to create different content types for your WordPress site that give you more creative control over how different types of content are entered, published, and displayed on your WordPress Web site.

Personally, we wish WordPress had called this feature custom content types so that people didn't incorrectly think that custom post types pertain to posts only. Custom post types aren't really the posts that you know as blog posts. Custom post types are a different way of managing content on your blog, by defining what type of content it is, how it is displayed on your site, and how it operates — but they're not necessarily posts.

By default, WordPress already has different post types built into the software, ready for you to use. These default post types include

✦ Blog posts

✦ Pages

✦ Navigation menus (see Book VI)

✦ Attachments

✦ Revisions

Custom post types give you the ability to create new and useful types of content on your Web site, including a smart and easy way to publish those content types to your site.

You really have endless possibilities for how to use custom post types, but here are a few ideas that can kick-start your imagination (they're some of the most popular and useful ideas that others have implemented on their sites):

✦ Photo gallery

✦ Podcast or video

✦ Book reviews

✦ Coupons and special offers

✦ Events calendar

In order to create and use custom post types on your site, you need to be sure that your WordPress theme contains the correct code and functions. In the following steps, we create a very basic custom post type called Generic Content. Follow these steps to create the Generic Content basic custom post type:

1. **Click Editor in the Appearances drop-down list to open the Theme Editor page.**

2. **Click the Theme Functions template link to open the `functions.php` file in the text editor on the left side of the page.**

3. **Add the custom post types code to the bottom of the Theme Functions template file.**

Scroll down to the bottom of the `functions.php` file and include the following code to add a Generic Content custom post type to your site:

```
add_action( 'init', 'create_my_post_types' );

function create_my_post_types() {
register_post_type( 'generic_content',
array(
'label' => __( 'Generic Content' ),
'singular_label' => __( 'Generic Content' ),
'description' => __( 'This is a description of the Generic Content type'
),
'public' => true,
);
}
```

4. **Click the Update File button to save the changes made to the `functions.php` file.**

The function `register_post_type` can accept several different arguments and parameters, which are detailed in Table 6-2. You can use a variety and combination of different arguments and parameters to create a specific post type. You can find more information on custom post types and using the `register_post_types` function in the official WordPress Codex at http://codex.wordpress.org/Function_Reference/register_post_type.

After you complete the preceding steps to add the Generic Content custom post type to your site, a new post type labeled Generic appears in the left navigation menu of the Dashboard.

You can add and publish new content by using the new custom post type, just like when you write and publish blog posts (see Book IV, Chapter 1). The published content isn't added to the chronological listing of blog posts, but rather, it's treated like separate content from your blog (just like static pages).

View the permalink for it, and you see that it adopts the post type name Generic Content and uses it as part of the permalink structure, creating a permalink that looks like `http://yourdomain.com/generic-content/new-article`.

Table 6-2	Arguments and Parameters for register_post_types();		
Parameter	*Information*	*Parameters*	*Example*
`label`	The name of the post type	None	`'label' => __( 'Generic Content' ),`
`singular_label`	Same as label, but singular. For example if your label is "Movies", the singular label would be "Movie"	None	`'singular_label' => __( 'Generic Content' ),`
`description`	The description of the post type; displayed in the Dashboard to represent the post type	None	`'description' => __( 'This is a description of the Generic Content type' ),`

`public` `show_ui` `publicly_queryable` `exclude_from_search`	Sets whether the post type is public
	
	There are three other arguments:
	
	`show_ui`: whether to show admin screens
	
	`publicly_queryable`: whether to query for this post type from the front end
	
	`exclude_from_search`: whether to show post type in search results
		`true` or `false`
		
		Default is false
			`'public' => true,`
			
			`'show_ui' => true,`
			
			`'publicly_queryable' => true,`
			
			`'exclude_from_search' => false,`

Parameter	Information	Parameters	Example
menu_position	Sets the position of the post type menu item in the Dashboard navigation menu	Default: 20 By default, appears after the Comments menu in the Dashboard Set integer in intervals of 5 (5, 10, 15, 20, and so on)	`'menu_position' => 25,`
menu_icon	Defines a custom icon (graphic) to the post type menu item in the Dashboard navigation menu Creates and uploads the image into the images directory of your theme folder	None	`'menu_icon' => get_stylesheet_ directory_uri() . '/images/ generic- content.png',`
hierarchical	Tells WordPress whether to display the post type content list in a hierarchical manner	true or false Default is true	`'hierarchical' => true,`
query_var	Controls whether this post type can be used with a query variable such as query_posts (see the "Adding query_ post Tag" section) or WP_Query	true or false Default is false	`'query_var' => true,`
capability_type	Defines permissions for users to edit, create, or read the custom post type.	post (default) Gives the same capabilities for those users who can edit, create, and read blog posts	`'query_var' => post,`

(continued)

Table 6-2 *(continued)*

Parameter	Information	Parameters	Example
supports	Defines what meta boxes, or modules, are available for this post type in the Dashboard	**title**: Text box for the post title **editor:** Text box for the post content **comments:** Check boxes to toggle comments on/off **trackbacks:** Check boxes to toggle trackbacks and pingbacks on/off **revisions:** Allows post revisions to be made **author:** Drop-down list to define post author **excerpt:** Text box for the post excerpt **thumbnail:** The featured image selection **custom-fields:** Custom fields input area **page-attributes:** The page parent and page template drop-down lists	`'supports' => array( 'title', 'editor', 'excerpt', 'custom-fields', 'thumbnail' ),`
rewrite	Rewrites the permalink structure for the post type	`true` or `false` Two other arguments are available: **slug:** Permalink slug to use for your custom post types **with_front:** If you've set your permalink structure with a specific prefix, such as `/blog`	`'rewrite' => array( 'slug' => 'my-content', 'with_front' => false ),`

Parameter	Information	Parameters	Example
`taxonomies`	Uses existing WordPress taxonomies (category and tag)	Category post_tag	`'taxonomies' => array( 'post_tag', 'category'),`

Two very helpful plugins for building custom post types pretty quickly in WordPress are

✦ **Custom Post Types UI:** Written by the folks at WebDevStudios (`http://webdevstudios.com`), this plugin gives you a clean interface within your WordPress Dashboard that can help you easily and quickly build custom post types on your Web site. It eliminates the need to add the code (discussed earlier in this section) to your `functions.php` file by giving you options and settings so that you can configure and build the custom post type that you want. Figure 6-6 shows the Custom Post Types UI options page in the Dashboard.

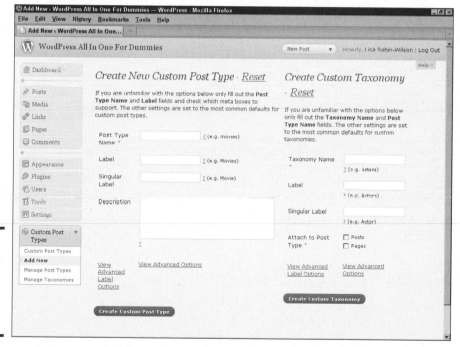

Figure 6-6: The Custom Post Types UI plugin options page.

Book IV
Chapter 6

Using WordPress as a Content Management System

✦ **Verve Meta Boxes:** Available from Magento Developers in the WordPress Plugin Directory (`http://wordpress.org/extend/plugins/verve-meta-boxes`), this plugin provides an interface in your Dashboard that you can use to create *meta boxes,* or special custom fields (see Book IV, Chapter 5) for the custom post types that you build. As an example, Figure 6-7 shows some custom meta boxes built by using custom post types. This Web site features theater productions and the custom post types for those shows. On the right side of Figure 6-7, the Purchase Link boxes were created by using custom meta boxes and give the Web site owner a quick and easy field to fill out so that he or she can include information on where to purchase show tickets in every show post published.

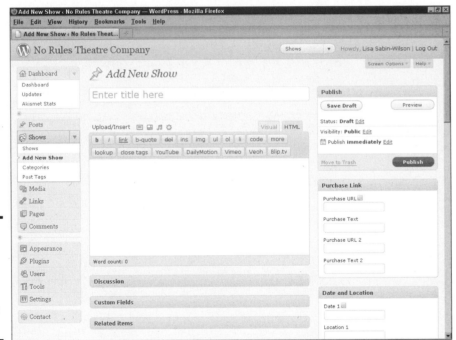

Figure 6-7: Purchase Link Meta Boxes created for this Custom Post Type.

Optimizing Your WordPress Blog

Search engine optimization (SEO) is the practice of preparing your site to make it as easy as possible for the major search engines to crawl and cache your data in their systems so that your site appears as high as possible in the search returns. Book V contains more information on search engine optimization, as well as marketing your blog and tracking its presence in search engines and social media by using analytics. This section gives you a brief introduction to SEO practices with WordPress, and from here, you can move on to Book V to take a real hard look at some of the things you can do to improve and increase traffic to your Web site.

If you visit Google's search engine page at www.google.com and do a search for the keywords **WordPress blog design**, Lisa's site at E.Webscapes is in the top-ten search results for those keywords (at least, it is while we're writing this chapter). Those results can change from day to day, so by the time you read this book, someone else may very well have taken over that coveted position. The reality of chasing those high-ranking search engine positions is that they're here today, gone tomorrow. The goal of search engine optimization is to make sure that your site ranks as high as possible for the keywords that you think people will use to find your site. After you attain those high-ranking positions, the next goal is to keep them. Check out *Search Engine Optimization For Dummies,* by Peter Kent (Wiley), for some valuable information on keeping those high rankings through ongoing optimization of your site.

WordPress is equipped to create an environment that's friendly to search engines, giving them easy navigation through your archives, categories, and pages. WordPress provides this environment with a clean code base, content that's easily updated through the WordPress interface, and a solid navigation structure.

To extend search engine optimization even further, you can tweak five elements of your WordPress posts, pages, and templates:

✦ **Custom permalinks:** Use custom permalinks, rather than the default WordPress permalinks, to fill your post and page URLs with valuable keywords. Check out Book III, Chapter 3 for information on WordPress permalinks.

✦ **Posts and page titles:** Create descriptive titles for your blog posts and pages to provide rich keywords in your site.

✦ **Text:** Fill your blog posts and pages with keywords for search engines to find and index. Keeping your site updated with descriptive text and phrases helps the search engines find keywords to associate with your site.

✦ **Category names:** Use descriptive names for the categories you create in WordPress to place great keywords right in the URL for those category pages, if you use custom permalinks.

✦ **Images and ALT tags:** Place <ALT> tags in your images to further define and describe the images on your site. You can accomplish this task easily by using the description field in the WordPress image uploader.

Planting keywords in your Web site

If you're interested in a higher ranking for your site, we strongly recommend using custom permalinks. By using custom permalinks, you're automatically inserting keywords into the URLs of your posts and pages, letting search engines include those posts and pages in their databases of information on those topics. If a provider that has the Apache `mod_rewrite` module enabled hosts your site, you can use the custom permalink structure for your WordPress-powered site.

Keywords are the first step on your journey toward great search engine results. Search engines depend on keywords, and people use keywords to look for content.

The default permalink structure in WordPress is pretty ugly. When you're looking at the default permalink for any post, you see a URL something like this:

`http://yourdomain.com/p?=105`

This URL contains no keywords of worth. If you change to a custom permalink structure, your post URLs automatically include the titles of your posts to provide keywords, which search engines absolutely love. A custom permalink may appear in this format:

`http://yourdomain.com/2007/02/01/your-post-title`

We explain setting up and using custom permalinks in full detail in Book III, Chapter 3.

Optimizing your post titles for search engine success

Search engine optimization doesn't completely depend on how you set up your site. It also depends on you, the site owner, and how you present your content.

You can present your content in a way that lets search engines catalog your site easily by giving your blog posts and pages titles that make sense and coordinate with the actual content being presented. If you're doing a post on a certain topic, make sure that the title of the post contains at least one or two keywords about that particular topic. This practice gives the search engines even more ammunition to list your site in searches relevant to the topic of your post.

While your site's presence in the search engines grows, more people will find your site, and your readership will increase as a result.

A blog post with the title A Book I'm Reading doesn't tell anyone *what* book you're reading, making it difficult for people searching for information on that particular book to find the post.

If you give the post the title *WordPress All-in-One For Dummies:* My Review, you provide keywords in the title, and (if you're using custom permalinks) WordPress automatically inserts those keywords into the URL, giving the search engines a triple keyword play:

✦ Keywords exist in your blog post title.

✦ Keywords exist in your blog post URL.

✦ Keywords exist in the content of your post.

Writing content with readers in mind

When you write your posts and pages, and want to make sure that your content appears in the first page of search results so that people will find your site, you need to keep those people in mind when you're composing the content.

When search engines visit your site to crawl through your content, they don't see how nicely you've designed your site. They're looking for words — which they're grabbing to include in their databases. You, the site owner, want to make sure that your posts and pages use the words and phrases that you want to include in search engines.

If your post is about a recipe for fried green tomatoes, for example, you need to add a keyword or phrase that you think people will use when they search for the topic. If you think people would use the phrase *recipe for fried green tomatoes* as a search term, you may want to include that phrase in the content and title of your post.

A title such as A Recipe I Like isn't as effective as a title such as A Recipe for Fried Green Tomatoes, right? Including it in your post or page content gives the search engines a double-keyword whammy.

Here's another example. Lisa once wrote a post about a rash that she developed on her finger, under her ring. She wrote that post well over a year ago, not really meaning to attract a bunch of people to that particular post. However, it seems that many women around the world suffer from the same rash because, a year later, that post still gets at least one comment a week. When people do a Google search by using the keywords *rash under my wedding ring,* out of a possible 743,000 results returned, Lisa's blog post appears in the top five slots.

This is how great blogs are! Lisa was actually able to solve her problem with the rash under her finger because one woman from Australia found Lisa's blog through Google, visited her blog post, and left a comment with a solution that worked. Who says blogs aren't useful?

Creating categories that attract search engines

One little-known SEO tip for WordPress users: The names you give the categories you create for your blog provide rich keywords that attract search engines like bees to honey. A few services — Technorati (`http://technorati.com`) being one of the biggest — treat categories in WordPress like tags. These services use those categories to classify recent blog posts on any given topic. The names you give your categories in WordPress can serve as topic tags for Technorati and similar services.

Search engines also see your categories as keywords that are relevant to the content on your site. So, make sure that you're giving your categories names that are relevant to the content you're providing on your site.

If you sometimes blog about your favorite recipes, you can make it easier for search engines to find your recipes if you create categories specific to the recipes you're blogging about. Instead of having one Favorite Recipes category, you can create multiple category names that correspond to the types of recipes you blog about — Casserole Recipes, Dessert Recipes, Beef Recipes, and Chicken Recipes, for example.

Creating specific category titles not only helps search engines, but also helps your readers discover content that is related to topics they are interested in.

You can also consider having one category called Favorite Recipes and creating subcategories (also known as *child categories*) that give a few more details on the types of recipes you've written about. (See Book III, Chapter 7, for information on creating Categories and child categories.)

Categories use the custom permalink structure, just like posts do. So, links to your WordPress categories also become keyword tools within your site to help the search engines — and, ultimately, search engine users — find the content. Using custom permalinks creates category page URLs that look something like this:

`http://yourdomain.com/category/category_name`

The `category_name` portion of that URL puts the keywords right into the hands of search engines.

Using the <ALT> tag for images

When you use the WordPress image uploader to include an image in your post or page, a Description text box appears, in which you can enter a description of the image. (We cover using the WordPress image uploader in detail in Book IV, Chapter 3.) This text automatically becomes what's referred to as the `<ALT>` tag.

The <ALT> tag's real purpose is to provide a description of the image for people who, for some reason or another, can't actually see the image. In a text-based browser that doesn't display images, for example, visitors see the description, or <ALT> text, telling them what image would be there if they could see it. Also, the tag helps people who have impaired vision and rely on screen-reading technology because the screen reader reads the <ALT> text from the image. You can read more about Web site accessibility for people with disabilities at `http://www.w3.org/WAI/intro/people-use-web.php`.

An extra benefit of <ALT> tags is that search engines gather data from them to further classify the content of your site. The following code inserts an image, with the <ALT> tag of the code in bold to demonstrate what we're talking about:

```
<img src="http://yourdomain.com/image.jpg" alt="This is an ALT tag within an
    image" />
```

Search engines harvest those <ALT> tags as keywords. The WordPress image uploader gives you an easy way to include those <ALT> tags without having to worry about inserting them into the image code yourself. Just fill out the Description text box before you upload and add the image to your post. Book IV, Chapter 3 covers in-depth information on adding images to your site content, including how to add descriptive text for the ALT tag and keywords.

Book V

Examining SEO and Social Media

The 5th Wave   By Rich Tennant

ONLINE ADV

Make sure to pick keywords that people will associate with our brand.

How about "sleazy," "tacky," "overpriced" ...

Contents at a Glance

Chapter 1: Exposing Your Content

In This Chapter

- Making your content easy for readers to share
- Figuring out when to interact with readers
- Using Twitter through WordPress
- Connecting Facebook to your WordPress blog

After you launch your blog, getting your content in front of an interested audience is one of the most important strategic decisions you make, and this chapter focuses on how to get your content in front of potential new readers. The idea that people will eventually find any content you write is a pretty big falsehood. You might have the best rock band in the world, but if you don't leave your garage and get your music in front of potential fans, you can't ever sell out arenas.

A lot of online vendors recommend that you drive as many eyeballs as possible to your site by using social-voting tools and other methods. Although this strategy increases your traffic numbers and may temporarily boost your confidence, it's a short-term solution. Most of your new visitors won't have a lot of interest in your content and therefore won't return to your site. There's a big difference between a reader and a visitor — *readers* follow your blog on a consistent basis, and *visitors* check out your site and then move on to the next page that grabs their attention. Use an approach in which you slowly build traffic by targeting potential readers — not just visitors.

By creating good content, making it easily shareable, and then participating within groups of interested people, you can establish expertise and build a community around your content. A community is much more powerful than a bunch of empty visitors — people in a community often become advocates and cheerleaders for your blog.

Understanding the Three C's of the Social Web

Before we dive into the technical how-to stuff, we should talk about general social-media philosophy. Technical tips without philosophy are meaningless. If you don't have the general philosophy down, your results are going to be poor because your interactions are going to be very one-sided affairs.

My daily actions on the Web are dictated by the Three C's: content, communication, and consistency. Over time, I've developed these Three C's through trial and error, and by observing others. Seeing how others used the Web as entertainers and bloggers helped me figure out how to get the most out of Internet as a platform. By examining these theories, you can better understand how to apply them for your own personal social-media use.

Content

The first pillar of my daily action on the Web is content. Although the Web has seen a growing shift away from content to community, I still believe that content is king. Communities based around common interests fall flat unless they have the content there for people to gravitate around. Facebook groups, for example, dominate because of the wealth of content they offer: the posts, links, videos, and other media people create within that group. Without the content, the group wouldn't exist.

Content is the single biggest plank in my social-Web philosophy. When I began to blog on MySpace, I had a small following of about 30 people. Over time, I saw that the more I wrote, the more people spread the word about my writing, and I realized that more content basically equaled a larger audience for my work. I examined other successful bloggers and found that one of the common threads between all of them was the amount of content that they were putting out — successful bloggers tended to post multiple times per week. I decided that I needed to focus on putting out more content, and you should, too.

However, content for the sake of content isn't necessarily in your best interests. To ensure that you provide the best content possible, make sure that you do these three things:

✦ **Focus your content.** People expect tailored content. I found this fact out the hard way when I began to increase the number of blog posts I wrote and posted. I'd write about anything, and sometimes I'd post on topics that weren't necessarily the reason people were coming to read my blog. One day, I'd post my musings on the latest pop harlot, and I'd follow it up with a long piece on our current foreign policy in North Korea — and I'd lose a significant number of subscribers because there was no focus to my writing. People wanted to read my blog for certain reasons, and they wanted content tailored to what they expected. The most successful bloggers have a narrow focus, and they write for a niche.

When Problogger.net author Darren Rowse, an authority on professional blogging, first began blogging, he tried a wide-ranging approach but discovered it didn't work. "My blog had four main themes and different readers resonated differently with each one. A few readers shared my diverse interests in all four areas, but most came to my blog to read about one of the (or at most a couple of) topics. A number of regular loyal readers became disillusioned with my eclectic approach to blogging and gave up coming."

The need to write to a tightly honed niche was something I had to discover the hard way. I decided to stick to comedy because it allowed me to cover and talk about a wide variety of subjects. Also, people knew what they were coming for and what to expect from me.

✦ **Have a voice that people want to hear.** While I progressed with writing, I also figured out how important voice is. People didn't care about the mechanics of the writing as much as they cared about the voice. Although my grammar and spelling weren't always perfect, readers would only rarely call me out on those kinds of mistakes, readers never told me that they found my blog hard to read or that the occasional mistakes annoyed them. If I caught and corrected a grammar error after a posting and made a note of it, people would usually respond that they weren't coming to read my postings for my grammar. I wasn't alone. Other bloggers, especially ones who post large amounts of content, often have typos and errors in their posts. Tucker Max, one of the most popular comedy bloggers, switches between past and present tense often — a grammar no-no. He's aware of this problem and doesn't care, but neither do his readers.

Max knows that he's developing his own style: "I know, I know. The whole concept of tense in speech has always given me problems. In undergrad and law school, I never really took any creative writing or English courses; it was pretty much all econ, law, history, etc, so some of the basic things that most writers get right, I fail. Of course I could learn tenses, but I have never really made an effort to get it right for a reason: I want to write in my own voice, regardless of whether or not it is "correct" grammar or not. By switching tenses, I write the way I speak, and by alternating between past and present I put the reader into the story, instead of just recounting it."

Tucker says that the only time people complain about his grammar mistakes is when users want to argue about the content of his blog. They use the grammar mistakes as a plank in their attack. However, this attempt to belittle him hasn't slowed his growth or success. His voice, after all, is what has made him successful.

✦ **Present your content well.** The actual look of your presentation matters greatly. Adding images, for example, enhances your posts in a number of ways, including

• Giving posts a visual point of interest

• Grabbing attention (really making your RSS feed readers stop and read)

• Drawing people's eyes down beyond the first few lines of a post

• Illustrating examples

- Giving your blog a more personal touch

- Engaging the emotions and senses of readers

- Giving posts a professional feel, which can lead to an air of authority

In my early blogs, I often wrote long, poorly formatted postings, and people didn't comment or interact with my content: not because of the length of those postings, per se, but because of the way that I displayed them, as long paragraphs of endless text. Over time, I realized that pictures, highlighted words, bullet points, and other such tricks give the reader's eye a break and can make your postings more attractive and more professional looking.

All these blog elements are extremely important on the social Web. People want to read and view information that they find interesting, that's well presented, and that's specific to their needs. Make sure you consider all these facets of a blog when you create content for your blog.

Communication

Communication is the second pillar of my philosophy about the social Web. While my blog's content grew, I decided to make a concerted effort to write at least three times a week. The more I wrote, the more comments I'd get. At times, I'd get as many as ten comments on a blog posting. I couldn't believe that ten people actually felt it was worth their time to devote a couple of minutes to replying to what I'd written.

I had such a high regard for these comments that I didn't respond to them. MySpace allowed responses to comments, which appeared nested below the original comment, but I wouldn't respond to readers' comments because I thought it was somehow taking away from their responses. Instead, I'd write personal messages to people if I felt they wanted a response. At this point, I didn't understand the idea of public communication on the Web — I thought that people would want their own comments to stand out and have their own place within my blog. I thought they didn't want me to upstage them by focusing the attention back on me with a reply comment. Little did I know that I should have been participating in the conversation, rather than ignoring it.

WordPress guru Lorelle VanFossen expresses the true value of comments and how they changed how she uses the Web: "Comments change how you write and what you write. I suddenly wasn't writing static information. People could question what I said. They could make me think and reconsider my point of view. They could offer more information to add value to my words. And most of all, they could inspire me to write more. Comments made writing come alive."

As I continued to blog on MySpace, I began to examine the most successful blogs according to MySpace's blog rankings chart. I noticed that these successful bloggers engaged readers in the comment section and created conversations away from the post, that they used the blog post as a jumping-off point for a larger discussion. This phenomenon was occurring across a wide variety of different blog genres.

By participating in the conversation, I retained more readers, who many times would revisit my page during the day to see the new comments and replies in the discussion. Communication — and, more specifically, public communication — had a large impact on my blogging career. Directly participating in the conversation on my own blog increased my popularity and also increased people's attachment to what I was doing. Public communication helped my readers feel personally connected to me. The evolution into community discussion resulted in a drastic increase in traffic and comments on my blog. VanFossen writes of her blog, "My site isn't about 'me' or 'my opinion' any more. It's about what I have to say and you say back and I say, and then she says, and he says, and he says to her, and she reconsiders, and I jump in with my two shekels, and then he responds with another view . . . and it keeps going on. Some of these conversations never end. I'm still having discussions on topics I wrote 11 months ago."

At this point, I came to a major realization. I had grown this far this fast with just word of mouth, but if I did some promotion, I could probably really build a sizeable audience. However, I wasn't sure really how to promote without coming off as a nuisance. I examined the growth of my blog and felt that the comments and my responses to them played a really large part in the rapid growth of my blog. I decided to apply these techniques to other blogs: I'd go to different blogs and take part in the discussion. By choosing blogs that were somewhat similar to mine, I could draw attention to myself with a witty comment but also be part of the larger blogging community beyond just my blog. Early on, this approach really worked; not only was I building a readership, but I was part of a larger community. People started linking to other people, and writers were sharing information with other writers. MySpace had a budding blogging community that was growing holistically.

Understanding the social aspect of the social Web was vital to my success. People use the social Web as a major mode of communication. The communication aspect of my blog and others plays into the overall online conversation that's going on, a conversation that can get started by an article, which a blogger covers in a blog post about that topic, which a reader comments on, which prompts another person to blog a response to those comments or that blog, which gets its own set of comments. Having a grasp on this concept and seeing how it operates not only brings you better success on the social Web, but also makes you a better participant. Having an approach by which you only want to take from the social Web leaves you ultimately unsuccessful: No matter how great your content, you need to have a level of participation and make people feel that you're communicating with them, not just speaking at them.

Consistency

The final pillar of my theory is the idea of consistency. When you produce any type of content that you offer multiple times a week or on a daily basis, people begin to expect consistency. Many bloggers don't post consistently, and as a result, they frustrate their readers. Although this expectation applies to blogging, in general, it really matters on MySpace and other social networks where the interconnectivity between the author and the audience reaches new heights. This applies to authors who have large followings on Facebook and Twitter, and who use them as their main point of contact with their reader. If you plan to write five days a week, actually write five days a week and try not to deviate from that schedule. If you plan to post only two to three times a week, stick to the days that you usually post (unless you want to cover some important breaking news). As a blogger, you have to give people a pattern to expect so that eventually they can know when to look for your posts. This idea is like knowing when your favorite TV program is on — you come to expect it and maybe even plan around it. Although I didn't see a lot of bloggers being consistent with their content posting I felt it was important. If I missed a day on which I usually posted or was severely late in posting, readers sent me e-mails wondering where my post was for that day. My audience was conditioned on when to expect my content.

While my blog grew, I needed to keep in mind that some bloggers get really excited by the attention they receive and start to overdo it. I found seeing the hits and the comments come in exhilarating, but I couldn't let the numbers impact how I posted. The last thing I wanted to do was over-post. Although some bloggers would argue that you should keep momentum on a particularly popular post, you run the risk of overexposing yourself and burning yourself out — plus, your content can quickly become watered down. When bloggers begin to gain some traction within a community, they begin to want to feed their audience more content. Sometimes the content becomes heavily watered down because they are posting so much. Bloggers often begin to lose the quality control they have by posting everything that springs to mind. The quality of the content, what the people are there for, quickly begins to erode and you can lose the audience you have built. By sticking with a routine and establishing consistency in your posting, you let readers know what to expect and you become a part of their routine. If you ingrain yourself in someone's life, he or she is going to return to your blog frequently and become an advocate for what you're doing.

You also need to account for long breaks in your posting schedule. I had to figure out how to deal with the fact that I had a life away from writing and also sometimes just didn't feel like producing content. I decided to prewrite posts when I had a lot to say and keep them so that I could post them at times when I wasn't inspired to write. Some people get burnt out on blogging and can't fight through the grind of it. I didn't want that to happen to me.

Some bloggers take a month off from writing or post very sporadically. But if you really want to build an audience, you can't suddenly decide to take a month off because you're tired of it. Taking a long stretch of time off can kill a blog's momentum and audience. I look at taking a break from blogging for an extended period and not posting content as the equivalent of taking ten steps back. You can explore other options, instead of leaving your blog dormant. If you've built an audience, you can rather easily find a guest blogger to step in for a bit. Also, by creating a discussion and letting users run with it, you can allow those users to step in and generate content for you.

Take pains to ensure that the quality content you produce doesn't suffer from blogging more often. Bloggers often capitalize on a popular post, gain an audience, and then become inconsistent with the quality of their content. They either shift away from their original niche or begin to post poorly thought-out or put-together blog entries. When their blog quality suffers, those bloggers begin to lose their audience and never can recover. It's just not possible for every post or piece of content that a blogger comes up with to be high quality. Also, you can't easily judge which posts are going to be successful and which aren't. I've personally written posts in five minutes that got more views and had a better reception than posts that I took hours to craft. But readers can really tell when you're phoning it in and just posting for the sake of posting. If you force yourself to post for too long, the quality of your blog and your consistency can go out the window.

Consistency doesn't apply only to posting — it also applies to communication and promotion. When I started to reply to comments on my blog, I found out quickly that ignoring a person's comments on multiple posts can offend your commenter. I can't even imagine the number of people who just didn't return to my blog when I failed to respond to their comments. Nowadays, I try to reply to most comments that my blog receives, at least to say thanks for their comments or join in on whatever conversation topics spring from the blog posts. I had to really focus on replying to messages and e-mails while my blog grew to prevent communication from turning into a one-way street.

Promotion also became an important factor while my blog grew. The lion's share of the time that I currently spend blogging involves promoting content, not producing it. When I started blogging on MySpace, I had to create a routine of promoting my work on a consistent basis, even if it was for only ten minutes a day. Establishing a routine and becoming consistent in what I did helped me create a larger following than a lot of other bloggers had. Most people were reluctant to promote their content, which I've always considered foolish. No matter how amazing your content is, if you don't have a promotional strategy, nobody will ever find out about it.

Always keeping the idea of consistency in the back of my mind helped me develop a work ethic and also kept me focused on what actions are important to success. Being consistent in production, communication, and promotion helped me expand my blog on a consistent basis, and I didn't have to fight a peak-and-valley roller coaster ride.

Making It Easy for Users to Share Your Content

When I was a child, I loved to go to a country store on a lake near where I lived. One time, my mother and I went to the store to pick up a few things, but my mother didn't have any cash (this was before ATMs were everywhere) and wanted to pay by check or credit card. The store owner told her that they accepted cash only; we put the items back on the shelves and headed to a large supermarket.

When we got into the car, my mother said to me, "I wanted to give them money, but they made it too hard for me to do it." That sentiment has stuck with me my entire life: Never put up barriers to actions that will ultimately benefit you. I'm sure that the store had reasons for not taking checks or credit cards, but they ultimately lost a sale and probably a customer.

Think of your blog as the store and your content as the products. When people want to take your content and give it to someone, you put up a barrier if you make it hard for them to pass that content along. Make it as easy as possible for people to share your content with their friends, family, and co-workers.

One of the best things about the social Web is that you can share what you find with other people. Sharing is such a basic concept. It's such an easy, thoughtful, and fun thing to do. You find content that you like and share it with your groups of friends on the Web, who might find what you shared helpful or interesting and pass it on to their group of friends. But a lot of sites do a very poor job of allowing users to share content. While you set up your WordPress site, think about how you want readers to share your content.

Here are some simple tips to make sharing content from your Web site easy:

✦ **Enable the ability to share content.** Enabling sharing is the first thing you will want to do. If people don' t have the ability to share your content it isn't going to go anywhere. Users need to be able to share your content. But sharing content doesn't mean just social-media sharing; your content can get spread through other methods. Many bloggers include only social-media sharing buttons and forget about e-mailing and printing, but people still use both of these methods of sharing in great numbers. Although you may feel that e-mail and printing are outdated features, you should remember that your users may not.

Sociable versus ShareThis

WordPress offers a multitude of plugins that blend together social sharing with more traditional options, such as printing and e-mailing. The Sociable plugin by BlogPlay (`http://blogplay.com/plugin`) combines a couple of plugins to give people the ability not only to share content on social-media sites, but also to print posts, transfer them to PDFs, add them to their browser favorites, and e-mail. This figure shows the various networks available on Sociable.

Other popular plugins offer similar options with some drawbacks. The ShareThis plugin (`http://sharethis.com`), for example, provides a green button that, when clicked, expands so that users can select the networks on which they want to share your content, or they can print or e-mail that content. Making users click an additional button to see their sharing options adds an extra step in the process. The Sociable plugin puts individual icons onto your posts, getting rid of the extra step that users must take to share your content through ShareThis.

Additionally, depending on the type of content you're producing and the audience you're writing for, a reader can easily overlook the ShareThis button, meaning that users may skim over and ignore your sharing option. In my own blogs, a lot more of my content gets shared when I present the reader with individual buttons instead of using a Share This button.

✦ **Don't overwhelm the user with choices.** I see sites that include too many sharing options all the time. The reader becomes overwhelmed and probably also has trouble finding the network that he or she uses.

Pick a few sharing sites to which you want to link, test them out, and cycle in new ones that people may use. Offer only a low number of sharing options at a time so that people can share your content easily. Determine which of these networks your content applies to. If you write celebrity gossip, your content might do better being seeded on sites that people can share quickly with their friends, such as Facebook or Twitter. If you write in-depth technical resources, a social bookmarking site such as Delicious might a better place to seed your content and bring your blog additional traffic. If you write about health and beauty, perhaps providing a sharing button to kirtsy (www.kirtsy.com) can get you traffic from people interested in those specific topics.

Make sure that the sharing options you give visitors apply to sites where your content makes sense. Don't be afraid to try different sites and study your statistics to see where readers are discovering your content. Many of these sites allow you to search by domain, so you can check to see how often people are sharing your Web site and what content, specifically, they're sharing.

✦ **Present the ability to share at the right time for your audience.** When to present the sharing buttons really depends on the type of content you're posting and the audience reading it. If you post a picture and include a comment below it, this could push your sharing buttons below the fold, so make sure that your major sharing options appear next to or above the content.

Below the fold refers to what doesn't appear in a user's Web browser unless the user scrolls down to view it. The term is taken from newspaper printing, in which some items appear below the fold on the front page.

To get some ideas about how best to deploy your sharing buttons, check out sites that are similar to yours and see where some of the more successful bloggers have done it.

✦ **Think about the user, not yourself.** Take this major lesson away from this section. Too many times, people get excited about the latest gadget or tool for their blogs. They get eager to try it out and excited to deploy it, but in the end, they aren't thinking about whether it can help the user and whether the user is going to enjoy it.

How you use the Web and how you navigate a blog can be completely different than how most other people use it. Review button use and where people are sharing your blog posts and also use tools such as Google Analytics and Crazy Egg to see how people interact with your page.

By using its site-overlay feature, Google Analytics allows you to see how often someone clicks various items on your Web site. You can sign up for Google Analytics for free and deploy it very easily. (You just need to paste the tracking code in your WordPress footer.)

To access the site-overlay feature from your Google Analytics Dashboard, follow these steps:

1. **On the left menu, click on the Content link.**

2. **Make sure that you're on the overview screen. You can do this by making sure that the Overview link is highlighted.**

3. **Click on the In-Page Analytics link under the Click Patterns heading on the right side of the screen.**

Now, on the home page of your site, little text boxes for the various links on your home page appear, displaying percentages (see Figure 1-1). The percentages within these text boxes reflect how popular the various links are within your site. If you navigate through your site while using the site-overlay feature, you can see, page by page, how people are interacting with your navigation, content, sharing features, and other content.

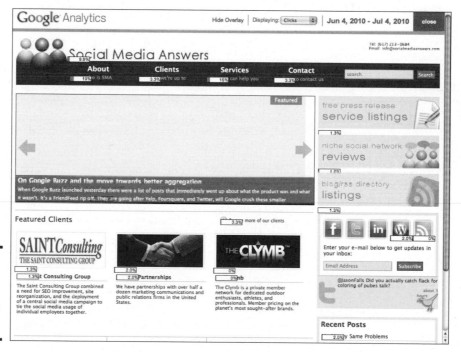

Figure 1-1:
Google
Analytics'
Site Overlay
feature.

Crazy Egg offers a free trial and a paid version that can create a heat map for your Web page. A heat map uses colors to show how "hot" or "cold" various sections of your site are. This map really allows you to analyze how people are interacting with your site. However, don't use the paid version of Crazy Egg until you have some solid traffic flowing into your Web site. Paying to analyze traffic when you have a low number of visits isn't the best use of your money.

✦ **Test, test, and test some more.** How to best lay out your sharing options on your site takes continual testing. You can't get it right the first time — or the first five times. Sometimes, it takes months to find the right mix.

Determining Where You Need to Participate

Communication is such an important part of social media, and communication is a two-way street. In social media, communication isn't a bullhorn; you need to interact with people. If you want the rewards of participation, you need to listen, as well as talk. This idea often gets lost when people start using social media to promote their content.

Determining who you want to interact with and where to interact with them is a large part of using social media in your marketing strategy. Finding the best communities in which you can participate and actively engage in conversations is the quickest way to build a loyal audience.

Although reaching out to audiences known for being receptive to your blog's content is a good strategy, you may find that you're following a well-trod path. Other bloggers may have already found success there. Don't be afraid to try out areas where others who have blogs similar to yours aren't participating if you think the audience is there. Be original and trail-blaze a little.

As a blogger, you often work as the marketing person for your own blog. In order to gain readership, you need to participate with your potential audience in communities where they are already participating. Additionally, you can really leverage participating in these communities if you understand the bloggers in your niche, work with them to possibly get a guest-blogging slot, or even get links from them in their blogrolls.

Taking the time to create a list of potential audiences goes a long way toward creating your own blog-marketing strategy. Your list should include social networks and message boards where you think that your content will be greeted with open arms, bloggers who work in the niche you participate in that you want to monitor, and users who have influence on other social networks (such as someone who has a large Twitter following in your niche, or your particular area of interest/expertise).

Some bloggers have actually purchased lists of other bloggers in their niche from marketing firms. Personally, I don't like to buy established lists or rely solely on a monitoring service. (We talk about social-media monitoring more in Chapter 5 of this minibook.) Although purchased lists might make for a good jumping-off point, a lot of lists are outdated or ignore important markets (such as large social networking, Twitter, or YouTube friends/followers).

The most important piece of research a person can do while constructing a list is to understand the niche to which they're building a readership in. Here are some items of interest that I look for when finding out about a niche:

✦ **Who's in the niche?** When I put together a list of bloggers to target, I feel like a detective. Each link on a blogroll or in a post seems like a clue. Start with a major blog in your niche and see where the blogroll leads, the links to commenters' blogs, and blogs that they mention in their content to get a wide view of the niche. Knowing who associates with whom and what circles people run in can help you discover a lot about a niche. You can determine who the power players are, as well as whether the niche is competitive about news or has a collegial atmosphere. This information helps you determine how you want to approach your outreach.

✦ **Is there a niche social-media site or group that acts as a connecting point for the community?** Often, in various groups, you can find one or more niche social-media sites that connect blogs together. These sites can provide you with a great resource for discovering some of the top blogs, and they may help you flesh out your list of bloggers quickly. Additionally, see whether you can get your blog listed on these types of sites. Most of these kinds of sites allow free submittals, and you can find forms to fill out or an e-mail address to which you can submit your content.

The site Milblogging.com is great example of a small niche community designed around a topic; in this case, a community of members of the military. This kind of online community might be a directory with social features, a Ning community, or a group on a large social network; whatever the case may be, you can often find large groups that have discussions within a niche. These niche sites can tell you what people in the niche you are targeting find important, what the hot topics are, and information about what other people are doing in this niche, such as pitches people have made to other bloggers.

Additionally, these sites feature the type of content that people in your niche may find interesting. I usually keep a Word document open or use Evernote to write down blogging ideas based on the conversations on these sites.

✦ **Are common discussions occurring throughout the community?** You can often discover opportunities to get your blog in front of new people or for topics to cover by looking for common threads within a niche.

Maybe the bloggers are talking about how PR people are pitching them, a charity cause that they all support, or an event that they regard as important. A common theme may give you information, opportunity, or direction on how you should approach this niche.

✦ **Do they use other media to have discussions?** Find out what other social-media sites people in this niche use. Maybe they use Twitter a lot, or maybe you see a high use of Facebook, LinkedIn, MySpace, FriendFeed, or YouTube. You may find secondary ways to reach this niche where you can build a following for your blog.

It pays to determine the social-media sites your niche prefers. Certain niches (such as wine bloggers) have taken to Twitter, but others have strong ties to Facebook or other social-networking sites. Leverage these sites when you pitch your blog to customers. They may prefer that method of connection.

In the end, you might think you can simply buy a list, slam together a bunch of search results into a spreadsheet, and then mass–e-mail everyone whom you want to contact. However, without studying how your niche operates, you can't create mutually beneficial relationships, you can't become a voice in the community, and you probably can't see a lot of success. Instead, you come off as an outsider just trying to push your message down the throats of these bloggers, and your campaign will have very poor results.

Finding Influencers

After you compile lists of bloggers you would like to target, you can begin to break the list down and determine who are the influencers in your niche, including people whom I like to call hidden influencers. *Hidden influencers* are people that have a large social imprint that doesn't necessarily show up on their blog. For example, some bloggers don't have a lot of commenters on their blog but their Twitter feed is followed by tens of thousands. Here are some ways to determine whether a blogger is an influencer:

✦ **Subscriber count:** A lot of bloggers who have large audiences display their subscriber numbers on their blogs. (See Figure 1-2.)

✦ **Comment count:** An active community and commentary group on a blog usually shows that the blog has a large readership. Be wary of blogs in which the author interacts with only two or three people. When an author only pays attention to a couple commenters, they usually have a pretty narrow vision. You want to target authors that participate with more people in their audience.

140,000 readers and counting

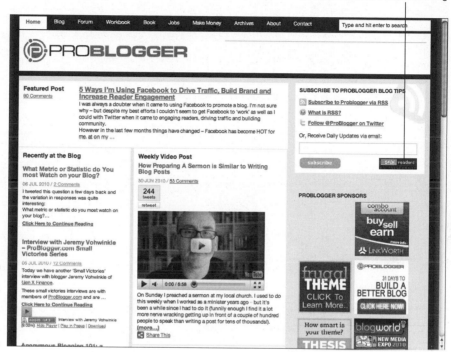

Figure 1-2:
Blog
subscriber
count.

✦ **Alexa/Compete:** Alexa (www.alexa.com) and Compete (www.compete.com) measure traffic to a site. They aren't 100 percent accurate, but they do a decent job of giving you a picture of the amount of traffic a site gets. I usually create a column on my list of bloggers where I record either the Compete or Alexa score, and how that score compares to the other bloggers or sites on the list.

✦ **Klout:** Klout (www.klout.com) helps you evaluate the influence of Twitter users. Sometimes, bloggers may have a very large reach on Twitter and are more active there than on their own blogs. Don't discount creating relationships with the twitterati.

✦ **PostRank:** PostRank (www.postrank.com) can act as a great evaluation service. It ranks the blogs you follow, and within these blogs, it ranks the individual top posts. Go back through your list and add a column for RSS feeds for each blog in your niche. After you gather that information, follow these steps to have PostRank automatically rate the blogs you follow:

1. **Go to www.postrank.com and click the Topics tab on the top of the page.**

2. **Log in to your PostRank account or set up a new account.**

3. **Click the My Subscriptions, link on the right side.**

4. **Click the Import tab.**

5. **From the Import Feed Using drop-down list, select Direct Input.**

6. **Paste your feeds into the text box that appears. The names of your feeds will automatically be detected.**

7. **Name this collection of feeds.**

You now have imported all the feeds of your niche in one place. To see the results, click the Topic tab on the right sidebar; your named list of imported topics appears. When you click the title of a topic, a list of all the blogs you entered appears, now ranked by PostRank. (See Figure 1-3.)

When you click the arrow on the right of the blog title, the top-ranked posts recently created by the blog appear in the new window. This feature allows you to see what content is popular in your niche.

By using PostRank, not only do you have the blogs ranked within your niche, but you also know the top posts of each blog based on traffic and social-media sharing. Pretty useful intelligence to have, no?

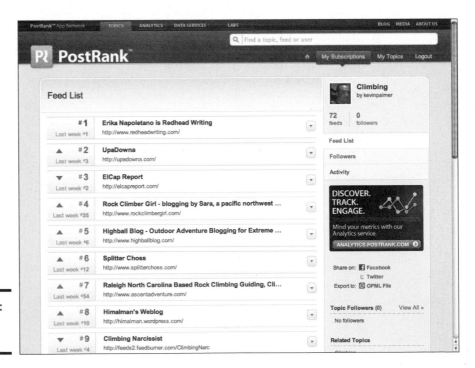

Figure 1-3: PostRank results.

After you identify the influencers, you want to attract them to your blog. If influencers read your blog, they may offer you guest-blogging spots, share your content, and form a relationship with you so that you can be mutually beneficial to each other.

In order to turn these influencers into readers, you can try multiple tactics, including the following:

+ **Comment on their blogs.** Reading and commenting on a popular blog can help you start to build your name in your niche — if you leave quality, well-thought-out comments, of course. Most blogs allow your username to link back to a Web site; make sure that you use this link as a way for people to find your blog.

  Not only can you get the attention of a popular blogger by engaging in conversation on his or her blog, you also get the attention of that blogger's readership. If the readers and commentators like your contribution, you can get additional traffic, new readers, and even potentially high rankings back links into your Web site; all because you left a comment on the blog.

+ **E-mail them.** Depending on the niche, top influencers might get slammed with e-mail, so this approach might not be the best way to reach out to someone. But it doesn't hurt to write a personal note that lets the blogger know about you and your blog, and perhaps offer to guest blog if he or she ever accepts posts from other bloggers. Make sure that the e-mail isn't all about you, which is the quickest way to turn someone off. Talk about their blog and show that you have knowledge about what they are writing about. Show that you have actually read their blog and demonstrate genuine interest in what they are doing.

+ **Interact with them on their platforms of choice.** Sometimes, influencers or popular bloggers participate in areas other than their blogs. They might use a message board, a forum, Twitter, Facebook, or another type of social-media site. Interacting with a blogger on his or her platform of choice can help you differentiate yourself from other bloggers.

+ **Link to them.** Linking to bloggers in the content you create — especially if you're posting rebuttals to their posts — can really get their attention.

When you use any of the tactics in the preceding list, the three C's (content, communication, and consistency) come into effect. When you communicate with these bloggers, you need to make sure that you have consistent content on your site. Trying to reach out to another blogger when you have only three posts total doesn't present the most credibility but after you've worked at it for a few months, doing blogger outreach can provide you with a good way to grow your audience.

Leveraging Twitter for Social-Media Success

Twitter has become one of the most effective ways for bloggers to build an audience. You can use Twitter to find people who have the same interests that you do, communicate with them, and steer a ton of traffic to your blog.

Building a Twitter profile into a successful tool to generate traffic is pretty straightforward. Just follow these steps:

1. **Make sure that your profile is completely filled out, including your picture.**

2. **Follow the three C's — content, communication, and consistency — when you post to Twitter.**

   By posting quality content consistently on Twitter, you *will* build an audience. Period. When you mix in the communication aspect and retweet the quality content of others, answer questions, and interact with other Twitter users, your profile will grow that much more.

3. **Find people who are interested in what you're writing about and interact with them.**

4. **Use a tool such as Follower Wonk (`www.followerwonk.com`) to find people whose profiles contain specific keywords that you're writing about.**

   You may want to follow and interact with these people.

Building your Twitter account by using automated tools

I hesitantly include this section because using automated tools is a fast way to get your account deleted by Twitter. Automated tools allow you to do mass additions or removals to your account. You can remove people that aren't active, that aren't following you, or allow you to target the friend's lists of other users to add them to your account. Using these mass adding-and-removal tools kind of goes against the spirit of the site where you are supposed to be discovering cool content not just mass promoting. So, I'm warning you right now, if you go down this path, you need to see losing your account as an acceptable risk. If you use the tool that I discuss in a logical and non-aggressive way, it can help you target and build an audience quickly.

I include automated tools in my discussion of building out your social media accounts because a lot of people use this technique, including people who shun them. (A lot of social media experts who deride these tools have used them to get where they are.) I don't believe in giving you half the information — you need to make this choice on your own.

However, if you go above the parameters I discuss in this section, and hyper-aggressively add people and then unfollow them on your account, Twitter will probably quickly ban you.

In order to target users on Twitter here are the steps you can take:

1. **Go to Refollow (`www.refollow.com`). (See Figure 1-4.)**

   Refollow.com is a great service, but it is no longer free. It used to be free but recent changes to the Twitter platform and their need to restructure their service has led to them asking for payment for their services.

2. **Log in to Refollow by using your Twitter account login information.**

3. **After you log in, you will see a control panel. On the right sidebar, below the Show Me title, select Users Who Are Following.**

4. **In the "Users Who are Following" box, type the name of the profile you want to evaluate.**

5. **At the top of the page, select the following check boxes:**

   • Not Following Me

   • I'm Not Following

   • Never Followed

   • Not Locked

   • With Picture

   • Tweeted in the Last 3 Days

6. **In the Exclude box below the check boxes, enter terms that you want to exclude from the search results.**

   Exclude some key profanity terms (you can figure them out yourself), Pics, Trump (a MLM scheme), Teeth (for teeth whitening products), Income, and Money. (These exclusions cut out the largest amount of spam on Twitter.)

7. **Choose to follow the users who showed up from the search by selecting Select Page on the right side, and then click the Follow button.**

   Refollow then adds these people to your Twitter account so that you are now following those 100 people.

   Don't follow more than 100 to 200 people a day. This tool allows you to follow up to 500, but if you follow that many people each day, Twitter will probably ban you after a few days.

Figure 1-4:
The Refollow
Dashboard.

You can use Refollow to find people who are following people within your niche and add them to your Twitter account so that they may notice your content. I advise only adding people once in a 24-hour period so you don't look like you are gaming the system. Once a week, unfollow everyone who isn't following you back to keep your following ratio even. You should not be following more people than are following you.

Updating Twitter from your WordPress blog

Getting back to WordPress (that's why you bought the book, right?), you can find tons of plugins to integrate Twitter into your WordPress blog. From how the tweets show up on your sidebar to integrating tweets into your comments, the WordPress community has tons of solutions to help you integrate Twitter into your blog.

These plugins change often, and I invite you to try different ones, depending on how you want to integrate Twitter into your site. But if you want to turn your WordPress Dashboard into more of a social-media command center, you can give yourself the ability to tweet right from your WordPress Dashboard.

Although tools such as Tweetdeck and Hootsuite are better designed for an active and strategic Twitter presence, having the ability to tweet from your WordPress Dashboard allows people to update all their social media from one spot. For people just getting started in social media, this integration makes your social-media use efficient and constantly reminds you to participate.

One of the better WordPress integration plugins for this purpose is Alex King's Twitter Tools (`http://wordpress.org/extend/plugins/ twitter-tools`). This installation allows you to tweet from your WordPress Dashboard, as well as create an archive page for all your tweets. And it can create a WordPress blog post of your daily tweets, among other features.

This plugin can also update your Twitter feed whenever you submit a new blog post. You can update Twitter about new blog posts by using Hootsuite, Feedburner, and other free tools, but going with the Alex King Twitter plugin allows you to use all these features through one plugin.

Engaging with Facebook

Facebook integration is another key strategy to consider when you're setting up your blog for the first time. First, integrate the Facebook-sharing feature within your blog, which can be done with the Share This or Add This plugin. With over 450 million users, Facebook is a must-have sharing option for any blog.

Next, decide how you want your blog to interact with Facebook. Are you writing a very personal blog? Then you might want to use a Facebook profile as your connecting place on Facebook. Some WordPress plugins (such as the Facebook Dashboard Widget) integrate a Facebook profile so that you can update your status right from the WordPress Dashboard.

However, if you don't want your Facebook account attached to your blog, you may want to consider creating a Facebook Fan page. A Fan page doesn't have the Dashboard controls that a profile does, but it allows you to leverage your social-media presence. By setting up a Facebook Fan page, you can deeply integrate the Facebook Like option, which allows users to Like your site and become a fan of your page with a couple of clicks. Integrating the like feature allows you to get exposure for your Web site through each of your fans' friends on Facebook.

When you have a Facebook Fan page, you can display a community widget on the side of your WordPress blog, letting everyone know who your fans are on Facebook. Basically, if a Facebook user likes your page, they can show up in this widget. Facebook offers a lot of different badges and Like-button integration in their Developers section at `http://developers.facebook.com/plugins`.

In this Developers section, you really can dig deep into how you want to integrate Facebook into your blog. You can display the friends of a visitor who likes your site, recommendations based on what the visitor's friends have liked, and numerous other combinations.

Chapter 2: Creating a Social-Media Listening Hub

In This Chapter

✔ Understanding why you need to monitor your brand

✔ Finding out which monitoring tools are right for you

✔ Cleaning and aggregating your monitoring data

✔ Turning your WordPress Dashboard into a listening post

his chapter focuses on the importance of social-media listening, the free monitoring services available for you to use, and how to integrate these sources into your WordPress installation so that you can turn your run-of-the-mill WordPress installation into a social-media listening hub.

A social-media listening hub is a collection of information from several sources, including mentions of your blog, keywords or topics that you write about, and even information about competitors. You can sign up for services that monitor these topics, such as Radian6 (www.radian6.com), Sysomos (www.sysomos.com), and hundreds of others. (For a complete list of monitoring services, check out http://socialmediaanswers. com/a-list-of-social-media-monitoring-tools). But most of these services cost money and give you another place to log in to — and you may not use this kind of service to its full capability. For a small business or an independent blogger, the investment (both time and financial) doesn't always make sense. By leveraging the power of the WordPress platform, you can easily cut down on both the time and financial commitment of monitoring platforms.

In this chapter, we walk you through determining what sources you should pull your data from, how to determine and search for the keywords you deem important, and how to integrate your search results into your WordPress Dashboard. Additionally, we look at some other tools that can help expand your monitoring practices.

Exploring Reasons for a Social-Media Listening Hub

When you begin to engage in the world of social media, one of the most important things you can do is monitor what Internet users are saying about your company, your blog, yourself, or your products. By investigating what Internet users are saying, you can find and participate in discussions about your blog or company, and come to an understanding about the way your community views your blog (or company). With this information, you can participate by responding to comments on other blogs, Twitter, or message boards, or by creating targeted content on your own blog.

The conversations happening about your area of interest or niche amount to really great intelligence. For a business, regardless of whether you participate in social media, social-media users are talking about your company, so you need to be aware what they're saying. If you're blogging about a particular topic, you can evolve your content by tracking what members of your niche are discussing about it.

Eavesdropping on yourself

By monitoring your niche you essentially can eavesdrop on thousands of conversations daily, and then pick and choose the ones in which you want to participate. The social-media listening hub you create allows you to follow various conversations going on through microblogging services such as Twitter, Facebook, blogs, news sites, message boards, and even comments on YouTube. If someone says something negative about you, you can respond quickly to fix the situation. You could make attempts step in and correct any misinformation being said about your business, blog, or area of interest. You could make sure that people are informed about what you're doing. This is the benefit of setting up a social-media monitoring hub.

Keeping tabs on your brand

Think about what keywords or phrases you want to monitor. Of course, you want to monitor your name, your blog/company name, and other keywords that are directly associated with you. Also, consider monitoring common misspellings and permutations of the name of your brand. The MSN Keyword Mutation Tool (`http://adlab.microsoft.com/Keyword-Mutation-Detection/`) can help you determine all the common spellings and usages of the keywords you are monitoring. When you try to figure out common misspellings for your brand, examine some of the terms used to find your page by using Google Analytics (`www.google.com/analytics`) or a paid tool such as Trellian Keyword Discovery Tool (`www.keyworddiscovery.com/search.html`).

For example, if LeBron James wanted to set up a monitoring service, he might use the following keywords: LeBron James, LuBron James, Le Bron James, Cleveland Cavaliers, and perhaps his nickname, King James. If he wanted to expand this service past direct mentions of him or his team, he could also include more general terms such as NBA Basketball or even Olympic Basketball. The general term NBA Basketball may be *too* general, though, producing too many results to monitor.

Additionally, you may want to view your blog or company through the lens of your customers: What terms do they associate with your company? Looking at your blog from other points of view can provide you with good ideas for keywords, but not always. Although you don't always want your company known for these terms and may not see yourself that way, getting the perspective of other people can open your eyes on how users view your blog or Web site.

Don't think of this process as just pulling in keywords, either. You can pull in multiple feeds, just like you do with an RSS reader, which allows you to monitor specific sites. So, if you concentrate on an industry, and a Web site deals specifically with your industry and has an active news flow pushed through an RSS feed, you might want to consider adding specific Web sites into the mix of feeds you run through WordPress.

The setup in WordPress that we describe in this chapter gives you the convenience of having everything in one place and can help you monitor your brand, company, or blog. The limitations of the WordPress platform mean that you can monitor only five different groupings, so you can't use this method as a replacement for an enterprise-monitoring tool for a large company. Additionally, if you own a restaurant, hotel, or bar, and want to pick up review sites such as Yelp and Trip Advisor, these tools can't do it. Most social-media monitoring tools don't count review sites as social media. Tools such as Reputation Ranger (http://reputationranger.com) can monitor ratings sites for a nominal monthly fee if you want to pay attention to those types of sites.

When your content changes, change what you're monitoring to match the evolution of what you're blogging about.

Exploring Different Listening Tools

You can find tons of different types of monitoring or listening tools that oversee the social-media space. If you work for a large company, you can use large, paid tools such as Radian 6 (www.radian6.com), Sysomos (www.sysomos.com), Alterian (www.alterian.com), Lithium (www.lithium.com), or others. Pricing for these tools runs from a few hundred dollars to the tens of thousands per month. Most individuals and small businesses can't make that investment. If you're one of the smaller guys, you can create your own monitoring service right in WordPress by importing free monitoring tools into your Dashboard to create a social-media listening hub.

Some monitoring tools pick up blog coverage, Twitter remarks, and message board comments. Others pick up content created around video and pictures. Try out these different monitoring services and determine which give you the best results and which make you feel the most comfortable. Then choose the best tools to create a good monitoring mix. One solution probably can't cover everything, so experiment with different combinations of tools.

Most, but not all, of these tools use Boolean search methods, so you need to understand how to narrow down your searches. If you want to combine terms, put an AND between two items (for example, cake AND pie). If you use OR, you can broaden your search — for example, to track common misspelling (MacDonalds OR McDonalds). Finally, if you want to exclude terms, you can use the NOT operator to exclude items from your search. Use NOT if you want to exclude a company or a blog with the same name that writes about a different topic (for example, Afghan NOT blanket, if you are blogging about Afghanistan).

Although some of the monitoring tools in the following sections don't apply to every type of Web site, we would include these tools in most monitoring setups.

Monitoring with Google Alerts

Most social-media experts widely consider Google Alerts (`www.google.com/alerts`) a must-use monitoring source for anyone dabbling in social media. Google Alerts allows the user to set up monitoring on news sites, blogs, pictures, videos, and groups. You can toggle the amount of results you see from 20 to 50; and you can choose how often they come in, either in real time, daily, or weekly. You can have Google deliver your alerts to your e-mail or via RSS.

Google Alerts isn't perfect, but it doesn't have many drawbacks. Some of the specialized searches (such as Boardreader, which targets message boards) pick up more around their areas of expertise than Google Alerts does, but in general, and compared to other tools, Google Alerts covers the widest range of content.

You can easily set up Google Alerts by following these steps:

1. **Navigate to `www.google.com/alerts` in your Web browser.**

A page loads, welcoming you to the Google Alerts Web site.

2. **In the Search Terms text box, type in the keyword or phrase that you want to monitor.**

   If you enter a phrase in which the words have to go together in that particular order, put the phrase in quotes.

3. **From the Type drop-down list, select the type of monitoring that you want to use.**

   The options send you different kinds of alerts:

   • *Everything:* All types of Internet content available

   • *News:* Only news sources

   • *Blogs:* Blog sources

   • *Discussions:* Discussion sources, such as social media

   We suggest that you select Everything so that you receive alerts in all areas of Internet content available on the Web. This gives you wider coverage in regards to your tool.

4. **Select the frequency of updates in the How Often drop-down list.**

   Because you'll receive the updates via RSS and not e-mail (which you set up in Step 6), you want the highest frequency possible. So, select As-It-Happens.

5. **From the Volume drop-down list, select the amount of items you want to appear in each update.**

   If you selected As-It-Happens in Step 4, you receive items in real time, so you don't need to specify the amount of items.

6. **Select your delivery type in the Deliver To drop-down list.**

   To make the delivery source an RSS feed, as opposed to an e-mail, select Feed.

7. **Click the Create Alert button.**

   Your Google Alert Management screen, where you can get the RSS feeds for all your Google Alerts, appears.

8. **To get the URL of the RSS feed, right-click the Feed hyperlink next to the orange RSS icon and select Copy Link Location from the pop-up menu that appears.**

9. **Paste the copied link location into a document in which you list all the feeds that you plan to aggregate later.**

10. **Repeat Steps 2 through 9 for all the terms you want to monitor.**

Before you start importing the feed into your WordPress Dashboard, you might want to receive the update via e-mail for a few days to test out the quality of the results you're getting. Starting with e-mails allows you to fine-tune the keywords you use and gives you the ability to test out and narrow down what you want to monitor. Doing this saves you the time of parsing all your RSS feeds, blending them all together, and then having to go back and edit everything because they are set up wrong. Using the e-mail as a test is a massive timesaver.

Tracking conversations with Social Mention

Social Mention (`http://socialmention.com`) allows users to track and measure what social-media users are saying about any topic. It measures over 100 social-media Web sites, including Twitter, Facebook, FriendFeed, YouTube, Digg, and others.

Social Mention also tracks the sentiment of posts. *Sentiment scores* refer to how the post was written — whether the post has a negative, neutral, or positive tone. Social Mention is the only free tool right now that features sentiment scoring.

You can set up monitoring on Social Mention by following these steps:

1. **Navigate to `http://socialmention.com` in your Web browser.**

   The Social Mention Web site loads in your browser window.

2. **In the text box on the main page, enter the search term you want to monitor and select where you want to monitor it from the drop-down list.**

   Don't click the Create an Alert link, which allows you to set up an e-mail alert.

   The options available in the drop-down list include

   - All
   - Blogs
   - Microblogs
   - Networks
   - Bookmarks
   - Comments
   - Events
   - Images
   - News
   - Videos
   - Audio
   - Questions

3. **Click the Search button.**

   A new screen appears, displaying the RSS feed for your search results on the right side of the page.

4. **Right-click the RSS Feed link next to the orange RSS icon and select Copy Link Location from the pop-up menu that appears.**

5. **Paste the link location into a document in which you list all the feeds that you plan to aggregate later.**

Social Mention is a little different than the other free tools because it has sentiment analysis built into its page. Although this information doesn't get pulled in via RSS feed, you still may want to occasionally look at it because it displays the sentiment around your site. Sentiment score rates content around your site by grading it positive, negative, and neutral. Although automated sentiment score is often imprecise, this gives you a good general idea of how your site is perceived. On the left side of Social Mention's search results, a few statistics around the search term you entered into the site search appear:

✦ **Strength:** The likelihood that users are talking about your term in social media; the higher number, the better for this measure.

✦ **Sentiment:** The ratio of positive mentions versus negative mentions of the search term.

✦ **Passion:** The measurement of people who mention your search term and those who do so repeatedly. A higher number means that people who mention that search term do it more than once on a regular basis.

✦ **Reach:** Based on the unique influence of authors who are generating content around your search term.

Below each statistical section, more detailed stats appear, which show how often users talk about your search term in social media and how many people are mentioning it. First, your Average Time Per Mention displays how often users talk about that phrase. Next, the Last Mention shows when your keyword was last mentioned in social media. Finally, the Number of Unique Authors who have talked about your search term appears, as well as the Number of Retweets.

Social Mention also shows the sentiment scores related to the search term you entered — the total positive mentions, neutral mentions, and negative mentions. If you scroll down the page, you can see bar graphs for the top keywords used, the top users covering this area, the top hashtags used on Twitter, and the sites that appear most frequently in your search.

Be careful about relying too heavily on automated sentiment analysis in both free and paid tools. The technology doesn't exist right now to automatically measure sentiment with high accuracy; use this analysis as a general picture, rather than an accurate description.

Listening to blogs with BlogPulse

BlogPulse (www.blogpulse.com) is an automated blog-monitoring service created by Nielsen. This tool doesn't get as much coverage as Technorati (see the following section) or other tools in this chapter, but it often catches blogs that other services don't.

Remember, this niche-monitoring tool monitors blogs only. It can't give you results from message boards or other social-media sites. You can compare the results you get from BlogPulse directly with the results you get from Technorati and make a choice between the two tools.

You can set up monitoring on BlogPulse by following these steps:

1. **Navigate to http://blogpulse.com.**

   The BlogPulse Web site loads in your browser window.

2. **Type your search term in the Search Blogosphere text box.**

   This text box appears in the upper-right corner of the page.

3. **Click the Go button.**

   After BlogPulse does the search, it takes you to a results page.

4. **Right-click the RSS Feed link next to the orange RSS icon and choose Copy Link Location from the pop-up menu that appears.**

   On the results page, where it says Search Results, an orange XML icon appears. They use the XML export rather than pure RSS but both types of data sources will work for what we are doing.

5. **Paste this link location into a document in which you list all the feeds that you plan to aggregate later.**

6. **Repeat Steps 2 through 5 to add as many BlogPulse monitoring terms as you want.**

Checking rank with Technorati

Technorati (http://technorati.com) seems like the old dog when you talk about all these different monitoring services because it's been around for so long! It was one of the first sites to monitor and rank the blogosphere. Although the site may have lost some of its luster to other products that are available, such as BlogPulse or even Google Alerts, at least try it out because Technorati was considered the top blog-data source for a long time. Users have encountered many problems when using the site, however, including its slow performance and occasional poor results.

But a lot of Technorati users swear by their results, so try it and compare it to other resources.

You can set up monitoring on Technorati by following these steps:

1. **Navigate to** `http://technorati.com`.

   The Technorati Web site loads in your browser window.

2. **Type the search term that you want to monitor in the Search Posts text box at the top of the screen, and then click the magnifying glass. When you click on the magnifying glass, your search results will appear.**

3. **Click the RSS icon in the menu bar of your browser, and then copy and paste the URL of your feed to your list.**

   Technorati recently introduced a partnership with IngBoo to do RSS services, which, to be honest, is a pain. It requires yet another step in trying to gather all this information together because you have to register for IngBoo's services as well. However, it is a service you may find useful.

Connecting conversations with BackType

BackType (`www.backtype.com`) is a real-time, conversational search engine, meaning that it tracks conversations in social media in real time. It indexes and connects millions of conversations from blogs, social networks, and other social media so that you can find out what people are saying about the topics that interest you. BackType started out monitoring blog comments and has continually expanded the width and scope of what it covers.

The strength of BackType is in its blog comments targeting, so try out the search function to see what it returns. BackType may not be a must-add tool because it is limited in scope, but if people online are talking about and referencing your brand or blog often in blog comments, you may find it a worthy source.

At the time of this writing, BackType is monitoring only tracks based on a specific URL as opposed to search terms, and has shut down its search engine until it's integrated into a larger platform. For example, if you wanted to monitor Google you would have to choose Google.com and not the search term Google. We include it because its new platform can potentially eclipse some of the other players in this space, so it's worth your time to check out.

Searching communities with Boardreader

Boardreader (`http://boardreader.com`) is a community search tool that does an excellent job when it comes to message boards and smaller communities. Although the other tools we talk about in the previous sections cover blogs, microblogging, and other common social-media platforms, Boardreader focuses on groups and message boards, which often get overlooked when it comes to social-media searches. Boardreader also has a fairly in-depth repository of historical social-media data with some sites going back for up to ten years.

We classify Boardreader as a must-add tool because its niche focuses on groups and message boards, where conversations have been happening much longer than just Facebook and Twitter. Many other monitoring tools often overlook these areas when talking about monitoring the Web, but you can find so many vibrant communities that are worth being a part of, in addition to monitoring what is being said about your blog or company.

To set up your Boardreader tracking, follow these steps:

1. **Navigate to `http://boardreader.com`.**

   The Boardreader Web site loads in your browser window.

2. **In the text box, type the search term that you want to monitor, and then click the Search button. The results appear when the screen refreshes.**

3. **Click the Show Tools link below the Search text box.**

   The RSS Feed link appears.

4. **Right-click the RSS Feed link next to the orange RSS icon and choose Copy Link Location from the pop-up menu that appears.**

5. **Paste this link location into a document in which you list all the feeds that you plan to aggregate later.**

6. **Repeat Steps 1 through 5 to search for and monitor as many different search terms as you want.**

Staying on top of conversations with Twitter Search

Twitter Search (`http://search.twitter.com`) provides the most accurate way to stay on top of the conversations happening on Twitter that use the keywords you want to monitor. Twitter Search is limited to only the Twitter platform. Although Twitter is clearly the most popular microblogging platform, competitors still exist. You may prefer to use a tool that monitors multiple microblogging Web sites, such as Twingly (discussed in the following section).

You can use the Twitter Search service to monitor conversations on Twitter by following these steps:

1. **Navigate to `http://search.twitter.com`.**

   The Twitter Search Web site loads in your browser window.

2. **In the text box, type the search term that you want to monitor, and then click the Search button.**

   The screen that appears displays the results of your search.

3. **Click Feed for This Query on the upper-right side of the page.**

   The RSS export page appears.

4. **Copy and paste the URL in the Web address bar of your browser to whatever list you are generating for terms.**

5. **Repeat Steps 1 through 4 for all the terms that you want to monitor.**

Microblog searching with Twingly

Twingly Microblog Search (www.twingly.com/microblogsearch) deals with real-time search microblogging and traditional blog search. Their microblog service also monitors conversations on other microblogging sites besides Twitter, such as Jaiku, Indentica, Bleeper, Bloggy, Crip, Koornk, Lareta, Linux Outlaws, Suffice to Say, TWIT Army, and YouAre.

Compare the results you get from Twingly with Twitter Search (see the preceding section), just to make sure that Twingly is picking up everything on Twitter. If it isn't, you can use Twitter Search and configure Twingly to pick up only the other microblogging sites. (See Figure 2-1.)

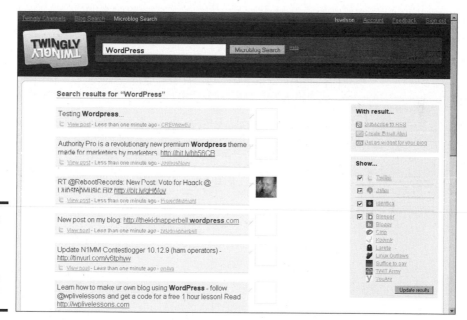

Figure 2-1:
Choosing
micro-
blogging
services to
monitor.

To monitor conversations by using Twingly, follow these steps:

1. **Navigate to www.twingly.com/microblogsearch.**

   The Twingly Microblog Search page opens in your browser window.

2. **In the text box, type the search term that you want to monitor, and then click the Microblog Search button. All the relevant search results appear.**

3. **On the right side of the screen, select the microblogging tools (refer to Figure 2-1) that you want to monitor, and then click Update Results.**

   This includes only the services that you want to monitor.

4. **On the right sidebar, right-click the Subscribe to RSS link next to the orange RSS icon and choose Copy Link Location from the pop-up menu that appears.**

5. **Paste this link location into a document in which you list all the feeds that you plan to aggregate later.**

6. **Repeat Steps 1 through 5 for all the terms you want to monitor.**

Creating Your Own Personal Monitoring Mix

After trying out the various monitoring services, you can create a mix of services to import into your WordPress Dashboard. You import the results of these monitoring services by leveraging RSS (Really Simple Syndication). You can combine different single RSS feeds into one RSS feed and create an organized setup for all the information you have to manage. For example if you have various RSS feeds from different sources around the keywords "cookies" you can combine them all into one RSS feed. Or if you want to combine various feeds based off sources, like all your Twitter RSS feeds, you can do that as well.

Look for the orange RSS icon that's usually found in the URL bar of your browser. Additionally, some sites offer an RSS export on the right sidebar or in the search bar for the site. Grab the address of all these feeds by clicking on the feed name and copying the feed URL from the browser.

For each search that you do on a monitoring service, you need to log the feed address. To make recording these addresses easy, open a spreadsheet or a document into which you can paste the various feeds. You can collect them in one place before you begin to splice them together (which we talk about in the following sections). Think of it as a holding area.

Grouping your monitoring results

After you copy the locations for all your RSS feeds in one document, you need to group those RSS feeds together. After you group these feeds, you splice them together to make one master feed per grouping (see the following section). Grouping your RSS feeds keeps your monitoring system nice and tidy, and allows you to more easily set up the WordPress Dashboard. Reorder the spreadsheet or Word document that you created into categories. You can import feeds into your WordPress Dashboard, so you can monitor what you want. If you're tracking a variety of keywords, you may want to put your feeds into groups. For example, Wendy's Restaurants could make these keyword groupings:

✦ **Grouping 1:** Your brand, products, and other information around your company

- Wendy's (the company name)
- Frosties (a prominent product name)
- Dave Thomas (a prominent person in the company)

✦ **Grouping 2:** Competitors

- McDonald's
- Burger King
- In-N-Out

✦ **Grouping 3:** Keyword-based searches (Burgers)

- Hamburgers
- Cheeseburgers

✦ **Grouping 4:** Keyword-based searches (Fast Food)

- Fast food
- Drive thru

✦ **Grouping 5:** Keyword-based searches (Chicken)

- Chicken sandwiches
- Chicken salad
- Chicken nuggets

In each of these groups, you place your Google Alerts feed, Twingly feed, and whatever other feeds you feel will provide information about that subject area. You can blend each group of feeds together into one master feed for that group and bring them into WordPress. Remember, WordPress limits you to five groups total. Any more than five groups slows down the Dashboard and is more than WordPress really can handle.

Grouping all these various feeds together gives you the most complete monitoring solution by covering multiple monitoring tools and blending them together. You get more coverage of your brand or blog than you would by just using Google Alerts, but on the downside, you may see some duplicates because of overlaps between the different services.

If you feel overwhelmed by duplicate search results, you can blend one feed that covers only your brand, or simplify setting up your monitoring even more and avoid blending the feeds by keeping one feed for each item. For example:

+ **General overview:** Google Alerts or Social Mention

+ **Message boards:** Board Reader

+ **Microblogging:** Twitter Search

Cleaning and combining your feeds

If you decide to blend your feeds together, you need to fine-tune them, and then splice them together. First, clean up the feeds to make them a little more targeted by using FeedRinse (www.feedrinse.com). To combine the cleaned feeds file, use xFruits (www.xfruits.com) to turn the file into a feed that you can bring into WordPress.

To clean your feeds by using FeedRinse and then combine it by using xFruits, follow these steps:

1. **Go to www.feedrinse.com.**

If you don't have an account, you need to set one up by clicking the Sign Up link on the FeedRinse home page. It takes just a few seconds and allows you to come back to edit these feed splices later. (See Figure 2-2.) After you sign up, remember to sign into FeedRinse in order to save your results.

2. **Click Add Feeds.**

A screen appears where you can bring in your feeds individually or by an OPML file. For our example, you bring in feeds individually, copy and paste the feed locations from the document you created of groups of feeds (see the preceding section). If you imported feeds into a feed reader such as Google Reader, you can import the entire OPML file to FeedRinse. (See Figure 2-3.)

Figure 2-2:
The
FeedRinse
sign-up
form.

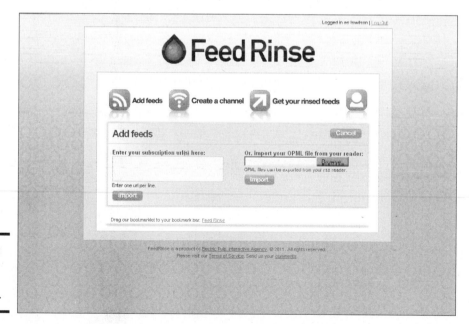

Figure 2-3:
Adding
feeds to
FeedRinse.

3. **Edit the contents of your feed.**

   If you didn't use Boolean search methods to narrow down the contents of your feed (which we suggest you do in the section "Exploring Different Listening Tools," earlier in this chapter) or you're still picking up terms in your results that don't relate to what you want to target, you can use the editing capabilities in FeedRinse to narrow down the contents of the feeds. Using FeedRinse editing really gives you a laser-focused feed. For each feed you import to FeedRinse, you can include or exclude posts based on the presence of selected keywords. If you want to monitor Caesars Palace in Las Vegas, for example, you can exclude all posts that mention Atlantic City or other locations. (See Figure 2-4)

4. **Click the Create a Channel icon. This will take you to a screen where you can name your feed.**

5. **Enter a name for your channel in the Give Your Channel a Name text box to keep track of it in the FeedRinse system.**

   After you enter a name for your channel, a drop-down list box appears with a plus-sign icon on the right.

6. **From the drop-down list, select the feed that you want to include in this channel, and then add it to the channel by clicking the plus-sign icon.**

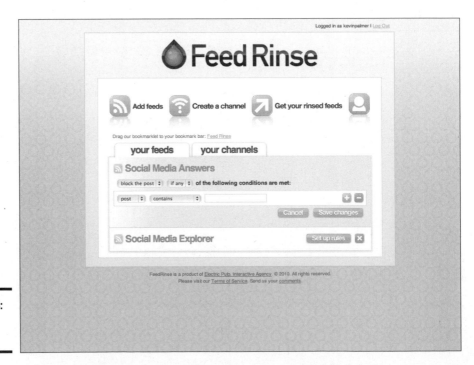

Figure 2-4:
Edit your
feeds.

7. **Repeat Step 6 to add all the feeds that you want. There is no limit to the number of feeds you can create.**

8. **After you add all the feeds to your channel, click the Save Changes button (see Figure 2-5).**

9. **Export your newly rinsed feed by clicking the Get Your Rinsed Feeds link, and then click the Copy Your Reading List Link button (see Figure 2-6).**

   Clicking this button combines the URLs of the new feeds before you import them into WordPress.

10. **Go to www.xfruits.com.**

11. **Click the Sign In link in the upper-right corner of the screen.**

   The Sign In page appears. If you don't have an account with xFruits, you need to sign up for one, which you can do on this page.

Figure 2-5:
Create a
channel.

Figure 2-6:
Export your
feeds.

12. **Fill in the appropriate text boxes and click the Sign Up or Sign In button.**

    A menu page appears, showing all the different xFruits RSS and OPML services.

13. **Choose the Aggregator RSS option.**

14. **Paste the URL that you copied in Step 9 into a Feed or OPML text box.**

15. **Enter a title for your feed in the Title text box.**

16. **(Optional) If you want make your feed public, add tags to it by typing them into the Tags text box.**

    When you make your feed public, other users can find it and use it.

17. **After you complete all the settings, click Aggregate My Feeds (see Figure 2-7).**

    Your feeds are now rinsed, exported to an OPML file, and combined into one RSS feed. The My xFruits screen appears, where it displays various feed combinations you've created. (See Figure 2-8.)

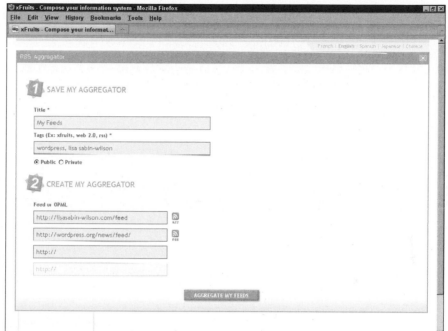

Figure 2-7:
Turning your
FeedRinse
file into RSS.

Figure 2-8:
Configuring
your file
export.

18. **Click the Aggregator RSS image, which is to the left of the list of latest blog posts for this section.**

This takes you to your new feed.

19. **Copy the URL in the Web browser and save it to a list to import to WordPress in the next step.**

That's the URL of your new feed! (See Figure 2-9.)

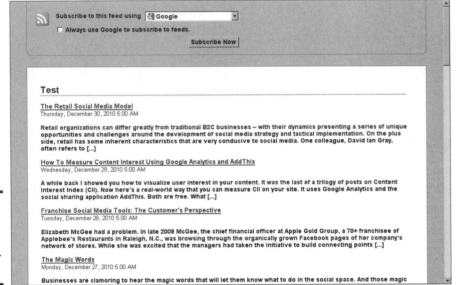

Figure 2-9:
Grabbing
the RSS file
from xFruits.
com.

20. **Repeat Steps 2 through 20 if you're setting up multiple feed groupings.**

For example, you might create one grouping about your competitors or different groupings based on different keywords.

Now that you have your feeds set up, you can bring them into the WordPress Dashboard.

Editing the Dashboard to Create a Listening Post

After you choose your data sources, clean up your feeds, and put them all in individual RSS feeds, you can finally bring them into WordPress and set up your social-media listening hub.

You can bring these RSS feeds into your Dashboard in two ways:

✦ **Edit your WordPress install by hand.** You can edit the trunk code (the core coding of WordPress), which WordPress provides in Trac at `http://core.trac.wordpress.org/browser/trunk//wp-admin/includes/dashboard.php`.

✦ **Use a plugin.** If you don't feel comfortable doing any type of editing to the code, you can just take the easy way out (or the most sane way) and use a plugin, which we recommend. Currently, I use the Dashboard Latest News plugin, which you can find in the plugin repository at `http://wordpress.org/extend/plugins/dashboard-last-news`.

Follow these steps to set up the Dashboard Last News plugin and configure it to create a social-listening Dashboard in WordPress.

1. **From the Plugins menu on the left side of your WordPress installation, choose Add New. This takes you to the form where you can search for new plugins.**

2. **In the Search text box, type** dashboard-last-news **and click Search Plugins.**

   The search results page appears.

3. **Search for the Dashboard-Last-News plugin and click the Install now link, which installs the plugin on your site.**

4. **After the installation is complete, activate the plugin by clicking Activate Plugin in the Installed Plugin menu that appears below the Plugin menu.**

5. **Click the Last News link in the Settings menu in the Dashboard.**

   A new menu appears, which you can use to select how many Dashboard widgets you want for your RSS.

6. **Select the number of Last News Dashboard widgets you want (up to five) in the drop-down menu on the Dashboard Last News page, and then click Update.**

7. **Click the Dashboard link in the menu on the left to go back to your Dashboard.**

   A Last News section that contains the widgets you created in step 6 appears in your Dashboard.

8. **To configure a widget, hover over the menu bar for that widget and, when the word Configure appears, click it.**

   The screen reloads, and you can now completely configure the widget.

9. **Enter a name for the widget in the Widget Title text box.**

You may want to name it according to the subject area it covers. The example dashboard has data coming in around Social Media and Design to go along with the terms we are monitoring.

10. **(Optional) Select the Image (Y/N) check box to add an image next to the individual search results in the widget.**

You may not want to include images because most of the images that are automatically pulled are voting option buttons or other feed image buttons, which don't add anything by having. Also, images slow down the load time.

11. **Select a number from the Lines to Display drop-down list, which specifies how many online entries that the monitoring tools have found that you want to appear in the widget.**

You can choose between 1 and 40.

12. **Paste the URL that you created in xFruits (as discussed in the preceding section) into the Fill the RSS or Atom URL Here text box and click Submit (see Figure 2-10).**

13. **Repeat Steps 8 through 12 for the other widgets on your Dashboard by using your other xFruits-generated feeds.**

Figure 2-10:
Configuring
the Last
News
widget.

Last News - 1   Cancel

Widget Title : Last News - 1

Image (y/n) : ☐   Feeds fields ? 3 ▾   Lines to display ?
10 ▾
Fill the RSS or Atom URL here :

Fill the RSS or Atom URL here :

Fill the RSS or Atom URL here :

(Submit)

After you have your feeds set up, you can configure the appearance of your WordPress Dashboard.

14. **Drag and drop the new widget boxes where you want them.**

15. **(Optional) Expand the number of columns and remove current widgets by clicking the Screen Options link in the upper-right corner of the Dashboard, and then selecting or deselecting the check boxes for the widgets in the drop-down list that appears.**

Chapter 3: Understanding Analytics

In This Chapter

✔ Understanding how analytics can tell you about your blog

✔ Choosing an analytics-tracking option

✔ Deciphering analytics terminology

✔ Working with Google Analytics

✔ Analyzing your WordPress blog posts with PostRank

*E*very business on the face of the Earth needs to figure out what works and what doesn't if it wants to succeed. Bloggers often know basic statistics about their blogs, such as the current number on their hit counters or how many people subscribe to their blogs. However, these stats just give you the big picture, and they don't really address why something is or isn't working.

You need to get at least a basic understanding of analytics if you want to leverage your blog to the fullest. The data provided by free programs such as Google Analytics can really help you grow as a blogger. In this chapter, we look at incorporating various data-measuring tools into your WordPress installation, deciphering what the data is telling you, and determining how to act on it.

Google Analytics provides you with a tremendous amount of information on your content. The goal of this chapter is to help you interpret the data, understand where your traffic is coming from, understand which of your content is the most popular among your visitors, know how to draw correlations between various data sets, and use this information to shape the content you write. This process may sound very geeky and accountant-like, but in reality, it gives you a road map that helps you improve your business.

Understanding the Importance of Analytics

I have an undergraduate degree in History, and I went to grad school for Digital Media Studies. This tells you that, besides the fact I targeted two worthless degrees, I'm not a fan of math and have avoided collegiate degrees that involve any type of math courses. In fact, I avoid math like my 7-year-old nephew avoids vegetables. People's eyes glaze over when they hear the word *analytics* followed by *stats,* any type of *percentages,* and anything that sounds like accountant-speak.

However, you should view analytics not as a bunch of numbers, but as a tool set that tells a story. It can tell you how people are finding your content, what content is most popular, and where users are sharing that content. Knowing what type of content is popular, where your site is popular (in which time zones, countries and states, for example), and even what time of day your posts get more readers is all pretty valuable information. Understanding your audience's interest in your content, as well as preferences for when and how to read your content, is important.

At one point in my life, I had a pretty popular humor blog. Through studying analytics and reactions to my content, I figured out that if I posted my blog between 9:30 a.m. and 10:00 a.m. EST, my posts garnered the most comments and got the most traffic throughout the day. When I posted after noon, my blog got about half as many comments and half as much traffic over a 24-hour period. Additionally, I saw that my site was getting shared and voted for on the social news site Reddit (`www.reddit.com`) more often than Digg, (`www.digg.com`), another social news site, so I replaced the Digg button with a Reddit button. This change increased the amount of traffic I received from Reddit because people had the visual reminder to share the post with their friends and vote the post as a favorite of theirs.

I was able to continue to drill down from there. Not only did I have the information on where my content was being shared, but I was also able to garner more information for analytics. Posts that had a picture mixed in with the first three paragraphs often had a lower bounce rate (the interval of time it takes for a visitor to visit my site, then 'bounce' away to a different site) than posts that had no picture at all. If I wrote the post while elevating my left leg and wearing a tinfoil helmet, I saw a 25 percent bump in traffic. (Okay, maybe that last one isn't true.)

Exploring the Options to Track Data

You have a lot of options when it comes to tracking data on your blog. Although Kevin prefers one specific solution, Google Analytics, we share with you some of the different options that you have. Analytics is popular because of its widespread use, the amount of content written on how to maximize it, and the fact that it is completely free.

Here are three popular tools:

✦ **StatCounter (`www.statcounter.com`):** StatCounter has both a free and a paid service. The paid service doesn't kick in until you get to 250K page views a month.

StatCounter (shown in Figure 3-1) uses the log generated by your server and gives you the ability to configure the reports to fit your needs. If you want to use a log file, you need to have a self-hosted blog and to know where your log file is to be stored. StatCounter requires a little more technical knowledge than your average analytics app because you have to deal with your log file instead of cutting and pasting a line of code into your site. The main advantage of StatCounter is that it is in real time, whereas Google Analytics always has a little bit of lag in its reporting.

✦ **WordPress.com Stats (`http://wordpress.org/extend/plugins/ stats`):** WordPress.com provides a pretty good stat package for its hosted-blog users. Shortly after launching, WordPress.com provided a WordPress Stats plugin that self-hosted users can use (see Figure 3-2). If you use this package, your stats appear on the WordPress Dashboard, but to drill down deeper into them, you need to access the stats on WordPress.com. The advantages of WordPress stats are that they are pretty easy to install and present a very simplified overview of your data. On the downside, they don't drill as deep as Analytics and the reporting isn't as in-depth. With Analytics you can customize numerous reports, which you can't do with WordPress stats.

Figure 3-1: StatCounter.

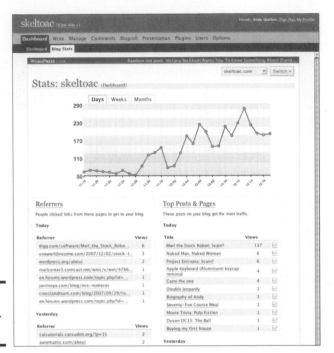

Figure 3-2:
WordPress.
com Stats.

✦ **Google Analytics (`www.google.com/analytics`):** Google Analytics can seem overwhelming when you sit down in front of it for the first time, but it has the most robust stats features this side of Omniture. (Omniture is an enterprise-level stats package.) Also, because Google has opened the analytics platform up to developers, some pretty cool innovations for bloggers and social-media people are on the way. This recent development gives you reason enough to try out the platform.

WordPress plugins (which we cover in the section "Signing Up and Installing Google Analytics on Your WordPress Site," later in this chapter) bring a simplified version of Google Analytics (see Figure 3-3) to your WordPress Dashboard (much like the WordPress.com Stats plugin). Most bloggers are very interested in the general statistics of their Web site but feel overwhelmed by Google Analytics. Even with some training, they still prefer to have their stats broken down in a much more digestible fashion. This plugin is for them: It allows for a good overview of their analytics information, including goals that bloggers can set up within analytics. Although the plugin doesn't offer everything that Google Analytics brings to the table, it provides more than enough so that users can see the overall health of their Web sites and monitor where their traffic is coming from, what posts are popular, and how people are finding their Web sites. Besides the Dashboard Stats Overview, this plugin gives a breakdown of traffic to each post, which is a nice added bonus because it gives you a breakdown of traffic to each of your posts daily.

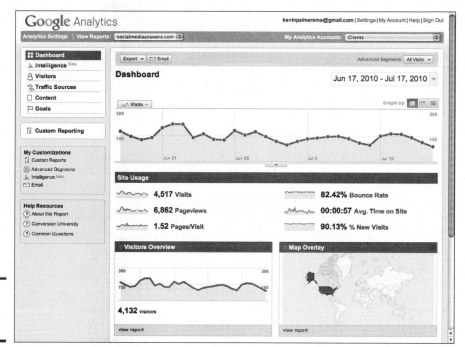

Figure 3-3:
Google
Analytics.

Understanding Key Analytics Terminology

One of the reasons that people find analytics programs so overwhelming is their obscure terminology and jargon. Here, we've taken the time to define some of the more popular terms (we even spent the time putting them in alphabetical order for you; you can thank us later):

✦ **Bounce rate:** The percentage of single-page visits or visits in which the person leaves your site from the entrance page. This metric measures visit quality — a high bounce rate generally indicates that visitors don't find your site entrance pages relevant to them.

   In the eyes of e-commerce, bounce rate speaks to the quality of your entrance page. The more compelling your landing pages, the more visitors stay on your site and convert into purchasers, subscribers, or whatever action you want them to complete. You can minimize bounce rates by tailoring landing pages to each ad that you run (in the case of businesses) or to the audience based on the referring (for example, if you create a special bio page for your Twitter profile). Landing pages should provide the information and services that the ad promises.

   When it comes to blogging, a high bounce rate from a social-media source (like a social news site like Digg) can tell you that users didn't find the content interesting, and a high bounce rate from search engines can mean that your site isn't what users thought they were getting. In blogging, having a low bounce rate really speaks to the quality of the content on your site. If you get a lot of search and social-media traffic, a bounce rate below 50 percent is a number you want to strive for.

✦ **Content:** The different pages within the site (the Content menu of Google Analytics breaks these pages down where they have their own statistics).

✦ **Dashboard:** The interface with the overall summary of your analytics data. It's the first page you see when you log in to Google Analytics.

✦ **Direct traffic:** When Web visitors reach your site by typing your Web address directly into their browsers' address bars. (Launching a site by a bookmark also falls into this category.) You can get direct-traffic visitors because of an offline promotion, repeat readers, word of mouth, or simply from your business card.

✦ **First-time unique visitor:** This metric tracks the number of visitors to your Web site who haven't visited prior to the time frame you're analyzing.

✦ **Hit:** Any request to the Web server for any type of file, not just a post in your blog, including a page, an image (JPEG, GIF, PNG, and so on), a sound clip, or any of several other file types. An HTML page can account for several hits: the page itself, each image on the page, and any embedded sound or video clips. Therefore, the number of hits a Web site receives doesn't give you a valid popularity gauge, but rather indicates server use and how many files have been loaded.

✦ **Keyword:** A database index entry that identifies a specific record or document. (That definition sounds way more fancy than a keyword actually is.) Keyword searching is the most common form of text search on the Web. Most search engines do their text query and retrieval by using keywords. Unless the author of the Web document specifies the keywords for his or her document (which you can do by using meta tags), the search engine has to determine them. (So you can't guarantee how Google indexes the page.) Essentially, search engines pull out and index words that it determines are significant. A search engine is more likely to deem words important if those words appear toward the beginning of a document and are repeated several times throughout the document.

✦ **Meta tag:** A special HTML tag that provides information about a Web page. Unlike normal HTML tags, meta tags don't affect how the page appears in a user's browser. Instead, meta tags provide information such as who created the page, how often it's updated, a title for the page, a description of the page's content, and what keywords represent the page's content. Many search engines use this information when they build their indexes, although most major search engines rarely index the `keywords` meta tag anymore because it has been abused by people trying to game search results.

✦ **Pageview:** A *page* is defined as any file or content delivered by a Web server that would generally be considered a Web document, which includes HTML pages (.html, .htm, .shtml), posts or pages within a WordPress installation, script-generated pages (.cgi, .asp, .cfm), and plain-text pages. It also includes sound files (.wav, .aiff, and so on), video files (.mov, .mpeg, and so on), and other nondocument files. Only image files (.jpeg, .gif, .png), JavaScript (.js), and Cascading Style Sheets (.css) are excluded from this definition. Each time a file defined as a page is served, or viewed in a visitors Web browser, a *pageview* is registered by Google Analytics. The pageview statistic is more important and accurate than a hit statistic because it doesn't include images or other items that may register hits to your site.

✦ **Path:** A series of clicks that result in distinct pageviews. A path can't contain non-pages, such as image files.

✦ **Referrals:** A *referral* occurs when a user clicks any hyperlink that takes him or her to a page or file in another Web site; it could be text, an image, or any other type of link. When a user arrives at your site from another site, the server records the referral information in the hit log for every file requested by that user. If the user found the link by using a search engine, the server records the search engine's name and any keywords used, as well. Referrals give you an indication of what social-media site, as well as links from other Web sites and blogs, are directing traffic to your blog.

✦ **Referrer:** The URL of an HTML page that refers visitors to a site.

✦ **Traffic sources:** This metric tells you how visitors found your Web site — either via direct traffic, referring sites, or search engines.

✦ **Unique visitors:** The number of unduplicated (counted only once) visitors to your Web site over the course of a specified time period. The server determines a unique visitor by using *cookies*, small tracking files stored in your visitors' browsers that keep track of the number of times they visit your site.

✦ **Visitor:** A stat designed to come as close as possible to defining the number of actual, distinct people who visit a Web site. The Web site, of course, can't really determine whether any one "visitor" is really two people sharing a computer, but a good visitor-tracking system can come close to the actual number. The most accurate visitor-tracking systems generally employ cookies to maintain tallies of distinct visitors.

Signing Up and Installing Google Analytics on Your WordPress Site

Because we've pretty much made the decision for you to use Google Analytics, in the following sections, we walk you through the necessary steps to sign up for Google Analytics, install it on your blog, and add the WordPress plugin to your site.

Signing up for Google Analytics

In order to sign up for Google Analytics, follow these steps:

1. **Go to: www.google.com/analytics and click the Sign Up Now button, which is located on the right side of the page, below the Access Analytics button.**

   A page where you can sign up for a Google account or sign in via an existing Google account appears. If you don't have a Google account, follow the link to sign up for one.

2. **Sign in via your Google account by entering your Google e-mail address and password in the text boxes and then clicking Sign In.**

   The first of a series of walk-through pages appears.

3. **Click the Sign Up button.**

4. **On the General Information page that appears (see Figure 3-4), enter the URL of your Web site and the name you want to call your account (this really doesn't matter; you can call it your Web site's name) in the appropriate text boxes, and select the country and time zone you're in from the drop-down lists.**

5. **After you fill out this information, click the Continue button.**

Figure 3-4: Entering your first URL in Google Analytics.

6. **On the Contact Information page that appears (see Figure 3-5), enter your first name and last name in the text boxes, and select the country or territory you reside in from the drop-down list.**

7. **After you complete this information, click the Continue button.**

   The page that appears displays the Google Terms of Service Agreement, which you have to accept.

8. **Select the check box to accept the Google Terms of Service Agreement.**

9. **Click the Edit Settings link below the terms of service.**

   After the terms of service, a new page appears where you can select how much of your analytics data is shared with Google. Read through this information and make an informed decision about how much of your data you want to make available. If you use Google Adwords (used for advertising on the Google search and content network), you may want to give permission to allow access to Google products but not third parties because you should be cautious about who has general data about your site after that data is entered in.

10. **Click the Create New Account button.**

    On the page that appears, Google Analytics provides you with your Google tracking code.

Figure 3-5:
The Contact
Information
page.

11. **Copy this code (see Figure 3-6) by selecting it and pressing Ctrl+C.**

Paste the Google tracking code into your WordPress blog in the following section. When you've added the tracking code on your site, click the Save and Finish button.

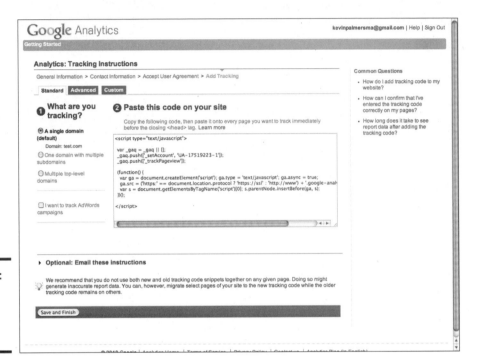

Figure 3-6:
Get your
Google
Analytics
code.

Installing the tracking code

After you set up your Google Analytics account and obtain the code to install in your WordPress site, you're ready for the installation. You can install Google Analytics pretty simply by following these steps:

1. **Go to your WordPress Dashboard and log in.**

If you have a theme framework, such as Genesis or Thesis, you can paste the code in the theme's Options page, or if you're using one of the many Google for WordPress plugins, you can paste the code in the Plugin Options page. However, we recommend that you paste the code directly into your footer (the `footer.php` template file within your theme) because this location works for pretty much all WordPress-designed sites.

2. **Click the Appearance menu in the Dashboard, and select Editor below the appearance menu header.**

   The Edit Themes page loads in your browser window.

3. **From the Templates menu on the right side of the Edit Themes page, click Footer. This shows you the coding for the footer in the text box on the left side.**

4. **Paste the Google Tracking code in the Footer Template file.**

   Paste the code that you copied by pressing Ctrl+V. Be sure to paste the code before the close body tag (</body>).

5. **Click Update File.**

   Figure 3-7 shows an example footer code.

You have to put this code *before* the close body tag, not after. If you put it after the close body tag, the code doesn't function.

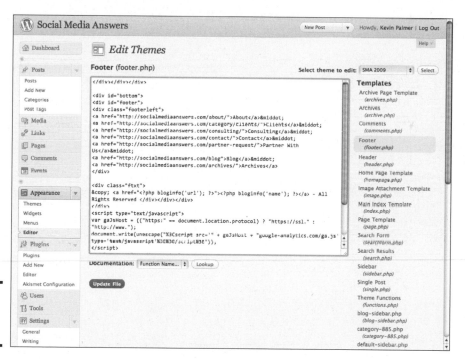

Figure 3-7:
An example footer code.

Verifying that you installed the code properly

After you install your code, check whether you installed it correctly. When you log back in to Google Analytics, your Dashboard appears (see Figure 3-8). A green check box in the Status column means that you're good to go. A stopwatch icon in that column means that the tracking code has been detected and is waiting for data to report. A yellow triangle (like the one in Figure 3-8) means that Google hasn't picked up the tracking code yet. Verification can take anywhere from minutes to hours, so if it isn't working correctly right away, don't panic. If you don't see the stopwatch icon within 24 hours, try to reinstall the code.

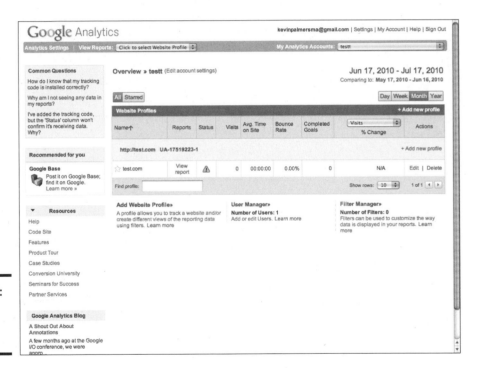

Figure 3-8:
Tracking code not working.

Installing and configuring the Analytics plugin

After you install Google Analytics on your WordPress site and make sure that the tracking code is working properly, you can install the plugin so that you can get a basic version of your stats right on your WordPress Dashboard. Just follow these steps:

1. **Log in to your WordPress account.**

Your WordPress Dashboard appears.

2. **From the Plugins menu, select Add New.**

   A search box appears so you can search for the plugin.

3. **In the Search text box, type** google analytics dashboard **and click the Install Now button.**

   This takes you to the plugin installation screen.

4. **Activate the plugin by clicking the Activate plugin button on the Plugin Installation menu.**

5. **On the WordPress Dashboard, select Google Analytics Dashboard in the Settings section.**

   The screen that pops up asks you to provide your log in information for Google Analytics.

6. **Enter your information and click Save Options to log in.**

   A configuration page appears (see Figure 3-9).

7. **From the Available Accounts drop-down list, select the analytics account from which you want to pull your stats.**

8. **(Optional) Select the check boxes to remove your password and authentication information from Google.**

   You select these check boxes if you want to deactivate the plugin. If you only select to forget password or forget authentication, you will have to log back in to the menu like in Step 6.

9. **Specify the level (or role, such as Administrator, Contributor, and so on) of WordPress users who can see the stats by selecting an option from the Dashboard Level drop-down list. This is good for blogs that have multiple authors.**

10. **Label your goals within analytics by entering the titles of your goals in the text boxes.**

    Goal labels can help people who are tracking specific metrics, such as sales, sign-ups, or other actions, to see if people are converting.

11. **Click Save Changes.**

    The plugin appears on your Dashboard.

12. **Drag and drop the plugin to the position you prefer.**

    Figure 3-10 shows a WordPress Dashboard with the Google Analytics plugin.

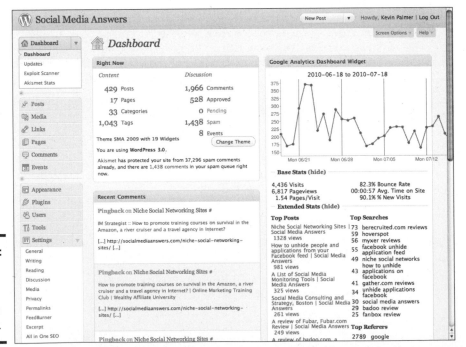

Figure 3-9:
The Google
Analytics
configu-
ration page.

Figure 3-10:
Google
Analytics
on your
WordPress
Dashboard.

Using the data from the plugin

After you install Google Analytics on your WordPress Dashboard, you can examine the data it provides. Your Dashboard displays two basic groups of stats:

✦ **A general overview:** The stats here include the amount of visits, pageviews, pageviews per visit, bounce rate, average time on site, and the percent of new visits. This information gives you a good overview of the base stats of your blog.

✦ **An extended stats section:** Stats here include the most popular post over the last 30 days, the top searches that found your site, and the top referrers. These stats show you the most popular content on your site, the ways people are finding your site, and the sources of your traffic. If you want get even more detailed information, go to the Posts section on WordPress (see Figure 3-11), where you can find per-page stats for each of your posts and pages. Each breakdown has a chart, number of pageviews, number of exits, and the number of unique pageviews.

By examining the two data sets, you can get a handle on the traffic that's coming to your blog. We recommend paying attention to the following questions:

✦ What posts are popular?

✦ Do the popular posts have a unique theme or type?

✦ Do long posts or short posts help increase traffic?

✦ Do videos, lists, or any other type of specific posts give you more traffic than the rest?

The answers to these questions can help you draw various conclusions and adapt your publishing schedule, content type, and writing style to optimize the popularity of your blog.

Figure 3-11:
A per-post
breakdown,
using
Google
Analytics for
WordPress.

Using PostRank with WordPress

PostRank (www.postrank.com) is a service that gathers data about blog posts, showing how many comments, tweets, bookmarks, and other various shares have been applied to those posts through social media. PostRank takes all this data, combines it with some analytics data, and then rates your post on a scale from 1 to 10.

Within the PostRank system, you can also rank blogs within your niche, subscribe to blogs, and even get expanded analytics (expanded analytics do cost a small monthly fee).

Combining the PostRank plugin with Google Analytics shows you the numbers related to how users view, share, or discuss your posts in various social-media outlets — and PostRank also shows you specifically where these discussions are taking place, which Google Analytics doesn't do. You can use this information to figure out how much your posts need to be shared to obtain the numbers you're seeing from Twitter, Delicious, and other services.

To install the PostRank plugin, follow these steps:

1. **Log in to your WordPress account.**

Your WordPress Dashboard appears.

2. **From the Plugins drop-down list, choose Add New.**

   The search menu appears so you can search for the plugin, using key-words of your choice.

3. **In the Search text box, type** postrank **and click Search Plugins.**

   A page of search results appears.

4. **Click Install next to the PostRank plugin.**

5. **After the installation is complete, Activate the plugin by clicking the Activate plugin button on the Plugin Installation page.**

6. **Select Postrank under the Settings section on the left sidebar.**

   Make sure that the two check boxes (Display PostRanks on Admin Pages and Display the PostRank Analytics Dashboard Widget) are checked so that the PostRank data appears on your Dashboard.

   The plugin widget appears on yourDashboard; click the Dashboard menu link to view your main Dashboard page to see the new PostRanks Widget.

7. **Drag and drop the widget to the position you prefer.**

   Figure 3-12 shows a WordPress Dashboard with the PostRank widget.

The PostRank plugin also allows you to see the per-post detail for each post on the Posts page in your Dashboard (click the Posts link in the Dashboard menu to view the Posts page).

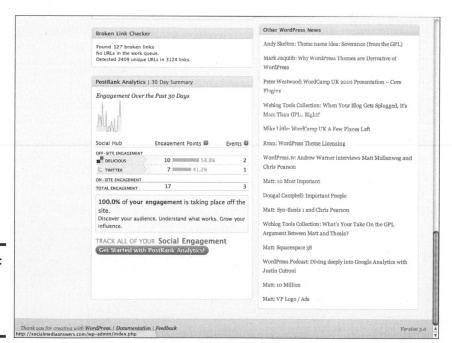

Figure 3-12:
The PostRank Dashboard widget.

Broken Link Checker

Found 127 broken links
No URLs in the work queue.
Detected 2409 unique URLs in 3124 links.

PostRank Analytics | 30 Day Summary

Engagement Over the Past 30 Days

Social Hub	Engagement Points 📊	Events 📊
OFF-SITE ENGAGEMENT		
DELICIOUS	10 ▪▪▪▪ 58.8%	2
TWITTER	7 ▪▪▪ 41.2%	1
ON-SITE ENGAGEMENT		
TOTAL ENGAGEMENT	17	3

100.0% of your engagement is taking place off the site.
Discover your audience. Understand what works. Grow your influence.

TRACK ALL OF YOUR **Social Engagement**
Get Started with PostRank Analytics!

Other WordPress News

Andy Skelton: Theme name idea: Severance (from the GPL)

Mark Jaquith: Why WordPress Themes are Derivative of WordPress

Peter Westwood: WordCamp UK 2010 Presentation – Core Plugins

Weblog Tools Collection: When Your Blog Gets Splogged, It's More Than GPL.. Right?

Mike Little WordCamp UK A Few Places Left

Ryan: WordPress Theme Licensing

WordPress.tv: Andrew Warner interviews Matt Mullenweg and Chris Pearson

Matt: 10 Most Important

Dougal Campbell: Important People

Matt: Syn-thesis 1 and Chris Pearson

Weblog Tools Collection: What's Your Take On the GPL Argument Between Matt and Thesis?

Matt: Squarespace 38

WordPress Podcast: Diving deeply into Google Analytics with Justin Cutroni

Matt: 10 Million

Matt: VP Logo / Ads

Thank you for creating with WordPress. | Documentation | Feedback
http://socialmediaanswers.com/wp-admin/index.php

Version 3.0

Chapter 4: Search Engine Optimization

In This Chapter

✔ Appreciating search engine optimization (SEO) benefits

✔ Improving your SEO with WordPress

✔ Getting your blog into good SEO shape

✔ Finding information about your niche

✔ Creating SEO-improvement strategies

Google, Yahoo!, Bing, and other search engines have a massive impact on a blog. Search engines can easily refer the largest amount of traffic to your site and, if dealt with properly, can help you grow a large audience in time. Often, bloggers don't discover the importance of search engine optimization (SEO) until their blogs have been around for a while. By taking the time to make sure that you're following SEO best practices from the get-go, you can reap the rewards of a consistent flow of search engine traffic.

If you've been blogging for a while and haven't been following the practices in this chapter, roll up your sleeves and dive back into your blog to fix some of the SEO practices that you may have overlooked (or just didn't know about) over the history of your blog. If you've been blogging for only a few months, this process doesn't take long; if you have a large backlog of content, well . . . pull up a chair — this fix is going to take a while. Either way, don't worry. You're in safe hands. This chapter helps you through the difficult task of optimizing your site for search engines.

Understanding the Importance of Search Engine Optimization

Talk about search engine optimization (SEO) usually puts most people to sleep. We're not going to lie: Hardcore SEO is a time-consuming job that requires a strong analytical mind. Casual bloggers, or even most small-business owners, don't need to understand all the minute details that go into SEO. However, everyone with a web site that desires traffic needs to get familiar with some of the basic concepts and best practices. Why, you ask?

One thousand pageviews. That's why.

Of course, you're not going to get 1,000 page views right off the bat by changing your SEO.

SEO deals with following best practices when it comes to blogging. By just following these simple guidelines and by using WordPress, you can increase search engine traffic to your blog. Period. To be honest, you probably won't rank number one in really tough categories just by following SEO best practices. But you definitely can increase your traffic significantly and improve your rank for some long-tail keywords. Long-tail keywords are keywords that aren't searched for often, but when you amass ranking for a lot of them over a period of time, the traffic adds up.

Bloggers want as many search results as possible on the first two pages of Google and other search engines to be from their blogs. (Most search-engine visitors don't go past the first two pages of Google.) This search-results aim is a more reasonable goal than trying to rank number one for a highly competitive keyword. If you really do want to rank number one in a competitive space, check out sites such as SEO Book (www.seobook.com) or SEOmoz (www.seomoz.org), which can help you achieve that difficult goal.

Outlining the Advantages That WordPress Presents for SEO

Using WordPress for your blogging platform or content management system, comes with some advantages, including that WordPress was designed to function well with search engines. Search engines can crawl the source code of a WordPress site pretty easily, which eliminates issues that a lot of Web programmers face when optimizing a site. The following list outlines some of WordPress's SEO advantages:

✦ **Permalinks:** URLs where your content is permanently housed. While your blog grows and you add more posts, the items on your front page get pushed off the front page of your blog and are replaced by recent content. Visitors can easily bookmark and share permalinks so that they can return to that specific post on your blog, so these old posts can live on. One of the technical benefits of WordPress is that it uses the Apache `mod_rewrite` module to establish the permalink system, which allows you to create and customize your permalink structure.

✦ **Pinging:** When you post new content, WordPress has a built-in pinging system that notifies major indexes automatically so that they can come and crawl your site again. This system helps speed up the indexing process and keeps your search results current and relevant.

✦ **Plugins:** The fact that WordPress is so developer friendly allows you to use the latest SEO plugins. Do you want to submit a sitemap to Google? There's a plugin for that. Do you want to edit the metadata around a post? There's a plugin for that. Do you want to alert Google News every time you post? Guess what . . . there's a plugin for that, too. With over 10,000 plugins available at press time, you can use an advanced and eager plugin ecosystem to help power your blog. We cover plugins in-depth in Chapter 5 of this minibook.

✦ **Theme construction:** SEO, social media, and design all go hand in hand. You can push a ton of people to your Web page by using proper SEO and robust social-media profiles, but if your blog has a confusing or poorly done design, visitors aren't going to stay. Likewise, a poorly designed site prevents a lot of search engines from reading your content.

In this situation, *poorly designed* doesn't refer to aesthetics — how your site looks to the eye. Search engines ignore the style of your site and your CSS, for the most part. But the structure, the coding, of your site can affect search engines that are attempting to crawl your site. WordPress is designed to accommodate search engines: It doesn't overload pages with coding so that search engines can easily access the site. A large percentage of WordPress themes have valid code (code that is up to standards based on the recommendations from `www.w3c.org`, The World Wide Web Consortium): Right from the start, having valid code allows search engines to access your site much more easily.

When you start changing your code or adding a lot of plugins to your site, check to see whether your code validates. Validated code means that the code on your Web site fits a minimum standard for browsers. Otherwise, you could be preventing search engines from easily crawling your sites.

If you want to check out whether your site validates, use the free W3C validator tool at `http://validator.w3.org`. (See Figure 4-1.)

Figure 4-1:
The W3C
Markup
Validation
Service.

Understanding How Search Engines See Your Content

Search engines don't care what your site looks like because they can't see what your site looks like; their crawlers care only about the content. The crawls care about the material in your blog, the way it's titled, the words you use, and the way you structure them.

You need to keep this focus in mind when you create the content of your blog. Your URL structure and the keywords, post titles, and images you use in posts all have an impact on how your blog ranks. Having a basic understanding about how search engines view your content can help you write content more attractive to search engines. Here are a few key areas to think about when you craft your content:

✦ **Keywords in content:** Search engines take an intense look at the keywords or combination of keywords you use. Keywords are often compared to the words found within links guiding people back to the post and in the title of the post itself to see if they match. The better these keywords align, the better ranking you get from the search engine.

✦ **Post title:** Search engines analyze the title of your blog post for keyword content. If you're targeting a specific keyword in your post and that keyword is mentioned throughout the post, mention it in the post title, as well. Also, both people and search engines place a lot of value on the early words of a title.

✦ **URL structure:** One of the coolest things about WordPress is the way it allows you to edit permalinks from within a post page. (See Figure 4-2.) You can always edit the URL to be slightly different from the automated post title so that it contains relevant keywords for search terms, especially if you write a cute title for the post.

For example, say you write a post about reviewing Facebook applications and title it "So Many Facebook Applications, So Little Time." You can change the URL structure to something much more keyword based — perhaps something like `facebook-applications-review`. This reworking removes a lot of the fluff words from the URL and goes right after keywords you want to target.

Figure 4-2:
Editing a
permalink.

✦ **Image titles and other image information:** Probably the single most-missed item Kevin sees when he begins helping a client with his or her SEO. You need to fill out the image information for your posts because this is a powerful way for people to discover your content and an additional piece of content that can tie keywords to your posts. (See Figure 4-3.) This information includes the filename of your image. Saving an image file to your site as `DS-039.jpg` offers nothing for readers or search engines, and thus has no value to search engines or for you because it doesn't contain a real keyword. Name a picture of a Facebook Application, for example, as `Facebook-application.jpg`. Leverage the keyword title and alt tags (alternative text added to the image within the HTML markup that tell search engines what the picture is) because they provide extra content for the search engines to see and using them can help you get a little more keyword saturation within your posts.

Figure 4-3: The Add an Image page.

Using links as currency

If content is king, then links are the currency that keeps the king in power. No matter how good a site you have, how great your content, and how well you optimize that content, you need links. Search engines assess the links flowing into your site for number and quality, and evaluate your Web site accordingly.

If a high-quality site that has a high Google Page Rank (a value from 0 to 10) features a link to your page, search engines take notice and assume that you have authority on a subject. Search engines consider these high-quality links more important than low-quality links. However, having a good amount of mid-quality links can help, as well. (This tactic, like many well-known approaches to improving site rank, is based only on trial and error. Google keeps its algorithm a secret, so no one knows for sure.)

Getting listed on a blogroll, having a pingback or trackback when a blogger mentions your content in their posts, or even leaving a comment on someone's blog can provide links back into your site. If you want to check out how many links you currently have coming into your site, go to Google and type **link:www.yoursite.com** into the search text box and click Google Search. You can also search for competitor's sites to see where they're listed and to what sites they're linked.

Although you do need to try and get other sites to link to your site (called outside links) because outside links factor into search engine algorithms, you can help your own ranking by adding internal links, as well. If you have an authoritative post on a particular subject, you should link internally to these posts or pages within your site. Take ESPN.com, for example: The first time it mentions an athlete in an article, it links to the profile of that athlete on the site. It essentially tells the search engines each time they visit ESPN.com that the player profile has relevancy, and the search engine indexes it. If you repeatedly link some of your internal pages that are gaining page rank to a profile page over a period of time, that profile page is going to garner a higher search engine ranking (especially if external sites are linking to it, too).

This internal and external linking strategy uses the concept of pillar posts (authoritative or popular), in which you have a few pages of content that you consider high value and try to build external and internal links into them so that you can get these posts ranked highly on search results.

Submitting to search engines and directories

After you get some content onto your Web site (the rule of thumb is usually ten posts or so), submit your blog to some search engines. Plenty of sites out there charge you to submit your site to search engines, but honestly, you can submit your site easily yourself. Also, with the help of some plugins (described in Book V, Chapter 5), you can get your information to search engines even more easily than you may think.

After you submit your Web site or sitemap, a search engine reviews it for search engine crawling errors; if everything checks out, you're on your way to having your site crawled and indexed. This process — from the submission of your site through its first appearance in search-engine results — can easily take four to six weeks. So be patient: Don't resubmit and don't freak out that search engines are never going to list your site. Give it time.

Not to be confused with search engines are Web site and blog directories. Directories can lead to a small amount of traffic, and some directories, such as dmoz (`www.dmoz.org`), actually supply information to search engines and other directories. The main benefit of getting listed in directories isn't really traffic, but rather the amount of backlinks (links to your site from other Web sites) you can build into your site.

Kevin has compiled a large list of blog/Web site directories at `http://socialmediaanswers.com/blog-directory-list-and-rss-directory-list`.

Although submitting your blog to directories may not be as important as submitting to search engines, you may still want to do it. Because filling out 40 or more forms is pretty monotonous, create a single document in which you prewrite all the necessary information: site title, URL, description, contact information, and your registration information. This template helps speed up the submission process to these sites.

Optimizing Your Blog under the Hood

Some optimization concepts really happen "under the hood" — you can't readily see these adjustments on your page, but they have an impact on how search engines deal with your content.

Metadata

The metadata on a Web site contains the information that describes to search engines what your site is about. Additionally, the information often contained in the metadata shows up as the actual search engine results in Google. The search engine pulls the page title and page description that appear in search results from the header of your blog. If you do nothing to control this information, Google and other search engines often pull their description from the page title and the first few sentences of a blog post.

Although the title and the first few sentences sound good in principle, they probably don't represent what your blog post is actually about. You probably don't sum up your post topic in the first two sentences of that post. Those first few lines likely aren't the best ad copy or the most enticing information. Thankfully, some plugins (such as the WordPress All in One SEO Pack plugin found in the WordPress plugin directory at `http://wordpress.org/extend/plugins/all-in-one-seo-pack`) allow you to control these details on a post and page level. Additionally, theme frameworks (see Book VI, Chapter 7) like Genesis or Thesis offer you more control over your SEO information.

Include descriptive page titles, descriptions, and targeted keywords for each post via these plugins or frameworks: This information has an impact on your results and often helps people decide to click the link to your Web site.

Robots.txt

When a search engine goes to your Web site, it first looks at your `robots.txt` file to get the information about what it should and shouldn't be looking for, and where to look.

You can alter your `robots.txt` file to direct search engines to the information that they should crawl and to give specific content priority over other content. Several plugins allow you to configure your `robots.txt` file, which we cover in Book V, Chapter 5.

Researching Your Niche

When you're working to improve your SEO, you can use a lot of publicly available data. This data can help you determine where you should try to get links and what type of content you may want to target. These two sites can help you get a general picture of the niche you're working in:

✦ **Google (www.google.com):** In the section "Using links as currency," earlier in this chapter, we tell you how you can find what types of links are flowing into a Web site by typing **link:www.*yoursite.com*** into the Google search text box and clicking Google Search. (Replace *yoursite.com* with the domain you want to target.) Google gives you a list of the sites linking to your site. By doing this search for other Web sites in your niche, you can find out the sources of their links — industry-specific directories you may not know about, places where they've guest blogged, or other resource sites that you may be able to get listed on.

This data gives you information about what to target for a link-building campaign.

✦ **SEMRush (www.semrush.com):** SEMRush (see Figure 4-4) offers both paid and free versions, and spending a few dollars for a month's access to the light version of the product can be a good investment. (The free version lets you look up only ten results at a time.) SEMRush allows you to see the terms for which other Web sites rank. Use this information to judge the health of the competitor's domain, the number of terms for which it ranks in Google's top 20, and the terms themselves.

You can use this information in a lot of different ways. For example, you can see what terms you might want to work into your content. SEMRush provides not only information about what terms search engines use to rank these sites, but also how competitive some of those keywords are with other web sites that are similar to yours.

Figure 4-4:
SEMRush.

Creating Search Engine Strategies

You can use the general concepts of why WordPress is good for SEO, the importance of your content, and researching your niche that we discuss in previous sections of this chapter when you set up your blog, write strategic content, and begin to build links into your Web site.

Setting up your blog

When setting up your blog, you are going to want to follow some best practices to make sure that your site is optimized for search engines. Some of these best practices include

✦ **Permalinks:** First, set up your permalink structure. Log in to your WordPress account and, on your sidebar, select Permalinks in the Settings section. The Permalink Settings page appears (see Figure 4-5). Select the Custom Structure radio button and type **/%*postname*%/** into the text box.

Making this change gives you a URL that contains just your domain and the title of your blog post. If you use a really focused category structure in which you've carefully picked out keywords, you may want to add the category to the URL. In that case, you enter **/%*category*%/%*postname*%/** in the text box.

Figure 4-5: The WordPress Permalinks Settings page.

Avoid using the default URL structure, which includes just the number of your post, and don't use dates in the URL. These numbers have no real value when doing SEO. WordPress by default numbers all your posts and pages with specific ID numbers. If you have not set up a custom permalink structure in WordPress, permalinks for your posts end up looking something like this: `http://yourdomain.com/?p=12` (where 12 is the specific post ID number). Although these numbers are used for many WordPress features, including exclusions of data and cus-tomized RSS feeds, you don't want these numbers in your URLs because they do not contain any keywords that describe what the post is about.

Also, if you already have an established blog and are just now setting up these permalinks, you must take the time to install a redirection plugin. You can find several of these plugins available in the Plugin section on WordPress.org. You must establish a redirection for your older posts so that you don't lose the links that search engines, like Google and Yahoo!, have already indexed for your site. One good redirection plugin to use is simply called Redirection, and can be found in the WordPress plugin directory here: `http://wordpress.org/extend/plugins/redirection`.

+ **Privacy:** You don't want your blog to fail to be indexed because you didn't set the correct privacy settings. In the WordPress Settings menu, click the Privacy link. In the resulting Privacy page, make sure that the I Would Like My Site to Be Visible to Everyone radio button is checked.

The other radio button, I Would Like to Block Search Engines, but Allow Normal Visitors, if checked, blocks search engines, which kind of defeats the purpose of everything we discuss in this chapter.

Improving your blog's design

After improving your setup in the back end of your blog, you will want to make some changes to your design so your blog works better with search engines. Some improvements you can make to your theme templates include

+ **Breadcrumbs:** Breadcrumbs, often overlooked when creating a Web site, provide the valuable navigation usually seen above the title on a blog post. (See Figure 4-6.) Breadcrumbs are pretty valuable for usability and search engine navigation. They allow the average user to navigate the site easily, and they help search engines determine the structure and layout of your site. A good plugin to use to create breadcrumb navi-gation is called Yoast Breadcrumbs and can be found in the WordPress plugin directory here: `http://wordpress.org/extend/plugins/breadcrumbs`.

Breadcrumbs

Figure 4-6:
Users and
search
engines can
follow the
breadcrumbs.

✦ **Validated code and speed:** If you're not a professional Web designer, probably you don't do a lot of coding to your site. So we don't go in-depth on the proper use of JavaScript or how best to optimize your code. But if you make some small edits to your WordPress installation or add a lot of code through widgets, do it properly by putting it directly into your CSS, rather than coding into your site. Coding these features properly helps improve the speed of your site, how quickly it loads, and how search engines crawl the site. Book VI contains a great deal of information about coding the templates in your theme; check out that book for more information about correct coding.

When it comes to improving site speed, proper code has a lot to do with the performance of your site. You can take other steps to help improve the speed of your site, such as installing caching plugins, such as the W3 Total Cache plugin (`http://wordpress.org/extend/plugins/w3-total-cache`). The quality of your hosting (Book II, Chapter 1), the size of your image files (make sure that you set image-file quality to Web standards), the amount of images you're using, and third-party widgets or scripts (like installing a widget provided by Twitter or Facebook) can all impact the speed and performance of your site. If you are putting special widgets developed by sites like blog catalog, traffic exchange sites, or banner exchange sites, these require information from other sites to load. Depending on these other sites for quick load times can often lead to slow loading times on your own site.

✦ **Pagination:** Another basic design feature often overlooked when setting up a site, *pagination* creates bottom navigation that allows people and search engines to navigate to other pages. (See Figure 4-7.) Pagination can really help both people and search engines navigate through your category pages.

Figure 4-7:
Pagination
in action.

Most themes don't have built-in pagination, so you have to add a plugin to accomplish this effect. A few of these kinds of plugins are on the market, and we recommend some in Book V, Chapter 5.

✦ **Avoid sidebar bloat:** If you have a *huge* blogroll, don't include it on your sidebar throughout the site. In fact, if you want to include something that huge, create a page for all your links; having them on your sidebar throughout the site slows down the speed in which the pages on your site loads in your visitors browser and with all these outbound links, it bleeds page rank all over the place. Remember: Links pass on authority, when you link to a site or a site links to you, the link is saying that your site has value for the keyword in the link. So evaluate the links that you have and think about whether you really want to link to that Web site.

Often, when bloggers start out, they sign up for every service under the sun, including Web sites that require you to place reciprocal links or banners on your Web page. All those links and banners quickly turn your Web site into a bad NASCAR car, and your site's performance degrades because it needs to load all those external codes. Be very picky about what you put into your sidebar.

Dealing with duplicate content

WordPress does have one major problem when it comes to SEO: It creates so many places for your content to live that duplicate content can confuse search engines. Thankfully, plugins and some basic editing easily take care of these issues.

First, take care of your archive page on your site, which is the page that displays archives such as category, date-based archives, and so on. You don't want your archive page to present full blog posts, only truncated versions (short excerpts) of your posts. Check your theme to see how your archive is presented. If your archive shows complete posts, see whether your theme has instructions about how to change your archive presentation. (We can't give you a single way to make this change because each theme is unique, but check out the information in Book VI; it is full of great information about tweaking and altering theme template files.)

Additionally, make sure that search engines aren't indexing all your archives by using a robots plugin. (We cover plugins in Book V, Chapter 5.) You want robots going through only your category archive, not the author index and other archives.

Creating an editorial SEO list/calendar

We're not going to take the fun out of blogging by telling you that you need to plan out your posts from now until the end of time. Still, it doesn't hurt to create a list of some of the keywords that your competitors rank for and some of the content they've discussed. Take that list and apply it to new posts, or write *evergreen content* (topics that aren't timely) centered around what you want to say. Planning out your blog can really help in figuring out what keywords you want to target when you want to write content to improve for ranking for targeted keywords.

If you feel that your blog is more news- or current-events oriented, create a reference list of keywords to incorporate into your newer posts so that you can rank for these targeted terms.

Establishing a routine for publishing posts on your site

Although you can't really call this high strategy, getting into the habit of posting content regularly on your site helps you get the basics down. Here are some things to keep in mind:

✦ **Properly title your post.** Make sure that your post includes the keyword or phrase for which you're trying to rank.

✦ **Fix your URL.** Get rid of stop words or useless words from your URL and make sure that the keywords you want to target appear in the URL of your post. *Stop words* are filler words such as *a, so, in, an*, and so on. For a comprehensive list of stop words, check out this list: `http://www.link-assistant.com/seo-stop-words.html`

✦ **Choose a category.** Make sure that you have your categories set up and that you properly place your post into the category it falls under. Whatever you do, don't use the uncategorized category — it brings no SEO value to the table.

✦ **Fill out metadata.** If you're using a theme framework, the form for metadata often appears right below the post window. If you aren't using a theme framework, you can use the All in One SEO Pack plugin (we talk about this plugin in a previous section). When activated, this plugin usually appears toward the bottom of your posting page. (See Figure 4-8.) Make sure that you completely fill out the title, description, keywords, and other information the plugin or theme framework asks for.

✦ **Properly tag posts.** You may want to get into the habit of taking the keywords from the All in One SEO Pack plugin and pasting them into the tags section of the post.

✦ **Fill out image info.** Take the time to completely fill out your image info when you upload pictures to your posts. Every time you upload an image to WordPress, a screen will appear in which you can fill in the URL slug, description, and alt text for the image you have uploaded.

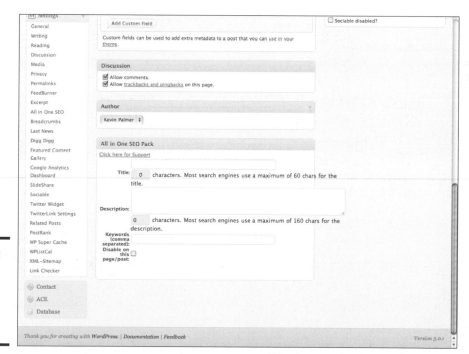

Figure 4-8:
The All in One SEO Pack's metadata form.

Creating a link-building strategy

In previous sections of this chapter, we tackle most of the onsite SEO strategy and concepts. In this section, we explain how you can start working on your off-page strategy. Here are some things to keep in mind:

✦ **Fill out your social media profiles.** As we discuss in Chapter 1 of this minibook, a lot of social-media sites pass on page rank through their profiles. These sites allow you to link to yours with a descriptive word and these major sites say that this link has value to search engines. Also, most profiles allow you to link to your Web site. Take the time to fill out your social-media profile properly and list your site in these profiles.

✦ **Use forum signatures.** If you participate in forums, you can easily generate traffic and earn some links to your Web site from other Web sites by including your site URL in your forum signature.

✦ **Examine your competitor's links.** See where your competitors or other people in your niche are getting links — directories, lists, guest blogs, friends? — and then try to get links on those sites. Try to determine the relationship and figure out whether you can establish a relationship with that site, as well.

✦ **Guest blog.** Find some of the top sites in your niche, and then ask them whether you can guest blog. Guest blogging gives you a link from a respected source, as well as builds a relationship with other bloggers. Also, guest blogging can't hurt your subscriber numbers; often, you see a bump after you guest blog on a large site.

✦ **Blog and Web site directory registration.** Directory registration, albeit a time-consuming affair, can often provide a large amount of backlinks into your site from respected sources.

✦ **Comment on other blogs.** A lot of blogs pass on page rank because the links in their comment section are live. Make sure that when you participate and engage other bloggers, you properly fill out your information before you post, including the URL to your site. Don't start posting inane comments on random blogs in order to get links — it is considered rude to do that to other bloggers and can lead to your blog being marked as spam in various commenting systems.

✦ **Participate in social bookmarking.** Getting involved in Reddit, Digg, and other social-bookmarking communities allows you to participate in social media with people who have similar interests, and you can build links into your site by submitting content to social-news and bookmarking sites.

Chapter 5: Exploring Popular SEO Plugins

In This Chapter

✔ **Using plugins for SEO best practices**

✔ **Breaking down your SEO configuration options**

✔ **Generating sitemaps**

✔ **Using redirect plugins**

✔ **Adding breadcrumbs and pagination**

You've made it this far, which means that you have the concepts of SEO down and the beginnings of your strategy properly mapped out: Now you need to install the tools. In this chapter, we go through some of the most popular SEO-related plugins. All these plugins have a good developer behind them and a good track record.

Several plugins in the WordPress plugin directory assist with SEO, so it's hard to decide which ones to use. In this chapter, we provide you with the plugins that are the most common, and the ones that we use ourselves, because they are some of the more-solid and reliable plugins available that bring good SEO results.

Exploring Must-Use Plugins for SEO Best Practices

Here are the plugins that we cover in this chapter:

✦ **All in One SEO Pack:** Gives the user complete control of the search-engine optimization of his or her blog.

✦ **Google XML Sitemaps:** Generates an XML sitemap that's sent to Google, Yahoo!, Bing, and Ask.com. When your site has a sitemap, site crawlers can more efficiently crawl your site. One of the added bonuses of the sitemap is that it notifies search engines every time you post.

✦ **Redirection:** Can help when you move from an old site to WordPress or when you want to change the URL structure of an established site. It allows users to manage 301 redirections (when the Web address of a page has changed, a 301 redirect tells search engines where they can find the new Web address of the page), track any 404 errors (errors that are displayed when you try to load a page that does not exist) that occur on the site, and manage any possible incorrect Web address (URL) issues with your Web site.

✦ **Yoast Breadcrumbs:** This plugin allows you to easily add breadcrumbs (covered in Chapter 4 of this minibook) to your site. On most sites, you just need to add a line of code to your template to make the breadcrumb navigation links display on your site.

✦ **WP-PageNavi:** In order to achieve pagination for your WordPress site, this plugin gives you the ability to display page links at the bottom of each archive page and/or category page.

✦ **Robots Meta:** Using the Robots Meta plugin gives you the ability to control how your site is crawled by the search engines, allowing you to hide content that you don't want to be noticed by search engine robots and to ensure that search engine crawlers see only what you want them to see. It helps eliminate duplicate content by preventing crawlers from indexing category, author, and tag pages, only focusing on your main content. Also, this plugin allows you to easily add the verification tools from Yahoo! Site Explorer, Bing's Webmaster Central, and Google's Webmaster Tools. If you don't want to edit your header, you can easily use this tool to add the various code that these search engines request you to use to verify your Web page.

All in One SEO Pack

We have a profound love for the All in One SEO Pack plugin, developed by our coauthor, Michael Torbert. This plugin makes everyone's life so much easier because it automates many SEO tasks for you. Out of all the plugins we cover, this one is an absolute must for your site. It gives you so much control over your search engine optimization, and it's very flexible.

This plugin breaks down each option on the configuration page, which allows you to preselect options right off the bat or make some changes to the plugin. We don't break down every option within the plugin because when you hover over any of the fields, the plugin gives in depth detail on what each field is, along with helpful inline help documentation for you. However, we do suggest that you make a few of changes, from the default settings, right from the start.

After you install this plugin on the All in One SEO Plugin Options page (check out Book VII, Chapter 2 for information on plugin installation), which you find when you click the All In One SEO link in the Settings menu on your Dashboard, scroll past the rows of advertisements that appear on this page and be sure that the Plugin Status radio button is set to Enabled. Below that radio button are three text boxes that you need to type information into — these three text boxes include

✦ **Home Title:** Type the title of your Web site in this box (this will be the same Site Title that you filled out in the General Settings page, as we discuss in Book III, Chapter 3).

✦ **Home Description:** Type a description of your Web site in this box (this will probably be the same as the Tag Line that you filled out in the General Settings page, as we discuss in Book III, Chapter 3).

✦ **Home Keywords (comma separated):** Type in multiple keywords that describe your site, and separate them each by commas. For example, if my site is about country music, my Home Keywords might look like this: *country music, guitar, southern, fiddle, Nashville*; just to name a few.

The Canonical URLs check box appears below the text boxes. It is checked by default and you should keep that default setting in place because canonical URLs assist with SEO by giving the search engines a definitive source URL for pages on your Web site. For example, when Google crawls a Web page, it sees the following four URLs:

✦ `www.example.com`

✦ `example.com`

✦ `www.example.com/index.html`

✦ `example.com/home.asp`

Although you may think that all these URLs are the same; technically, they're all different. In the *canonicalization process,* Google chooses which one of those URLs best represents your site from that group. When selecting to use canonical URLs in the All In One SEO plugin, you are telling Google which URL you want them to choose.

Make sure that you select the Canonical URLs check box. (See Figure 5-1.) Selecting this check box prevents duplicate-content issues by giving you control over the canonical URLs and forcing the search engines to index only one URL per page on your Web site.

Most of the remaining options that are selected, by default, should work fine for your site. However, you should select the Use No Index for Archives and Use No Index for Tag Archives check boxes to make sure that the search engines are not indexing your archives pages, which would provide the search engines with duplicate content that they have already indexed.

After you make all your selections, click the Update Options button at the bottom of the page.

The following is a screenshot of the All in One SEO Pack configuration page:

Click on option titles to get help!

Field	Value
Plugin Status:	⦿ Enabled ○ Disabled
Home Title:	Social Media Consulting and Strategy, Boston | Social Media Answers
Home Description:	Boston based Social Media Answers creates social media strategies for business as well as partnering with PR and Marketing firms to handle
Home Keywords (comma separated):	social media, social networking, blogging, social media consulting, video, podcasting, reviews, information, social media marketing
Canonical URLs:	☑
Rewrite Titles:	☑
Post Title Format:	%post_title% | %blog_title%
Page Title Format:	%page_title% | %blog_title%
Category Title Format:	%category_title% | %blog_title%
Archive Title Format:	%date% | %blog_title%
Tag Title Format:	%tag% | %blog_title%
Search Title Format:	%search% | %blog_title%
Description Format:	%description%
404 Title Format:	Nothing found for %request_words%
Paged Format:	– Part %page%

socialmediaanswers.com/wp–admin/options-general.php?p...

Figure 5-1: The All in One SEO Pack configuration page.

You can use the All in One SEO Pack right out of the box, without changing any of the default options that are already set for you: If you aren't confident in fine-tuning it, you don't have to do it. But don't forget to put in the proper information for your home page on the Options page of the plugin; this includes your home page title, description, and keywords.

XML Sitemap Generator for WordPress

You can use XML Sitemap Generator (http://wordpress.org/extend/plugins/google-sitemap-generator) right out of the box with very little configuration. After it is installed, you do need to tell the plugin to create your sitemap for the first time. You can accomplish this easy task by following these steps:

1. **Click the XML Sitemap link in the Settings menu on your Dashboard.**

   The XML Site Generator for WordPress options page appears in your browser window (see Figure 5-2).

2. **Locate the top module titled:** *The sitemap wasn't generated yet.*

3. **Click the link labeled Click Here To Tell the Plugin to Build Your Sitemap.**

The XML Site Generator for WordPress page refreshes and the This Sitemap Wasn't Generated Yet module is replaced with the Result of the Last Build Process module, and the date your sitemap was last generated is displayed.

4. **(Optional) View your sitemap in your browser.**

Click the first sitemap link in the top module, or you can visit the following address: `http://yourdomain.com/sitemap.xml` (where *your domain.com* is your actual domain).

You will never need to visit your sitemap, or maintain it. The XML Sitemap Generator maintains the file for you. Every time you publish a new post or page on your Web site, the plugin automatically updates your sitemap with the information and notifies major search engines, like Google, Bing, and Ask.com that you have updated your site with new content. Basically, the plugin sends an invitation to the search engines to come to your site and index your new content in their search engines.

Having a Google Webmaster account is also something you can do to further assist Google in finding and indexing new content on your site. If you don't already have one, you can sign up for one at Google.com (visit `http://google.com`, click the sign in link at the top right, then click the Create an account now link and follow the steps to create a new Google account). After you sign in to your Google Account, you can set up the Google Webmaster tools and add your sitemap to Google.

In the Basic Options section of the XML Sitemap Generator for WordPress plugin page (see Figure 5-2), select every check box you see there except for *Enable Manual Sitemap Building via GET Request, Enable MySQL Standard Mode,* and *Use This Only If You're Getting MySQL Errors* options, as they are not necessary unless you are experiencing errors with the plugin — in which case, you should contact the plugin developer and report the problems you are experiencing (contact information for the plugin developer is available on the plugin page in the WordPress plugin directory; for this plugin, you can find it here: `http://wordpress.org/extend/plugins/google-sitemap-generator`).

All the other default settings are fine for you to use, so leave those as is. In the Sitemap Content section, select the following check boxes: Include Homepage, Include Posts, Include Static Pages, Include Categories, and Include the Last Mortification Time. Making these selections allows for your site to get crawled by the search engines the most efficient way.

Figure 5-2:
XML
Sitemap
Generator
for
WordPress
settings.

Redirection

If you're redoing the URL (Permalink) structure of your site or moving a site to WordPress from another blogging platform, like Blogger or Typepad, you really need to use the Redirection plugin (`http://wordpress.org/extend/plugins/redirection`). Redirection allows you to maintain the links that are currently coming into your site by rerouting (or redirecting) people coming in through search engines and other existing links going to the new permalink. If you change URLs, you need to reroute/redirect old links to maintain the integrity of incoming traffic from Web sites and search engines that are still using the old page URL.

Using Redirection is a pretty simple process: Put the old URL in the Source URL text box and the new URL in the Target URL text box, and then click the Add Redirection button. (See Figure 5-3.)

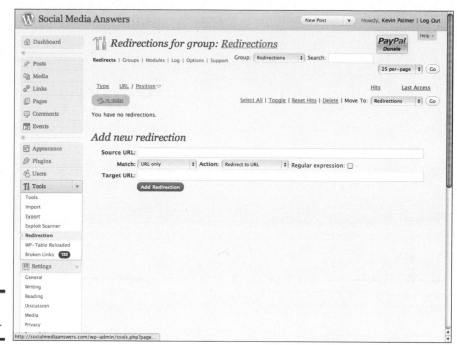

Figure 5-3:
Redirection.

Yoast Breadcrumbs

Yoast Breadcrumbs adds navigation breadcrumbs (covered in Chapter 4 of this minibook) to your site. Although you can install and activate the plugin like any other plugin, you need to go through a few extra steps to get the breadcrumbs to show up on your page. For most standard WordPress themes you need to add the following code into the template where you want the plugin to appear (see Book VI if you need assistance with editing template files):

```php
<?php if ( function_exists('yoast_breadcrumb') ) {
   yoast_breadcrumb('<p id="breadcrumbs">','</p>');
} ?>
```

WP-Page Navi

In order to create page navigation links underneath your blog posts and archive listings for sites that have numbered pages, you need to install this WP-Page Navi plugin (http://wordpress.org/extend/plugins/wp-pagenavi). (See the settings in Figure 5-4.) This plugin provides a better user experience for your readers by making it easier for them to navigate through your content, and allowing search engines to easily go through your Web page and index your pages and posts. After you install and activate the plugin, you need to insert the following code into your Main Index template (`index.php`):

```
<?php wp_pagenavi(); ?>
```

The `wp_pagenavi();` template tag needs to be added on a line directly after The Loop. Please go to Book VI, Chapter 3 for extensive discussion of The Loop in the Main Index template file to find out where, exactly, you need to add this line of code.

Installing this code gives you the lower navigation. You can experiment with where you want to place the `wp_pagenavi()` code in your template file to give you the type and look and feel you want. Additionally, you can control the look of the plugin by providing styling in your CSS (`style.css`) theme file for the WP-PageNavi plugin display, or you can have the plugin insert it's default CSS into your regular CSS by unchecking the Use Pagenavi.css? option.

Figure 5-4:
WP-Page
Navi
settings.

Robots Meta

Similar to the All in One SEO Pack plugin (see "All in One SEO Pack," earlier in this chapter), the Robots Meta plugin (`http://wordpress.org/extend/plugins/robots-meta`) gives you a breakdown of each menu option and the impact that it has on your site. This plugin, however, isn't ready to go out of the box, like many of the other plugins we discuss in this chapter. To use it, you need to consider how your SEO works on your site and what content you want the search engines to index. If you want to base your search results on your categories (we recommend this approach if you have a lot of content in categories based off popular keywords), make sure that robots doesn't scroll your subpages.

We can't offer any recommendations for setting up this plugin — the choices are too specific to you and your site needs. (See Figure 5-5.) Just go through and think about each choice and how it pertains to your blog and configure the settings that you feel work best for your individual Web site.

Figure 5-5:
Robots
Meta
configu-
ration.

Book VI

Customizing the Look of Your Site

Contents at a Glance

Chapter 1: Examining the Default Theme: Twenty Ten

In This Chapter

✔ Discovering Twenty Ten's layout features

✔ Tweaking your header and background colors

✔ Installing custom navigation menus

✔ Exploring widgets on your Web site

*B*undled with the release of WordPress 3.0 in June 2010 is the new default theme, Twenty Ten. Since 2005, the default theme was Kubrick, but the community and core development team realized that an update or replacement that reflected a new design and built-in functionality for the new WordPress features was needed desperately.

Although nothing was technically wrong with Kubrick — after all it was and is still being used on thousands of WordPress sites — the look and functionality had not kept pace with the rapid development of WordPress. Think of it this way: WordPress was rocking in a new era and needed some hip new clothes to look the part!

The resulting community effort was Twenty Ten, a powerful theme with drop-down menu navigation, header and background image uploaders, multiple-page templates, widget-ready areas, and parent-child theme support. These features make Twenty Ten an excellent base for many of your theme customization projects. This chapter takes you through all the features of the default Twenty Ten theme including layouts, editing the header graphic and background colors, installing and using custom navigation menus, and using widgets on your site to add some great features.

Exploring the Layout and Structure

The Twenty Ten theme is meant to offer a clean design style that is highly customizable for the millions of WordPress users who just want a simple look for their site that focuses on their content. As such, the font treatments are sharp and easy to read. Many of the new built-in theme features allow the user to make simple yet elegant tweaks to the theme, including uploading new feature images and adjusting the background colors. Figure 1-1 shows the Twenty Ten WordPress default theme.

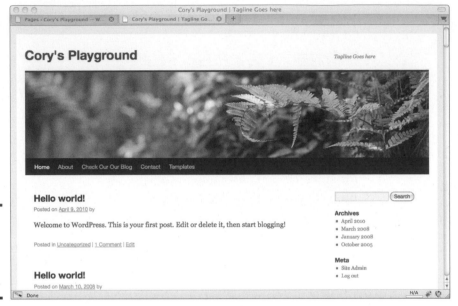

Figure 1-1:
The default
theme for
WordPress,
Twenty Ten.

The Twenty Ten theme's distinctive layout features include

✦ **Two column default layout:** The two-column layout — one of the most
   common layouts for blogs and used more and more on general Web
   sites — is the default in Twenty Ten and includes a content area on
   the left, a widget-ready sidebar on the right, and a footer area with four
   widget-ready spaces. Figure 1-2 shows the standard two-column layout.

✦ **One-column page layout:** Twenty Ten's one-column layout can be
   applied to WordPress Pages via the page template feature. This one-
   column layout, shown in Figure 1-3, comes in very handy for such pages
   as product sales pages, e-mail subscription form pages, photography or
   portfolio pages, and other content that you don't want bothered by dis-
   tractions on the sidebar.

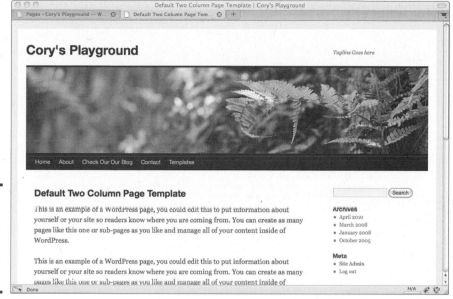

Figure 1-2:
The Twenty Ten theme's standard two-column layout.

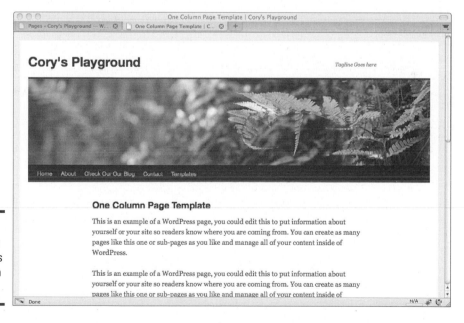

Figure 1-3:
The Twenty Ten theme's one-column layout.

✦ **Widget-ready areas:** By default, the footer in the Twenty Ten theme is widgetized so that the footer expands to show any content you add to any of the four widget-ready areas. Figure 1-4 shows the footer space with sample widget content. When this theme is activated in the WordPress Widgets panel, the widget-ready areas are labeled First Footer Widget Area, Second Footer Widget Area, Third Footer Widget Area, and Fourth Footer Widget Area, as shown in the theme design from left to right. Later in this chapter, you discover how to apply the footer widgets to your site.

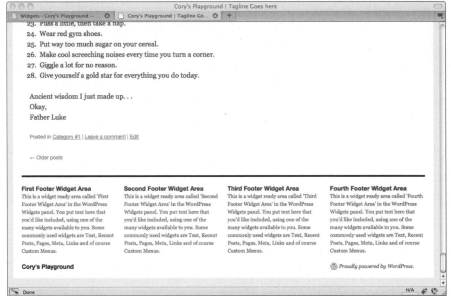

Figure 1-4:
The Twenty Ten theme's footer widget area.

To apply Twenty Ten's one-column layout to a new WordPress Page, follow these steps:

1. **On the WordPress Dashboard, choose Pages⇨Add New.**

   You can also edit an existing Page and apply the one-column page layout by using these steps.

2. **Add your page title and content into the corresponding areas.**

   Book IV, Chapter 1 takes you through the steps of writing and publishing a post or a page in WordPress.

3. **Choose Templates ⇨One Column, No Sidebar.**

   The Templates drop-down menu is located under the Page Attributes heading on the right side of the Add New Page screen.

The Twenty Ten theme only has one page template. In some themes, you may see multiple page template options in this menu.

4. **Click the Publish button.**

   This saves your new page and publishes it to your site with the One Column, No Sidebar page template assigned to it.

Customizing the Header Image

Another great feature in Twenty Ten is the header uploader, which allows you to upload new and unique custom header graphics for your WordPress site. Twenty Ten comes preloaded with eight default header images. To install one, follow these steps:

1. **On the WordPress Dashboard, choose Appearance⇨Header.**

   On the Custom Header page, the settings for the header image feature appear.

2. **Scroll to the Default Images section, which shows the available header images.**

3. **Select the radio button next to the header image you like.**

4. **Click the Save Changes button.**

   Figure 1-5 shows the default header images.

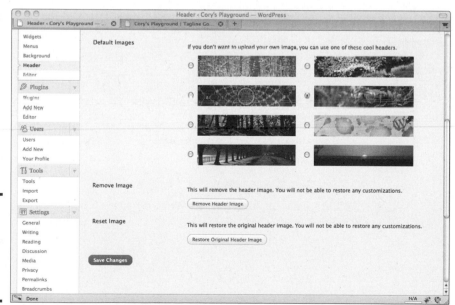

Figure 1-5: The Twenty Ten theme's default header images.

Although the default header images are acceptable, you most likely will want something unique for your blog. The uploader allows you to choose a custom header image easily. Just follow these steps:

1. **On the WordPress Dashboard, choose Appearance⇨Header.**

The Custom Header page loads in your browser window.

2. **Scroll to the Upload Image section shown in Figure 1-6.**

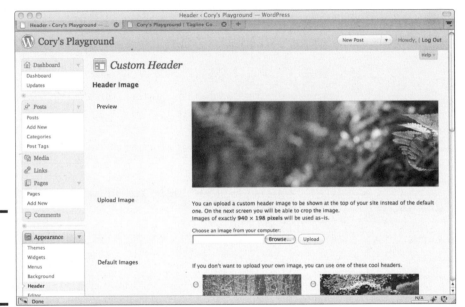

Figure 1-6:
Twenty
Ten's
header
uploader.

3. **Click the Choose File button.**

A window pops up asking you to select an image from your computer's hard drive.

4. **Select the image you want to use.**

5. **Click the Open button.**

6. **Click the Upload button.**

Your image uploads to your Web server and the Crop Header Image page appears.

7. **Use the image crop tool to resize your header image.**

To resize and crop your image, drag one of the eight boxes located at the corners and the middle of each side of the image. You can also click within the image and move the entire image up or down to get the optimal placement and cropping effect that you want.

The Twenty Ten theme's default header size is 940 x 198 pixels. Generally, uploading a new header image already cropped in an image-editing program to that exact size is best. However, if your image is larger, you can use the built-in cropping feature to fit the image in the default space after you upload the header, as shown in Figure 1-7.

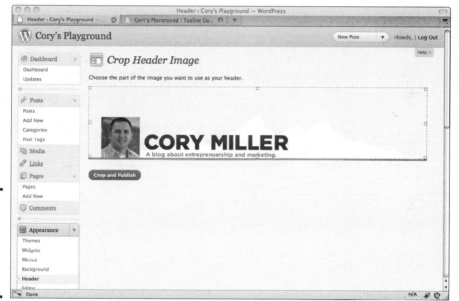

Figure 1-7: Cropping the header image in the Twenty Ten theme.

8. **Click the Crop and Publish button.**

This loads the Custom Header page in the Dashboard and displays your new header image.

9. **Click the Save Changes button.**

This saves the changes you made to the header image and publishes it to your site.

Customizing the Background Color

After you explore the header image settings, you may want to pick a background color or image that complements your header. With the Background options in the Twenty Ten theme, you can. Here's how:

1. **In the WordPress Dashboard, choose Appearance➪Background.**

The Custom Background page opens in your Dashboard, displaying all the options for the custom background feature.

2. **In the Display Options section, enter the HTML color value for your desired background color in the Color field.**

Color values are defined in HTML and CSS by six-digit hexadecimal codes starting with the # sign, such as #000000 for black or #FFFFFF for white. (As noted in Book VI, Chapter 4, adjusting hexadecimal colors is one of the easiest ways to tweak the colors in your theme for a new look.)

Alternatively, you can click the Select a Color link to access a color picker and select just the right color you want, as shown in Figure 1-8. The color picker automatically provides the six-digit hexadecimal code for your color choice.

3. **Click the Save Changes button.**

This saves your changes and applies them to your site.

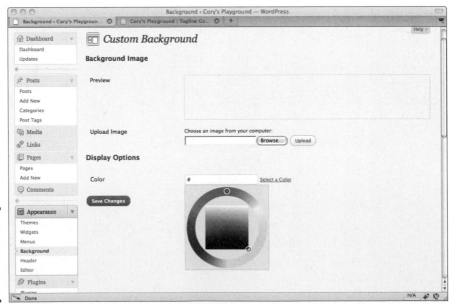

Figure 1-8: The Twenty Ten theme's background options.

If you want something a little more substantial for your background than just a simple color, you can also upload an image to use as a background on your Web site. A background image adds some flair to your site. To upload a new background graphic, simply follow these steps:

1. **On the WordPress Dashboard, choose Appearance⇨Background.**

The Custom Background page loads in your Dashboard.

2. **Scroll to the Upload Image section (refer to Figure 1-8).**

3. **Click the Choose File button.**

A window pops up asking you to select an image from your computer's hard drive.

4. **Click the Upload button, as shown in Figure 1-9.**

**Book VI
Chapter 1**

Examining the
Default Theme:
Twenty Ten

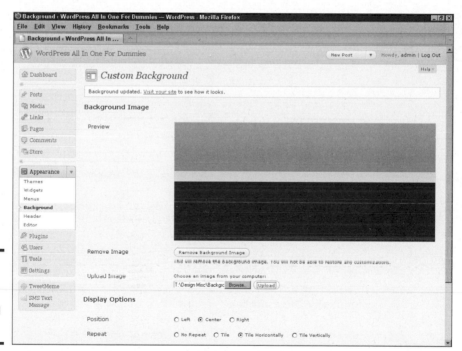

Figure 1-9:
Twenty
Ten's
background
uploader.

After you upload a background image, new display options appear (see Figure 1-10) that allow you to place your image exactly how you desire. Select any of these features and the Preview window shows you how your background image will display.

Figure 1-10:
Background
image
display
options.

✦ **Position:** This is where you want the image placed or pinned with options for image to start at the left side, center, or right side of the theme background.

✦ **Repeat:** This sets how you want the image to tile or repeat across the page. If you want one image without tiling, set Repeat to No Repeat.

✦ **Attachment:** This sets whether the background image scrolls with the page in the browser or is fixed in one place no matter where the page is in the browser.

✦ **Color:** This sets the solid color that will display behind your background image

After you finalize your selections, click the Save Changes button and view your site for the exact look.

If you upload the wrong image from your computer or the image doesn't look the way you hoped, there's a convenient Remove Background Image button on the Custom Background page. Using this button completely removes the image from the Custom Background settings and allows you to start over with a different image.

Including Custom Navigation Menus

Navigational menus are vital parts of your site's design. They tell your site visitors where to go and how to access important information or areas on your site. The Menus feature released in WordPress 3.0 was an extremely significant addition to the already powerful software that allowed greater control over the navigational areas.

Similar to the way the drag-and-drop WordPress Widgets feature enables users to tweak areas of their sites without having to know a lot of code, the new Menus feature offers an easy way to add and reorder a variety of navigational links to your site, as well as create secondary menu bars (if your theme offers multiple menu areas).

Additionally, the Menus feature improved WordPress further by allowing users to easily create more traditional Web sites, which sometimes need multiple and more diverse navigational areas than a typical blog layout uses or needs.

Twenty Ten comes with the appropriate code in the navigation menus that make use of this robust feature. (By default, Twenty Ten offers only one menu navigation area to include a custom menu.)

To create a new navigation menu in Twenty Ten, follow these steps:

1. **In the WordPress Dashboard, click Appearance⇨Menus.**

   The Menus page loads in your Dashboard.

2. **Enter a menu name in the Menu Name field and then click Create Menu, as shown in Figure 1-11.**

   After you create your new custom menu, the gray modules to the left become active for you to add new links to your custom menu.

3. **In the Theme Locations module, choose your new menu from the Primary Navigation drop-down menu and click Save.**

   This activates your new menu in the theme for display on your site. As noted in the Theme Locations module, the Twenty Ten theme supports only one custom menu, defined as Primary Navigation.

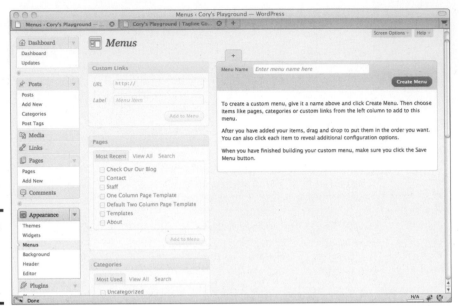

Figure 1-11:
The
WordPress
Menus
page.

4. **Add menu items, such as custom links, pages, and categories, to your new menu.**

   Items you can add to your menu include the following:

   - *Pages:* To include existing pages in your menu, scroll to the Pages module (shown in Figure 1-12) and click the pages you want to include. After you do that, click Add to Menu and then click Save Menu.

   - *Categories:* To include existing categories in your menu, scroll to the Categories module (shown in Figure 1-12) and click the categories you want to include. After you do that, click Add to Menu and then click Save Menu.

   - *Custom Links:* You can add links to sites that exist outside your Web site, such as your Twitter or Facebook profile pages. Scroll to the Custom Links module (shown in Figure 1-13). In the URL field, type the Web address you want to direct people to. In the Label field, add the word or phrase the menu displays for people to click. Then click Save to Menu.

5. **Click Save Menu to add your custom menu to your theme.**

   Be sure to click Save Menu after you make any significant change to your custom menu, such as reordering or adding new menu items so they are reflected on your site.

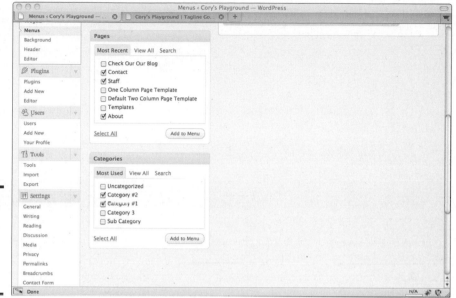

Figure 1-12: Selecting categories to add to the custom menu.

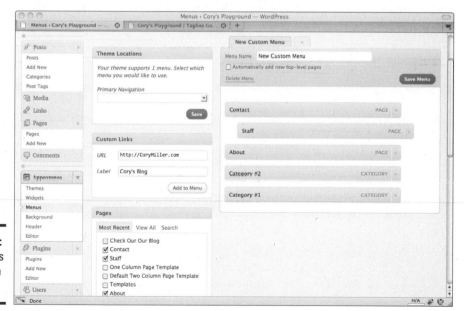

Figure 1-13: Adding links to a custom menu.

After you save your navigation menu, you can use the drag-and-drop interface to rearrange your menu, as shown in Figure 1-14. Additionally, you can create subpages under top-level menu items by moving menu items slightly to the right beneath the top-level menu items. Not cluttering up the navigation bar and organizing content logically can be handy for sites with lots of page content.

You can also create multiple custom menus and add them to your theme through widget areas by using the Custom Menu widget, navigation areas if your theme supports multiple menu areas, or additional menu areas by inserting the WordPress template tag directly into your theme's template files.

Figure 1-14: The drag-and-drop interface of the WordPress Menus feature.

Enhancing Your Web Site with Widgets

WordPress widgets are very helpful tools built in to the WordPress.com application. They allow you to arrange the display of content in your blog sidebar, such as your blogroll(s), recent posts, and monthly and category archive lists. With widgets, arrange and display the content in the sidebar of your blog without having to know a single bit of PHP or HTML.

In this case, Widget areas are the regions in your theme that allow you to insert and arrange content (such as a list of your recent blog posts or links to your favorite sites) or custom menus, by dragging and dropping (and editing) available widgets (shown on the WordPress Dashboard's Widget page) into those corresponding areas.

Many widgets offered by WordPress (and those added sometimes by WordPress themes and plugins) provide drag-and-drop installation of more advanced functions normally available only if you wrote code directly into your theme files.

Choose Widgets on the Appearance menu in the Dashboard. The Widgets page displays the available widgets. This feature is a big draw because it lets you control what features you use and where you place them without having to know a lick of code.

To explore the Twenty Ten theme's widget-ready areas, choose Appearance➪ Widgets on the WordPress Dashboard. The Widgets page displays Primary Widget Area, Secondary Widget Area, First Footer Widget Area, Second Footer Widget Area, Third Footer Widget Area, and Fourth Footer Widget Area, as shown in Figure 1-15. The corresponding widget areas that can be edited in the Twenty Ten theme through the WordPress Dashboard are shown in Figure 1-15.

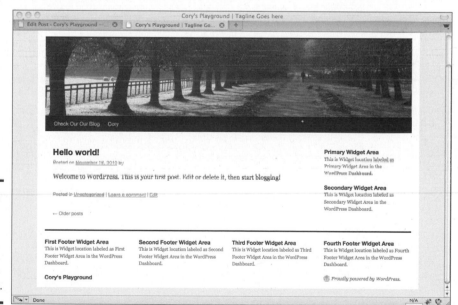

Figure 1-15: This page displays available widgets and widget-ready areas.

Adding widgets to your sidebar or footer

To add widgets to your sidebar and footer, you drag and drop widgets from the Available Widgets section to the desired widget area. For example, to add a Search box to the right sidebar of the default layout, drag the Search widget from the Available Widgets section to the Primary Widget Area, as shown in Figure 1-16.

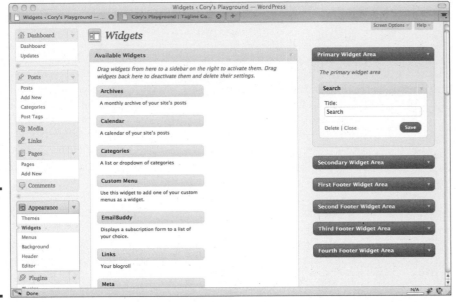

Figure 1-16: Adding a widget to the Primary Widget Area.

The Widgets page lists all the widgets that are available for your WordPress site. On the right side of the Widgets page are the sidebar and footer areas designated in your theme. You drag your selected widget from the Available Widgets section into your chosen widget area on the right.

To add a new widget to your sidebar, follow these steps:

1. **Find the widget you want to use.**

   The widgets are listed in the Available Widgets section. For the purpose of these steps, choose the Recent Posts widget (see Figure 1-17).

2. **Drag and drop the widget into the Primary Widget Area section on the right side of the page.**

   The widget is now located in the Primary Widget Area section, and the content of the widget now appears on your site in the sidebar.

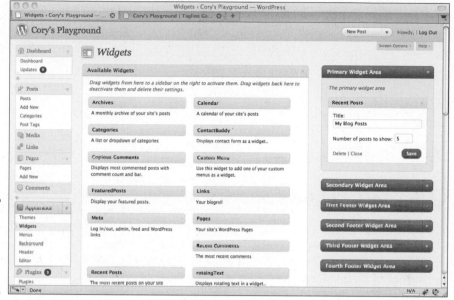

**Book VI
Chapter 1**

Examining the
Default Theme:
Twenty Ten

Figure 1-17:
Editing the
Recent
Posts
widget.

3. **Click the arrow to the right of the widget title.**

Options for the widget appear. Each widget has different options that you can configure. The Recent Posts widget, for example, lets you configure the title, as well as the number of recent posts you want to display (refer to Figure 1-17). The default is set to 5; the maximum allowed is 15.

4. **Select your options and click the Save button.**

The options you've set are saved. Click the Close link.

5. **Arrange your widgets in the order you want them to appear in on your site by clicking a widget and dragging it above or below another widget.**

Repeat this step until your widgets are arranged the way you want them.

To remove a widget from your sidebar, click the arrow to the right of the widget title and then click the Delete link. WordPress removes the widget from the right side of the page and places it back in the Available Widgets list. If you want to remove a widget, but want WordPress to remember the settings that you configured for it, instead of clicking the Delete link, simply drag the widget into the Inactive Widget areas on the right side of the Widgets page, at the bottom of the page. This stores the widget and all the settings for future use.

After you select and configure your widgets, click the Visit Site button at the top of your WordPress Dashboard (to the right of your site name), and your blog's sidebar matches the content (and order of the content) of the Widgets page sidebar. How cool is that? You can go back to the Widgets page and rearrange the items, as well as add and remove items, to your heart's content.

The number of options available for editing a widget depends on the widget. Some have a number of editable options; others simply let you write a title for the widget area. As shown in Fig. 1-17, the Recent Posts widget has two options: one for editing the title of the widget and one to determine how many recent posts to display.

Using the Text widget

The Text widget is one of the most highly used and useful WordPress widgets because it allows you to add text and even HTML code into widget areas without editing the theme's template files. Therefore, you can designate several types of information on your site by including your desired text within it.

Here are some examples of how the Text widget can be used and why it's such an important and popular feature:

✦ **Add an e-mail newsletter subscription form.** Add a form that allows your site visitors to sign up for your e-mail newsletter. Because this often involves HTML, the Text widget is especially helpful.

✦ **Display business hours of operation.** Display the days and hours of your business operation where everyone can easily see them.

✦ **Post your updates from social networks.** Many social-networking sites like Twitter and Facebook offer embed codes to display your updates on those sites directly on your Web site. They often include JavaScript, HTML, and CSS, which you can easily embed with the Text widget.

✦ **Announce special events and notices.** If your organization has a special sale, announcement about a new staff member, or important notice about inclement weather closings, you can use the Text widget to post this information to your site in just a few seconds.

The WordPress Text widget doesn't allow you to include PHP code of any kind. Because of the nature of this widget, it doesn't execute PHP code, such as special WordPress template tags or functions (like the ones you find in Book VI, Chapter 3). There is, however, a great plugin called the Advanced Text Widget that does allow you to insert PHP code within it. You can download the Advanced Text Widget from the WordPress Plugin Directory at `http://wordpress.org/extend/plugins/advanced-text-widget`. (More information about using and installing WordPress plugins is found in Book VII.)

To add the Text widget, follow these steps:

1. **On the WordPress Dashboard, choose Appearance⇨Widgets.**

2. **Scroll to the Available Widgets section.**

3. **Drag and drop the Text widget to the desired widget area.**

   The Text Widget opens.

4. **Add a widget headline in the Title field and any desired text in the text area, as shown in Figure 1-18.**

5. **After you finish, click Save and then click the Close link.**

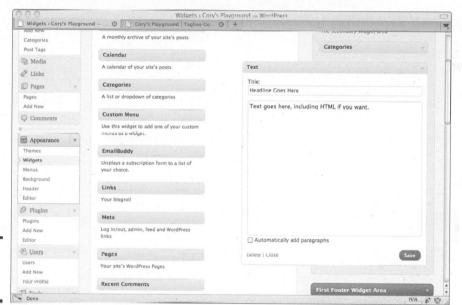

Figure 1-18:
The Text
widget.

Using the RSS widget

The RSS widget allows you to pull headlines from almost any RSS feed, including recent headlines from your other WordPress blogs or sites. You can also use it to pull in headlines from news sites or other sources that offer RSS feeds. This is commonly referred to as *aggregation,* which means that you're gathering information from a syndicated RSS feed source to display on your site.

After you drag and drop the RSS widget to the appropriate widget area, the widget opens and you can enter the RSS Feed URL you want to display. Additionally, you can easily tweak other settings, as shown in Figure 1-19, to add information into the widget area for your reader.

Follow these steps to add the RSS widget to your blog:

1. **Add the RSS widget to your sidebar on the Widgets page.**

   Follow the steps in the "Adding widgets to your sidebar or footer" section, earlier in this chapter, to add the widget.

2. **Click the arrow to the right of the RSS widget's name.**

   The options you can configure for the RSS widget appear.

3. **In the Enter the RSS URL Here text box, type the RSS URL of the blog you want to add.**

   You can usually find the RSS Feed URL of a blog listed in the sidebar.

4. **Type the title of the RSS widget.**

   This title is what will appear in your blog above the links from this blog. If Lisa wanted to add the RSS feed from her personal blog, for example, she would type **Lisa Sabin-Wilson's blog**.

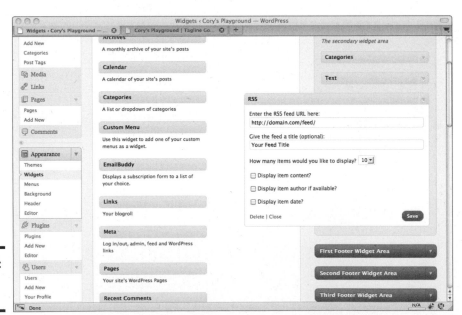

Figure 1-19:
The RSS
widget.

5. **Select the number of items to display.**

   The drop-down menu gives you a choice of 1–20. Select the number of items from the RSS feed that you want to display on your site.

6. **(Optional) Select the Display the Item Content check box.**

   Selecting this check box tells WordPress that you also want to display the content of the feed (usually, the content of the blog post from the feed URL). If you want to display only the title, leave the check box unselected.

7. **(Optional) Select the Display Item Author, If Available check box.**

   Select this option if you want to display the author's name with the item's title.

8. **(Optional) Select the Display Item Date check box.**

   Select this option if you want to display the date the item was published with the item's title.

9. **Click the Save Changes button.**

   WordPress saves all the options and reloads the Widgets page with your RSS widget intact.

Chapter 2: Finding and Installing WordPress Themes

In This Chapter

✔ Understanding free theme options

✔ Exploring things to avoid with free themes

✔ Installing, previewing, and activating your new theme

✔ Discovering premium theme options

WordPress themes are simply a group of files, called templates, bundled together that, when activated in WordPress, determine the look and basic function of your site. (We talk more about templates files in Book VI, Chapter 3.)

Because themes set the design style of your site, including how content displays on it, they are the first and most basic way of customizing your site to fit your unique needs. One of the most amazing things about the WordPress community is the thousands of free themes that are available — and the new ones released each week.

Although finding one WordPress theme among thousands of options can be challenging, it's a fun adventure, and you can explore the various designs and features to, ultimately, find the right theme for you and your site. In this chapter, you discover the options for finding and installing free themes on your WordPress site. We also discuss premium theme options and tell you a few things to avoid.

Getting Started with Free Themes

With thousands of free WordPress themes available, and new ones appearing all the time, your challenge is to find the right one for your site. Here are a few things to remember while you explore (also see the nearby sidebar, "Are all WordPress themes free?," for information about free versus premium themes):

✦ **Free themes are excellent starting places:** We encourage first-time WordPress users to find a couple of free themes and use them as starting points for understanding how themes work and what you can do with them. Testing free themes, their layouts, and options helps you identify what you want in a theme.

✦ **You'll switch themes frequently:** Typically, you'll find a WordPress theme that you adore and then, a week or two later, you'll find another theme that fits you or your site better. Often, you won't stay with your initial choice. Something new will pop up on your radar screen. Eventually, you'll want to stick with one that fits your needs best and doesn't aggravate visitors because of constant changes.

✦ **You get what you pay for:** Although a plethora of free WordPress themes exist, largely, you receive limited or no support for them. Free themes are often a labor of love. The designers have full-time jobs and responsibilities and often release these free projects for fun, passion, and a desire to contribute to the WordPress community. Therefore, you should not expect (or demand) support for these themes. Some designers maintain very active and helpful forums to help users but, often, those are rare. Just be aware that, with free themes, you're on your own.

✦ **Download themes from reputable sources:** Themes are essentially pieces of software. Therefore, they can contain things that could be scammy, spammy, or potentially harmful to your site or computer. Therefore, it's vital that you do your homework by reading online reviews and downloading themes from credible, trusted sources. For new users, the best place to find free WordPress themes is the WordPress Free Themes Directory (see Figure 2-1) at `http://wordpress.org/extend/themes`.

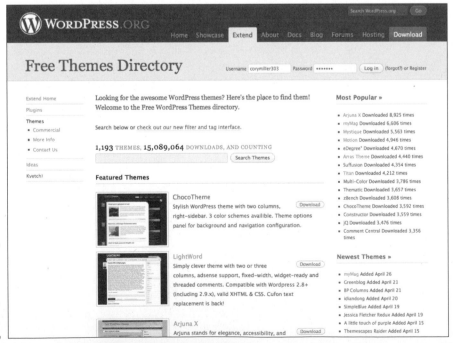

Figure 2-1:
The most trusted resource for free themes.

Are all WordPress themes free?

Not all WordPress themes are created equal, and it's important for you, the user, to know the difference between free and premium themes:

✔ **Free:** These themes are free, period. You can download and use them on your Web site at absolutely no cost. It's a courtesy to include a link to the designer in the footer of your blog — but you can remove that link if you want to.

✔ **Premium:** These themes cost money. You usually find premium themes available for download only after you've paid anywhere from $10 to $500. The designer feels that these themes are a cut above the rest and, therefore, are worth the money you spend for them. Generally, you aren't allowed to remove any designer credits that appear in these themes, and you aren't allowed to redistribute the themes. (**Note:** You *won't* find premium themes in the WordPress Themes Directory.) We provide information on where to find premium themes at the end of this chapter.

Understanding What to Avoid with Free Themes

Although free themes are great, you want to avoid some things when finding and using free themes. As with everything on the Web, themes have the potential to be abused. Although free themes were conceived to allow people (namely designers and developers) to contribute work to the WordPress community, they've also been used to "game the system" and wreak havoc for users. As such, you need to understand what to watch out for and what to avoid.

Here are some things to avoid when searching for free themes:

✦ **Spam links:** Many free themes outside the WordPress Free Themes Directory include links in the footer or sidebars that can be good or bad. The good uses of these links are designed to credit the original designer and possibly link to her Web site or portfolio. This practice — a nice reward to the creators — should be observed because it increases the designer's traffic and clients. Spam links, however, aren't links to the designer's site; they're links to sites you may not ordinarily associate with or endorse on your site. The best example is a link in the footer that links to odd, off-topic, and uncharacteristic keywords or phrases, such as *weight loss supplement* or *best flower deals*. Mostly, this spam technique is used to increase the advertised site's search engine ranking for that particular keyword by adding another link from your site or, worse, to take your site visitor who clicks it to a site unrelated to the linked phrase.

✦ **Hidden and malicious code:** Unfortunately, one abuse reported in the WordPress community has been hidden and malicious code within a theme that can produce spam links, security exploits, and abuses on your WordPress site. Hackers install code in various places that run this type of malware. Unscrupulous theme designers can, and do, place code in theme files that inserts hidden malware, virus links, and spam. Sometimes, you see a line or two of encrypted code that looks like it's just part of the theme code. Unless you have a great deal of knowledge of PHP, you may not know that the theme is infected with dangerous code.

✦ **Lack of continued development:** WordPress software continues to improve with each new update. Two or three times a year, WordPress releases new software versions, adding new features and security patches and numerous other updates. Sometimes, a code function will be superseded or replaced, causing a theme to break because it hasn't been updated for the new WordPress version. Additionally, to use new features added to WordPress, because the software adds new features, the theme will need to be updated accordingly. Because free themes typically come without any warranty or support, one thing you should look for, especially if a theme has many advanced back-end options, is whether the developer is actively maintaining the theme for current versions of WordPress. This typically is more of an issue with plugins than themes, but it's worth noting.

✦ **Endlessly searching for free themes:** Avoid searching endlessly for the perfect theme — trust me, you won't find it. You may find a great theme and then see another with a feature or design style you wish the previous theme had, but the new theme lacks certain other features. Infinite options can hinder you making a final decision. Peruse the most popular themes on the WordPress Free Themes Directory, choose five that fit your criteria, and then move on. You always have the option to change a theme later.

The results of these unsafe theme elements can range from simply annoying to downright dangerous, affecting the integrity and security of your computer and/or hosting account. For this reason, the WordPress Themes Directory is considered a safe place from which to download free themes. WordPress designers develop these themes and upload them to the theme directory, and the folks behind the WordPress platform vet each theme. In the official directory, themes that contain unsafe elements simply aren't allowed.

The WordPress Themes Directory isn't the only place on the Web to find free WordPress themes, but it's the place to find the most functional and *safe* themes available. Safe themes contain clean code and basic WordPress functions that are considered fundamental requirements in a theme to ensure that your WordPress blog functions with the minimum requirements. The WordPress.org Web site lists the basic requirements that theme designers have to meet before their theme is accepted into the themes directory; you can find that listing of requirements at `http://wordpress.org/extend/themes/about`. We highly recommend that you stick to the WordPress Themes Directory for free themes to use on your site; you can be certain those themes do not contain any unsafe elements or malicious code.

Installing a Theme

After you find a WordPress theme, you can install the theme on your WordPress site via FTP or the WordPress Dashboard.

To install a theme via FTP, follow these steps:

1. **Download the theme file from the Theme Directory.**

Typically, theme files are provided in a compressed format, or Zip file.

(I discuss how you can peruse the WordPress Free Themes Directory from your WordPress installation in the next section.)

2. **Unzip or extract the theme's Zip file.**

You see a new folder on your desktop, typically labeled with the corresponding theme name (revisit Book II, Chapter 2 if you need to refresh yourself on how to use FTP Protocol).

3. **Upload the theme folder to your Web server.**

Connect to your hosting server via FTP and upload the extracted theme folder into the /wp-content/themes folder on your server (see Figure 2-2).

Figure 2-2:
Upload and
download
panels in
FTP.

To install a theme via the Dashboard's theme installer, follow these steps:

1. **Download the theme file from the Theme Directory to your desktop.**

    Typically, theme files are provided in a compressed format, or Zip file. Using this method, you do not extract the Zip file because the theme installer does that for you.

2. **Log in to your WordPress Dashboard and choose Appearance⇨Themes.**

    The Manage Themes panel appears.

3. **Click the Install Themes tab.**

    The Install Themes panel appears and displays a submenu of links.

4. **Click the Upload link.**

    The panel displays a utility to upload a theme in Zip format.

5. **Upload the Zip file you downloaded in Step 1.**

    Click the Browse button, and then locate and select the Zip file you stored on your computer.

6. **Click the Install Now button.**

    WordPress unpacks and installs the theme in the appropriate directory for you. Figure 2-3 shows the results of installing a theme via this method.

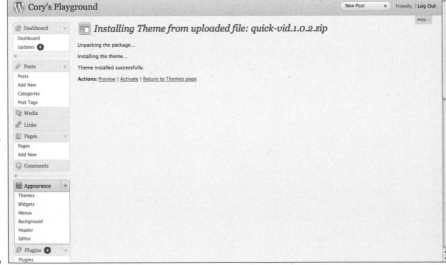

Figure 2-3: Installing a theme via the Dashboard's theme installer.

Browsing the free themes

Finding free themes via the Install Themes tab is extremely convenient because it lets you search the Free Themes Directory from your WordPress site. Start by choosing Appearance⇨Themes on the WordPress Dashboard and click the Install themes tab, as shown in Figure 2-4.

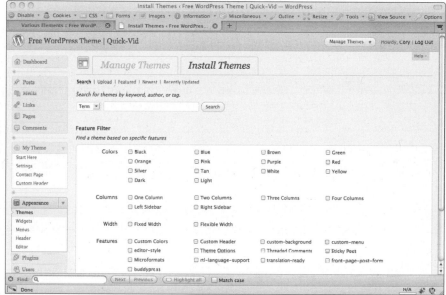

Figure 2-4: The Install Themes tab, where you can search for and find free themes from your Dashboard.

After you navigate to the Install Themes tab, you see the following submenu links:

✦ **Search:** If you know the name of a free theme, you can easily search for it here by keyword, author, or tag to find the exact theme you want. You can also refine your search based on specific features within the themes, including color, layout, and subject (such as "Holiday").

✦ **Upload:** You use this link to upload themes you downloaded from other sources.

✦ **Featured:** If you don't have a theme in mind, this page shows you some of the more popular themes out there. We recommend you install and test-drive one of these for your site's first theme.

✦ **Newest:** As the name indicates, these are themes recently added to the Free Themes Directory.

✦ **Recently Updated:** While WordPress improves, many themes need updating or new features added. This option shows you what themes were updated recently.

After you find the theme that you want, click the Install link below the theme screenshot.

Previewing and activating a theme

After you upload a theme via FTP or the theme installer, you can preview and activate your desired theme.

 The WordPress Theme Preview option allows you to look at your site without actually activating the theme on your site. If you have a site that's receiving traffic, it's best to preview any new theme before activating it to ensure you'll be happy with its look and functionality. If you're trying to decide between several new theme options, you can preview them before changing your live site.

To preview your new theme, follow these steps:

1. Log in to your WordPress Dashboard and choose Appearance⇨Themes.

The Manage Themes page appears and displays your current (activated) theme and any themes that are installed in your /wp-content/themes directory on your Web server.

2. Preview the theme you want to use.

Click the Preview link beneath the theme name; a preview of your blog using the theme appears.

3. Choose whether to activate the theme.

Click Activate in the top-right corner to go live with your new theme, or close the preview by clicking the Close button in the top-left corner, as shown in Figure 2-5.

To activate a new theme without previewing, follow these steps:

1. Log in to your WordPress Dashboard and choose Appearance⇨Themes.

The Manage Themes page appears and displays your current (activated) theme and any themes that are installed in your /wp-content/themes directory on your Web server.

2. Find the theme you want to use and click the Activate link beneath the theme name.

The theme immediately becomes live on your site, as shown in Figure 2-6.

Figure 2-5:
A WordPress
theme
preview.

Figure 2-6:
An active
theme on a
WordPress
site.

Exploring Premium Theme Options

Thousands of free WordPress themes are available, but you might also want to consider premium (for purchase) themes for your site. The cliché "you get what you pay for" is something often quoted when referring to free services or products, including WordPress and free themes.

Typically, when you download and use something free, there's no recourse for assistance with the product or service. Requests for help generally go unanswered. Therefore, your expectations should be lower because you aren't paying anything. When you pay for something, you usually assume that you have support or service for your purchase and the product is high (or acceptable) quality.

For instance, WordPress is available free. However, despite an active support forum, there's no guarantee or promise of getting support while using the software. Moreover, you have no right to demand service.

Here are some things to consider when contemplating a premium theme. Additionally, we selected the commercial companies listed later in this chapter based on these criteria:

✦ **Selection:** Many theme developers offer a rich and diverse theme selection, including themes designed for specific niche industries, topics, or uses (such as video, blogging, real estate, or magazine themes, for example). Generally, you can find a good solid theme to use for your site from one source.

✦ **Innovation:** To differentiate them from their free counterparts, premium themes include innovative features, such as theme settings or advanced options that extend WordPress to help you do more.

✦ **Great design with solid code:** Although many beautiful free themes are available, premium themes are professionally coded, beautifully designed, cost thousands of dollars, and require dozens of hours to build, which simply isn't feasible for many free theme developers.

✦ **Support:** Most commercial companies have full-time support staff to answer questions, troubleshoot issues, and point you to resources beyond their support. Often, premium theme developers spend more time helping customers troubleshoot issues outside the theme products. Therefore, purchasing a premium theme often provides a dedicated support community to question about advanced issues and upcoming WordPress features; otherwise, you're on your own.

✦ **Stability:** No doubt, you've purchased a product or service from a company only to find later that they've gone out of business. If you choose to use a premium theme, we highly encourage you to purchase a theme from an established company with a solid business model, a record of accomplishment, and a dedicated team devoted to building and supporting quality products.

Although some free themes have some, or all of, the features in the preceding list, for the most part, they don't. Keep in mind that just because a designer calls a theme premium doesn't mean that the theme has passed through any kind of quality review. One designer's view of what constitutes a premium theme can, and will, differ from the next.

Fully investigate any theme before you spend your money on it. Some things to check out before you pay:

✦ E-mail the designer who is selling the premium theme and ask about a support policy.

✦ Find people who've purchased the theme and contact them to find out their experiences with the theme and the designer.

✦ Carefully read any terms that the designer has published on his site to find any restrictions that exist with licensing.

✦ If the premium theme designer has a support forum, ask whether you can browse through the forum to find out how actively the designer answers questions and provides support. Are users waiting weeks to get their questions answered? Or does the designer seem to be on top of support requests?

✦ Search Google for the theme and the designer. Often, users of premium themes post about their experiences with the theme and the designer. You can find a lot of positive and, potentially, negative information about the theme and the designer before you buy.

These developers are doing some amazingly innovative things with WordPress themes, and we highly recommend you explore their offerings:

✦ **iThemes (`http://ithemes.com`):** Shown in Figure 2-7, iThemes emphasizes business WordPress themes that use WordPress as a full-fledged and powerful content management system. Their pride and joy is iThemes Builder, which is more a build-a-WordPress Web site tool than a typical theme.

✦ **StudioPress (`http://studiopress.com`):** Shown in Figure 2-8, StudioPress has a great team, paid support moderators, and a big selection of WordPress themes. Their highlight project is Genesis Theme Framework, which provides six layout options, search engine optimization, and automatic theme updates.

Figure 2-7: iThemes.com, provider of premium WordPress themes.

Figure 2-8: StudioPress offers premium themes and a support forum.

✦ **WooThemes (http://woothemes.com):** Shown in Figure 2-9, WooThemes has a wide selection of high-quality themes with excellent theme options and support. Their highlight theme is Canvas, a highly customizable theme that has more than 100 options to personalize your site via a theme options panel.

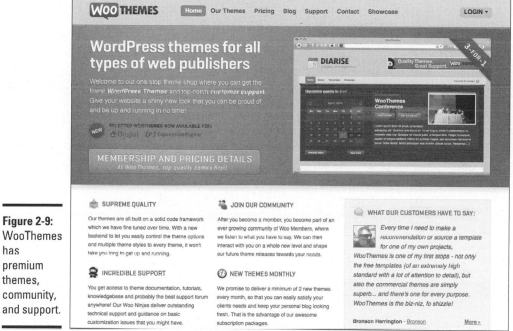

Book VI Chapter 2

Finding and Installing WordPress Themes

Figure 2-9: WooThemes has premium themes, community, and support.

✦ **Press75 (http://press75.com):** Shown in Figure 2-10, Press75 offers a number of niche themes for photography, portfolios, and video. Check out the Social Life and Video Elements themes for great examples.

✦ **Headway Themes (http://headwaythemes.com):** Shown in Figure 2-11, Headway's signature theme is Headway, which offers drag-and-drop layout editing and advanced, easy-to-use styling options.

You can't find, preview, or install premium themes by using the Add New Themes feature on your WordPress Dashboard (covered in a previous section of this chapter). You can only find, purchase, and download premium themes from a third-party Web site. After you find a premium theme you like, you need to install it via the FTP method we cover in the earlier "Installing a Theme" section. You can find a very nice selection of premium themes on the WordPress Web site at http://wordpress.org/extend/themes/commercial.

Figure 2-10: Press75 offers premium themes, demos, and theme packages.

Figure 2-11: Headway Themes has some unique layouts.

Chapter 3: Exploring the Anatomy of a Theme

In This Chapter

✔ **Examining the theme's stylesheet**

✔ **Exploring template tags**

✔ **Making widget areas**

✔ **Understanding the main template files**

This chapter breaks down the parts that make up your WordPress theme. Understanding your theme allows you greater flexibility when you customize it. Many of the problems we see people encounter with their theme, such as not knowing which files edit certain functions of their site, comes from lack of understanding all the pieces.

There are those who like to get their hands dirty (present company included!). If you're one of them, you need to read this chapter. WordPress users who create their own themes do so in the interest of:

✦ **Individuality:** Having a theme that no one else has. (If you use one of the free themes, you can pretty much count on the fact that at *least* a dozen other WordPress blogs will have the same look as yours.)

✦ **Creativity:** Displaying your own personal flair and style.

✦ **Control:** Having full control of how the blog looks, acts, and delivers your content.

Many of you aren't at all interested in creating your own templates for your WordPress blog, however. Sometimes, it's just easier to leave matters to the professionals and to hire an experienced WordPress theme developer to create a custom look for your WordPress Web site or to use one of the thousands of free themes provided by WordPress designers (see Chapter 2 of this minibook).

Creating themes does require you to step into the code of the templates, which can be a scary place sometimes — especially if you don't really know what you're looking at. A good place to start is to understand the structure of a WordPress blog. Separately, the parts won't do you any good. But when you put them together, the real magic begins! This chapter covers the basics of doing just that, and near the end of the chapter, you find specific steps to put your own theme together.

 You don't need to know HTML to use WordPress. If you plan to create and design WordPress themes, however, you need some basic knowledge of HTML and Cascading Style Sheets (CSS). For assistance with HTML, check out *HTML 4 For Dummies,* 5th Edition, by Ed Tittel and Mary Burmeister, or *HTML, XML, and CSS Bible,* 3rd Edition, by Bryan Pfaffenberger, Steven M. Schafer, Chuck White, and Bill Karow (both published by Wiley).

Starting with the Basics

A WordPress theme is a collection of WordPress templates made up of WordPress template tags. When we refer to a WordPress *theme,* we are talking about the group of templates that makes up the theme. When we talk about a WordPress *template,* we are referring to only one of the template files that contain WordPress template tags. WordPress template tags make all the templates work together as a theme (more about this topic later in the chapter). These files include

- ✦ **The theme's stylesheet:** (`style.css`) The stylesheet provides the theme's name, as well as the CSS rules that apply to the theme. (Later in this chapter we go into detail about how stylesheets work.)

- ✦ **The main index template:** (`index.php`) The index file is the first file that will be loaded when a visitor comes to your site. It contains the HTML as well as any PHP code needed on your home page.

- ✦ **An optional functions file:** (`functions.php`) This optional file is a place where you can add additional functionality to your site via PHP functions.

Template and functions files end with the `.php` extension. *PHP* is the scripting language used in WordPress, which your Web server recognizes and interprets as such (Book II, Chapter 3 covers additional details on the PHP language that you will find helpful). These files contain more than just scripts, though. The PHP files also contain HTML, which is the basic markup language of Web pages.

Within this set of PHP files is all the information your browser and Web server need to make your Web site. Everything from the color of the background to the layout of the content is contained in this set of files.

The difference between a template and a theme can cause confusion. *Templates* are individual files. Each template file provides the structure in which your content will display. A *theme* is a set of templates. The theme uses the templates to make the whole site.

Understanding where the WordPress theme files are located on your web server gives you the ability to find and edit them, as needed. You can view and edit WordPress theme files, using two different methods, by following these steps:

1. **Connect to your Web server via FTP, and have a look at the existing WordPress themes on your server.**

The correct location is /wp-content/themes/. When you open this folder, you find the /twentyten theme folder.

If a theme is uploaded to any folder other than /wp-content/themes, it won't work.

2. **Open the folder for the Twenty Ten theme (/wp-content/themes/ twentyten), and look at the template files inside.**

When you open the Twenty Ten theme folder (see Figure 3-1), you see several files. At minimum, you find these five templates in the default theme:

- *Stylesheet* (style.css)
- *Header template* (header.php)
- *Main Index* (index.php)
- *Sidebar template* (sidebar.php)
- *Footer template* (footer.php)

These files are the main WordPress template files, and we discuss them in more detail in this chapter. There are several template files, however, and you should try to explore all of them if you can. Take a peek inside and see the different template functions they contain. These filenames are the same in every WordPress theme.

3. **Log in to your WordPress Dashboard in your Web browser window and click the Editor link on the Appearance menu to look at the template files within a theme.**

This page lists the various templates available within the active theme. (Figure 3-2 shows the templates in the default Twenty Ten theme.) A text box on the left side of the screen displays the contents of each template, and this box is also where you can edit the template file(s). To view and edit a template file, click the template name in the list on the right side of the page.

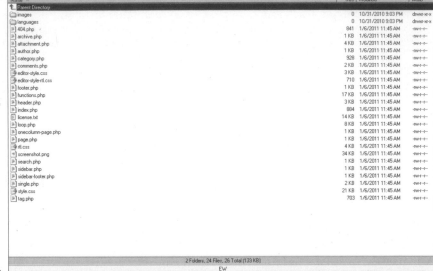

Figure 3-1:
WordPress themes in the `/wp-content/themes` folder on your Web server.

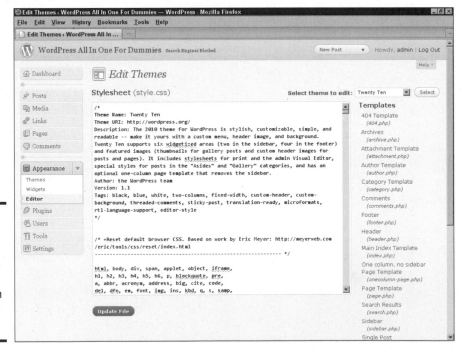

Figure 3-2:
A list of templates available in the default Twenty Ten WordPress theme.

The Edit Themes page also shows the template tags within the template file. These tags make all the magic happen in your blog; they connect all the templates to form a theme. The next section of this chapter discusses these template tags in detail, showing you what they mean and how they function.

Below the text box on the Edit Themes page is a drop-down menu labeled Documentation. Click the arrow on the right side of the menu, and a list drops down that contains all the template tags used in the template you are currently viewing. This list is helpful when you edit templates, and it gives you some insight into some of the different template tags used to create functions and features within your WordPress theme.

Understanding the Stylesheet

Every WordPress theme includes a `style.css` file. A browser uses this file, commonly known as the *stylesheet*, to style the theme. Style can include text colors, background images, and the spacing between elements on the site. The stylesheet targets areas of the site to style by using CSS IDs and classes. *CSS IDs* and *classes* are simply means of naming a particular element of the site. IDs are used for elements that only appear once on a page, while classes can be used as many times as you need. Although this file references *style,* it contains much more information about the theme.

At the very beginning of the `style.css` file, a comment block known as the *stylesheet header* passes information about your theme to WordPress. *Comments* are code statements included only for programmers, developers, and any others who read the code. Computers tend to ignore comment statements entirely, but WordPress uses the stylesheet header to get information about your theme. In CSS, comments always begin with a forward slash (/) followed by a star (*), and end with a star followed by a forward slash (*/). The following code shows an example of the stylesheet header for the Twenty Ten theme:

```
/*
Theme Name: Twenty Ten
Theme URI: http://wordpress.org/
Description: The 2010 default theme for WordPress.
Author: the WordPress team
Version: 1.0
Tags: black, blue, white, two-columns, fixed-width, custom-header, custom-
    background, threaded-comments, sticky-post, translation-ready, microformats,
    rtl-language-support, editor-style
*/
```

Figure 3-3 shows how Twenty Ten looks when activated.

**Book VI
Chapter 3**

**Exploring the
Anatomy of a Theme**

Figure 3-3:
This shows the currently active theme, Twenty Ten. The title and information are taken directly from the style.css header.

If you make modifications to the stylesheet header, the changes reflect in the WordPress Dashboard on the Themes page located in the Appearance menu.

Themes must provide this information in the stylesheet header, and no two themes can have the same information. Two themes with the same name and details would conflict in the theme selection page. If you create your own theme based on another theme, make sure that you change this information first.

Below the stylesheet header are the CSS styles that drive the formatting and styling of your theme.

Chapter 4 of this minibook goes into detail about CSS, including some examples that you can use to tweak the style of your existing WordPress theme — check it out!

Exploring Template Tags, Values, and Parameters

Some people are intimidated when they look at template tags. Really, they're just a simple bit of PHP code that you can use inside a template file to display information dynamically. Before starting to play around with template tags in your WordPress templates, it's important to understand what makes up a template tag and why.

WordPress is based in PHP (a scripting language for creating Web pages) and uses PHP commands to pull information from the MySQL database. Every tag begins with the function to start PHP and ends with a function to stop PHP. In the middle of those two commands lives the request to the database that tells WordPress to grab the data and display it.

A typical template tag looks like this:

```
<?php get_info(); ?>
```

This entire example tells WordPress to do three things:

+ Start PHP (`<?php`).
+ Use PHP to get information from the MySQL database and deliver it to your blog (`get_info();`).
+ Stop PHP (`?>`).

In this case, `get_info` is the actual tag function, which grabs information from the database to deliver it to your blog. What information is retrieved depends on what tag function appears between the two PHP commands. As you may notice, there's a lot of starting and stopping of PHP throughout the WordPress templates. The process seems as though it would be resource intensive, if not exhaustive — but it really isn't.

For every PHP command you start, you need a stop command. Every time a command begins with `<?php`, somewhere later in the code is the closing `?>` command. PHP commands that aren't structured properly cause really ugly errors on your site, and they've been known to send programmers, developers, and hosting providers into loud screaming fits.

Understanding the basics

If every piece of content on your site were hard-coded, it wouldn't be easy to use and modify. Template tags allow you to add information and content dynamically to your site. One example of adding information by using a template tag is the `the_category` tag. Instead of typing all the categories and links that each post belongs in, you can use the `the_category()` tag in your template to automatically display all the categories as links.

Using template tags prevents duplication of effort by automating the process of adding content to your Web site.

When you use a template tag, you're really telling WordPress to do something or retrieve some information. Often, template tags are used to fetch data from the server and even display it on the front end. More than 100 template tags are built into WordPress, and the tags vary greatly in what they can accomplish. A complete list of template tags can be found in the WordPress Codex at `http://codex.wordpress.org/Template_Tags`.

Template tags can be used only inside of PHP blocks. The PHP blocks can be opened and closed as many times as needed in a template file. When opened, the server knows that anything contained in the block is to be translated as PHP. The opening tag (`<?php`) must be followed, at some point, by the closing tag (`?>`). All blocks must contain these tags. A template tag is used in the same way that PHP functions are. The tag is always text with no spaces (may be separated by underscores or dashes), opening and closing brackets, and a semicolon. The following line of code shows you how it all looks:

```
<?php template_tag_name(); ?>
```

PHP is a fairly advanced coding language, and has many built-in functions for you to use. If you are not a PHP developer, I recommend that you keep it simple when you're attempting to add custom PHP. All code must be semantically perfect or it will not work. Always read your code to make sure that you entered it correctly.

Some template tags can be used only inside the loop so check the Codex for details. You can find out more about the loop in the section titled "Examining the Main Index and The Loop."

Using parameters

Because a template tag is a PHP function, you can pass parameters to the tag. A *parameter* is simply a variable that allows you to change or filter the output of a template tag. There are three types of template tags in WordPress:

✦ **Tags without parameters:** Some template tags don't require any options, so they don't need any parameters passed to them. For example, the `is_user_logged_in()` tag doesn't accept any parameters because it only returns `true` or `false`.

✦ **Tags with PHP function–style parameters:** Template tags with PHP function-style parameters accept parameters that are passed to them by placing one or more values inside the function's parentheses. For example, if you're using the `bloginfo()` tag, you can filter the output to just the description by using

```
<?php bloginfo('description'); ?>
```

If there are multiple parameters, the order in which you list them is very important. Each function sets the necessary order of its variables, so double-check the order of your parameters.

Always place the value in single quotes, and separate multiple parameters by commas.

✦ **Tags with query string–style parameters:** Template tags with query string–style parameters allow you to change the values of just the parameters you require. This is useful for template tags that have a large number of options. For example, the `wp_list_pages()` tag has 18 parameters. Instead of using the PHP function–style parameters, this function allows you to get to the source of what you need and give it a value. For example, if you want to list all your WordPress pages except for page 24, you use

```php
<?php wp_list_pages('exclude=24'); ?>
```

Query string–style parameters can be the most difficult to work with because they are generally dealing with the template tags that have the most possible parameters.

Table 3-1 helps you understand the three variations of parameters used by WordPress.

Table 3-1	Three Variations of Template Parameters	
Variation	*Description*	*Example*
Tags without parameters	These tags have no additional options available. Tags without parameters have nothing within the parentheses.	`the_tag();`
Tags with PHP function-style parameters	These tags have a comma-separated list of values placed within the tag parentheses.	`the_tag ('1,2,3');`
Tags with query-string parameters	These types of tags generally have several available parameters. This tag style enables you to change the value for each parameter without being required to provide values for all available parameters for the tag.	`the_tag ('parameter= true);`

The WordPress Codex, located at `http://codex.wordpress.org`, has every conceivable template tag and possible parameter known to the WordPress software. The tags and parameters that I share with you in this chapter are the ones used most often.

Customizing common tags

Because template tags must be used inside the PHP template files, they can easily be customized with HTML. If you're using the PHP tag `wp_list_pages()`, for example, you could display it in an HTML unordered list so that the pages are easily accessible to the users, like this:

```
<ul>
<?php wp_list_pages(); ?>
</ul>
```

This displays all the pages that you created in WordPress as an unordered list. If you had the pages About, Blog, and Content, it would be displayed like this:

✦ About

✦ Blog

✦ Contact

Another example is titles. For proper search engine optimization, you should always put page titles in H1 HTML tags, like this:

```
<h1 class="pagetitle">
<?php the_title(); ?>
</h1>
```

Digging deeper into the WordPress Codex

One of the best resources you can use for expanding your knowledge of WordPress is the WordPress Codex (`http://codex.wordpress.org`) shown in Figure 3-4. The Codex offers details, information, and examples for all theme templates, template tags, and theme creation in general. We use it when working on a theme because it has extensive and up-to-date information about functions and template tags.

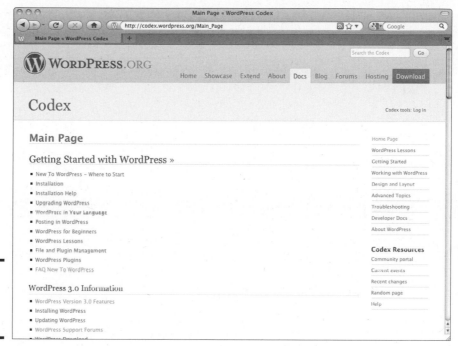

Figure 3-4:
The
WordPress
Codex.

Creating New Widget Areas

Many themes are *widget-ready,* meaning that you can insert widgets into them easily. *Widgets* allow you to add functionality to your sidebar without having to use code. Some common widget functionalities include displaying recent posts, displaying recent comments, adding a search box for searching content on a site, and adding static text. Even widget-ready themes have their limitations, however. You may find that the theme you chose doesn't have widget-ready areas in all the places you want them. However, you can make your own.

Registering your widget

To add a widget-ready area to the WordPress Dashboard Widget interface, you must first register the widget in your theme's functions.php file by adding the following code:

```
register_sidebar( array (
'name' => __( 'Widget Name'),
'id' => 'widget-name',
'description' => __( 'The primary widget area'),
'before_widget' => '<li id="%1$s" class="widget-container %2$s">',
'after_widget' => "</li>",
'before_title' => '<h3 class="widget-title">',
'after_title' => '</h3>',
) );
```

Within that code, you see seven different *arrays*. An array is a set of values that tells WordPress how you would like your widgets handled and displayed:

✦ **name:** This name is unique to the widget and is displayed on the Widgets page in the Dashboard. It is helpful if you register several different widgetized areas on your site.

✦ **id:** This is the unique ID given to the Widget

✦ **description:** This is a text description of the Widget. The text that gets placed here will display on the Widgets page in the Dashboard.

✦ **before_widget:** This is the HTML markup that gets inserted directly before the widget. It is helpful for CSS styling purposes.

✦ **after_widget:** This is the HTML markup that gets inserted directly after the widget.

✦ **before_title:** This is the HTML markup that gets inserted directly before the widget title.

✦ **after_title:** This is the HTML markup that gets inserted directly after the widget title.

You can insert this code directly beneath the first opening PHP tag (<?php). It is sometimes helpful to hit the return key to add a few extra lines when you are adding code. The extra empty lines around your code are ignored by the browser, but can greatly increase readability of the code.

Even though you use register_sidebar to register a widget, widgets do not have to appear in a sidebar. Widgets can appear anywhere you want them to. This code snippet registers a widget named Widget Name in the WordPress Dashboard. Additionally, it places the widget's content in an element that has the CSS class of widget, and puts <h4> tags around the widget's title.

Widgets that have been registered in the WordPress Dashboard are ready to be populated with content. In your site's Dashboard, on the right under the Appearance tab, you will see a page titled Widgets. There, you can now see the new widget area you have just registered.

Displaying new widgets on your site

When a widget-ready area is registered with the WordPress Dashboard, you can display the area somewhere on your site. A very common place for widget-ready areas is in the sidebar.

To add a widget-ready area in your sidebar, pick a location within the sidebar and then locate that area in the HTML, which can vary from theme to theme. Many times, theme authors will create their own sidebar.php file, and you can add this code there. After you find the area in the HTML, add the following code to the template:

```php
<?php dynamic_sidebar('Widget Name'); ?>
```

This displays the contents of the widget that you previously registered in the admin area.

Simplifying customization with functions

You may find that the simple code doesn't accomplish all the functionality that you need. For example, you may want to style the widget's title separate from the content. One solution is to create a custom PHP function that gives you a few more options. First, open `functions.php`. To create a function, you insert the following code directly below the opening `<?php` tag:

```php
function add_new_widget_location( $name ) {
if ( ! function_exists( 'dynamic_sidebar' ) || ! dynamic_sidebar(
$name ) ) : ?>
<div class="widget">
<h4><?php echo $name; ?></h4>
<div class="widget">
<p>This section is widgetized. If you would like to
add content to this section, you may do so by using the Widgets
panel from within your WordPress Admin Dashboard. This Widget
Section is called "<strong><?php echo $name; ?></strong>"</p>
</div>
</div>
<?php endif; ?>
<?php
}
```

In the function above, the first part checks to see whether a widget is assigned to this area. If so, the widget displays. If not, a message with the name of the widget area displays, which allows users to distinguish the widget area they want to add widgets to. Now if you want to display a widget by using this method, you go to the desired template file and insert the following code where you want the widget to appear:

```php
<?php add_new_widget_location('Widget-Name'); ?>
```

Exploring common problems

A common problem when creating widget areas is forgetting the admin side. Although people successfully create the widget in the PHP template where they want it, they often fail to make it to the `functions.php` to register the new widget area as described.

Another common problem is omitting the widget code from the `functions.php` file. If you're adding widget areas to an existing site, you need to add the widget code to the bottom of the list of widgets in the `functions.php` file.

Failure to do so causes the widget areas to shift their contents. This places your widgets out of order, causing you to have to redo them on the Widgets page in the WordPress Dashboard.

Examining the Main Index and The Loop

Your theme is required to have only two files. The first is `style.css`. The other is a main index file, known in WordPress as `index.php`. The `index.php` file is the first file WordPress tries to load when someone visits your site. Extremely flexible, `index.php` can be used as a stand-alone file or include other templates. The Main Index template drags your blog posts out of the MySQL database and inserts them into your blog. This template is to your blog what the dance floor is to a nightclub — where all the action happens.

The filename of the Main Index template is `index.php`. You can find it in the `/wp-content/themes/twentyten/` folder.

The first template tag in the Main Index template calls in the Header template, meaning that it pulls the information from the Header template into the Main Index template, as follows:

```
<?php get_header(); ?>
```

Your theme can work without calling in the Header template, but it will be missing several essential pieces — the CSS and the blog name and tagline, for starters.

The Main Index template in the Twenty Ten theme calls in three other files in a similar fashion:

✦ `get_template_part( 'loop', 'index' );` — this function calls in the template file named: `loop.php`.

✦ `get_sidebar();` — this function calls in the template file named: `sidebar.php`.

✦ `get_footer();` — this function calls in the template file named: `footer.php`.

Each of these three functions and template files is covered in upcoming sections of this chapter.

The concept of *calling in* a template file by using a function or template tag is exactly what the Main Index template does with the four functions for the header, loop, sidebar, and footer templates explained later in this section.

Generally, one of the important functions of the main index is to contain The Loop. In WordPress, The Loop displays posts and pages on your site. Any PHP or HTML that you include in The Loop will repeat for each of your posts that it displays. The Loop is a function that WordPress uses to display the posts, and pages, on your site. The Loop has a starting point and an ending point; anything placed in between is used to display each post, including any HTML, PHP, or CSS tags and codes.

Here's a look at what the WordPress Codex calls "The World's Simplest Index."

```php
<?php
get_header();
if (have_posts()) :
  while (have_posts()) :
    the_post();
    the_content();
  endwhile;
endif;
get_sidebar();
get_footer();
?>
```

**Book VI
Chapter 3**

Exploring the
Anatomy of a Theme

First, the template starts by opening the php tag. Next, it includes the header, meaning that it retrieves anything contained in the header.php file and displays it. Now the good stuff starts happening. The Loop begins with the while (have_posts()) : bit. Anything between the while and the endwhile repeats for each post that displays. The number of posts that displays is determined in the settings section of the WordPress Dashboard.

If your blog has posts (and most do, even when you first install it), WordPress proceeds with The Loop, starting with the piece of code that looks like this:

```php
if (have_posts()) :
  while (have_posts()) :
```

This code tells WordPress to grab the posts from the MySQL database and display them on your blog page.

Then The Loop closes with this tag:

```php
  endwhile;
endif;
```

Near the beginning of the Loop template, there is a template tag that looks like this:

```php
if (have_posts()) :
```

To read that template tag in plain English, it says: If [this blog] has posts.

If your blog meets that condition (that is, if it has posts), WordPress proceeds with The Loop and displays your blog posts. If it does meet that condition (that is, it does not have posts), WordPress displays a message that no posts exist.

When The Loop ends (at the `endwhile`), the index template goes on to execute the files for sidebar and footer. Although it is simple, The Loop is one of the core functions of WordPress.

Misplacement of the `while` or `endwhile` statements causes The Loop to break. If you're having trouble with The Loop in an existing template, check your version against the original and see whether the `while` statements are misplaced.

In your travels as a WordPress user, you may run across plugins or scripts with instructions that say something like this: "This must be placed within The Loop." That's The Loop that we discuss in this section, so pay particular attention. Understanding The Loop arms you with the knowledge you need for tackling and understanding your WordPress themes.

The Loop is no different from any other template tag; it must begin with a function to start PHP, and it must end with a function to stop PHP. The Loop begins with PHP and then makes a request: "While there are posts in my blog, display them on this page." This PHP function tells WordPress to grab the blog post information from the database and return it to the blog page. The end of The Loop is like a traffic cop with a big red stop sign telling WordPress to stop the function completely.

You can set the number of posts displayed per page in the Reading Settings page in the WordPress Dashboard. The Loop abides by this rule and displays only the number of posts per page that you've set.

WordPress uses other template files besides the main index, such as the header, sidebar and footer templates. The next section gives you a closer look at a few of them.

Header template

The Header template for your WordPress themes is the starting point for every WordPress theme because it tells Web browsers the following:

+ The title of your blog
+ The location of the CSS

✦ The RSS feed URL

✦ The blog URL

✦ The tagline (or description) of the blog

In many themes, the first elements in the header are a main image and the navigation. These two elements are usually in the header.php because they load on every page and rarely change. The following statement is the built-in WordPress function to call the header template:

```
<?php get_header(); ?>
```

Every page on the Web has to start with a few pieces of code. In every header.php file in any WordPress theme, you'll find these bits of code at the top:

✦ The DOCTYPE (which stands for *document type declaration*) tells the browser which type of XHTML standards you're using. The Twenty Ten theme uses <!DOCTYPE html>, which is a declaration for W3C standards compliance mode and covers all major browser systems.

✦ The <html> tag (*HTML* stands for *Hypertext Markup Language*) tells the browser which language you're using to write your Web pages.

✦ The <head> tag tells the browser that the information contained within the tag shouldn't be displayed on the site; rather, it's information about the document.

In the header template of the Twenty Ten, these bits of code look like the following example, and you should leave them intact:

```
<!DOCTYPE html>
<html <?php language_attributes(); ?>>
<head>
```

On the Edit Themes page, click the Header template link to display the template code in the text box. Look closely, and you see that the <!DOCTYPE html> declaration, <html> tag, and <head> tag show up in the template.

The <head> tag needs to be closed at the end of the Header template, which looks like this: </head>. You also need to include a fourth tag, the <body> tag, which tells the browser where the information you want to display begins. Both the <body> and <html> tags need to be closed at the end of the template, like this: </body></html>.

Using bloginfo parameters

The Header template makes much use of one WordPress template tag in particular: `bloginfo();`.

What differentiates the type of information that a tag pulls in is a *parameter*. Parameters are placed inside the parentheses of the tag, enclosed in single quotes. For the most part, these parameters pull information from the settings in your WordPress Dashboard. The template tag to get your blog title, for example, looks like this:

```
<?php bloginfo('name'); ?>
```

Table 3-2 lists the various parameters you need for the `bloginfo();` tag and shows you what the template tag looks like. The parameters in Table 3-2 are listed in the order of their appearance in the Twenty Ten `header.php` template file, and pertain to the `bloginfo();` template tag only.

Table 3-2	Tag Values for bloginfo();	
Parameter	*Information*	*Tag*
`charset`	Character settings set in Settings/General	`<?php bloginfo ('charset'); ?>`
`name`	Blog title, set in Settings/General	`<?php bloginfo ('name'); ?>`
`descrip-tion`	Tagline for your blog, set in Settings/General	`<?php bloginfo ('description'); ?>`
`url`	Your blog's Web address, set in Settings/General	`<?php bloginfo ('url'); ?>`
`stylesheet_url`	URL of primary CSS file	`<?php bloginfo ('stylesheet url'); ?>`
`pingback_url`	Displays the trackback URL for your blog on single post pages	`<?php bloginfo ('pingback_url'); ?>`

Creating title tags

Here's a useful tip about your blog's `<title>` tag: Search engines pick up the words used in the `<title>` tag as keywords to categorize your site in their search engine directories.

The `<title></title>` tags are HTML tags that tell the browser to display the title of your Web site in the title bar of a visitor's browser window.

Search engines love the title bar. The more you can tweak that title to provide detailed descriptions of your site (otherwise known as search engine optimization or SEO), the more the search engines will love your Blog site. Browsers will show that love by giving your site higher rankings in their results. For more information and tips on SEO with WordPress, see Book V.

The blog `<title>` tag is the code that lives in the Header template between these two tag markers: `<title></title>`. In the default Twenty Ten theme, this bit of code looks like this (don't let this code scare you! we promise we'll break it down for you!):

Book VI Chapter 3

Exploring the Anatomy of a Theme

```php
<title><?php
    /*
     * Print the <title> tag based on what is being viewed.
     */
    global $page, $paged;

    wp_title( '|', true, 'right' );

    // Add the blog name.
    bloginfo( 'name' );

    // Add the blog description for the home/front page.
    $site_description = get_bloginfo( 'description', 'display'
    );
    if ( $site_description && ( is_home() || is_front_page() )
    )
        echo " | $site_description";

    // Add a page number if necessary:
    if ( $paged >= 2 || $page >= 2 )
    echo ' | ' . sprintf( __( 'Page %s', 'twentyten' ), max(
    $paged, $page ) );

    ?></title>
```

It may help for us to put this example into plain English. The way the Twenty Ten Header template displays the title is based on the type of page that is being displayed — and it shrewdly uses SEO to help you with the browser powers that be. Table 3-3 breaks down what's happening.

Table 3-3	Title Tags and What They Do	
Title Tags and Parameters	*Tags Used*	*What Is Displayed in the Title Bar*
`wp_title( '|',` `true, 'right' );`	`wp_title`	Displays the title of the page you are viewing with a separator bar, "|" to the right of the title.
`bloginfo` `( 'name' );`	`bloginfo` `( 'name' );`	Displays the name of your site to the right of the title of the page.
`$site_description =` `get_bloginfo` `( 'description',` `'display' );` `if ( $site_` `description &&` `( is_home() || is_` `front_page() ) )` `echo "	$site_` `description";`	`$site_` `description =` `get_bloginfo` `( 'description',` `'display' );` `is_home()` `is_front_page()`	If the reader is viewing the home, or front, page of your site; the site description is displayed to the right of the page title.
`if ( $paged >= 2 ||` `$page >= 2 )echo` `'	' . sprintf` `(__('Page %s',` `'twentyten'),` `max($paged,` `$page));`	Conditional statement, in plain English, reads: if this is paged, then display the page number.	If the reader is viewing page 2, 3, 4, and so on of an archive page, the title bar will display the page number to the right of the page title.

The title bar of the browser window always displays your blog name unless you're on a single post page. In that case, it displays your blog title plus the title of the post on that page.

Within some of the WordPress template tags, such as the `<title>` tag in the earlier example, you may notice some weird characters that look like a foreign language. You may wonder what `&raquo;` is, for example. It isn't part of any PHP function or CSS style. Rather, it's a *character entity* — a kind of code that enables you to display a special character in your blog. The `&raquo;` character entity displays a double right-angle quotation mark.

Displaying your blog name and tagline

The default Twenty Ten theme header displays your blog name and tagline on the top of your site, on every page.

You can use the `bloginfo();` tag plus a little HTML code to display your blog name and tagline. Most blogs have a clickable title, which is a site title that takes you back to the main page when it's clicked. No matter where your visitors are on your site, they can always go back home by clicking the title of your site in the header.

To create a clickable title, use the following code:

```
<a href="<?php bloginfo('url'); ?>"><?php bloginfo('name'); ?></a>
```

The `bloginfo('url');` tag is your main blog Internet address, and the `bloginfo('name');` tag is the name of your blog (refer to Table 3-1). So the code creates a link that looks something like this:

```
<a href="http://yourdomain.com">Your Blog Name</a>
```

The tagline generally isn't linked back home. You can display it by using the following tag:

```
<?php bloginfo('description'); ?>
```

This tag pulls the tagline directly from the one that you set up on the General Settings page in your WordPress Dashboard.

This example shows how WordPress is intuitive and user-friendly; you can do things such as changing the blog name and tagline with a few keystrokes in the Dashboard. Changing your options in the Dashboard creates the change on every page of your site — no coding experience required. Beautiful, isn't it?

In the Twenty Ten templates, these tags are surrounded by tags that look like these: `<h1></h1>` or `<h4></h4>`. These tags are `<header>` tags, which define the look and layout of the blog name and tagline in the CSS of your theme. We cover CSS further in Chapter 4 of this minibook.

Sidebar template

The sidebar template in WordPress has the file name: `sidebar.php`. The sidebar is usually found on the left or right side of the main content area of your WordPress theme (in the Twenty Ten theme, the sidebar is displayed to the right of the main content area). It is a good place to put useful information about your site, such as a site summary, advertisements, or testimonials.

Many themes use widget areas in the sidebar template. This allows you to display content easily on your WordPress pages and posts. The following statement is the built-in WordPress function to call the sidebar template:

```
<?php get_sidebar(); ?>
```

This code calls the Sidebar template and all the information it contains into your blog page.

Footer template

The footer template in WordPress has the file name: `footer.php`. The footer is generally at the bottom of the page, and contains brief reference information about the site. This usually includes copyright information, template design credits, and a mention of WordPress. Similarly to the Header and Sidebar templates, the Footer template gets called into the Main Index template through this bit of code:

```
<?php get_footer(); ?>
```

This code calls the Footer and all the information it contains into your blog page.

The default Twenty Ten theme shows the site title and a statement that says "Proudly powered by WordPress." You can use the footer to include all sorts of information about your site; however, you don't have to restrict it to small bits of information.

Examining Other Template Files

To make your Web site work properly, WordPress uses all the theme files together. Some, such as the header and footer, are used on every page. Others, such as the comments template (`comments.php`), are used only at specific times, to pull in specific functions.

When someone visits your site, WordPress uses a series of queries to determine which templates to use.

Many more theme templates can be included in your theme. Here are some of the other template files you might want to use:

✦ **Comments template (`comments.php`):** The Comments template is required if you plan to host comments on your blog; it provides all the template tags you need to display those comments. The template tag used to call the comments into the template is `<?php comments_ template(); ?>`.

✦ **Single Post template (single.php):** When your visitors click the title or permalink of a post you published to your blog, they're taken to that post's individual page. There, they can read the entire post, and if you have comments enabled, they see the comments form and can leave comments.

✦ **Page template (page.php):** You can use a Page template for static pages in your WordPress site.

✦ **Search Results (search.php):** You can use this template to create a custom display of search results on your blog. When someone uses the search feature to search your site for specific keywords, this template formats the return of those results.

✦ **404 template (404.php):** Use this template to create a custom 404 page, which is the page visitors get when the browser can't find the page requested and returns that ugly 404 Page Cannot Be Found error.

The templates in the preceding list are optional. If these templates don't exist in your WordPress themes folder, nothing breaks. The Main Index template handles the display of these items (the single post page, the search results page, and so on). The only exception is the Comments template. If you want to display comments on your site, you must have that template included in your theme.

Customizing Your Blog Posts with Template Tags

This section covers the template tags that you use to display the body of each blog post you publish. The body of a blog post includes information such as the post date and time, title, author name, category, and content. Table 3-4 lists the common template tags you can use for posts, available for you to use in any WordPress theme template. The tags in Table 3-4 work only if you place them within The Loop (covered earlier in this chapter and found in the loop.php template file).

Table 3-4	Template Tags for Blog Posts
Tag	*Function*
get_the_date();	Displays the date of the post.
get_the_time();	Displays the time of the post.
the_title();	Displays the title of the post.
the_permalink();	Displays the permalink (URL) of the post.
get_the_author();	Displays the post author's name.
the_author_link();	Displays the URL of the post author's site.

(continued)

Table 3-4 *(continued)*

Tag	Function
`the_content('Read More...');`	Displays the content of the post. (If you use an excerpt [below], the words *Read More* appear and are linked to the individual post page.)
`the_excerpt();`	Displays an excerpt (snippet) of the post.
`the_category();`	Displays the category (or categories) assigned to the post. If the post is assigned to multiple categories, commas will separate them.
`comments_popup_link ('No Comments', 'Comment (1)', 'Comments(%)');`	Displays a link to the comments, along with the comment count for the post in parentheses. (If no comments exist, it displays a *No Comments* message.)
`next_posts_link ('&laquo; Previous Entries')`	Displays the words *Previous Entries* linked to the previous page of blog entries.
`previous_posts_link ('Next Entries &raquo;')`	Displays the words *Next Entries* linked to the next page of blog entries.

The last two tags in Table 3-4 aren't like the others. You don't place these tags in The Loop; instead, you insert them after The Loop but before the `if` statement ends. Here's an example:

```
<?php endwhile; ?>
<?php next_posts_link('&laquo; Previous Entries') ?>
<?php previous_posts_link('Next Entries &raquo;') ?>
<?php endif; ?>
```

Putting It All Together

Template files can't do a whole lot by themselves. The real power comes when they're put together.

Connecting the templates

WordPress has built-in functions to include the main template files, such as `header.php`, `sidebar.php`, and `footer.php`, in other templates. An `include` function is a custom PHP function that is built in to WordPress, allowing you to retrieve the content of another template file and display it along with the content of another template file. Table 3-5 shows the templates and the function to include them.

Table 3-5	Template Files and Include Functions
Template Name	*Include Function*
header.php	`<?php get_header(); ?>`
sidebar.php	`<?php get_sidebar(); ?>`
footer.php	`<?php get_footer(); ?>`
search.php	`<?php get_search_form(); ?>`
comments.php	`<?php comments_template(); ?>`

If you want to include a file that doesn't have a built-in `include` function, you need a different piece of code. For instance, if you want to add a unique sidebar to a certain page template, you could name the sidebar file `sidebar_page.php`. To include that in another template, you would use the following code:

```
<?php get_template_part('sidebar_page.php'); ?>
```

In this statement, the PHP `get_template_part` function looks through the main theme folder for the `sidebar_page.php` file and displays the sidebar.

In this section, you put together the guts of a basic Main Index template by using the information on templates and tags we provide so far in this chapter. There seem to be endless lines of code when you view the `loop.php` template file in the Twenty Ten theme, so we've simplified it for you with the following steps. These steps should give you a basic understanding of the WordPress Loop and common template tags and functions that you can use to create your own.

You create a new WordPress theme, using some of the basic WordPress templates. The first steps in pulling everything together are as follows:

1. **Connect to your Web server via FTP, click the wp-content folder, and then click the themes folder.**

This folder contains the themes that are currently installed in your WordPress blog. (Go to Book II, Chapter 2 if you need more information on FTP.)

2. **Create a new folder, and call it `mytheme`.**

   In most FTP programs, you can right-click and choose New Folder. (If you aren't sure how to create a folder, refer to your FTP program's help files.)

3. **In your favored text editor (like Notepad for the PC or Textmate for the Mac) create and save the following files with the lines of code we provide for each:**

   - **Header template:** Create the file with the following lines of code then save it with the filename: `header.php`:

```
<!DOCTYPE html PUBLIC "-//W3C//DTD XHTML 1.0 Transitional//EN"
  "http://www.w3.org/TR/xhtml1/DTD/xhtml1-transitional.dtd">
<html xmlns="http://www.w3.org/1999/xhtml" <?php language_
  attributes(); ?> />

<head profile="http://gmpg.org/xfn/11">
<meta http-equiv="Content-Type" content="<?php bloginfo('html_type');
  ?>;
charset=<?php bloginfo('charset'); ?>" />

<title><?php bloginfo( 'name' ); ?> <?php if ( is_single() ) { ?>
  &raquo; Blog Archive <?php } ?>
<?php wp_title(); ?></title>

<link rel="stylesheet" href="<?php bloginfo( 'stylesheet_url' ); ?>"
  type="text/css" media="screen" />
<link rel="pingback" href="<?php bloginfo( 'pingback_url' ); ?>" />

<?php if ( is_singular() ) wp_enqueue_script( 'comment-reply' ); ?>
<?php wp_head(); ?>
</head>
<body <?php body_class() ?>>
<div id="page">
<div id="header">
<h1><a href="<?php bloginfo('url'); ?>"><?php bloginfo('name');
  ?><?a></h1>
<h2><?php bloginfo('description'); ?></h2>
</div>
<div id="main">
```

   - **Theme Functions:** Create the file with the following lines of code and then save it with the filename: `functions.php`:

```
<?php
if ( function_exists('register_sidebar') ) register_sidebar(array('nam
  e'=>'Sidebar',
));
?>
```

     The Theme Functions file registers the widget area for your site so that you are able to add widgets to your sidebar by using the available WordPress widgets from the Widget page in the Dashboard.

- **Sidebar template**: Create the file with the following lines of code and then save it with the filename: `sidebar.php`:

```
<div id="side" class="sidebar">
<ul>
<?php if ( !function_exists('dynamic_sidebar') || !dynamic_
  sidebar('Sidebar') ) : ?>
<?php endif; ?>
</ul>
</div>
```

The code here tells WordPress where you want the WordPress widgets to display in your theme; in this case, widgets are displayed in the sidebar of your site.

- **Footer template:** Create the file with the following lines of code and then save it with the filename: `footer.php`:

```
</div>
<div id="footer">
<p>&copy; Copyright <a href="<?php bloginfo('url'); ?>"><?php
  bloginfo('name'); ?></a>. All Rights Reserved</p>
</div>
<?php wp_footer(); ?>
</body>
</html>
```

- **Stylesheet:** Create the file with the following lines of code and then save it with the filename: `style.css` (more CSS is covered in Chapter 4 of this minibook — this example gives you just some very basic styling to create your sample theme):

```
/*
Theme Name: My Theme
Description: Basic Theme from WordPress All In One For Dummies example
Author: Lisa Sabin-Wilson
Author URI: http://lisasabin-wilson.com
*/

body {
font-family: verdana, arial, helvetica, sans-serif;
font-size:16px;
color: #555;
background: #eee;
}

#page {
width: 960px;
margin: 0 auto;
background: white;
border: 1px solid silver;
}
```

```
#header {
width: 950px;
height: 100px;
background: black;
color: white;
padding: 5px;
}

#header h1 a {
color: white;
font-size: 22px;
font-family: Georgia;
text-decoration: none;
}

#header h2 {
font-size: 16px;
font-family: Georgia;
color: #eee;
}

#main {
width: 600px;
float:left;
}

#side {
width: 220px;
margin: 0 15px;
float:left;
}

#footer {
clear:both;
width: 960px;
height: 50px;
background: black;
color: white;
}

#footer p {
text-align:center;
padding: 15px 0;
}

#footer a {
color:white;
}
```

Using the tags provided in Table 3-4, along with the information on The Loop and the calls to the Header, Sidebar, and Footer templates provided in earlier sections, you can follow the next steps for a bare-bones example of what the Main Index template looks like when you put the tags together.

When typing templates, be sure to use a text editor such as Notepad or TextEdit. Using a word processing program such as Microsoft Word opens a whole slew of problems in your code. Word processing programs insert hidden characters and format quotation marks in a way that WordPress can't read.

Now that you have the basic theme foundation, the last template file you need to create is the Main Index template. To create a Main Index template to work with the other templates in your WordPress theme, open a new window in a text-editor program and then follow these steps. (Type the text in each of these steps on its own line. Press the Enter key after typing each line so that each tag starts on a new line.)

1. **Type** `<?php get_header(); ?>`.

   This template tag pulls the information in the Header template of your WordPress theme.

2. **Type** `<?php if (have_posts()) : ?>`.

   This template tag is an `if` statement that asks, "Does this blog have posts?" If the answer is yes, it grabs the post content information from your MySQL database and displays the posts in your blog.

3. **Type** `<?php while (have_posts()) : the_post(); ?>`.

   This template tag starts The Loop.

4. **Type** `<a href="<?php the_permalink(); ?>"><?php the_title(); ?></a>`.

   This tag tells your blog to display the title of a post that's clickable (linked) to the URL of the post.

5. **Type** `Posted on <?php the_date(); ?> at <?php the_time(); ?>`.

   This template tag displays the date and time when the post was made. With these template tags, the date and time format are determined by the format you set in the Dashboard.

6. **Type** `Posted in <?php the_category(','); ?>`.

   This template tag displays a comma-separated list of the categories to which you've assigned the post — *Posted in: category 1, category 2,* for example.

7. **Type** `<?php the_content('Read More..'); ?>`.

   This template tag displays the actual content of the blog post. The `'Read More..'` portion of this tag tells WordPress to display the words *Read More,* which are clickable (hyperlinked) to the post's permalink, where the reader can read the rest of the post in its entirety. This tag applies when you're displaying a post excerpt, as determined by the actual post configuration in the Dashboard.

8. **Type** `Posted by: <?php the_author(); ?>`.

   This template tag displays the author of the post in this manner: *Posted by: Lisa Sabin-Wilson.*

9. **Type** `<?php comments_popup_link('No Comments',` `'1 Comment', '% Comments'); ?>`.

   This template tag displays the link to the comments for this post, along with the number of comments.

10. **Type** `<?php endwhile; ?>`.

    This template tag ends The Loop and tells WordPress to stop displaying blog posts here. WordPress knows exactly how many times The Loop needs to work, based on the setting in the WordPress Dashboard. That's exactly how many times WordPress will execute The Loop.

11. **Type** `<?php next_posts_link('&laquo; Previous` `Entries'); ?>`.

    This template tag displays a clickable link to the previous page of blog entries, if any.

12. **Type** `<?php previous posts link('&raquo; Next` `Entries'); ?>`.

    This template tag displays a clickable link to the next page of blog entries, if any.

13. **Type** `<?php else : ?>`.

    This template tag refers to the `if` question asked in Step 2. If the answer to that question is no, this step provides the `else` statement — IF this blog has posts, THEN list them here (Step 2 and Step 3), or ELSE display the following message.

14. **Type** `Not Found. Sorry, but you are looking for something` `that isn't here.`

    This is the message followed by the template tag that is displayed after the `else` statement from Step 13. You can reword this statement to have it say whatever you want.

15. **Type** `<?php endif; ?>`.

    This template tag ends the `if` statement from Step 2.

16. **Type** `<?php get_sidebar(); ?>`.

    This template tag calls in the Sidebar template and pulls that information into the Main Index template.

17. **Type** `<?php get_footer(); ?>`.

    This template tag calls in the Footer template and pulls that information into the Main Index template. ***Note:*** The code in the `footer.php` template ends the `<body>` and the `<html>` tags that were started in the Header template (`header.php`).

When you're done, the display of the Main Index template code looks like this:

```php
<?php get_header(); ?>
<?php if (have_posts()) : ?>
 <?php while (have_posts()) : the_post(); ?>
 <div <?php post_class() ?> id="post-<?php the_ID(); ?>">
    <a href="<?php the_permalink(); ?>"><?php the_title(); ?></a>
    Posted on: <?php the_date(); ?> at <?php the_time(); ?>
    Posted in: <?php the_category(','); ?>

    <?php the_content('Read More..'); ?>
    Posted by: <?php the_author(); ?> | <?php comments_popup_link('No
    Comments', '1 Comment', '% Comments'); ?>
</div>

<?php endwhile; ?>
<?php next_posts_link('&laquo; Previous Entries') ?>
<?php previous_posts_link('Next Entries &raquo;') ?>
<?php else : ?>
Not Found
Sorry, but you are looking for something that isn't here.
<?php endif; ?>
<?php get_sidebar(); ?>
<?php get_footer(); ?>
```

18. **Save this file as** index.php, **and upload it to the** mythemes **folder.**

In Notepad, you can save it by choosing File⇨Save As. Type the name of the file in the File Name text box, and click Save.

19. **Activate the theme in the WordPress Dashboard, and view your blog to see your handiwork in action!**

Our Main Index template code has one template tag that is explained in Chapter 6 in this minibook: `<div <?php post_class() ?> id="post-<?php the_ID(); ?>">`. This tag helps you create some interesting styles in your template by using CSS, so check out Chapter 6 to find out all about it!

This very simple and basic Main Index template that you just built does not have the standard HTML mark up in it, so you will find that the visual display of your blog differs somewhat from the default Twenty Ten theme. This example was used to give you the bare-bones basics of the Main Index template and The Loop in action. Chapter 4 of this minibook goes into detail about the use of HTML and CSS to create nice styling and formatting for your posts and pages.

Using additional stylesheets

Often, a theme uses multiple stylesheets for browser compatibility or consistent organization. If you use multiple stylesheets, the process for including them in the template is the same as any other stylesheet.

To add a new stylesheet, create a directory in the root theme folder called css. Next, create a new file called `mystyle.css` within the css folder. To include the file, you must edit the `header.php` file. The example below shows the code you need to include in the new CSS file.

```
<link rel="stylesheet" href="<?php bloginfo('stylesheet_directory');
?>/css/mystyle.css" type="text/css" media="screen" />
```

Chapter 4: Customizing Your Theme

In This Chapter

✔ **Personalizing your header and background graphics**

✔ **Customizing with site with CSS**

✔ **Modifying your theme with CSS and HTML**

✔ **Customizing basic elements for uniqueness**

✔ **Exploring additional resources**

Customizing your WordPress theme's overall look with unique graphics and colors is one of the most fun and exciting aspects of tweaking WordPress themes. We enjoy taking one of our favorite, easily customizable themes, and personalizing it with some simple changes to make it unique. (For more information on finding an existing theme, read Book VI, Chapter 2.)

After you find an existing free (or premium) WordPress theme that suits your needs, the next step is personalizing the theme through some of the following techniques:

✦ **Plugging in your own graphics:** The easiest way to make a theme your own is through a graphical header that includes your logo and matching background graphics.

✦ **Adjusting colors:** You might like the structure and design of your theme, but want to adjust the colors to match your own tastes or brand look. You can do this in the CSS, too.

✦ **Adding/changing fonts:** You may want to change the font, or *typography,* on your site by using different font types, sizes, or colors. You can edit these display properties in the CSS.

Often, the customization process is one of trial and error. You'll mix and match different elements, tweaking and tinkering with graphics and CSS until you achieve design perfection. In this chapter, you explore the easiest ways to customize your WordPress theme through graphics and CSS.

Changing Your Background Graphic

Using background graphics is an easy way to set your site apart from others that use the same theme. A background graphic for your site can be compared to finding just the right desktop background for your computer. You can choose from a variety of background graphics for your site the way you can for your computer desktop, such as photography, abstract art, and repeatable patterns.

You can find ideas for new and different background graphics by checking out some of the CSS galleries on the Web, such as `http://cssdrive.com` and `http://csselite.com`. Sites like these should be used for inspiration only, not theft. Be careful when using images from outside sources. You only want to use graphics and images that you have been given the right (through express permission or licenses that allow you to reuse) to use on your sites. For this reason, we suggest purchasing graphics from reputable sources. Three of our favorite online graphic sites include:

✦ **iStockphoto (`http://istockphoto.com`):** An extensive library of stock photography, vector illustrations, video and audio clips, and Flash media. You can sign up for an account and search through libraries of image files to find the image that suits you, or your client, best. The files that you use from iStockphoto aren't free; you do have to pay for them — and be sure that you read the license for each image you use from them. They have several different licenses. The cheapest one is their Standard License, which has some limitations. For example, you can use an illustration from iStockphoto in one Web site design, but you cannot use that same illustration in a theme design that you intend to sell multiple times (say in a premium theme marketplace). Be sure to read the fine print!

✦ **Dreamstime (`http://dreamstime.com`):** Dreamstime is a major supplier of stock photography and digital images. Sign up for an account and search through their huge library of digital image offerings. Dreamstime does offer free images, at times — so keep your eyes out for those! Also, Dreamstime has different licenses for their image files that you need to pay close attention to, but one nice feature is their Royalty Free licensing option. This option allows you to pay for the image one time and then use the image as many times as you like; however, you can't redistribute the image in the same Web site theme repeatedly, such as in a template that's sold to the public.

✦ **Graphic River (`http://www.graphicriver.net`):** Graphic River offers stock graphic files from Photoshop images, design templates, textures, vector graphics, and icons, to name just a few. Their selection is vast, and the cost to download and use their graphic files are minimal. As with all graphic and image libraries, be sure to read their terms of use or any licensing attached to each of the files to make sure you are legally abiding by their terms.

Another great resource for finding free graphics and more is Smashing Magazine at `http://smashingmagazine.com`. You'll find hundreds of links and resources to free and, often, reusable graphics, such as textures and wallpapers for your site.

To best use background graphics, you must answer a few simple questions:

✦ **What type of background graphic do you want to use?** For example, do you want a repeatable pattern or texture or an image like a black-and-white photograph of something in your business?

✦ **How do you want the background graphic to display in your browser?** Do you want to tile or repeat your background image in the browser window or pin it to a certain position no matter what size your guest's browser is?

The answers to those questions determine how you install a background graphic in your theme design.

When working with graphics on the Web, we recommend using GIF, JPG, or PNG image formats. For images with a small number of colors (such as charts, line art, logos, and so on), GIF format works best. For other image types (screenshots with text and images, blended transparency, and so on), use JPG or PNG.

For Web design, the characteristics of each image file format can help you decide which file format you need to use for your site. The most common image file formats and characteristics include:

✦ **.jpg:** Suited for use with photographs and smaller images used in your Web design projects. Although the `.jpg` format compresses with lossy compression, you can adjust compression when you save a file in a `.jpg` format. That is, you can choose the degree, or amount, of compression that will occur from 1 to 100. Usually, you won't see a great deal of image quality loss with compression levels 1 through 20.

✦ **.png:** Suited for larger graphics used in Web design, like the logo or main header graphic that helps brand the overall, visual look of the Web site. A `.png` file uses lossless image compression; therefore, no data loss occurs during compression, which creates a cleaner, sharper image. You can also create and save a `.png` file on a transparent canvas; `.jpg` files must have a white canvas or some other color that you designate.

✦ **.gif:** Compression of a `.gif` file is lossless; therefore, the image renders exactly the way you design it, without loss of quality. However, `.gif` files compress with lossless quality when the image uses 256 colors, or less. For images that use more colors (higher quality), `.gif` isn't the greatest format to use. We recommend using the `.png` format, instead.

Uploading an image for background use

If you want to change the background graphic in your theme, follow these steps:

1. **Upload your new background graphic via FTP to the images folder in your theme directory.**

Typically, the images folder can be found at `wp-content/themes/themename/images`.

2. **On the WordPress Dashboard, choose Appearance⇨Editor.**

The Theme Editor page displays.

3. **Click the Stylesheet (`style.css`) link on the right side of the page.**

The `style.css` template opens in the text editor box on the left side of the Theme Editor page.

4. **Scroll down to find the `body` CSS selector.**

We discuss CSS selectors later in this chapter, but the following code segment is a sample CSS snippet from the Twenty Ten theme. (How the `body` selector is defined differs from theme to theme.)

```
body {
    background: #f1f1f1;
}
```

5. **Edit the background property values.**

Change this:

```
background: #f1f1f1;
```

To this:

```
background-color: #FFFFFF;
background-image: url('images/newbackground.gif');
```

In the above example, we added a new background image (`newback ground.gif`) to the existing code and changed the color code to white (#FFFFFF).

6. **Click the Update File button to save the stylesheet changes you made.**

Your changes are saved and applied to your theme. Figure 4-1 shows a preview of the new background on the test site without any positioning.

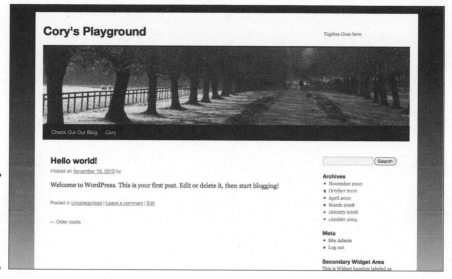

Figure 4-1:
A new
background
image on
a blog.

Positioning, repeating, and attaching images

After you upload a background graphic, you can use CSS background properties to position it how you want it. The main CSS properties — `background-position`, `background-repeat`, and `background-attachment` — help you achieve the desired effect. Table 4-1 describes the CSS background properties and their available values for changing them in your theme stylesheet.

Table 4-1	CSS Background Properties		
Property	*Description*	*Values*	*Example*
back-ground-position	Determines the starting point of your background image on your Web page	bottom center	background-position: bottom center;
		bottom right	
		left center	
		right center	
		center center	

(continued)

Table 4-1 *(continued)*

Property	Description	Values	Example
back-ground-repeat	Determines whether your background image will repeat or tile	repeat (repeats infinitely) repeat-y (repeats vertically) repeat-x (repeats horizontally) no-repeat (does not repeat)	background-repeat: repeat-y;
back-ground-attach-ment	Determines whether your background image is fixed or scrolls with the browser window	fixed scroll	background-attachment: scroll;

In the previous section, we upload a new background graphic, newback-ground.gif. You can explore positioning it with some of the values provided in Table 4-1. If you're a visual person, you'll enjoy testing and tweaking values to see the effects on your site.

Say your goal is to *tile,* or repeat, the background image horizontally (see Figure 4-2), or across the browser screen from left to right so that it scales with the width of the browser on any computer. To achieve this, we open the stylesheet again and change

```
background: #f1f1f1;
```

to

```
background: #FFFFFF;
background-image: url(images/newbackground.gif);
background-repeat: repeat-x;
```

If your goal is to display a fixed image that does not scroll or move when your site visitor moves the browser, then you can use the background-position, background-repeat, and background-attachment properties to display it exactly how you want it to appear.

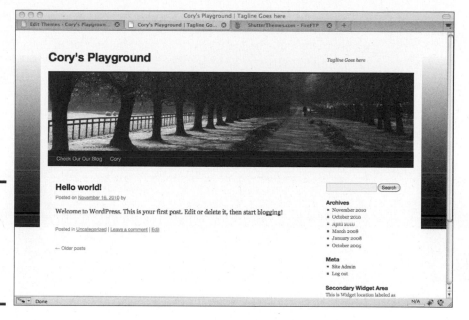

Book VI
Chapter 4

Customizing
Your Theme

Figure 4-2:
A background image repeating across the x-axis.

In Figure 4-3, the image is pinned to top left and fixed, so wherever the browser moves, the image stays in that exact place. To achieve the look, change `background: #f1f1f1` in your stylesheet to

```
background: #FFFFFF;
background-image: url(images/newfixedbackground.gif);
background-position: top left;
background-attachment: fixed;
background-repeat: no-repeat;
```

As you can see from these examples, changing the background graphic by using CSS has a number of options that depends on your creativity and design style more than anything else. But properly leveraged, you can use this to take your design to the next level for yourself and your clients.

Changing Your Header Graphic

Creating unique header graphics is one of the fastest ways to personalize a site and make it unique. The header graphic is typically the strongest graphic design element. Positioned at the top of your theme, a header graphic often includes a logo or other information about your site or business.

Here are some elements you might include in your header graphic:

✦ **Business name or logo:** This sounds obvious, but the header graphic is the prime way to identify the site. If you don't have a logo, this can be as simple as stylizing your business name, but your brand identity needs to be prominent and polished in the header graphic.

✦ **Profile photos:** If it's for a blog, or an independent professional's site, say for a real estate agent, you might want to include a studio-quality profile photo of the person to help your site guests know who they're dealing with and to add a touch of warmth.

✦ **Taglines, important slogans, and keywords:** Use the header area to tell your site visitors something about your site or business.

✦ **Contact information:** If you're doing a small business Web site, including phone and address information is vital.

✦ **Background images:** Be creative with the header image behind all this information. Use a pattern or graphic that matches your brand colors and doesn't distract attention from the vital information you want to communicate.

Most new WordPress themes, particularly premium themes, allow you to upload new header graphics over existing ones easily from the WordPress Dashboard. Sometimes this is called a Custom Header Uploader script or feature. This feature allows you to turn off HTML overlay text and use only graphics for your header, too.

You can personalize your header graphic the following ways:

✦ Replace or overwrite the theme's existing header image with an appropriate image of your choosing.

✦ Use a repeating graphic pattern.

Using a repeating graphic pattern is similar to using a repeating background image, which we discuss in the earlier "Positioning, repeating, and attaching images" section. In this section, we explain how to find and replace your existing header image (in the free Quick-Vid theme from iThemes) by using the Custom Header feature found in many WordPress themes. Figure 4-3 shows the Quick-Vid theme's default header image.

Figure 4-3:
The default
header of
the free
Quick-Vid
theme from
iThemes.

Considering the image dimensions

Generally, you want to replace the existing header image with an image that
has the exact width and height dimensions. To determine the dimensions of
the existing image, find the default header graphic and open it in an image-
editing program, such as Adobe Photoshop. Create (or crop) your new
header graphic to the same dimensions (in pixels) to minimize problems
when adding the image to your theme.

I find Photoshop Elements is a handy design software tool for basic image
editing. It has significantly fewer features than its bigger and older brother,
Photoshop, but for most image-editing jobs, it does great for a fraction of
the price.

Uploading a header image

Depending on your theme, replacing an existing header image is a fast
and efficient way of making changes — you simply upload the graphic and
refresh your site.

The WordPress Custom Header feature is included in many of the popular themes. To add a new header graphic in your theme with the Custom Header feature, follow these steps:

1. **On the WordPress Dashboard, choose Appearance⇨Custom Header.**

   The Custom Header page appears (shown in Figure 4-4) where you can adjust your header area, add or remove text, and upload new graphics.

2. **Select No on the Display Text option and then click Save Changes.**

   Because you are uploading only a header graphic, you do not want the default HTML text to show.

3. **Upload your new header graphic by clicking the Browse button in the Upload Image section.**

   If your image isn't sized to the specifications given, you'll be asked to crop it to fit.

4. **Refresh your site and see how your new header graphic looks.**

   Figure 4-5 shows Cory's photo, site name, and tagline in the new header graphic.

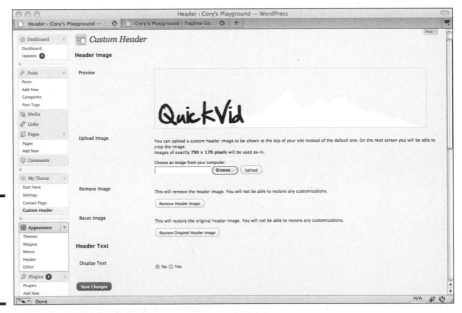

Figure 4-4: The WordPress Custom Header feature.

Figure 4-5:
The Quick-
Vid theme
with a new
header
image.

Personalizing Your Theme with CSS

Cascading Style Sheets (CSS) are part of every WordPress theme. The primary way of personalizing your theme with CSS is through your theme's default stylesheet (`style.css`). Through a comment block (shown in Figure 4-6), your theme's `style.css` file tells WordPress the theme name, the version number, and the author, along with other information.

With CSS changes to your theme's stylesheet you can apply unique styling, such as different fonts, sizes, and colors, to headlines, text, links, and borders, and adjust the spacing between them too. With all the CSS options available, you can fine-tune the look and feel of different elements with simple tweaks.

To explore your theme's stylesheet, choose Appearance➪Editor on the WordPress Dashboard. By default, your theme's main stylesheet (`style.css`) should appear. If not, look at the far right side of the WordPress Dashboard under the Templates heading and scroll down to find the Styles heading and click the Stylesheet file, as shown in Figure 4-7.

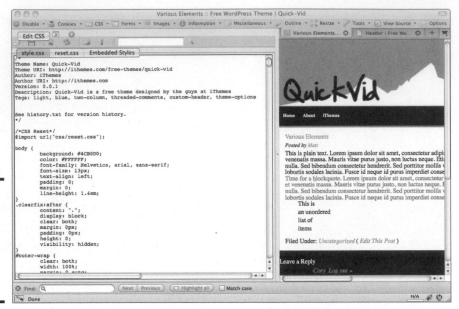

Figure 4-6:
The comment block of a typical WordPress stylesheet.

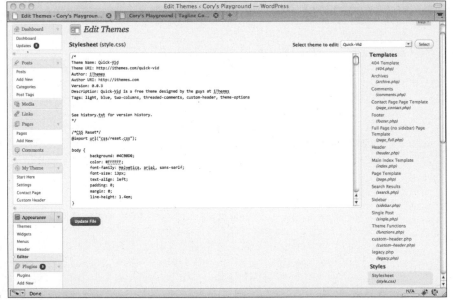

Figure 4-7:
Shows the list of files contained in the Quick-Vid theme, separated by Templates and Styles.

Making changes to the stylesheet or any other theme file can cause your site to load the theme improperly. Be careful what you change here. When you make changes, ensure you're on a playground or sandbox site so that you can easily restore your original file and don't permanently affect a "live" or important site. We also recommend saving an original copy of the stylesheet in a text program, such as Notepad (for the PC) or TextMate (for the Mac), so you can find the original CSS and copy and paste it back into your stylesheet if necessary.

Knowing some key CSS concepts can help you personalize your theme's stylesheet. CSS is simply a set of commands that allows you to customize the look and feel of your HTML markup. Some common commands and tools we discuss are selectors, IDs and classes, properties and values, and more. You use these commands to customize HTML to display your design customizations.

CSS selectors

Typically, CSS *selectors* are named for the corresponding HTML elements, IDs, and classes that you want to style with CSS properties and values. Selectors are very important in CSS because they are used to "select" elements on an HTML/PHP page so that they can be appropriately styled.

With CSS, you can provide style (such as size, color, and placement) to the display of elements on your blog (such as text links, header images, font size and colors, paragraph margins, and line spacing). *CSS selectors* contain names, properties, and values to define which HTML elements in the templates you will style with CSS. Table 4-2 lists some basic global CSS selectors.

Table 4-2		Basic Global CSS Selectors	
CSS Selector	*Description*	*HTML*	*CSS Example*
body	Contains the elements of the overall site style	`<body>`	`body {font-family: Georgia}`
a	Sets the attributes for hyperlinks within your site	`<a href="http://wordpress.org">WordPress</a>`	`a {color: blue}`

(continued)

Table 4-2 *(continued)*

CSS Selector	Description	HTML	CSS Example
h1, h2, h3, h4, h5, h6	Headings or headlines	`<h1>My main title</h1>`	`h1 {color: black}`
block quote	Defines how indented text is styled	`<blockquote> "A journey of a thousand miles begins with a single step." </blockquote>`	`blockquote {font-style: italic}`
p	Sets formatting for paragraphs	`<p>My first paragraph says to keep writing</p>`	`p {color: #000}`

If you were to assign a style to the h1 selector, it will affect all <h1> tags in your HTML. Sometimes you want this, but sometimes you want to affect only a smaller subset of elements.

CSS IDs and classes

With CSS IDs and classes, you can define more elements to style. Generally, IDs are used to style one broader specific element (like your header section) on your page. Classes style, define, and categorize more specifically grouped items (like alignment of images and text, widgets, or links to posts).

✦ **CSS IDs** are identified with the hash mark (#). For example, #header indicates the header ID. There can only be one element identified with an ID.

✦ **CSS classes** are identified with a period (.). For example, .alignleft indicates aligning an element to the left.

Table 4-3 lists some CSS IDs and classes.

Table 4-3		CSS IDs and Classes Examples		
CSS IDs and Classes	Description	HTML		CSS Example
`#header`	Identifies the header section of your theme	`<div id= "header">`		`#header {back ground: #000}`
`#footer`	Identifies the footer section of your theme	`<div id= "footer">`		`#footer {back ground: #ccc}`
`.wp-caption-text`	Identifies the WordPress image caption	`<p class="wp-caption-text"> This is a caption</p>`		`.wp-caption-text {color: #000}`
`.align left`	Identifies the left alignment feature in WordPress	`<img class= "alignleft" src="http:// yourdomain.com/ photo.jpg" />`		`.align left {float: left}`

CSS properties and values

CSS properties are assigned to the CSS selector name. You also need to provide values for the CSS properties to define the style elements for the particular CSS selector you're working with.

For example, the body selector that follows defines the overall look of your Web page; `background` is a property and `#DDDDDD` is the value, and `color` is a property and `#222222` is the value.

```
body {
background:#DDDDDD;
color: #222222;
}
```

Every CSS property needs to be followed by a colon (`:`), and each CSS value needs to be followed by a semicolon (`;`).

Understanding that properties are assigned to selectors, as well as your options for the values, makes CSS a fun playground for personalizing your site. You can experiment with colors, fonts, font sizes and more to tweak the visual look of your theme.

Understanding Basic HTML Techniques

HTML can help you customize and organize your theme. To understand how HTML and CSS work together, think of it this way: If a Web site were a building, HTML is the structure (the studs and foundation) and CSS is the paint.

HTML contains the elements that CSS provides the styles for. All you have to do to apply a CSS style is use the right HTML element. Here is a very basic block of HTML that we can break down for this example:

```
<body>
<div id="content">
<h1>Headline Goes Here</h1>
<p>This is a sample sentence of body text. <blockquote>The journey
of a thousand miles starts with the first step.</blockquote> I'm
going to continue on this sentence and end it here. </p>
<p>Click <a href="http://corymiller.com">here</a> to visit my
website.</p>
</div>
</body>
```

All HTML elements must have opening and closing tags. Opening tags are contained in less-than (<) and greater-than (>) symbols. Closing tags are the same, except they are preceded by a forward-slash (/).

For example:

```
<h1>Headline Goes Here</h1>
```

Note that the HTML elements must be properly nested. In line four of the example above, a paragraph tag is opened (`<p>`). Later in that line, a block quote is opened (`<blockquote>`) and nesting inside the paragraph tag. When editing this line, you could not end the paragraph (`</p>`) before you ended the block quote (`</blockquote>`). Nested elements must close before the elements they are nested within close.

Finally, proper *tabbing,* or indenting, is important when writing HTML, mainly for readability so you can quickly scan through code to find what you're looking for. A good rule is that if you didn't close a tag in the line above, indent one tab over. This allows you to see where each element begins and ends. It can also be very helpful when diagnosing problems.

For more in-depth tutorials on HTML, see w3schools.com's HTML section at `http://www.w3schools.com/html/default.asp`.

Changing Basic Elements for a Unique Look

When you understand the basic concepts about personalizing your site with graphics and CSS, you begin to see how easy changing the look and feel of your site is with these tools. The next few sections explore some of our favorite ways to accomplish an interesting design presentation or a unique and creative look.

Background colors and images

Changing the background image can completely change the feel of your site. However, you can also use background colors and images for other elements in your theme.

Background techniques include using solid colors and repeating gradients or patterns to achieve a subtle yet polished effect. (***Note:*** Use colors that accent the colors of your logo and don't hamper text readability.)

You can add CSS background colors and image effects to the following areas of your theme:

✦ Post and page content sections

✦ Sidebar widgets

✦ Comment blocks

✦ Footer area

Font family, color, and size

You can change the fonts in your theme for style or for readability purposes. We've seen typographic (or font) design experts use simple font variations to achieve amazing design results. You can use fonts to separate headlines from body text (or widget headlines and text from the main content) to be less distracting. Table 4-4 lists some examples of often-used font properties.

Table 4-4		Fonts
Font Properties	*Common Values*	*CSS Examples*
`font-family`	`Georgia, Times, serif`	`body {font-family: Georgia; serif;}`
`font-size`	`px, %, em`	`body {font-size: 14px;}`
`font-style`	`Italic, underline`	`body {font-style: italic;}`
`font-weight`	`bold, bolder, normal`	`body {font-weight: normal}`

The Web is actually kind of picky about how it displays fonts, as well as what kind of fonts you can use in the `font-family` property. Not all fonts display correctly on the Web. To be safe, here are some commonly used font families that display correctly in most browsers:

✦ **Serif fonts:** Times New Roman, Georgia, Garamond, Bookman Old Style

✦ **Sans-serif fonts:** Verdana, Arial, Tahoma, Trebuchet MS

Font Color

With more than 16 million different HTML color combinations available, you can find just the right shade of color for your project. After some time, you'll memorize your favorite color codes. Knowing codes for different shades of gray can help you quickly add an extra design touch. For example, you can use the shades of gray listed in Table 4-5 for backgrounds, borders on design elements, and widget headers.

Table 4-5	My Favorite CSS Colors
Color	*Value*
White	#FFFFFF
Black	#000000
Gray	#CCCCCC
	#DDDDDD
	#333333
	#E0E0E0

You can easily change the color of your font by changing the `color` property of the CSS selector you want to tweak. You can use hexadecimal codes to define the colors.

You can define the overall font color in your site by defining it in the body CSS selector like this:

```
body {
color: #333;
}
```

Font Size

To tweak the size of your font, change the `font-size` property of the CSS selector you want to tweak. Generally, the following units of measurement determine font sizes:

✦ **px (pixel):** Increasing or decreasing the number of pixels increases or decreases the font size (12px is larger than 10px).

✦ **pt (point):** As with pixels, increasing or decreasing the number of points affects the font size (12pt is larger than 10pt).

✦ **% (percentage):** Increasing or decreasing the percentage number affects the font size (50% is the equivalent to 7 pixels; 100% is the equivalent to 17 pixels).

In the default template CSS, the font size is defined in the body tag in pixels, like this:

```
font-size: 12px;
```

Putting all three elements (font-family, color, and font-size) together in the <body> tag styles the font for the entire body of your site. Here's how the elements work together in the <body> tag of the default template CSS:

```
body {
font-size: 12px;
font-family: Georgia, "Bitstream Charter", serif;
color: #666;
}
```

Serif fonts have little tails, or curlicues, at the edges of letters. (This book's text is in a serif font.) Sans-serif fonts have straight edges and no fancy styling. (The heading in Table 4-4 uses a sans-serif font — look ma, no tails!)

When you want to change a font family in your CSS, open the stylesheet (style.css), search for property: font-family, change the values for that property, and then save your changes.

In the default template CSS, the font is defined in the <body> tag like this:

```
font-family: Georgia, "Bitstream Charter", serif;
```

Borders

Using CSS borders can add an interesting and unique flair to elements of your theme design. (See Figure 4-8.) Table 4-6 illustrates common properties and CSS examples for borders in your theme design.

Table 4-6	Common Border Properties	
Border Properties	*Common Values*	*CSS Examples*
border-size	px, em	body {border-size: 1px; }
border-style	solid, dotted, dashed	body {border-style: solid}
border-color	Hexadecimal values	body {border-color: #CCCCCC}

Figure 4-8:
A dashed
15px black
border.

Finding Additional Resources

There may come a time when you want to explore customizing your theme further. Here are some recommended resources:

- ✦ **WordPress Codex (`http://codex.wordpress.org`):** Official WordPress documentation
- ✦ **W3Schools (`http://w3schools.com`):** A free and comprehensive online HTML and CSS reference
- ✦ **WebDesign.com (`http://webdesign.com`):** A premium library of WordPress video tutorials and training
- ✦ **Smashing Magazine (`http://smashingmagazine.com`):** Numerous tips and tricks for customizing a WordPress theme

Chapter 5: Understanding Parent and Child Themes

In This Chapter

✓ Defining the relationship between parent and child themes

✓ Tweaking child themes with styles

✓ Customizing child themes with images

✓ Modifying child themes with template files

*U*sing a theme exactly as a theme author released it is great. If a new version is released that fixes a browser compatibility issue or adds features offered by a new version of WordPress, a quick theme upgrade is very easy to do.

However, there's a good chance you'll want to tinker with the design, add new features, or modify the theme structure. If you modify the theme, you won't be able to upgrade to a newly released version without modifying the theme again.

If only you could upgrade customized versions of themes with new features when they're released. Fortunately, child themes give you this best-of-both-worlds theme solution.

This chapter explores what child themes are, how to create a child theme–ready parent theme, and how to get the most out of using child themes.

Customizing Theme Style with Child Themes

A WordPress theme consists of a collection of template files, stylesheets, images, and JavaScript files. The theme controls the layout and design that your visitors see on the site. When such a theme is properly set up as a parent theme, it allows a *child theme,* or a subset of instructions, to override its files. This ensures a child theme can selectively modify the layout, styling, and functionality of the parent theme.

The quickest way to understand child themes is by example. In this section, you create a simple child theme that modifies the style of the parent theme.

Currently, the default WordPress theme is Twenty Ten. Figure 5-1 shows how the Twenty Ten theme appears on a sample site.

You likely have Twenty Ten on your WordPress site, and Twenty Ten is child theme–ready; therefore, it's a great candidate for creating an example child theme. To keep the names simple, we call the new child theme TwentyTen Child (original, we know).

Creating a child theme

Like regular themes, a child theme needs to reside in a directory inside the `/wp-content/themes` directory. The first step to creating a child theme is to add the directory that will hold it. For this example, create a new directory called `twentyten-child` inside the `/wp-content/themes` directory.

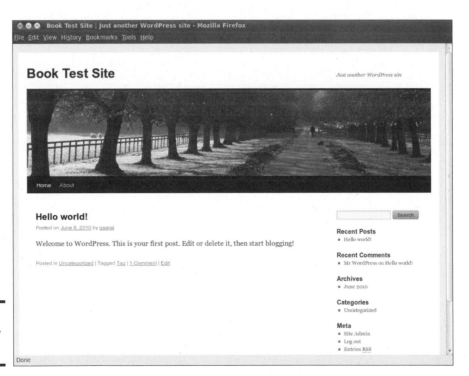

Figure 5-1:
The Twenty Ten theme.

To register the `twentyten-child` directory as a theme and to make it a child of the Twenty Ten theme, create a `style.css` file and add the appropriate theme headers. To do this, type the following code into your favorite code or plain-text editor, such as Notepad for the PC or TextMate for the Mac, and save the file as `style.css`.

```
/*
Theme Name: TwentyTen Child
Description: My magnificent child theme
Author: Cory Miller
Version: 1.0
Template: twentyten
*/
```

Typically, you'll find the following headers in a WordPress theme:

+ **Theme Name:** The theme user sees this name in the back end of WordPress.

+ **Description:** This header provides the user any additional information about the theme. Currently, it only appears on the Manage Themes page (Appearance⇨Themes).

+ **Author:** This header lists one or more theme authors. Currently, it is only shown in the Manage Themes page (Appearance⇨Themes).

+ **Version:** The version number is very useful for keeping track of outdated versions of the theme. It is always a good idea to update the version number when modifying a theme.

+ **Template:** This header changes a theme into a child theme. The value of this header tells WordPress the directory name of the parent theme. Because our child theme uses Twenty Ten as the parent, our `style. css` needs to have a `Template` header with a value of `twentyten` (the directory name of the Twenty Ten theme).

Now activate the new TwentyTen Child theme as your active theme. (If you need a reminder on how to activate a theme on your site, check out Book VI, Chapter 2.) You should see a site layout similar to the one shown in Figure 5-2.

Figure 5-2 shows that the new theme doesn't look quite right. The problem is that the new child theme replaced the `style.css` file of the parent theme, yet the new child theme's `style.css` file is empty.

You could just copy and paste the contents of the parent theme's `style. css` file, but that would waste some of the potential of child themes.

Figure 5-2:
The
TwentyTen
Child theme.

Loading a parent theme's style

One of the great things about CSS is how rules can override one another. If you list the same rule twice in your CSS, the rule that comes last takes precedence.

For example:

```
a {
color: blue;
}

a {
color: red;
}
```

This example is overly simple, but it nicely shows what we're talking about. The first rule says that all links ('a' tags) should be blue; whereas, the second one says that links should be red. Because CSS says that the last instruction takes precedence, the links will be red.

Using this feature of CSS, you can inherit all the styling of the parent theme and selectively modify it by overriding the rules of the parent theme. But how can you load the parent theme's `style.css` file so that it inherits the parent theme's styling?

Fortunately, CSS has another great feature that helps you do this with ease. Just add one line to the TwentyTen Child theme's `style.css` file as in the listing below.

```
/*
Theme Name: TwentyTen Child
Description: My magnificent child theme
Author: Cory Miller
Version: 1.0
Template: twentyten
*/
@import url('../twentyten/style.css');
```

A number of things are going on here, so let me break it down piece by piece:

✦ **@import:** This tells the browser to load another stylesheet. Using this allows you to pull in the parent stylesheet quickly and easily.

✦ **url('...'):** This indicates that the value is a location and not a normal value.

✦ **('../twentyten/style.css');:** This is the location of the parent stylesheet. Notice the `/twentyten` directory name. This needs to be changed to match the `Template` value in the header so that the appropriate stylesheet is loaded.

Figure 5-3 shows how the site appears after updating the child theme's `style.css` file to match the listing.

Customizing the parent theme's styling

Your TwentyTen Child theme is set up to match the parent Twenty Ten theme. Now you can add new styling to the TwentyTen Child theme's `style.css` file. A simple example of how customizing works is to add a style that converts all h1, h2, and h3 headings to uppercase.

```
/*
Theme Name: TwentyTen Child
Description: My magnificent child theme
Author: Cory Miller
Version: 1.0
Template: twentyten
*/
@import url('../twentyten/style.css');

h1, h2, h3 {
text-transform: uppercase;
}
```

Figure 5-4 shows how the child theme looks with the code additions applied — getting better, isn't it?

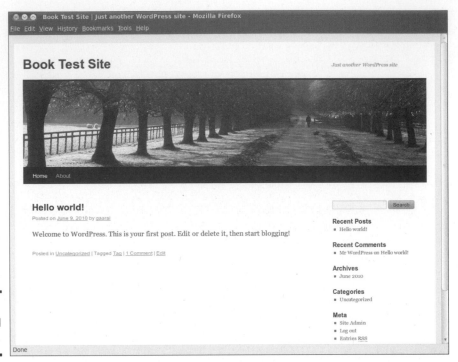

Figure 5-3:
The updated child theme.

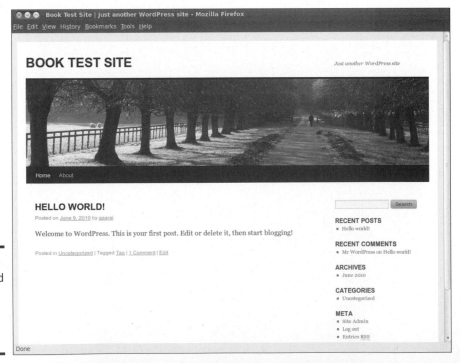

Figure 5-4:
The updated child theme with uppercase headings.

As you can see, with just a few lines in a `style.css` file, you can create a new child theme that adds specific customizations to an existing theme. Not only was it quick and easy to do, you didn't have to modify anything in the parent theme to make it work. Therefore, when upgrades to the parent theme are available, you can upgrade the parent to get the additional features without having to make your modifications again.

Customizations that are more complex work the same way. Simply add the new rules after the import rule that adds the parent stylesheet.

Using images in child theme designs

Many themes use images to add nice touches to the design. Typically, these images are added to a directory named `images` inside the theme.

Just as a parent theme may refer to images in its `style.css` file, your child themes can have their own images directory. The following are examples of how these images can be used.

Using a child theme image in a child theme stylesheet

Including a child theme image in a child theme stylesheet is common. To do so, you simply add the new image to the child theme's `images` directory and refer to it in the child theme's `style.css` file. To get a feel for the mechanics of this process, follow these steps:

1. **Create an `images` directory inside the child theme's directory.**

2. **Add an image to use into the directory.**

   For this example, add an image called `body-bg.png`. We used a simple gradient that we created in an image editor.

3. **Add the necessary styling to the child theme's `style.css` file, as follows:**

   ```
   /*
   Theme Name: TwentyTen Child
   Description: My magnificent child theme
   Author: Cory Miller
   Version: 1.0
   Template: twentyten
   */
   @import url('../twentyten/style.css');
   body {
   background: url('images/body-bg.png');
   }
   ```

With a quick refresh of the site, you see that the site now has a new background. Figure 5-5 shows the results clearly by using the browser's zoom feature to make the site smaller.

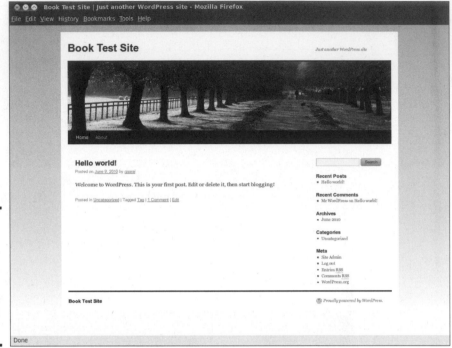

Figure 5-5:
The
TwentyTen
Child
theme after
editing the
background
image.

Using a parent theme image in a child theme stylesheet

Child theme images are acceptable for most purposes. Sometimes, however, you're better off using images supplied by the parent theme. You could just copy the parent theme image to the child theme, but that would prevent the child theme from matching the parent theme if the parent theme image ever changes. Fortunately, you can refer to an image in the parent theme with the `@import` rule the same way you can reference the parent theme's `style.css` file.

In the footer of the Twenty Ten design, a WordPress logo appears beside the phrase "Proudly powered by WordPress," as shown in Figure 5-6. This is a parent theme image.

In this example, we want to add the logo image in front of each widget title in the sidebar. Because the logo image already exists inside the parent, we can simply add a customization to the child theme's `style.css` file to make this change, as follows:

```
/*
Theme Name: TwentyTen Child
Description: My magnificent child theme
Author: Cory Miller
Version: 1.0
Template: twentyten
*/

@import url('../twentyten/style.css');

.widget-title {
background: url('../twentyten/images/wordpress.png') no-repeat
left center;
padding-left: 20px;
line-height: 16px
}
```

Save the file and refresh the site. Now we're showing our WordPress pride. (See Figure 5-7.)

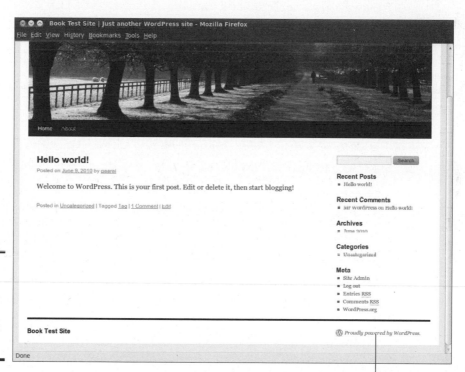

Figure 5-6:
The WordPress logo in the Twenty Ten footer.

WordPress logo

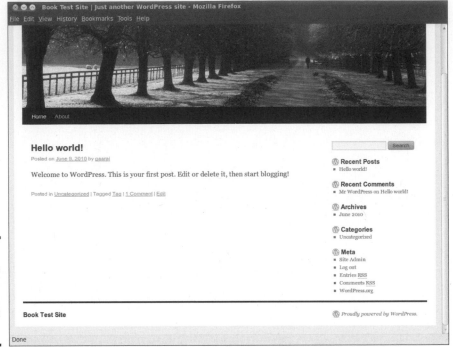

Figure 5-7:
Showing the
WordPress
logo before
each widget
title.

Using a child theme image in a parent theme stylesheet

Looking at the previous examples, you might wonder whether replacing an image used in the parent's stylesheet with one found in the child theme's directory is possible. That would require a change to the parent theme's stylesheet, and the idea behind a child theme is to avoid changes to the parent, so no, that isn't possible. However, you can override the parent theme's rule to refer to the child theme's new image by simply creating an overriding rule in the child theme's stylesheet that points to the new image.

Taking our WordPress pride from the previous customization a step further, the WordPress logo in the footer is much too small. We can do better — with a larger logo.

Fortunately, a 58-x-69-pixel WordPress button appears on the WordPress.org Logos and Graphics page (`http://wordpress.org/about/logos`).

After adding the desired logo to your child theme's images directory as
wp-button.png, the following style.css file replaces the WordPress logo
on the parent theme's footer with the new WordPress button:

```
/*
Theme Name: TwentyTen Child
Description: My magnificent child theme
Author: Cory Miller
Version: 1.0
Template: twentyten
*/
@import url('../twentyten/style.css');
#site-generator a {
background-image: url('images/wp-logo-blue.png');
}
#site-info {

width: 650px;

}

#site-generator {

width: 270px;

}

#site-generator a {

background: url('images/wp-button.png') right center no-repeat;

line-height: 59px;

padding: 0 63px 10px 0;

float: right;

}
```

Book VI
Chapter 5

Understanding
Parent and Child
Themes

Notice how some rules beyond just the background were modified in order
to override parent theme styling that didn't work well with the new background. Now your child theme shows your WordPress pride loud and clear.
The new look, shown in Figure 5-8, looks quite nice if you ask me.

You cannot directly replace parent theme images. Rather, you must provide
a new image in the child theme and override the parent's styling to refer to
this new image.

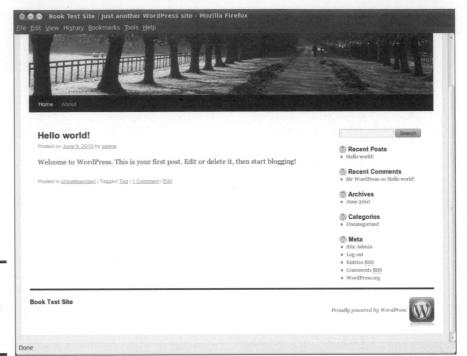

Figure 5-8: The new WordPress footer button.

Modifying Theme Structure with Child Themes

The preceding section showed how to use a child theme to modify the stylesheet of an existing theme. This is tremendously powerful. A talented CSS developer can use this technique to create an amazing variety of layouts and designs.

However, this is just the beginning of the power of child themes. Although every child theme overrides the parent theme's `style.css` file, the child theme can override the parent theme's template files, too. However, child themes aren't limited to just overriding template files; when needed, child theme's can also supply their own template files.

Template files are PHP files that WordPress runs to render different views of the site. A site view is the type of content being looked at. Examples of different views are home, category archive, individual post, and page content.

Some examples of common template files are `index.php`, `archive.php`, `single.php`, `page.php`, `attachment.php`, and `search.php`. (You can read more about available template files, including how to use them, in Chapter 3 of this minibook.)

You might wonder what purpose modifying template files of a parent theme serves. Although modifying the stylesheet of a parent theme can allow for some very powerful control over the design, it can't add new content, modify the underlying site structure, or change how the theme functions. To get that level of control, you need to modify the template files.

Overriding parent template files

When both the child theme and parent theme supply the same template file, the child theme file is used. It is this process of replacing the original parent template file that is referred to as *overriding*.

Although overriding each of the theme's template files can defeat the purpose of using a child theme — because updates to those template files won't enhance the child theme — sometimes, producing a needed result makes doing so necessary.

The easiest way to customize a specific template file in a child theme is to copy the template file from the parent theme folder to the child theme folder. After the file is copied, it can be customized as needed, and the changes will reflect in the child theme.

A good example of a template file that can be overridden is the `footer.php` file. Customizing the footer allows for adding site-specific branding.

Adding new template files

A child theme can override existing parent template files, but it can supply template files that don't exist in the parent, too. Although you may never need your child themes to do this, this option can open possibilities for your designs.

For example, this technique proves most valuable with page templates. The Twenty Ten theme has a page template named One Column, No Sidebar. Although you might expect this page template to create a full-width layout for the content, it doesn't. Instead, it simply removes the sidebar and centers the content, as shown in Figure 5-9.

This isn't a design flaw. The layout was intentionally set up this way to improve readability. However, we like to have a full-width layout option so that we can embed a video, add a forum, or add other content that works well with full width. To add this feature to your child theme, simply add a new page template and the necessary styling to the `style.css` file.

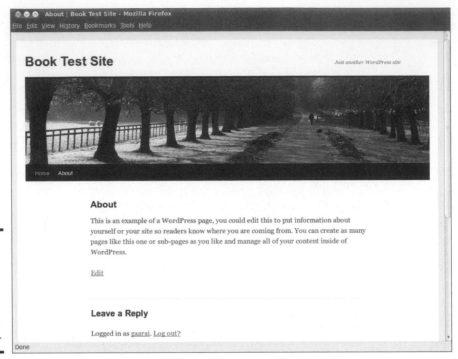

Figure 5-9:
The One
Column,
No Sidebar
page
template in
Twenty Ten.

A good way to create a new theme page template is to copy an existing one and modify it as needed. In this case, copying the `onecolumn-page.php` file of the parent theme to a new file, called `fullwidth-page.php`, is a good start. After a few customizations, the `fullwidget-page.php` file looks like this:

```php
<?php
/**
 * Template Name: Full width, no sidebar
 */
get_header(); ?>
<div id="container" class="full-width">
<div id="content" role="main">
<?php if ( have_posts() ) while ( have_posts() ) : the_post(); ?>
<div id="post-<?php the_ID(); ?>" <?php post_class();
?>>
<h1 class="entry-title"><?php the_title();
?></h1>
<div class="entry-content">
<?php the_content(); ?>
<?php wp_link_pages( array( 'before' => '<div
class="page-link">' . __( 'Pages:', 'twentyten' ), 'after' =>
'</div>' ) ); ?>
<?php edit_post_link( __( 'Edit', 'twentyten'
), '<span class="edit-link">', '</span>' ); ?>
```

```
</div><!-- .entry-content -->
</div><!-- #post-## -->
<?php comments_template( '', true ); ?>
<?php endwhile; ?>
</div><!-- #content -->
</div><!-- #container -->
<?php get_footer(); ?>
```

The key modification is changing the `one-column` class in the `div` with an `id` of `container` to the `full-width` class. This new class allows the page template to be styled without modifying other site styling.

The styling change to make this work is quick and easy. Simply add the following lines after the `@import` rule in the child theme's `style.css` file:

```
.full-width #content {
margin-right: 20px;
}
```

Switching to the new Full Width, No Sidebar page template produces the layout shown in Figure 5-10.

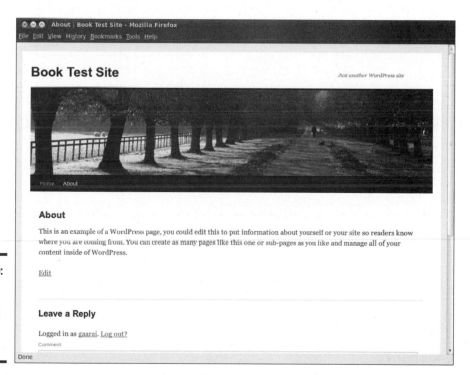

Figure 5-10:
The new
Full Width,
No Sidebar
page
template.

Removing template files

You may be asking why you would want to remove a parent's template file. That's a good question. Unfortunately, the Twenty Ten theme doesn't provide a good example of why you would want to do this. Therefore, you must use your imagination a bit.

Imagine that you're creating a child theme built off a parent theme called Example Parent. Example Parent is well designed, and a great child theme was quickly built off it. The child theme looks and works exactly the way you want it to, but there's a problem.

The Example Parent theme has a `home.php` template file that provides a highly customized non-blog home page. This works very well, but it isn't what you want for the site. You want a standard blog home page. If the `home.php` file didn't exist in Example Parent, everything would work perfectly.

There isn't a way to remove the `home.php` file from Example Parent without modifying the theme, so you have to use a trick. Instead of removing the file, override the `home.php` file and have it emulate `index.php`.

You may think that simply copying and pasting the Example Parent `index.php` code into the child theme's `home.php` file is a good approach. Although this works, there is a better way: You can tell WordPress to run the `index.php` file so that changes to `index.php` are respected. This single line of code inside the child theme's `home.php` is all that is needed to replace `home.php` with `index.php`:

```php
<?php locate_template( array( 'index.php' ), true ); ?>
```

The `locate_template` function does a bit of magic. If the child theme supplies an `index.php` file, then it is used. If not, then the parent `index.php` file is used.

This produces the same result that removing the parent theme's `home.php` file would have. The `home.php` code is ignored and the changes to `index.php` are respected.

Modifying the functions.php file

Like template files, child themes can provide a Theme Functions template, or `functions.php` file. Unlike template files, the `functions.php` of a child theme does not override the file of the parent theme.

When a parent theme and a child theme each have a `functions.php` file, both the parent and child `functions.php` files run. The child theme's `functions.php` file runs first and then the parent theme's `functions.php` file runs. This is intentional because it allows the child theme to replace functions defined in the parent theme. However, this only works if the functions are set up to allow this.

The Twenty Ten `functions.php` file defines a function called `twentyten_setup`. This function handles the configuration of many theme options and activates some additional features. Child themes can replace this function to change the default configuration and features of the theme, too.

The following lines of code summarize how the `functions.php` file allows this to happen:

```
if ( ! function_exists( 'twentyten_setup' ) ).
function twentyten_setup() {
// removed code
}
endif;
```

Wrapping the function declaration in the `if` statement protects the site from breaking in the event of a code conflict and allows a child theme to define its own version of the function.

In the TwentyTen Child theme, you can see how modifying this function affects the theme. Add a new `twentyten_setup` function that adds post thumbnails support to the TwentyTen Child theme's `functions.php` file.

```
<?php
function twentyten_setup() {
add_theme_support( 'post-thumbnails' );
}
```

The result of this change is the child theme no longer supports other special WordPress features, such as custom editor styling, automatic feed link generation, internationalization and location, and so on.

The take-away from this example is that a child theme can provide its own custom version of the function because the parent theme wraps the function declaration in an `if` block that checks for the function first.

Preparing a Parent Theme

WordPress has made it very easy for theme developers to make parent themes. WordPress does most of the hard work; however, a theme developer must follow some rules for a parent theme to function properly.

The words *stylesheet* and *template* have been used numerous times in many different contexts. Typically, *stylesheet* refers to a CSS file in a theme and *template* refers to a template file in the theme. However, these words also have specific meaning when working with parent and child themes. You must understand the difference between a stylesheet and a template when working with parent and child themes.

In WordPress, the active theme is the stylesheet and the active theme's parent is the template. If the theme doesn't have a parent, then the active theme is both the stylesheet and the template.

Originally, child themes could only replace the `style.css` file of a theme. The parent provided all the template files and `functions.php` code. Thus, the child theme provided style and the parent theme provided the template files. The capabilities of child themes expanded in subsequent versions of WordPress, making the use of these terms for parent and child themes somewhat confusing.

Imagine two themes: Parent and Child. The following code is in the Parent theme's `header.php` file and loads an additional stylesheet provided by the theme.

```
<link type="text/css" rel="stylesheet" media="all" href="<?php
bloginfo('stylesheet_directory') ?>/reset.css" />
```

The `bloginfo` function prints information about the blog configuration or settings. This example uses the function to print the URL location of the stylesheet directory. The site is hosted at `http://example.com` and the Parent is the active theme. The above code produces the following output.

```
<link type="text/css" rel="stylesheet" media="all"
href="http://example.com/wp-content/themes/Parent/reset.css" />
```

If the child theme is activated, the output would be

```
<link type="text/css" rel="stylesheet" media="all"
href="http://example.com/wp-content/themes/Child/reset.css" />
```

The location now refers to the `reset.css` file in the Child theme. This could work if every child theme copies the `reset.css` file of the Parent theme, but requiring child themes to add files in order to function isn't good design. The solution is simple, however. Instead of using the `stylesheet_directory` in the `bloginfo` call above, use `template_directory`. The code looks like this:

```
<link type="text/css" rel="stylesheet" media="all" href="<?php
bloginfo('template_directory') ?>/reset.css" />
```

Now, all child themes will properly load the parent `reset.css` file.

When developing, use `template_directory` in stand-alone, parent themes and `stylesheet_directory` in child themes.

Chapter 6: Digging into Advanced Theme Development

The previous chapters of this minibook describe WordPress themes and using their structure to build your site. Delving into deeper topics can help you create flexible themes that offer users options to control the theme.

Whether you're building a theme for a client, the WordPress.org theme directory, or yourself, adding advanced theme features can make theme development easier and faster with a high-quality result. With these advanced theme concepts and tools, you can build robust, dynamic themes that allow for easier design customization and offer a variety of layout options.

Beyond just tools and methods of advanced theme development, this chapter provides some development practices that help projects succeed.

Getting Started with Advanced Theming

Before themes were added to WordPress, customizing the design of the site meant modifying the main WordPress `index.php` file and the default `print.css` file. Version 1.5 added the first theme support and rudimentary child theme support. Over time, WordPress began to support other features, such as custom headers, custom backgrounds, and featured images.

Additionally, the capabilities of themes have grown steadily. Incremental improvement — beginning with a small, simple starting point and improving it over time — works very well in theme development. By developing incrementally, you can build a theme from start to completion from an existing, well-tested theme (most themes are part of a larger incremental improvement process) and maximize your development time. I can't think of a single theme I've developed that wasn't built on another theme.

There isn't a need to develop each theme from scratch. Choosing a good starting point will make a big difference on how quickly you can get your project off the ground.

Finding a good starting point

Choosing a solid starting point to build your latest and greatest theme design on can be time consuming. Although exploring all the available themes in detail is tempting, I find exhaustive searches waste more time than they save.

Typically, I begin with the most current theme unless there's a more suitable one. Because the design and capabilities of the theme were recently implemented, modifying it to meet the current project's needs is faster than rediscovering all the nuances of an older, unfamiliar theme.

You might wonder whether we ever build themes off other designers' themes. We did. These days, if a new theme comes out that shows how to integrate some new feature, we play around with the theme to understand the concept but always go back to one of our themes to implement the modification. The reason for this is simple. If we can implement the feature into our own design, we have a much better appreciation for how it works. Allowing someone else's code or design to do the heavy lifting can place a limitation on how we use that feature.

If you are new to theme development and haven't produced a theme of your own, we highly recommend starting with the WordPress default theme, Twenty Ten (see Chapter 1 in this minibook for a full analysis of the Twenty Ten theme). This theme is developed for helping new theme developers discover how themes work.

I use this approach in the examples in this chapter. Unless otherwise noted, all the examples are built off the WordPress default Twenty Ten theme.

Customizing the theme to your needs

After you select a theme for your project, you should create a copy of the theme. This way you can look at the unmodified version in case you accidentally remove something that causes the theme or design to break.

When we find code and styling that we don't believe we need anymore, we comment it out rather than deleting it. This removes the functionality but still allows us to add it back in if we change our mind.

A line of code can be commented out by adding `//` in front of it. For example:

```
// add_editor_style();
```

CSS can be commented out by wrapping a section in `/*` and `*/`. For example:

```
/*#content {
 margin: 0 280px 0 20px;
}
*/
#primary,
#secondary {
 float: right;
/* overflow: hidden;
*/
 width: 220px;
}
```

When you start finalizing the theme, go through the files and remove any blocks of commented styling and code to clean up your files.

Adding New Template Files

In Chapter 3 of this minibook, I introduce the concept of template files and give you an overview of the template files available to you. In Chapter 5, we explain the idea of overriding template files with child themes. The following sections explore some advanced uses of template files.

Although you rarely need to use all these techniques, being fluent in your options gives you flexibility to address specific needs quickly when they come up.

Creating named templates

WordPress recognizes three special areas of a theme: header, footer, and sidebar. The `get_header`, `get_footer`, and `get_sidebar` functions default to loading `header.php`, `footer.php`, and `sidebar.php`, respectively. Each of these functions also supports a name argument to allow you to load an alternate version of the file. For example, running `get_header('main')` causes WordPress to load `header-main.php`.

You might wonder why you would use a name argument when you could just create a template file named whatever you like and load it directly. The reasons for using the `get_header`, `get_footer`, or `get_sidebar` functions with a name argument are

✦ Holding to a standard naming convention that other WordPress developers can easily understand

✦ Automatically providing support for child themes to override the parent theme's template file

✦ Offering a fallback that loads the unnamed template file if the named one doesn't exist

In short, use the name argument feature if you have multiple, specialized header, footer, or sidebar template files.

This named template feature can be used with the Theme Options discussed in the "Exploring Theme Options" section, later in this chapter, to allow users to easily switch between different header, footer, and sidebar styles. On the Theme Options page, you can give the user the ability to choose the specific header, footer, or sidebar template file he or she wants, giving them an easy way to change the layout or design of the site. A good example of content you could add to a different sidebar file can be found in the nearby Query posts for category content sidebar, which discusses displaying a list of recent posts and filing them in a specific category in the sidebar of your site.

Query posts for category content

WordPress makes it possible to pull in very specific types of content on your Web site through the `query_posts();` template tag. You place this template tag before The Loop, and it lets you specify which category you want to pull information from. If you have a category called WordPress, and you want to display the last three posts from that category on your front page, in your blog sidebar, or somewhere else on your site, you can use this template tag.

The `query_posts();` template tag has several parameters that let you display different types of content, such as posts in specific categories, content from specific pages/posts, or dates in your blog archives. The `query_posts();` tag lets you pass many variables and parameters; it's not just limited to categories either, you can use it for pages, posts, tags and more. Visit the WordPress Codex at `http://codex.wordpress.org/Template_Tags/query_posts` and read about this tag's options.

To query the posts on your blog to pull out posts from just one specific category, you

can use the following tag with the associated arguments for the available parameters. This example tells WordPress to query all posts that exist on your site and list the last five posts in the Books category:

```php
<?php query_posts('showposts=5&category_
        name=books;); ?>
```

Simply place this code on a line above the start of The Loop; you can use it in a sidebar to display clickable titles of the last five posts in the Books category. (When clicked, the reader is taken to the individual post page to read the full post.)

```php
<?php query_posts('showposts=5&category_
        name=books;); ?>
<?php if (have_posts()) : while (have_
        posts()) : the_post(); ?>
<strong><a href="<?php the_permalink()
        ?>" rel="bookmark"
        title="Permanent Link to
<?php the_title_attribute(); ?>"><?php
        the_title(); ?></a></strong>
<?php the_excerpt(); endwhile; endif; ?>
```

Creating and using template parts

Template parts are relatively new (they were added in version 3.0). A template part is very similar to the header, footer, and sidebar templates except that you aren't limited to just header, footer, and sidebar.

The get_header, get_footer, and get_sidebar functions allow for code that's duplicated in many of the template files to be placed in a single file and loaded by using a standard process. The purpose of template parts is to offer a new standardized function that can be used to load sections of code specific to an individual theme. Using the concept of template parts, sections of code that add a specialized section of header widgets or display a block of ads can be placed in individual files and easily loaded as a template part.

Template parts are loaded by using the get_template_part function. The get_template_part function accepts two arguments: slug and name. The slug argument is required and describes the generic type of template part to be loaded, such as loop. The name argument is optional and selects a specialized template part, such as post.

A call to get_template_part with just the slug argument will try to load a template file with a file name of slug.php. Thus, a call to get_template_part('loop') will try to load loop.php, and a call to get_template_part('header-widgets') will try to load header-widgets.php. See a pattern here? *Slug* refers to the name of the template file, minus the .php extension, because WordPress already assumes that it's a PHP file.

A call to get_template_part with both the slug and name arguments will try to load a template file with a filename of slug-name.php. If a template file with a filename of slug-name.php doesn't exist, then WordPress will try to load a template file with a filename of slug.php. Thus, a call to get_template_part('loop', 'post') will first try to load loop-post.php followed by loop.php if loop-post.php doesn't exist; a call to get_template_part('header-widgets', 'post') will first try to load header-widgets-post.php followed by header-widgets.php if header-widgets-post.php doesn't exist.

The Twenty Ten theme offers a good example of the template part feature in use. It uses a template part called loop to allow The Loop to be put into individual files.

The Loop is the section of code found in most theme template files that uses a PHP while loop to loop through the set of post, page, and archive content (to name a few) and display it. The presence of The Loop in a template file is crucial for a theme to function properly. A section of Chapter 3 in this minibook examines The Loop.

Twenty Ten's `index.php` template file shows a template part for The Loop in action:

```
<?php get_header(); ?>
    <div id="container">
        <div id="content" role="main">
            <?php get_template_part('loop', 'index'); ?>
        </div><!-- #content -->
    </div><!-- #container -->
    <?php get_sidebar(); ?>
    <?php get_footer(); ?>
```

Loading The Loop by using a template part, Twenty Ten cleans up the `index.php` code considerably when compared to other themes. This cleanup of the template file code is just the icing on the cake. The true benefits are the improvements to theme development.

Twenty Ten's `index.php` template file calls for a template part with a slug of `loop` and a name of `index`. Because Twenty Ten doesn't supply a `loop-index.php` file, `loop.php` is used. This allows a child theme (child themes are discussed at length in Chapter 5 of this minibook) to supply a `loop-index.php` file to customize just The Loop for `index.php`. A child theme can do this without having to supply a customized `index.php` file because of Twenty Ten's use of template parts and using both arguments of the `get_template_part` function.

With Twenty Ten's code for the header, Loop, sidebar, and footer placed into separate files, the template files become much easier to customize for specific uses. This can be seen by comparing the `page.php` to the `onecolumn-page.php` template files:

The `page.php` listing:

```
<?php get_header(); ?>
    <div id="container">
        <div id="content" role="main">
            <?php get_template_part('loop', 'page'); ?>
        </div><!-- #content -->
    </div><!-- #container -->
    <?php get_sidebar(); ?>
    <?php get_footer(); ?>
```

The `onecolumn-page.php` listing:

```
/* Template Name: One column, no sidebar */
    <?php get_header(); ?>
    <div id="container" class="one-column">
        <div id="content" role="main">
            <?php get_template_part('loop', 'page'); ?>
        </div><!-- #content -->
    </div><!-- #container -->
    <?php get_footer(); ?>
```

Other than the `onecolumn-page.php` having the `Template Name` comment at the top, allowing it to be used as a page template (discussed in the upcoming "Using page templates" section), the only difference is that `page.php` has the `get_sidebar` function call and `onecolumn-page.php` adds a `one-column` class to the `container` div. With just these modifications and a few styling rules added for the `one-column class`, the theme now has a page template that doesn't have a sidebar.

You might wonder how the preceding example shows the value of template parts if it is really about the `get_sidebar` function. Although the `get_sidebar` function is the feature of the previous example, the unsung hero is the `get_template_part` function.

Before template parts, the full Loop code would be duplicated in the `page.php` and `onecolumn-page.php` files. This means that a modification to the `page.php` file's Loop code would also require the same modification to the `onecolumn-page.php` file. Imagine if you had to make the same modification to five template files. Repeatedly making the same modifications quickly becomes tiring and each modification increases the chance of making mistakes. Using a template part means that the modification needs to be made only one time.

Looking at the `page.php` and `onecolumn-page.php` example, the `get_template_part` call allows for easily creating as many customized page templates as needed without having to duplicate The Loop code. Without the duplicate code, the code for The Loop can be easily modified in one place.

When you start duplicating sections of code in numerous template files, place the code in a separate file and use the `get_template_part` function to load it where needed.

Exploring content-specific standard templates

The template files discussed so far span a wide scope of site views specific to the view and not the content. For example, the `category.php` template file applies to all category archive views but not to a specific category, and the `page.php` template file applies to all page views but not to a specific page. However, you can create template files for specific content and not just the view.

Four content-specific template types are available: author, category, page, and tag. Each one allows you to refer to specific content by the term's ID (an individual author's ID, for instance) or by the *slug*.

The slug discussed in this section differs from the slug argument of the `get_template_part` function described in the preceding section. For this section, slug refers to a post, page, or category slug (to name a few), such as a Press Releases category having a slug of `press-releases` or a post titled "Hello World" having a slug of `hello-world`.

**Book VI
Chapter 6**

Digging into
Advanced Theme
Development

For example, imagine that you have an About Us page with an `id` of `138` and a slug of `about-us`. You can create a template for this specific page by creating a file named either `page-138.php` or `page-about-us.php`. In the same way, if you want to create a template specific to an awesome author named Cory with an `id` of 7 and a slug of `cory`, you can create a file named either `author-7.php` or `author-cory.php`.

Creating a template by using the slug can be extremely helpful for making templates for sites that you don't manage. If you want to share a theme that you created, you could create a `category-featured.php` template, and this template would automatically apply to any category view that has a slug of `featured`.

Using categories as the example, the file naming convention is as follows:

✦ A template with the filename `category.php` is a catchall (default) for the display for all categories (alternatively, a template with the filename of `archives.php` will display categories if a `category.php` does not exist).

✦ Add a dash and the category ID number to the end of the filename (shown in Table 6-1) to specify a template for an individual category.

✦ Alternatively, you can add a dash and the category slug to the end of the filename (shown in Table 6-1) to define it as a template for that particular category. For example, if you have a category called Books, the category slug is `books`; the individual category template file would be named `category-books.php`.

✦ If you don't have a `category.php`, an `archives.php`, or `category-#.php` file, the category display pulls from the Main Index template (`index.php`).

Table 6-1 gives you some examples of file naming conventions for category templates.

Table 6-1 Category Template File Naming Conventions

If the Category ID or Slug Is . . .	*The Category Template Filename Is . . .*
1	`category-1.php`
2	`category-2.php`
3	`category-3.php`
`books`	`category-books.php`
`movies`	`category-movies.php`
`music`	`category-music.php`

Because creating a template by using slugs is so useful (and because an ID is only relevant to a specific site), you might wonder why the id option exists. The short answer is that the id option existed before the slug option; however, it is still valuable in specific instances. You can use the id option for a content-specific template without worrying about the customization breaking when the slug changes. This is especially helpful if you set up the site for someone and can't trust that he or she will leave the slugs alone (such as changing a category with a slug of news to press-releases).

Using page templates

Although the page-slug.php feature is very helpful; sometimes, requiring the theme's user to use the name you choose for a specific feature is too difficult or unnecessary. Page templates allow you to create a stand-alone template (just like page.php or single.php) that the user can selectively use on any specific page he or she chooses. As opposed to the page-slug.php feature, a page template can be used on more than one page. The combined features of user selection and multiple uses make page templates a much more powerful theme tool than page-slug.php templates.

**Book VI
Chapter 6**

**Digging into
Advanced Theme
Development**

For more on page templates, refer to Chapters 1, 3, and 5 in this minibook.

To make a template a page template, simply add Template Name: Descriptive Name to a comment section at the top of the template file. For example, the following code is the beginning of the onecolumn-page. php page template file in the Twenty Ten theme:

```php
<?php
/**
 * Template Name: One column, no sidebar
 *
 * A custom page template without sidebar.
 *
 * The "Template Name:" bit above allows this to be selectable
 * from a dropdown menu on the edit page screen.
 *
 * @package WordPress
 * @subpackage Twenty_Ten
 * @since Twenty Ten 1.0
 */
```

This registers the template file as a page template and adds One Column, No Sidebar to the Page Attributes module's Template drop-down, as shown in Figure 6-1. (Check out Book 4, Chapters 1 and 2 for information on publishing pages and using the Page Attributes options.) Using a template on a static page is a two-step process: Upload the template, and tell WordPress to use the template by tweaking the page's code.

Figure 6-1:
Add New
Page in the
Dashboard
Showing
Page
Attributes
for Page
Template
Assignment.

By providing a robust set of page templates, you can offer users of your theme an easy-to-use set of options for formatting their pages. Although these options can be used only for pages, named header, footer, sidebar, and template parts can be used to offer users options on other site views.

Adding Theme Support for Built-In Features

The WordPress core offers a number of great tools that can be easily added to a theme to give the theme more customization options. WordPress provides you with several built-in features that give you the ability to enhance your site and theme. This section covers five of the most popular features, including:

✦ Custom navigation menus

✦ Custom post types

✦ Custom taxonomies

✦ Post formats

✦ Featured images

Each of these features are part of the WordPress core; however, they aren't activated by default. When we say that you're "adding theme support," what we mean is that you are activating a built-in feature in your theme. Therefore, when you're travelling around the WordPress community, whether it's in a support forum or at a WordCamp event, and you hear someone say the theme supports a certain feature, you can smile because you know exactly what he is talking about.

Activating support for these features in the theme you are using involves a few steps:

✦ **Core Function:** Add support for the feature in your theme by including the core function in your theme's Theme Functions template file (`functions.php`).

✦ **Template Function:** Add the necessary function tags in your theme template(s) to display the features on your Web site.

✦ **Templates:** In some cases, you can create feature-specific templates to create enhancements to your site.

The following sections take you through each feature. You add the core function to your theme, add the function tags to your templates and, if indicated, create a feature-specific template in your theme that will handle the added features.

Adding support for custom menus

We think the WordPress menu-building feature is a great tool that WordPress offers to theme developers. Before the addition of this tool, theme developers implemented their own menu solution, creating a huge number of themes with navigation customization requiring coding and a small set of themes with very different ways of handling navigation. Creating complex, multi-level menus on your WordPress site takes just a few steps, as outlined in this section.

A *navigation menu* is a listing of links that displays on your site. These links can be links to pages, posts, or categories within your site, or they can be links to other sites. Either way, you can define navigation menus on your site with the built-in Custom Menus feature in WordPress.

It's to your advantage to provide at least one navigation menu on your site so that readers can see everything your site has to offer. Providing visitors with a link — or several links — keeps with the point-and-click spirit of the Web.

The Twenty Ten theme already supports menus. Looking at Twenty Ten's `functions.php` file, you can see that the following lines of code handle registering the theme's menu:

```
// This theme uses wp_nav_menu() in one location.
register_nav_menus( array(
 'primary' => __( 'Primary Navigation', 'twentyten' ),
) );
```

This registers a single navigation area with a theme location name of `primary` and a human-readable name of Primary Navigation. With the Twenty Ten theme active, choose Appearance⇨Menus.

Core menu function and template tags

The Custom Menu feature is already built in to the default Twenty Ten WordPress theme, so you don't have to worry about preparing your theme for it. However, if you're using a different theme, adding this functionality is easy:

1. **Choose Appearance⇨Editor and then click the Theme Functions template file (`functions.php`).**

   The Theme Functions template opens in the text editor on the left side of the Edit Themes page.

2. **Type the following function on a new line in the Theme Functions template file:**

   ```
   // ADD MENU SUPPORT
   add_theme_support( 'nav-menus' );
   ```

3. **Click the Update File button to save the changes to the template.**

   This template tag tells WordPress that your theme can use the Custom Menu feature, and a Menus link now displays on the Appearance menu in the Dashboard.

4. **Open the Header template (`header.php`).**

   Click the Header link on the Edit Themes page to open the Header template in the text editor on the left side of the Edit Themes page.

5. **Add the following template tag by typing it on a new line in the Header template (`header.php`):**

   ```
   <?php wp_nav_menu(); ?>
   ```

   This template tag is needed so the menu you build by using the Custom Menu feature will display at the top of your Web site. Table 6-2 gives the details on the different parameters you can use with the `wp_nav_menu();` template tag to further customize the display to suit your needs.

6. **Click the Update File button at the bottom of the page to save the changes you made to the Header template.**

Table 6-2	Common Tag Parameters for wp_nav_menu();		
Parameter	*Information*	*Default*	*Tag Example*
`id`	The unique ID of the menu (because you can create several menus, each has a unique ID number)	Blank	`wp_nav_menu( array( 'id' => '1' ) );`
`slug`	The menu name in slug form (for example, `nav-menu`)	Blank	`wp_nav_menu( array( 'slug' => 'nav-menu' ) );`
`menu`	The menu name	Blank	`wp_nav_menu( array( 'menu' => 'Nav Menu' ) );` or `wp_nav_menu('Nav Menu');`
`menu_class`	The CSS class used to style the menu list	Menu	`wp_nav_menu( array( 'menu_class' => 'mymenu' ) );`
`format`	The HTML markup used to style the list (either an unordered list (`ul/li`) or `div` class)	`div`	`wp_nav_menu( array( 'format' => 'ul' ) );`

(continued)

Table 6-2 *(continued)*

Parameter	Information	Default	Tag Example
`fallback_cb`	The parameter that creates a fallback if a custom menu doesn't exist	`wp_page_menu` (the default list of page links)	`wp_nav_menu( ' fallback_cb' => 'wp_page_menu') ;`
`before`	The text that displays before the link text	None	`wp_nav_menu( array( 'before' => 'Click Here' ) );`
`after`	The text that displays after the link text	None	`wp_nav_menu( array( 'after' => '&raquo;' ) );`

Figure 6-2 shows the default Twenty Ten theme with a navigation menu (Home, About, and Blog) beneath the theme's header graphic.

A menu called Main was created in the WordPress Dashboard. (See Chapter 1 in this minibook to create menus in the WordPress Dashboard.) The template tag used in the theme to display the menu looks like this:

```
<?php wp_nav_menu('Main'); ?>
```

The HTML markup for the menu is generated as an unordered list, by default, and looks like this:

```
<ul id="menu-main" class="menu">
<li id="menu-item-53" class="menu-item menu-item-type-custom menu-item-object-
    custom menu-item-53"><a href="/">Home</a></li>
<li id="menu-item-51" class="menu-item menu-item-type-post_type menu-item-object-
    page menu-item-51"><a href="http://localhost/wpdemo/blog/">Blog</a></li>
<li id="menu-item-52" class="menu-item menu-item-type-post_type menu-item-object-
    page menu-item-52"><a href="http://localhost/wpdemo/about/">About</a></li>
</ul>
```

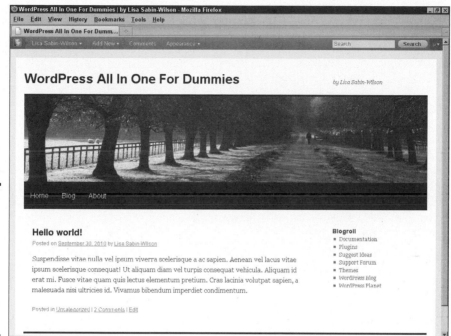

Figure 6-2:
The Twenty
Ten theme
displayed
on Lisa's
site with a
navigation
menu below
the header.

Notice, in the HTML markup, the `<ul id="menu-main" class="menu">` line defines the CSS ID and class.

The ID reflects the name that you give your menu. Because the menu is named Main, the CSS ID is `menu-main`. If the menu was named Foo, the ID would be `menu-foo`. By assigning menu names in the CSS and HTML markup, WordPress allows you to utilize CSS to create different styles and formats for your different menus.

When developing themes for either yourself or others to use, make sure that the CSS you define for the menus can do things like account for subpages by creating drop-down menus. There are several different ways to accomplish this; Listing 6-1 gives you just one example — a block of CSS that you can use to create a nice style for your menu. (This CSS example assumes that you have a menu named "Main"; therefore, the HTML and CSS markups use `menu-main`).

Listing 6-1:   Sample CSS for Drop-down Menu Navigation

```
#menu-main {
....width: 960px;
....font-family: Georgia, Times New Roman, Trebuchet MS;
....font-size: 16px;
```

(continued)

Listing 6-1 *(continued)*

```
....color: #FFFFFF;
....margin: 0 auto 0;
....clear: both;
....overflow: hidden;
....}

#menu-main ul {
....width: 100%;
....float: left;
....list-style: none;
....margin: 0;
....padding: 0;
....}

#menu-main li {
....float: left;
....list-style: none;
....}

#menu-main li a {
....color: #FFFFFF;
....display: block;
....font-size: 16px;
....margin: 0;
....padding: 12px 15px 12px 15px;
....text-decoration: none;
....position: relative;
....}

#menu-main li a:hover, #menu-main li a:active, #menu-main .current_page_item a,
     #menu-main .current-cat a, #menu-main .current-menu-item {
....color: #CCCCCC;
....}

#menu-main li li a, #menu-main li li a:link, #menu-main li li a:visited {
....background: #555555;
....color: #FFFFFF;
....width: 138px;
....font-size: 12px;
....margin: 0;
....padding: 5px 10px 5px 10px;
....border-left: 1px solid #FFFFFF;
....border-right: 1px solid #FFFFFF;
....border-bottom: 1px solid #FFFFFF;
....position: relative;
....}

#menu-main li li a:hover, #menu-main li li a:active {
....background: #333333;
....color: #FFFFFF;
....}

#menu-main li ul {
....z-index: 9999;
....position: absolute;
....left: -999em;
....height: auto;
....width: 160px;
....}
```

```
#menu-main li ul a {
....width: 140px;
....}

#menu-main li ul ul {
....margin: -31px 0 0 159px;
....}

#menu-main li:hover ul ul, #menu-main li:hover ul ul ul, #menu-main li.sfHover ul
    ul, #menu-main li.sfHover ul ul ul {
....left: -999em;
....}

#menu-main li:hover ul, #menu-main li li:hover ul, #menu-main li li li:hover
    ul, #menu-main li.sfHover ul, #menu-main li li.sfHover ul, #menu-main li li
    li.sfHover ul {
....left: auto;
....}

#menu-main li:hover, #menu-main li.sfHover {
....position: static;
....}
```

Book VI
Chapter 6

Digging into
Advanced Theme
Development

The CSS you use to customize the display of your menus will differ; the example in the preceding section is just that, an example. After you get the hang of using CSS, you can try different methods, colors, and styling to create a custom look of your own. (Additional information about Basic HTML and CSS is found in Chapter 4 of this minibook).

Displaying custom menus using widgets

You don't have to use the `wp_nav_menu()`; template tag to display the menus on your site because WordPress also provides a Custom Menu widget that you can add to your theme, allowing you to use widgets, instead of template tags, to display the navigation menus on your site. This is especially helpful if you've created multiple menus for use in and around your site in various places. Have a look into Chapter 4 in this minibook for more information on using WordPress widgets.

Your first step is to register a special widget area for your theme to handle the Custom Menu widget display. To do this, open your theme's `function.php` file and add the following lines of code:

```
// ADD MENU WIDGET
if ( function_exists('register_sidebars') )
....register_sidebar(array('name'=>'Menu',));
```

These few lines of code create a new Menu widget area on the Widgets page in your Dashboard. You can drag the Custom Menu widget into the Menu widget to indicate that you want to display a custom menu in that area. Figure 6-3 shows the Menu widget area with the Custom Menu widget added.

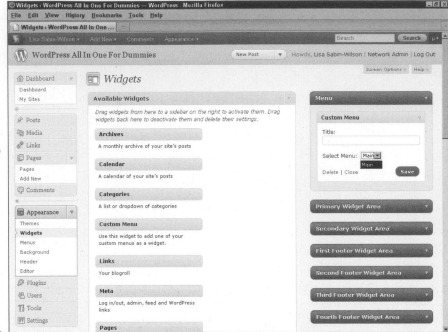

Figure 6-3:
Figure 6-3:
Widgets
page
displaying a
new Menu
widget
area with
the Custom
Menu
widget
added.

To add the widget area to your theme, open the Theme Editor
(Appearance⇨Editor), open the `header.php` file, and add these lines of
code in the area in which you want to display the Menu widget:

```
<ul>
<?php if ( !function_exists('dynamic_sidebar') || !dynamic_sidebar('Menu') ) : ?>
<?php endif; ?>
</ul>
```

These lines of code tell WordPress that you want information contained in
the Menu widget area to display on your site.

Adding support for custom post types

Custom post types and custom taxonomies have expanded the CMS capabilities of WordPress and are likely to become a big part of plugin and theme
features as more developers become familiar with their use. *Custom post
types* allow developers to create new content types separate from posts and
pages, such as movie reviews or recipes. *Custom taxonomies* allow developers to create new types of content grouping separate from categories and
tags, such as genres for movie reviews or seasons for recipes.

Posts and pages are nice generic containers of content. A *page* is timeless content that has a hierarchal structure — a page can have a parent (forming a nested, or hierarchal, structure of pages). A *post* is content that is listed in linear (not hierarchal) order based on when it was published and organized into categories and tags. What happens when you want a hybrid of these features? What if you want content that doesn't show up in the post listings, displays the posting date, and doesn't have either categories or tags? Custom post types are created to satisfy this desire to customize content types.

By default, WordPress already has different post types built in to the software, ready for you to use. The default post types include

**Book VI
Chapter 6**

Digging into
Advanced Theme
Development

✦ Blog posts

✦ Pages

✦ Menus

✦ Attachments

✦ Revisions

Custom post types give you the ability to create new and useful types of content on your Web site, including a smart and easier way to publish those content types to your site.

The possibilities for the use of custom post types are endless. To kick-start your imagination, here are some of the more popular and useful ideas that others have implemented on sites:

✦ Photo gallery

✦ Podcast or video

✦ Book reviews

✦ Coupons and special offers

✦ Events calendar

Core custom post type function

To create and use custom post types on your site, you need to be sure that your WordPress theme contains the correct code and functions. The following steps create a very basic and generic custom post type called Generic Content. Follow these steps to create the same basic custom post type:

1. **Open the Theme Functions template file (`functions.php`).**

   Choose Appearance➪Editor to open the Theme Editor page. Then click the Theme Functions template link to open the `functions.php` file in the text editor.

2. **Add the custom post types code to the bottom of the Theme Functions template file.**

   Scroll to the bottom of the `functions.php` file and include the following code to add a Generic Content custom post type to your site:

   ```
   // ADD CUSTOM POST TYPE
   add_action( 'init', 'create_post_type' );
   function create_post_type() {
     register_post_type( 'generic-content',
       array(
         'labels' => array(
           'name' => __( 'Generic Content' ),
           'singular_name' => __( 'Generic Content' )
         ),
         'public' => true
       )
     );
   }
   ```

3. **Click the Update File button to save the changes made to the `functions.php` file.**

The `register_post_type` function can accept several arguments and parameters, which are detailed in Table 6-3. You can use a variety and combination of different arguments and parameters to create a specific post type. You can find more information on Custom Post Types and using the `register_post_types` function in the WordPress Codex at `http://codex.wordpress.org/Function_Reference/register_post_type`.

If you really don't feel up to writing this code in the Theme Functions template file, there is a nifty plugin developed for WordPress called Custom Post Types UI, written by Brad Williams of WebDevStudios (`http://webdevstudios.com`). This plugin provides you with an interface in your WordPress Dashboard that simplifies the creation of custom post types on your site and completely bypasses the need to create the code in the Theme Functions template file (`functions.php`). You can find the plugin at `http://wordpress.org/extend/plugins/custom-post-type-ui`.

After you complete the steps to add the generic content post type to your site, the Generic Content post type appears on the left navigation menu in the Dashboard, as shown in Figure 6-4.

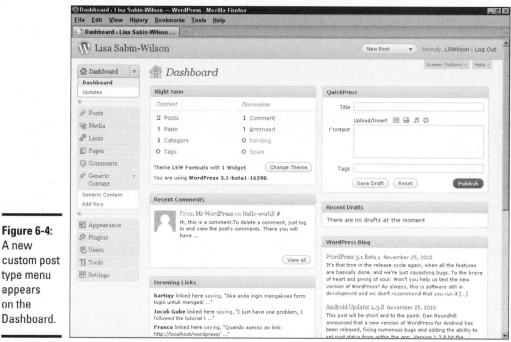

**Book VI
Chapter 6**

Digging into
Advanced Theme
Development

Figure 6-4:
A new
custom post
type menu
appears
on the
Dashboard.

You add and publish new content using the new custom post type the same way you do when you write and publish blog posts. The published content isn't added to the chronological listing of blog posts; it's treated as separate content, just like static pages.

Generic Content is part of the permalink structure, and the permalink looks similar to `http://yourdomain.com/generic-content/new-article`.

Table 6-3   **Arguments and Parameters for register_post_types();**

Parameter	Information	Parameters	Example
label	A plural descriptive name for the post type	None	'label' => __('Generic Content'),
labels	An array of descriptive labels for the post type	Default is empty and is set to the label value	'name' => __('Generic Content'),
		name	
		singular_name	
		add_new	
		add_new_item	
		edit_item	
		new_item	
		view_item	
		search_items	
		not_found	
		not_found_in_trash	
		parent_item_colon	
		menu_name	
description	The description of the post type; displayed in the Dashboard to represent the post type	None	'description' => __('This is a description of the Generic Content type'),

Parameter	Information	Parameters	Example
public	Sets whether the post type is public;	true or false; Default is false	'public' => true,
show_ui	The three other arguments are		'show_ui' => true,
publicly_ queryable	**show_ui**: Show admin screens		'publicly_ queryable' => true,
exclude_ from_search	**publicly_query-able**: Query for this post type from the front end		'exclude_from_ search' => false,
show_in_nav_ menus	**exclude_from_ search**: Show post type in search results		'show_in_nav_ menus' => true
menu_ position	Sets the position of the post type menu item in the Dashboard navigation menu	Default 20; By default, custom post types appear after the Comments menu in the Dashboard	'menu_position' => 25,
		Set integer in intervals of five (5, 10, 15, 20, and so on)	
menu_icon	Defines a custom icon (graphic) to the post type menu item in the Dashboard navigation menu	None	'menu_icon' => get_stylesheet_ directory_uri() . '/images/ generic-content. png',
	Creates and uploads the image into the images directory of your theme folder.		

(continued)

Table 6-3 *(continued)*

Parameter	Information	Parameters	Example
`hierarchical`	Tells WordPress whether to display the post type content list in a hierarchical manner	`true` or `false`; Default is true	`'hierarchical' => true,`
`query_var`	Controls whether this post type can be used with a query variable such as `query_posts` (see previous section) or `WP_Query`	`true` or `false`: Default is false	`'query_var' => true,`
`capability_type`	Defines permissions for users to edit, create, or read the custom post type	`post` (default); Gives the same capabilities for those who can edit, create, and read blog posts	`'query_var' => post,`
`capabilities`	Tells WordPress what capabilities are accepted for this post type	Default: empty; the `capability_type` value is used. **edit_post**: allows post type to be edited **read_post**: allows post type to be read **delete_post**: allows post type to be deleted	`'capabilities' => edit_post,`
`map_meta_cap`	Tells WordPress whether to use the default internal meta capabilities.	`true` or `false`; Default is false	`'map_meta_cap' => true,`

Parameter	Information	Parameters	Example
supports	Defines what meta boxes, or modules, are available for this post type in the Dashboard	**title**: Text box for the post title	`'supports' => array( 'title', 'editor', 'excerpt', 'custom-fields', 'thumbnail' ),`
		editor: Text box for the post content	
		comments: Check boxes to toggle comments on/off	
		trackbacks: Check boxes to toggle trackbacks and pingbacks on/off	
		revisions: Allows post revisions	
		author: Drop-down box to define post author	
		excerpt: Text box for the post excerpt	
		thumbnail: The featured image selection	
		custom-fields: Custom fields input area	
		page-attributes: The page parent and page template drop-down menus	

(continued)

Table 6-3 *(continued)*

Parameter	Information	Parameters	Example

`rewrite`	Rewrites the permalink structure for the post type	`true` or `false`;
		
		Two other arguments are available:
		
		`slug`: Permalink slug to prepend to your custom post types
		
		`with_front`: If you've set your permalink structure with a specific prefix such as `/blog`
			`'rewrite' =>`
			`array( 'slug' =>`
			`'my-content',`
			`'with_front' =>`
			`false ),`

`has_archive`	Tells WordPress whether to enable post archives for this post type	`true` or `false` Default is false (if `true`, WordPress uses the post type name as it's slug in the permalink URL)	`'has_archive' =>` `true,`
`can_export`	Tells WordPress whether this post type can be exported using the built-in content exporter	`true` or `false` Default is true	`'can_export' =>` `false,`

`taxonomies`	Uses existing WordPress taxonomies (category and tag)	Category `post_tag`	`'taxonomies'`
			`=> array(`
			`'post_tag',`
			`'category'),`

Listing 6-2 gives you a real-world example that Lisa used on a site she developed called No Rules Theatre, which you can see at http://norules theatre.org. This site uses a custom post type called Shows to create custom content for the shows that the theatre produces each season. Reference the parameters and information provided in Table 4-2 while reading the lines of code in Listing 6-2 to see how the custom post types for the No Rules Theatre site were created and applied.

Listing 6-2:   Real World Custom Post Type Example from norulestheatre.org

```
// ADD CUSTOM POST TYPE: SHOWS
add_action( 'init', 'create_my_post_types' );
function create_my_post_types() {
....register_post_type( 'shows',
....array(
....'labels' => array(
....'name' => __( 'Shows' ),
....'singular_name' => __( 'Show' ),
....'add_new' => __( 'Add New Show' ),
....'add_new_item' => __( 'Add New Show' ),
....'edit' => __( 'Edit' ),
....'edit_item' => __( 'Edit Show' ),
....'new_item' => __( 'New Show' ),
....'view' => __( 'View Show' ),
....'view_item' => __( 'View Show' ),
....'search items' => __( 'Search Shows' ),
....'not_found' => __( 'No shows found' ),
....'not_found_in_trash' => __( 'No shows found in Trash' ),
....'parent' => __( 'Parent Show' ),
....),

....'public' => true,
....'show_ui' => true,
....'publicly_queryable' => true,
....'exclude_from_search' => false,
....'menu_position' => 10,
....'menu_icon' => get_stylesheet_directory_uri() . '/img/nrt-shows.png',
....'hierarchical' => true,
....'query_var' => true,
....'rewrite' => array( 'slug' => 'shows', 'with_front' => false ),
....'taxonomies' => array( 'post_tag', 'category'),
....'can_export' => true,
....'supports' => array(
....'post-thumbnails',
....'excerpts',
....'comments',
....'revisions',
....'title',
....'editor',
....'page-attributes',
....'custom-fields')
....)
....);
}
```

In the previous section we discuss Custom Menus, and in Chapter 1 of this minibook, we show you how to add custom menus in the Dashboard. Chapter 1 states the three modules WordPress gives you to add menus from are Custom Links, Pages, and Categories. On the Custom Menu page in the WordPress Dashboard, click the Screen Options tab at the top right of that page; the check box next to Post Types enables your custom post types in the Menus you create.

Custom post type templates

By default, custom post types utilize the `single.php` template in your theme. That is unless you create a specific template for your custom post type if you find the regular WordPress `single.php` template too limiting for your post type.

The preceding section has the code to build a simple Generic Content custom post. After that is added, a Generic Content menu appears in the WordPress Dashboard. Choose Generic Content➪Add New and publish a new post to add some content for testing. In this example, a new Generic Content type with a title of Test and a slug of `test` is added. Because the Generic Content type doesn't have a specific template, it uses the `single.php` template, and resulting posts look no different from a standard one.

If you get a Not Found page when you try to go to a new custom post type entry, reset your permalink settings. Choose Settings➪Permalinks on the WordPress Dashboard and then click Save Changes. This forces WordPress to reset the permalinks, which adds the new custom post type link formats in the process.

To build a template specific for the Generic Content post type, add a new template named `single-`*posttype*`.php` where *posttype* is the first argument passed to the `register_post_type` function from the preceding section. For this example, the single template file specific to Sample Post Type is `single-generic-content.php`. Any modifications made to this template file will only appear for instances of the Generic Content post type.

Tying this together with the section on template parts from earlier in this chapter, a basic structure for `single-generic-content.php` for the Twenty Ten theme is

```
<?php get_header(); ?>
<div id="container">
    <div id="content" role="main">
        <?php get_template_part('loop', 'generic-content'); ?>
    </div><!-- #content -->
</div><!-- #container -->
<?php get_sidebar(); ?>
<?php get_footer(); ?>
```

By using the template part, creating a file called `loop-generic-content.php` allows for easy customization of The Loop for the Generic Content post type entry.

Adding Support for Custom Taxonomies

Similar to how having posts and pages as content options can be limiting, sometimes categories and tags just aren't enough. The example of a movie review custom post type might need a variety of new taxonomies or grouping options. Organizing movie reviews by director, movie star, review rating, film genre, and MPAA rating allows visitors to the site to view different groupings of reviews that might interest them. Like the custom post type example, this example creates a very simple taxonomy to test custom taxonomy–specific templates. For this example, a new post taxonomy called Sample Taxonomy is created.

**Book VI
Chapter 6**

Digging into
Advanced Theme
Development

To register this new taxonomy, you use the `register_taxonomy` function. Adding the following code to the bottom of your theme's `functions.php` file registers the new sample taxonomy custom taxonomy specifically for WordPress built-in posts, adds a new Posts➪Sample Taxonomy admin menu entry to manage the Sample Taxonomy entries, and adds sample taxonomy options to the editor for posts.

```
register_taxonomy( 'sample-taxonomy', 'post', array( 'label' -> 'Sample Taxonomy'
    ) );
```

This function call gives the new custom taxonomy an internal name of `sample-taxonomy`, assigns the new taxonomy to Posts, and gives the taxonomy a human-readable name of Sample Taxonomy.

After adding this code to your theme, you can create and assign Sample Taxonomies when creating a new post or editing an existing post. For this example, you could add a new sample taxonomy with a name of Testing to an existing post and update the post.

With the Testing taxonomy added, you can now visit `example.com/sample-taxonomy/testing` to get the archive page for the new sample taxonomy.

If you get a Not Found page or don't get an archive listing when you try to go to a specific sample taxonomy entry's archive, resave your permalink settings. Choose Settings➪Permalinks on the WordPress Dashboard and then click Save Changes. This forces WordPress to reset the permalinks, which adds the new custom taxonomy link formats in the process.

Adding a new template file called `taxonomy-sample-taxonomy.php` allows for adding a template specific to this new custom taxonomy. Like you can with categories and tags, you can add a template that is specific to a single custom taxonomy entry. Therefore, a template specific to a sample taxonomy with a slug of `testing` would have a filename of `taxonomy-sample-taxonomy-testing.php`.

Custom Taxonomies is a feature that will appeal to only a specific type of site that deals, mainly, in niche areas of content. Sites that want to really drill down navigation and grouping options for their content. You can find more about custom taxonomies in the WordPress Codex at `http://codex.wordpress.org/Function_Reference/register_taxonomy`.

Adding support for post formats

Introduced in version 3.1 of WordPress, the Post Formats feature allows you to designate a different content display and style for certain types of designated posts. Unlike custom post types, you aren't able to create different post formats because WordPress has already assigned them for you — it's up to you what post format, if any, you want to use in your theme.

Here are the nine types of WordPress post formats:

✦ **Aside:** A very short post that shares a random thought or idea. Typically, an aside is shared without a post title or any category/tag designations; it's simply a random, one-off thought — not a full post — shared on your blog.

✦ **Audio:** A post that shares audio files or podcasts. Usually, audio posts have very little text and include a built-in audio player so visitors can click and listen.

✦ **Chat:** A transcript of an online conversation that can be formatted to look like a chat (or Instant Message) window.

✦ **Gallery:** A gallery of clickable images, where clicking an image opens a larger version of the photo. Often, galleries do not contain text (but may have a title) and are used for only the display of a gallery.

✦ **Image:** A post that shares a single image. The image may, or may not, have text or a caption to go with the post.

✦ **Link:** A post that provides a link you find useful and want to share with your readers. These post formats often contain a title and, sometimes, a short bit of text that describes the link.

✦ **Quote:** A post that displays a quotation on your blog. Often, users will include a byline, or the quote's source.

✦ **Status:** A short status update, usually limited to 140 characters or less (think Twitter!).

✦ **Video:** A post that displays a video, usually embedded within a video player (say YouTube) so your readers can play the video without leaving your site.

This list of post format types is all there is; you only have nine designated post formats. You can use one or all of them in your theme, depending on your specific needs.

A good, real-world example of post formats is found at Lisa's Web site (http://lisasabin-wilson.com). Lisa's site, shown in Figure 6-5, cleanly separates the formats in the menu navigation and in the individual post styling and icons that he uses to designate the formats.

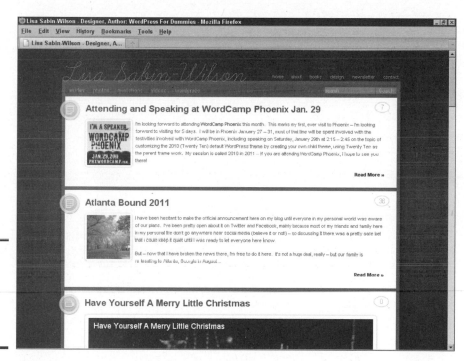

Figure 6-5:
Post
formats at
brian
gardner.
com.

If you find that your site needs a different type of post format that is not currently available, consider adding it as a custom post type.

Post class defined

In the default Twenty Ten theme, examine the code for the `loop.php` template. About ¾ the way in, you see a line of code that looks like this:

```
<div id="post-<?php the_ID(); ?>" <?php
        post_class(); ?>>
```

The cool part of that template tag is the `post_class()` section. This template tag tells WordPress to insert specific HTML markup in your template that allows you to use CSS to make custom styles for sticky posts, categories, tags, and post formats.

For example, a post has the following options set:

✔ Stick this post to the front page

✔ Filed in a category called WordPress

✔ Tagged with News

By having the `post_class()` tag in the template, WordPress inserts HTML markup that allows the use of CSS to style sticky posts, or posts assigned to specific tags, categories, or post formats, differently. WordPress inserts the following HTML markup for the post:

```
<div class="post sticky category-
            wordpress tag-news">
```

Likewise, for post formats, if a post is published using the Images post format, the `post_class()` tag in the template contains the following HTML markup indicating that this post should be formatted for an image display:

```
<div class="post type-post format-image">
```

Add this information to the CSS and HTML information provided to you in Chapter 3 of this minibook, and you see how you can use CSS along with the `post_class();` tag to provide custom styles for each post type on your site and unique styles for the different categories and tags you use in your posts.

Core post format function

To add support for post formats in your theme, you need to add the core function call to your Theme Functions template file (`functions.php`). After you follow these few steps to make it happen, you'll see the magic that occurs on the Add New Post page in your WordPress Dashboard! Here's how to add post formats support in your theme:

1. **Choose Appearance⇨Editor on your Dashboard.**

The Edit Themes page appears.

2. **Open the Themes Function file in the text editor.**

The link for the Theme Functions template file is on the right side of the Edit Themes page. Clicking this link opens the Theme Functions template file (`functions.php`) in the text editor on the left side of the Edit Themes page.

3. **Add the following function on a new line:**

```
add_theme_support( 'post-formats', array( 'aside', 'chat', 'gallery',
    'image', 'link', 'quote', 'status', 'video', 'audio' ) );
```

4. **Click the Update File button to save the changes made to the**
`functions.php` **file.**

In Step 3, the code sample adds all nine post formats to the theme. You don't have to use all nine; you can include only the formats that you think you will use in your theme and leave the rest.

You won't notice an immediate change to your site when you save your new Theme Functions template file with the Post Formats support added. To see what WordPress added to your site, you need to visit the Add New Post page (Posts➪Add New).

The change is subtle, but if you follow the steps to add post format support, you see a Format item in the Publish module on the right side of the page, as shown in Figure 6-6. Click the Edit link to the right of Format to designate a format for your post. In Figure 6-6, see all nine post format options listed. You also see a tenth format option, Standard (or Default), which is used when you don't select a specific format for your post.

**Book VI
Chapter 6**

**Digging into
Advanced Theme
Development**

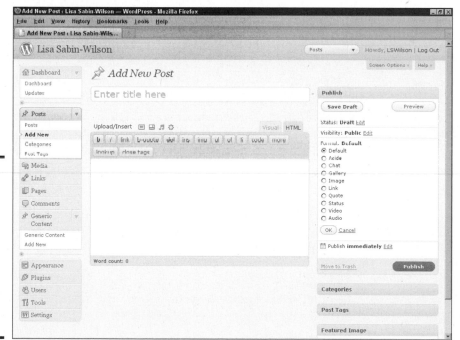

Figure 6-6:
Adding post format support to your theme gives you a Format option on the Add New Post page.

Template tags for post formats

Adding Post Format support to your theme isn't enough. If you're going to add post format support, you really should provide some unique styling for each type of format; otherwise, your post formats will look like your blog posts and the point of adding them to your theme will be lost.

You can display your post format two ways:

✦ **Content:** For each format, you can designate what content you want to display. For example, if you don't want to display a title for your Asides format, you leave out the template tag that calls it, but leave the tag in for your Video post format.

✦ **Style:** Utilizing the HTML markup that is provided by the `post_class();` tag, your formats each have a CSS class assigned to them. Use those CSS classes to provide unique styles for fonts, colors, backgrounds, and borders to each of your post formats. The nearby "Post class defined" sidebar discusses how to use HTML and CSS to create custom styles in your template.

Adding unique styles for your post formats starts with creating the content designations you want to display for each format. Earlier in this section is a list of nine post formats and some ideas on what you can do to display them on your site. The possibilities are endless and it's really up to you. Refer to Chapter 3 of this minibook for more information on the content-related template tags you can use in these areas. The following steps take you through the creation of a very simple, stripped-down Main Index file (`index.php`):

1. **Open your favorite text editor, such as Notepad (for PC) or TextMate (for Mac).**

2. **Type** `<?php get_header(); ?>`.

This function includes all the code from your theme's `header.php` file.

3. **Type the following two lines:**

```
<?php if (have_posts()) : ?>
<?php while (have_posts()) : the_post(); ?>
```

These two lines of code indicate the beginning of The Loop (discussed in Chapter 3 of this minibook).

4. **Type** `<div id="post-<?php the_ID(); ?>" <?php post_class(); ?>>`.

This line provides HTML and CSS markup, using the `post_class();` function that provides you with unique CSS classes for each of your post formats (see the "Post class defined" sidebar).

5. **Type** `<?php`.

This initiates the start of a PHP function.

6. Type the following lines to provide content for the Asides post format:

```
if ( has_post_format( 'aside' )) {
echo the_content();
}
```

7. Type the following lines to provide content for the Gallery post format:

```
elseif ( has_post_format( 'gallery' )) {
echo '<h3>';
echo the_title();
echo '</h3>';
echo the_content();
}
```

8. Type the following lines to provide content for the Image post format:

```
elseif ( has_post_format( 'image' )) {
echo '<h3>';
echo the_title();
echo '</h3>';
echo the_post_thumbnail('image-format');
echo the_content();
}
```

9. Type the following lines to provide content for the Link post format:

```
elseif ( has_post_format( 'link' )) {
echo '<h3>';
echo the_title();
echo '</h3>';
echo the_content();
}
```

10. Type the following lines to provide content for the Quote post format:

```
elseif ( has_post_format( 'quote' )) {
echo the_content();
}
```

11. Type the following lines to provide content for the Status post format:

```
elseif ( has_post_format( 'status' )) {
echo the_content();
}
```

12. Type the following lines to provide content for the Video post format:

```
elseif ( has_post_format( 'video' )) {
echo '<h3>';
echo the_title();
echo '</h3>';
echo the_content();
}
```

13. Type the following lines to provide content for the Audio post format:

```
elseif ( has_post_format( 'audio' )) {
echo '<h3>';
echo the_title();
echo '</h3>';
echo the_content();
}
```

Book VI
Chapter 6

Digging into
Advanced Theme
Development

14. **Type the following lines to provide content for all other (Default) posts:**

    ```
    else {
    echo '<h3>';
    echo the_title();
    echo '</h3>';
    echo the_content();
    }
    ```

15. **Type** ?>.

    This line ends the PHP function.

16. **Type** </div>.

    This closes the HTML div tag opened in Step 4.

17. **Type** <?php endwhile; else: ?> <?php endif; ?>.

    This closes the endwhile and if statements that were opened in Step 3.

18. **Type** <?php get_sidebar(); ?>.

    This function calls in the code included in the sidebar.php file of your theme.

19. **Type** <?php get_footer(); ?>.

    This function calls in the code included in the footer.php file of your theme.

20. **Save your file as** index.php.

    Upload it into your theme folder, replacing your existing index.php file.

Listing 6-3 displays the full code for your new index.php file.

Listing 6-3:   A Simple Post Formats Template

```php
<?php get_header(); ?>
<?php if (have_posts()) : ?>
<?php while (have_posts()) : the_post(); ?>
<div id="post-<?php the_ID(); ?>" <?php post_class(); ?>>
<?php

if ( has_post_format( 'aside' )) {
....echo the_content();
}

elseif ( has_post_format( 'gallery' )) {
....echo '<h3>';
....echo the_title();
....echo '</h3>';
....echo the_content();
}
```

```php
elseif ( has_post_format( 'gallery' )) {
....echo '<h3>';
....echo the_title();
....echo '</h3>';
....echo the_content();
}

elseif ( has_post_format( 'image' )) {
....echo '<h3>';
....echo the_title();
....echo '</h3>';
....echo the_post_thumbnail('image-format');
....echo the_content();
}

elseif ( has_post_format( 'link' )) {
....echo '<h3>';
....echo the_title();
....echo '</h3>';
....echo the_content();
}

elseif ( has_post_format( 'quote' )) {
....echo the_content();
}

elseif ( has_post_format( 'status' )) {
....echo the_content();
}

elseif ( has_post_format( 'video' )) {
....echo '<h3>';
....echo the_title();
....echo '</h3>';
....echo the_content();
}

elseif ( has_post_format( 'audio' )) {
....echo '<h3>';
....echo the_title();
....echo '</h3>';
....echo the_content();
}

else {
....echo '<h3>';
....echo the_title();
....echo '</h3>';
....echo the_content();
}
?>
</div>
<?php endwhile; else: ?>
<?php endif; ?>
<?php get_sidebar(); ?>
<?php get_footer(); ?>
```

The example in Listing 6-3 is a very simple one and doesn't include a whole lot of HTML markup or CSS classes. Therefore, you can focus on the code bits that are required to designate and define different content displays for your post formats. You can see, in Listing 6-3, that some of the formats contain the template tag to display the title: `the_title();` and others do not — but they all contain the template tag to display the content of the post: `the_content();`. As mentioned previously, you can play with different content types and markup that you want to add to your post formats.

By coupling your template additions for post formats with the `post_class();` tag that adds special CSS classes and markup for each post format type, you can customize the display of each post format to your heart's content.

Adding support for post thumbnails

The WordPress feature called Post Thumbnails (also known as Featured Images) takes a lot of the work out of associating an image with a post and using the correct size each time. A popular way to display content in WordPress themes includes a thumbnail image with a short snippet (excerpt) of text — the thumbnail images are consistent in size and placement within your theme. Prior to the inclusion of post thumbnails in WordPress, users would have to open their image in an image-editing program (such as Photoshop) and crop and resize their image to the desired size; or use fancy scripts that would resize images on the fly, which tend to be resource intensive on Web servers, so it wasn't an optimal solution. How about a content management system that will crop and resize your images for you to the exact dimensions that you specify? Yep, WordPress does that for you, with just a few adjustments.

By default, when you upload an image, WordPress creates three versions of your image based on dimensions that are set in your Dashboard (choose Settings⇨Media):

✦ **Thumbnail size:** Default dimensions are 150px x 150px

✦ **Medium size:** Default dimensions are 300px x 300px

✦ **Large size:** Default dimensions are 1024px x 1024px

Therefore, when you upload an image, you actually end up with four sizes of that image stored on your Web server: thumbnail, medium, large, and the original image. Images are cropped and resized proportionally and, typically, when you use them in your posts, you can designate which size you would like to use in the image options of the uploader. (See Book IV, Chapter 4 for a refresher on uploading images in WordPress.)

Within the WordPress image uploader, you can designate a particular image as the featured image of the post, and then, using the Featured Images function that you add to your theme, you can include template tags to display your chosen featured image with your post. This is helpful for creating magazine- or news-style themes that are popular with WordPress sites. Figure 6-7 displays Lisa's personal blog (`http://lisasabin-wilson.com`) where she uses post thumbnails and featured images to display a thumbnail associated with each post excerpt on her home page.

Figure 6-7: Post thumbnails in use at lisasabin-wilson.com.

Also covered in this section is adding support for different image sizes, other than the default image sizes that are set on the Media Settings page in your Dashboard. This is helpful when you have sections of your site where you want to display a much smaller thumbnail, or a larger version of the medium-sized thumbnail that's not as big as the large size.

Core post thumbnails function and template tag

Adding support for post thumbnails includes one line of code added to your Theme Functions template file (`functions.php`):

```
add_theme_support( 'post-thumbnails' );
```

After you add this line of code to your Theme Functions template file, you can use the Featured Image feature for your posts. You can designate featured images by using the function in the WordPress image uploader. The function is also an option on the Add New Post page, where you write and publish your posts.

After you add featured images to your posts, make sure that you add the correct tag in your template(s) so the featured images display on your site in the area you want them to display. Open your `index.php` template, for example, and include the following line of code to include the default thumbnail-size version of your chosen featured image in your posts:

```
<?php if ( has_post_thumbnail() ) { the_post_thumbnail('thumbnail'); ?>
```

The first part of that line of code checks whether a featured image is associated with the post; if there is, the image displays; if a featured image doesn't exist for the post, the code returns nothing. You can also include the other default image sizes (set in your Media Settings page in the Dashboard, as shown in Figure 6-8) for medium-, large-, and full-sized images by using these tags:

```
<?php if ( has_post_thumbnail() ) { the_post_thumbnail('medium'); ?>
```

```
<?php if ( has_post_thumbnail() ) { the_post_thumbnail('large'); ?>
```

```
<?php if ( has_post_thumbnail() ) { the_post_thumbnail('full'); ?>
```

Figure 6-8: The Media Settings page in the Dashboard.

Adding custom image sizes for post thumbnails

If the predefined, default image sizes in WordPress (thumbnail, medium, large, and full) don't satisfy you, and there's an area on your site that you want to display images with dimensions that vary from the default, WordPress makes it relatively easy to add custom image sizes in your Theme Functions template file. You then use the `the_post_thumbnail` function to display it in your theme.

You are not limited on what sizes you can add for your images, and this example shows you how to add a new image size of 600px x 300px. Add this line to your Theme Functions template file (`functions.php`) beneath the `add_theme_support('post-thumbnails')` function you added:

```
add_image_size( 'custom', 600, 300, true);
```

This code tells WordPress that it needs to create an additional version of the images you upload, and to crop and resize it to the dimensions of 600px x 300px. Notice the four parameters in the `add_image_size` function:

✦ **Name ($name):** Gives the image size a unique name that you can use in your template tag. For example, the image size in the example above uses the name `'custom'`.

✦ **Width ($width):** Gives the image size a width dimension in numbers. In our example, the width is defined as `'600'`.

✦ **Height ($height):** Gives the image size a height dimension in numbers. In our example, the height is defined as `'300'`.

✦ **Crop ($crop):** This parameter is optional and tells WordPress whether it should crop the image to exact dimensions or do a soft proportional resizing of the image. In our example, the parameter is set to `'true'` (accepted arguments: true or false).

Adding the custom image size to your template to display the featured image is the same as adding default image sizes. The only difference is the name of the image set in the parentheses of the template tag. The custom image size in our example uses the following tag:

```
<?php if ( has_post_thumbnail() ) { the_post_thumbnail('custom'); ?>
```

Exploring Theme Options

One of the key features of an advanced theme is a Theme Options page. A Theme Options page allows the theme user to supply information to the theme without having to modify the theme files. Although a single-use theme could have this information hard-coded into the theme, it's an inelegant solution. If the theme is used more than once or is managed by a non-developer, having an easy-to-change setting on the back end allows changes to be made quickly and easily.

Use a Theme Options page when the information is specific to the user and not the theme design. Web analytics code (such as visitor tracking JavaScript from Google Analytics or Woopra) is a good example of this user-specific information. Because hundreds of analytics providers exist, most analytics providers require the JavaScript code to be customized for the specific site. The theme could have a number of different header and footer files, providing easy-to-use theme options. Adding JavaScript code to the header and the footer rather than requiring theme file modifications can make using your theme much easier.

Advanced uses of a Theme Options page vary widely and include design editors, color pickers, font options, and settings to modify the theme layout (switch a sidebar from one side of the theme to another, for example). The options offered depend on the project and the design. Early in the design process, consider what a user may want to modify.

Understanding theme options basics

Before jumping into the code, you should understand some basic concepts of how theme options work.

Before WordPress version 2.8, adding options to your theme required the developer to code the entire process, including providing an input form to accept the options, storing the options in the database, and retrieving the options from the database to use them. Fortunately, things have gotten much better. Some work is still required, but adding options is much easier now.

To let the user access the theme options, an input form is required. This process requires the most work because the form still needs to be manually created and managed. The form will need to be added to the back end so the user can access it. Adding a new option to the Appearance menu allows the user to find the Theme Options page. Fortunately, WordPress offers an easy-to-use function called add_theme_page. To have WordPress manage as much as possible for you, the code will need to tell WordPress to store the data. The register_setting function can handle this.

Building a simple theme options page

Now that you know what pieces you need to build the Theme Options page, you can jump into the code. Open a plain-text editor and enter the code in Listing 6-4.

Listing 6-4:   The Theme Options Page

```
<?php
function cm_theme_options_init(){                                            a2
 register_setting( 'cm_theme_options', 'theme_options' );                    a3
}
add_action( 'admin_init', 'cm_theme_options_init' );                         a5
function cm_theme_options_menu() {                                           a6
 add_theme_page( 'Theme Options', 'Theme Options', 'manage_options',
    'cm_theme_options', 'cm_theme_options_page' );                          a7
}
add_action( 'admin_menu', 'cm_theme_options_menu' );                         a9
function cm_theme_options_page() {                                           a10
 ?>
 <div class="wrap">                                                          a12
```

```
<?php screen_icon(); ?>                                               a13
<h2>Theme Options</h2>                                               a14
<form method="post" action="options.php">                           a15
<?php settings_fields( 'cm_theme_options' ); ?>                     a16
<?php $options = get_option( 'theme_options' ); ?>                 a17
<table class="form-table">                                          a18
<tr valign="top">                                                   a19
<th scope="row">Checkbox</th>                                       a20
<td><input name="theme_options[checkbox]" type="checkbox" value="1" <?php
    checked('1', $options['checkbox']); ?> /></td>                 a21
</tr>
<tr valign="top"><th scope="row">Text</th>                          a23
<td><input type="text" name="theme_options[text]" value="<?php echo
    $options['text']; ?>" /></td>                                  a24
</tr>
<tr valign="top">                                                   a26
<th scope="row">Text Area</th>                                      a27
<td><textarea name="theme_options[text_area]"><?php echo $options['text_area'];
    ?></textarea></td>                                             a28
</tr>
</table>
<p class="submit"><input type="submit" class="button-primary" value="<?php _e
    ( 'Save Changes' ); ?>" /></p>                                 a31
</form>
</div>
<?php
}
?>
```

**Book VI
Chapter 6**

**Digging into
Advanced Theme
Development**

Here's a brief explanation of what the various lines do:

a2   This creates a new function that calls `register_setting`, the function that tells WordPress about the need to store data.

a3   This tells WordPress that you are creating a new settings group called `cm_theme_options`. The `theme_options` argument sets the WordPress options name used to store and retrieve the theme options. You'll want to change these to be unique to your theme so that you don't accidentally load or save over settings from other themes or plugins.

a5   The new `cm_theme_options_init` function needs to be called to work. This line causes the function to be called during the `admin_init` action, which is a good action to use to run functions that need to be called on each admin page load.

a6   This new function handles registering the new menu entry that will show your form.

a7   The `add_theme_page` function adds a new menu entry under the Appearance menu. In order, the arguments are page title (shows in the title bar of the browser), menu entry name, required access level to visit the page, the variable name of the page (this needs to be unique for the page to work), and the function that should be run when visiting the menu location. This last argument (`cm_theme_options_page` in the example) is the name of the function that holds the options form.

a9 The new `cm_theme_options_menu` function needs to be called to work. This line causes the function to be called during the `admin_menu` action, which is when new menu entries should be added.

a10 This new function produces the input form for editing the theme options.

a12 Wrapping a form in the `wrap` class applies WordPress's default formatting.

a13 This outputs the Appearance icon in front of the heading that follows.

a14 This adds a title to the theme options page.

a15 Starts the HTML form with an action that points to `options.php` and handles saving the data.

a16 The `settings_fields` adds some hidden inputs that allow the options to save properly. The `cm_theme_options` argument must match the first argument passed to the `register_setting` function. If this function is missing, or if the argument does not match the first argument of the `register_setting` function, the options will not save properly.

a17 This line loads the saved theme options into the `$options` variable. The `theme_options` argument must match the second argument passed to the `register_setting` function.

a18 Giving the table a class of `form-table` applies WordPress's default form styling.

a19–a20 Starts a new row to hold the first option and adds a description row header (the content inside the `th` tag). As indicated by the description, this option will be a generic check box input.

a21 Adds the check box input. The `checked` function from WordPress handles outputting the required HTML if a checked state was previously saved. The `theme_options[checkbox]` portion matches the second argument passed to the `register_setting` function followed by the name of the specific option (in this case, `checkbox`). The `$options['checkbox']` loads the specific option from the `$options` array.

a23 Starts a new row to hold another option and adds a description row header (the content inside the `th` tag). As indicated by the description, this option will be a generic text input.

a24 Adds the text input. The `echo` outputs the existing value so that it pre-populates the input. The `theme_options[text]` portion matches the second argument passed to the `register_setting` function followed by the name of the specific option (in this case, `text`). The `$options['text']` loads the specific option from the `$options` array.

a26–a27 Starts a new row to hold another option and adds a description row header (the content inside the `th` tag). As indicated by the description, this option will be a generic text area input.

a28 Adds the text area input. The `echo` outputs the existing value so that it pre-populates the input. The `theme_options[text_area]` portion matches the second argument passed to the `register_setting` function followed by the name of the specific option (in this case, `text_area`). The `$options['text_area']` loads the specific option from the `$options` array.

a31 Adds a button with a description of `Save Changes`. Giving the input a class of `button-primary` and wrapping it in a `p` tag with a class of `submit` applies WordPress's default button styling.

To load this file, you need to add a line of code to the theme's `functions.php` file. Edit the `functions.php` file, and add the following line at the bottom of the file:

```
require_once( 'theme-options.php' );
```

Choose Appearance⇨Theme Options. The Theme Options page appears, as shown in Figure 6-9.

**Book VI
Chapter 6**

Digging into Advanced Theme Development

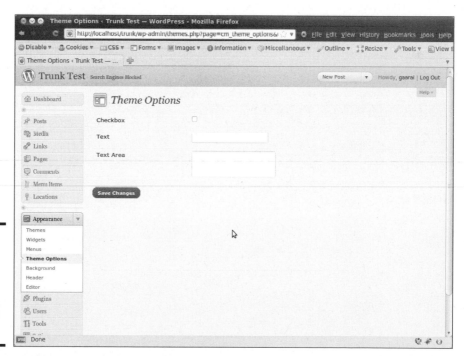

Figure 6-9: The new Theme Options page in the WordPress back end.

Using theme options in the theme

Compared to setting up a theme options page, using the stored options is very easy. To make it easier, add the following code — a quick function that makes using the options as simple as a single function call — to your theme's `functions.php` file:

```php
<?php
function get_theme_option( $option_name ) {
    global $theme_options;
        if ( ! isset( $theme_options ) )
            $theme_options = get_option( 'theme_options' );
        if ( isset( $theme_options[$option_name] ) )
            return $theme_options[$option_name];
    return '';
}
?>
```

The `get_theme_option` function takes an option name as its only argument and returns that option's value. For example, to get the check box option value, simply call `get_theme_option('checkbox')`.

If your theme has a section that can be enabled and disabled by a theme option check box, a section of code such as the following works very well:

```php
<?php if ( get_theme_option('checkbox') ) : ?>
    <!-- example code -->
<?php endif; ?>
```

Typically, text or text area options output user-provided content. By using a check to see whether an option has a value, your theme can offer a default set of text that can be overridden by text entered into a theme option:

```php
<div class="footer-right">
    <?php if ( get_theme_option('text') ) : ?>
        <?php echo get_theme_option('text'); ?>
    <?php else : ?>
        <p>Sample Theme by Cory Miller</p>
    <?php endif; ?>
    <p>Powered by <a
href="http://wordpress.org">WordPress</a></p>
</div>
```

Chapter 7: Using Theme Frameworks to Simplify Customization

In This Chapter

✔ Getting familiar with theme frameworks

✔ Exploring popular theme frameworks

✔ Recognizing common framework features

As theme development for WordPress became a more complex task, theme designers began to realize that they were using the same snippet of code and functions repeatedly to accomplish the same tasks in every theme they built. When it came time for them to upgrade their theme (for example, when WordPress released a new version with new features), they found themselves updating the same functions, adding the same features over and over to several themes they had developed. This is how theme frameworks were born. Essentially, a theme framework is a single theme that is a foundation for other themes to be built from.

In Chapter 5 of this minibook, we discuss child themes, including how to build them. With theme frameworks, the parent theme (the framework) contains all the WordPress functions and template tags, and you can build child themes on top of them. The nice thing about this setup is that the original theme developer has to update only one theme, the framework, to provide upgrades to all their theme offerings (the child themes).

Frameworks come with the tools developers can use to make a custom theme with great efficiency. Using a framework that provides these tools is much faster than building your own tools every time you want to modify a standard theme.

In this chapter, we explore some of the popular theme frameworks and the tools these frameworks contain that make them appealing to developers who want to create a custom theme.

Understanding Theme Frameworks

Many theme frameworks are available in the WordPress market. The goal of these frameworks is to allow users to create custom Web sites and themes without requiring them to be expert programmers. Creating custom layouts, designs, and functionality can be difficult, and theme frameworks bridge the gap for beginning users.

At its core, a theme framework is still just a WordPress theme. You install it and activate it just like any other theme. The real power of theme frameworks is usually found through theme options, child themes, and layout customization. One of the most important parts of using theme frameworks is starting with the right one for your project.

When you install a theme framework, you might be surprised to find limited or no styling in the theme. Generally, theme frameworks are meant to be blank canvases that you easily fill with your own color styles. The goal for a framework is to get out of your way when developing. By doing so, it allows you to utilize tools that are provided instead of having to remove a lot of unnecessary elements and styling.

Think of it like a toolbox. All the tools you need are packaged nicely inside. You only take out the tools that you need for a given project.

Discovering Popular Frameworks

Many theme frameworks are available from a variety of sources. Here's a look at a few of the more popular theme frameworks.

Theme Hybrid

The Theme Hybrid framework (see Figure 7-1) features 15 custom page templates and 8 widget-ready areas. Additionally, six child themes are available from the Theme Hybrid Web site at `http://themehybrid.com`. Theme Hybrid also supports a series of add-on plugins that are specific to this theme. These add-ons include such features as a Tabs plugin, Hooks plugin, and Page Template packs. The Hooks plugin in particular can be very handy for developers who are unfamiliar with PHP programming because it provides you with a graphical interface to latch into hooks, which we explore later in this chapter.

Theme Hybrid, its child themes, and all its add-on plugins are available free. You can download them from `http://themehybrid.com` or from WordPress Extend at `http://wordpress.org/extend`.

Key features:

✦ Theme Options menu

✦ Supports child themes

✦ Add-on plugins extend functionality

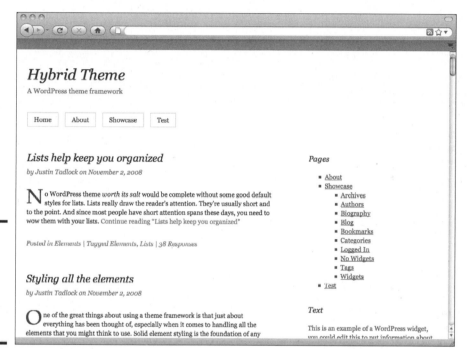

Figure 7-1:
A home page with a new installation of Theme Hybrid.

Carrington

The Carrington theme's developers set out to create a framework that would allow them to stop re-creating the same key features every time they needed to make an advanced WordPress theme. (See Figure 7-2.) By doing this for themselves, they created a tool that others can now use for theme development. Carrington takes a different approach from many other theme frameworks; it doesn't use the parent/child theme relationship. Instead, Carrington uses a unique system of template files to determine how different types of content display in your theme. This approach helps prevent bugs in code because there is less code. Carrington's developers offer several themes built from the base framework. Check out their Web site at `http://carringtontheme.com`.

The Carrington theme's features include

✦ Unique template file system

✦ Fast development of complex themes

✦ Predeveloped themes using the framework

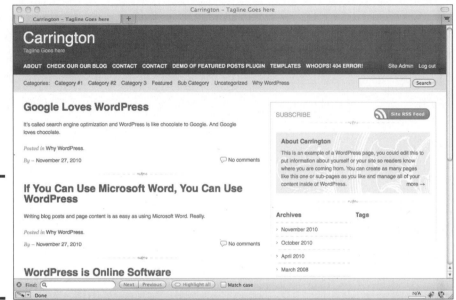

Figure 7-2:
A home page with a new installation of Carrington.

Thematic

Thematic (see Figure 7-3) features 13 widget-ready areas, grid-based layout samples, and styling for many popular plugins. About 20 child themes are available directly from the Thematic Web site, as are many more from third-party sources. Downloading Thematic won't cost you a dime. You can download the theme free at `http://themeshaper.com/thematic`. A large number of child themes are available free as well, while others are commercially supported.

The Thematic theme's features include

✦ Theme Options menu

✦ Supports child themes

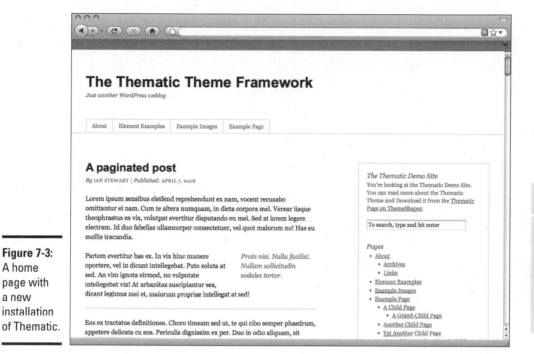

Figure 7-3:
A home
page with
a new
installation
of Thematic.

Genesis

Genesis (see Figure 7-4) includes six default layout options, a prerelease security audit from WordPress lead developer Mark Jaquith, and a comprehensive array of SEO settings. Another great feature of Genesis is a built-in theme store in the WordPress Dashboard that allows you to easily choose, purchase, and activate one of more than 18 child themes. Like other frameworks, Genesis has some theme-specific plugins that add functionality. Genesis can be purchased from StudioPress (http://studiopress.com) for $79.95 and includes one child theme. Additional child themes are available for $24.95.

The Genesis theme's features include

✦ Theme Options menu

✦ Supports child themes

✦ Add-on plugins to extend functionality

✦ Six default layout options

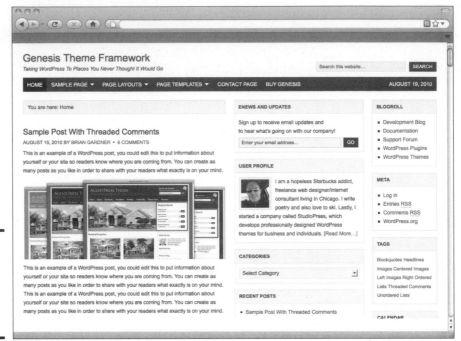

Figure 7-4:
A home
page with
a new
installation
of Genesis.

iThemes Builder

iThemes Builder (see Figure 7-5) sports a built-in layout editor that allows for infinite combinations of layouts. Widget areas can be created on the fly in the layout editor with no limit to the number you can create. Other key features include a style manager to customize the look of the site, a slew of in-theme SEO options, and integration with popular plugins like BuddyPress. You can purchase a copy of iThemes Builder from iThemes at `http://ithemes.com/purchase/builder-theme`. The price is $127 for unlimited sites and includes over 15 child themes.

Key features:

✦ Theme Options menu

✦ Supports child themes

✦ Add-on plugins to extend functionality

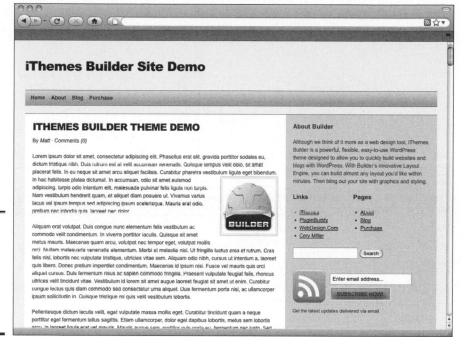

Figure 7-5:
A home
page with
a new
installation
of iThemes
Builder.

Headway

Headway's layout combinations are virtually limitless, thanks to a what-you-
see-is-what-you-get (WYSIWYG) style editor for creating layouts. The visual
editor allows you to drag and drop parts of your theme (known in Headway
as Leafs) and resize them to fit your needs. Headway also features a built-in
design manager that allows you to select colors and images for your sites
design. Headway, shown in Figure 7-6, can be purchased from `http://hcad`
`waythemes.com` for $87 for use on up to two sites, or $164 for use on unlimited sites.

The Headway theme's features include

✦ Drag-and-drop layout editor

✦ Built-in design manager

✦ Infinite widget areas

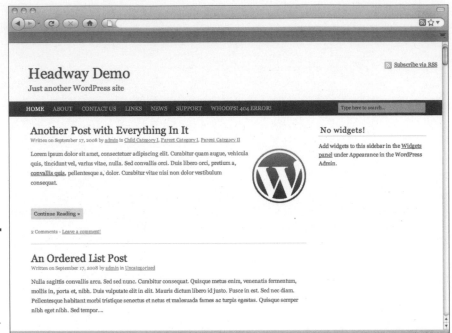

Figure 7-6:
A home
page with
a new
installation
of Headway.

Common Framework Features

Theme frameworks offer a host of features to make your life easier when it comes to building a Web site. Individual frameworks offer many unique features, but also share a common set of features. These common features generally allow for faster and easier development of your WordPress Web site.

Theme functions

Most themes include a `functions.php` file that contains functions for the theme, but some theme frameworks take this to the next level. They offer customization options using these functions that rival many plugins.

In the Genesis theme, a custom function allows users to create new widget areas. The `genesis_register_sidebar()` function, which takes care of the heavy lifting for widgetizing a new area, gives you some options to easily customize it. Below is an example of how you might use this function in your theme's `functions.php` file:

```
genesis_register_sidebar(array(
    'name'=>'My New Widget',
    'description' => 'This widget is new.',
    'before_title'=>'<h4 class="mywidget">',
    'after_title'=>'</h4>'
));
```

This function allows you to enter a few customizations into the function, such as a name for your widget, a description, and any HTML that you want to appear before and after your widget.

Many standard themes also provide functions that are used in the theme, but theme frameworks offer many additional custom functions that the theme doesn't. The custom functions help you make the theme do exactly what you need for a specific site.

Theme functions can vary greatly, so most theme authors have ample documentation through their site or forums where you can get more information about available functions.

Hooks

Many theme frameworks provide hooks to allow you to access and modify features of the theme. Hooks can seem a little advanced to many users, but with a little practice, hooks are quite efficient at modifying a theme. Theme frameworks provide hooks to allow you to latch in to functions of the theme and call or modify them at a specific time.

The two types of hooks are

✦ **Action:** Events during the loading of the theme when you can latch in a specific function. For example, if you want one of your functions to execute at the same time a file in the theme is loaded, you can use an action to hook the function to that file's load.

✦ **Filter:** Allows you to modify data while it passes to the theme or to the browser screen. Some theme frameworks allow you to filter the classes the theme applies to elements.

An example of modifying your theme with hooks can be found in iThemes Builder. For example, consider the hook to add meta data: `builder_add_meta_data`. This can be useful for SEO in your theme.

To add custom meta output, the default function can be replaced with a custom one. To do that, remove the existing action and add your own, like this:

```php
<?php
remove_action('builder_add_meta_data','builder_seo_options');
add_action('builder_add_meta_data','my_custom_builder_seo_options');
?>
```

The default SEO options were removed with `remove_action` and replaced with a new function called `my_custom_builder_seo_options`. Now, you need to define what `my_custom_builder_seo_options` will do.

```
<?php
function my_custom_builder_seo_options() {
    /*Add custom seo options here.*/
}
?>
```

This creates a basic PHP function where you can define what custom SEO options you want in the theme.

Because many frameworks have 100 or more hooks, most of them provide documentation (through their Web sites or forums) of what hooks are available, what each hook does, and what parameters are available to modify how the hook works.

Child themes

Some frameworks choose to allow you to modify the theme by using child themes (find out more about the parent/child theme relationship in Chapter 5 of this minibook). Child themes can be as simple as a stylesheet, but derive their power from the parent theme's template and function files.

Like a regular theme, a huge advantage of using a child theme is to protect any customizations you make from being overwritten if a newer version of the theme comes out. For frameworks, this is especially important because changes to the core theme may be more frequent than regular themes due to the need to add more hooks, functions, or options over time.

From the list of frameworks above, Theme Hybrid, Thematic, Genesis, and iThemes Builder all extend their frameworks through child themes. Many frameworks provide child themes free; others build child themes to sell.

Layout options

The ability to change the layout of a framework is important for many users. Different frameworks use different methods of achieving this. Some use template files to allow the reorganization of the layout; others provide an interface to create layouts from scratch.

Headway, for example, provides a unique layout editor, as shown in Figure 7-7. The layout of the theme is created through a drag-and-drop interface that allows you to organize, size, and style the layout in one location.

Styling

Many theme frameworks incorporate methods that let you customize the style of the Web site without needing to know CSS. (See the section on CSS and stylesheets in Chapter 4 of this minibook.) Frameworks that use a what-you-see-is-what-you-get (or WYSIWYG) style editor, such as Headway, allow you to easily match your theme's colors and design to your branding. Additionally, many editors include color pickers so you don't have to use hexadecimal values to choose colors.

Other common elements that can be styled are borders, fonts, and headers.

Figure 7-7:
Headway's layout editor.

Customizing Theme Frameworks

You may find that you are changing the same elements every time you set up a Web site using a theme framework. Here is a list of where to start when customizing a theme framework for a Web site:

✦ **Add a custom header or logo image.** Adding a nice header graphic to a site makes it look unique from the beginning. If graphics aren't your specialty, use a good designer for your header graphic. This crucial element will catch your visitors' eyes as soon as they hit the page.

✦ **Change the colors of the background and links to match the header and branding of the site.** Many frameworks provide a simple interface to do this; others require you to open the `style.css` file to change the color. Either way, changing the background and link colors to match the site adds cohesiveness throughout the branding of the site.

✦ **Consider the home page layout:** This is based on what the site is trying to achieve. If you want the site to focus on the blog, you might place it on the front page with a left or right sidebar. If your site is more static, you might create a layout with many widget areas on the home page that display things from around the site. The home page is the landing point for many of your site's visitors, so it's important to consider its layout early in the process.

✦ **Decide how to lay out the inside pages and blog post pages.** The pages are just as important as the home page. The form and function of the page and blog post layouts needs to be well planned to accommodate for the parts of the site that you want every user to see. These might include ads in the sidebar or an e-mail newsletter sign-up at the bottom of every post. In the case of pages, you might include information on your products and services in the sidebars and feature areas.

✦ **Add a contact form to the site:** Don't overlook one of those most vital items to install on almost every site. Some of the frameworks listed above offer built-in contact forms that you can add to any page.

If your theme framework doesn't offer a built-in contact form, many free plugins include this functionality, such as ContactBuddy from PluginBuddy. com and Contact Form 7 from ContactForm7.com. If you're looking for a more robust form plugin, Gravity Forms by Rocket Genius (`http://GravityForms.com`) is one of the best form creation plugins. It is a premium plugin but well worth the price.

Book VII

Using and Developing Plugins

The 5th Wave   By Rich Tennant

"Well, here's your problem. You're running applications written in C# on a B♭ server."

Contents at a Glance

Chapter 1: Introducing WordPress Plugins

In This Chapter

✓ Customizing WordPress with plugins

✓ Comparing plugins to themes

✓ Finding and installing WordPress plugins

✓ Comparing and evaluating WordPress plugins

✓ Using popular free plugins

By itself, WordPress is a very powerful program for Web publishing, but by customizing WordPress with *plugins* — add-on programs that give WordPress almost limitless ways to handle Web content — you can make it even more powerful. You can choose any plugins you need to expand your online possibilities. Plugins can turn your WordPress installation into a full-featured gallery for posting images on the Web, an online store to sell your products, a user forum, or a social-networking site. WordPress plugins can be simple, adding (say) a few minor features to your blog, or they can be complex enough to change your entire WordPress site's functionality.

This chapter explores WordPress plugins, what they do, how you find them, and how you install them.

Extending WordPress with Plugins

You've probably seen pocketknives with interchangeable blades or other tools (saws, forks, corkscrews, you name it). Plugins are the WordPress equivalent of those. You just choose the ones you want to install. Plugins can simply provide new features or they can change the way that WordPress works. Whether you choose a plugin to jazz up your WordPress blog or to hot-rod your whole Web site, you can do it without having to know anything about the underlying software code.

For example, if you have a WordPress blog and you want to add complex, fancy content (such as video), you can install a plugin to handle that content. If you have a WordPress Web site for your business and you want to create a form for visitors to use when they contact you, multiple plugins can do that job.

Identifying core plugins

Core plugins (or *canonical* plugins) are new to WordPress. Each one delivers a set of features approved by the contributing developers at WordPress who wrote the main WordPress software. They're intended to provide the most requested features that would be useful to the majority of WordPress users. Core plugins seek to keep those features closely integrated with WordPress, resulting in a streamlined integration that makes them easy to use. Currently, only two core plugins are included in the WordPress software by default:

✦ **Akismet:** This plugin is essential for combating comment spam on your site. Akismet is the answer to comment and trackback spam. Matt Mullenweg of Automattic says Akismet is a "collaborative effort to make comment and trackback spam a non-issue and restore innocence to blogging, so you never have to worry about spam again" (from the Akismet Web site at `http://akismet.com`). In Book III, Chapter 5 we take you through the steps of activating and setting up Akismet on your site.

✦ **Hello Dolly:** This plugin isn't necessary to make your blog run smoothly, but it adds some extra fun. Activate the Hello Dolly plugin on the Manage Plugins page in your WordPress Dashboard. When you activate it, your WordPress blog greets you with a different lyric from the song "Hello, Dolly!" each time. The Hello Dolly plugin is primarily included as a teaching tool to give budding plugin developers a framework for a simple plugin to help them launch their own plugin development efforts.

What makes core plugins different from the thousands of independently contributed plugins available within the WordPress Plugin Directory? Core plugins are included with the WordPress software that you download from the WordPress Web site. Therefore, every WordPress user gets these plugins without having to download them separately. You can choose whether to use the plugins by turning them on or off the way that you would any other plugin.

Core plugins have been around since the origin of WordPress. The very first core plugin was Hello Dolly by Matt Mullenweg, the founder of WordPress. This core plugin is still included with every download of WordPress. Matt describes the Hello Dolly plugin as "not just a plugin, it symbolizes the hope and enthusiasm of an entire generation summed up in two words sung most famously by Louis Armstrong: "Hello, Dolly". When activated, Hello Dolly randomly displays a lyric from the song "Hello, Dolly!" in the upper-right corner of your WordPress administration screen. This may not seem very useful to you and, in fact, it may not be useful to the majority of WordPress users, but the purpose behind the plugin is to provide WordPress plugin developers a simple example of how to write a plugin. This is Matt's method of providing WordPress users an example of a simple plugin.

Hello Dolly has been undeniably successful, spawning more than 40 similar plugins that take the concept and elaborate on it. Some of those plugin developers have gone on to write other successful, more complex plugins.

The Hello Dolly plugin is not the only core plugin in WordPress. Every copy of WordPress includes the Akismet plugin, also by Matt Mullenweg. Akismet is a spam-filtering solution that checks every comment made on your WordPress blog to determine whether the comment is spam. Akismet is only one of two plugins that require a WordPress.com API key, obtained free by signing up for a WordPress.com account.

An *API key* is a special numeric code that is unique to you (similar to a license code or a password) and used by software to identify you as an authorized user.

Figure 1-1 shows the core plugins installed with WordPress version 3.0.

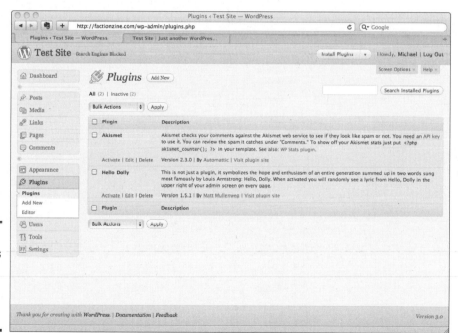

Figure 1-1:
Core plugins
installed
with
WordPress
version 3.0.

Additional WordPress core plugins are still in development, but expect to see them included with a future version of WordPress; so currently, there are only the two: Akismet and Hello Dolly.

Distinguishing between themes and plugins

Software developers often use *themes* (collections of visual features, such as fonts, colors, and layout specifications) when they customize software to establish a consistent look and feel. Some developers argue about themes and plugins — what they are, whether they're the same thing, and what they're for. To us, a theme governs the look and feel of your WordPress blog or Web site; a plugin makes the site work the way you want.

Here's a quick look at the differences between a WordPress theme and a plugin:

✦ A theme is a collection of template files that allow you to change the appearance of your WordPress blog or Web site. These files govern the layout, design, and presentation without affecting the underlying WordPress software. You can change your theme at any time without changing the WordPress software or any of the features you applied through WordPress plugins.

✦ A plugin is a collection of files that creates a program or tool to extend the features and behavior of WordPress. Any plugin can be downloaded from the WordPress Plugin Directory to provide some new feature for the administrator or users of your WordPress site. Changing a theme should not affect features of applied plugins and, similarly, changing a plugin should not affect the look and feel of your site applied by your chosen theme.

Here are some good things to remember when using plugins or themes:

✦ You may want to change your blog's theme but keep its functionality as is. If you added all your blog's features by using plugins, no problem. If you tweaked a theme to achieve some of the features (say, the tracking of statistics on visitors to your blog), those features will disappear when you change the theme.

✦ If you want to use themes to provide features for your blog, then you can only choose themes that do what you have in mind. If you use plugins to take care of the blog's chores, you can select any theme you want. The look and feel you're trying to achieve becomes a separate issue.

When themes get fancier to deliver knockout visual features, they stray into the range of tasks that plugins do best. Stick with themes for the visual appeal and plugins for the working features.

Finding free plugins to use on your site

Okay (you may be asking), where do I find all these mind-bogglingly useful plugins? Good news: The geniuses at WordPress have made plugins *really* easy to find by putting them all in one place. Every plugin that is approved for use with WordPress is located in one central directory. You can access the plugins two ways:

✦ **Online:** The WordPress Plugin Directory is located at `http://word press.org/extend/plugins`. To install a free plugin, follow these steps:

1. *Navigate to* `http://wordpress.org/extend/plugins` *in your browser.*

    You see the searchable Plugin Directory, as shown in Figure 1-2.

2. *Enter the name of the plugin (or a search term relevant to the plugin or a feature you're looking for) in the search box and then click the Search Plugins button.*

    The directory lists all plugins that match your query. You can also sort your search query by selecting one of the radio buttons underneath the search box: Relevance (default), Newest, Recently Updated, Most Popular or Highest Rated. Additionally, WordPress. Org lists plugins on the right side of the page by: Most Popular, Newest Plugins and Recently Updated to help you find plugins that may interest you.

Book VII Chapter 1

Introducing WordPress Plugins

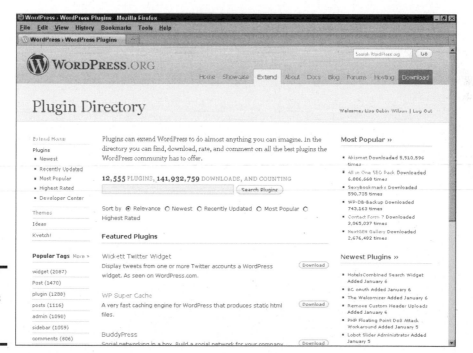

Figure 1-2:
WordPress Plugin Directory.

The Most Popular plugins have the greatest number of users and have been downloaded most often by users. In the Plugin Directory, they're grouped because the majority of WordPress users want to find them easily.

All plugins are tagged with keywords; the most popular tags are listed along the left side, as shown in Figure 1-3.

Popular Tags More >

widget (2087)

Post (1470)

plugin (1288)

posts (1116)

admin (1090)

sidebar (1059)

comments (806)

images (723)

twitter (660)

page (645)

google (636)

links (613)

image (568)

Figure 1-3: Plugin Directory showing popular tags.

✦ **Finding Plugins within the WordPress Dashboard:** To do this, follow these steps:

1. *Click the Add New link under the Plugins menu in your Dashboard.*

   This loads the Install Plugins page where you can search for plugins, as shown in Figure 1-4.

   When searching for, and finding, plugins in the Dashboard, you use the same method you used at the WordPress web site in their Plugin Directory. Ever since WordPress provided the plugin search in the Dashboard, most users don't use the WordPress Web site anymore. We provide it here as a method you can use, however, in case you find yourself in a situation where you cannot access your WordPress Dashboard (if your Web site is down, for example).

2. *On the Install Plugins page, click the Upload link at the top.*

   The Install Plugins page reloads with a form that allows you to browse your computer for a plugin .zip file that you previously downloaded from the WordPress Plugin Directory; upload it and WordPress installs it for you, automatically.

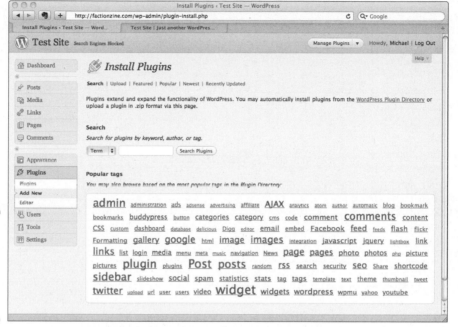

Figure 1-4:
Installing plugins within the WordPress Dashboard.

3. *Choose Plugins⇨Add New to access the WordPress.org Plugin Directory from the Install Plugins page.*

   Every plugin on the WordPress site is searchable from the Install Plugins page. Plugins are also listed by Featured, Popular, Newest, and Recently Updated categories. Popular Tags gives you shortcuts to the most-used tags for particular plugins with just a click of the links that are displayed at the top of the page.

4. *When you find a plugin you're looking for, click its link to view its details.*

   A description of the plugin appears in a pop-up window with a number of tabs at the top. These tabs can vary with each plugin and could include Installation, FAQ (Frequently Asked Questions), Screenshots, Stats, and Notes. Each tab provides important information about the plugin, as shown in Figure 1-5.

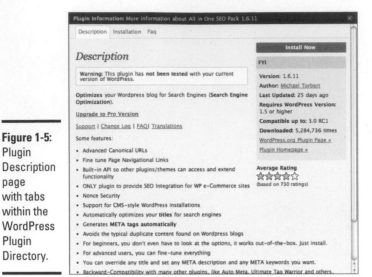

Figure 1-5:
Plugin
Description
page
with tabs
within the
WordPress
Plugin
Directory.

The FYI box on the right provides useful information, such as the version of the plugin, when the plugin was updated, what versions of WordPress are compatible with the plugin, and links to the author's Web site, as shown in Figure 1-6.

Figure 1-6:
FYI box
on the
plugin page
within the
WordPress
Plugin
Directory.

The rating section below the FYI box displays the average rating the plugin has received from its users, as shown in Figure 1-7. (For more on finding plugins via the WordPress Dashboard, see Chapter 2 of this minibook.)

If you don't have a WordPress.org account, we highly recommend that you get one. It's free, very useful, and gives you access to the WordPress.org support forums (where you can post support questions) and other resources (some of which we introduce in the next section). Sign up at `http://word press.org/support/register.php`.

Figure 1-7:
Rating
section
on the
plugin page
within the
WordPress
Plugin
Directory.

Average Rating
☆☆☆☆☆
(based on 730 ratings)

Comparing free and premium plugins

Everybody loves free stuff. Users love WordPress not only because it's a great program for Web publishing, but also because it's free and support is free. If everyone loves free plugins that enhance WordPress blogs and Web sites, why offer premium plugins? Why aren't all plugins free? The answer is complicated and undoubtedly contentious.

WordPress developers like to contribute code and plugins that help the WordPress community and contribute new capabilities to a great project. However, WordPress developers have to make a living and pay their bills. Professional developers contribute a lot to WordPress and make a living from WordPress by creating many of the best themes and plugins. As a WordPress user, you want the best. Why not pay a few bucks for something that is really good and (often) includes updates and support?

Plugins are available two ways:

✦ **Free plugin/premium plugin:** You get a certain set of features free and additional features for a price. Many of the best-known software companies follow this model.

✦ **Premium support:** Open source software companies realize that an issue with WordPress and similar software is access to good support and, therefore, develop premium support programs to offer access to good technical support for a price. Many plugin and theme developers use this model to benefit the community. With this model, many developers provide a membership program where the user pays a set fee upfront for support for a specified time frame (for example, $50 for one year of support, requiring you to renew your membership to continue obtaining support for another year, and so on).

Open source software can be copied, modified, and redistributed by anyone without having to pay to do so. Think of it as being similar to buying a CD, copying the disc, making changes to the music, and then reselling the music to your friends without having to pay any fees to the original artist. Check out Book I, Chapter 2 for a rundown about open source software, along with the GPL licensing of WordPress and how it applies to the work that plugin and theme developers do.

The great news is that you can choose between free plugins and premium plugins that don't cost much, and the choices will only grow as the community grows. Consider premium plugins when you need extra support or additional features, and reward your plugin developers for the job they do and their contribution to the WordPress community.

Evaluating plugins on the fly

How do you know that a plugin does what it's supposed to do? You can evaluate a plugin several ways but, unfortunately, none is foolproof. The most reliable way to tell whether a plugin is good is to examine the source code, but not everyone has that kind of programming knowledge. If you're a stranger to programming and short on time, however, you can still evaluate a plugin by other means. Here are some simple methods to help you determine whether WordPress users are using a plugin successfully:

✦ **Look at the popularity of the plugin.** Every plugin in the WordPress Plugin Directory shows the plugin's number of downloads (see Figure 1-8). The number might not equate to the number of satisfied users, but it's not a bad rough measure.

If the downloads are less than a thousand, exercise caution, especially if the plugin has been in the repository a long time. However, a plugin in the repository for a year and downloaded only 30 times might not be a bad plugin; the plugin might be a niche feature that's not popular.

Figure 1-8: Downloads for a plugin within the Plugin Directory.

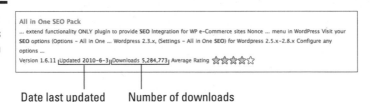

All in One SEO Pack

... extend functionality ONLY plugin to provide **SEO** Integration for WP e-Commerce sites Nonce ... menu in WordPress Visit your **SEO** options (Options – All in One ... Wordpress 2.3.x, (Settings – All in One **SEO**) for Wordpress 2.5.x–2.8.x Configure any options ...

Version 1.6.11 | Updated 2010–6–3 | Downloads 5,284,773 | Average Rating ★★★★☆

Date last updated   Number of downloads

✦ **Look at when the plugin was updated.** This number shows in the plugin directory, too (refer to Figure 1-8). If the plugin hasn't been updated in several years, it might no longer be maintained, or the developer stopped supporting it. Good plugin developers should release regular updates to their plugins because WordPress isn't a static application; it's ever changing. Plugin developers should update their plugins when major changes to WordPress occur.

✦ **Look at the plugin version.** If it shows *Alpha* or *Beta* in the version, the plugin is being tested and may have bugs that could affect your site; you may want to wait until the plugin has been thoroughly tested and released as a full version.

The WordPress community has no standard for numbering plugin versions but, generally, the higher the version number, the more *mature* (that is, tested and stable) the plugin is. Figure 1-9 shows a plugin within the repository with *Beta* in the version.

Figure 1-9:
Version number for a plugin within the Plugin Directory.

Edit Comments

This release: August 30, 2005 Version: 0.3 **Beta** Edit Comments is a simple WordPress plugin that allows commenters to edit their own comments. To edit a comment, a user must have the same IP address as the user that made the comment and they must also ...

Version 0.3 beta Updated 2005–9–1 Downloads 5,283 Average Rating ☆☆☆☆☆

✦ **Look at the number of downloads per day.** Shown on the Stats tab of the plugin's page (see Figure 1-10). Again, this is not a foolproof method, but the Downloads Per Day graph may indicate that people are using the plugin with some success.

Figure 1-10:
Download history for a plugin within the Plugin Directory.

All in One SEO Pack

Description Installation Faq Stats

Download

Downloads Per Day

30,000

50,000

40,000

20,000

0

2008-07-28 2008-09-13 2008-10-30 2008-12-16 2009-02-01 2009-03-20 2009-05-06 2009-06-22 2009-08-08 2009-09-24 2009-11-10 2009-12-27 2010-02-12 2010-03-31 2010-05-17

FYI

Version: 1.6.11
Other Versions »
Last Updated: 2010–6–3
Requires WordPress Version: 1.5 or higher
Compatible up to: 3.0 RC1
Author Homepage »
Plugin Homepage »
Donate to this plugin »

Forums Posts 🔊
Development Log 🔊

Compatibility

WordPress 3.0

+ Plugin 1.6.11

= **Works!**

32 people say it works.
11 people say it's broken.

Log in to vote

History

Today	3,643
Yesterday	5,030
Last Week	53,187
All Time	5,284,798

✦ **Use the ratings on the plugin's page.** Can be used as a (partial) guide to what people think of the plugin. If the plugin's average is five stars but is rated by only two people, this approach may not help. However, if 200 people give the plugin five stars, you have a better indication that users like the plugin.

If you have a free WordPress.org account, you can log in and rate the plugin. Although subjective, if used correctly, the ratings are a great guide for whether the plugin is good.

✦ **Use the "See what others are saying" section.** Posts from a plugin's Forums page appear on the right side of the plugin's page, as shown in Figure 1-11. Both good and bad (but hopefully not ugly) comments appear. This is probably the best feedback you're going to find on whether the plugin does its job well.

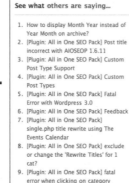

Average Rating

★★★★☆
(730 ratings)

See what others are saying...

1. How to display Month Year instead of Year Month on archive?
2. [Plugin: All in One SEO Pack] Post title incorrect with AIOSEOP 1.6.11
3. [Plugin: All in One SEO Pack] Custom Post Type Support
4. [Plugin: All in One SEO Pack] Custom Post Types
5. [Plugin: All in One SEO Pack] Fatal Error with Wordpress 3.0
6. [Plugin: All in One SEO Pack] Feedback
7. [Plugin: All in One SEO Pack] single.php title rewrite using The Events Calendar
8. [Plugin: All in One SEO Pack] exclude or change the 'Rewrite Titles' for 1 cat?
9. [Plugin: All in One SEO Pack] fatal error when clicking on category
10. [Plugin: All in One SEO Pack] preg_replace issue

Figure 1-11: Comments section for a plugin within the Plugin Directory.

Combining the methods is a good way to determine whether the plugin works as advertised.

The methods described here for evaluating plugins are no substitute for thoroughly testing a plugin. (Remember to test plugins on a development copy, not the online version of your blog or Web site.) Additionally, testing the plugin is good practice, unless you're familiar enough with the code and the developers that bugs or security issues seem unlikely.

Getting Started with Popular Free Plugins

Okay, here's a no-cost way to jump into the world of plugins: a list of five popular free plugins in the WordPress Plugin Directory.

✦ **Google XML Sitemaps:** Everyone who wants a blog or Web site indexed correctly by major search engines should use this plugin. A sitemap makes it easier for the search engines to see the structure of your Web site and know where to look for your content. The Google XML Sitemaps plugin is one we cover in Book V, Chapter 5 — read up on the features and benefits this plugin has to offer.

✦ **All in One SEO Pack:** This plugin *optimizes* your WordPress blog or Web site for search engines. In other words, it makes it as easy as possible for search engines to find and use your site. It has a multitude of features you can use to help make your blog or Web site more search-engine –friendly.

✦ **Contact Form 7:** If you want to create simple-but-flexible forms to put on your Web site, this great plugin offers many features, including Captcha, spam filtering, and file uploading.

✦ **WordPress.com Stats:** This plugin from the creators of WordPress shows you simple statistics on your page views, popular posts, and incoming traffic. This plugin requires an API key, which you can get by signing up for a free WordPress.com account at `http:// en.wordpress.com/signup`.

✦ **NextGEN Gallery:** This plugin has many handy features for managing your photos and images, such as a Flash slide show, sortable albums, image tags, and customizable templates. Even though WordPress includes a media library and gallery, this is a very valuable and popular plugin.

Try 'em, kid, the first ones are free (in fact, all of these are). These free plugins are among the 9,000-plus examples of the species in the WordPress Plugin Directory. Happy hunting!

Try each of these plugins out on a development copy of your WordPress blog or Web site and explore the features that they offer. Then visit the WordPress Plugin Directory at `http://wordpress.org/extend/ plugins` and click the Most Popular link to try more popular plugins.

All in One SEO Pack

The All in One SEO Pack plugin is one of the most popular plugins in the WordPress Plugin Directory (based on downloads). This plugin installs a complex set of features that help any WordPress blog or Web site administrator get better results from search engines, such as Bing, Google, and

Yahoo!. Many of the features are for experienced users, but the plugin still offers much that a beginner can do to optimize a blog or Web site for searches.

Because of the size and growth of the World Wide Web, most blogs and Web sites rely on their search engine listing to be found. Many of the visitors to your blog or Web site probably arrived via a Google search. Optimizing your WordPress site to make it easier for search engines to find you can increase your visitors and make your blog or Web site more successful in reaching an audience.

Many of the features provided in the All in One SEO Pack plugin are covered in Book V, Chapter 5. Be sure to head there to find out about the features of this plugin. Figure 1-12 shows the All in One SEO Pack Plugin Options page in the WordPress Dashboard.

The All in One SEO Pack plugin for WordPress is available as a free plugin at the WordPress Plugin Directory. You can install it either by downloading the file from the WordPress Directory or by clicking the Install Now link under Add New Plugins in the WordPress Dashboard.

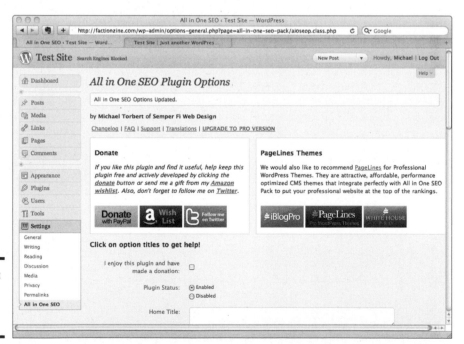

Figure 1-12: All in One SEO Pack options.

Subscribe to Comments

The Subscribe to Comments plugin is a popular free plugin that allows anyone commenting on a WordPress blog to sign up for an e-mail notification of subsequent comments or entries. This feature allows visitors to your site to follow the thread of comments on a blog post. For many blogs, this helps visitors see when someone responds to their comment or posts something new that they may want to comment on.

This plugin includes a full-featured subscription manager that commentators can use to unsubscribe to certain posts, block all notifications, or even change their notification e-mail address.

After the plugin is installed and activated, users see the Notify Me of Followup Comments via E-mail check box below the Leave a Reply section of a blog post, as shown in Figure 1-13. Users can leave a comment and check this box to receive e-mail notifications of later comments.

AJAX Edit Comments

The AJAX Edit Comments plugin is a very powerful plugin that lets administrators manage which visitors can edit their comments and what sorts of edits they can make. Additionally, it provides administrators with a comprehensive toolkit for managing comments.

Figure 1-13: Subscribing to comments regarding a WordPress blog post.

This premium plugin can't be found in the WordPress Plugin Directory. It's only available for purchase at www.ajaxeditcomments.com. For a low price, this plugin provides good support and a money-back guarantee.

The AJAX Edit Comments plugin allows visitors to your WordPress blog or Web site to edit their comments, saves you time from editing bad comments, and resolves the issue of being unable to correct a typo in a comment. Originally, this feature was part of WordPress until it was removed some time ago. However, it was quickly replaced by this full-featured plugin, which makes the tasks much easier to manage. The AJAX Edit Comments plugin has evolved into a very powerful and easy-to-use comment manager. Some features found in this premium plugin include

✦ Controlling which users, including anonymous users, can edit their comments.

✦ Editing comments after additional comments are posted.

✦ Editing the name, e-mail address, and any URLs that appear with the comments.

✦ Allowing users to request that comments be deleted.

✦ Allowing administrators to moderate comments from within the blog or Web site.

✦ Allowing administrators to move comments made to the wrong post.

✦ Blacklisting comments and removing spam links within comments.

✦ Providing a few nice sets of graphic icons that display on your site; the plugin gives you several icon sets to choose from.

Figure 1-14 shows the AJAX Edit Comments plugin.

Twitter Tools

Twitter Tools is a free plugin that integrates your WordPress blog or Web site and your Twitter account so that your tweets are pulled into your WordPress site as blog posts and your blog posts appear as tweets on Twitter. Figure 1-15 shows the interface for creating a tweet within the WordPress Dashboard.

The lines between blogs and Web sites and social-media sites are blurring. People are using social-media sites to 'microblog'— or hold conversations with their followers in readers in short bursts of conversation (usually in 140 characters, or less, such as with Twitter), whereas blogs are usually reserved for more-lengthy discussion of topics in the form of articles published to their Web site. Integration between WordPress and social media is a good thing for many WordPress users, and plugins social-media integration features are showing up in the WordPress Plugin Directory. This trend will undoubtedly continue.

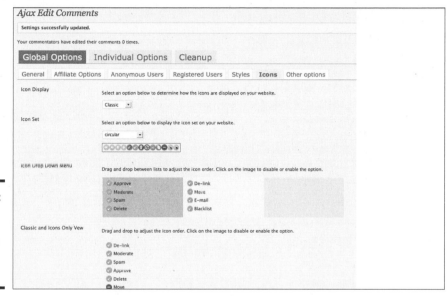

Figure 1-14: AJAX Edit Comments plugin main options screen.

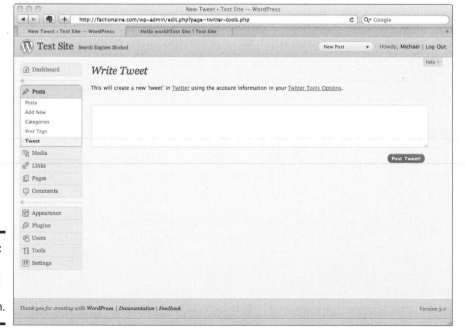

Figure 1-15: Creating a tweet using the Twitter Tools plugin.

The Twitter Tools plugin is a full-featured integration option that's easy to use, supports shortcode within sidebar widgets, and employs template tags if you aren't using widgets. There's even a method to allow developers to extend the plugin's features.

Many WordPress users install this essential plugin on every site.

Contact Form 7

The Contact Form 7 plugin is great for creating and managing simple forms within WordPress. Forms can include contact pages where a visitor can enter his name and contact details and write a comment or question, or they can be questionnaires that ask for feedback on something you published on your blog or Web site. We love forms as a method to gather standard information and Contact Form 7 provides this in an easy-to-use WordPress plugin. You can install this plugin from your WordPress Dashboard by searching for *Contact Form 7* on the Install plugins page, or you can download it from the WordPress Plugins Directory here: `http://wordpress. org/extend/plugins/contact-form-7`.

Creating a form in Contact Form 7 is easy. You can include a number of field types on your form, such as the following:

✦ Text line

✦ Paragraph box

✦ Drop-down choices

✦ Check boxes

✦ Radio buttons

✦ E-mail address field

✦ Question and answer field

✦ File upload field

Contact Form 7 also supports Captcha, the method for preventing automated spamming by requesting that anyone submitting a form enter a series of characters displayed in an image.

Comprehensive documentation and user guides for the plugin and good support forums appear on the plugin Web site.

Chapter 2: Installing and Activating Plugins

In This Chapter

- ✔ Installing WordPress plugins via the Dashboard
- ✔ Manually installing WordPress plugins
- ✔ Upgrading plugins
- ✔ Activating and deactivating plugins
- ✔ Uninstalling plugins

*W*ordPress is an extremely versatile Web publishing solution. However, plugins can extend the WordPress features to do almost anything you want, except perhaps write your Web content. But how can you make use of the nearly 10,000 plugins found in the WordPress Plugin Directory? How do you remove plugins you no longer find useful? Fortunately, WordPress makes these tasks easy. In this chapter, we explore how to install, activate, deactivate, and uninstall plugins.

Installing WordPress Plugins via the Dashboard

The administrative interface for WordPress is Dashboard, which is easy to reach and intuitive to use. Simply pull up your favorite Web browser and enter the URL for your WordPress Web site or blog followed by /wp login.php. For example, if your WordPress blog uses the URL http://www.mywordpressblog.com, you type **http://www.mywordpressblog.com/wp-login.php**.

On your WordPress installation's login page, enter your administrator username and password.

Always make sure that you change the default administrator account username from Admin to something unique you can remember to ensure greater security of your WordPress installation.

To find plugins in the WordPress Dashboard:

1. **Log in to your WordPress Dashboard.**

The Dashboard page appears, as shown in Figure 2-1.

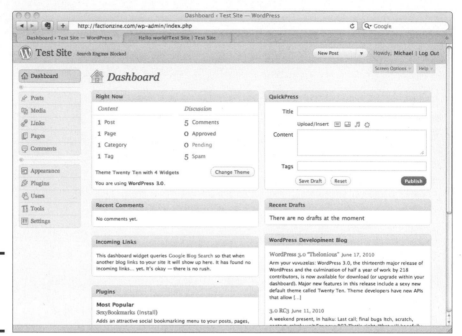

2. **Choose Plugins⇨Add New.**

The Install Plugins page appears, as shown in Figure 2-2. On this page are a number of selections, including a search box. Typing a term in this box and clicking the Search Plugins button searches the WordPress Plugins Directory for plugins that match the term.

At the top of the Install Plugins page, you find links for the following options:

- *Search:* The page where you can search for plugins within the directory.

- *Upload:* This page provides you with a means to upload a plugin directly into WordPress. We discuss this page in more detail later in this chapter.

- *Featured:* This page displays a selection of plugins featured by WordPress as great plugins you may want to try out.

- *Popular:* This page shows the most popular plugins based on criteria selected by WordPress.

Figure 2-2:
The Install Plugins page.

- *Newest:* This page shows the most recently added plugins within the repository.

- *Recently Updated:* This page shows the plugins most recently updated by their developer.

Each of these pages provides you with easy access to plugins that you may want to try without you having to search for them. Explore each of these pages at your leisure; you may find some great plugins this way.

At the bottom of the Install Plugins page is a selection of keywords, as shown in Figure 2-3. When you click a keyword, WordPress displays all the plugins tagged with the keyword. For example, clicking *gallery* shows all plugins tagged with that keyword, such as NextGen Gallery, a very popular plugin.

Figure 2-3:
Keywords at the bottom of the Install Plugins screen.

Use keywords to find popular plugins among WordPress users without having to search by term or plugin name.

After you find a plugin you like, you can easily find great plugins to install. Within the Dashboard, this is a very simple process:

1. **Click the Details link underneath the title of the plugin you want to install, as shown in Figure 2-4.**

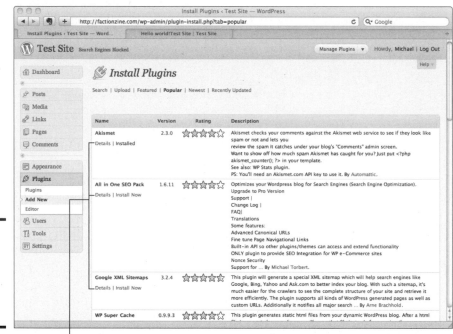

Figure 2-4: Plugins listed on the Install Plugins page.

Details link

The Plugin Information window, which provides a description of the plugin, appears with a number of tabs at the top, as shown in Figure 2-5.

2. **Click the Installation tab to view the installation instructions.**

Read the installation instructions before you proceed. Each plugin's installation and activation differs.

3. **Return to the Description tab and then click the Install Now button to install your plugin.**

The Installing Plugin page appears, with a message stating whether your plugin installed successfully, as shown in Figure 2-6.

Figure 2-5:
The Plugin Information window.

Book VII Chapter 2

Installing and Activating Plugins

If you see anything other than a successful message, you need to follow the support instructions on the Plugin Information window. This may include an FAQ tab or a Support link. Always make note of any error messages you see.

Figure 2-6:
The Installing Plugin page.

4. **Choose Plugins⇨Plugins to verify that your plugin installed successfully.**

   Your plugin should appear on the Plugins page's All list, as shown in Figure 2-7.

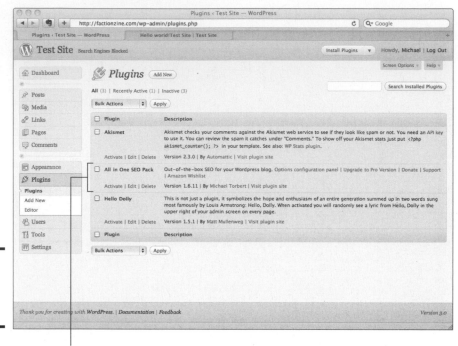

Figure 2-7:
List of
installed
plugins.

New plugin appears

Manually Installing Plugins

It is not often that you find that you need to install a WordPress plugin because WordPress makes it so easy to install plugins through the Dashboard — however, we cover this method of installing plugins for you in this chapter so that you're familiar with the mechanics of downloading, unpacking, uploading, activating, and using a plugin in WordPress just in case you ever need do it manually. This method isn't as easy as installing a plugin through the Dashboard, but the instructions below provide you an alternative installation method when you need it.

The first thing you need to know when manually installing a plugin is how to connect to the server where your WordPress installation is located via an FTP application. If you don't know how to do so, talk to your hosting provider. We also cover FTP extensively in Book II, Chapter 2 if you need a refresher.If you know how to connect to your server via FTP, the instructions below shouldn't be difficult:

1. **Download your plugin from the WordPress Plugin Directory at www. wordpress.org/extend/plugins.**

   If the plugin doesn't appear in the directory, use a search engine to find the Web site where you can download the plugin. Many WordPress developers have a Web site where you can download their plugin.

2. **After you download the plugin, check to see whether it's in a compressed format (often a Zip file). If so, "unzip" the file to access the uncompressed files.**

   Sometimes the plugin comes in Zip format; if it does, then you can use a free Web application to unzip your plugin.

3. **With the plugin saved to your local computer, connect to your server using your preferred FTP application.**

4. **Navigate to the wp-content folder within the WordPress installation for your Web site or blog.**

   The location of your WordPress installation can differ with every hosting provider. Make sure that you know the location before you proceed. Check out Book II, Chapters 2 and 4 for information on where the WordPress installation is located on your Web server.

5. **In the wp-content directory, find the plugins directory. Add your plugin to this location using your preferred FTP application (see Book II, Chapter 2).**

   Congratulations! Your plugin is installed and it can now be activated through the WordPress Dashboard by clicking the Plugins menu item and then clicking the Activate link that appears underneath the title of the plugin you just installed.

Upgrading Plugins

From time to time, WordPress plugin developers release new versions of their plugins. These new versions may be released to fix problems with the plugin, add new functionality, or make use of new features in the latest version of WordPress. Whatever the reason, you can expect to upgrade at least a couple of your plugins over the course of using WordPress.

You can upgrade plugins two easy ways: automatically and manually. Additionally, WordPress tells you which plugins need upgrading, as shown in Figure 2-8.

Book VII Chapter 2

Installing and Activating Plugins

Figure 2-8:
List of installed plugins you can upgrade.

Upgrading automatically

In the latest version of WordPress, upgrading plugins is easier than ever before. On the Dashboard, a new WordPress Updates page (Dashboard➪Updates) shows all available updates and includes an Update Plugins button for upgrading plugins with one click, as shown in Figure 2-9.

Figure 2-9:
The WordPress Updates page.

Update Plugins buttons

Here's how to upgrade your plugins automatically:

1. **Log in to the WordPress Dashboard and click Plugins on the Dashboard menu.**

If plugin upgrades are available, a number in a dark circle appears on the Plugins menu, as shown in Figure 2-10.

Figure 2-10:
Plugins menu showing that upgrades are available.

2. **On the Plugins page, scroll to a plugin that displays "There is a new version of *plugin* available," as shown in Figure 2-11.**

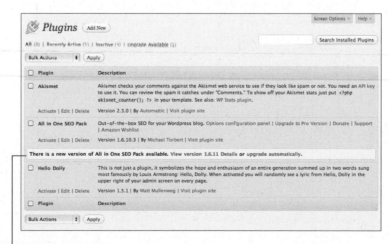

Figure 2-11:
List of installed plugins showing that a plugin upgrade is available.

New version message

3. **Click the Upgrade Automatically link.**

   After the upgrade, the "Plugin Reactivated Successfully" message displays.

   If you see anything other than a successful message, you need to follow the support instructions on the Plugin page found in the WordPress Plugin Directory (on the Plugins page, find the plugin you need support for and then click the Visit plugin site link — that will take you directly to the plugin page in the WordPress Plugins Directory). This may include a FAQ tab or a Support link. Always make note of any error messages you see.

Upgrading manually

The steps to upgrade a plugin manually are similar to upgrading a plugin automatically, requiring FTP access to the server where your WordPress installation is hosted.

1. **Download the latest version of the plugin from the WordPress Plugin Directory or the plugin developers Web site.**

2. **Connect to your server via an FTP application and go to the `plugins` directory in the `wp-content` directory.**

   You should see a folder with the same name as the plugin you want to upgrade.

3. **Rename this folder so that you have a backup if you need it.**

   Any memorable name, such as *plugin-old* should suffice.

4. **Upload the new version of your plugin via FTP to your server so that it's in the `wp-content/plugins` folder.**

5. **Log in to the WordPress Dashboard and activate your upgraded plugin.**

If you made any changes to the configuration files of your plugin before your upgrade, you need to make those changes again after the upgrade. If you need to back out of the upgrade, you can just delete the new plugin directory and rename the folder from *plugin-old* to *plugin*.

Activating and Deactivating Plugins

When you install a plugin within WordPress, the plugin must be activated, or switched on before it can be used. This simple one-click process can be done within the WordPress Dashboard.

1. **Log in to the WordPress Dashboard and choose Plugins.**

   Make sure that you see all the plugins; if not, click the All link under the Plugins page title.

2. Scroll to the plugin you want to activate.

The Activate link appears beneath the name of your plugin, as shown in Figure 2-12.

Figure 2-12:
List of installed plugins showing plugins that need activating.

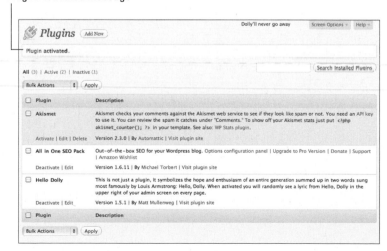

Activate links

3. Click the Activate link.

The Plugins page appears with a message confirming that the plugin was activated, as shown in Figure 2-13.

Plugin Activated message

Figure 2-13:
The Plugins page showing the Plugin Activated message.

To deactivate a plugin, follow the same steps, but instead of clicking the Activate link, click the Deactivate link, as shown in Figure 2-14.

Deactivate link

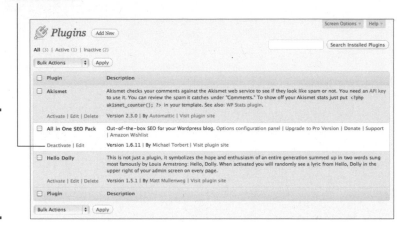

Figure 2-14:
The
Deactivate
link on the
Plugins
page.

The process of activating and deactivating plugins is very simple and easy to do within the WordPress Dashboard. Remember to watch for error messages and follow the plugin developer's support instructions when you need help.

Uninstalling Plugins

You may find that you no longer have need for a plugin or that you have to remove some plugins from your WordPress installation. Too many plugins can drain system resources and make WordPress very slow. The number of plugins you can install and activate before you see performance problems depends on the server you are using or your hosting provider.

When you need to uninstall a plugin, the process is just as painless as installing a plugin. Like installing a plugin, you can uninstall a plugin automatically via the Dashboard or manually.

Uninstalling automatically

To uninstall a plugin using the WordPress Dashboard, follow these steps:

1. **Log in to the Dashboard and click Plugins in the menu.**

2. **On the Plugins page, locate the plugin you want to uninstall.**

TIP

Make sure that you have deactivated the plugin before proceeding.

The Delete link appears beneath the name of your plugin, as shown in Figure 2-15.

Delete links

Figure 2-15:
The Delete
links on
the Plugins
page.

3. **Click Delete.**

The Delete Plugin page appears, asking you to confirm whether you want to delete the plugin, as shown in Figure 2-16.

Figure 2-16:
Deleting
plugin
files on
the Delete
Plugin page.

Delete Plugin

You are about to remove the following plugin:

• **All in One SEO Pack** by *Michael Torbert*

Are you sure you wish to delete these files?

(Yes, Delete these files) (No, Return me to the plugin list)

Click to view entire list of files which will be deleted

**Book VII
Chapter 2**

Installing and
Activating Plugins

4. **Click the Yes, Delete These Files button if you want to proceed. Otherwise, click the No, Return Me to the Plugin List button.**

The Plugins page appears with a message confirming that the plugin was deleted successfully, as shown in Figure 2-17.

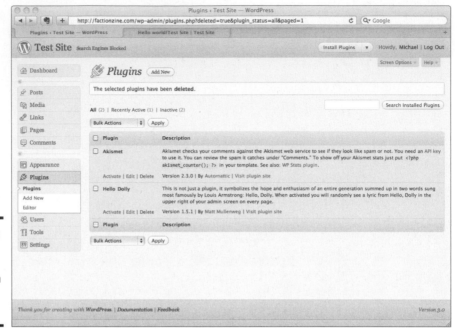

Figure 2-17:
The plugin-deleted message on the Plugins page.

If you see anything other than a successful message, you need to follow the support instructions in the Plugin Information window. This may include an FAQ tab or a Support link. Always make note of any error messages you see.

Uninstalling plugins manually

If you can't access the WordPress Dashboard or successfully uninstall the plugin from within the Dashboard, you can use a manual method. To uninstall a plugin manually, you need FTP access to your server. To uninstall a plugin from WordPress manually:

1. **Connect to your server via an FTP application and open the `plugins` folder in the `wp-content` directory.**

2. **Locate the folder for the plugin you want to uninstall and simply delete the folder.**

3. **If prompted to confirm that you want to delete the folder, click Yes.**

Always make backups of your `wp-content` folder before changing or deleting anything. After you delete a plugin with this method, there's no way to recover it unless you have a backup. For help with backups, consult your hosting provider.

Chapter 3: Exploring Plugin Options and Settings

In This Chapter

✓ Discovering plugin options management

✓ Exploring widgets

✓ Determining what to do when something goes wrong

✓ Finding technical support

*M*anaging plugins can easily be the most enjoyable or the least enjoyable part of your WordPress experience. In this regard, there are essentially two types of plugins: *plug and play* and *plug and configure*. The first allows you to "set it and forget it," or simply activate the plugin and immediately see it work. The latter requires configuration, which could involve modifying the settings, or in some cases, inserting code into your WordPress configuration files. Fortunately, in most instances, this isn't nearly as complicated as it sounds.

Almost every WordPress plugin has options pages. In this chapter we outline two examples: the WP Super Cache and WordPress.com Stats plugin. Not every plugin is going to work and do what you want it to do upon activation, so you need to be sure to look to see if there is an options setting page for the plugins you install, and then go through those options to be sure that you configured the plugin to work the way you want it to on your site. In this chapter, we walk you through some of the most common methods for setting plugin options and explore how WordPress plugin developers make their plugins work for you.

Discovering Global and Page/Post Specific Settings

By now, you've discovered that plugins can vary widely in scope, location, and configuration. Some plugins have settings that affect your entire WordPress site; others have settings that apply only to individual blog posts or Web pages.

Here is an example of the steps you would take to modify the settings or configurations using a plugin called Maintenance Mode (`http://word press.org/extend/plugins/maintenance-mode`). This plugin gives you the ability to display an "Under Construction" message on your WordPress site, and is a perfect example of using global settings.

Refer to Chapter 2 in this minibook for instructions on how to install a plugin on your WordPress Web site; using those instructions, install and activate the Maintenance Mode plugin. When installed, a Maintenance Mode link appears in the Settings menu on the Dashboard; click that link to load the plugin settings page for the Maintenance Mode plugin, as shown in Figure 3-1. On the Maintenance Mode settings page, you can alter the title and message that displays on your site within the Title and Message text fields.

Figure 3-1: The Maintenance Mode plugin settings page.

When visitors view your WordPress site, they see a customized message letting them know that your site is under construction, an example of plugin settings that apply globally, or to the entire site (rather than just one post or page, in particular).

Only visitors to your WordPress site who are not logged in see the message. An administrator logged into WordPress will continue to see your site as normal.

Advanced Plugin Configuration

In this section, we explore two plugins that require slightly more advanced configuration: WP Super Cache and WordPress.com Stats. Both of these plugins have advanced configurations — that is, they aren't a "set it and forget it" type of plugin, as users do need to perform additional configuration in order for the plugin to work on their site.

WP Super Cache

We recommend this plugin for every WordPress site because it helps shorten the time it takes for your site visitors to pull up the site in their browsers by serving static HTML files rather than dynamically generating the WordPress pages they see each time.

For the best performance results with this plugin, make sure that PHP Safe mode is disabled on your web server, and that the Apache modules `mod_mime` and `mod_rewrite` are installed. If you are unsure whether Safe mode is disabled, or if your server already has these Apache modules, check with your Web hosting provider. Additionally, you can ask your hosting provider to tweak the server configurations for these as well — unless you own the server or have a dedicated server configuration, it's likely that you do not have the necessary system administrator access to the Web server to make these configurations yourself.

After installing and activating WP Super Cache (check Chapter 2 of this mini-book for a refresher on installing and activating plugins), the plugin needs to be configured in order to enable caching on your site; Figure 3-2 shows the disabled status of WP Super Cache just below the Plugins title. Click the plugin admin page link to visit the WP Super Cache plugin settings page in your Dashboard.

Now comes the tricky part. After you click the Plugin Admin Page link to access the plugin settings page, WP Super Cache attempts to make certain changes to files on your web server. Depending on your server settings and file permissions, it may or may not be able to make these changes automatically. Some of these changes include

✦ **Creating an `advanced-cache.php` file:** If you get the message that looks like this:

```
Warning! /wp-content/advanced-cache.php does not exist or cannot be
    updated
```

the plugin tried to create a file called `advanced-cache.php` and was unable to. That's fine; you can make adjustments to the folder permissions on your web server so that the plugin can create the file:

1. Using your favorite FTP program, navigate to your blog's root directory (the directory that has `wp-admin` *and* `wp-content`*).*

2. *Make the* `wp-content` *directory writable by changing the directory permissions to 777 (see Book II, Chapter 2 for information on changing file and folder permissions via FTP).*

3. *Back in your WordPress Dashboard, refresh the WP Super Cache Settings page.*

   The warning message should no longer appear.

Make sure that you change the `/wp-content` folder permissions back to 755 so that the directory is not publically writable. You accomplish this via your FTP program, just as you did when you changed the permissions to 777 in the previous steps.

✦ **Configuring the `wp-config.php` file:** You may get the message

```
Error: WP_CACHE is not enabled in your wp-config.php file
```

To remedy this problem, use your FTP software to edit the `wp-config.php` file you used when you set up your WordPress blog. Add the following line:

```
define('WP_CACHE', true);
```

Save the file and upload it to the server, overwriting the old file. After you refresh your WP Super Cache Settings page again, you should no longer see the error message.

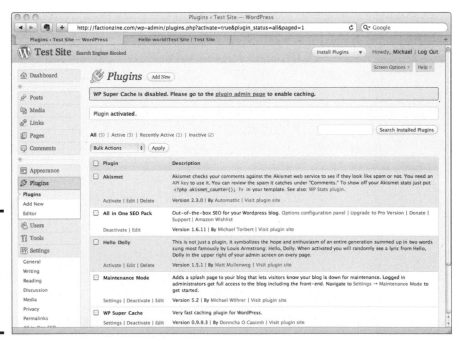

Figure 3-2:
WP Super
Cache
needs to be
configured
to enable
caching.

✦ **Enabling caching:** For basic use of WP Super Cache, select the Caching On radio button under the Caching heading on the WP Super Cache Settings page to enable caching on your site and then click the Update Status button. Caching is not enabled by default when you activate the plugin, so taking this step to enable caching is important to use this plugin.

✦ **Modifying the `.htaccess` file:** You may get a message telling you that your `.htaccess` file needs to be updated, as shown in Figure 3-3.

To resolve this issue, either modify the permissions of your `.htaccess` file to writable (777) or manually copy and paste the code given on the WP Super Cache Settings page to the top of your original `.htaccess` file. After you paste the code and resave the `.htaccess` file, refresh the WP Super Cache Settings page and click the Update Mod Rewrite Rules button. Be sure to go back to the Web server directory in your FTP program and reset the file permissions on your `.htaccess` file to its previous permissions (probably 755 or 644) to retain security on that file.

✦ **Enabling Super Cache Compression:** On the WP Super Cache Settings page, click the Advanced tab to load the advanced settings in your browser window. Click the box to the left of the Compress page so they're served more quickly to visitors to enable compression. By default, compression is disabled because some Web hosting providers have problems with compressed files — when you enable compressions, if you experience problems with the loading of your Web site, go back and disable compression and contact your Web hosting provider to find out if they can assist with the handling of compressed files on your Web server.

Figure 3-3:
Cannot
update
.htaccess.

For most blogs, configuring WP Super Cache with the basic settings is good enough. For some WordPress sites, however, other configurations are required, particularly those sites that receive a large amount of traffic and interaction from their visitors. *Cache Preload* is an option that you find under the Preload tab on the WP Super Cache Settings page — you can set WP Super Cache to preload mode, which creates a static file for every published post and page on your site to non-logged-in, or unknown, users. Cache Preload is an option that high-traffic sites should enable to increase the speed of the Web site.

Another advanced feature is preventing the caching of particular pages. For instance, if you have a WordPress page with dynamically served content, such as a forum, you don't want your page to be cached; otherwise, visitors would see new forum posts only when the cache refreshes. For example, say you have a forum whose pages use an address that begins with `mywebsite.com/forum/`. In the Accepted Filenames & Rejected URIs section under the Advanced tab on the WP Super Cache Settings page, enter `/forum/` in the text box and click the Save Strings button. Any time someone visits a page with the word `forum` in the URL — that is, any forum page — he or she sees the live dynamically served page rather than a cached one. This is shown in Figure 3-4.

> Add here strings (not a filename) that forces a page not to be cached. For example, if your URLs include year and you dont want to cache last year posts, it's enough to specify the year, i.e. '/2004/'. WP-Cache will search if that string is part of the URI and if so, it will not cache that page.
>
> ```
> wp-.*\.php
> index\.php
> /forum/
> ```
>
> (Save Strings »)

Figure 3-4:
Rejected
URIs.

WordPress.com Stats

This plugin provides fairly comprehensive statistics about your Web site traffic, such as the number of visits, where your visitors are coming from and what content they are viewing on your Web site, in a condensed format, which makes it easy to quickly review general visitors' data for different parts of your WordPress site.

To install and activate the plugin, follow these steps:

1. **In your WordPress Dashboard, choose Plugins⇨Add New.**

   On the Install Plugins page, use the keywords *WordPress.com Stats* to search for and find the plugin, created by Automattic.

2. **Click the Install Now link to install the WordPress.com Stats plugin.**

   A confirmation window pops up asking if you really want to install the plugin. Click OK.

3. Click the Activate Plugin link on the Installing Plugin page.

This activates the plugin on your site and takes you to the Plugins page in your Dashboard. Figure 3-5 shows the status of the WordPress.com Stats plugin activated within the list of plugins on the Plugins page in your Dashboard. Note the message at the top of the page saying that the WordPress.com Stats needs your attention.

WordPress.com stats plugin message

Figure 3-5: WordPress.com Stats needs to be configured.

4. Click the WordPress.com Stats link within the status message (refer to Figure 3-5).

This loads the WordPress.Com Stats page. (See Figure 3-6.)

5. Enter your WordPress.com API key in the API key text box.

If you don't have an API key, you need to sign up for a WordPress.com account at `http://wordpress.com`. Create your account and then click the Edit My Profile link in the menu to visit your Profile page in the WordPress.com Dashboard. On the profile page, click the API Key and Other Personal Settings link, which loads the Personal Settings page. Copy your API key from the top of that page and paste it in the API key text box in your WordPress Dashboard and be sure to click the Save button.

WordPress.com Stats

The WordPress.com Stats Plugin is not working because it needs to be linked to a WordPress.com account.

Enter your WordPress.com API key to link this blog to your WordPress.com account. Be sure to use your own API key! Using any other key will lock you out of your stats. (Get your key here.)

API Key: [   ]

(Save »)

Figure 3-6: The WordPress. com Stats plugin.

Congratulations! The WordPress.com Stats plugin is properly configured and will show you lots of great information about the visitorsto your WordPress blog or Web site.

Widget Settings

In a world of graphical user interfaces, WordPress fits right in with its system of widgets that allow users to add content and information to their Web sites without having to touch a single line of code in their WordPress templates. Book VI, Chapter 1 discusses the use of widgets, in-depth, whereas Book VI, Chapter 3 discusses how to add widget areas to your WordPress theme template files. Plugin developers can create widgets that work with their plugin so you can add the plugin information on your site anywhere you have a widget (sidebar) area.

Depending on your particular theme, adding a new widget to your WordPress site removes the default widgets your theme has set up for you.

Each plugin's widgets have greatly differing options for their display and functionality. The following list examines several WordPress plugins that create their own widgets for you to use:

✦ **WP e-Commerce (`http://wordpress.org/extend/plugins/ wp-e-commerce`):** Adds a full-featured shopping cart solution to your WordPress Web site. One feature this plugin provides is the ability to use several widgets included with this plugin, such as:

 • **Product Categories:** Displays a list of product categories on your site

 • **Product Specials:** Displays information on product specials on your site

 • **Shopping Cart:** Displays shopping cart information on your site, such as products added to the shopping cart, a running tally of product prices and quantities, and so on

- **Latest Products:** Displays a list of the latest products on your site

- **Price Range:** displays a range of prices for products on your site.

- **Product Donations:** lists products that are flagged as donated products on your site.

- **Product Tags:** Displays a tag cloud of tags assigned to products on your site

After you install (search for the WP e-Commerce plugins in Plugins⇨Add New inyour Dashboard) and activate the plugin (see Book VI, Chapter 1) on your WordPress site, click the Widgets link under the Appearance menu in your WordPress Dashboard. Figure 3-7 displays a few of the new widgets added to your WordPress Dashboard after the WP e-Commerce plugin has been installed and activated.

The information that the widgets display on your site is dependent upon the product information that you already set up within the WP e-Commerce plugin options. Because this is an e-Commerce plugin, it enables you to add products to sell on your site, so the widgets enable you to display specific information about those products. Check out more information about the WP e-Commerce plugin on their official Web site at: `http://www.instinct.co.nz/e-commerce`.

**Book VII
Chapter 3**

Exploring Plugin
Options and
Settings

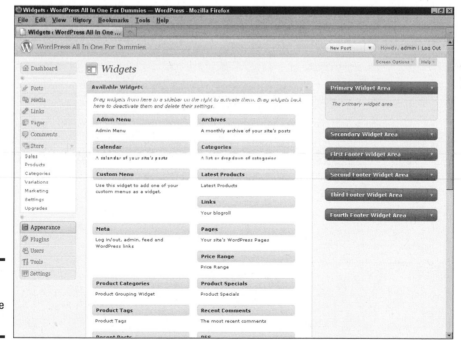

Figure 3-7:
The WP
e-Commerce
plugin.

It is possible to change the displayed title of each of the three widgets, along with various other options, through editing the widget options — see Book VI, Chapter 1 for more information about editing widget options. For instance, the Shopping Cart widget allows you to set it to appear to the user only when there are products in the cart. The Product Categories widget allows you to designate different groups to display, or to show the groups as thumbnail images.

Configure each widget to your preference, click the Save button for each widget, and then navigate to your Web site's home page. You now have a dynamically generated sidebar widget for your site's store, as shown in Figure 3-8.

✦ **SMS Text Message (`http://wordpress.org/extend/plugins/sms-text-message`):** This plugin allows your visitors to subscribe to and receive updates via text message on their phone.

To set up this plugin, follow these steps:

1. **Search for SMS Text Message in Plugins➪Add New in your Dashboard.**

   Install and activate the SMS Text Message plugin (see Book VII, Chapter 1 for information on installing and activating plugins).

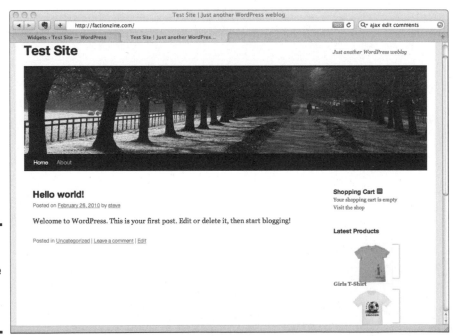

Figure 3-8:
The WP e-Commerce plugin's widget display.

2. **Visit the Widgets page by going to Appearance⊅Widgets in your Dashboard.**

3. **Drag the SMS Text Message widget to the right widget area.**

   Unlike WP e-Commerce, the SMS Text Message widget doesn't have options in Appearance⊅Widgets. Figure 3-9 shows the SMS Text Message widget placed in the Primary Widget Area on the Widgets page.

4. **Choose SMS Text Message⊅Options on the WordPress Dashboard menu on the left.**

   The SMS Text Message Options page appears, shown in Figure 3-10, with four options you can configure.

Figure 3-9:
The SMS
Text
Message
widget.

Book VII
Chapter 3

Exploring Plugin
Options and
Settings

Figure 3-10:
The SMS
Text
Message
Options
page.

5. **Set your widget header and footer. Make sure to change the From e-mail address to your Web site's address, so that replies from subscribers go directly to you.**

   Optionally, you can also modify the maximum number of characters allowed for each text message.

6. **Save your settings, navigate to your Web site's home page, and click the refresh button.**

You now have an SMS subscription widget on your blog, as shown in Figure 3-11.

✦ **Subscribe2:** Similar to SMS Text Message, the Subscribe2 plugin provides an e-mail subscription management system.

To set up this plugin, follow these steps:

1. **Search for Subscribe2 in Plugins⇨Add New in your Dashboard.**

   Install and activate the Subscribe2 plugin (see Chapter 2 of this minibook for information on installing and activating plugins).

2. **Choose Settings⇨Subscribe2 on the WordPress Dashboard menu.**

3. **Under the Appearance subheading (see Figure 3-12), select the Enable Subscribe2 Widget check box.**

4. **Click Save at the bottom of the page.**

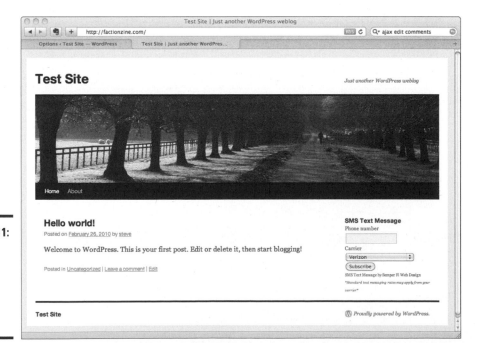

Figure 3-11: The SMS Text Message plugin's widget display.

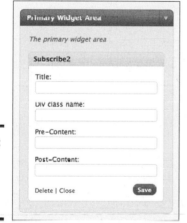

Figure 3-12: Enabling the Subscribe2 plugin's widget.

Appearance

Set default Subscribe2 page as ID: | About ⬍ |

Set the number of Subscribers displayed per page: 25 <u>Edit</u>

☐ Show a link to your subscription page in "meta"?

☑ Show the Subscribe2 button on the Write toolbar?

☐ Enable Subscribe2 Widget?

5. **Choose Appearance⇨Widgets and drag the Subscribe2 widget to the right widget area.**

   You can modify the widget title and add text before or after the content of the widget. In this options panel, you can even designate a CSS class for this widget's `div` for additional styling, as shown in Figure 3-13 in the Primary Widget Area.

Primary Widget Area ⌄

The primary widget area

Subscribe2

Title:

Div class name:

Pre-Content:

Post-Content:

Delete | Close   Save

Figure 3-13: Subscribe2 widget configuration.

6. **Configure the settings as desired and then click Save.**

   When you navigate to your home page and refresh, your subscription widget appears how you configured it.

   Site admins see something different than readers see in the widget. This smart widget shows unsubscribed users a subscription form and shows subscribed users a link to their personal subscription settings.

Setting Up a Test Site

Because WordPress changes so often, it is useful to create a test site on which we can install and run the WordPress software and plugins to test them before applying them to our regular, live Web site.

If you depend on your WordPress Web site for your income or business, having things run smoothly at all times is very important. Because installing or upgrading new plugins can sometimes have disastrous effects, you want to maintain a mirror of your WordPress installation on a test site. There are several ways to create a test environment, and everyone will have his own preferences. Here are the basics:

1. Find out whether your hosting provider gives you the ability to create subdomains.

Generally, most hosting providers give you this option. We use the cPanel hosting account manager to create this subdomain, but your hosting account might offer you a different management tool, such as NetAdmin or Plesk.

A *subdomain* is the second level of your current domain that can handle unique content separately from content in your main domain. Subdomains operate underneath your main domain, and can function as a wholly different section of your site, independent from your existing domain name.

For an example of a subdomain on Lisa's domain, `ewebscapes.com`, see Steps 3 and 4 where Lisa created the subdomain `http://testing.ewebscapes.com`. The prefix `testing` in that Web address (or URL) is a subdomain that branches off `ewebscapes.com`, which when set up, handles completely different content than content currently installed on her main domain.

2. Log in to your cPanel (or hosting account manager tool provided to you).

3. Locate and then click the Subdomains icon in the cPanel interface.

The Subdomains page within cPanel appears, as shown in Figure 3-14.

4. Type the name of your subdomain in the Subdomain text box.

For the purposes of making this straightforward and easy, type **testing** in the text box.

5. On the drop-drop menu, choose the name of the domain on which you want to add the subdomain.

In Figure 3-14, the drop-down menu shows the domain `ewebscapes.com`. Lisa created the subdomain on this domain, so her new subdomain is `http://testing.ewebscapes.com`.

A unique folder name for your new subdomain appears in the Document/Root text box. Don't alter this text because this tells your Web server where to install the necessary WordPress files.

6. **Click the Create button.**

It takes a few seconds, but the page refreshes and displays a message that the new subdomain has been created, as shown in Figure 3-15.

Now that you have a subdomain set up on your hosting account, you can install WordPress into the folder that was created when you added the subdomain. For example, if you created a subdomain called `testing`, then the folder on your Web server you'll install into will be the `/testing/` folder. For the steps to install WordPress, check out Book II, Chapter 4.

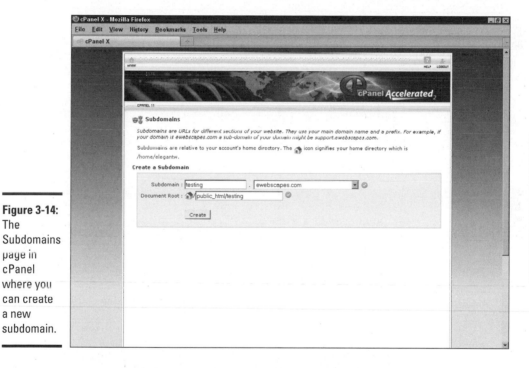

Figure 3-14: The Subdomains page in cPanel where you can create a new subdomain.

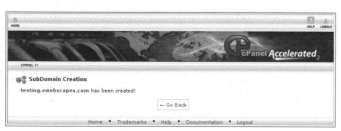

Figure 3-15: Successful subdomain creation message in cPanel.

After you have WordPress installed on your test domain, you can import the content from your live site using the WordPress import feature that we present in Book II, Chapter 7. After the content is imported, you have a carbon copy of your live site on your test domain where you can install different plugins and test different configurations first, before making those changes to your live site.

Finding Technical Support

Everyone who uses plugins has had this happen at some point: They find the perfect plugin but have no idea how to use it. What can you do when you can't figure out how to use the plugin or a plugin just doesn't seem to work for you at all?

Here are some resources to look up to resolve plugin issues.

✦ **Google.** Google is your primary resource. One trick is to do a site search on a Web site you know may have the solution to your problem. For instance, you can type this in the Google search field: *site:wordpress.org/ support/ plugin won't activate* to search the WordPress Forums page for the phrase, "plugin won't activate."

✦ **Search WordPress.org support forums.** Every day, countless WordPress enthusiasts volunteer hours of their time assisting people with general WordPress troubles and plugin-specific problems.

✦ **Contact the plugin developer.** Most, but not all, plugin developers maintain documentation about their plugins. This may be found either on the plugin's page in the Plugin Directory at `http://wordpress.org/ extend/plugins` or on the author's Web site. Many plugin authors also run a support forum for their plugins. If the provided documentation is not sufficient or nonexistent, you can reach out to the developer directly.

Before contacting a plugin developer directly, make sure that you have exhausted all other means of figuring out the problem yourself, as the developer likely receives a great deal of support requests.

✦ **Hire a WordPress consultant.** Sometimes you just want to pay an expert to solve your issues quickly. Codepoet.com has a list of verified WordPress consultants who make a living helping people with their WordPress problems.

Chapter 4: Modifying Existing Plugin Code to Your Liking

In This Chapter

✔ Troubleshooting problems with a plugin

✔ Locating plugin and theme conflicts

✔ Exploring plugin interaction with WordPress

✔ Finding functions within a plugin

✔ Identifying plugin functionality and output

Considering what WordPress plugins are — add-on programs that provide limitless possibilities to extend WordPress — and considering how many plugins there are — over 10,000 in the WordPress Plugin Directory — likely, you can find a plugin that does what you want. However, what if that plugin meets only part of your requirements? What if it's a good starting point but requires some work to get it to do what you need? Thankfully, if it's in the WordPress Plugin Directory, then it's licensed in a way that you can alter the code for your own purposes. You can even redistribute the changed plugin as long as you comply with the GPLv2 license.

So where do you start? How do you go about taking someone else's plugin and modifying it for your own purposes? In this chapter, we explore basic plugin code, describe how to tell what the code does, and explain how to find and fix problems in that code.

Troubleshooting Plugin Problems

As you can imagine, with over 10,000 plugins in the WordPress Plugin Directory, not every plugin is tested with every version of WordPress and every plugin and theme out there. There are billions of combinations of WordPress plugins; any combination might present a code conflict between two plugins or a plugin and a theme. Locating problems with a plugin takes some knowledge of PHP and basic error checking.

When attempting to troubleshoot a problem, having a methodical approach with a set of defined steps to follow is best. Start by documenting what the problem is and what caused it. Ask yourself some simple questions:

✦ **Does anyone else have this problem?** You can find the answer by going to the Forums page on WordPress.org or the plugin developer's support forum if he or she provides one. Figure 4-1 shows the Forums page for the All in One SEO Pack plugin. Search these support forums (and Google) to see whether anyone else has reported the problem and provided a resolution. If the problem is common, someone has identified a fix that you can implement.

Sometimes problems are the result of a bug in the plugin code that will be fixed in a revision. However, if the problem is present only on your installation of WordPress, or if any fixes that worked for others don't work for you, then move onto the next four questions.

✦ **Does an error message display in your WordPress Dashboard or on your Web site?** If an error message displays, search the support forums and Google for the error. Sometimes the error will provide a filename and line number of the code that is causing the problem, as shown in Figure 4-2. Locate the line in the file and check the code for syntax errors.

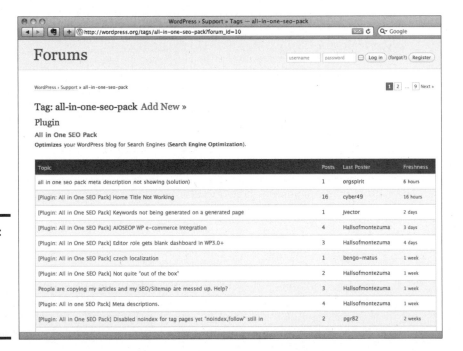

Figure 4-1: The All in One SEO Pack plugin's Forums page.

Figure 4-2:
A PHP error
message
with the
affected
filename
and line
number.

> Screen Options ▾   Help ▾
>
> 🔌 *Plugins* (Add New)
>
> Plugin could not be activated because it triggered a fatal error.
>
> **Parse error**: syntax error, unexpected '}' in **/home2/wordpre1/public_html/factionzine/wp-content/plugins/my-plugin/my-plugin.php** on line **15**

✦ **What changed before the problem appeared?** Problems don't just appear. Something causes the problem, and identifying that cause is your primary focus. If something was changed, document what that was and, if possible, reverse the change to see whether it resolves the problem. If it's as simple as uninstalling a plugin or theme that you just added, the problem could be a conflict between your site and the new plugin or theme. A solution is to find a different plugin or theme that doesn't cause a conflict with your site.

✦ **Does the problem affect the front end (your Web site) or just the back end (Dashboard)?** After you determine what changed, ask what the problem affected. This can help you identify the code within the plugin that's at fault. Some code affects the front end, some affects the back end, and some affects both.

When troubleshooting problems with plugins:

1. **Revert to the default theme.**

The WordPress version 3.0 default theme is Twenty Ten. Revert to this theme to see whether the problem goes away. If it does, the problem probably lies in a conflict between your theme and the plugin.

2. **Deactivate all other plugins.**

If you have other plugins installed in WordPress, deactivate them to see whether the problem disappears. If it does, the problem probably is a conflict between your plugin and another installed plugin. To determine which plugin, activate each plugin one at a time until the problem reappears.

Always back up your WordPress database before changing anything. Use a backup plugin, such as BackupBuddy (`http://ewebscapes.com/back upbuddy`), and keep your backup in a safe location so that you can restore from it later if you need to.

If you're unable to locate the cause of the problem by reverting your installation of WordPress to the default, then you could be looking at a conflict between the plugin and WordPress. If this is the case, you can try installing the plugin on a new, clean install of the latest version of WordPress in a different location. If the problem doesn't reappear, reinstall the latest version of WordPress on the site where you are having the problem and add your plugin, theme, and all the other plugins.

Sometimes, you won't get an error message; instead, you see a blank screen. This can have several causes. Conflicts in the code between plugins, themes, or the WordPress core could cause PHP issues where the process just stops running and nothing is sent to the browser. Typically, in a published plugin or theme, this won't be the issue. You're more likely to encounter this while developing and debugging your own (or another privately developed) plugin. Most often, the "White Screen of Death" is caused by insufficient server memory per instance of PHP. You can correct this by increasing the allotted memory for PHP instances. However, some hosts don't allow you to increase memory yourself and require you to contact them. Otherwise, you can address the problem by opening your `wp-config.php` file and finding this line:

```
define('DB_COLLATE', '');
```

Then add this line directly underneath, on its own line:

```
define('WP_MEMORY_LIMIT', '96M');
```

Adjust the memory from 96MB as needed. Even if your host allows you to increase the memory allotment, most likely, there's a limit on how high you can set it.

Back up your WordPress database before doing anything so drastic and make sure to back up your `wp-content` directory using FTP and the `wp-config.php` and `.htaccess` files because these contain important information you will need when you reinstall WordPress.

Reinstalling WordPress on a live site should be considered only as a last resort and only if you are comfortable with restoring a WordPress site with content. Consider using a different plugin as an alternative to reinstalling your WordPress site. After all, if the problem is a conflict between the plugin and WordPress, the plugin might not have been tested very well and could contain other bugs.

Locating Plugin and Theme Conflicts

Conflicts that occur between a plugin and a theme are common, especially where a theme takes on some of the functionality usually performed by a plugin. Locating these conflicts can be difficult and requires some understanding of PHP and how themes work in WordPress.

A *theme* is a collection of templates and CSS files that control the look of your WordPress site. However, themes can perform complex actions, such as SEO and image display. This functionality can conflict with plugins that perform the same tasks.

When identifying a conflict between your theme and your plugin, look for an error message, which can point to a specific line in a file. If no error message displays in either the WordPress Dashboard or on the front end of your site, you need to identify the specific element that is broken. To do this, duplicate your live site on the test site that you set up in Book VII, Chapter 3 and follow these steps (after you have things working correctly on your test site, you can apply the changes to your live site — this way, you're doing all your testing first in an environment that does not affect the live site):

1. **Deactivate all plugins except the one causing the conflict with your theme.**

2. **Remove all widgets from widget areas.**

   These can be common causes of conflicts.

3. **Test your site in several browsers to see whether the problem affects only a particular browser.**

4. **Comment out any changes you may have made to the theme or plugin files, including changes to CSS stylesheets.**

5. **Check for any errors appearing in the browser's Error Console.**

   Figure 4-3 shows the error console in Firefox.

Figure 4-3: The error console in Mozilla Firefox.

6. **Use an error-checking tool, such as the Web Developer add-on for Mozilla Firefox.**

7. **Disable JavaScript in your browser and see whether the problem is still present.**

Using browser-based Web developer tools, such as Firebug or the Web Developer add-on, can be extremely useful in troubleshooting problems on the front end. These tools are free and come with good documentation. Figure 4-4 shows both tools installed in Mozilla Firefox.

After you identify the cause of the problem, report it by using the WordPress.org Forums page or the plugin developer's own support forum. Seek help from the WordPress community before trying to resolve the problem yourself. Finally, always report any bugs and fixes you find to the plugin developer because this can help others with the same issue.

Figure 4-4: The Firebug and Web Developer add-ons in Mozilla Firefox.

Exploring Plugin Interaction with WordPress

WordPress plugins use an Application Programming Interface (API) provided within WordPress to make plugin development easier. The API provides *hooks,* which are means of calling pieces of functionality built into the WordPress core application. For example, in the core of WordPress is functionality for publishing a post. If a plugin wants to execute that functionality, it uses an action hook to call and execute the publish post functionality.

The two types of hooks in the API are

> ✦ **Action hooks:** WordPress launches these hooks at specific points during execution of PHP code or as specific events occur.
>
> ✦ **Filter hooks:** WordPress launches these hooks to modify text before it's added to the database or sent to the browser screen.

A complete list of action hooks available for plugin development can be found in the WordPress documentation at `http://codex.wordpress.org/Plugin_API/Action Reference`. A complete list of filter hooks can be found at `http://codex.wordpress.org/Plugin_API/Filter_Reference`.

Understanding action hooks

To explore a simple action hook within the API, we analyze the Hello Dolly plugin by Matt Mullenweg. When activated, the Hello Dolly plugin randomly displays a lyric from the song "Hello Dolly!" by Louis Armstrong in the upper right of every page in the WordPress Dashboard.

The following code in the Hello Dolly plugin calls the action hook `admin_head`.

```
add_action('admin_head', 'dolly_css');
```

The action hook `admin_head` runs in the HTML <head> section of the WordPress Dashboard. The function in the plugin that is hooked into `admin_head` is `dolly_css`. This function is defined in the plugin as shown:

```
function dolly_css() {
    $x = ( is_rtl() ) ? 'left' : 'right';
    echo "
    <style type='text/css'>
    #dolly {
        position: absolute;
        top: 4.5em;
        margin: 0;
        padding: 0;
        $x: 215px;
        font-size: 11px;
    }
    </style>
    ";
}
```

The function `dolly_css` simply echoes the HTML code between the
`<style></style>` tags to the browser. This is one method of delivering style
code to the browser. Another would be to put the style code in a plugin-specific
stylesheet and call the stylesheet so that the stylesheet loads in the header
of the Web site when it is loaded in a browser window. Figure 4-5 shows the
`<style>` code added to the `<head>` section of the WordPress Dashboard.

Figure 4-5:
Source
code of the
Dashboard
showing
Hello Dolly's
style code.

This is a very basic example of how a plugin uses the hooks provided by the WordPress plugin API to access certain core functionality within WordPress. Without this hook, you must write a function that duplicates a process that WordPress is already performing.

Understanding filter hooks

To demonstrate the use of a filter hook, we stay with the Hello Dolly theme. This time, look at the Fancy Dolly plugin (`http://wordpress.org/extend/plugins/fancy-plugin`). The developer has taken the Hello Dolly plugin and expanded its functionality to add a sidebar widget where you can enter text for random display rather than the lyrics to "Hello Dolly!."

The following code calls the `widget_title` filter hook:

```
apply_filters('widget_title', $instance['title'] );
```

The `apply_filter` is calling the `widget_title` filter hook. As you might imagine, this outputs the title of the widget to the browser. Figure 4-6 shows the widget title for the Hello Dolly widget on the front end of a Web site.

Book VII Chapter 4

Modifying Exisiting Plugin Code to Your Liking

Figure 4-6:
A widget title displayed on a Web site.

The function that is hooking into the `widget_title` filter hook is
`$instance['title']`, which is defined in the Fancy Dolly plugin as a form:

```
function form( $instance ) {
    /* Set up some default widget settings. */
    $defaults = array( 'title' => 'We love you Dolly', 'dtext' => 'Hello, Dolly
    Well, hello, Dolly
    It\'s so nice to have you back where you belong
    You\'re lookin\' swell, Dolly');
    $instance = wp_parse_args( (array) $instance, $defaults ); ?>
<p>
<label for="<?php echo $this->get_field_id( 'title' ); ?>">Title:</label>
<input id="<?php echo $this->get_field_id( 'title' ); ?>" name="<?php echo $this-
    >get_field_name( 'title' ); ?>" value="<?php echo $instance['title']; ?>"
    style="width:100%;" />
</p>
<p>
<label for="<?php echo $this->get_field_id( 'dtext' ); ?>">Text (each row will be
    displayed randomly, use Notepad to copy and paste):</label>
<textarea rows="16" cols="80" id="<?php echo $this->get_field_id( 'dtext' ); ?>"
    name="<?php echo $this->get_field_name( 'dtext' ); ?>" value="<?php echo
    $instance['dtext']; ?>"><?php echo $instance['dtext']; ?></textarea>
</p>
<?php
    }
```

The form has some default text already inserted, but it provides two fields —
`title` and `dtext` — in which you can enter your own text. The plugin then
randomly displays your text in the widget area of your Web site. Figure 4-7
shows the widget form where you can replace the default text with your own.

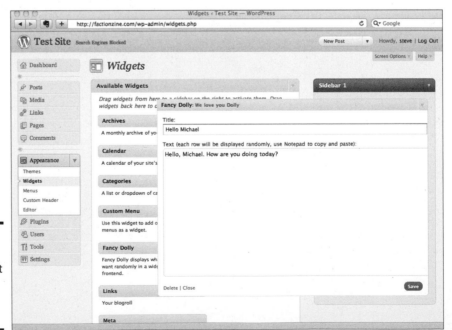

Figure 4-7:
The Fancy
Dolly widget
displaying
the input
form.

Figure 4-8 shows the text displaying in the widget area of the Web site.

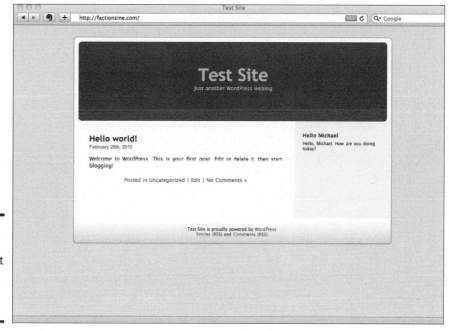

Figure 4-8:
The Fancy
Dolly widget
displaying
text on a
Web site.

Identifying Functions within a Plugin

In a previous section, we explore how plugins interact with WordPress by using the plugin API. Here, we show you how functions are defined in a plugin. In PHP, a *function* is a predefined set of commands carried out when the function is called. It's the same in WordPress; some functions are common PHP functions, and some functions are specific to WordPress. We discuss how to hook into these functions through the plugin API so that you can call existing commands instead of having to write them over again in your plugin. However, you can also write your own functions and call them in your plugin.

So how do you identify functions within a plugin? Here's an example from the Hello Dolly plugin; this code function is found at the bottom, as the last line of the plugin file: `hello.php`:

```
add_action('admin_head', 'dolly_css');
```

The WordPress Codex documentation describes the `add_action` function as having the following arguments, or parameters:

```
add_action( $tag, $function_to_add, $priority, $accepted_args );
```

✦ *$tag* is the name of the action you want to hook onto.

✦ *$function_to_add* is the name of the function you're calling.

✦ *$priority* is an optional value that represents how important the function is. The default is 10, a lower number makes the function run earlier, and a higher number makes the function run later.

✦ *$accepted_args* is the number of arguments your function takes. This is optional, and the default is 1.

In PHP code, the dollar sign, $, simply tells PHP that the word appearing directly after it is a variable that is defined. In our example, $tag is a variable that is defined in the add_action function.

The code in our example uses add_action to hook the dolly_css function to the admin_head action. Therefore, the dolly_css function must be defined somewhere in the plugin and must look like this:

```
function dolly_css() {
}
```

Between the {} brackets is the set of commands that carry out when the function is called. This function is called when WordPress runs admin_head. You see the set of commands for the dolly_css function earlier in this chapter, in the "Understanding action hooks" section.

This simple example outputs *Hello* in the head of the Web site:

```
add_action('wp_head', 'my_function');
function my_function() {
   echo "Hello";
}
```

Both add_action and add_filter contain a *$tag,* which is the name of the hook in the plugin API, and a *$function,* which is then defined in the plugin using function *function_name*() { }.

Identifying Functionality and Output

Actions and filters hook our functions to WordPress plugin API commands. By now, you should have an understanding of how this works and how it looks in a plugin file. In generic terms, WordPress plugins have two distinct purposes:

✦ **Functions:** Defined within the plugin code through a combination of actions and hooks; essentially, functions define what the plugin does.

✦ **Output:** What is displayed on your site as a result of the plugin function(s). For example, if the plugin function(s) makes calls to the database to retrieve a certain type of post (for instance, from a certain category or tag) from your content, the output is how those posts then get displayed on your site for your readers to see. Plugins can also use HTML markup and CSS to provide basic styling for the output.

Members of the WordPress community eager to learn more often ask how to go about dissecting a WordPress plugin, possibly to modify its internal functionality or even its output. In Book VII, Chapter 5, we discuss providing an API specific to your plugin. You can determine a plugin function, as well as how it outputs the result of the functions on your Web site by taking a look at the source code of the plugin.

When digging into an existing plugin that you'd like to alter, you want figure out what action and filter hooks it's using. Some plugins make this easy by putting most or all of the calls to hooks at the bottom of a file (often the primary plugin file). We use a plugin called TweetMeme Retweet Button as an example of how you can look into the source code of the plugin and make alterations. The TweetMeme Retweet Button plugin can be installed automatically through your WordPress Dashboard or downloaded at `http://wordpress.org/extend/plugins/tweetmeme`. Scroll to the bottom of `tweetmeme.php` and look for the `add_action()` and `add_filter()` functions:

**Book VII
Chapter 4**

**Modifying Existing
Plugin Code to Your
Liking**

```
// Only all the admin options if the user is an admin if(is_admin()){
    add_action('admin_menu', 'tm_options');      add_action('admin_init', 'tm_
    init'); }
// Set the default options when the plugin is activated
function tm_activate(){      add_option('tm_where',
'before');      add_option('tm_rss_where', 'before');
add_option('tm_source');      add_option('tm_style',
'float: right; margin-left: 10px;');
add_option('tm_version', 'large');
add_option('tm_display_page', '1');
add_option('tm_display_front', '1');
add_option('tm_display_rss', '1');
add_option('tm_ping', 'on');
add_option('tm_hashtags', 'on'); }
add_filter('the_content', 'tm_update', 8);
add_filter('get_the_excerpt', 'tm_remove_filter', 9);
add_action('publish_post', 'tm_ping', 9);
add_action('wp_head', 'tm_head');
register_activation_hook( __FILE__, 'tm_activate');
```

We can see most of the hooks the plugin uses (`admin_menu`, `admin_init`, `the_content`, `get_the_excerpt`, `publish_post`, `wp_head`) grouped nicely into one section. By now, you should know what most of these hooks do. If not, that's okay, too. You can look up literally hundreds of hooks on the WordPress Codex, which has plain English descriptions of many WordPress hooks:

✦ WordPress Filter Hooks: `http://codex.wordpress.org/Plugin_API/Filter_Reference`

✦ WordPress Action Hooks: `http://codex.wordpress.org/Plugin_API/Action_Reference`

By analyzing what hooks the plugin uses, you can determine how that plugin interfaces with WordPress to pass the results of its code to the rest of the WordPress system. For instance, TweetMeme calls the `tm_ping()` function on the `publish_post` action. The `publish_post` action hook always runs within WordPress whenever a post is published. From this line, we can deduce that an examination of the `tm_ping()` function will tell us what additional functionality occurs on this action.

Search for `function tm_ping`; you find the following lines of code:

```
function tm_ping($post_id) {
// do we have curl
    if ((get_option('tm_ping') != 'off') &&
      function_exists('curl_init')) {         $url = get_permalink($post_id);
      // create a new cURL resource         $ch = curl_init();          // set URL
      and other appropriate options          curl_setopt($ch, CURLOPT_URL, 'http://
      api.tweetmeme.com/ping.php?url=' . urlencode($url));          curl_setopt($ch,
      CURLOPT_CONNECTTIMEOUT, 2);          curl_setopt($ch, CURLOPT_TIMEOUT, 3);
      curl_setopt($ch, CURLOPT_RETURNTRANSFER, 1);          // grab URL and pass it
      to the browser          curl_exec($ch);          // close cURL resource, and
      free up system resources          curl_close($ch);
}
    }
```

When publishing or editing a post, the TweetMeme plugin uses `curl` to ping the TweetMeme API with the appropriate URL of the current post.

Everything inside a plugin contained in a function runs only when that plugin is called. Typically, action and filter hooks are contained in a function. Otherwise, the code will run sooner than necessary or not work at all.

Starting with the hooks at the bottom of the file makes it easier to follow the path of the plugin's functionality. We see that `tm_init()` is called on the `admin_init` action, `tm_options` is called on the `admin_menu` action, and so on.

Say you want to modify the styling of the TweetMeme button. To locate this part of the code, a logical place to start is the `the_content` filter, because the TweetMeme Retweet Button plugin outputs the TweetMeme button within the post content on your site:

```
add_filter('the_content', 'tm_update', 8);
```

From here, follow the path to the tm_update function. In this function, the button output comes from the $button variable, which is generated by the tm_generate_button() function:

```
$button = tm_generate_button();
```

The tm_generate_button function finally uncovers the code for the actual output of the button. The Tweetmeme.com domain delivers the button via an iframe, which is an HTML page embedded in your site, using the HTML <iframe> markup tag. In this function, you can change the button to an image that you host, change the dimensions of the elements in the div, or make any other modifications you prefer in order to change the output of the button as it appears on your Web site.

Editing Plugin Files

When editing, or altering, plugin files, you need to take care and make sure that you keep a backup of the original file, just in case you make any mistakes in coding. You can restore the original by uploading the backup that you kept, initially. You can do this by simply downloading the plugin files from your Web server via FTP before making any changes to the plugin files.

Additionally, WordPress provides you with a handy plugin editor feature. You can visit the Plugin Editor page in your Dashboard to edit plugin files:

1. **Click the Editor link under the Plugins menu in your Dashboard.**

The Plugin Editor page displays in your Web browser.

2. **Select the plugin you want to edit.**

In the Select Plugin to Edit drop-down menu, select the plugin you want to edit.

3. **Click the Select button.**

The Edit Plugins page refreshes with the primary plugin file of the plugin you selected displayed in the text box on the left side of the page.

4. **Select the plugin file you want to edit.**

The right side of the Edit Plugins page displays a list of links to the files included within the plugin you selected in Step 2. The primary plugin file is always the one that is displayed, first, in the text edit box on the left (the primary plugin file is the one that contains the initial action hooks and filters).

5. **Make your desired alterations to the plugin in the text box editor.**

Be sure to click the Update File button at the bottom of the Edit Plugins page in order to save and apply your changes.

Book VII
Chapter 4

Modifying Existing Plugin Code to Your Liking

The nice thing about the built-in plugin editor is that it has a fail-safe built in. The fail-safe feature comes into play if you make any errors when you edit plugins. For example, if your code syntax is wrong (you've misplaced a ; or " markers, or failed to close your PHP functions correctly), WordPress will notice that you've made an error in editing the code and will automatically deactivate the plugin so it doesn't cause errors or problems on your web site. Figure 4-9 displays the Edit Plugins page in the WordPress Dashboard with an error message telling you that the plugin has been deactivated because changes made to the plugin caused a fatal error.

In Chapter 2 of this minibook, we provide information about the automatic upgrade feature for plugins. It is important for you to know that when you upgrade a plugin in WordPress, the upgrade feature replaces the existing plugin files with the new, upgraded ones. It stands to reason, then, that any changes or alterations you made to the plugin file disappear when you upgrade the plugin in the future.

To avoid this, when you alter a plugin, rename the plugin and plugin folder, and then place it in its own folder in the /wp-content/plugins/ directory on your Web server. This saves your changes against future upgrades of the same plugin by essentially creating your own plugin based on the original one.

Figure 4-9:
Error
message
on the Edit
Plugins
page when
a plugin has
been altered
incorrectly.

Using the TweetMeme Retweet Button plugin we mention previously in this chapter, the following steps take you through how to rename the files to protect them from upgrade changes in the future:

1. **Connect to your Web server with your favored FTP program.**

    Book II, Chapter 2 covers FTP information, if you need a refresher here.

2. **Locate the `/wp-content/plugins/` folder in your WordPress installation.**

    Book II, Chapter 4 shows you how to locate your WordPress installation location.

3. **Download the `/tweetmeme-button/` folder.**

    This is the folder that contains the files for the TweetMeme Retweet Button plugin. All plugins in your `/wp-content/plugins` directory have their own, individual folder.

4. **Create a new folder in the `/wp-content/plugins` directory called: `/my-tweetmeme-button`.**

5. **Upload the contents of the `/tweetmeme-button/` plugin folder you downloaded in Step 3 to the new `/my-tweetmeme-button/` folder created in Step 4.**

6. **Go to Plugins⇨Editor in your WordPress Dashboard.**

7. **Change the name of the TweetMeme Retweet Button plugin in the plugin editor.**

    At the top of the `tweetmeme.php` file you see the following lines of code that define the plugin name and description:

    ```
    /*
    Plugin Name: TweetMeme Retweet Button
    Plugin URI: http://tweetmeme.com/about/plugins
    Description: Adds a button which easily lets you retweet your blog posts.
    Version: 1.8.2
    Author: TweetMeme
    Author URI: http://tweetmeme.com
    */
    ```

    Edit the `Plugin Name: TweetMeme Retweet Button` to: `My TweetMeMe Retweet Button` then click the Update File button, to save your changes.

8. **Visit the Plugins page in your Dashboard: Plugins⇨Plugins.**

9. **Click the Deactivate link under the TweetMeME Retweet Button plugin.**

    This deactivates the original TweetMeMe plugin.

10. Click the Activate link under the My TweetMeMe Retweet Button.

This activates your copy of the TweetMeMe Retweet Button plugin that you can now safely make your edits to, without worrying about the plugin code getting written over when upgrades occur.

 After following the preceding steps, leave a copy of the original TweetMeMe Retweet Button (or whichever plugin you chose to copy and edit) installed, but deactivated, in your WordPress installation. This way, you will still receive notifications in your Dashboard when there is a new upgrade available to the original plugin, allowing you to go through the same process of copying and editing the upgraded version to make sure that you are using the most up-to-date version of the original plugin functions on your site.

Chapter 5: Creating Simple WordPress Plugins from Scratch

In This Chapter

✔ Creating a valid plugin

✔ Filtering content

✔ Adding shortcodes and widgets

✔ Creating a plugin settings page

*W*ordPress plugins are one of the greatest parts of WordPress. As open source software, a developer can extend WordPress functionality through plugins and themes, and WordPress provides a great API (Application Program Interface) to do so. Using WordPress's built-in action hooks and filter hooks, you can create just about any functionality you can imagine. In this chapter on creating simple plugins, we assume that you have basic PHP knowledge.

This All-in-One doesn't turn you into a PHP programmer or MySQL database administrator; Book II, Chapter 3 gives you a glimpse of how PHP and MySQL work together to help WordPress build your Web site. If you're interested in finding out how to program PHP or become a MySQL database administrator, check out *PHP and MySQL For Dummies* by Janet Valade (Wiley).

Often, WordPress users are tempted to edit the core code of WordPress rather than write a plugin to achieve the desired functionality. This isn't recommended because it makes upgrading difficult and can cause various problems, including serious security issues.

When writing a plugin, you can develop it by using a simple text editor, such as Notepad (Windows) or TextEdit (Mac). However, writing a plugin on a server with WordPress installed is best because you can easily and efficiently test during development.

Understanding Plugin Structure

All that is required for WordPress to see a plugin is a PHP file in the `wp-content/plugins` directory of the site with some special information at the top of the file. This information at the top of a plugin file, typically referred to as a plugins header, is what WordPress looks for when determining which plugins are installed on the site. A freshly installed WordPress site makes a good starting point to understand how this works in practice.

Inspecting WordPress's default plugins

WordPress installs with two plugins by default: Akismet and Hello Dolly. Looking at the files for each of these plugins will help you understand how you can structure your own plugins.

Inside a fresh WordPress site's `wp-content/plugins` directory, you find a directory named `/akismet` and two files named `hello.php` and `index.php`. The `hello.php` file is for the Hello Dolly plugin and has the following text at the top of the file.

```
<?php
/**
 * @package Hello_Dolly
 * @version 1.5.1
 */
/*
Plugin Name: Hello Dolly
Plugin URI: http://wordpress.org/#
Description: This is not just a plugin, it symbolizes the hope and
    enthusiasm of an entire generation summed up in two words sung most
    famously by Louis Armstrong: Hello, Dolly. When activated you will
    randomly see a lyric from <cite>Hello, Dolly</cite> in the upper
    right of your admin screen on every page.
Author: Matt Mullenweg
Version: 1.5.1
Author URI: http://ma.tt/
*/
```

The section in bold is the plugin header, which tells WordPress about the plugin. If this section is removed, the Hello Dolly plugin will no longer be available because WordPress no longer recognizes it as a plugin. The Plugin Name, Plugin URI, and Description sections of the plugin header are referred to as fields. We discuss the fields and their use in Chapter 6 of this minibook.

Open the `index.php` file in the `/wp-content/plugins/` folder and you see the following few lines of code:

```
<?php
// Silence is golden.
?>
```

Because this file doesn't have a plugin header, it isn't a plugin. It's in the plugins directory to prevent people from going to *domain.com*/wp-content/plugins (where *domain.com* is your site's domain name) to get a full listing of all the plugins on your site. Because the `index.php` file doesn't output anything, people trying to get a listing of your plugins will simply see a blank screen.

All that remains now in the `/wp-content/plugins` directory is the `/akismet` directory. Inside this directory are three PHP files: `admin.php`, `akismet.php`, and `legacy.php`. If you open up each file, you will see that only the `akismet.php` file contains the plugin header.

```
/*
Plugin Name: Akismet
Plugin URI: http://akismet.com/
Description: Akismet checks your comments against the Akismet Web service
    to see if they look like spam or not. You need an <a href="http://
    akismet.com/get/">API key</a> to use it. You can review the spam it
    catches under "Comments." To show off your Akismet stats just put
    <code>&lt;?php akismet_counter(); ?&gt;</code> in your template. See
    also: <a href="http://wordpress.org/extend/plugins/stats/">WP Stats
    plugin</a>.
Version: 2.4.0
Author: Automattic
Author URI: http://automattic.com/wordpress-plugins/
License: GPLv2
*/
```

Because the `akismet.php` file has the plugin header, the `/akismet` directory is recognized by WordPress as a plugin. If the `akismet.php` file is removed, the Akismet plugin disappears from the listing of available plugins in your WordPress installation (Dashboard⇨Plugins).

Looking at the setup of these two default plugins tells you two very important things about the way that a plugin is structured.

✦ The file that has the plugin header can be in the plugins directory by itself or contained in a directory inside the plugins directory.

✦ The plugin header follows a standard format.

Knowing the requirements

Looking at the way the default plugins are set up gives you an idea of how to set up your plugins, but knowing all the requirements would be nice so you don't make mistakes. The reality is that there are very few requirements on how you must set up your plugin.

Requirement 1: Plugin header

The plugin header is what allows WordPress to recognize your plugin. Without this key piece of information, your plugin will not show up as an available plugin and you will be unable to activate it.

While there are many fields in the plugin header, only Plugin Name is required. For example, the following is a valid plugin header.

```
/*
Plugin Name: Example Plugin
*/
```

Of course, providing additional information can be very helpful, but if you're quickly making a plugin for yourself, the plugin name is all that is required.

Requirement 2: Correct placement of main plugin file

The main plugin file (the one with the plugin header) must be either in the `/wp-content/plugins` directory or inside a directory immediately inside the `/wp-content/plugins` directory.

Examples of valid locations for the main plugin PHP file:

✦ `wp-content/plugins/example.php`

✦ `wp-content/plugins/example/example.php`

Examples of invalid locations for the main plugin PHP file:

✦ `wp-content/example.php`

✦ `wp-content/plugins/example/lib/example.php`

You cannot place the main plugin file too deep. WordPress will only look in the `/wp-content/plugins` directory and inside the first level of the directories contained in `/wp-content/plugins`, but no deeper.

Following best practices

The requirements are very lax and allow you to set up your plugin any way you want. You can name the main plugin file and plugin directory anything you like. You can even put multiple main plugin files inside a single directory. However, just because you can, doesn't mean that you should. The following are some best practices to help keep some consistency.

Best Practice 1: Always use a plugin directory

Hello Dolly doesn't reside in a directory because it's simple enough to need only one file. However, all plugins should reside in their own directory, even if they need only one file.

When creating a plugin, a single file may be enough to do what you need, but further development may require adding more files. It is better to start with the plugin in a directory instead of restructuring it later.

Moving or renaming a main plugin file deactivates the plugin because WordPress stores the plugins activation state based upon the path to the main plugin file.

Do yourself and any users of your plugin a favor and always place your plugins inside a directory.

Best Practice 2: Use meaningful, unique names

When doing any WordPress development (whether for a plugin or theme), you must always keep in mind that your code shares space with code from other people (other plugin developers, WordPress core developers, theme developers, and so on). This means that you should never use simple names for anything; the name of your plugin should be unique.

You might think that naming your plugin "Plugin" allows you to move past the boring stuff and onto development, but it just makes things difficult to keep track of. If your plugin produces a widget that displays a listing of recent movie reviews, "Michael Torbert's Movie Reviews Widget" is much more meaningful than "Widget Plugin."

Best Practice 3: Match the plugin and plugin directory names

Make sure that your plugin's directory name makes it easy to find the plugin in the `/wp-content/plugins` directory.

Going with the preceding example, having Michael Torbert's Movie Reviews Widget in a `widget` directory will make finding the widget difficult. The directory name doesn't have to match exactly, but it should make sense. Some good directory names for this example are `/movie-reviews-widget`, `/mt-movie-reviews-widget`, or `/movie-reviews`.

Best Practice 4: Don't use spaces in directory or filenames

Although modern desktop operating systems can handle directories and files that have spaces in the name, some Web servers can't. A good practice is to use a hyphen (-) in place of a space when naming files and directories. In other words, use `movie-reviews-widget` rather than `movie reviews widget`.

Avoiding spaces in file and directory names will save you many headaches.

Best Practice 5: Consistent main plugin filenames

Although you can name the plugin main file anything, coming up with a consistent naming scheme that you use throughout your plugins can be a good idea.

The most popular naming scheme is to match the main plugin PHP filename to the plugin directory name. For example, the main plugin file for a plugin directory called `/movie-reviews` is `movie-reviews.php`. The problem with this naming scheme is that it doesn't mean anything. Plugin filenames should always indicate the plugin's purpose. The purpose of the `movie-reviews.php` file is clearer when you know that many developers name the main plugin file the same as the plugin directory.

Another naming scheme is to use a consistent filename across all plugins. For example, naming the main plugin file `init.php` indicates that the file is used to initialize the plugin (`init` is the abbreviation for initialize). The name `init.php` makes the purpose of the file clear regardless of the plugin name or purpose.

Creating Your First Plugin

When developing something new, taking very small steps is usually best. This way, if something breaks, the problem is clear. Doing a large number of new things at one time makes finding where something went wrong difficult.

Sticking with this concept, the first plugin we help you create in this chapter is a plugin that can be activated and deactivated but doesn't do anything. In other words, a fully functional plugin shell that's ready for code to be added.

Because this plugin is an example and won't really do anything, we named it Example: Do Nothing.

Setting up the plugin files

For this plugin, all that you need is a main plugin file. Following the best practices from earlier in this chapter, this file is placed in its own directory by following these quick steps:

1. **Connect to your Web server via FTP.**

   Check out Book II, Chapter 2 for a refresher on using FTP.

2. **Browse to the `/wp-content/plugins` directory in your WordPress installation directory.**

   If you're unsure where your WordPress installation directory is located, flip to Book II, Chapter 4 where we cover installing WordPress on your Web server.

3. **Create a new directory within `/wp-content/plugins` called `/example-do-nothing`.**

   Most FTP programs allow you to right-click with your mouse and choose Add New Folder or Add New Directory.

4. **Create an empty `.php` file with the filename `init.php`.**

   Use your favorite text editor, such as Notepad for PC or TextMate for Mac, to open a new file and then save it with the filename `init.php`.

5. **Upload your blank `init.php` file to `/wp-content/plugins/example-do-nothing`.**

   Your plugin directory and plugin file are set up. In the next section, you add code to the `init.php` plugin file.

Adding the plugin header

Open the `init.php` file you created in the previous section (most FTP programs have built-in text editors that allow you to right-click the file with your mouse and choose Edit) and add the following lines of code to create the plugin header:

```
<?php
/*
Plugin Name: Example: Do Nothing
Description: This plugin does nothing. It is an example of how to create
    a valid WordPress plugin.
*/
```

 Adding the closing `?>` tag at the end of a PHP file is optional at this point. Leaving it out is helpful because it prevents accidentally adding code after it, which may cause the PHP code to break.

Adding a plugin description isn't necessary, but it makes the purpose of the plugin clear to anyone who reads your code. Additionally, the plugin description displays on the Plugins page in your Dashboard to give users a good idea of what the purpose of your plugin is. When developing, you wind up with many plugins that were used for simple tests or are unfinished. Having solid names and descriptions adds order to the chaos so that important code isn't forgotten or accidentally deleted.

Be sure to save the `init.php` file and upload it to your `/wp-content/plugins/example-do-nothing` directory on your Web server.

Testing the plugin

After modifying the `init.php` file and saving it in the `/wp-content/plugins/example-do-nothing` directory, visit your WordPress Dashboard and click Plugins to view the Plugins page in your Dashboard. Your new plugin is listed with the title Example: Do Nothing, as shown in Figure 5-1.

Click the Activate link directly beneath the title. The Plugins page displays a *Plugin activated* message, which indicates the Example: Do Nothing plugin was activated in your WordPress install. Although your new plugin doesn't "do" anything, you have a simple WordPress plugin with the correct file structure, naming conventions, and headers.

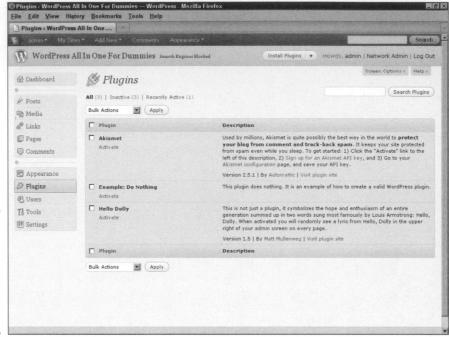

Figure 5-1:
The Plugins page showing the sample plugin in the list.

Fixing Problems

Even though we start simply, potentially, a number of things could go wrong. If you're having problems, delete what you have and start over and follow our previous directions carefully. If you still have problems, this section covers some common issues and gives you solutions that you can try to fix them.

White screen of nothingness

A common problem when doing plugin development is making a change and finding that every attempt to load the site in your browser window results in a blank white screen. A code error is breaking WordPress when it tries to run your plugin code.

A quick way to fix this is to rename your `/wp-content/plugins/example-do-nothing` plugin directory on your Web server to something like `/wp-content/plugins/old.example-do-nothing`. This causes automatic deactivation of the plugin because WordPress won't be able to locate it.

Before changing the name back, go to the Plugins page in your Dashboard. A message at the top of the page states *The plugin example-do-nothing/init.php has been deactivated due to an error: Plugin file does not exist.*

This confirms that WordPress fully deactivated the broken plugin; you should be able to load your Web site successfully without seeing the dreaded white screen of nothingness. After this, you can change the filename back, fix your problem, and try again. If the plugin is still broken, WordPress prevents the plugin from activating and gives you details about the error.

Unexpected output error

When you activate a plugin in your Dashboard and see an error message on the Plugins page about unexpected output, it means that you have code or text within the main plugin PHP file that is outside of a `<?php ?>` code block. We cover PHP programming in Book II, Chapter 3 and explain that every PHP function must start with a command that tells your Web server to initiate (or start) PHP. If your plugin file is missing the `<?php` line, an error about unexpected output occurs and WordPress doesn't activate your plugin.

If your plugin activates, have some fun and try to create this error so you will know it when you see it. Intentionally create the error by following these steps:

1. **Connect to your Web server via FTP.**

2. **Browse to the `/wp-content/plugins/example-do-nothing` directory.**

3. **Open the `init.php` file in your text editor.**

4. **Remove the `<?php` line from the top of the `init.php` file.**

5. **Save the `init.php` file.**

6. **Upload the file to the `/wp-content/plugins/example-do-nothing` directory.**

When you try to activate the Example: Do Nothing plugin, the following message displays at the top of the Plugins page: */* Plugin Name: Example: Do Nothing Description: This plugin does nothing. It is an example of how to create a valid WordPress plugin. */*.

WordPress also displays an error message on the Plugins page (see Figure 5-2), directly beneath the Plugins header: *The plugin generated 138 characters of unexpected output during activation. If you notice "headers already sent" messages, problems with syndication feeds or other issues, try deactivating or removing this plugin.*

All this fuss because of a missing `<?php` line.

Plugin name   Unexpected output error message

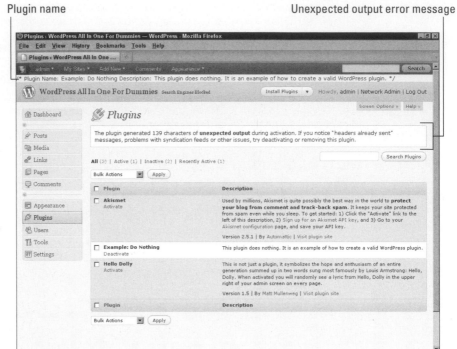

Figure 5-2:
Unexpected
output error
message
displayed on
the Plugins
page.

Filtering Content

Now that you know how a plugin is created, it's time to have some fun and create a WordPress plugin that actually does something, and in the process, discover more basics of WordPress plugin development.

A powerful feature of WordPress is its numerous filters. By latching code to a filter, you can modify information as it flows through WordPress, and therefore modify the information WordPress displays or stores.

Imagine that you have a habit of using contractions far too often. Your readership mocks you and your penchant for the commoner practice of merging words together. At night, you worry about whether you missed an instance of *it's*, *we're*, or *I'll*.

It is causing you to lose sleep. You tried listening to the self-help tapes, you review every word and you have been to therapy to find the deep-seated cause of your craving for contractions. Despite your best efforts and the constant ridicule, you cannot help but sound like an etiquette contrarian.

Fortunately, there is a cure. With a simple filter and a bit of code, your grammatical ailment can be disguised easily with a simple WordPress plugin that you create in the next section of this chapter.

Setting up the plugin structure

The plugin we create in this section is Example: Contraction Compulsion Correction that will reside in a directory called `/example-contraction-compulsion-correction` with a main plugin file named `init.php`. Apply the same steps to create the directory and main plugin file as you did in the "Creating Your First Plugin" section, earlier in this chapter.

Add the following plugin header to the top of the main plugin (`init.php`) file:

```
<?php
/*
Plugin Name: Example: Contraction Compulsion Correction
Description: This plugin cannot solve your contraction issues, but it can
    hide them by fixing them on the fly.
*/
```

Save the `init.php` file and then visit the Plugins page in your Dashboard. The Example: Contraction Compulsion Correction plugin appears there, as shown in Figure 5-3.

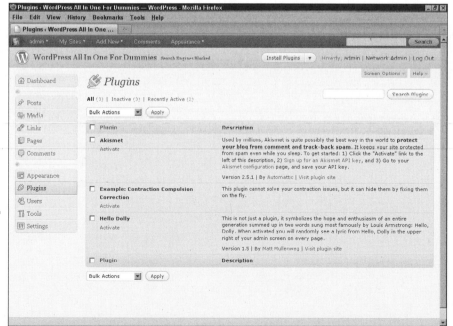

Figure 5-3: The Plugins page showing your new plugin in the list.

Using curly brackets (complex syntax)

You see curly brackets within code. Curly brackets (referred to as *complex syntax in the PHP Manual:* `http://www.php.net/manual/en/language.types.string.php`) serve to open and then close the function definition, or expression. For example, the code samples in the preceding steps name the function `function my_filter_the_content ($content)`. An open curly bracket, indicating the start of the function expression, immediately follows that line. Immediately after the two lines, `$content="Test content replacement.";` and `return $content`, that are the expression for the function, is the closing curly bracket that indicates the end of the function expression. Without these curly brackets, your code will not work correctly. Check out the entire PHP manual online at `http://php.net/manual` to brush up on correct PHP code syntax, including when you need to use single quotation versus double quotation marks and the importance of the semi colon (`;`).

Testing the filter

The filter we use here is the `the_content` filter. To make sure that this has the desired effect, we use the filter to replace all the content in your blog posts and pages with a simple message. If the filter works as expected, you can expand it to hide the contractions that you published in your posts (or pages).

The `the_content` filter is just one of hundreds of available filters in WordPress. You can find information about filters in the WordPress.org Codex (`http://codex.wordpress.org/Plugin_API/Filter_Reference`).

Follow these steps to include the `the_content` filter in your plugin, which will replace all the content on your Web site (posts and pages) with a single phrase. (We change this in the following section to filter the contractions out of your published content.)

1. **Connect to your Web server via FTP.**

2. **Browse to this directory /wp-content/plugins/-contraction-compulsion-correction.**

3. **Open the init.php file in your text editor.**

4. **Type the following lines of code at the end of the file (after the plugin header):**

```
function my_filter_the_content($content) {
```

```
$content = "Test content replacement.";
return $content;
}
add_filter('the_content','my_filter_the_content');
```

5. **Save your `init.php` file and upload it to the `/wp-content/ plugins/-contraction-compulsion-correction` folder.**

The last line of code in Step 4 tells WordPress to apply the filter after the plugin is activated. The earlier lines of code define the function (`function my_filter_the_content ($content)`) with a variable ($content), define the $content variable (`$content = "Test content replacement.";`), and tell WordPress to return $content ($content was defined in the second line) within the body of your published posts and pages. (Check out the nearby "Using curly brackets (complex syntax)" sidebar about using correct PHP syntax.)

With the `the_content` filter in place in your plugin, visit the Plugins page in your Dashboard and activate the Example: Contraction Compulsion Correction plugin. After activation, view any post or page on your Web site. The result: *Test content replacement* replaces the content of that entry. Your new plugin is filtering content on your Web site (see Figure 5-4). In the next section, we apply the real filter that fulfills the purpose of the plugin we're creating.

**Book VII
Chapter 5**

Creating Simple
WordPress Plugins
from Scratch

Figure 5-4:
Your plugin
filters
content on
your Web
site.

Replacing contractions in your content

To replace all the contractions within your content with the full phrases or words, the following steps take you through the process of changing the code in the init.php plugin file:

1. **Connect to your Web server via FTP.**

2. **Browse to the /wp-content/plugins/-contraction-compulsion-correction directory.**

3. **Open the init.php file in your text editor.**

4. **Remove the following lines of code:**

   ```
   function my_filter_the_content($content) {
   $content = "Test content replacement.";
   return $content;
   }
   add_filter('the_content','my_filter_the_content');
   ```

5. **Type the following lines of code at the end of the file (after the plugin header):**

   ```
   function my_filter_the_content($content) {
   $replacements = array(
   "isn't" => "is not",
   "we'll" => "we will",
   "you'll" => "you will",
   "can't" => "cannot",
   );
   foreach($replacements as $search => $replace) {
   $search = str_replace("'","&#8217;",$search);
   $content = str_replace(ucfirst($search),ucfirst($replace),$content);
   $content = str_ireplace($search,$replace,$content);
   }
   return $content;
   }
   add_filter('the_content','my_filter_the_content');
   ```

6. **Save your init.php file and upload it to the /wp-content/ plugins/-contraction-compulsion-correction folder.**

To do the replacement, an array holds the text to search for and to use as the replacement. The array defines the words you're replacing within your content and loops to make all the replacements. In our example, *isn't* is replaced with *is not, we'll* is replaced with *will not*, and so on. Of course, this example only covers a small subset of the contractions. You will have to modify the example to fit your specific contraction compulsions.

The observant developer will notice that there is much more than just a simple replacement going on in the loop. We also use the `str_replace` function, which replaces all occurrences of the search string with the replacement string.

The first replacement (`$search = str_replace("'","&#8217;",$search);`) is needed because WordPress changes single quotes to a fancy version represented by `"&#8217;"`. This searches for the instances of the single quote, and then `$content = str_replace("'","&#8217;",$content);` replaces the single quote in the content. This allows the replacements array to have normal-looking searches with regular single quotes.

The third search and replace statement (`$content = str_replace(ucfirst($search),ucfirst($replace),$content);`) replaces content matches that have an uppercase first letter with a replacement that also has an uppercase first letter.

The last search and replace statement: (`$content = str_ireplace($search,$replace,$content);`) does a non–case-sensitive search to replace all remaining matches with the lowercase version of the replacement.

To test your contraction replacement plugin, follow these steps:

1. **Log in to your Dashboard.**

2. **Visit the Add New Post page (Posts⇨Add New).**

   The Add New Post page loads in your Dashboard where you can write and publish a new post (see Book IV, Chapter 1).

3. **Type a title for your post in the Title text field.**

4. **Type this line of text in the post editor:** *Isn't it grand that we'll soon be sailing on the ocean blue? You'll see. We'll have a great time. I can't wait.*

   Notice the contractions *Isn't, we'll, You'll, We'll* and *can't*. Figure 5-5 shows our Add New Post page with this phrase added.

5. **Publish your post by clicking the Publish button.**

   Figure 5-6 displays the post on our Web site with the contractions replaced with the appropriate words, as defined in our plugin function.

Figure 5-5:
The Add
New Post
page
with the
contractions
in place.

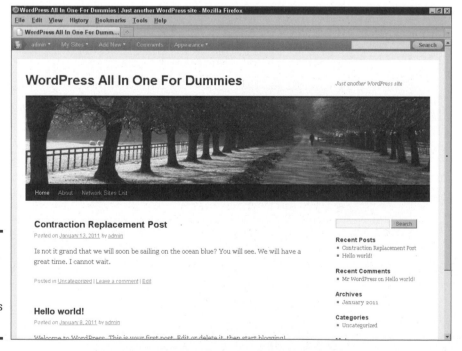

Figure 5-6:
The
published
posts with
contractions
replaced.

Creating Shortcodes

You can use the `the_content` filter to add new sections of content to posts and pages. For example, you can add a form for subscribing to new posts. However, this type of all-or-nothing method of adding content often adds content where it isn't wanted. Using a shortcode is often a much better solution because it offers flexibility and ease of use.

Shortcodes, introduced in WordPress 2.5, can be employed for a wide variety of uses. WordPress includes a shortcode, `[gallery]`, which you can add to any post to display a gallery of images assigned to that post in place of the shortcode. (See Book IV, Chapter 4 on adding photo galleries to you posts.) Many plugins (such as a forum or contact form plugin) use shortcodes to allow the plugin users to designate specific pages for the plugin front end to appear. They can surround sections of content, allowing the code that powers the shortcode to modify the content.

The main features of a shortcode include

✦ A shortcode can stand by itself. The `[gallery]` shortcode (built into WordPress) is a good example of this; simply adding `[gallery]` to the content of a page or post is all that is needed to allow the shortcode to insert a gallery of uploaded images and display them within the body of a post or page.

✦ A shortcode can support arguments that pass specific information to the code that powers the shortcode. For example, `[gallery width="400" caption="My Venice Vacation"]`.

✦ Shortcodes can be used around a section of content the way HTML tags can. This allows for the code that powers the shortcode to modify specific sections of content, such as `[code lang="php"]<?php the_title(); ?>[/code]`. The "code" shortcode doesn't exist by default in WordPress. We build it in the upcoming "Building a simple shortcode" section.

Setting up the plugin structure

This plugin, Example: My Shortcodes, will reside in a directory called `/example-my-shortcodes` with a main plugin file named `init.php`.

The reason for the relatively generic name is that we will use this plugin to create multiple shortcodes. To get started, the following plugin header is added to the `init.php` file. (Follow the same steps you took earlier in this chapter to create the directory and main plugin file.)

```php
<?php
/*
Plugin Name: Example: My Shortcodes
Description: This plugin provides the digg and code shortcodes.
*/
```

Building a simple shortcode

In many ways, shortcodes are coded like filters (similar to the way we did earlier in this chapter) except that with shortcodes, the content to be filtered is optional. For this shortcode, we won't worry about content filtering or shortcode attributes. This shortcode is about familiarizing you with the shortcode concept.

The shortcode we create in this section is named *digg*. Adding this shortcode to a post displays a Digg This Post link that allows that post to be submitted to digg.com, a site for keeping track of interesting links.

Creating a shortcode requires two things:

✦ **Shortcode function:** A function that will handle the creation of the shortcode and a call to the add_shortcode function.

✦ **Shortcode arguments:** The add_shortcode function accepts two arguments: the name of the shortcode and the function used by the shortcode.

To get started with your shortcode, add the following code to the end of the Example: My Shortcodes plugin's init.php file.

```
function my_digg_shortcode() {
return "<p><a href='http://digg.com/submit?url=".urlencode(get_
    permalink())."&bodytext=".urlencode(get_the_title())."'>Digg This
    Post</a></p>";
}
add_shortcode('digg','my_digg_shortcode');
```

 HTML links have to follow some rules because only certain characters are permitted. The urlencode function used for both get_permalink and get_the_title ensures that the information added to the link results in a valid link being created.

After the changes are saved, make sure that the plugin is active and then add a post that has [digg] in the content. If everything works properly, you should see a Digg This Post link in place of the shortcode when viewing the post on your Web site (see Figure 5-7).

Shortcodes can be displayed depending on specific criteria. It's easy to modify the [digg] shortcode to display the Digg This Post link if an individual post is being viewed rather than a listing, such as the home page or a category archive. The following code shows an updated my_digg_shortcode function that uses the `is_single` template tag function to return an empty string if an individual post is not being viewed:

```
function my_digg_shortcode() {
if(!is_single()) return '';

return "<p><a href='http://digg.com/submit?url=".urlencode(get_
    permalink())."&bodytext=".urlencode(get_the_title())."'>Digg This
    Post</a></p>";
}
add_shortcode('digg','my_digg_shortcode');
```

Notice the exclamation point (`!`) in front of the `is_single` function call. In PHP language, the exclamation point means *not*. Therefore, the `if` statement translates to "if the current view is not a single post, return an empty string." Because the `if` statement fails when the view is a single post, the original functionality of returning the Digg This Post link is used. The function fires only when a visitor is viewing a single, individual post page, not when they are viewing any other type of page (such as a static page or a category archive page).

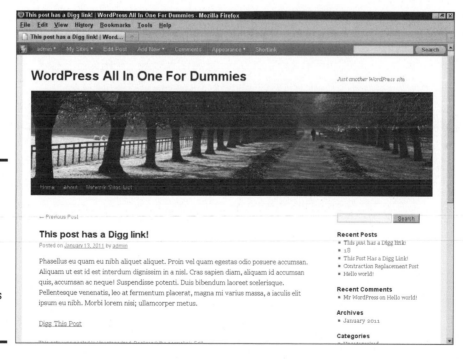

Figure 5-7:
Digg This
Post link
added to
a post,
using the
Example:
My
Shortcodes
[digg]
shortcode.

Book VII
Chapter 5

Creating Simple
WordPress Plugins
from Scratch

Using shortcode attributes

By using attributes, the shortcode output can be customized to meet specific needs without having to rewrite an existing shortcode or create a new one.

The [digg] shortcode, from thepreceding section, is a good example of how an attribute can be used to customize the shortcode output. Notice that the generated digg.com link includes bodytext=. The text added after bodytext= is the default description text for the submitted link, which is the text that displays on your site. The shortcode sends the title of the post (get_the_title). Using an attribute, this behavior can be made default while allowing the user to supply a customized description.

To add the attribute support, the my_digg_shortcode function needs to be updated again. Update the function to match the following:

```
function my_digg_shortcode($attributes=array()) {
if(!is_single()) return '';

$attributes=shortcode_atts(
array('description'=>get_the_title()),
$attributes
);
extract($attributes);

return "<p><a href='http://digg.com/submit?url=".urlencode(get_
    permalink())."&bodytext=".urlencode($description)."'>Digg This
    Post</a></p>";
}
add_shortcode('digg','my_digg_shortcode');
```

We should discuss a few changes. The first change is the addition of the $attributes argument to the my_digg_shortcode function declaration. Without this argument, the shortcode function is unable to receive any of the attributes set on the shortcode. The =array() ensures that the $attributes variable is set to an empty array if the shortcode doesn't have any attributes set.

The call to the shortcode_atts function passes in an array of default attribute values and merges these defaults with the attributes used in the actual shortcode. It then stores this resulting array back to the $attributes variable. Without this section, the attributes will not have a default value. It's a good idea to set the defaults, even if the default is an empty string.

The extract function takes the array of attributes and breaks the information into individual plugins. In this example, it creates the $description variable because that is the used attribute. If a shortcode uses title and id attributes, then using extract will create $title and $id variables.

Finally, because the $description variable holds the description that should be used, the get_the_title function call in the returned string is replaced with the $description variable.

Update your shortcode in the body of your test post (see Figure 5-8) to use this new description attribute. For example:

```
[digg description="Shortcodes are awesome!"]
```

After saving the post changes, view the updated post, hover on the Digg This Post link, and you should see a link with the following format:

```
http://digg.com/submit?url=http://domain.com/testing-short
codes/&bodytext=Shortcodes+are+awesome!
```

Adding content to shortcodes

The final piece of the shortcodes puzzle is content. By wrapping a shortcode around a section of content, the shortcode function can modify the content in creative ways.

Going back to the earlier example given for using content with shortcodes, the example we present in this section creates a new shortcode called code. The purpose of this shortcode is to allow designated sections of content to be formatted as code.

To get the new code shortcode running, add the following to the bottom of your plugin init.php file.

**Book VII
Chapter 5**

**Creating Simple
WordPress Plugins
from Scratch**

```php
function my_code_shortcode($attributes=array(),$content='') {
if(empty($content)) return '';

$attributes=shortcode_atts(
array('lang'=>''),
$attributes
);
extract($attributes);

$content=str_replace("</p>\n<p>","\n\n",$content);
$content=str_replace('<p>','',$content);
$content=str_replace('</p>','',$content);
$content=str_replace('<br />','',$content);

$style='white-space:pre;overflow:auto;';
$style.='font:"Courier New",Courier,Fixed;';

if('php'==$lang) {
$style.='background-color:#8BD2FF;color:#FFF;';
}
else if('css'==$lang) {
$style.='background-color:#DFE0B0;color:#333;';
}
else {
$style.='background-color:#EEE;color:#000;';
}

return "<pre class='$lang' style='$style'>$content</pre>";
}
add_shortcode('code','my_code_shortcode');
```

Before digging into how everything works, save the changes to the plugin and add the following shortcodes to a post:

```
[code]This is a basic code test[/code]

[code lang="php"]<?php echo "This is PHP code."; ?>[/code]

[code lang="css"]p { color:#FFF; }[/code]
```

Figure 5-8 shows that these shortcodes produce some fixed-space boxes with different background colors and styling to contain the code.

Figure 5-8: Code added to a post, using the code shortcode.

Now that it's clear what the shortcode is doing, we can tear apart the function to find out how it works. The first line for the [code] shortcode looks like this:

```
function my_code_shortcode($attributes=array(),$content='') {
```

Just as it was important to add the $attributes variable to the function declaration to get access to the shortcode attributes, adding the $content variable is needed to access the content of the shortcode. The next line in our code shortcode looks like this:

```
if(empty($content)) return '';
```

This line states that if the $content variable is empty, the function returns an empty string because going any further with empty content is unnecessary. The next five lines of the code are

```
$attributes=shortcode_atts(
array('lang'=>''),
$attributes
);
extract($attributes);
```

As with the [digg] shortcode, from the previous section, the shortcode_atts function is used to establish some base defaults. By default, the lang attribute is an empty string. The extract function is then used to fill out the $lang variable. The next four lines contain the str_replace function, which we discuss in the "Replacing contractions in your content" section, earlier in this chapter:

```
$content=str_replace("</p>\n<p>","\n\n",$content);
$content=str_replace('<p>','',$content);
$content=str_replace('</p>','',$content);
$content=str_replace('<br />','',$content);
```

This set of str_replace function calls allows for proper handling of multi-line content by the [code] shortcode. The problem is that WordPress always tries to add the <p> (paragraph) and
 (line break) HTML markup tags even when it shouldn't. The str_replace calls replace the separation of two <p> tag sections with two new lines (a new line is represented by the \n code) and then remove all the remaining <p> and <br /> tags inserted by WordPress. This allows the content to display properly when it is wrapped in a <pre> (preformat for code) tag.

The next two lines of the shortcode deal with CSS styling:

```
$style='white-space:pre;overflow:auto;';
$style.='font:"Courier New",Courier,Fixed;';
```

The $style variable stores the basic CSS styling for the [code] shortcode output, and the next few lines add styles for specific types of code:

```
if('php'==$lang) {
$style.='background-color:#8BD2FF;color:#FFF;';
}
else if('css'==$lang) {
$style.='background-color:#DFE0B0;color:#333;';
}
else {
$style.='background-color:#EEEEEE;color:#000;';
}
```

**Book VII
Chapter 5**

Creating Simple
WordPress Plugins
from Scratch

This set of conditional code determines the background and text color based on the lang attribute used in the shortcode — php receives a blue background with white text, css receives a khaki background with dark text, and the default is a gray background with black text.

The last line of the function returns the shortcode output by wrapping the content in a <pre> HTML markup tag. The <pre> tag uses the generated style and adds the $lang as a class. The addition of the class allows for more customization through a stylesheet:

```
return "<pre class='$lang' style='$style'>$content</pre>";
```

While not everyone needs to display code on their site, this example gives you a large set of options when creating new shortcodes. Through creative use of attributes, content handling, and WordPress's built-in functions, you can create very powerful tools that make managing your site much easier.

Adding Widgets

Widgets are individual features you can add to theme sidebars. Widgets can add a simple site search, display a calendar, list the most recent posts, and show RSS feed updates. These features just scratch the surface of what widgets offer and what widgets are capable of.

WordPress 2.8 introduced a new widget API that makes widget creation very easy. If you tried creating widgets in the past and gave up because of the difficulty of making them work properly, it's time to try widget creation again.

Coding a simple widget

The format for setting up filters and shortcodes are very similar. Add a function that performs a specific task and then use either `add_filter` or `add_shortcode` to register the function as a filter or shortcode.

Widgets are a bit different. Instead of creating one function and registering it, widgets are a collection of functions packaged in a container called a *class*. The class is registered as a widget using the `register_widget` function.

Like shortcodes, multiple plugins can be housed in a single plugin file. However, because the code for some of these widgets gets lengthy, each widget will be its own plugin.

The widget plugin we define in the following steps creates a widget that you can use on the Widgets page of your Dashboard (Appearance➪Widgets) to show a widget in your sidebar that displays "You are logged in as *Name*" or "Welcome Guest" depending on whether you are logged in.

This plugin, Example: My User Widget, creates a widget called My User Widget. As you did in the previous examples, create a plugin directory in the `/wp-content/plugins` directory by adding a new folder called `/example-my-user-widget` and add an empty `init.php` file that will serve as your main plugin PHP file and then follow these steps to create the sample plugin:

1. **Open this file in your text editor: `init.php`.**

2. **Create the plugin header by adding this code to the top of the `init.php` file:**

```
<?php
/*
Plugin Name: Example: My User Widget
Description: This plugin provides a simple widget that shows the name of
    the logged in user
*/
```

3. **Press the Enter key and type the next line of code:**

```
class My_User_Widget extends WP_Widget {
```

This creates a new class called `My_User_Widget`. This new `My_User_Widget` class is based off (and extends) the structure of the existing `WP_Widget` class.

A class is a way of grouping a set of functions and a set of data into a logical group. In this case, everything that is in the `My_User_Widget` class is specific to just the My User Widget widget. Making modifications to this class will not affect any other widgets on your site.

The `WP_Widget` class is the central feature of WordPress's Widget API. This class provides the structure and most of the code that powers widgets. When the `My_User_Widget` class extends the `WP_Widget` class, the `My_User_Widget` class automatically gains all the features of the `WP_Widget` class. This means that only the code that needs to be customized for the specific widget needs to be defined because the `WP_Widget` class handles everything else.

4. **Press Enter and type the following lines of code in the `init.php` file:**

```
function My_User_Widget() {
parent::WP_Widget(false,'My User Widget');
}
```

The `My_User_Widget` function has the same name as the `My_User_Widget` class. A PHP class function that has the same name as the class is a *constructor*. This function is called automatically when the class code is run (for widgets, WordPress automatically runs the registered widget code behind the scenes). Constructors run necessary initialization code so that the class behaves properly.

The line of code the `My_User_Widget` function runs hands control to the `WP_Widget` class constructor. By calling `parent::WP_Widget`, the `My_User_Widget` class can tell WordPress about the new widget. In this instance, the `My_User_Widget` says that the default base ID should be used (this is the `false` argument and defaults to the lowercase version of the class name, `my_user_widget`, in this case) and that the widget's name is My User Widget.

5. **Press Enter and type the following line of code in the `init.php` file:**

```
function widget($args) {
```

The `widget` function displays the widget content. This function accepts two parameters: `$args` and `$instance`. For this example, only `$args` is needed. We discuss `$instance` when we create the next widget.

6. **Press Enter and type the following lines of code in the `init.php` file:**

```
$user=wp_get_current_user();
if(!isset($user->user_nicename)) {
$message='Welcome Guest';
}
else {
$message="You are logged in as {$user->user_nicename}";
}
```

This code finds out information about the current user and sets a message to display that's dependent on whether the user is logged in. This is determined by checking the `$user` variable. If the `$user->user_nicename` variable is not set, then the user isn't logged in.

7. **Press Enter and type the following lines of code in the `init.php` file:**

```
extract($args);
echo $before_widget;
echo "<p>$message</p>";
echo $after_widget;
}
}
```

The `$args` variable contains a number of important details about how the sidebar wants widgets to be formatted. It's passed into the "extract" function to pull out the settings into stand-alone variables. The four main variables used are `$before_widget`, `$after_widget`, `$before_title`, and `$after_title`. Because this widget does not have a title, the title variables are not used. The `$before_widget` variable should always be echoed out before any widget content, and the `$after_widget` variable should always be echoed out after the widget content.

8. **Press Enter and type the following lines of code in the `init.php` file:**

```
function register_my_user_widget() {
register_widget('My_User_Widget');
}
add_action('widgets_init','register_my_user_widget');
```

To register a widget with WordPress (so WordPress recognizes it as a widget), use the `register_widget` function and pass it the name of the `widget` class.

Although calling the `register_widget` immediately after the class definition would be nice, it isn't that simple. The code of the widget that includes the different functions must run before the widget can be registered. When code needs to run at specific times, the code is placed in a function and the `add_action` function is used to have WordPress run the function at a specific time.

These specific points in time are *actions*. For widget registration, we want to use the `widget_init` action. This action happens after WordPress finishes setting up the code necessary to handle widget registrations, while being early enough for the widget to be registered in time.

With this final piece in place, the widget is ready for use. When you are done, the entire code block looks like this:

```php
<?php
/*
Plugin Name: Example: My User Widget
Description: This plugin provides a simple widget that shows the name of
    the logged in user
*/
class My_User_Widget extends WP_Widget {
function My_User_Widget() {
parent::WP_Widget(false,'My User Widget');
}
function widget($args) {
$user=wp_get_current_user();
if(!isset($user->user_nicename)) {
$message='Welcome Guest';
}
else {
$message="You are logged in as {$user->user_nicename}";
}
extract($args);
echo $before_widget;
echo "<p>$message</p>";
echo $after_widget;
}
}
function register_my_user_widget() {
register_widget('My_User_Widget');
}
add_action('widgets_init','register_my_user_widget');
```

Before WordPress 2.8, widget code had to manage everything by itself. To allow a widget to be used more than once, complex and bug-prone code needed to be produced and maintained. Fortunately, the `WP_Widget` class handles this seamlessly. Widget developers no longer need to worry about single-use or multi-use widgets because all widgets coded to use the `WP_Widget` class automatically become multi-use widgets.

With this final piece in place, the widget is ready for use. Open the Widgets page in your Dashboard (Appearance➪Widgets); you see a new widget called My User Widget.

Adding an options editor to a widget

Although some widgets work properly without any type of customization, most widgets need at least the ability for the user to supply a title for the widget. Thanks to the `WP_Widget` class, adding options to a widget is easy.

The My User Widget example made use of the `widget` function to display the widget's content. This addition to the widget code uses two additional functions to handle the widget options. The `form` function displays the HTML form inputs that allow the user to configure the widgets options. The `update` function allows the widget code to process the submitted data to ensure that only valid input is saved.

In this example, you create a basic clone of WordPress's Text widget. Although a bit simple, this will allow you to focus on the process of using widget options without getting caught up in the details of a complex widget concept.

Time to start coding, so set up the plugin environment by creating a new directory in your `/wp-content/plugins` called `/example-my-text-widget` and include a blank `init.php` file as your main plugin PHP file. The plugin you're creating in this section is Example: My Text Widget, which creates a widget called My Text Widget.

Follow these steps to create the `init.php` file for your Example: My Text Widget plugin:

1. **Open the `init.php` file in your text editor.**

2. **Create the plugin header by adding this code to the top of the `init.php` file:**

```
<?php
/*
Plugin Name: Example: My Text Widget
Description: This plugin provides a basic Text Widget clone complete with
    widget options
*/
```

3. **Press Enter and type the following line of code in the `init.php` file:**

```
class My_Text_Widget extends WP_Widget {
```

As with the My User Widget in thepreceding section, this widget is created by extending WordPress' `WP_Widget` class. This new widget's class is `My_Text_Widget`.

4. **Press Enter and type the following lines of code in the `init.php` file:**

```
function My_Text_Widget() {
$widget_ops=array('description'=>'Simple Text Widget clone');
$control_ops=array('width'=>400);
parent::WP_Widget(false,'My Text Widget',$widget_ops,$control_ops);
}
```

The constructor for this plugin is a bit different this time. The `parent::WP_Widget` function is still called to set up the widget, but two more arguments are given: `$widget_ops` and `$control_ops`. These two arguments allow a variety of widget options to be set. The `$widget_ops` argument can set two options: `description` and `classname`. The description shows under the name of the widget in the widgets listing. The `classname` option sets what class the rendered widget uses.

5. **Press Enter and type the following line of code in the init.php file:**

```
function form($instance) {
```

The form class function displays an HTML form that allows the user to set the options used by the widget. The $instance variable is an array containing the current widget options. When the widget is new, this $instance variable is an empty array.

6. **Press Enter and type the following line of code in the init.php file:**

```
$instance=wp_parse_args($instance,array('title'=>'','text'=>''));
```

Remember how the shortcode plugins used the shortcode_atts function to merge default options with ones from the shortcode? The wp_parse_args in this example performs the same task by merging the existing $instance options with default option values.

7. **Press Enter and type the following line of code in the init.php file:**

```
extract($instance);
```

The extract function is used to pull the title and text options in the $instance variable into the standalone variables $title and $text.

8. **Press Enter and type ?>.**

By using the close PHP tag, ?>, we can more easily display a large amount of HTML without having to constantly echo out each line.

9. **Press Enter and type the following lines of code in the init.php file:**

```
<p>
<label for="<?php echo $this->get_field_id('title'); ?>">
<?php _e('Title:'); ?>
<input
  class="widefat"
  type="text"
  id="<?php echo $this->get_field_id('title'); ?>"
  name="<?php echo $this->get_field_name('title'); ?>"
  value="<?php echo esc_attr($title); ?>"
/>
</label>
</p>
```

The block of HTML displays the title input.

Notice the $this->get_field_id and $this->get_field_name function calls. These functions are provided by the WP_Widget class and produce the needed id and name values specific to this widget instance. To use these functions, simply pass in the name of the option that is used, title in this case.

The _e('Title:'); section simply prints out Title:. The reason it is wrapped in a call to the _e function is that the _e function allows the text to be translated into other languages.

The value attribute of the input tag sets what the default value of the field is. Because we want this to be populated with the current title, the

$title variable is echoed in this attribute. Before echoing, the $title variable is passed through the esc_attr function, which allows the text to be properly formatted for use as an attribute value. If the esc_attr isn't used, some values in the title, such as a double-quote, could break the HTML.

10. **Press Enter and type the following lines of code in the `init.php` file:**

```
<textarea
  class="widefat"
  rows="16"
  id="<?php echo $this->get_field_id('text'); ?>"
  name="<?php echo $this->get_field_name('text'); ?>"
>
<?php echo esc_attr($text); ?>
</textarea>
```

This block of HTML displays the textarea input that allows the user to input the text that she wants to display. The only difference between this input and the previous one is that the textarea and text inputs have a different format and that this input does not have a description.

11. **Press Enter and type** <?php.

The form HTML is complete, so the open PHP tag, "<?php", is used to switch back to PHP code.

12. **Press Enter and type** }.

This closes the form function.

13. **Press Enter and type the following line of code in the `init.php` file:**

```
function update($new_instance,$old_instance) {
```

The update class function processes the submitted form data. The $new_instance argument provides the data submitted by the form. The $old_instance argument provides the widget's old options.

14. **Press Enter and type the following line of code in the `init.php` file:**

```
$instance=array();
```

First, a new empty array variable, $instance, is created. This variable will store the final options values.

15. **Press Enter and type the following lines of code in the `init.php` file:**

```
$instance['title']=strip_tags($new_instance['title']);
$instance['text']=$new_instance['text'];
```

Store the title and text options from the $new_instance variable into the $instance variable. The title option is run through the strip_tags function so that no HTML tags are stored in the title option.

16. **Press Enter and type the following line of code in the `init.php` file:**

```
return $instance;
```

The "update" function works like a filter function. The data is passed in, it can be manipulated as desired, and then the final value is returned.

After seeing how this function works, you might wonder why creating the $instance variable was needed. While using $new_instance directly would be more simple, it also could produce unexpected results. It is possible for unexpected data to come through as part of the $new_instance variable. By creating the $instance variable and only assigning known options to it, you can be assured that you know exactly what data is stored for the widget and that your code has had a chance to clean it up.

17. Press Enter and type }.

Close the "update" function.

18. Press Enter and type the following line of code in the init.php file:

```
function widget($args,$instance) {
```

The widget class function is the same as before, but it now has the $instance argument. The $instance argument stores the options set for the widget.

19. Press Enter and type the following lines of code in the init.php file:

```
extract($args);
extract($instance);
```

Use the extract function on both $args and $instance to populate easy-to-use variables for each.

20. Press Enter and type the following line of code in the init.php file:

```
$title=apply_filters('widget_title',$title,$instance,$this->id_base);
```

Remember that in a previous section when we assembled The Example: Contraction Compulsion Correction plugin, we added the add_filter function to add a function to be used as a filter. The apply_filters in this example function is how those filter functions are used. This line of code translates to *Store the result of the* widget_title *filters in the* $title *variable.* Each filter is passed the $title, $instance and $this->id_base variables. Every widget that has a title should have this line of code so that filters have a chance to filter all widget titles.

21. Press Enter and type the following lines of code in the init.php file:

```
echo $before_widget;
if(!empty($title)) echo $before_title . $title . $after_title;
echo $text;
echo $after_widget;
```

Finally, after getting everything set, we are ready to display the widget. As with the previous widget, the $before_widget variable is echoed before the rest of the widget content and the $after_widget variable is echoed after all the other widget content. Because this widget supports a title, there is now the addition of the $before_title and $after_title variables that, like the $before_widget and $after_widget variables, come from the $args argument passed to the function. The if statement

ensures that the title displays only if the title isn't empty (remember, !
means "not").

22. Press Enter and type }.

This closes the widget function class.

23. Press Enter and type }.

This closes the `My_Text_Widget` class.

24. Press Enter and type the following lines of code in the `init.php` file:

```
function register_my_text_widget() {
register_widget('My_Text_Widget');
}
add_action('widgets_init','register_my_text_widget');
```

Register the widget. Note how the `My_Text_Widget` argument of the
`register_widget` function matches the name of this widget's class.

When you are finished with thepreceding steps, the entire block of code
looks like this when all put together in your `init.php` file:

```
<?php
/*
Plugin Name: Example: My Text Widget
Description: This plugin provides a basic Text Widget clone complete with
    widget options
*/

class My_Text_Widget extends WP_Widget {

function My_Text_Widget() {
$widget_ops=array('description'=>'Simple Text Widget clone');
$control_ops=array('width'=>400);
parent::WP_Widget(false,'My Text Widget',$widget_ops,$control_ops);
}

function form($instance) {

$instance=wp_parse_args($instance,array('title'=>'','text'=>''));

extract($instance);

?>

<p>
<label for="<?php echo $this->get_field_id('title'); ?>">
<?php _e('Title:'); ?>
<input
  class="widefat"
  type="text"
  id="<?php echo $this->get_field_id('title'); ?>"
```

```
      name="<?php echo $this->get_field_name('title'); ?>"
      value="<?php echo esc_attr($title); ?>"
  />
  </label>
  </p>

  <textarea
    class="widefat"
    rows="16"
    id="<?php echo $this->get_field_id('text'); ?>"
    name="<?php echo $this->get_field_name('text'); ?>"
  >
  <?php echo esc_attr($text); ?>
  </textarea>

  <?php

  }

  function update($new_instance,$old_instance) {

  $instance=array();

  $instance['title']=strip_tags($new_instance['title']);
  $instance['text']=$new_instance['text'];

  return $instance;

  }

  function widget($args,$instance) {

  extract($args);
  extract($instance);

  $title=apply_filters('widget_title',$title,$instance,$this->id_base);

  echo $before_widget;
  if(!empty($title)) echo $before_title . $title . $after_title;
  echo $text;
  echo $after_widget;

  }
  }

  function register_my_text_widget() {
  register_widget('My_Text_Widget');
  }
  add_action('widgets_init','register_my_text_widget');
```

With this final piece in place, the widget is ready for use. Open the Widgets page in your Dashboard (Appearance➪Widgets); you see a new widget ready for you to use called My Text Widget that, when expanded, has a Title field and text box for the user to configure and add content to, as shown in Figure 5-9.

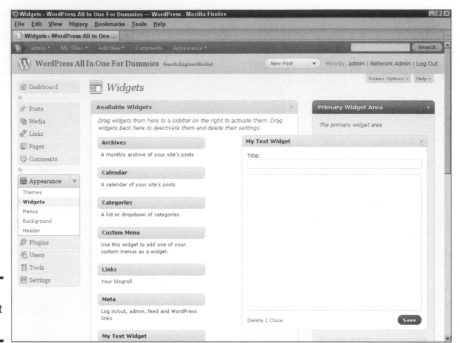

Figure 5-9:
The My Text
Widget.

Building a Settings Page

Many plugins offer a settings page that allows the user to customize plugin options. The options offered by a settings page varies from a few check boxes, drop downs, or text inputs to multiple advanced editors that allow the user to build data sets, set up forums, or do advanced content management. Although this section focuses on building a simple settings page, you can expand the concept to fill any type of need that your plugin has.

When reduced to a bare minimum, a basic settings page consists of code that displays the page, stores the settings, and adds the page to the WordPress admin menu. The plugin created in this section will give you a solid foundation that you can use to build your own plugin settings pages.

Setting up the plugin structure

The plugin you create in this section is Example: Settings Page. To get started with this plugin, create a new plugins directory named /example-settings-page. All the files for this plugin go in this new directory. That's right, *files*. We're going to change up the structure a little bit in this plugin by adding multiple plugin files to the plugin directory.

As plugins get larger, having everything in one file quickly becomes hard to manage. A good practice is to separate different functionality into separate files. Similar to the way the init.php file is named because it *initializes* the plugin, the other files used by the plugin should be named so the purpose of each file is easy to discern when looking at the filenames.

This new plugin will have the following files, so go ahead and create five blank files and name them with the filenames given here:

✦ **init.php:** Contains the plugin header and will load the other needed plugin files

✦ **settings-page.php:** Holds the settings page code

✦ **default-settings.php:** Sets the default values used for the settings

✦ **msp-form-class.php:** Provides a class that makes adding form inputs easy

✦ **settings-functions.php:** Provides functions to load and save the settings

By dividing the plugin code into logical groups, each of which have their own file, the code becomes much easier to maintain. With this type of setup, as new features are added to the plugin, they can easily be isolated to their own files.

All the files must be created before the plugin will function. To start, add the following code to your plugin's init.php file:

```php
<?php
/*
Plugin Name: Example: Settings Page
Description: This plugin is offers a solid starting point for building
    settings pages
*/

require_once(dirname(__FILE__).'/default-settings.php');
require_once(dirname(__FILE__).'/msp-form-class.php');
require_once(dirname(__FILE__).'/settings-functions.php');
require_once(dirname(__FILE__).'/settings-page.php');
```

The require_once function loads another PHP file. If the file isn't found, a fatal error occurs and the plugin doesn't function. Therefore, trying to activate the plugin at this point causes the plugin to fail. This is good because it prevents the plugin from activating when needed files are missing, which can happen if an incomplete upload of the plugin files occurs.

There are four primary functions to load other PHP code: include, include_once, require, and require_once. The include functions will not cause a fatal error if there is a problem loading the requested file, while the require functions will. The functions that add _once will not load the file if the file has been loaded already. This helps prevent accidentally loading a file multiple times, which can break the code or cause unexpected behavior.

Directly underneath the `require_once` functions, add the following line:

```
dirname(__FILE__).'/default-settings.php'
```

This section of code finds the full path to the `default-settings.php` file. We recommend loading the file by referring to its full path because it avoids issues with some server setups.

That's all the `init.php` file needs for this plugin. You can now save and upload the file to your plugin directory at `/wp-content/plugins/example-settings-page`. When you add new features to the plugin, add new files to hold these features and use a `require_once` call to load each one.

Adding a new Admin menu entry

Add the following lines of code to the `settings-page.php` file that you created at the beginning of this section:

```php
<?php

function msp_add_admin_menu() {
add_options_page(
   'Example Settings Page',
   'Example Settings',
   'manage_options',
   'msp-example-settings-page',
   'msp_display_settings_page'
);
if(isset($_POST['msp_save'])) {
   add_action("admin_head-$page",'msp_save_settings_handler');
}
}
add_action('admin_menu','msp_add_admin_menu');
```

This code adds a new link in the Dashboard⇨Settings menu titled Example Setting. The `add_options_page` function is the key to adding this new menu. The following list describes what each argument in this function does.

- ✦ **Example Settings Page:** The first argument sets the title of the page. The browser, not the settings page, displays this title.

- ✦ **Example Settings:** The second argument is the name of the menu. The space is limited, so try to keep the name short.

- ✦ **manage_options:** The third argument is the capability that the user must have in order to see and access the menu. For settings pages, the `manage_options` capability is typically the best choice as only administrators have this capability by default. `edit_others_posts` can be used to allow administrators and editors, whereas, `edit_published_posts` can be used for administrators, editors, and authors.

✦ **msp-example-settings-page:** The fourth argument is a name that WordPress uses internally to navigate to the page. Make sure that this is a unique name or you can run into problems with other plugins. The msp at the front of the name stands for *My Settings Page*. Consistently using a prefix in this manner helps prevent duplicate name issues.

✦ **msp_display_settings_page:** The fifth argument is the name of the function that is called when the page is viewed. As with the fourth argument, make sure that this is unique to your plugin. Notice the msp prefix is used here, too.

Just as the register_widget function cannot be called when a plugin first loads, the add_options_page function also must wait until WordPress is ready before it can be called. To call the function when WordPress is ready, it's wrapped in a function that's called when the admin_menu action is run.

Other than registering the new admin menu, this code also does a check that adds a page-specific action if form data with a msp_save variable has been submitted. When this action fires, the msp_save_settings_handler function will process and save the submitted form data.

Creating a settings form

There are as many ways to set up a settings form as there are stars in the sky. Well, maybe not quite that many, but we're sure that the numbers are close. Most of these methods use large sections of repeated code for each individual input.

This form shows how each type of HTML form input type can be integrated into your settings form. Instead of manually coding each input, which is time consuming and error prone, a set of functions is provided that make adding new inputs very easy.

Open your plugin settings-page.php file and follow these steps to add the code that handles the HTML form input for your settings page:

1. **Open this file in your text editor: settings-page.php**

2. **Add the following line of code at the bottom of the settings-php file:**

```
function msp_display_settings_page() {
$form=new MSP_Form(msp_get_settings());
?>
```

The msp-form-class.php file, which we will create later, contains a new class called MSP_Form. This class accepts an array of settings to assign the initial values of the form inputs. The settings come from the msp_get_settings function, which will be defined in the settings-functions.php file (covered in the next section).

When using a class like this, a variable stores an *object*. In this case, the object is stored in a variable called $form. Later in this form code, the $form variable will be used to easily add new form inputs by using the functions provided by the MSP_Form class.

3. **Press Enter and type the following lines of code:**

```
<?php if(isset($_GET['updated'])) : ?>
<div id="message" class="updated fade">
  <p><strong>Settings saved.</strong></p>
</div>
<?php endif; ?>
```

When the form data is saved, the page redirects to a new settings page link that contains a variable named updated. So, this section of code displays a *Settings saved* message when this redirect happens, confirming to the user that their settings changes are saved.

4. **Press Enter and type the following lines of code:**

```
<div class="wrap">
<?php screen_icon(); ?>
<h2>Example Settings Page</h2>
```

This section simply follows the page structure used by WordPress's built-in editors so that your settings page fits in with the style of WordPress.

5. **Press Enter and type the following line of code:**

```
<form method="post" action="<?php echo $_SERVER['REQUEST_URI']; ?>">
```

Many settings pages use code that submits the form data to the options.php page built into WordPress. To have a bit more control over how the data is saved, this settings page form sends the data back to itself, allowing this plugin's code to have full control over how the data is stored.

6. **Press Enter and type the following line of code:**

```
<?php wp_nonce_field('msp-update-settings'); ?>
```

The wp_nonce_field function is part of the nonce system of WordPress. Nonces protect a site against attackers. All your WordPress-managed forms should use nonces and use them properly. The key is to have the wp_nonce_field function call (with a unique attribute to identify the form's purpose) inside the HTML form tags and a call to check_admin_referer (that uses a matching attribute) before any action is taken with the form data. The check_admin_referer call can be found in the msp_save_settings_handler function at the end of this file's code.

7. **Press Enter and type the following code:**

```
<table class="form-table">
<tr valign="top">
<th scope="row"><label for="text">Text</label></th>
<td>
```

```
<?php $form->add_text('text'); ?>
</td>
</tr>
<tr valign="top">
<th scope="row"><label for="textarea">Text Area</label></th>
<td>
<?php $form->add_textarea('textarea'); ?>
</td>
</tr>
```

This is the table structure commonly used in editors throughout WordPress, using the HTML markup to create tables. It is simple and easy to expand to have new options. I typically just copy a single row, paste a few copies, and then modify each copy to have a new input when I expand my forms.

The call to the `$form->add_text` function is what adds the text input to the form. This function accepts an argument that defines what the name of the setting is, *text* in this case. The `textarea` section of the code follows the same format as this section.

8. **Press Enter and type the following lines of code:**

```
<tr valign="top">
<th scope="row">Multi-Checkbox</th>
<td>
<label title="1">
<?php $form->add_multicheckbox('multicheckbox','1'); ?> 1
</label><br />
<label title="2">
<?php $form->add_multicheckbox('multicheckbox','2'); ?> 2
</label><br />
<label title="3">
<?php $form->add_multicheckbox('multicheckbox','3'); ?> 3
</label><br />
<label title="4">
<?php $form->add_multicheckbox('multicheckbox','4'); ?> 4
</label>
</td>
</tr>
```

This section makes use of the `MSP_Form` class' `add_multicheckbox` function to create a form input that allows multiple values to be stored in a single setting. The second argument used for this function sets the value that the specific check box has. When loading data from this type of setting, the values of the checked inputs will be stored in an array.

9. **Press Enter and type the following lines of code:**

```
<tr valign="top">
<th scope="row">Radio</th>
<td>
<label title="Option 1">
<?php $form->add_radio('radio','1'); ?>
Option 1
</label>
<br />
<label title="Option 2">
<?php $form->add_radio('radio','2'); ?>
Option 2
```

```
</label>
<br />
<label title="Option 3">
<?php $form->add_radio('radio','3'); ?>
Option 3
</label>
</td>
</tr>
```

This section makes use of the `MSP_Form` class's `add_radio` function to create a form input using radios buttons. It uses the same format as the `multicheckbox` inputs from Step 8. The second argument is used to set the value used for the individual input. Unlike the `multicheckbox` inputs, the data loaded for a radio setting is a string and not an array.

10. **Press Enter and type the following lines of code:**

```
<tr valign="top">
<th scope="row"><label for="select">Select</label></th>
<td>
<?php
$options = array(
  '1'=>'Option 1',
  '2'=>'Option 2',
  '3'=>'Option 3',
);
?>
<?php $form->add_select('select',$options); ?>
</td>
</tr>
</table>
```

Select inputs can be very difficult to code by hand. The `MSP_Form` class makes adding a select input very easy. First, create an associative, or *named,* array. A named array sets the key to be used for each value. In other words, each array input looks like `'1'=>'Option 1'`, where 1 is the value to be stored for that setting and *Option 1* is the description to show for that value. Then the named array is passed in as the second argument to the `add_select` function.

11. **Press Enter and type the following lines of code:**

```
<p class="submit">
<input type="submit" name="msp_save" class="button-primary" value="Save
    Changes" />
</p>
```

Note the `msp_save` value used for the submit button's name. This is the name used to check for a settings form submission toward the top of this file.

12. **Press Enter and type the following lines of code:**

```
<?php $form->add_used_inputs(); ?>
</form>
</div>
```

This call to `add_used_inputs` is very important for handling the submitted form data.

13. **Press Enter and type the following lines of code:**

```php
<?php
}
function msp_save_settings_handler() {
check_admin_referer('msp-update-settings');
$settings=MSP_Form::get_post_data();
msp_update_settings($settings);
}
```

The `msp_save_settings_handler` completes the `settings-page. php` code. First, the nonce set inside the form is checked with the `check_admin_referer` to ensure that proper use of nonces is used. The `MSP_Form` class function `get_post_data` is used to store that submitted settings into the `$settings` variable. These settings are then passed to the `msp_update_settings` function (defined in the `settings-functions.php` file) to save the settings.

When you finish, the code in your entire `settings-page.php` file looks like this:

```php
<?php

function msp_add_admin_menu() {
add_options_page(
  'Example Settings Page',
  'Example Settings',
  'manage_options',
  'msp-example-settings-page',
  'msp_display_settings_page'
);
if(isset($_POST['msp_save'])) {
  add_action("admin_head-$page",'msp_save_settings_handler');
}
}
add_action('admin_menu','msp_add_admin_menu');

function msp_display_settings_page() {
$form=new MSP_Form(msp_get_settings());
?>
<?php if(isset($_GET['updated'])) : ?>
<div id="message" class="updated fade">
  <p><strong>Settings saved.</strong></p>
</div>
<?php endif; ?>
<div class="wrap">
<?php screen_icon(); ?>
<h2>Example Settings Page</h2>
<form method="post" action="<?php echo $_SERVER['REQUEST_URI']; ?>">
<?php wp_nonce_field('msp-update-settings'); ?>
<table class="form-table">
<tr valign="top">
<th scope="row"><label for="text">Text</label></th>
<td>
<?php $form->add_text('text'); ?>
</td>
</tr>
<tr valign="top">
<th scope="row"><label for="textarea">Text Area</label></th>
```

```
<td>
<?php $form->add_textarea('textarea'); ?>
</td>
</tr>
<tr valign="top">
<th scope="row"><label for="checkbox">Checkbox</label></th>
<td>
<?php $form->add_checkbox('checkbox'); ?>
</td>
</tr>
<tr valign="top">
<th scope="row">Multi-Checkbox</th>
<td>
<label title="1">
<?php $form->add_multicheckbox('multicheckbox','1'); ?> 1
</label><br />
<label title="2">
<?php $form->add_multicheckbox('multicheckbox','2'); ?> 2
</label><br />
<label title="3">
<?php $form->add_multicheckbox('multicheckbox','3'); ?> 3
</label><br />
<label title="4">
<?php $form->add_multicheckbox('multicheckbox','4'); ?> 4
</label>
</td>
</tr>
<tr valign="top">
<th scope="row">Radio</th>
<td>
<label title="Option 1">
<?php $form->add_radio('radio','1'); ?>
Option 1
</label>
<br />
<label title="Option 2">
<?php $form->add_radio('radio','2'); ?>
Option 2
</label>
<br />
<label title="Option 3">
<?php $form->add_radio('radio','3'); ?>
Option 3
</label>
</td>
</tr>
<tr valign="top">
<th scope="row"><label for="select">Select</label></th>
<td>
<?php
$options = array(
  '1'=>'Option 1',
  '2'=>'Option 2',
  '3'=>'Option 3',
);
?>
```

```php
<?php $form->add_select('select',$options); ?>
</td>
</tr>
</table>
<p class="submit">
<input type="submit" name="msp_save" class="button-primary" value="Save
    Changes" />
</p>
<?php $form->add_used_inputs(); ?>
</form>
</div>
<?php
}
function msp_save_settings_handler() {
check_admin_referer('msp update-settings');
$settings=MSP_Form::get_post_data();
msp_update_settings($settings);
}
```

Configuring default settings

A nice feature of this settings form code is that default settings can be set easily. These default settings are loaded even if the settings form hasn't been saved, allowing for reliable use of the defaults.

To set up the defaults, add the following code to a new file and save it as default-settings.php in your /example-settings page plugin directory:

Book VII
Chapter 5

Creating Simple
WordPress Plugins
from Scratch

```php
<?php
function msp_get_default_settings() {
  $defaults=array(
    'text'    => 'Sample Text',
    'textarea' => 'Sample Textarea Text',
    'checkbox' => '1',
    'multicheckbox' => array('2','3'),
    'radio'    => '2',
    'select'   => '3',
  );
  return $defaults;
}
```

By modifying the $defaults array, new default values can be added, removed, or modified easily. The format for this type of array is 'setting_name'=>'setting_value', where setting_name is the name of the setting and setting_value is the default value you want to use for that setting.

Adding settings functions

The settings functions manage loading and saving settings. Both functions are optimized for performance and reliability. Add the following code to a new file and save it as `settings-functions.php` in your `/example-settings-page` plugin directory:

```php
<?php
function msp_get_settings($name=null) {
static $settings=null;

if(is_null($settings)) {
$settings=get_option('msp-example-settings');
if(!is_array($settings)) $settings=array();

$defaults=msp_get_default_settings();
$settings=array_merge($defaults,$settings);
}

if(is_null($name)) return $settings;
if(isset($settings[$name])) return $settings[$name];
return '';
}

function msp_update_settings($settings) {
update_option('msp-example-settings',$settings);

$redirect_url=array_shift(explode('?',$_SERVER['REQUEST_URI']));
$redirect_url.='?page='.$_REQUEST['page'].'&updated=true';

wp_redirect($redirect_url);
}

$all_settings=msp_get_settings();
$text=msp_get_settings('text');
```

By calling the function with no argument, all the settings are returned. When you pass a setting name, the value for just that setting is returned.

The `msp_update_settings` function accepts a new array of settings to be saved. After the settings are saved, a new redirect link with the "updated" variable is built that displays the *Settings saved* message. WordPress's `wp_redirect` function then redirects the site to this new link.

Creating the MSP_Form class

The `MSP_Form` class code is quite lengthy. It is well worth the effort as it makes form building very easy.

Add the following code to a new file and save it as `msp-form-class.php` in your /`example-settings-page` plugin directory:

```php
<?php
class MSP_Form {
var $inputs=array();
var $settings=array();
function MSP_Form($settings=array()) {
if(is_array($settings)) $this->settings=$settings;
}
function add_used_inputs() {
$value=implode(',',array_unique($this->inputs));
$this->add_hidden('___msp_form_used_inputs',$value);
}
function get_post_data() {
if(!isset($_POST['___msp_form_used_inputs'])) {
return $_POST;
}
$data=array();
$inputs=explode(',',$_POST['___msp_form_used_inputs']);
foreach((array)$inputs as $var) {
$real_var=str_replace('[]','',$var);
if(isset($_POST[$real_var])) {
$data[$real_var]=stripslashes_deep($_POST[$real_var]);
}
else if($var!=$real_var) {
$data[$real_var]=array();
}
else {
$data[$real_var]='';
}
}
return $data;
}

// $form->add_text('name');
function add_text($name,$options=array()) {
if(!isset($options['class'])) $options['class']='regular-text';
$this->_add_input('text',$name,$options);
}
function add_textarea($name,$options=array()) {
$this->_add_input('textarea',$name,$options);
}
function add_checkbox($name,$options=array()) {
if($this->_get_setting($name)) $options['checked']='checked';
$this->_add_input('checkbox',$name,$options);
}
function add_file($name,$options=array()) {
$this->_add_input('file',$name,$options);
}
function add_password($name,$options=array()) {
$this->_add_input('password',$name,$options);
}
```

```
// $form->add_select('num',array('1'=>'One','2'=>'Two'));
function add_select($name,$values,$options=array()) {
$options['values']=$values;
$this->_add_input('select',$name,$options);
}


// $form->add_radio('type','extended');
function add_radio($name,$value,$options=array()) {
if($this->_get_setting($name)==$value) $options['checked']='checked';
$options['value']=$value;
$this->_add_input('radio',$name,$options);
}
function add_multicheckbox($name,$value,$options=array()) {
$setting=$this->_get_setting($name);
if(is_array($setting) && in_array($value,$setting)) {
$options['checked']='checked';
}
$options['value']=$value;
$this->_add_input('checkbox',"{$name}[]",$options);
}
function add_hidden($name,$value,$options=array()) {
$options['value']=$value;
$this->_add_input('hidden',$name,$options);
}


// $form->add_submit('save','Save');
function add_submit($name,$description,$options=array()) {
$options['value']=$description;
$this->_add_input('submit',$name,$options);
}
function add_button($name,$description,$options=array()) {
$options['value']=$description;
$this->_add_input('button',$name,$options);
}
function add_reset($name,$description,$options=array()) {
$options['value']=$description;
$this->_add_input('reset',$name,$options);
}


// $form->add_image('imagemap','http://domain.com/img.gif');
function add_image($name,$image_url,$options=array()) {
$options['src']=$image_url;
$this->_add_input('image',$name,$options);
}


// This function should not be called directly.
function _add_input($type,$name,$options=array()) {
$this->inputs[]=$name;
$settings_var=str_replace('[]','',$name);
$css_var=str_replace('[','-',str_replace(']','',$settings_var));

if(!is_array($options)) $options=array();
$options['type']=$type;
$options['name']=$name;
if(!isset($options['value']) && 'checkbox'!=$type) {
$options['value']=$this->_get_setting($settings_var);
}
```

```
if('radio'==$type || $settings_var!=$name) {
if(empty($options['class'])) $options['class']=$css_var;
}
else {
if(empty($options['id'])) $options['id']=$css_var;
}

$scrublist=array($type=>array());
$scrublist['textarea']=array('value','type');
$scrublist['file']=array('value');
$scrublist['dropdown']=array('value','values','type');

$attributes = '';
foreach($options as $var => $val) {
  if(!is_array($val) && !in_array($var,$scrublist[$type]))
  $attributes.="$var='".esc_attr($val)."' ";
}

if('textarea'==$options['type']) {
  echo "<textarea $attributes>";
  echo format_to_edit($options['value']);
  echo "</textarea>\n";
}
else if('select'==$options['type']) {
  echo "<select $attributes>\n";
  if(is_array($options['values'])) {
  foreach($options['values'] as $val=>$name) {
  $selected=($options['value']==$val)?' selected="selected"':'';
  echo "<option value=\"$val\"$selected>$name</option>\n";
  }
  }
  echo "</select>\n";
}
else {
  echo "<input $attributes />\n";
}

}

// This function should not be called directly.
function _get_setting($name) {
if(isset($this->settings[$name])) {
return $this->settings[$name];
}
return '';
}

}
```

You can use 13 functions to add inputs to a form. The following shows an example of how to use each one:

```
$form->add_text('setting_name');
$form->add_textarea('setting_name');
$form->add_checkbox('setting_name');
$form->add_file('setting_name');
$form->add_password('setting_name');
```

```
$form->add_select('setting_name',array('1'=>'One','2'=>'Two'));
$form->add_radio('setting_name','value_1');
$form->add_radio('setting_name','value_2');
$form->add_multicheckbox('setting_name','value_1');
$form->add_multicheckbox('setting_name','value_2');
$form->add_hidden('setting_name','value');
$form->add_submit('setting_name','value');
$form->add_button('setting_name','value');
$form->add_reset('setting_name','value');
$form->add_image('imagemap','http://domain.com/img.gif');
```

A feature that all the form input functions support is an optional last parameter to set additional HTML tag attributes to the final output. Here is an example of a block of code that sets additional HTML markup to the final output:

```
$form->add_text('setting_name',array('class'=>'regular-text code'));
$form->add_text('setting_name',array('style'=>'width:250px;font-
    size:2em;'));
$form->add_textarea('setting_name',array('rows'=>'10','cols'=>'30'));
$form->add_checkbox('setting_name',array('checked'=>'checked'));
```

This adds the class `regular-text` and `code` to the first text input, adds inline styling to control the width and font size of the second text input, uses 10 rows and 30 columns for the `textarea` input, and forces the `checkbox` to always be checked on page load for the last input.

This last optional argument can be used on any of the inputs to set needed tag attributes. By using this last argument in creative ways, you can always rely on using the input form functions rather than coding inputs by scratch.

Testing the plugin

After you have the files entered, you're ready to activate the Example: Settings Page plugin.

Because the code is divided, if you get an error about not being able to activate the plugin, note which file and line number had the error. This will help you quickly fix your error.

After activating the plugin, visit your Dashboard and go to Settings⇨Example Settings to see the settings form in action, as shown in Figure 5-10. Notice how the form is populated by the default values you set. These default values are set the first time the `msp_get_settings` function is called. Therefore, even if the user has never gone to your settings page, the defaults will be available. In addition, when you add new settings and update the defaults to have these new settings, those new defaults will also automatically become available.

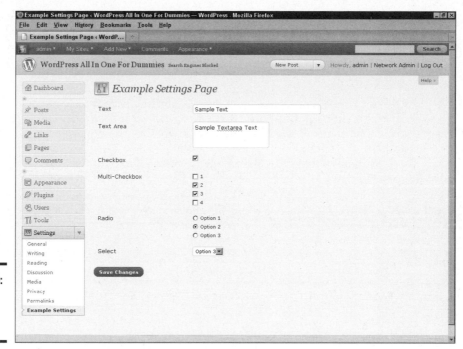

**Book VII
Chapter 5**

Creating Simple
WordPress Plugins
from Scratch

Figure 5-10:
Example
Settings
page.

After testing out the settings options, pop into the `settings-page.php` file and try adding new settings. When you have the new settings, make sure you update the `$defaults` array in `default-settings.php`.

This plugin can be extended with code from another one of the example plugins. To load the settings, simply use the `msp_get_settings` function.

For example, the `widget` function from the Example: My User Widget plugin you created earlier in this chapter could be updated to make use of two settings, `guest_message` and `user_message`.

```
function widget($args) {
$user=wp_get_current_user();
if(!isset($user->user_nicename))
$message=msp_get_settings('guest_message');
else
$message=msp_get_settings('user_message').$user->user_nicename;

extract($args);

echo $before_widget;
echo "<p>$message</p>";
echo $after_widget;
}
```

Plugin development has helped WordPress give users the ability to extend the basic WordPress installation via functions and features provided by useful plugins. The contributions of plugin code from thousands of people around the world built up a platform capable of amazing things.

With the variety of plugins you developed through the course of this chapter, you already have a solid set of starting points for your own plugin developments. Apply a little creativity and effort into making one of the plugins your own, and you'll be amazed at what can be done.

You have the tools. Now show the world what you can do.

Chapter 6: Exploring Plugin Development Best Practices

In This Chapter

✔ **Exploring best practice options**

✔ **Naming, filing, and locating your plugin**

✔ **Internationalizing your plugin**

During the eight years the WordPress platform has been around (since 2003), thousands of WordPress plugins have been developed. As with any method or technique, the practice of WordPress plugin development has improved and standards have emerged from the developer community as the best ways, or best practices, for developing WordPress plugins. This involves making sure that you not only have the necessary functions in place to make your plugin do what you want, but also standard techniques to ensure that your plugin includes all the essentials, such as localization (translation), security, speed, and compatibility.

This chapter looks at the standards for WordPress plugin development and provides you with a checklist, of sorts, to ensure that your plugin has covered all the bases before you release it for public consumption.

Attending to the Basics

In this chapter, you discover how to use a plugin template to deal with some of the programming you will use repeatedly as a plugin developer. You must also include some basic information within your plugin so that the users of your plugin identify the plugin easily. Standard practices also exist for the elements that should be included in your plugin if you intend to submit it to the official WordPress Plugin Directory at http://wordpress.org/extend/plugins. Plugins submitted to the directory are reviewed and vetted by WordPress developers to make sure that your plugin has all the necessary elements, is formatted correctly, and meets the standards of practice for all plugins.

Among these necessary elements — the basics — is a short snippet of code at the top of your plugin file that identifies seven important identifying characteristics of your plugin:

✦ **Plugin Name:** The identifying name of your plugin. Obviously, giving your plugin a unique and appropriate name is a good start so that it's easily identifiable in the WordPress Plugin Directory and the list of plugins available on a user's Dashboard. Because people who use WordPress will most likely install several plugins in their installation of WordPress, you want to make sure that your plugin has a unique name, and preferably a name that describes, in just a few words, what your plugin is.

For example, say you're writing a plugin that allows people to connect their blog to the Twitter service. Would naming your plugin My Great Plugin make sense? On the other hand, is giving the plugin a name like WordPress Twitter Connect more helpful? The first name may go far to serve your ego but is utterly useless from a user's standpoint. Create plugin titles that make sense to the user and make the function of the plugin easily identifiable.

✦ **Plugin URI:** The Web address of the Web page that displays a full description of your plugin (and, perhaps, support forums and a history of the plugin, including a change log and instructions on how to use it).

✦ **Description:** A brief description of what the plugin does. This plugin description also displays in the WordPress Dashboard (to the right of the plugin name) and gives users a brief description of what the plugin does and why they should use it.

If you intend to submit your plugin to the WordPress Plugin Directory, the words you use in the description and title will identify your plugin in search results there. Therefore, when writing the description of your plugin, use terms that will help users find your plugin easily. When people search for a particular term in the directory, all the plugins with that term in either the title or description will appear.

Figure 6-1 displays the WordPress Plugin Directory search results page for the term *Twitter;* the titles and descriptions all contain *Twitter* and help identify the plugin in the search results.

✦ **Version:** The plugin's unique version number (that is, 1.0, 2.0, and so on). Most likely, the first time you release your plugin, you'll identify it as version 1.0. Each time you release an update to the plugin, you change the version; and the extent of the changes determines the version number you use. Small changes to the plugin, such as styling improvements or the correction of a small bug, necessitate a point release, such as 1.2. However, if your new release includes many features that greatly extend the functions of the original release, you would probably consider it a major release and version it 2.0.

In Book I, Chapter 3, we discuss the WordPress development and release cycle as it pertains to the WordPress software. Within that chapter, you find information about the various versions of WordPress, how and why different version numbers exist, and point releases versus major releases.

The version numbers are up to you, of course; this is simply a standard practice by many developers who release software in order to keep their versions organized.

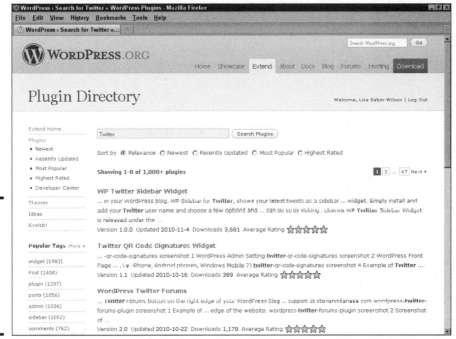

Figure 6-1:
The
WordPress
Plugins
Directory
search
results for
Twitter.

✦ **Author:** Your name and the names of any developers who helped you create this plugin.

✦ **Author URI:** The Web address of the plugin author's Web site.

✦ **License:** The name of the license under which your plugin is released. (The accepted license here is GPLv2, which is the license under which WordPress is released. For more information on GPL licensing, including how it pertains to your plugin development practices, see Book I, Chapter 2).

The necessary code to include these seven items looks like this:

```php
<?php
/*
Plugin Name: Your Plugin Name
Plugin URI: Web Address of your Plugin
Description: A brief description of the Plugin.
Version: Version Number
Author: Name(s) of the plugin Author(s)
Author URI: Web Address of the plugin author(s) Web site
License: License name (ie: GPL2)
*/
?>
```

It is customary to include a licensing statement in the header of your plugin that indicates adherence to the GPLv2 license. This statement is easy to include and formatted like this:

```php
<?php
/*  Copyright 2011 WordPress Twitter Connect Lisa Sabin-Wilson

    This program is free software; you can redistribute it and/or modify it under
      the terms of the GNU General Public License, version 2, as published by the
      Free Software Foundation.

    This program is distributed in the hope that it will be useful,
    but WITHOUT ANY WARRANTY; without even the implied warranty of
    MERCHANTABILITY or FITNESS FOR A PARTICULAR PURPOSE.  See the
    GNU General Public License for more details.

    You should have received a copy of the GNU General Public License
    along with this program; if not, write to the Free Software
    Foundation, Inc., 51 Franklin St, Fifth Floor, Boston, MA  02110-1301  USA
*/
?>
```

Figure 6-2 shows the Plugins page, displaying plugin names and descriptions.

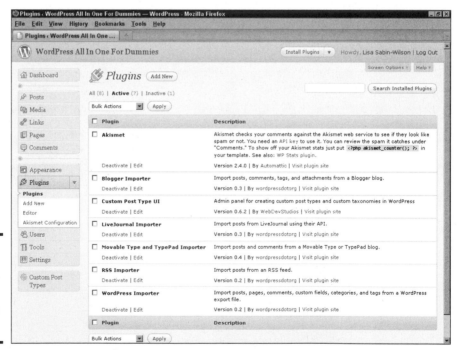

Figure 6-2:
The
WordPress
Plugins
page on the
Dashboard.

Creating a readme.txt File

If you are planning to submit your plugin to the WordPress Plugin Directory, you must also include a standard `readme.txt` file. This is a required file and your plugin won't be accepted to the Plugin Directory without it. The format of this text file is important because it contains necessary information about your plugin that users can open and read, as well as information that displays on your plugin's page within the Plugin Directory. The information in this file includes required and optional elements, as described in Table 6-1.

Table 6-1	Required and Optional Elements for the readme.txt Plugin File	
Component	*Required or Optional*	*Description*
Plugin Name	Required	The name of your plugin.
Contributors	Required	Comma separated list of contributors' wordpress.org usernames.
Tags	Required	Comma separated list of keywords that describe the plugin.
Requires at least:	Required	The lowest WordPress version number your plugin works with.
Tested up to:	Required	The highest WordPress version number you've successfully tested your plugin on.
Stable Tag	Required	Indicates the subversion tag of the latest stable version of your plugin. If no stable tag is provided, it is assumed `trunk` is stable.
Short Description	Required	A brief description of your plugin, no longer than 150 characters.
Long Description	Optional	A longer description of your plugin, with no limit on character length.
Donation Link	Optional	A Web address for your donations page.
Installation Instruction	Optional	A description of how the user will install your plugin.
Frequently Asked Questions	Optional	A Q&A to guide users on the use of your plugin.
Change Log	Optional	A history of changes made to your plugin.

(continued)

Table 6-1 *(continued)*

Component	Required or Optional	Description
First Screenshot Description	Optional	The first screenshot should be named `screenshot-1.jpg` (or `.png`, or `.gif`) and placed in the directory of your `readme.txt` file.
Second Screenshot Description	Optional	The second screenshot should be named `screenshot-2.jpg` (or `.png` or `.gif`) and placed in the same directory as your `readme.txt` file.
Video	Optional	If you have video instructions on how to use your plugin, include the Web address here.
Arbitrary Section	Optional	Provide any other information here about your plugin.

An example of a properly formatted `readme.txt` file looks like this (this one contains all the required components):

```
=== WordPress Twitter Connect ===
Contributors: LSWilson
Tags: twitter, social media
Requires at least: 2.7
Tested up to: 3.0
Stable tag: trunk

Submits your WordPress blog posts to your Twitter account when you publish.

== Description ==

Use this plugin to automatically submit your blog posts to your Twitter account
    when you hit the publish button. You can also submit your blog posts to
    multiple Twitter accounts, specified in the WordPress Twitter Connect options
    page in your Dashboard.

== Installation ==

Extract the zip file and just drop the contents in the wp-content/plugins/
    directory of your WordPress installation and then activate the Plugin from
    Plugins page.
```

If you're concerned about whether your plugin's `readme.txt` file adheres to the expectations of the WordPress Plugin Directory, use the WordPress validator tool (`http://wordpress.org/extend/plugins/about/validator`) to validate the file. This tool tells you whether your `readme.txt` file contains all the necessary components and information. If you're still having problems, there is a very handy `readme.txt` file generator located at `http://sudarmuthu.com/wordpress/wp-readme` that helps you generate a valid `readme.txt` file for your plugin by making sure that the basic requirements are met, as described in the previous sections.

Internationalizing or Localizing Your Plugin

WordPress users exist across the United States, Russia, Japan, Germany, and all points in between. Therefore, the next person to download and use your plugin may not speak the same language you do. So if you wrote and distributed your plugin in English, it may be useless to the next person to download it if he only speaks German. However, the WordPress software has internationalization built into it, which means it can be *localized,* or translated, into different languages.

You aren't translating the file into different languages, unless you want to. Rather, you're providing a mechanism of support for people who will want to provide translation for your plugin through the creation of .mo (machine object) files (discussed later in this chapter). Many people in different countries create (and have created) .mo files for the translation of WordPress into different languages; by providing localization for your plugin, you're enabling them to translate your plugin text, as well. (If you're interested in translating WordPress into a different language, check out this resource page in the WordPress Codex at http://codex.wordpress.org/Translating_WordPress.)

Using GetText Functions for Text Strings

WordPress provides you with two main localization functions: __ and _e. These functions use the GetText translation utility installed on your Web server. These two functions let you wrap plain text into strings of text to be translated. You need to account for two types of text strings in your plugin file:

✦ **HTML:** Example: `<h1>`*Plugin Name*`</h1>`

To wrap HTML text strings within the GetText function call, you would wrap it using the _e function like this:

```
<h1><?php _e('Plugin Name', 'plugin-name'); ?></h1>
```

This tells PHP to echo (_c) or display the string of text on your Web browser screen, but adds the benefit of using the GetText function, which allows for that string of text to be translated.

✦ **PHP:** Example: `<?php comments_number('No Responses', 'One Response', '% Responses' );?>`

To wrap PHP text strings with the GetText function, you would wrap it using the __ function, like this:

```
<?php comments_number(__('No Responses',plugin-name),('One Response',
    'plugin-name'),( '% Responses', 'plugin-name') );?>
```

Unlike the echo function(_e), the __ function is used when you need to add a string of text to an existing function call (in this case, comments_number()).

Avoid slang when writing your text strings in your plugin file. Slang is significant to only a certain demographic (age, geographic location, and so on) and may not translate well into other languages.

The second argument within the `GetText` string for the PHP text string example is `plugin-name`. This defines the domain of the text and tells `GetText` to return the translations only from the dictionary supplied with that domain name. This is the *plugin text domain* and most plugin authors use the name of their plugin (separated by hyphens) as the definer here. Use the text domain in your `GetText` functions toensure that `GetText` pulls the dictionary you supply instead of attempting to pull the text from the core WordPress language files, because some of the text you provide in your plugin is unique and, most likely, won't exist within the WordPress core language files.

In a plugin file, you define the text domain like this:

```
$my_translator_domain  = PLUGIN-NAME;
$my_translator_is_setup = 0;
function fabfunc_setup(){
  global $my_translator_domain, $my_translator_is_setup;
  if($my_translator_is_setup) {
    return;
  }
  load_plugin_textdomain($my_translator_domain,
      PLUGINDIR.'/'.dirname(plugin_basename(__FILE__)),
      dirname(plugin_basename(__FILE__)));
}
```

These lines of code simply tell WordPress where your plugin file is located (the text domain), which, in turn, informs WordPress where your `.pot`, or translation file, is for your specific plugin.

Creating the POT file

After you create your plugin and include all text strings within the `GetText` functions of __ and _e, you need to create a `.pot` (portable object template) file, which contains translations for all the strings of text that you wrapped in the `GetText` functions. Typically, you create the `.pot` file in your own language, in a special format, thereby, allowing other translators to create their own `.po (portable object)`, or an `.mo` (machine object) file in their language, using yours as the guide to translate by.

The `.pot` file is the original translation file and the `.po` file is a text file that includes your original text (from the `.pot`) along with their translation; or they can use an `.mo` file, which is basically the same as a `.po` file. However, while `.po` files are written in plain text meant to be human readable, `.mo` files are complied to make it easy for computers to read. Most Web servers will use `.mo` files to provide translations for `.pot` files.

WordPress has an extensive `.pot` file that you can use as a template for your own. You can find it and download it at `http://svn.automattic.`

com/wordpress-i18n/pot/trunk/wordpress.pot. Additionally, .pot files can be translated into .mo files using free translation tools available online, such as Poedit: http://www.poedit.net, which is a free tool that takes the original .pot file and the provided translations in a .po file and merges them into a compiled .mo file for your Web server to deliver the translated text.

The .pot file begins with a *header* section, which contains required information about what your translation is for. The .pot header section looks like this:

```
# LANGUAGE (LOCALE) translation for WordPress.
# Copyright (C) 20114 WordPress contributors.
# This file is distributed under the same license as the WordPress package.
# FIRST AUTHOR <YOU@YOUREMAIL.COM>, 2011.
#
#, fuzzy
msgid ""
msgstr ""
"Project-Id-Version: WordPress VERSION\n"
"Report-Msgid-Bugs-To: \n"
"POT-Creation-Date: 2011-01-01 12:00-0600\n"
"PO-Revision-Date: 2011-01-01 12:00-0600\n"
"Last-Translator: YOUR FULL NAME <YOU@YOUREMAIL.COM>\n"
"Language-Team: LANGUAGE <EMAIL@EMAIL.COM>\n"
"MIME-Version: 1.0\n"
"Content-Type: text/plain; charset=CHARSET\n"
"Content-Transfer-Encoding: 8bit\n"
```

All the capitalized, italicized information in this code example are placeholders. Replace these terms with your own information.

The format of the .pot file is specific and needs to contain the following information:

✦ **File Name:** The name of the file in which the text string exists. For example, if the plugin file is wordpress-twitter-connect.php, you need to include that filename in this section.

✦ **Line of code:** The exact line number of the text string in question.

✦ **msgid:** The source of the message, or the exact string of text that you included within one of the GetText functions, either __ or _e.

✦ **msgstr:** A blank string where the translation (in the subsequent .pot files) is inserted.

For your default .pot file, to format a text string using the GetText function (<h1><?php _e('WordPress Twitter Connect'); ?></h1>), which exists on line two (2) in the wordpress-twitter-connect.php plugin file, you include three lines in the .pot file that look like this:

```
#: wordpress-twitter-connect.php:2
msgid: "WordPress Twitter Connect"
msgstr: ""
```

You need to go through all the text strings in your plugin file that you wrapped in the GetText functions and define them in the .pot file in the format provided. Now, if anyone wants to create a .po file for your plugin in a different language, he or she simply copies their language translation of your .pot file between the quotation marks for the msgstr: section for each text string included in the original .pot file.

All .pot and .po (or .mo) files need to be included in your plugin folder in order for the translations to be delivered to your Web site. Figure 6-3 shows the directory structure of the popular WordPress All In One SEO Pack plugin, you can see the original .pot file, along with the translated .mo files listed within the /wp-content/plugins/all-in-one-seo-pack/ plugin folder.

You, or other translators, can create unlimited .mo files for several different languages. Make sure that you name the language file according to the standardized naming conventions for the different languages. For example, the French .mo file for the wordpress-twitter-connect.php plugin is wordpress-twitter-connect-fr_FR.mo. The naming convention for the languages is language_*COUNTRY*.mo.

A full list of language codes can be found at http://en.wikipedia.org/wiki/ISO_639, and a full list of country codes can be found at http://en.wikipedia.org/wiki/ISO_3166-1_alpha-2.

Name	Size	Modified	Attrib
🔺 Parent Directory			
📁 images	0	1/6/2011 6:16 PM	drwxr-xr-x
📄 aioseop.class.php	98 KB	1/6/2011 6:16 PM	-rw-r--r--
📄 aioseop_options.php	0	1/6/2011 6:16 PM	-rw-r--r--
📄 all_in_one_seo_pack.php	46 KB	1/6/2011 6:16 PM	-rw-r--r--
📄 all_in_one_seo_pack.pot	14 KB	1/6/2011 6:16 PM	-rw-r--r--
📄 all_in_one_seo_pack-bg_BG.mo	18 KB	1/6/2011 6:16 PM	-rw-r--r--
📄 all_in_one_seo_pack-bg_NO.mo	4 KB	1/6/2011 6:16 PM	-rw-r--r--
📄 all_in_one_seo_pack-cs_CZ.mo	13 KB	1/6/2011 6:16 PM	-rw-r--r--
📄 all_in_one_seo_pack-da_DK.mo	4 KB	1/6/2011 6:16 PM	-rw-r--r--
📄 all_in_one_seo_pack-de_DE.mo	13 KB	1/6/2011 6:16 PM	-rw-r--r--
📄 all_in_one_seo_pack-es_ES.mo	4 KB	1/6/2011 6:16 PM	-rw-r--r--
📄 all_in_one_seo_pack-fr_FR.mo	5 KB	1/6/2011 6:16 PM	-rw-r--r--
📄 all_in_one_seo_pack-he_IL.mo	4 KB	1/6/2011 6:16 PM	-rw-r--r--
📄 all_in_one_seo_pack-hu_HU.mo	8 KB	1/6/2011 6:16 PM	-rw-r--r--
📄 all_in_one_seo_pack-it_IT.mo	10 KB	1/6/2011 6:16 PM	-rw-r--r--
📄 all_in_one_seo_pack-ja.mo	15 KB	1/6/2011 6:16 PM	-rw-r--r--
📄 all_in_one_seo_pack-nl_NL.mo	13 KB	1/6/2011 6:16 PM	-rw-r--r--
📄 all_in_one_seo_pack-pl_PL.mo	12 KB	1/6/2011 6:16 PM	-rw-r--r--
📄 all_in_one_seo_pack-pt_BR.mo	13 KB	1/6/2011 6:16 PM	-rw-r--r--
📄 all_in_one_seo_pack-ru_RU.mo	15 KB	1/6/2011 6:16 PM	-rw-r--r--
📄 all_in_one_seo_pack-tr_TR.mo	14 KB	1/6/2011 6:16 PM	-rw-r--r--
📄 all_in_one_seo_pack-uk.mo	5 KB	1/6/2011 6:16 PM	-rw-r--r--
📄 all_in_one_seo_pack-zh_CN.mo	12 KB	1/6/2011 6:16 PM	-rw-r--r--
📄 all_in_one_seo_pack-zh_TW.mo	13 KB	1/6/2011 6:16 PM	-rw-r--r--
📄 readme.txt	3 KB	1/6/2011 6:16 PM	-rw-r--r--

1 Folder, 24 Files, 25 Total, 1 Selected (0 bytes)

EW

Figure 6-3:
All In One SEO Pack plugin files with both .pot and .mo translation files.

Chapter 7: Plugin Tips and Tricks

In This Chapter

✔ Using a plugin template

✔ Making your plugin pluggable

✔ Enhancing plugins with CSS and JavaScript

✔ Custom post types

✔ Exploring little-known useful hooks

✔ Using custom shortcodes

*W*hen you have a WordPress plugin or two under your belt, you'll discover that you want to interact with many more parts of WordPress. WordPress is constantly coming out with new functionality, and with it, new API hooks. This chapter discusses some of this functionality and offers you some ways to extend your use of WordPress plugins. Because this functionality involves some simple programming skills, we assume (for the purposes of this chapter) that you have some basic PHP and WordPress plugin development knowledge.

Using a Plugin Template

When you start writing WordPress plugins, you find that you spend a significant amount of time rewriting the same things. Typically, most plugins have the same basic structure and are set up the same way, meaning that they all deal with settings pages, storing options, and interacting with particular plugins, among other things. You eventually conclude that a valuable use of your time is to create a template for all the plugins to save you hours of work each time you start a new plugin.

Such a template varies from person to person, and to you, depending on programming styles, preferences, and the types of plugins the developer wants to include. For instance, if you often write plugins that use your own database tables, you should include this in your template. Similarly, if your plugins almost never require options pages, leave those out of your template.

When making a template, keep in mind your personal plugin preferences and tendencies.

To create your own template, determine what functionality and structure your plugins usually contain. Follow these steps:

1. **Create your file structure.**

   As you write more plugins, you find yourself repeating the same general filenames. If you find that you're including enough JavaScript and CSS in your plugins to necessitate their own files or directories, include these in your template. For example, if you're using a lot of JavaScript or CSS, you could modify the file structure of your plugin template to look something like the one shown in Figure 7-1.

Figure 7-1: Recommended file structure for a plugin.

2. **Determine what functionality you generally have in your plugins.**

   If you usually contain masses of code in a class, you can set up a basic class for your plugin template. Likewise, if your plugins typically have a single options page or a system of top-level and submenu pages, you can set up a general template.

3. **Create your primary plugin PHP file.**

   Usually, this file just contains some general `add_action` calls, file includes, and other general initializations (check out Chapter 5 of this minibook for information on `add_action` calls and other plugin functions). If you always call certain actions, like registering a plugin function to be run when the plugin is activated (`register_activation_hook`) and adding a menu item for the plugin in the Dashboard (`admin_menu`), set them up in your primary plugin PHP file template.

   ```php
   <?php
   $myInstance = new myPlugin();

   add_action('register_activation_hook','my_activation_plugin');
   add_action('admin_menu',array($myInstance, 'admin_menu'));

   ?>
   ```

4. **Set up the functions you use most often in the body of your primary plugin PHP file, after you add them in Step 3.**

The line of code used here: function my_activation_plugin, was added in Step 3 through the use of the add_action hook. In your plugin template, you define any scripts your plugin uses by adding this function, which then fires when a user activates the plugin:

```php
<?php

function my_activation_plugin(){
//plugin activation scripts here
}
?>
```

5. **(Optional) Create your basic class structure.**

To do this, you might add a few lines of code that resemble the following:

```php
<?php
class myPlugin {
    var $options = ;
    var $db_version = '1';
    function myPlugin() {
    add_action('admin_init',array($this,'admin_init');
    }
    function admin_init(){
        //admin initializations
    }
    function process_options($args,$data){
        //process our options here
    }
    function admin_menu(){
        //code for admin menu
    }
    function __construct(){
        //PHP 5 Constructor here
    }
} //end class
?>
```

Obviously, your class template may be more detailed than that, depending on your particular coding styles and the types of plugins you like to write.

In addition to these steps, you might want to set up a basic plugin options page, along with plugin options management scripts. Everyone uses different techniques for such things as processing plugin options, and after you determine your particular type, include the basic format in your template. As your programming style, WordPress, or your interest in different types of plugins changes over time, you will find that your template needs change, too. Make sure that you update your template.

Programmers like to spend their efforts solving problems, writing beautiful code, and achieving awesome functionality. Doing grunt work repeatedly to set up the same basic structure in every plugin takes our energy away from writing beautiful code poetry. Practice these concepts and watch your coding efficiency improve for all your future plugins!

Making Your Plugin Pluggable

The WordPress API provides a great solution for hooking in and extending or modifying its functionality. Sometimes, however, you may find that it would be useful to hook into another plugin, rather than WordPress itself, and extend or modify its functionality instead.

Here's an example of making your plugin pluggable: an issue about interaction (or lack of) between WP e-Commerce (`http://getshopped.org`) and the All in One SEO Pack plugin. All in One SEO Pack, among other things, adds a custom document title, description, keywords, and canonical URL to each page on a WordPress site. People often ask how to have their plugin modify this information before it displays onscreen. Forum plugins and shopping cart plugins particularly have this need, which All in One SEO Pack could easily satisfy if it would just provide a method of accessing its functionality, which it has — read on.

WP e-Commerce (and other plugins with similar functionality) creates its own virtual pages for product listings, and so on, all contained on a single WordPress page. For example, if you define `http://mywebstore.com/shop` as the WordPress page WP e-Commerce uses, `http://mywebsite.com/shop/product-name` and all other product pages are dynamically created by the WP e-Commerce plugin, and are outside the reach of other WordPress plugins. So, WordPress, and by extension, the All in One SEO Pack plugin, doesn't know about them. You can see the problem this would create for SEO purposes; WordPress and All in One SEO Pack would think that all these product pages are really the same page as the shop page, with the same titles, canonical URL, and so on. Code could have been written into the plugin to compensate for the needs of the WP e-Commerce, but that would be never ending, as there are infinite possibilities for other plugins that may need to hook into the All in One SEO Pack functions. So, the All in One SEO Pack API was born.

The WP e-Commerce plugin has an important need to hook into the document title, meta description, meta keywords, and canonical URL that the All in One SEO Pack plugin produces. Because WordPress and All in One SEO Pack weren't aware of the generated product pages, they all had the same canonical URL, which is detrimental for SEO purposes. The fix was simple. In the All in One SEO Pack plugin, after the canonical URL is generated, and immediately before printing it to the screen, the `apply_filters` function is used on the variable. This allows WP e-Commerce to use `add_filter` to hook in and filter the canonical URL, returning the appropriate URL for that page. That is, in the All in One SEO Pack plugin, they added the following:

```
function prepare_canonical_url(){
    $canonical_url = my_determine_canonical_url_function();
    $new_canonical_url = apply_filters( 'aioseop_canonical_url',$canonical_url);

    return $new_canonical_url;
}
```

This returns the value of the canonical URL and lets another plugin filter it, if desired, prior to returning the final value.

The part you can now add in the primary WP e-Commerce plugin file (at the end of the file before the closing `?>`) is just as simple, and works the same way `add_filter` does for hooking into the WordPress API.

```
add_filter('aioseop_canonical_url','wpec_change_canonical_url');

function wpec_change_canonical_url($old_url){
    $new_url = determine_current_product_page_url($old_url);
    return $new_url;
}
```

This provides a simple solution to allow other plugins (and themes) to hook into a plugin, without the need to add code specific to any one plugin.

Enhancing Plugins with CSS and JavaScript

As you have discovered by now, there are many ways to add functionality to a plugin. In this section, we look at two methods, CSS styling and JavaScript. You may never develop a plugin that uses either, but it's still useful to understand how these can be included. Chances are you may need this at some point, so it's a good reference for any budding plugin developer to have.

Calling stylesheets within a plugin

Controlling how your plugin's output looks onscreen (whether in the WordPress Dashboard or on the front end of the Web site or blog) is best controlled through a stylesheet. If you've been around Web design and HTML, you're probably familiar with CSS (Cascading Style Sheets). Nearly every styling aspect for a Web site is controlled by a stylesheet, and WordPress is no exception. If you want to read the authoritative guide to stylesheets, visit the W3C.org Web site at http://www.w3.org/Style/css. (For more on CSS, see Book VI.)

You can use a single stylesheet to control how your Plugin Options page looks in the Dashboard, how your plugin widget looks in the Dashboard, or how your plugin displays information on the front-end Web site.

Create and use a separate stylesheet for the plugin within the Dashboard and the plugin's display on the front end because the stylesheets are called at different times. The back-end stylesheet is called when you are administering your site in the WordPress Dashboard; whereas, the front-end stylesheet is called when a user visits the Web site. Additionally, it makes management of styling easier and cleaner.

The best practice for adding stylesheets within your plugin is to create a `/styles` directory, for example, `/my-plugin/styles`. Place your stylesheets for the back end and front end inside this directory, as shown in Figure 7-2.

Figure 7-2: The file structure for a plugin showing stylesheets.

To call a stylesheet from your plugin, you should use the built-in WordPress `wp_enqueue_style` function because it creates a queuing system in WordPress for loading stylesheets only when they are needed, instead of on every page. Additionally, it has support for dependencies so you can specify whether your stylesheet depends on another that should be called first. This queuing system is used for scripts, too. Moreover, the `wp_enqueue_scripts` function does the same for scripts, which we discuss a little later in this section.

Let's look at some practical examples using `wp_enqueue_style`.

Say you're creating a gallery plugin to display images on your Web site. You want your gallery to look nice, so you want to create a stylesheet that controls how the images display. Here's how to call that stylesheet in your plugin using a simple function and action hook (these lines of code get added to your primary plugin PHP file at the end, just before the closing `?>` tag):

1. **Create a function in your primary plugin PHP file to register your stylesheet and invoke `wp_enqueue_style`.**

```
function add_my_plugin_stylesheet() {
    wp_register_style('mypluginstylesheet', '/wp-content/plugins/
      my-plugin/styles/site-style.css');
    wp_enqueue_style('mypluginstylesheet');
}
```

2. Use the `wp_print_styles` action hook and call your function.

```
add_action( 'wp_print_styles', 'add_my_plugin_stylesheet' );
```

Here's a breakdown of the hooks in the function:

✦ **The `wp_register_style` function registers your stylesheet for later use by `wp_enqueue_style`.**

```
wp_register_style( $handle, $src, $deps, $ver, $media )
```

The function has a number of parameters; the first is $handle, which is the name of your stylesheet.

$handle must be unique. You cannot have more than one stylesheet with the same name in the same directory.

The second parameter is $src, the path to your stylesheet from the root of WordPress. In this case, it's the full path to the file within the plugin's styles directory.

The remaining parameters are optional. To find out more about them, read the WordPress documentation on this function at `http://codex.wordpress.org/Function_Reference/wp_register_style`.

✦ **The `wp_enqueue_style` function queues the stylesheet.**

```
wp_enqueue_style( $handle, $src, $deps, $ver, $media )
```

The $handle parameter is the name of your stylesheet as registered with `wp_register_style`. The $src parameter is the path, but you don't need this parameter because you registered the stylesheet path already. The remaining parameters are optional and explained in the WordPress documentation on this function at `http://codex.wordpress.org/Function_Reference/wp_enqueue_style`.

✦ **The action hook that calls the function uses `wp_print_styles` to output the stylesheet to the browser.**

Figure 7-3 shows the plugin stylesheet being called in the <HEAD> section of the site source code.

Figure 7-3:
Source
code of a
Web site
showing
the plugin
stylesheet
being
called.

Another example uses a stylesheet for the plugin's admin interface, which controls how your plugin option page within the Dashboard will appear. These lines of code also get added to your plugin's primary PHP file (just prior to the closing `?>` tag):

```
add_action('admin_init', 'myplugin_admin_init');

function myplugin_admin_init() {
   wp_register_style('mypluginadminstylesheet', '/wp-content/plugins/my-plugin/
   admin-styles.css');
   add_action('admin_print_styles' 'myplugin_admin_style');
   function myplugin_admin_style() {
      wp_enqueue_style('mypluginadminstylesheet');
   }
}
```

This example uses some hooks that are specific to the WordPress Dashboard:

✦ The action hook calls `admin_init`. This makes sure that the function is called when the Dashboard is accessed. The callback function is `myplugin_admin_init`.

✦ The function registers the stylesheet, using `wp_register_style`.

✦ An action hook calls the `myplugin_admin_style` function. The `admin_print_styles` hook is used because it's specific to the WordPress Dashboard display.

✦ Our function then queues the stylesheet, using `wp_enqueue_style`.

Figure 7-4 shows the plugin stylesheet being called in the source code of the Plugin Options page in the Dashboard.

Figure 7-4:
The source code of the Plugin Options page in the Dashboard showing the plugin stylesheet being called.

Calling JavaScript within a plugin

After using the `wp_register_style` and `wp_enqueue_style` functions to call stylesheets within a plugin, you can see how similar functions can call JavaScript, which has many uses within a plugin.

JavaScript can control functionality within a form or display something with an effect. WordPress comes with some JavaScript in the core that you can call in your plugin or you can write your own. Like stylesheets, it's best to store JavaScript in a separate subdirectory within your plugin; for example, `/my-plugin/javascript`.

Instead of using `wp_register_style` and `wp_enqueue_style` to register and queue JavaScript, you must use `wp_register_script` and `wp_enqueue_script`. They work in much the same way and have much the same parameters. Here's an example to be added to your plugins primary PHP file, near the end before the closing `?>` tag:

```
if ( !is_admin() ) {
   wp_register_script('custom_script','/wp-content/plugins/my-plugin/javascript/
     custom-script.js',);
   wp_enqueue_script('custom_script');
}
```

Immediately, you notice that the `wp_enqueue_script` function loads scripts in the front end of your Web site and in the Dashboard. Because this can cause conflicts with other scripts used by WordPress in the Dashboard display, the "if is not" (`!is_admin`) instruction tells the plugin to load JavaScript only if it's not being loaded in the Dashboard. This code loads `custom-script.js` only on the front end of the Web site (that is, what your site visitors see). You could add a more specific conditional `if` instruction to load JavaScript only on a certain page.

If you want to load the JavaScript in wp-admin, the action hook `admin_init` loads your callback function when `wp-admin` is accessed and the `admin_print_script` function outputs the script to the browser, just like the stylesheet example.

Custom Post Types

One of the most confusing features of WordPress is custom post types. It is also a useful, powerful, and easy feature to implement and use after you understand how it works. WordPress has five default post types:

✦ **Post:** The most commonly used post type. Content appears in a blog in reverse sequential time order.

✦ **Page:** Similar to a post, but pages don't use the time-based structure of posts. Pages can be organized in a hierarchy and have their own URLs off the main site URL.

✦ **Attachment:** This special post type holds information about files uploaded through the WordPress Media upload system.

✦ **Revisions:** This post type holds past revisions of posts and pages as well as drafts.

✦ **Nav Menus:** This post type holds information about each item in a navigation menu.

A post type is really a type of content stored in the `wp_posts` table in the WordPress database. The post type is stored in the `wp_posts` table in the `post_type` column. The information in the `post_type` column differentiates each type of content so that WordPress, a theme, or a plugin can treat the specific content types differently.

When you understand that a post type is really just a method to distinguish how different content types are used, you can investigate custom post types.

Say you have a Web site about movies. Movies have common attributes — actors, directors, writers, and producers. But say you don't want to store your movie information in a post or a page because it doesn't fit either content type. This is where custom post types become useful. You can create a custom post type for movies and apply the common attributes of actors, directors, and so on. A theme can handle movies differently than a post or a page by having a custom template for the movies post type and create different styling attributes and templates for the movies post type. You can search and archive movies differently than you can with posts and pages.

Here's how to create a simple custom post type in WordPress by adding these lines of code into the Theme Functions template file (located in the theme file and called functions.php):

```
add_action('init','create_post_type');
function create_post_type() {
  register_post_type( 'movies',
    array(
      'labels' => array(
        'name' => ('Movies'),
        'singular_name' -> ('Movie'),
        'rewrite' => array('slug' -> 'movies'),
      ),
      'public' => true,
    )
  );
}
```

Let's see what's going on in the code:

✦ The first line is the action hook. This uses 'init' so that it's called on the front end and in the Dashboard to display the custom post type in both.

✦ The callback function starts with the register_post_type function and the custom post type name. This is what creates the custom post type and gives it properties.

✦ Next is an array of arguments that are the custom post type properties.

✦ The 'labels' arguments include the name that displays on the Dashboard menu, the name that will be used (Movies), and what is used for the slug in the URL to the posts(http://yourdomain.com/ movies, for example) in this custom post type.

✦ The 'public' argument controls whether the custom post type displays in the Dashboard.

Figure 7-5 shows how the Custom Post Type page and menu item look in the Dashboard.

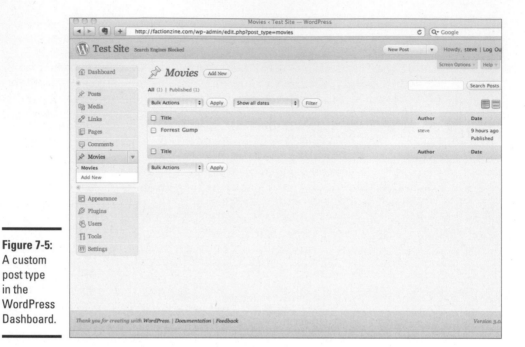

Figure 7-5:
A custom post type in the WordPress Dashboard.

Figure 7-6 shows a custom post type on a Web site.

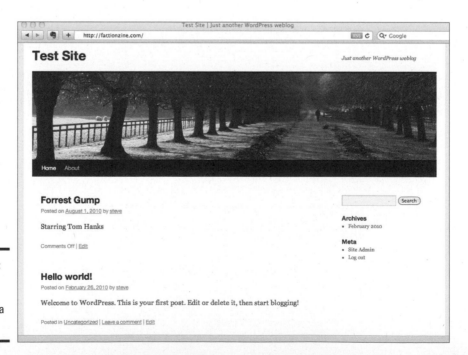

Figure 7-6:
A custom post type shown on a Web site.

Many other arguments associated with `register_post_type` give this function its real power. For full documentation on all the arguments and the use of this function, check out `http://codex.wordpress.org/Function_Reference/register_post_type`. (Custom post types are also discussed in detail in Book VI, Chapter 6.)

Using Custom Shortcodes

One of the most common inefficiencies with plugins is when a plugin wants to add information within the body of a post or page. The plugin developer manually creates a bloated filtering function, hooks into `the_content` (the function tag that calls the body of the content from the database and delivers it to your web site), and filters it in an attempt to find the appropriate spot to display the information. Fortunately, WordPress has a built-in solution for this. Using the shortcode API, your users can easily choose where in a given post to display the information your plugin is providing them.

The basic premise is that you have a string of data that your plugin dynamically generates, and you want your users to determine where in each post and page it displays. From your users' perspective, they will type a shortcode like this within the body of their content in order to display information from a plugin:

```
[myshortcode]
```

On the developer side, you just use the `add_shortcode` function and add it to your primary plugin PHP file:

```
<?php add_shortcode($tag, $func); ?>
```

The `add_shortcode` function accepts two parameters: The `$tag` parameter is the string that users will type within the body of their content to make a call to the plugin shortcode (from the previous example: `[myshortcode]` is what the users type, so your `$tag` parameter would be: `myshortcode`. The `$func` parameter is your callback function (a function that you still need to define with in the body of your primary plugin PHP file, covered in the next section) that returns the output of the called shortcode.

We jump right into a basic usage example, and then we look at some more complex ones. The shortcode function gets added to your primary plugin PHP code, near the bottom, before the closing `?>` tag:

```
add_shortcode('myshortcode','my_shortcode');

function my_shortcode(){
    return "this is the text displayed by the shortcode";
}
```

In this example, you added the shortcode hook: `add_shortcode` `('myshortcode', 'my_shortcode');` and you gave definition to the function (`$func`) called `my_shortcode` by telling WordPress to output the text: This is the text displayed by the shortcode.

All your user has to do is type **[myshortcode]** somewhere in the body of his post/page editor (in the Dashboard, Post⮞Add New), as shown in Figure 7-7. When users view the site, the shortcode the user entered in the body of their post is now translated by WordPress and displays the returned value, or output, of the shortcode function, as shown in Figure 7-8.

Shortcode names must be unique to your own plugin, so you may want to give it a name that is specific to your plugin. For example, if your plugin is called "Super SEO Plugin," you could name your shortcode: `[superseoplugin code]` in an attempt to make sure that no other plugin uses your shortcode. Another plugin using a shortcode with the same name will cause a conflict.

Shortcodes can include arguments to be passed into the shortcode function.

```php
<?php
add shortcode('myshortcode','my_shortcode');

function my_shortcode($attr, $content){
    return 'My name is ' . $attr['first'] . $attr['last'];
}
```

Figure 7-7: Post editor showing a simple shortcode.

Calling this with

```
[myshortcode first="John" last="Smith"]
```

outputs *My name is John Smith.*

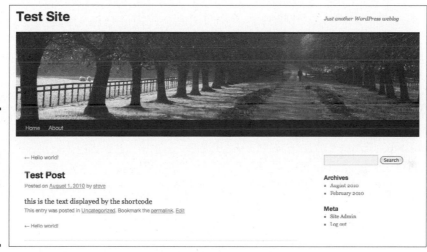

Figure 7-8:
The shortcode is replaced by the returned value of the shortcode function.

Adding Functionality to Profile Filters

WordPress provides four contact methods by default: AIM, Yahoo! IM, and Jabber/Google Talk. These are, of course, extensible, meaning that you can easily add new contact methods through the use of filters. It's painless to add more, and you can even add on a little extra functionality while you're at it.

Users fill out their profile data in the WordPress Dashboard by going to Users➪Your Profile (see Book III, Chapter 1). User profile fields are stored in the WordPress database in the user_metadata table and you can easily fetch them by using `get_the_author_meta('aim')` and print them with `the_author_meta('aim')`. If you add a Twitter Contact Info field, it appears in profiles, and you can use `the_author_meta('twitter')` template tags in your theme to print the account name.

Figure 7-9 shows the Twitter Contact Info field in a profile within the WordPress Dashboard.

Twitter contact field

Figure 7-9:
Custom
Twitter
profile field,
as shown
in the
Dashboard.

the_author_meta() template tag has a hook called the_author_
{$field}, where the PHP variable `$field` is the requested meta field
assigned to each contact type in the user profile files, such as `aim` in the
above example. These dynamic hooks are powerful because they allow you
to narrow your target.

In this example, we use the dynamic `the_author_twitter` hook to
change the result from "lisasabinwilson" to <a href="http://
twitter.com/lisasabinwilson">@lisasabinwilson</a>. When you
call the_author_meta('twitter') in your theme, you get a clickable link
to Lisa Sabin-Wilson's Twitter profile. Start by entering the following lines of
code in your Theme Functions file (functions.php) in your active theme
folder (add this code toward the bottom of the file before the closing ?>
tag):

```
/**
 * Add Twitter to the list of contact methods captured via profiles.
 */
function my_add_twitter_author_meta( $contact_methods ) {
$contact_methods['twitter'] = 'Twitter';
return $contact_methods;
}

add_filter( 'user_contactmethods', 'my_add_twitter_author_meta' );

/**
 * Convert staff Twitter accounts to links to twitter.com.
 */

function my_link_author_twitter_accounts( $value ) {
if ( strlen( $value ) ) {
$url = esc_url( 'http://twitter.com/' . $value );
$value = '<a href="' . $url . '">@' . esc_html( $value ) . '</a>';
}
return $value;
}
add_filter( 'the_author_twitter', 'my_link_author_twitter_accounts' );
```

Correcting Hyperlink Problems

Most Web sites use underline to style hyperlinks. When producing content in WordPress, highlighting words and phrases quickly to add hyperlinks can lead to hyperlinking (and underlining) the spaces before and after your anchor text.

For some, this is enough to convince them to hide underlines for hyperlinks, even though that may not be desired.

Here's a quick snippet that filters through blog post content and ensures that you don't have any spaces on the wrong side of the tag or between a closing tag and punctuation. Add this in your Theme Functions (functions.php) file:

```
/**
 * Prevents underlined spaces to the left and right of links.
 *
 * @param string $content Content
 * @return string Content
 */

function my_anchor_text_trim_spaces( $content ) {
// Remove spaces immediately after an <a> tag.
$content = preg_replace( '#<a([^>]+)>\s+#', ' <a$1>', $content );
// Remove spaces immediately before an </a> tag.
$content = preg_replace( '#\s+</a>#', '</a> ', $content );
// Remove single spaces between an </a> tag and punctuation.
```

```
$content = preg_replace( '#</a>\s([.,!?;])#', '</a>$1', $content );
return $content;
}
add_filter( 'the_content', 'my_anchor_text_trim_spaces' );
```

HTML ignores more than one space in a row (also more than one tab character and line break), unless you're using the `pre` element or nonbreaking space entities (` `). Therefore, even if your converted text contains two consecutive spaces, the browser won't show it any differently.

Book VIII

Running Multiple Sites with WordPress

Contents at a Glance

Chapter 1: An Introduction to Multiple Sites

In This Chapter

✔ **Discovering where multiple sites began**

✔ **Exploring what you can do with multiple sites**

✔ **Configuring your Web server**

*1*n this chapter, we introduce you to the multisite feature that's built into the WordPress software. The multisite feature allows you, the site owner, to add and maintain multiple blogs within one, single installation of WordPress. This feature was introduced in WordPress version 3.0. Prior to that, if you wanted to run multiple WordPress blogs with one installation of the software, you needed to use different software called WordPress MU (Multi User). In this chapter, you discover how the multisite feature works and why you might want to use it. You also explore how to configure and set up your Web server environment for use with the multisite feature.

With the network features enabled, users of your network can run their own sites within your installation of WordPress. They also have access to their own Dashboard with the options and features you read about in the previous minibooks. Heck, it's probably a good idea to buy a copy of this book for the members of your network so they can become familiar with the WordPress Dashboard and features, too. At least have a copy on hand so people can borrow yours!

Exploring the Merge from Multiuser to Network

Running multiple sites under one installation of WordPress was not always possible. From August 2005 until July 2010, there was a completely separate software package called WordPress MU. In July 2010, the codebase of WordPress MU and WordPress merged, meaning that the features of

WordPress MU were included in the WordPress software, rendering the WordPress MU software package obsolete. The merger of codebases brought several advantages, including

+ **One codebase:** Having the multisite feature available in one piece of software completely eliminates user confusion on which version of WordPress they need to use. Now, you use the same software package regardless of whether you want to use the multisite feature. If you do, just a few minutes of configuration can make it happen.

+ **Bug fixes:** WordPress MU was not as popular as the original WordPress software; therefore, the MU project didn't attract as many developers to contribute code, fixes, and additional feature development. When the merge occurred in July 2010, the multisite feature gained the massive WordPress developer community, making bug fixes and new features a quicker and easier process.

+ **Easier interface:** If you worked with MU, you know what we mean here. The interface and Dashboard features for the multisite feature in WordPress is much easier to work with, mainly because it works in tandem with the other WordPress settings and features you're already familiar with.

In the past, the WordPress codebase would be updated and those changes would be rolled over to WordPress MU with any additional fixes. Occasionally, WordPress MU users had to wait two to four weeks or longer for updates. Because the number of users familiar with WordPress MU was far less than WordPress, feedback for bugs was also slow. Even though more than 95 percent of the two codebases were identical, the remaining code in WordPress MU did the bulk of the work maintaining multiple blogs.

Understanding the Difference between Sites and Blogs

With the merger of WordPress MU and WordPress came a name change. Each additional blog under WordPress MU is now a site. But, what's the difference?

Largely, it's one of perception. Everything functions the same, but people can see greater possibilities when they no longer think of each site as "just" a blog. Now, WordPress can be so much more:

+ With the addition of the Domain Mapping plugin (see Chapter 6 in this minibook), you can manage multiple sites with different, and unique, domain names. None of them has to be a blog. They can have a blog element, or just use pages and have a static site.

✦ The built-in options let you choose between subdomains or subfolder sites when you install the network. If you install WordPress in the root of your Web space, you will get `subdomain.yourdomain.com` (if you choose subdomains) or `yourdomain.com/subfolder` (if you choose subfolders). Chapter 2 of this minibook discusses the differences and advantages.

After you choose the kind of sites you want to host and create those sites, you can't change them later on. These sites are served virtually, meaning that they do not exist as files or folders anywhere on the server. They only exist in the database. The correct location is served to the browser by using rewrite rules in the `.htaccess` file.

✦ The main, or parent, site of the network can also be a landing page of the entire network of sites, showcasing content from other sites in the network and drawing in visitors further.

Discovering When You Should Use the Network Feature

Determining whether to use the multisite feature depends on user access and posting. Each site in the network, although sharing the same codebase and users, is still a self-contained unit. Users still have to access the back end of each site to manage options or post to that site. A limited amount of general options is network-wide, and posting is not one of them.

You can use multiple sites in a network to give the appearance that only one site exists. Put the same theme on each site, and the visitor doesn't realize that they are separate. This is a good way to separate sections of a magazine site, using editors for complete sections (sites) but not letting them access other parts of the network or the back end of other sites.

Usually, for multiple users to post to one site, WordPress is sufficient. The multiuser part of the WordPress MU name did not refer to how many users, really. MU was always a bit of a misnomer and an inaccurate depiction of what the software actually did. A *network of sites* is a much closer description.

Another factor to consider is how comfortable you are with editing files directly on the server. Setting up the network involves access to the server directly, and ongoing maintenance and support for your users can often lead to the network owner doing the necessary maintenance, which is not for the faint of heart. Generally, you should use a network of sites in the following cases:

✦ **You want multiple sites and one installation.** You're a blogger or site owner who wants to maintain another site, possibly with a subdomain or a separate domain, all on one Web host. You're comfortable with some edits to files, you want to work with one codebase to make site maintenance easier, and most of your plugins and themes are accessible to all the sites. You can have one login across the sites and manage each site individually.

✦ **You want to host blogs or sites for others.** This is a little more involved. You want to set up a network where users can sign up for their own sites or blogs underneath (or part of) your main site and you maintain the technical aspects for them.

Because all files are shared, some aspects have been locked down for security purposes. One of the most puzzling for new users is the suppression of errors. Most PHP errors (say you installed a faulty plugin or incorrectly edited a file) do not output messages to the screen. Instead, what appears is what we like to call the White Screen of Death.

Knowing how to find and use error logs and do general debugging are skills needed when you are managing your own network. Even if your Web host will set up the ongoing daily or weekly tasks for you, managing a network can be a steep learning curve.

When you enable the network, the existing WordPress site becomes the main site in the installation.

Although WordPress can be quite powerful, in the following situations the management of multiple sites has its limitations:

✦ **One Web account is used for the installation.** You cannot use multiple hosting accounts.

✦ **You want to post to multiple blogs at one time.** WordPress will not do this by default.

✦ **If you choose subdirectory sites, the main site will regenerate permalinks with `/blog/` in it to prevent collisions with subsites.** There are existing plugins available to strip this.

WordPress MU had quirks in the software. The www was stripped from the domain name, for example, and you couldn't install on just an IP address or by using only localhost as the name. These issues are addressed in WordPress 3.0.

Setting Up the Optimal Hosting Environment

This chapter assumes that you already have the WordPress software installed and running correctly on your Web server, and that your Web server meets the minimum requirements to run WordPress.

Before you enable the WordPress multisite feature, you need to determine how you are going to use the feature. You have a couple of options:

✦ Manage just a few of your own WordPress blogs or Web sites.

✦ Run a full-blown blogging network with several hundred different blogs and multiple users.

If you are planning to run just a few of your own sites with the WordPress multisite feature, then your current hosting situation is probably well suited. However, if your plans are to host a large network with hundreds of blogs and multiple users, you should consider contacting your host and increasing your bandwidth, as well as the disk space limitations on your account.

The best example of a large blog network with hundreds of blogs and users (actually, more like millions) is the hosted service at WordPress.com (http://wordpress.com). At WordPress.com, people are invited to sign up for an account and start a blog using the network feature within the WordPress platform on the WordPress server. When you enable this feature on your own domain and enable the user registration feature, you are inviting users to

✦ Create an account.

✦ Create a blog on your WordPress installation (on your domain).

✦ Create content by publishing blog posts.

✦ Upload media files such as photos, audio, and video.

✦ Invite friends to view their blog, or to sign up for their own account.

In addition to the necessary security measures, time, and administrative tasks that go into running a community of blogs, you have a few more things to worry about. Creating a community will increase the resource use, bandwidth, and disk space on your Web server. In many cases, if you go over the allotted limits given to you by your Web host, you will incur great cost. Make sure that you anticipate your bandwidth and disk space needs before running a large network on your Web site! (Don't say we didn't warn you.)

Checking out shared versus dedicated hosting

Many WordPress Network communities start with grand dreams of being a large and active community. Be realistic on how your community will operate in order to make the right hosting choice for yourself and your community.

Small blogging communities can be easily handled using a shared-server solution, whereas larger, more active communities should really consider a dedicated-server solution for operation. The difference between the two lies in their names:

✦ **Shared-server solution:** You have one account on one server that has several other accounts on it. Think of this as apartment living. One apartment building has several apartments for multiple people to live, all under one roof.

✦ **Dedicated-server solution:** You have one account. You have one server. That server is dedicated to your account, and your account is dedicated to the server. Think of this as owning a home where you don't share your living space with anyone else.

A dedicated-server solution is a more expensive investment for your blog community, while a shared-server solution is the most economical. Your decision on which solution to go with for your WordPress Network blogging community will be based on your realistic estimates of how big and how active your community will be. You can move from a shared-server solution to a dedicated-server solution if your community gets larger than you expected; however, starting with the right solution for your community from day one is easier.

Exploring subdomains versus subdirectories

The WordPress network feature gives you two different ways to run a network of blogs on your domain. You can use the subdomain option or the subdirectory option. The most popular option (and recommended structure) sets up subdomains for the blogs created by your WordPress Network. With the subdomain option, the username of the blog appears first, followed by your domain name. With the subdirectory option, your domain name appears first, followed by the username of the blog. Which one should you choose? The choice is yours. You can see the difference in the URLs of these two options by comparing the following examples:

✦ A **subdomain** looks like this: `http://username.yourdomain.com`

✦ A **subdirectory** looks like this: `http://yourdomain.com/username`

Apache mod_rewrite

Apache (`http://httpd.apache.org`) is Web server software that's loaded and running on your Web server. Not everyone has access to Apache files, however. Usually, the only person who has access to those files is the Web server administrator. (This is usually your Web host.) Depending on your own Web server account and configuration, you may or may not have access to the Apache software files.

The Apache module that's necessary in order for the WordPress Network to create nice permalink URLs is called `mod_rewrite`.

This must be configured so that it's active and installed on your server.

You or your Web host can make sure that the Apache `mod_rewrite` is activated on your server; open the `httpd.conf` file and verify that the following line is included within:

```
LoadModule rewrite_module /
libexec/mod_rewrite.so
```

If it isn't, type that line on its own line and save the file. You will probably need to restart Apache before the change takes effect.

While the network is being set up, tables are added (to the database) that contain information about the network, including the main site URL. If you're developing a site or want to change the domain later, you need to change every reference to the domain name in the database. Look at Book II, Chapter 3 to find more about the WordPress database structure, including how data is stored in tables, as well as the use of popular database administration tool called phpMyAdmin to manage, view and edit database tables.

Choosing Linux, Apache, MySQL, and PHP server snvironments

A network of sites works best on a LAMP (Linux, Apache, MySQL and PHP) server with the `mod_rewrite` Apache module enabled. Mod_rewrite is an Apache module that builds URLs that are easier to read (also, see the nearby "Apache mod_rewrite" sidebar for more information). In WordPress, this is used for permalinks. If your install uses any permalink other than the default, `?p=123`, then you're okay. Your Web host can help you determine if your Web server allows this. It is a requirement for setting up the WordPress multisite feature (more information on permalink structure can be found in Book III, Chapter 3).

For the purposes of this chapter, we stick to the LAMP server setup because it is most similar to the average Web host, and most widely used.

**Book VIII
Chapter 1**

An Introduction to
Multiple Sites

Remember that the Apache `mod_rewrite` module is required for WordPress multisites. If you do not know if your current hosting environment has this module in place, drop an e-mail to your hosting provider and ask. They will be able to answer that question for you (in addition to installing the module for you in the event that your server does not yet have it).

Networks also work well on Nginx and Lightspeed servers; however, many users have reported having much difficulty on IIS (Windows) servers. Therefore, we don't recommend setting up WordPress, with multisite features, on a Windows server environment.

Subdomain sites work by way of a virtual host entry in Apache, also known as a wildcard subdomain. On shared hosts, your Web hosting provider support team will have to enable this for you, or they may already have done so for all accounts. It is best to ask your hosting provider before you begin. In these situations, the domain you use for your install must be the default domain in your account. Otherwise, the URLs of your subsites will fail to work properly or to have a folder name in the URL.

Some hosts may require you to have a dedicated IP address, but this is not a specific software requirement for a WordPress network to function.

Before proceeding with the final steps in enabling the WordPress multisite feature, you need to get a few items in order on your Web server. You also need to make a decision about how the multiple blogs within your network will be handled. These configurations need to be in place in order to run the WordPress Network successfully.

In the next section, you edit and configure Apache server files. If you can perform the configurations in this section yourself (and if you have access to the Apache configuration files), this section is for you. If you don't know how, are uncomfortable with adjusting these settings, or don't have access to change the configurations in your Web server software, you need to ask your hosting provider for help or hire a consultant to perform the configurations for you. We can't stress enough that you should not edit the Apache server files yourself if you aren't comfortable, or don't fully understand what you are doing. Web hosting providers have support staff to help you with these things, if you need it — take advantage of that!

Adding a virtual host to the Apache configuration

You need to add a hostname record pointing at your Web server in the DNS configuration tool available in your Web server administration software (like WebHost Manager (WHM), a popular Web host administration tool). The hostname record looks like this: *.*yourdomain.com* (where *yourdomain.* *com* is replaced with your actual domain name). Follow these steps to enable the wildcard subdomains in Apache:

1. **Log in as the root user to your server.**

2. **Open the `httpd.conf` file or the `vhost include` file for your current Web account.**

3. **Find the virtual host section for your domain.**

4. **Add the wildcard subdomain record next to the domain name.**

   It will look like this:

   ```
   ServerAlias yourdomain.com *.yourdomain.com
   ```

5. **Save the file.**

6. **Restart Apache.**

You will also need to add a wildcard subdomain DNS record. Depending on how your domain is set up, this can be done at your registrar or your Web host. If you simply pointed to your Web host's nameservers, then you can add more DNS records at your Web host in the Web server administration interface, such as WHM (Web Host Manager).

You also should add a `CNAME` record with a value of `*`. CNAME stands for "Canonical Name" and is a record stored in the DNS settings of your Apache Web server that tells Apache you would like to associate a new subdomain with the main account domain. Applying the value of `*` tells Apache to send any subdomain requests to your main domain, and from there, WordPress looks up that sudbomain in the database to see whether it exists.

Networks require a great deal more server memory (RAM) than typical WordPress sites (not using the multisite feature), simply because multisites are generally bigger, have a lot more traffic, and use up more database space and resources because multiple sites are running (as opposed to just one with regular WordPress). You aren't simply adding instances of WordPress. You're multiplying the processing and resource use of the server when you run the WordPress multisite feature. Although smaller instances of a network run okay on most Web hosts, you may find that when your network grows, you need more memory. We generally recommend that you start with a hosting account that has access to at least 256MB of RAM (memory).

For each site created, nine additional tables are added to the single database. Each table has a prefix similar to `wp_BLOG-ID_tablename` (where `BLOG-ID` is a unique ID assigned to the site).

The only exception to this is the main site. Its tables remain untouched, and remain the same as you saw in Book II, Chapter 3. With WordPress multi-sites, all new installations will leave the main blog tables untouched, and number additional site tables sequentially, with every new site that is added to the network.

Much discussion about the database layout has occurred in Trac, WordPress's codebase management system, and in the WordPress. org forums. Although it may seem unwieldy, it will scale appropriately. Limitations on database size have more to do with the server and database management tools. The average users build a small to medium-sized network, which usually needs no more than a VPS account.

Chapter 2: Setting Up and Configuring Network Features

In This Chapter

✓ **Enabling the network**

✓ **Configuring the network installation**

✓ **Disabling the network**

*T*his chapter covers how to find the files you need to edit the network, how to enable multiple sites in the network, and how to remove the network should you no longer want to have multiple sites in your WordPress install.

By default, access to network settings is disabled to ensure that users don't set up their network without researching all that the setup entails. Setting up a network is more than configuring options or turning on a feature. Before enabling and setting up a network, be sure that you read Chapter 1 of this minibook.

What you need:

✦ Backups of your site

✦ Access to the `wp-config.php` file for editing

✦ Enabled wildcard subdomains if you're using subdomains

Enabling the Network Feature

You need to enable access to the network menu so you can set up the network and allow the creation of multiple sites. Follow these steps:

1. **Connect to your Web server via FTP.**

   If you need a refresher on FTP, refer to Book II, Chapter 2.

2. **Locate the `wp-config.php` file in the root or `/public_html` directory of your Web site.**

   This file is with the main WordPress files.

3. **Open the `wp-config.php` file for editing in your favorite text editor.**

For Windows users, Notepad will do. For Macs, use TextMate.

4. **Find the line that reads `define('DB_COLLATE', '');`.**

Click at the end of that line. Press Enter and a new, blank line is created.

Some FTP clients let you right-click the filename on the server and choose Edit to edit the file within your FTP program, depending on which program you are using.

5. **Type** `define('WP_ALLOW_MULTISITE', true );`.

This line of code tells WordPress that you intend to use the multisite feature; additionally, it activates the Network option under the Tools menu in your WordPress Dashboard (covered later in this chapter).

6. **Save the `wp-config.php` file and upload it to your Web site.**

When you log in to the Dashboard of WordPress, you see the Network submenu under Tools, as shown in Figure 2-1.

Figure 2-1:
The
Network
menu.

Choosing this menu item will show the Create a Network admin page, covered in the next section. You will also see a reminder to deactivate all your plugins before continuing with network setup.

Before you begin your edits, make a copy of your `wp-config.php` file and keep it in a safe place on your computer.

Exploring the Difference between Subdirectories and Subdomains

Before you start setting up the network, the Create a Network page lets you choose the URL format of sites you are adding beneath the Addresses of Sites in your Network heading. By default, these sites are in subdomain format (`subdomain.yourdomain.com`) or subdirectory (`yourdomain.com/subdirectory`) format.

Figure 2-2 shows both choices displayed via radio buttons.

Figure 2-2:
Choosing
subdomains
or subdirec-
tories.

In some cases, depending to your setup, your choice here may be limited. WordPress does some autodetection with information about your installation and may prevent you from choosing an option that won't work with your setup.

Table 2-1 explains some of the situations you may encounter.

Table 2-1	Common Network Setup Situations
Situation	*Format*
Site URL is different than Home URL.	Network cannot be enabled.
Site URL is `http://localhost`.	Subdirectories only.
Site URL is an IP address.	
WordPress is installed in a folder (for example, `http://domain.com/wp`).	
Install is more than 30 days old.	Subdomains only.
WordPress is installed in the root of the domain (`http://domain.com`).	Subdomains are default, can choose either.

Site addresses generate in a similar way. They don't really exist and you won't see these site addresses in your directory structure on your Web server because they are served to the browser *virtually* when that site is requested. From a technical standpoint, subdomains require an extra step in server setup for the wildcards. Chapter 1 in this minibook covers setting up wildcard subdomains on the server side. Subdomains are somewhat separated from the main domain, at least in terms of content. Subdirectories, on the other hand, are part of the main domain, as if they were a page off the main site.

The terms *subdirectory* and *subfolder* are interchangeable, but we stick to *subdirectory* for the purposes of this book.

Because each site's URL is saved in its tables in the database, after you pick which subsites you want to create, you cannot switch this without reinstalling the network.

Each site format offers certain search engine optimization benefits. Search engines read subdomains as separate sites on your Web host; therefore, they maintain their page rank and authority and multiple results for your domain are listed. Subdirectories are read as pages or sections off your main domain, help the main domain's page rank and authority, and provide one result for your domain in search engines.

If you want your extra sites to have separate domain names, you still need to pick one of these options. Chapter 6 of this minibook covers top-level domains.

Installing the Network on Your Site

The Network Details heading on the Create a Network page has options filled in automatically. The server address, for example, is pulled from your installation and isn't editable. The network title and administrator e-mail address are pulled from your installation database, too, because your initial WordPress site is the main site in the network. Clicking the Install button causes WordPress to create new network tables in the database. The page refreshes and the Create a Network of WordPress Sites page appears, as shown in Figure 2-3.

From the Create a Network of WordPress Sites page, follow these steps to install the multisite feature after you install the network. ***Note:*** These steps require that you edit Web server files, so be sure to have your text editor program handy.

1. **Create a directory on your Web server called `blogs.dir`.**

In your WordPress installation directory is a folder labeled `/wp-content/`. In that folder, create your new directory, which stores all the uploaded media (photos, videos, audio, and other media) within the network sites on your domain. The entire path should look similar to `/public_html/wp-content/blogs.dir`.

Most FTP programs allow you to create a new directory (or a new folder) by right-clicking in the Web server window and choosing Make New Directory. For more information about FTP, see Book II, Chapter 2.

2. **Add the network-related configuration lines to the `wp-config.php`.**

On the Create a Network of WordPress Sites page, WordPress gives you up to seven lines of configuration rules that need to be added to the `wp-config.php` file. The first line includes the line you added earlier in this chapter: `define('multisite', true );`. You can skip that line, copy the rest of the lines, and then paste them beneath the `define('multisite', truc);` line in your `wp-config.php`. The lines of code you add look like this:

```
define( 'SUBDOMAIN_INSTALL', true );
$base = '/ ';
define( 'DOMAIN_CURRENT_SITE', 'localhost' );
define( 'PATH_CURRENT_SITE', '/' );
define( 'SITE_ID_CURRENT_SITE', 1 );
define( 'BLOG_ID_CURRENT_SITE', 1 );
```

Figure 2-3:
The Create a Network page.

**Book VIII
Chapter 2**

**Setting Up and
Configuring
Network Features**

These lines of code provide configuration settings regarding subdomains, the base URL of your Web site, and your Web site's current path. Additionally, it assigns a unique ID of 1 to your Web site and blog for the main installation site of your multisite network.

The lines of code on the Create a Network of WordPress Sites page are unique to your installation of WordPress and specific to your site setup so make sure that you copy the lines of code from your installation.

3. **Add the rewrite rules to the `.htaccess` file on your Web server.**

   WordPress gives you up to 13 lines of code that you need to add to the `.htaccess` file on your Web server in the WordPress installation directory. The lines look something like this:

   ```
   RewriteEngine On
   RewriteBase /
   RewriteRule ^index\.php$ - [L]

   # uploaded files
   RewriteRule ^([_0-9a-zA-Z-]+/)?files/(.+) wp-includes/ms-files.
       php?file=$2 [L]

   # add a trailing slash to /wp-admin
   RewriteRule ^([_0-9a-zA-Z-]+/)?wp-admin$ $1wp-admin/ [R=301,L]

   RewriteCond %{REQUEST_FILENAME} -f [OR]
   RewriteCond %{REQUEST_FILENAME} -d
   RewriteRule ^ - [L]
   RewriteRule ^[_0-9a-zA-Z-]+/(wp-(content|admin|includes).*) $1 [L]
   RewriteRule ^[_0-9a-zA-Z-]+/(.*\.php)$ $1 [L]
   RewriteRule . index.php [L]
   ```

In Chapter 1 of this minibook, we discuss the Apache `mod_rewrite` module. You must have it installed on your Web server to run the WordPress multisite feature. The rules you add to the `.htaccess` file on your Web server are `mod_rewrite` rules. They need to be in place so that your Web server tells WordPress how to handle things, such as permalinks for blog posts and pages, media, and other uploaded files. Without these rules in place, the WordPress multisite feature will not work correctly.

4. **Copy the lines of code from the Create a Network of WordPress Sites page, open the `.htaccess` file, and paste the lines of code there.**

   Completely replace the rules that already exist in that file.

5. **Save the `.htaccess` file and upload it to your Web server.**

6. **Return to the Dashboard and click the Dashboard link at the top of the menu navigation.**

   You may be asked to log in to WordPress again because you have changed some of the browser cookie-handling rules in the `wp-config.php` and `.htaccess` files.

Completion of the installation steps activates a Network Admin menu item in the upper-right menu of links in your WordPress Dashboard. The Network Admin section is where you, as the site owner, administer and manage your multisite WordPress network. (See Chapter 3 of this minibook.)

Disabling the Network

At some point, you may decide that running a network of sites isn't for you, and you may find that you want to disable the multisite feature completely. Before disabling the network, you want to save any content from the other sites by making a full backup of your database and any files that exist in the /wp-content/blogs.dir/ folder. Book II, Chapter 7 has detailed information about backing up your site if you need a refresher.

The first step is to restore the original wp-config.php file and .htaccess files that you saved earlier. This causes your WordPress installation to stop displaying the Network Admin menu and the extra sites.

You may also want to delete the tables that were added, which permanently removes the extra sites from your installation. Book II, Chapter 3 takes you through the WordPress database, including using a popular database administration tool called phpMyAdmin. You can use that tool to delete the multisite tables from your WordPress database when you want to deactivate the feature. The extra database tables that are no longer required when you aren't running the WordPress multisite feature include

✦ **wp_blogs:** This database table contains one record per site and is used for site lookup.

✦ **wp_blog_versions:** This database table is used internally for upgrades.

✦ **wp_registration_log:** This database table contains information on sites created when a user signs up, if they chose to create a site at the same time.

✦ **wp_signups:** This database table contains information on users who signed up for the network.

✦ **wp_site:** This database table contains one record per WordPress network.

✦ **wp_sitemeta:** This database table contains network settings.

Additionally, you can delete any database tables that have blog IDs associated with them. These tables start with prefixes that look like wp_1_, wp_2_, wp_3_, and so on.

WordPress adds new tables each time you add a new site to your network. Those database tables are assigned a unique number, incrementally.

Dealing with Common Errors

Occasionally, you might enter a configuration setting incorrectly or change your mind about the kind of network you require. If you installed WordPress, enabled the network, and then want to move it to a new location, you will encounter errors when changing the URL. The proper method is to move WordPress first, disable the network if you installed it, and then enable the network at the new location.

To change from subdomains to subfolders or vice versa, follow these steps:

1. **Delete the extra sites, if any were created.**

2. **Edit `wp-config.php`, changing the value of `define( 'SUBDOMAIN_INSTALL', true );` to `define( 'SUBDOMAIN_INSTALL', false );`**

   To switch from subdomains to subdirectories, change `false` to `true`.

3. **Save the `wp-config.php` file and upload it to your Web site.**

4. **Visit the Dashboard of WordPress and choose Settings⇨Permalink and click the Save Changes button.**

   This saves and resets your permalink structure settings and flushes the internal rewrite rules, which are slightly different in subdomains than they are in subdirectories.

This process can't be done if you want to keep extra sites.

Chapter 3: Becoming a Network Admin

In This Chapter

✔ Getting familiar with the Network Admin menu

✔ Managing your network

✔ Preventing spam blogs

After you enable the WordPress network option and become a network admin, you can examine the various settings that are available to you, and go over the responsibilities you have while running a network.

As a network admin, you can access the Network Admin menu, which includes a number of submenus, to manage the sites in your network, as well as the overall settings for your network. This chapter discusses the menu items and options on the Network Admin page, guides you in setting network options, and discusses the best ways to prevent spam and spam blogs (splogs).

Exploring the Network Admin Menu

When you visit the Dashboard after activating the multisite feature, you see the Network Admin menu in the upper-right side of the Dashboard, as shown in Figure 3-1. WordPress has separated the Network Admin features from the rest of the regular Dashboard features to make it easier for you to know which part of your site you are managing. For example, if you are performing items that maintain your main Web site, such as publishing posts or pages, creating/editing categories, and so on, you'll work in the regular Dashboard (see Book III). However, if you're managing any one of the network sites, plugins, and themes for the network sites or registered users, you will work in the Network Admin section of the Dashboard.

Network Admin link

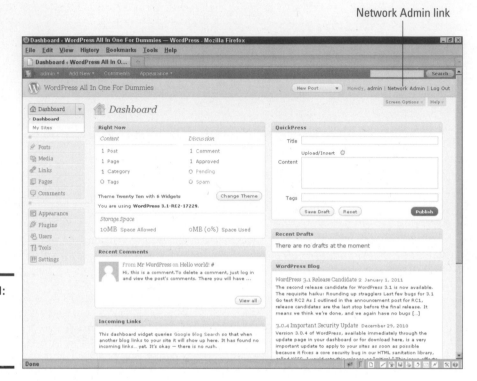

Figure 3-1:
The
Network
Admin
menu.

The distinct differences between the Site Admin Dashboard and the Network Admin Dashboard, and subsequent menu features, are important. WordPress tries its best to assume which features you're attempting to work with; however, if you find yourself getting lost in the Dashboard and cannot find a menu or feature that you're used to seeing, double-check to make sure that you're working in the correct section of the Dashboard.

The Network Admin page (see Figure 3-2) looks similar to the regular WordPress Dashboard we discuss in Book III. Notice, however, that the modules shown on the Network Admin Dashboard pertain to the network of sites and give you options to create a new site, create a new user, and search existing sites and users. Obviously, you won't perform this search if you don't have any users or sites yet. However, this function is extremely useful when you have a community of users and sites within your network.

The Network Admin Dashboard is configurable, just like the regular Dashboard; you can move the modules around and edit the settings of the modules. Refer to Book III, Chapters 1 and 2 for more information about arranging the Dashboard modules to suit your tastes.

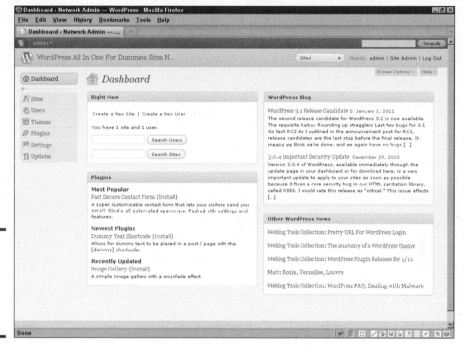

Figure 3-2:
The
Network
Admin
Dashboard
page.

The Search Users feature allows you to search usernames and user e-mail addresses. If you search for the user *Lisa,* for instance, your results will include any user whose username or e-mail address contains *Lisa* — so you can receive multiple returns when using just one search word or phrase. The Search Sites feature returns any blog content within your community that contains your search term, too.

The Network Admin page has two links near the top of the page that are very useful:

✦ **Create a New Site:** Click this link to create a new site within your network. When clicked, the Sites page appears where you can add a new site. We cover how to do this in the upcoming "Sites" section.

✦ **Create a New User:** Click this link to create a new user account within your community. When clicked, the Users page appears where you can add a new user to your community. We cover how to do this in the upcoming "Users" section.

Additionally, the Network Admin page gives you a real-time count of how many sites and users you have in your network, which is nice-to-know information for any network admin.

Managing Your Network

As mentioned, the Network Admin Dashboard has its own set of unique menus separate from the regular Site Admin Dashboard. Those menus are located on the left side of the Network Admin Dashboard. This section goes through each menu item and provides you with explanations and instructions on how to work with the settings and configurations to help you manage your network, sites, and users.

The full list of menus available on the Network Admin Dashboard includes

✦ **Sites:** View a list of the sites in your network, along with details about them.

✦ **Users:** See detailed info about current users in your network.

✦ **Themes:** View all the currently available themes to enable or disable them for use in your network.

✦ **Plugins:** Manage (activate/deactivate) themes for use on all sites within your network.

✦ **Settings:** Configure global settings for your network.

✦ **Updates:** Upgrade all sites in your network with one click.

All the items in the Network Admin Dashboard are important, and you will use them frequently throughout the life of your network. Normally, we would take you through each of the menu items in order so it's easy for you to follow along in your Dashboard; however, performing some preliminary configurations on your network before you do anything else is important. Therefore, the following section starts with the Settings menu and then takes you through the other menu items in order of appearance in the Network Admin Dashboard.

Settings

When you click the Settings menu link in the Network Admin Dashboard, the Settings page loads in your browser window. The Settings page contains several sections of options for you to configure to set up your network the way you want to.

Operational settings

The operational settings, shown in Figure 3-3, are Network Name and Network Admin Email:

✦ **Network Name:** This is the name for your overall network of sites. This name is included in all communications regarding your network, including e-mails that new users receive when they register a new site within your network. Type your desired network name in the text box provided.

✦ **Network Admin Email:** This is the e-mail address correspondence that your Web site is addressed from, including all registration and sign-up e-mails that new users receive when they register a new site or user account within your network. Enter the e-mail that you want to use for these purposes in the text box provided.

Registration settings

The Registration Settings section (see Figure 3-4) allows you to control aspects of allowing users to sign up to your network. The most important option is whether to allow open registration.

Figure 3-3:
The Operational Settings section on the Network Settings page.

Figure 3-4:
The Registration Settings on the Network Settings page.

Book VIII
Chapter 3

Becoming a
Network Admin

From one of the following options, decide how you want registrations to be handled on your network:

✦ **Registration is Disabled:** Disallows new user registration completely. When selected, this option prevents people who visit your site from registering for a user account.

✦ **User Accounts May Be Registered:** Gives people the ability to create only a user account; users will not be able to create a blog within your network.

✦ **Logged In Users May Register New Sites:** Allows only existing users — those who are already logged in — to create a new blog within your network. This also disables new user registration completely. You would use this option if you don't want just anyone registering for an account. Instead, you (as the site administrator) can add new users at your discretion.

✦ **Both Sites and User Accounts Can Be Registered:** Gives users the ability to register an account and a site on your network during the registration process.

These options apply only to outside users. As a network admin, you can create new sites and users any time you want by using the options in the Network Admin Dashboard. (See the information about creating new users in the upcoming "Users" section.)

The remaining options under the Registration Settings heading are as follows:

✦ **Registration Notification:** When this option is checked, an e-mail is sent to the network admin every time a user or a site is created on the system, even if the network admin creates the new site.

✦ **Add New Users:** Choose Yes or No to show whether you want to allow your community blog owners (individual site admins) to add new users to their own community blog via the Users page within their individual dashboards.

✦ **Banned Names:** By default, WordPress bans several usernames from being registered within your community, including *www, web, root, admin, main, invite, administrator,* and so on. For good reason, you don't want a random user to register a username, such as *admin,* because you don't want that person misrepresenting himself as an administrator on your site. You can enter an unlimited amount of usernames that you do not want to allow on your site in the Banned Names text box.

✦ **Limited Email Registrations:** You can limit sign-ups based on e-mail domains by filling in this text box one e-mail per line. If you have open registrations but you limited the e-mail addresses, anyone who tries to sign up who doesn't match a domain on the list will be unable to register. This is an excellent option to use in a school or corporate environment where you're providing students or employees e-mail addresses and sites.

✦ **Banned Email Domains:** This feature, the reverse of the above, blocks all sign-ups from a particular domain, which can be useful in stopping spammers. For example, you can enter **gmail.com** in the field, and anyone trying to sign up with a Gmail address will be denied.

New site settings

The New Site Settings section is a configurable list of items that populates default values when a new site is created. The list includes the values that display in welcome e-mails, on a user's first post page, and on a new site's first page, as shown in Figure 3-5.

✦ **Welcome Email:** The e-mail text that owners of newly registered sites in your network receive when their registration is complete. There is a default message that you can leave in place, if you like. Or, you can type the text of the e-mail you want new site owners to receive when they register a new site within your Network.

A few variables you can use in this e-mail aren't explained entirely on the Site Options page, including

- SITE_NAME: Inserts the name of your WordPress site
- BLOG_URL: Inserts the URL of the new member's blog
- USERNAME: Inserts the new member's username
- PASSWORD: Inserts the new member's password
- BLOG_URLwp-login.php: Inserts the hyperlinked login URL for the new member's blog
- SITE_URL: Inserts the hyperlinked URL for your WordPress site

✦ **First Post:** This is the first, default post that displays on every newly created site in your network. WordPress provides you with some default text that you can leave in place, or you can type your desired text in the provided text box that you want to appear in the first post on every site that's created in your community.

You can use this area to provide useful information about your site and services. This also serves as a nice guide for new users because they can view that post in their Dashboard, on the Edit Post page, to see how it was entered and formatted and then use that as a guide for creating their own blog posts. You can also use the variables mentioned in the bullet points in "Welcome Email" to have WordPress automatically add some information for you.

✦ **First Page:** Similar to the First Post setting, this default text for a default page displays on every newly created site in your network. (The First Page text box does not include default text; if you leave it blank, no default page is created.)

✦ **First Comment:** This default comment displays on the first default post on every newly created site within your network. Type the text that you want to appear in the first comment on every site that's created in your community.

✦ **First Comment Author:** Type the name of the author of the first comment on new sites in your network.

✦ **First Comment URL:** Type the Web address (URL) for the author of the first comment; this links (via hyperlink) the first comment author's name to the URL you type here.

New Site Settings	
Welcome Email	Dear User, Your new SITE_NAME site has been successfully set up at: BLOG_URL You can log in to the administrator account with the following information: The welcome email sent to new site owners.
Welcome User Email	Password: PASSWORD LOGINLINK Thanks! --The Team @ SITE_NAME The welcome email sent to new users.
First Post	Welcome to <a href="SITE_URL">SITE_NAME</a>. This is your first post. Edit or delete it, then start blogging! The first post on a new site.
First Page	The first page on a new site.
First Comment	

Figure 3-5:
New Site Settings on the Network Settings page.

Upload settings

The Upload Settings section (see Figure 3-6) defines global values pertaining to the type of files you will allow the site owners within your network to upload using the file upload feature on the WordPress Write Posts and Write Page areas (see Book III, Chapter 4). The check boxes shown in the Media Upload Buttons under the Upload Settings section are deselected, by default. To give your network site owners the ability to upload files, place a check mark next to the name of each media type:

✦ Images

✦ Videos

✦ Music

Enabling the file types will display the upload icons above the post box on the Write Page and Write Post pages in the users Dashboard (see Book III,

Chapter 4 for information on uploading files). In some situations, you may decide to disallow certain file types, so disabling a file type removes that file type's icon from the post editor.

The next option in the Upload Settings section is Site Upload space. The amount is in megabytes (MB), and the default storage space is 10MB. This amount of hard drive space is what you give users to store the files they upload to their blogs. If you want to change the default storage space, type a number in the text box provided.

The Upload File Types text field defines the types of files that you, as the network admin, will allow site owners to upload to their sites in their Dashboard. Users cannot upload any file types that do not appear in this text box. By default, WordPress includes the following file types: `.jpg`, `.jpeg`, `.png`, `.gif`, `.mp3`, `.mov`, `.avi`, `.wmv`, `.midi`, `.mid`, and `.pdf`. You can remove any default file types and add new ones.

The final option under Upload Settings defines the Max Upload file size. This amount is in kilobytes (K), and the default file size is 1500K. This means that a user cannot upload a file that is larger than 1500K. Adjust this number as you see fit by typing a new number in the text box provided.

Figure 3-6:
Upload
Settings on
the Network
Settings
page.

Upload Settings	
Media upload buttons	☐ Images ☐ Videos ☐ Music The media upload buttons to display on the "Write Post" page. Make sure you update the allowed upload file types below as well.
Site upload space	☑ Limit total size of files uploaded to 10 MB
Upload file types	jpg jpeg png gif mp3 mov avi wmv midi mid pdf
Max upload file size	1500 KB

Menu settings

The Plugins menu is disabled within the Dashboard of all network sites (except for the network admin's), as shown in Figure 3-7. However, the network admin always has access to the Plugins menu. If you leave this option unselected, the Plugins page will be visible to users on their own site dashboard. Place a check mark in the box to enable the Plugins menu for your network users. For more information about using plugins with WordPress, see Book VII.

When you have completely finished configuring the settings on the Network Settings page, do not forget to click the Save Changes button at the bottom of the page, underneath the final Menu Settings section (see Figure 3-7). If you navigate away from the Network Settings page without clicking the Save Changes button, none of your configurations will be saved, and you'll need to go through the entire process again.

Figure 3-7:
The
Network
Options
page's
Menu
Settings
section.

Menu Settings

Enable administration   ☐ Plugins
menus

Save Changes

Sites

Clicking the Sites menu item on the Network Admin Dashboard takes you to the Sites page where you can manage your individual sites. Although each site in the network has its own Dashboard for basic tasks, such as posting, changing themes, and so on, the Sites page is where you create and delete sites and make edits to properties of the sites within your network. Editing information from this page is handy when you have issues accessing a site's back-end Dashboard.

The Sites page also lists all the sites within your network. The listing shows the following statistics about each community site:

✦ **Path:** The site's path in your network. For example, in Figure 3-8, you see a site listed with the path /newsite/. This means that the site's domain is newsite.*yourdomain.com* if you're using a subdomain setup, or *yoursite.com*/newsite if you're using a subdirectory setup).

✦ **Last Updated:** The date the site was last updated (or published to).

✦ **Registered:** The date the site was registered in your network.

✦ **Users:** The username and e-mail address associated with the user(s) of that site.

When you hover on the pathname of a site in your network, you see a handy listing of links that will help you manage the site. Figure 3-8 shows the options that appear beneath a site listing when you hover your mouse on a site name in the list.

The management options for network sites, shown in Figure 3-8, are as follows:

✦ **Edit:** A link to the Edit Site page (see Figure 3-9) where you can change aspects of each site.

✦ **Dashboard:** A link to the Dashboard of the site.

✦ **Deactivate:** Click this link to mark the site for deletion in your network; after clicking the Deactivate link, a message displays in a pop-up window that asks you to confirm your intention to deactivate the site. Click the Yes button to confirm. The user's site will display a message stating that the site has been deleted. This action can be reversed by revisiting the Sites page and clicking the Activate link that appears underneath the site pathname (the Activate link only appears underneath sites that are marked as Deactivated).

✦ **Archive:** Click this link to archive the site in your network, which prevents visitors from viewing the site and displays "This site has been archived or suspended." This action can be reversed by revisiting the Sites page and clicking the Unarchive link that appears beneath the site's pathname. (The Unarchive link only appears beneath sites that are archived.)

✦ **Spam:** Clicking this link marks the site as spam and blocks the users from being able to access the dashboard. It also displays a message stating, "This site has been archived or suspended". This action can be reversed by revisiting the Sites page and clicking the Not Spam link that appears underneath the site's pathname (the Not Spam link only appears underneath sites that are marked as Spam).

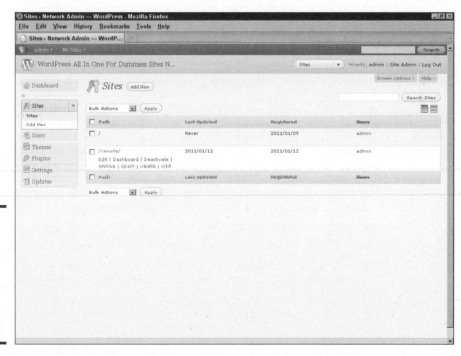

Figure 3-8:
Individual
Site
Manage-
ment
Options on
the Sites
page.

✦ **Delete:** Click this link to delete the site from your network of sites permanently. Although you see a confirmation screen that asks you to confirm your intention to delete the site, when done, you cannot reverse this decision.

✦ **Visit:** Click this link to visit the live site in your Web browser.

Figure 3-9:
The Edit Site
Page.

Generally, you only use the Edit Site page (refer to Figure 3-9) when the settings are unavailable from the Dashboard of that particular site, by configuring the options that appear underneath each of the four tabs on the Edit Sites page, as shown in Figure 3-9:

✦ **Info:** Under this tab, you can edit the sites domain, path, registered date, updated date and attributes (Public, Archived, Spam, Deleted, Mature).

✦ **Users:** Under this tab, you can manage the users that are assigned to the site, as well as add new users to the site under the Add New User section.

✦ **Themes:** Under this tab, you can enable themes for this site. This is particularly useful if you have themes that aren't network enabled (see the upcoming "Themes" section) because all the themes that aren't enabled within your network are listed under the Themes tab, which allows you to enable themes on a per-site basis.

✦ **Settings:** the settings under this tab cover all the database settings for the site that you are editing. Editing these settings is rare because as the network admin, you have access to each user's Dashboard and can make any changes to the site's configuration settings there.

Also in the Sites menu in the Network Admin Dashboard, you see a link called Add New — click that link to load the Add New Site page in your Network Admin Dashboard (Figure 3-10). You can create a new site from the Add New Site page, as shown in Figure 3-10. Fill in the Site Address, Site Title, and Admin Email fields and then click the Add Site button to add the new site to your network. If the admin e-mail you enter is associated with an existing user, the new site is assigned to that user in your network. If the user doesn't exist, a new user is created and an e-mail is sent with a notification. The site is immediately accessible. The e-mail the user receives contains a link to their site, a login link and their username and password.

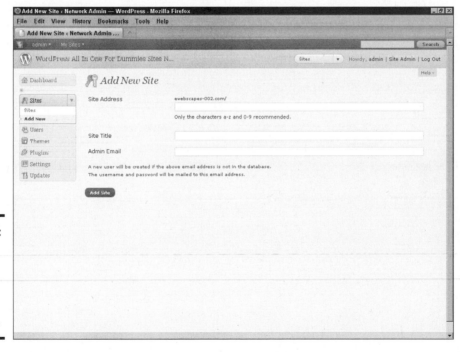

Figure 3-10:
The Add New Site page in the Network Admin Dashboard.

Users

Clicking the Users menu link in the Network Admin Dashboard takes you to the Users page where you see a full listing of members, or users, within your network. The Users page (see Figure 3-11) lists the following information about each user:

+ **Username:** The login name the member uses when she logs in to her account in your community.

+ **Name:** The user's real name, taken from her profile. If the user has not provided her name in her profile, this column will be blank.

+ **E-mail:** The e-mail address the user entered when she registered on your site.

+ **Registered:** The date when the user registered.

+ **Sites:** If you enable sites within your WordPress Network, this lists any sites the user is a member of.

Similar to the Sites page, you can add and delete users to the network, and manage users, by clicking the Edit or Delete links that appear under their names when you hover on them with your mouse (the same way you do with sites on the Sites page).

To delete a user, you simply hover over the username in the list that appears on the Users page. Click the Delete link and a new screen appears with a page telling you to transfer this user's posts and links to another user account (most likely, yours). Then click the Confirm Deletion button and WordPress removes the user from the network, permanently — this action is irreversible, so be certain about your decision before you click that button!

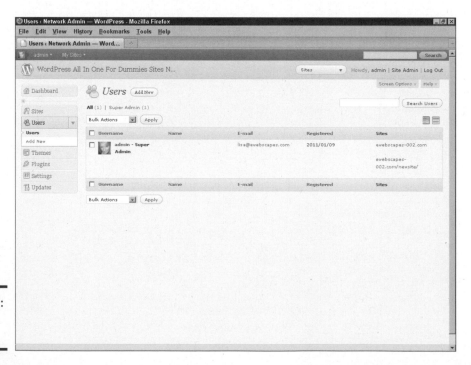

Figure 3-11:
The Users page.

You can also edit a user's profile information by clicking the Edit link that appears when you hover your mouse on his name on the Users page. Clicking that link takes you to the Edit User page, shown in Figure 3-12, where you are presented with several options, which just happen to (mostly) be the very same options and setting that you configured for your own profile information back in Book III, Chapter 3.

The only difference with the Edit User page within the Network Admin Dashboard is the setting labeled Super Admin — deselected by default. However, if you select this box, you grant this user network admin privileges for your network. This means that the user has the exact same access and permission as you.

At the time of this writing, the terms *super admin* and *network admin* are interchangeable. When WordPress merged the WordPress MU code base with the regular WordPress software, the term they used to describe the network admin was *super admin*. Now, network admin is the standard term; however, areas within the Network Admin Dashboard and regular Dashboard still use *Super Admin* as a label. We will most likely see that change in the very near future because WordPress will realize the discrepancy and update later versions of the software.

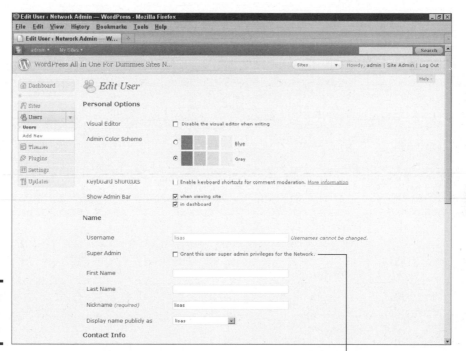

Figure 3-12:
The Edit
Users page.

The Super Admin setting

Also in the Users menu in the Network Admin Dashboard, you see a link called Add New — click that link to load the Add New User page in your Network Admin Dashboard (Figure 3-13).

You can add a new user from the Add New User page, by filling in the username and e-mail of the user you want to add and then clicking the Add User button. The new user is sent an e-mail notification alerting them of the new account, along with the site URL, their username and password (randomly generated by WordPress at the time the user account is created).

Figure 3-13:
The Add
New User
page in the
Network
Admin
Dashboard.

Add New User

Username

Email

Username and password will be mailed to the above email address.

Add User

Themes

When a network is enabled, only users with network admin access have permission to install themes, which are shared across the network. You can review details on how to find, install, and activate new themes with your WordPress installation in Book VI, Chapters 1 and 2. After you install a theme, you must enable it in your network in order for the theme to appear in the Appearance menu of each site, where users in your network can activate it on their site. To access the Network Themes page (shown in Figure 3-14), click the Themes link under the Themes menu on the Network Admin Dashboard.

In Chapter 5 of this minibook, we show you how to enable a theme on a per-site basis.

Plugins

Most WordPress plugins will work on your network. There are, however, some special plugins and some special considerations for using plugins with a network.

First, if you need a refresher on how to find, install, and activate plugins in WordPress, page back through and find Book VII, Chapters 1 and 2 for this information.

Figure 3-14:
The
Network
Themes
page.

Browse to the Plugins page in your WordPress Network Admin Dashboard by clicking the Plugins link under the Plugins menu. You find that the Plugins page is just as we describe in Book VII, Chapter 1, but you could easily miss one very small, subtle difference if you don't know where to look. Check out Figure 3-15 below the name of the plugin. Do you see the Network Activate link? That is the big difference between plugins listed in the regular Dashboard and the Network Admin Dashboard. As the network admin, you can enable certain plugins to be activated globally, across your entire network. This means that all sites in your network will have the network-activated plugin features available. (Plugins that you activate on the regular Dashboard {under Site Admin} are only activated and available for *your* main Web site.)

Earlier in this chapter in the Settings: Menu Settings section, if you select the Plugins menu, then users see the plugins listed on their Plugins page in their Dashboard. In their list of plugins, they only see the plugins that you have not network activated; rather, they see a list of all the plugins you installed in your WordPress installation, but none of them are activated on that user's site. The user has the ability to activate, and deactivate, those plugins as they desire.

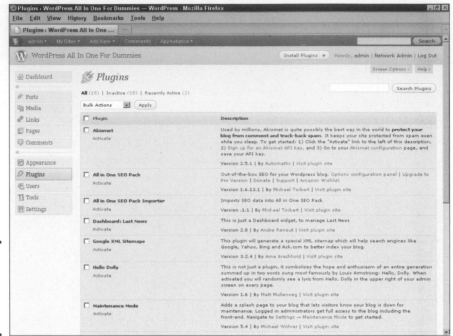

Figure 3-15:
The
Network
Plugins
page.

Network admins are the only people who can install new plugins on the site; regular users within the network do not have that kind of access (unless you made them a network admin in their User settings).

Also located in the Plugins menu in the Network Admin Dashboard are two other links: Add New and Editor. This is where you can add and install new plugins by searching the WordPress Plugin Directory within your Dashboard (we cover this in Book VII, Chapters 1 and 2), and the Editor link gives you access to the Plugin Editor, covered in Book VII, Chapter 4.

Updates

Clicking the Updates link on the Network Admin Dashboard menu gives you access to the WordPress Updates page, which takes you through the same process of upgrading your WordPress installation software as we describe in Book II, Chapter 6. (In fact, the page looks the same as the one we show you in Book II, Chapter 6.) However, with a network site, WordPress takes the extra step of upgrading all sites within your network so they all use the same, upgraded feature sets.

If the process of upgrading network sites stalls or stops, the URL of the last site upgraded displays on the WordPress Updates page. The network admin can access the dashboard of the site where the upgrade stopped, which usually clears up the issue. A user accessing their site Dashboard after an upgrade also triggers this process.

Stopping Spam Sign-Ups and Splogs

If you choose to have open sign-ups in which any member of the public can register and create a new site on your network, at some point, automated bots run by malicious users and spammers will visit your network sign-up page and attempt to create one, or multiple, sites in your network. They do so by automated means, hoping to create links to their sites or fill their site on your network with spam posts. This kind of spam blog or site is a *splog*.

Spam bloggers don't hack your system to take advantage of this; they call aspects of the sign-up page directly. You can do a few simple things to slow them down considerably or stop them altogether.

In the earlier "Registration settings" section, we go over a few options, including areas in which you can specify e-mail addresses to allow or block. The Add New Users check box (refer to Figure 3-4) stops many spammers when unchecked. When spammers access the system to set up a spam site, they often use the Add New Users feature to create many other blogs via programs built in to the bots.

Spammers often find your site via Google Search for the link to the sign-up page. You can stop Google and other search engines from crawling your sign-up page by adding `rel=nofollow,noindex` on the sign-up page link. Wherever you add a link to your sign-up page, inviting new users to sign up, the HTML code you use to add the `nofollow,noindex` looks like this:

```
<a href="http://yoursite.com/wp-signup.php" rel="nofollow,noindex ">Get your own
    site here</a>
```

You can add this to any page or widget area as a normal link to instruct legitimate visitors to sign up for a site in your network.

Plugins can help stop spam blogs, too. The Moderate New Blogs plugin interrupts the user sign-up process and sends you (the network admin) an e-mail notification that a user has signed up for a blog. You can then determine whether the blog is legitimate. Download the plugin at `http://wordpress.org/extend/plugins/moderate-new-blogs`.

The Hashcash plugin was written to stop spam comments, mainly, but does also prevent spam sign-ups on a WordPress site, with, or without, the network feature activated. You can get the plugin at `http://wordpress.org/extend/plugins/wp-hashcash`. This plugin checks to make sure that the sign-up page was opened within a browser window, and not accessed directly.

The Cookies for Comments plugin (available at `http://wordpress.org/extend/plugins/cookies-for-comments`) leaves a cookie in a visitor's browser. If the sign-up page is visited, the plugin checks for the cookie. If there isn't a cookie, the sign-up fails. Be sure to check the installation directions on this because it requires a `.htaccess` file edit.

If persistent spammers still manage to sign up despite using the plugins above, you can block them by their IP address. A post on the BuddyPress forums instructs you how to add rules to your `.htaccess` file to block spam attempts. You can see the instructions at `http://ewebscapes.com/block-spam`.

Chapter 4: Management of Users and Access Control

In This Chapter

✓ **Understanding default user management**

✓ **Changing default user behavior**

✓ **Exploring user access to site features**

*I*n Chapter 3, we discuss the new Network Admin menu you now have access to in your Dashboard to manage aspects of your network. In this chapter, we explain how users are managed across the network, including how you can change some of the default management options to suit your needs. One of the hardest things for new network admins to understand is that although each site is managed separately, users are global.

That is, after a user logs in, he is logged in across the entire network, has the ability to comment on any site that has enabled the Must Be Logged in to Comment feature in their Discussion Settings page (Book III, Chapter 3). The user can visit the Dashboard of the main site in the install to manage his profile information and access the Dashboard⇨My Sites menu to reach sites that they administer. The user also registers at the main site, and not at individual sites in the network.

Setting Default User Permissions

When you enable the network, new site and new user registrations are turned off, by default. However, the Network Admin can add new sites and users from the Network Admin Dashboard. To let users sign up for your network, complete the following steps:

1. **Click the Network Admin link at the top of the Dashboard and then click the Settings menu link.**

   The Settings page loads in your browser window.

2. **In the Registration Settings section, select the User Accounts May Be Registered option (as shown in Figure 4-1).**

   This allows users to register on your network, assigns them to the main site as a Subscriber, but doesn't allow them to create a new site of their own.

3. **Click the Save Changes button at the bottom of the page.**

By selecting the option: *Both sites and user accounts can be registered* on the Network Admin Settings page, you allow users not only to register a new account, but also give them the option to create a new site on your network.

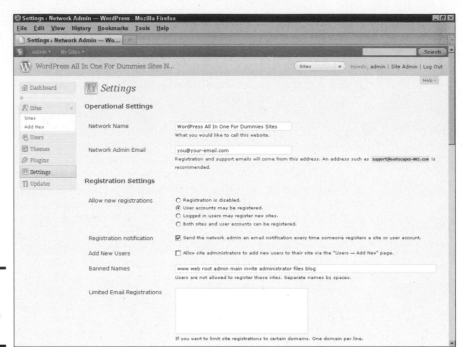

Figure 4-1: User registration options.

User registration

When signing up, users are directed to the main site of the installation and then added to one of the child sites. This site may be their site (if they choose to have a site when registering) or an existing site. If it's any existing site other than the main site, the user must be manually added to that site by the Network Admin, or the user who owns the site (if you have enabled the option under the Network Admin Settings to allow site admins to add new users to their sites).

The registration page (see Figure 4-2) is located at `http://yourdomain.com/wp-signup.php`. This sign-up page bypasses the WordPress registration page described in Book III, Chapter 4.

Figure 4-2:
The network
sign-up
page.

After filling out the form, the user will receive an e-mail with a link to activate her account. When she does so, she can immediately log in and manage her details; she is directed to her primary site, which is the main site or Dashboard site if she has no site to administer.

Users can also be added to existing sites in the network. The Network Admin can always assign users to specific sites on a per-case basis. When Network Admins set up a network, the Allow Site Administrators to Add New Users to Their Site via the "Users à Add New" Page setting (shown in Figure 4-3) allows them to add other users in the network to their sites. Although the Add New Users setting is turned off by default, you can enable it by selecting the box on the Settings page in the Network Admin Dashboard.

Controlling access to sites

The Network Admin has a list of all the sites on the network; by default, other users cannot find other sites in the network. Unless you, the Network Admin, add such ability via plugins, a user cannot navigate from one child site to the next. The only list provided to a user is the Dashboard⇨My Sites menu shown in Figure 4-4.

Figure 4-3:
Allowing users to add other users to their site.

The Add New Users setting

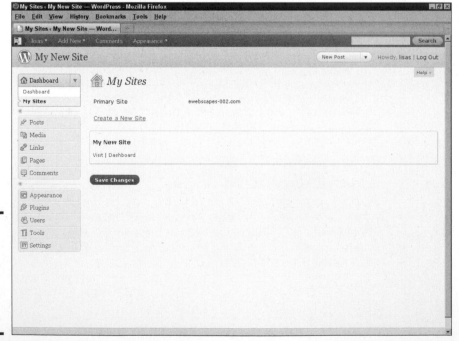

Figure 4-4:
The My Sites page shows sites the user administrates.

The My Sites page lists only sites the user is the administrator of, not sites on which the user has a lesser role. Additionally, the My Sites menu has a link for the user to create more sites (if the Network Admin has allowed it via the Network Admin⇨Settings menu).

By default, users can create no sites or an unlimited number of sites. You can limit the number of sites a user can create by installing the Limit Blogs per User plugin.

Follow these steps to limit the amount of sites your users can create:

1. **Click the Network Admin link located at the top right of your Dashboard.**

2. **Click Plugins⇨Add New.**

   This loads the Install Plugins page in your Network Admin Dashboard.

3. **In the Search field, add the name of the plugin: Limit Blogs per User.**

   Be sure that you have 'term' selected in the drop-down menu to WordPress Knows to Search by Terms (Not by Author or Tag).

4. **Click the Search Plugins button.**

   This reloads the Install Plugins page with a return list of plugins that match the terms you entered in the search field in Step 3 — locate and click the Install Now link for the *Limit Blogs per User* plugin by Brajesh Singh.

5. **Click the Network Activate link on the Installing Plugin page.**

   This action activates the Limit Blogs per User plugin on your network.

6. **Choose Network Admin⇨Settings.**

   Scroll to the bottom of the Settings page to the Limit Blog Registrations per User heading (shown in Figure 4-5) and enter the number of sites that you want to limit your network users to (the value of 1 allows users to create no more than 1 site, and so on — additionally a value of 0, or leaving the field empty, will allow users to create an unlimited number of sites in your network).

Importing users

You may have an existing pool of users you want to add to the network; for example, if you had a Web site before your network existed where you collected registrations or sign-ups (even newsletter programs give you a downloadable list of users you can use to import into your network). The Bulk Import Users plugin, available at `http://wpmututorials.com/plugins/bulk-import-users`, can be used with some plugins mentioned later in this chapter to assign users to various sites in the network. Figure 4-6 shows the Bulk Import Members page with instructions for importing a list of users. Currently, there is no default method of importing users into WordPress without the use of plugins.

Figure 4-5:
The Limit Blog Registrations per User option.

Figure 4-6:
The Bulk Import Users plugin.

Changing Defaults

Depending on your specific needs, you may find yourself wanting to change how users are added to sites, as subscribers, within your network. For example, by default, users cannot add themselves to a random network site without making the request to the Network Admin, or the site administrator of the site they want to be added to. This may work fine for most sites, but if you want your users to be able to register with existing sites within your network, then read on because this section is for you.

Site-specific sign-up

For many people, signing up to the main site and then needing to be added to a child site can be confusing. Plugins, however, can make the process easier and less confusing for visitors.

If you want existing users to have the ability to add themselves to existing sites on the network, the Add Users widget plugin, available in the WordPress Plugins Directory at http://wordpress.org/extend/plugins/add-users-sidebar-widget, will allow them to do so. Install this as a regular plugin, which we outline in Book VII, Chapters 1 and 2.

When the network is activated, the plugin adds a widget on the Widgets page of every users Dashboard (Dashboard⇨Appearance⇨Widgets) called the Add Users widget. Drag the widget to the appropriate sidebar to display it on the sidebar of the site where you want users to add themselves. (If you need a refresher on how to use widgets, see Book VI, Chapter 1.) Site administrators who have added the widget to their site now display a welcome message in their sidebar with a button labeled "Add Me!" that users can click to allow them to register for the site they are visiting (see Figure 4-7).

 If the user is not logged in to the network, the welcome message will then display: If you want to add yourself to this site, please log in., so remember, only users who are already network members, and are logged in, can add themselves to network sites using the Add Users widget plugin.

Changing roles on sign-up

When added to a network or a site, a user is assigned the role of Subscriber, by default. You may want to assign a different role to the user and automatically add him to your other sites in the network. (Book III, Chapter 4 explains roles and permissions.)

When a user signs up for his own site, for example, you may want to assign him a non-administrator role. For example, you may want to set his role to Editor, to restrict the menus the user has access to in the Dashboard and to prevent him from being able to use some of the functionality of WordPress. A Network Admin may want to have new site owners sign up as editors for the sites, giving them less permissions in the their Dashboard.

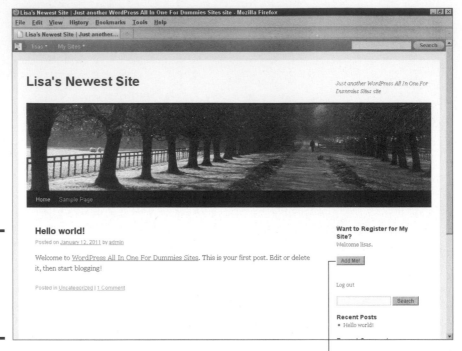

Figure 4-7:
The Add
Users
widget on
the front of
the site.

Add Me! button

The Multisite User Management plugin at `http://wordpress.org/extend/plugins/multisite-user-management` allows you to set a role other than administrator for new users who choose to have a site of their own, and also allows you to set new user roles on other sites within your network (such as the default Subscriber role).

Locking down menus

Certain user roles have certain permissions (which we outline in Book III, Chapter 4) that give users access to various menus in their Dashboard. However, you may want to have increased granular control and close areas that you do not want users to access.

User management plugins exist but, generally, aren't written to be used across a network. So far, the only ones we've tried are on a site-by-site basis, meaning that the user role set on that site will need to be changed again on another site in the network.

Access to menus can be limited via the Menus plugin available at `http://wordpress.org/extend/plugins/menus`.

Exploring Default Site Settings

Default settings can control user access to various such things as menus, themes, and the Dashboard. The next few sections discuss these settings in detail.

Private blogs

The Site Visibility setting on the Privacy Settings page in the regular Dashboard (as well as your users' Dashboard) controls the privacy of that particular site. However, just because you set the main site (the Network Admin's site) to private, does not mean that every site in your network is private — each user must toggle her own privacy settings on the Privacy page in her Dashboard. To access the Privacy Settings page, choose Settings⟳Privacy, as shown in Figure 4-8.

By default, sites are visible to everyone, including search engines and other bots. By selecting the second option, search engines and bots cannot crawl the site at all. Additionally, if you use plugins to create a visible list of network sites — any sites that are marked private will not display in such public lists. Individual plugins should be tested to verify that they observe the privacy setting.

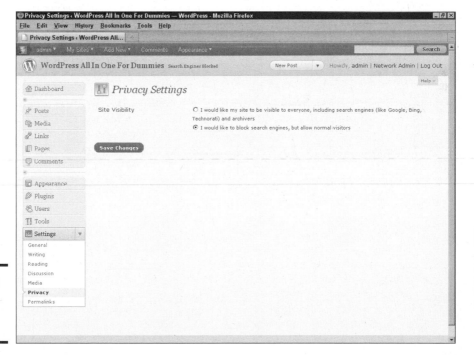

Figure 4-8:
Default
privacy
settings.

Enabling plugins

Because users cannot add or edit plugins, the Plugins menu is disabled by default. The Network Admin can still access the Plugins page via the Network Admin Dashboard Plugins menu link — but other administrators cannot.

To enable the Plugins menu for site administrators, follow these steps:

1. **Choose Network Admin⇨Settings.**

2. **Scroll to the Menu settings section.**

   The check box for the Plugins menu is empty, designating that users will not see the menu regardless of their user role.

3. **Check the box to make the Plugins menu available to site administrators, as shown in Figure 4-9.**

Figure 4-9:
Enabling the Plugins menu for site administrators.

4. **Save your selection by clicking the Save Changes button, as shown in Figure 4-9.**

Similarly, a Network Admin must enable any themes installed on the network before a site administrator can choose the theme from the Appearance menu. We explain this in Chapter 3 of this minibook.

Chapter 5: Using Network Plugins and Themes

In This Chapter

✔ Understanding theme management

✔ Understanding network-wide plugins

✔ Finding network-wide and Must-Use plugins

When you add new plugins and themes to your WordPress installation, you add new functionality and aesthetics. However, you don't just multiply your choices; the possibilities become endless. For example, you can gather and display information from across the network or have the same features available to everyone. You can choose to have the same theme on all sites or different themes. Not only can you manage plugins and themes on a global level, you also have site-specific control.

In this chapter, we cover having certain functionality appear across the network and having certain plugins active by default on all sites for all users. We also cover controlling access to different themes for different sites.

One of the interesting features of a network is the extensive use of the `mu-plugins` folder. In this chapter, we describe exactly how this folder processes plugin code. We also cover the Network Activate link on the Plugins page, which is very similar to the Activate link but has important differences.

When you have a single installation of WordPress on a single site, the Activate link on the plugin page turns that plugin on for that site (see Book VII, Chapters 1 and 2). When you have multiple sites in a network, the activate link works the same way for the site you activate the plugin on.

Network Admins will see a *Network Activate* link on the Plugins page in the Network Admin Dashboard, which activates the plugin on all sites in the network. This will simply turn the plugin on for all network sites. It will not allow you to manage plugin options globally unless the plugin itself was coded to do so. A list of network activated plugins will be shown in the Plugins page in the Network Admin Dashboard (Network Admin➪Plugins).

This chapter doesn't cover installing plugins and themes. We cover plugins in Book VII, Chapter 2 and themes in Book VIII, Chapter 2.

Using One Theme on Multiple Sites

In certain situations (for example, when a Network Admin wants consistent branding/design across their entire network), each site in a network is used as a subsection of the main site. Some WordPress networks are set up as a magazine-style design on their main site and populate the content on their site with different posts from sites within their network, aggregating all the content to the main site in the network. You can see an example of this on a new blog on the WordPress.com network called FoodPress (`http://foodpress.com`), as shown in Figure 5-1.

FoodPress is a site run by Automattic, the company who owns WordPress.com, and their goal is to highlight posts from within the WordPress.com network that are about food and cooking. When you visit that site, you'll notice that all the post title links point to different blogs within their network. Although, WordPress.com allows the administrators of their network sites to use different designs, so the branding across sites is not consistent with the main FoodPress site — we use this example here of a magazine-style theme that aggregates content from within their network.

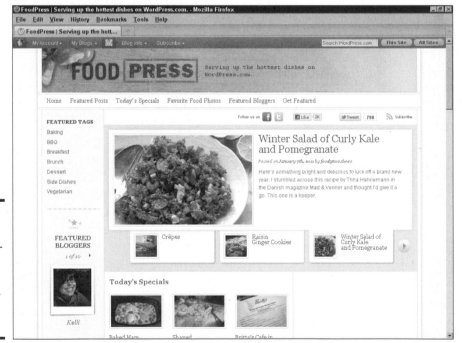

Figure 5-1: FoodPress, a magazine-style site in the WordPress.com network.

Although each site in the network operates separately from the main (Network Admin) site, some Network Admins want each site to look the same as the main site because it ties into the main site visually, through design and branding, and provides a consistent experience for visitors to any site within a network. You may have a custom theme specially made for the main site in your network, with added features to display network-wide content. It may make sense for you to create a theme that is used on all sites within your network (other than your main site) that is created from the same design, with the same color scheme and graphics to provide that consistent look; if consistency and network branding is your goal.

In Book VI, you read about how WordPress accesses themes stored on the Web server. When the network is enabled, these themes are shared among all sites, and available with the site administrator's Dashboard. If a change to a theme file is made, every site in the network using that theme experiences the change because only one copy of the theme is being served. When a theme is enabled, it appears in the administrator's Dashboard on the Manage Themes page (Dashboard⇨Appearance⇨Themes). Users can choose to activate this theme so it displays on the front side of the site. The Network Admin must activate a theme for use across all sites in a network by clicking the Network Enable link under the Theme name in the Network Admin Dashboard (Network Admin⇨Themes).

The main network site could have 20 different themes installed in the main WordPress installation; however, if the Network Admin has not enabled them for use across the entire network, then site administrators will not see network-disabled themes in their Dashboards and therefore, will not be able to use them on their site.

If a consistent network design is what you're after, you will run into a few troubles with the WordPress network because, by default, no matter what themes you have activated, the default WordPress Twenty Ten theme is the theme that gets activated whenever new sites are created within your network. It would be nice for WordPress to provide you with a global setting in the Network Admin Dashboard that would allow Network Admins to assign the default theme to every site that is created; however, that is currently not the case, unless you want to edit some code in the WordPress configuration file (which we do cover in a later section in this chapter).

There is, however, a wonderful plugin that adds a simple item in the Network Admin⇨Settings options called Default Theme. Simply, it gives Network Admins the option to assign a default theme to be the theme displayed on newly created sites.

The Default Theme plugin is not a free plugin, unfortunately; rather, it is available from the development group at WPMU Dev at `http://ewebscapes.com/wpmu-premium`. In order to access the plugin, you do need to purchase membership to their site — however, do not let that deter you.

The WPMU Dev membership gives you access to hundreds of WordPress network-related plugins and themes for one annual membership — we recommend them highly and feel their membership is worth every penny spent. After you have your WPMU Dev membership; you can begin downloading any one of hundreds of plugins and themes for your WordPress network. You can purchase membership by visiting their site at `http://ewebscapes.com/wpmu-premium`.

Enabling themes for individual sites

You may have a customized theme for one member site that you don't want other sites within the network to use, or have access to. Each site on the network is editable by Network Admins, who can do some basic tasks, such as enabling or disabling themes, or adding new themes to the network, without leaving their own Dashboard. If you want to have a theme available for use on only one site, and not available for other sites to choose, follow these steps:

1. **Click the Network Admin link in the upper-right corner of your Dashboard and then click the Sites menu link.**

   The Sites page appears, showing a list of all sites across the network, sorted by creation date, as shown in Figure 5-2.

2. **Hover your mouse cursor over the site you want to enable a theme for and then click the Edit link.**

   The Edit Site page displays in your Dashboard.

3. **Click the Themes tab on the Edit Sites page.**

   This changes the display on the Edit Sites page to show a list of themes that can be enabled for the site you are editing (see Figure 5-3).

4. **Click the Enable link for the theme you want to enable for the site you are editing.**

   The Edit Site page refreshes with the Theme tab still active and displays a message stating that the theme has been enabled.

5. **Your selected theme is now enabled on the site.**

   Repeat these steps for any sites that you want to enable a theme on.

Figure 5-2:
A list of sites on the network.

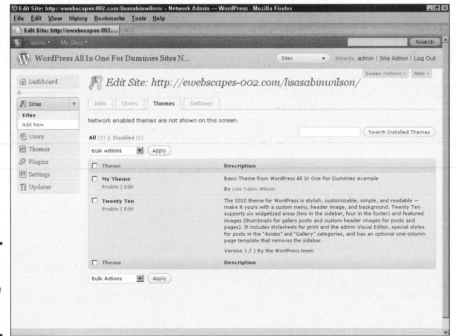

Figure 5-3:
The Edit Site with the Themes tab active.

Installing themes for network use

Installing a theme for use on your network is the same process we outline in Book VI, Chapter 2, with an extra step: You have to enable each theme in the Network Admin Dashboard to activate it on the Appearance menu in the individual site administrators Dashboard for sites within your network to use. Here's how to enable a theme so all your site owners can use it on their sites:

1. **Click the Network Admin link in the upper-right corner of your Dashboard and then click the Themes menu link.**

   The Themes page displays with a list of installed themes, as shown in Figure 5-4. Each theme installed in the `/wp-content/themes` folder is listed on this page.

2. **Click the Network Enable link.**

   Enabling a theme on the Themes page in the Network Admin causes it to appear in the list of available themes within each network site Dashboard (but does not change his active theme, it merely makes this theme available for his use).

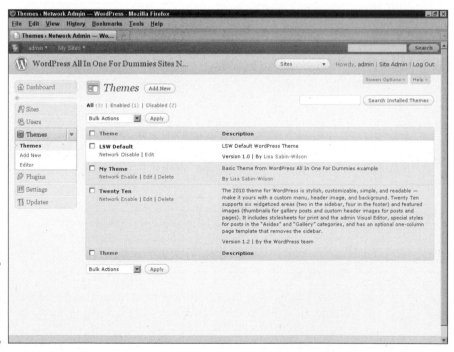

Figure 5-4: A list of themes on the network.

3. **Repeat these steps to enable more themes on your network.**

   Anytime you install a new theme in your main WordPress installation does not mean that it's available for use network-wide. As the Network Admin, you always have to enable the theme first, before your site owners can use it.

Setting the default theme for sites

When a new site is created on the network, by default, it displays the Twenty Ten theme provided within WordPress. If you want to use a different theme as the default for all new sites created, you can accomplish this by adding a define statement in the wp-config.php file of your WordPress installation. (Check out Book II, Chapter 5 to familiarize yourself with the wp-config.php file you're working with in this section.)

Install your theme on the server, which we outline in Book VI, Chapters 1 and 2. You may also want to enable the theme network-wide, as outlined in the preceding section. This isn't a necessary step, but if you have other themes available, and if the active theme is disabled, a user who switches away from that theme will not be able to switch back to it.

Because the Twenty Ten WordPress theme is already the default, we use another popular WordPress theme called Hybrid (by Justin Tadlock: http://wordpress.org/extend/themes/hybrid) as the theme we want to set as the default theme for all sites within the network:

1. **Log in to your Web server via FTP, and then locate and open the .wp-config.php file to edit it.**

   Refer to Book II, Chapter 2 for a refresher on using FTP, and Book II, Chapter 4 to discover where you'll find the wp-config.php file on your Web server.

2. **Open the wp-config.php file in your favorite text editor.**

   It is a good idea to save a copy of your original wp-config.php file before editing it: Do this by downloading a copy to your local computer hard drive so you have a working copy of wp-config.php saved and safe, in case you make any mistakes or typos in the next few steps.

3. **Locate the following line of code in the wp-config.php file: define ('WPLANG', '');**

   You will find this line toward the bottom of the file; scroll until you locate it. When you find it, place your mouse cursor at the end of that line and click, and then hit the Enter key on your keyboard. This adds a new, blank line directly underneath it.

4. **Type: `define('WP_DEFAULT_THEME', 'hybrid');`**

   This one line of code tells WordPress to use the Hybrid theme as the default theme for all new sites within your network.

5. **Save the `wp-config.php` file and upload it to your Web server.**

   The `hybrid` in quotes refers to the theme's folder name on the Web server. The name within the quotes should be identical to the folder name where the theme files reside. All new sites created now display the Hybrid theme.

Gathering and Displaying Network-wide Content

Depending on your needs, you may want to gather content from sites across your network to display on the front page of the main site (such as with the FoodPress example we provide at the beginning of this chapter). Although some plugins will do this for you, you can accomplish this by placing a few lines of code in your theme template file.

The main page of your network is controlled by the theme that is active in your regular Dashboard under Apperance➪Themes. You can customize this theme with some code samples in the next section to suit your particular needs.

Adding Posts from Network Sites

One of the best ways to pull visitors into your site is to display a short list of headlines from posts made by other sites within your network. With a single WordPress site, this simply is handled by the Recent Posts widget. When running a network, however, there's no built-in way to pull a list of posts from across all the sites in your network. However, the Recent Global Posts widget plugin available from the folks at WPMU Premium Dev can do this for you quickly and efficiently, and includes a handy widget to make it easy for you to add recent posts from across your network of sites to your main Web site.

As we mention in an early part of this chapter, plugins from WPMU Dev Premium are not free, and you cannot access them from the official WordPress Plugins Directory. You first need to pay for and register a membership at their site: `http://ewebscapes.com/wpmu-premium`

After you have your membership, log in and download the Recent Global Posts Widget plugin here: `http://premium.wpmudev.org/project/recent-global-posts-widget`.

Listing network sites

To list all the sites in the network, use the Multi-Site Site List Shortcode plugin available for free from the WordPress Plugin Directory: `http://wordpress.org/extend/plugins/multi-site-site-list-shortcode`. You install this plugin just as you do any other plugin in WordPress; see Book VII, Chapters 1 and 2 for information on installing WordPress plugins.

To use the information this plugin provides, you must include a `shortcode` that the plugin developer provides, within the body of a page, or a post, published to your main site. The most common and useful method is to create a page that includes the plugin `shortcode`. To list all network sites, follow these steps. In this example, I use the default Twenty Ten theme:

1. **Log in to the WordPress Dashboard on the main site.**

2. **Choose Pages⇨Add New.**

3. **Fill in a title for your page.**

   Something like: Network Sites List

4. **Add this short code in the body of your page:**

   ```
   [site-list]
   ```

5. **Publish the page.**

   When you visit the front end of your site, you will see a page with your new title in the menu. Clicking this shows the visitor the list of sites in the network, as shown in Figure 5-5.

Figure 5-5:
A page showing the list of network sites.

The Multi-Site Site List Shortcode plugin also gives you a settings page where you can select sites that you would like to hide from the listing of sites. You can find the Multi-Site Site List Shortcode Options page by clicking Settings⇨Multi-Site Site List within your regular Dashboard. The Multi-Site Site List Shortcode Options page is shown in Figure 5-6.

Displaying user comments

When running multiple sites, you may also want to display a list of the most recent comments from across the network. The Diamond Multsite widgets plugin (available at http://wordpress.org/extend/plugins/diamond-multisite-widgets) lets you do just that.

Install the plugin as outlined in Book VII, and click the Network Activate link. Visit the Appearance ⇨Widgets menu in the Dashboard area of your site to load the Widgets page, and you see that a new widget has been added called Diamond Recent Comments.

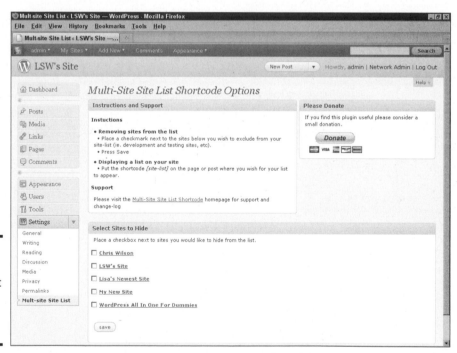

Figure 5-6:
The Multi-Site Site List Shortcode Options page.

Drag this widget to the sidebar of your choosing and it will display a list of the most recent comments from every site on the entire network. The widget has configurable options; if you expand the Diamond Recent Comments widget, you see that there are several optional settings that allow you to configure:

✦ **Widget Title:** This is the title that is displayed on your site, above the widget information.

✦ **Cache Expire Time:** In seconds, it's the time frame in which the plugin will refresh the comments displayed with this widget.

✦ **Comments Count:** Enter the maximum number of comments you want to display.

✦ **Exclude Blogs:** Place a check mark next to the name of the site that you want to exclude comments from.

✦ **Whitelist:** Place a check mark next to the name of the site(s) that you want to always include comments from.

✦ **Format String:** Enter the format for how you want the comments to display on your site by typing in the strings of text shown directly beneath this option (see Figure 5-7).

Diamond Recent Comments widgets options

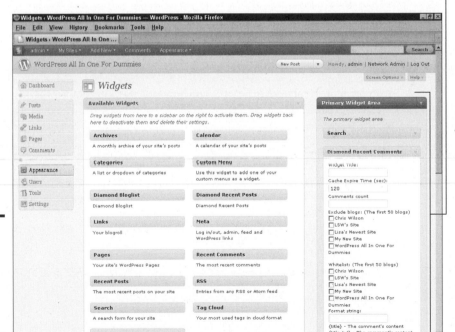

Figure 5-7:
The Diamond Recent Comments widget options.

✦ **Avatar Size:** Enter the size of the comment author's avatar for display on your site.

✦ **Default Avatar URL:** Enter the Web address to the graphic/image file you want to display as the default avatar (for comment authors who do not have one).

✦ **Default "Read More" link text:** Enter the text that you want the Read More link to display (by default, the widget displays the words "Read More" as the direct link to the comment).

✦ **DateTime Format:** Enter the date and time format that you prefer.

Be sure to click the Save button within the widget to save all the settings you created here.

Sitewide tags and categories

The Sitewide Tags plugin pulls information from every new post on each site and reproduces it on a site that the plugin creates in your network called the Tags Blog site, which is a site in your network that aggregates the posts from every site. You may also set Tags Blog as the main site in your network so that all new posts appear on the front page.

The plugin pulls and reposts almost all content from a post on another network site, including the title, content, tags, categories, and author information. At this time, however, it doesn't pull the post thumbnail or the comments.

By default, this plugin is set to create a new site called Tags Blog and saves up to 5,000 posts before it, automatically, removes older ones. Each post it aggregates retains its original permalink (the full URL to the post), and all post meta (the post's original author, the date and time it was published, and any categories and tags assigned to the post).

All the aggregated posts from across the network are saved and published to one site; the Tags Blog are then are displayed as if theses posts were posted to a single site. Each new post is saved to the Tags Blog site when it's created. Users or visitors can then search the Tags Blog site and see tags from across the network, search all aggregated posts across the network, see posts by all network authors — the possibilities for network-wide aggregation and display are quite useful.

Because the original permalink of the post is retained, search engines will not read these aggregated posts as duplicate content, and thereby any page rankings or SEO juice is retained by each site.

You can find the plugin at `http://wordpress.org/extend/plugins/wordpress-mu-sitewide-tags` or you may also install it by using the built-in plugin installer.

After you install the plugin, activate it on the network by moving it to the `mu-plugins` folder (the mu-plugins folder is discussed later in this chapter). When moved to this folder on the server, the plugin will be automatically activated and start working.

After you activate the plugin, you need to enable it. Visit the Settings page in your Network Dashboard (Network Admin⇨Settings) and scroll to the bottom of the page. Figure 5-8 shows the Global Tags option, where you enable the Tags Blog on your network by selecting the Enabled check box in the Global Tags section.

Figure 5-8:
Check box
to enable
Tags Blog.

Global Tags

Tags Blog   ☑ **Enabled**

After you click the Save Changes button on the Settings page, scroll back down to the bottom of the page and you see the Global Tags section has changed and provides you with new options (see Figure 5-9), including

✦ **Tags Blog:** Enabled: This creates a site named tags and aggregates all posts to this site.

✦ **Blogname:** The name you want to assign to the Tags Blog. Using this option will cause the Tags Blog to be created.

✦ **Post to Main Blog:** Select this option to have WordPress push posts from all network sites to the main site in the network. With this option selected, the Tabs Blog is not created and the plugin uses your main site to aggregate the network content to, instead.

✦ **Max Posts:** Set to 5,000 by default. Beyond that, the plugin will delete older posts from the Tags Blog site, automatically.

✦ **Include Pages:** Check to enable, this will also include any pages users create on their network sites, and push them to the assigned tags blog.

✦ **Privacy:** Whether the Tags Blog site can be indexed by search engines.

✦ **Non-public blogs:** When enabled, this will aggregate posts from sites that have changed their privacy setting under Settings ⇨ Privacy to non-public.

✦ **Post meta:** If you are using a plugin or a theme on some or all of the network sites that creates custom files, you may enter those field names here so those values will also be pulled to the tags blog.

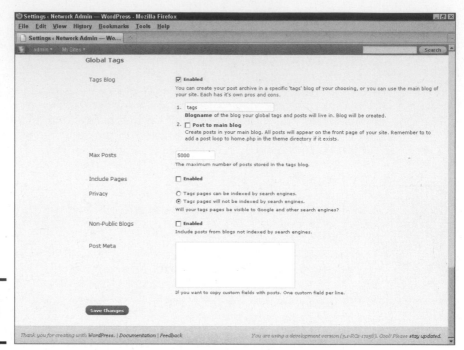

Figure 5-9:
Global tags
options.

Using and Installing Network-wide Plugins

Network-wide plugins perform an action globally across all sites in the network. Sometimes, you might see these referred to as *sitewide plugins,* which
is old WordPress MU terminology (pre-WordPress version 3.0). Because
you're working with one codebase, only one copy of a plugin is needed. All
sites within the network use the same copy.

Any changes made to this copy affect every site within your network.

A special breed of plugins — the "Must-Use" plugins — get installed into
the /wp-content/mu-plugins folder on your Web server. Any plugin file
placed inside this folder runs as if it were part of WordPress. The plugins
in this folder automatically execute, without the need for activation in your
Dashboard.

You cannot access the files in this folder from the back WordPress
Dashboard. If you use the Install Plugins page (Plugins⇨Add New) to find
and install a Must-Use plugin, you may be required to move the plugin files
from the plugins folder to the mu-plugins folder. The plugin's readme.
txt file will always state if the plugin needs to be moved into the Must-Use
(mu-plugins) folder.

Generally, plugins placed in the `/wp-content/mu-plugins` folder are for network-wide features or customizations that users can't disable. An example of this would be a custom-branded login page on each site in your network. If a plugin design adds a new menu item, the menu item will appear as soon as the plugin is placed in the `/wp-content/mu-plugins` folder, without further need for activation in the Dashboard.

Not all plugins placed in the `/wp-content/mu-plugins` folder appear in the plugins list (Plugins⇨Plugins) because they all don't require activation. After you create the `/wp-content/mu-plugins` folder via FTP or your Web host's control panel, a new link — Must-Use — appears on the Plugins page, as shown in Figure 5-10.

You still control plugin settings on a per-site basis; you must visit the back end of each site if you want to alter any settings provided by the plugin.

The main *Must-Use* plugin file needs to be placed in the `/wp-content/mu-plugins` folder, not in a subfolder. If multiple files are needed, some plugins use a file with a command to include the subfolder so the code executes. Figure 5-10 shows a list of installed Must-Use plugins.

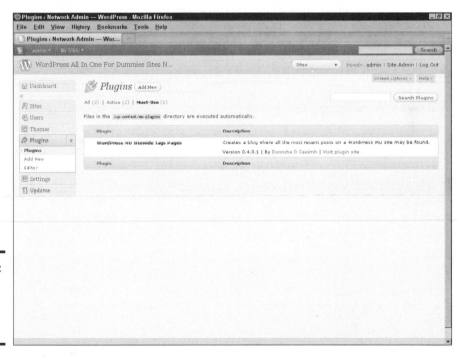

Figure 5-10:
The Must-Use link on the Plugins page.

Here's how to create the `/wp-content/mu-plugins` folder and install a network-wide plugin:

1. **Connect to your Web server via FTP.**

2. **Navigate to the /wp-content folder.**

   You see the subdirectories `plugins` and `themes`.

3. **Using your FTP program, create a mu-plugins subdirectory.**

   Most FTP programs will allow you to right-click with your mouse and choose to add a new folder.

4. **Upload the plugin file — not the plugin folder — to the /wp-content/ mu-plugins folder on your Web server.**

   The plugin immediately runs on your install. Generally speaking, the only plugins that go in this folder are ones in which the plugin's instructions (typically found in the `readme.txt` file) explicitly state to do so.

Discovering Handy Network Plugins

Although some of the network plugins we suggest in this section may not be suitable for all networks, we recommend these plugins because we find them most useful. In the list below, we cover each plugin and any special instructions it might require.

You can find network plugins that take advantage of WordPress's multisite functionality in the WordPress Plugin Directory at `http://wordpress.org/extend/plugins`. Usually, Multisite plugins are tagged with certain keywords within the directory to help you find them better, such as *wpmu*, *wordpressmu*, *multisite*, and *network*.

When you click on the linked tags in the directory for these terms, you are taken directly to a URL for a page that lists the related plugins, such as

✦ `http://wordpress.org/extend/plugins/tags/multisite`

✦ `http://wordpress.org/extend/plugins/tags/network`

✦ `http://wordpress.org/extend/plugins/tags/wpmu`

Additionally, you can find more plugins via search engines and by asking on the Forums page (`http://wordpress.org/support`).

Chapter 6: Using Multiple Domains within Your Network

In This Chapter

✔ Introducing domain mapping

✔ Understanding how to map domains

✔ Advanced usage

*W*ith a network of multiple sites easily available in WordPress, many people have expressed the desire to run multiple sites on their own separate domain names through one install. Prior to the network feature being added to the WordPress software, users could only run one site per installation of the software. Now, it is possible to run several different sites under one installation of WordPress by activating the network feature, which we discussed in Chapters 4 and 5 of this minibook.

In this chapter, we discuss using multiple domains and a feature called Domain Mapping, that enables you to run not only multiple sites, but also multiple sites with their own, unique domain name that is not tied to the main site installation domain.

Introducing Domain Mapping

Domain mapping means telling your Web server which domains you want WordPress to answer to, and which site you want shown to the visitor when they request that domain. This process is more than domain forwarding or masking because the URLs for your posts will have the full domain name in them. Instead of the child site being in `secondsite.yourdomain.com` format, it can be `myotherdomain.com`.

Domain mapping isn't possible in certain instances, however. If your WordPress install is in a subfolder and this folder is part of the URL, then any mapped domain will also contain this folder name. In that case, it would be better to move the install so that it isn't in a subfolder.

You also need to access your Web host's control panel (where you manage DNS records on your Web server) and the control panel for your domain name registrar, which is often a different company.

The network install, by default, lets you choose between a subfolder setup and a subdomain setup. This step is still required before you can specify a domain for that site. We cover how to enable the network in Chapter 2 of this minibook. Please ensure that the network is set up and functioning properly before you attempt to map domains.

Parking or pointing domains

You need to set up your Web server to accept any incoming requests for the domain you want to map and the location to send them to. On cPanel-based Web hosts, this is referred to as *domain parking*. We use cPanel here because it's quite popular and available on many Web hosts.

Follow these steps to park a domain on your Web hosting account via cPanel:

1. **Log in to your Web site's cPanel.**

   The address is provided by your Web host and usually available at `http://yourdomain.com/cpanel`.

2. **In the Domains section, click the Parked Domains icon, as shown in Figure 6-1.**

   The Parked domains page displays in your browser window that lists any domains you have parked, if you have previously parked any, and provides a form to enter a new domain.

Figure 6-1:
The Parked
Domains
icon in
cPanel.

3. **In the Create a New Parked Domain section, enter the domain name you want to map.**

   The domain is directed to the root folder of your Web site, which is where your WordPress install should be located. If it isn't, please follow the steps provided in the next section.

4. **Click Add Domain.**

   The screen refreshes and presents you with a page similar to Figure 6-2. The domain you added is shown in a list under Domains, which indicates successful parking of the domain you entered in Step 4.

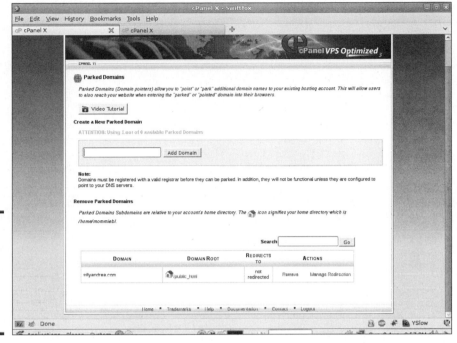

Figure 6-2:
The Parked
Domains
page
showing
a parked
domain.

Other Web hosts may refer to domain parking as *pointing* or *mirroring*. You may need to ask your Web host support team which area you need to do this in. You're using a `ServerAlias` directive for the mapped domains, telling the Web server to send all requests for the mapped domain to the domain where WordPress is installed.

If the domain you're using for your WordPress network installation isn't the main domain of the Web site, but an add-on domain, you have to do a slightly different process to park the domain. Because you can't tell a parked domain to go anywhere other than the root folder, you need to choose the Addon Domains feature.

Follow these steps to create an Addon Domain in your Web hosting cPanel:

1. **Log in to your Web site's cPanel.**

In the Domains section, click the Addon Domains icon, as shown in Figure 6-3. The Addon Domains page appears.

2. **Enter the new domain name you want to map in the New Domain Name field.**

The other fields, Subdomain/FTP Username, and Document Root get auto-populated by your Web server; do not alter the information your Web server populates for the Subdomain/FTP Username, as this field is setting the username you will use to connect when you need to use FTP.

Figure 6-3:
The Addon
Domains
icon in
cPanel.

3. **In the Document Root field, enter the folder location of your WordPress network installation.**

   Figure 6-4 shows the Create an Add-on Domain information filled in.

4. **Click Add Domain to save your changes.**

   The Addon Domains page refreshes, and your new domain appears under the Addon Domains section.

Figure 6-4:
Create an
Add-on
Domain in
cPanel.

Domain name server records

To instruct the domain name registrar where to send the domain name to, you need to edit the domain nameserver (DNS) records. A common domain name registrar is GoDaddy, whose domain registration account interface we use in the following steps. To edit the name server records, follow these steps:

1. **Log in to your domain name registrar.**

2. **Click the domain name management tools.**

Figure 6-5 shows the information for the domain to map.

3. **Click the Set Nameservers link in the Nameservers section.**

4. **Type the nameservers for your Web host where your WordPress install is located, and save your changes.**

This tells servers around the world that your domain "lives" at this Web server location. Nameserver changes may take up to 24 hours to propagate across the Internet.

Figure 6-5:
The domain name records of a mapped domain.

Installing the Domain Mapping Plugin

Before you can map the domain, you need to install the WordPress MU Domain Mapping plugin to help handle this in WordPress. The Domain Mapping plugin doesn't do any setup on the server side; it helps rename the site and takes care of any login issues.

1. **Download the plugin from `http://wordpress.org/extend/ plugins/wordpress-mu-domain-mapping`.**

2. **Unzip the plugin on your local computer.**

   Inside are two php files: `domain-mapping.php` and `sunrise.php`.

3. **Open your FTP program and navigate to your Web site's `wp-content` folder.**

   If you need a reminder on how to do this, see Chapter 1 of this minibook.

4. **Upload the `sunrise.php` file directly into the `/wp-content` folder.**

5. **Inside the `/wp-content`, there may be a folder called `/mu-plugins`. If there isn't, use your FTP program to create this folder.**

6. **Upload the `domain-mapping.php` file into the `/mu-plugins` folder.**

   Figure 6-6 shows how these files look on the server. From here, you need to add a line to your `wp-config.php` file.

Figure 6-6: A look at the `/wp-content/plugins` folder that contains the `sunrise.php` file.

7. **Download a copy of your `wp-config.php` file by using your FTP vprogram.**

8. **Open `wp-config.php` on your computer with a text editor and add the following line under the `define( 'MULTISITE', true );` line.**

   ```
   define( 'SUNRISE', 'on' );
   ```

9. **Save the file and upload it to your Web site.**

   The plugin is immediately available (and running) on your network. All you need to do is set up the options and map a domain to a site. Two new items are added to the Super Admin menu: Domain Mapping and Domains. On the user administrator side, a new Domain Mapping item appears on the Tools menu.

The network admin will need to activate domain mapping on the Domain Mapping page (Network Admin⇨Domain Mapping) before a user can map a domain by enabling the Domain Mapping feature.

Obtaining your IP address

An *IP address* is a number assigned to every Web site and computer connected to the Internet. This number is used in domain mapping to help direct Internet traffic to the appropriate site in your network. You can find the IP address of your Web site three ways: Your Web host provider can tell you, the address may appear in some place within the Web host's control panel, and you can visit an IP lookup Web site. Such Web sites can tell you the IP of your Web site when you provide your domain name. To find your address with an IP lookup Web site, follow these steps:

1. **Visit Network Solutions' WHOIS feature located at `www.network solutions.com/whois/index.jsp`.**

2. **Enter the domain name of your Web site and then click Search.**

3. **Write down the IP address it shows.**

Figure 6-7 displays the IP address of mommieblogs.com.

Figure 6-7: WHOIS record revealing the IP address of mommie blogs.com.

4. **In your WordPress Dashboard, choose Network Admin⇨Domain Mapping, enter your IP address, and click Save.**

Mapping a domain to a site

To map a domain to a site in your network, here's what you need to do:

1. **Navigate to the child site you want to map.**

2. **Log in to the Dashboard of that child site.**

3. **Choose Tools➪Domain Mapping.**

   The Domain Mapping page appears, as shown in Figure 6-8.

4. **Enter the domain name you want to map to this site.**

   The check box indicates whether the domain is the primary domain for this site and is used only if you want to map multiple domains to the site. Only one domain can be the primary domain and used in the URL. Any other domains mapped to this site redirect to the primary domain.

5. **Click the Add button to save your changes.**

   The site now appears when you enter the mapped domain URL in your Web browser address bar.

This plugin also lets the network admin map a domain to a site without visiting the site's Dashboard. You can do this by choosing Network Admin➪Domains. (See Figure 6-9.) *Note:* You need to know the ID number of the site you want to map.

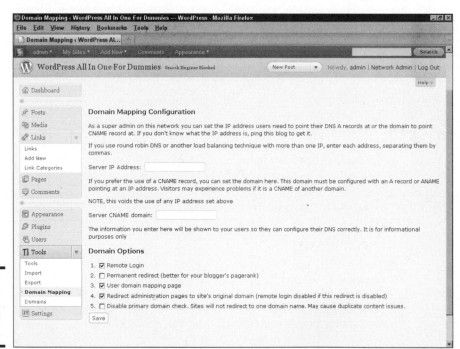

Figure 6-8:
Mapping a domain to a user's site.

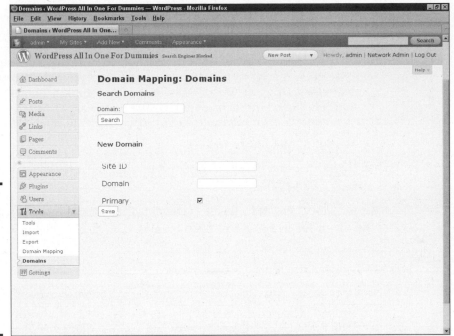

Book VIII
Chapter 6

Figure 6-9:
The Domain
Mapping:
Domains
page maps
domains
from a
single
location.

Mapping a Large Volume of Domains

On some enterprises, you may need to map a large volume of domains to the WordPress network, for example if you have 10-100, or more, domains. Adding each domain to the server with a `ServerAlias` directive is not only time consuming but, as the list grows, the server slows while reading all the domains.

The time necessary to add these domains can be shortened considerably by using a wildcard host. To use a wildcard host, you need to access your Web site via a terminal or via SSH with the root user. This is only available on VPS or dedicated hosts. The ideal situation for using a wildcard host is when the main installation of WordPress is the default domain on the server. A quick way to check if your WordPress main installation domain is the default domain on your Web server is to type your IP address in your browser address bar. If your main WordPress site displays in your browser, then you know that you can proceed with using a wildcard host. If it does not, you will need to obtain a dedicated IP address from your Web hosting provider — contact them to set that up for you.

Using Multiple
Domains within
Your Network

Apache configuration

Adding a wildcard host to your Web server requires that you access the Apache configuration files on your Web server. This section assumes that you have access to those files; if you do not, contact your Web hosting provider to either provide you with the access you need, or ask them to complete the steps for you to add the wildcard host to your account.

Here's how you set this feature up:

1. **Log in to your Web site with the root user via a terminal.**

2. **Navigate to the configuration files in the folder located at `/etc/httpd/` by typing**

   ```
   cd /etc/httpd/
   ```

3. **Open the `httpd.conf` file by typing**

   ```
   vi httpd.conf
   ```

   Page down in the file until you see the vhost section. Find the vhost section that contains the information about your WordPress installation and the main domain of your network (depending on the number of domains hosted on your server, there may be several vhost entries in the `httpd.conf` file — be sure that you're editing the vhost that contains the main domain of your WordPress install.)

4. **Press the Insert key to begin editing the file.**

5. **Comment out the lines and place the wildcard as shown.**

   ```
   <VirtualHost *:80>
   ```

6. **Save the changes by pressing the Esc key, typing `:wq`, and then pressing Enter.**

7. **On the command line, restart Apache by typing**

   ```
   /etc/init.d/apache restart
   ```

You can now map domains in volume by using the following steps:

1. **Log in to your domain name registrar.**

2. **Click the domain name management tools for the domain you want to map.**

3. **Click the Total DNS records; refer to Figure 6-5.**

4. **Locate the A records at the top of the page.**

   Insert the IP address of your WordPress network. (We show you how to obtain this in the section "Obtaining your IP address," earlier in this chapter.)

Figure 6-10 shows an A record and the Web server's IP address it points to. The domain is sent to that IP address regardless of nameserver.

5. **Choose Network Admin⇨Domains from your WordPress Dashboard.**

   The Domain Mapping: Domains page appears, as shown in Figure 6-11.

6. **Enter the ID of the site you want to map.**

   You can get the ID number from the Sites page (Super Admin⇨Sites).

7. **Enter the domain name you want to map to this site.**

8. **Click Save.**

   The page refreshes and shows you a list of mapped domains.

There is no longer any need to park or point domains at the Web host. The server is instructed to take any domain name request and send it to the WordPress network. WordPress associates the mapped domain with the correct site.

Figure 6-10:
Domain A records.

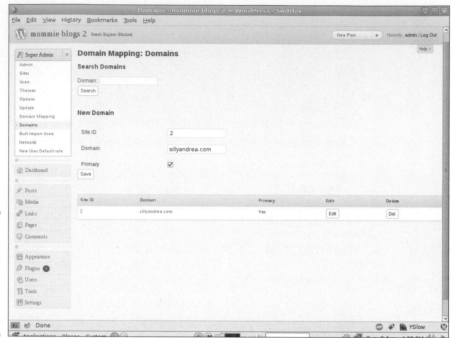

Figure 6-11:
Mapping a domain from the Domain Mapping: Domains page.

Hiding the original installation domain

The domain mapping plugin mentioned earlier in the "Installing the Domain Mapping Plugin" section lets you to access the child site by the original location regardless of whether it's a subdomain site or a subfolder site, so you can use domain mapping no matter which set up you chose for your network (subdomains or subdirectories). The domain mapped for the child site is also the domain used on all uploaded media files, which maintains consistency for the site.

In some cases, users may want to hide the original installation domain; for example, if your main installation domain is an obscure looking domain like: http://00954-yourvpsdomain-ba.com, you probably want to hide that domain from showing simply because its not a domain that is easily remembered, or one that will be used, by visitors to your site. If you want to hide the original installation domain, here's how you can do so:

1. **Choose Network Admin⇨Sites.**

The Edit Site page appears in your Network Admin Dashboard.

2. **Hover over the name of the site you want to edit and click the Edit link that appears, as shown in Figure 6-12.**

   The Edit Site page displays in your browser window.

3. **Find all instances of the original domain name and change them to the new mapped domain.**

   Be sure to click on each of the tabs on the Edit Site page (Info, Users, Themes, and Settings) to change the original domain name to the new mapped domain wherever it appears on the Edit Site page. Keep any folder names intact.

4. **Save your changes by clicking the Save Changes button, as shown in Figure 6-13.**

Your mapped site is now inaccessible at the original child site name (the subdomain or subfolder) and any references to it have been changed. Previous links within the body of posts, however, aren't updated automatically, so you need to edit the posts manually to change the links to reflect your newly mapped domain.

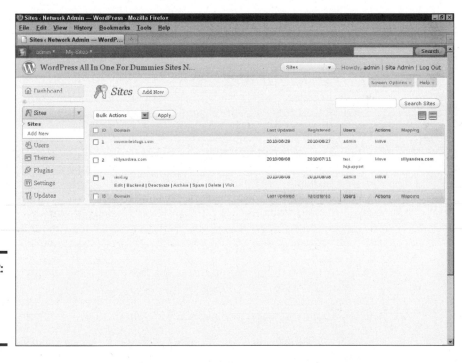

Figure 6-12:
The Edit link for individual sites.

Figure 6-13:
The Edit Site
page in the
Network
Admin
Dashboard.

Setting Up Multiple Networks

Multiple networks are supported in the WordPress codebase, but there is no built-in menu or interface in the Dashboard. Running multiple networks in one install is an advanced feature that allows you to have another network in the same installation acting as a second independent network of sites. It can use its fully qualified domain name or a subdomain. The extra networks inherit the same type of sites. If your original network was installed by using subdomain sites, the extra network will also have subdomain sites. The network admin carries over to the new network, too. Additionally, you can add other network admins to the second network who will not have Network Admin access on the original network.

The plugin that helps you do this is WP Multi Network (available at `http://wordpress.org/extend/plugins/wp-multi-network`). You install and manage the WP Multi Network plugin in a way that's similar to how you install and manage the Domain Mapping plugin. The domain for the new network still needs to be parked on the install, but the creation of the network is done later on the Network options page after you install the WP Multi Network plugin. You cannot take an existing site on the network and turn it into a second network. You must set up a new site when the new network is created. Figure 6-14 shows the options screen for the WP Multi Network plugin.

Figure 6-14:
The
Networks
page in the
Network
Admin
Dashboard.

To create a new network, fill in the fields shown on the Networks page in Figure 6-14:

✦ **Network Name:** This refers to the name of the network you are creating (example: My New Network).

✦ **Domain:** The domain name you will use for this new network (example: `mynewnetwork.com`).

✦ **Path:** The server path your new network will use (example: `/home/mynewnetwork/public_html/`).

✦ **Site Name:** The name of the site that will serve as the main site in this network (example: Network Main Site).

When you are done, click the Create Network button at the bottom of the Network page, and WordPress creates your new network that you are now able to assign child sites to.

Index

Special Characters and Numerics

A

Internet

Blogging For Dummies,
3rd Edition
978-0-470-61996-4

eBay For Dummies,
6th Edition
978-0-470-49741-8

Facebook For Dummies,
3rd Edition
978-0-470-87804-0

Web Marketing
For Dummies,
2nd Edition
978 0-470-37181-7

WordPress
For Dummies,
3rd Edition
978-0-470-59274-8

Language & Foreign Language

French For Dummies
978-0-7645-5193-2

Italian Phrases
For Dummies
978-0-7645-7203-6

Spanish For Dummies,
2nd Edition
978-0-470-87855-2

Spanish
For Dummies,
Audio Set
978-0-470-09585-0

Math & Science

Algebra I
For Dummies,
2nd Edition
978-0-470-55964-2

Biology For Dummies,
2nd Edition
978-0-470-59875-7

Calculus For Dummies
978-0-7645-2498-1

Chemistry For Dummies
978-0-7645-5430-8

Microsoft Office

Excel 2010 For Dummies
978-0-470-48953-6

Office 2010 All in One
For Dummies
978-0-470-49748-7

Office 2010 For Dummies,
Book + DVD Bundle
978-0-470-62698-6

Word 2010 For Dummies
978-0-470-48772-3

Music

Guitar For Dummies,
2nd Edition
978-0-7645-9904-0

iPod & iTunes For
Dummies, 8th Edition
978-0-470-87871-2

Piano Exercises
For Dummies
978-0-470-38765-8

Parenting & Education

Parenting For Dummies,
2nd Edition
978-0-7645-5418-6

Type 1 Diabetes
For Dummies
978-0-470-17811-9

Pets

Cats For Dummies,
2nd Edition
978-0-7645-5275-5

Dog Training For Dummies,
3rd Edition
978-0-470-60029-0

Puppies For Dummies,
2nd Edition
978-0-470-03717-1

Religion & Inspiration

The Bible For Dummies
978-0-7645-5296-0

Catholicism For Dummies
978-0-7645-5391-2

Women in the Bible
For Dummies
978-0-7645-8475-6

Self-Help & Relationship

Anger Management
For Dummies
978-0-470-03715-7

Overcoming Anxiety
For Dummies,
2nd Edition
978-0-470-57441-6

Sports

Baseball
For Dummies,
3rd Edition
978-0-7645-7537-2

Basketball
For Dummies,
2nd Edition
978-0-7645-5248-9

Golf For Dummies,
3rd Edition
978-0-471-76871-5

Web Development

Web Design
All-in-One
For Dummies
978-0-470-41796-6

Web Sites
Do-It-Yourself
For Dummies,
2nd Edition
978-0-470-56520-9

Windows 7

Windows 7
For Dummies
978-0-470-49743-2

Windows 7
For Dummies,
Book + DVD Bundle
978-0-470-52398-8

Windows 7 All
For Dummi
978-0

Apple & Macs

iPad For Dummies
978-0-470-58027-1

iPhone For Dummies,
4th Edition
978-0-470-87870-5

MacBook For Dummies, 3rd
Edition
978-0-470-76918-8

Mac OS X Snow Leopard For
Dummies
978-0-470-43543-4

Business

Bookkeeping For Dummies
978-0-7645-9848-7

Job Interviews
For Dummies,
3rd Edition
978-0-470-17748-8

Resumes For Dummies,
5th Edition
978-0-470-08037-5

Starting an
Online Business
For Dummies,
6th Edition
978-0-470-60210-2

Stock Investing
For Dummies,
3rd Edition
978-0-470-40114-9

Successful
Time Management
For Dummies
978-0-470-29034-7

Computer Hardware

BlackBerry
For Dummies,
4th Edition
978-0-470-60700-8

Computers For Seniors
For Dummies,
2nd Edition
978-0-470-53483-0

PCs For Dummies,
Windows
7 Edition
978-0-470-46542-4

Laptops For Dummies,
4th Edition
978-0-470-57829-2

Cooking & Entertaining

Cooking Basics
For Dummies,
3rd Edition
978-0-7645-7206-7

Wine For Dummies,
4th Edition
978-0-470-04579-4

Diet & Nutrition

Dieting For Dummies,
2nd Edition
978-0-7645-4149-0

Nutrition For Dummies,
4th Edition
978-0-471-79868-2

Weight Training
For Dummies,
3rd Edition
978-0-471-76845-6

Digital Photography

Digital SLR Cameras &
Photography For Dummies,
3rd Edition
978-0-470-46606-3

Photoshop Elements 8
For Dummies
978-0-470-52967-6

Gardening

Gardening Basics
For Dummies
978-0-470-03749-2

Organic Gardening
For Dummies,
2nd Edition
978-0-470-43067-5

Green/Sustainable

Raising Chickens
For Dummies
978-0-470-46544-8

Green Cleaning
For Dummies
978-0-470-39106-8

Health

Diabetes For Dummies,
3rd Edition
978-0-470-27086-8

Food Allergies
For Dummies
978-0-470-09584-3

Living Gluten-Free
For Dummies,
2nd Edition
978-0-470-58589-4

Hobbies/General

Chess For Dummies,
2nd Edition
978-0-7645-8404-6

Drawing
Cartoons & Comics
For Dummies
978-0-470-42683-8

Knitting For Dummies,
2nd Edition
978-0-470-28747-7

Organizing
For Dummies
978-0-7645-5300-4

Su Doku For Dummies
978-0-470-01892-7

Home Improvement

Home Maintenance
For Dummies,
2nd Edition
978-0-470-43063-7

Home Theater
For Dummies,
3rd Edition
978-0-470-41189-6

Living the
Country Lifestyle
All-in-One
For Dummies
978-0-470-43061-3

Solar Power Your Home
For Dummies,
2nd Edition
978-0-470-59678-4